FIDDLER'S GREEN

The Great Squandering: 1921–2010

A History of the British Merchant Navy

Other Books in the Series:

Full of adventure, heroism and skullduggery, this series covers the period from Tudor times to the present day via the Seven Years War, slavery, the American Rebellion, the Napoleonic Wars, Empire, Depression, and two world wars.

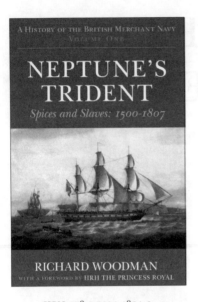

ISBN 978 0 7524 4814 5

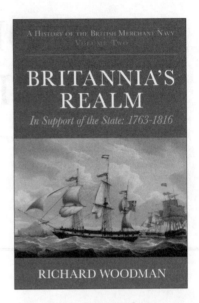

ISBN 978 0 7524 4819 0

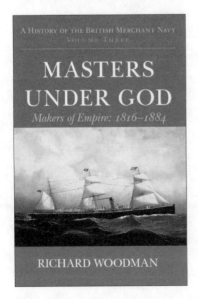

ISBN 978 0 7524 4820 6

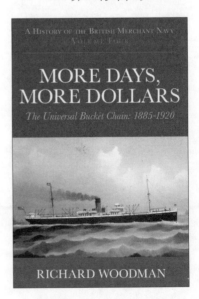

ISBN 978 0 7524 4821 3

A History of the British Merchant Navy
Volume Five

FIDDLER'S GREEN

The Great Squandering: 1921–2010

RICHARD WOODMAN

The History Press

Wrap me up in my tarpaulin jacket,

No more on the docks I'll be seen,

Just tell my old shipmates,

I'm taking a trip, mates,

And I'll see you one day on Fiddler's Green.

Traditional

First published 2010
Reprinted 2010

The History Press
The Mill, Brimscombe Port
Stroud, Gloucestershire, GL5 2QG
www.thehistorypress.co.uk

© Richard Woodman, 2010

The right of Richard Woodman to be identified as the Author
of this work has been asserted in accordance with the
Copyrights, Designs and Patents Act 1988.

British Library Cataloguing in Publication Data.
A catalogue record for this book is available from the British Library.

ISBN 978 0 7524 4822 0

Typesetting and origination by The History Press
Printed in India

CONTENTS

Brangwyn's drawing shows the tedium of discharging timber. The dockers were to strike in wartime and resist change afterwards. Neither circumstance endeared them to the seafarers whose ships they loaded and discharged. (© Courtesy of Lloyd's Register of Shipping)

INTRODUCTION

'Only Four Inches from Death'

In this final volume recording the history of the British Merchant Navy, we come to its end. What remains today is something different from what helped make Great Britain the world's first superpower. The 'whale' that had defeated the 'elephant' of Napoleonic France, Imperial and Nazi Germany was to be killed from within. There is no high climacteric, only the sad and somewhat shameful narrative of decline.

Of the five volumes I have written, this last has been the most difficult because it touches modern times, a period not yet to be regarded as a fit and proper subject for historical discourse. Much of what follows lies within living memory; I was myself at sea in cargo-liners for a part of it and such personal experience makes objectivity difficult – some will say impossible. And yet the subject could not have been abandoned earlier, for it is in its finality that culmination and tragedy lie: this is a real story, with a beginning, a middle and – alas – an end. My close association with merchant shipping was small enough for me to avoid writing a memoir, but my later career at sea in public service spanned many years alongside the ailing Merchant Navy; I have, therefore, a distinct and at least partially objective perception of its death throes. Others have contributed to this perspective.

The great movements to which British merchant shipping contributed so much – imperial, commercial, social – have filled earlier volumes but they consolidated the successes of a score of companies and produced a new breed of shipowner, a magnate; remote, secretive and – converted by titles and honours – patrician. But such was the size and diversity of the British merchant marine, that alongside these great men's conglomerates there remained the small entities, owning a few tramp-steamers or a dozen cargo ships on scheduled lines.

The impact of the two world wars that disturbed the peace of the first half of the twentieth century and the Depression that fell between them had an odd effect upon British merchant shipping. It was widely and justifiably perceived at the end of the First World War that the country owed its survival to what had by then become – in compliment to its war service – 'the Merchant Navy', and to the rough, unpolished diamonds that very largely adorned it. Much of this success had been hard won and its ultimate triumph had necessarily implicated the state, victory not coming until a dedicated Ministry of Shipping – which had co-opted expertise from the industry itself – had assumed responsibility for the management of the merchant fleet. Until this improved state of affairs occurred, along with the scandalously belated introduction of convoy, British merchant shipping had been compelled to accept a high level of attrition, mostly from German submarines, with little or no protection from the Royal Navy.

After the First World War the Government returned the supervision and regulation of shipping to the Mercantile Marine Department of the Board of Trade, a ministry of state with many other less important responsibilities. In the following years, merchant shipping was largely subject to the caprice of the markets. This, to some extent, suited the shipowner; content with having done his patriotic duty during the late war, he returned to making money. There was nothing wrong with this; it was what shipowners did, and the service they provided was of benefit to both Great Britain and the wider world. When it came, the Depression was an opportunity to some, a disaster to others.

During the second great conflict fewer mistakes were made than in the first. Convoy was introduced immediately and, after some initial tribulations, the whole matter of supply was consolidated under the Ministry of War Transport. In the immediate post-war world, with Great Britain strapped by its debt to the United States and under political pressure to divest itself of its imperial burden, the Merchant Navy attempted recovery. Many new ships were built but in shipyards exhausted by war. Under-capitalised, old fashioned in their methods, employing a workforce clinging to increasingly outdated working practices and blind to the rising power and innovation of foreign builders, British shipbuilding slid into inexorable decline.

The shipowner observed this with a keen eye. To competition from the traditional maritime states of Europe, the United States and Japan, new threats were now added. The merchant fleets of the Comecon allies of the Warsaw Pact, secure under the domination of the Union of Soviet Socialist Republics were one source of competition, to which were added the smaller but growing mercantile marines of newly independent, ex-colonial states.

To much of this, successive British Governments after 1964 seemed indifferent. For the shipowner, the consequences of all this were as plain as they were ineluctable. If a British merchant fleet was to survive at all, it would have to shrink, and it was not a shipowner's job to preserve a strategic asset; it was his job to satisfy his backers. As ship-owning became less profitable he 'diversified', a process that often entailed odd outcomes; others simply 'got out' of shipping altogether. Those that remained played for higher stakes. Immense investment was required, among other things, to convert to containerisation but despite initial promise, the temptation of short-term profits to shareholders prevailed, terminating Britain's role as a world carrier.

Operating in a global marketplace, centuries before the term was coined or the notion grasped, the increasingly expensive British seafarer discovered that in a conflict of capital and labour the former is always the winner. He and his fellows were cast off to fend for themselves – one of the great mass workforces that had been an integral part of the Industrial Revolution to be abandoned. That he was preceded by the shipbuilders, the foundry men, the dockers, the fishermen, and would be followed by the miners, and others, was cold consolation.

As it had always done, the Merchant Navy rallied to the colours when the Falkland Islands were invaded and, as it had always done, it accepted attrition. But, as also always happened, once the conflict was over, global economic forces completed what the antipathy between capital and labour had begun and Government neglect had encouraged. British merchant shipping sank into obscurity.

The interplay of economic and political events, from wars to oil crises, the revolution which cast off break-bulk general cargoes in favour of containerisation and the integrated transport system, changed the very scenery of the country itself. Ports no longer existed in the middle of cities. London's quays and warehouses stood empty, awaiting the imaginative property developer. Shipping slid quietly downstream to Tilbury, Sheerness and Felixstowe far beyond. Southampton returned to its origins and became an out port of London. With trans-Atlantic trade shrunk and shipbuilding in terminal decline, Liverpool and Glasgow withered, though the former revived somewhat later, dealing in bulk cargoes of scrap and other post-industrial detritus. The lesser ports of the west coast followed suit, those on the east coats of England and Scotland flourished as oil and gas were prospected for and produced from the seabed of the North and Norwegian Seas, but these were new specialities and part of another story.

Some few of the incidents connected with the last years of the period under review glitter with the vigour of those of an earlier age but, at the end, the British seem to have given up the sea. Indeed the end itself is a surprise of sorts, being inconceivable for an island nation which subsists on commerce and the carriage of goods. If this last volume has a polemic ring about it, then so be it; in my own lifetime our national attitude to the sea and seafaring has undergone an incredible transformation in defiance of the lessons of history and setting at nought the endeavours of our predecessors. We are now where we were when it all started five centuries ago.

Finally, a confession: space limits my account of the Second World War, work which I, among others, have undertaken elsewhere. I have, however, lingered over less well-known events but, insofar as the Second World War is concerned, I have outlined the state's assumption of control over the private fleets of some of its citizens, and told something of the story of the Merchant Navy at war. This is all that space permits. Nevertheless, it is important to note that of the 2,850 Allied and neutral merchant ships torpedoed by German U-boats, 2,520 were sunk in the North Atlantic. On the other hand, 650 U-boats were lost at sea, 522 of them in the Atlantic and Indian Oceans, but predominantly the former. Some 600 years before Christ the Greek Anarcharsis declaimed that 'those who go to sea are only four inches from death'. The seafarer is never far from danger, though this is never truer than in wartime; between 1939 and 1945 statistically he ran a greater risk than his fellows in the armed forces. The fact is that the importance of the maritime war and the contribution made by merchant ships, cannot be overemphasised: it was absolutely vital to the survival of this nation and to the final victory of the Allies.

ACKNOWLEDGEMENTS

Many people have helped me write this history, particularly this last volume. Such generous assistance raises expectations; I hope I have not dashed those of anyone to whom I have turned for help, and that I have remembered them all. While it may seem invidious to do so, I must single out a few for special mention as they have been exceptionally kind in giving of their experience and wisdom. For help with the general history of shipping, George Swaine, Captain Brian McManus and Michael Grey, have proved both invaluable and indefatigable. Captain Peter Hore RN and Peter Nash of The Society for Nautical Research, have been instrumental in assisting with funding for some of the illustrations. For the free use of pictures Michael Charles, proprietor of the British Mercantile Marine Memorial Collection, and the marine artists Robert Lloyd, James Pottinger, John Morris and Malcolm Armstrong have been exceptionally generous. For advice on negotiating some difficult shoal waters, Captain Peter Adams, Martin Barraclough, Chris Bourne, Andrew Craig-Bennett, Jim Davis, Michael Everard, Captain Aris Finiefs, Max Gladwin, Nicolas Lampe, George Monk, Bernard de Neumann, Captain Ken Owen, The Lord Sterling, Dr Roderick Suddaby, Douglas Potter and William Thompson are all warmly thanked. For her help in locating some books on my behalf, Alison Harris of The Marine Society has earned my deep gratitude, as has Paul Ridgway whose advice, assistance and promotion of the project have been greatly appreciated. Many others have helped with information, sourced pictures or granted permission to use images or material. They include Alexander Aiken, Captain Roger Barker, Sir Michael Bibby, Charlotte Bleasdale, Quentin Bone and the Family Estate of Muirhead Bone, Captain Tim Charlesworth, Nick Cutmore, Martin Dick, Captain Patrick Duff, Michael Duggan, Captain Goddard, Paul Heaton, Martin Muncaster and Mike Stammers. For anecdotes, memoirs, yarns and information, I am indebted to John Ager, Captain John Bray, Captain John Burton, Captain John Burton-Hall, Robert Bushnell, Heather Cowan, Peter Cowdell, Captain Peter Elphick, Commodore Ian Gibb, Captain Duncan Glass, Professor Richard Goss, The Lord Greenway, Graham Hall, Vanessa Harrison, Elizabeth Hodges, Captain Frank Holden, P.M. Heaton, Robert Hunter, David Hutchings, John Johnston-Allen, Ian Johnston, Herbert Jones, Captain John Joyce, Professor Alston Kennerley, Captain Peter King, Cdr Christopher Lee RNR, Andrew Linington, Captain Michael Lloyd, Richard Lothian, Captain Brian Lucy, Malcolm MacKenzie, William MacLachlan, David Mole, Tom Offord, Captain Overland, Dr Sarah Palmer, Captain Bill Richards, Dennis Richards, John Robinson,

Captain Simon Robinson, Philip Roche, Louis Roskell, Captain Malcolm Rushan, Dr Ann Savours, Herbie Smith, Captain Ian Smith, Captain John Snape, Fraser Stuart, Captain Chris Sturke, H.S. Taylor, Captain Ian Tew, David Thomas, Captain Barry Thompson, Rosie Thurston, Peter Villiers, Philip Wake, Richard Walsh, Captain Donald Watt, William Whately, John Woodger, Donald Wright and Harry Wright. I cannot omit the Merchant Mariners of Wight, who collectively pooled their reminiscences to produce background information, and to whom I also extend my thanks.

It would be both unjust and discourteous not to record my debt to the many authors, both quick and dead, whose words I have quoted or whose books I have consulted over many years. To any whom I have unwittingly failed to acknowledge, I offer my apologies. Among these, and without listing their many titles, I must mention those stalwart supporters of the Merchant Navy, Roy Fenton and John Clarkson architects of the *Ships in Focus* series, Duncan Haws and Norman Middlemiss whose monographs on Merchant Fleets have been invaluable. In similar vein, further thanks must go to Richard Osborne and his colleagues of the World Ship Society. To all of these and their many enthusiastic associates I express my sincere thanks. Captain Joshua Garner has been a good friend to the series, nudging me continually throughout its writing and mining nuggets of information on my behalf. It is appropriate to say that his rescue of the tombstone of Podmore Williams was a worthy and compassionate act.

My thanks go to the industrious and tolerant team at The History Press, especially Amy Rigg, and to my agent Barbara Levy for her help and warm encouragement. My wife Chris has always supported me in all my voyages, of which the writing of this history has been by far the longest and most ambitious. For this reason the entire work is dedicated to her.

Richard Woodman
Harwich, 2010

One curiosity of Japan's arming in the 1920s was the lingering of the pier-head painter. They had died out in the west after the war, made obsolescent by the camera. H. Shimidzu, however, continued to provide ship-portraits, such as the Blue Funnel liner *Helenus*, built in 1913 but seen here off Mount Fuji, or off Fuliyama in 1926. (© Courtesy of The British Mercantile Marine Memorial Collection)

ONE

'CONFLICTING INTERESTS
AND ENTANGLEMENTS'

British Shipping in the Long Slump, 1921–1938

The 1920s and 1930s were turbulent decades. The extreme mortality among the armies ranged against each other between 1914 and 1918 had a permanent genetic impact. The surviving troops returning to Germany, joining their mutinous naval brothers, found a country under the unforgiving sanctions of the victors, paving the way for the eventual rise of the Nazis. Italy rapidly turned Fascist, though retaining a strong left-wing faction. Russia had collapsed into the arms of the Communist Party, raising the 'Red Spectre' of global Bolshevism, and the Austro-Hungarian Empire disintegrated, leading to instability and national factionalism in its wake among a plethora of small, helpless states. The Ottoman Empire had also fallen apart, creating new nations lacking in cohesion and drawing France and Britain into entanglements in the Middle East that haunt us yet.

Among the victors, the United States of America, widely seen as the saviour of the Western democracies under President Woodrow Wilson, grasped new possibilities in the post-war exhaustion of Great Britain and France. Having become the world's creditor, the United States reverted to isolationism, Congress refusing to ratify Wilson's idealistic vision of a League of Nations that, arising from the perceived failure of The Hague Peace Conferences of 1899 and 1907, would regulate international affairs. Wilson defined the League's purpose in his Fourteen Points – four more than the Ten Commandments, Clemenceau wryly noted during the Versailles negotiations – compromising the League's effectiveness.[1]

Britain's commitment to her alliance with France and her position as guarantor of Belgian neutrality violated by Germany had greatly weakened her, marking the beginning of a fateful retreat from maritime power, a remarkable and self-inflicted wound which would prove mortal to British merchant shipping. In sending an

Expeditionary Force to the Western Front at the behest of her allies – principally France – the British Imperial General Staff abandoned the tried and tested policy of relying upon sea power.

> By not adhering to her oceanic strategy and isolation from the Continent, *faute de mieux*, Britain became the linchpin and paymaster of the Allies, expending over £23 billion at 1914 prices. Thus by 1919, when ironically the Empire was at its greatest extent, victory was a bitter fruit. Financially exhausted and losing 750,000 men from these small islands alone, Britain still had to face a continent irretrievably ruined by the war.[2]

Elsewhere independence movements were growing in the 'white' Dominions and in the Indian subcontinent so that, although the tide of White colonisation was still flooding, particularly in Africa, the tug of the inevitable ebb was already making itself manifest. As for the people of Great Britain, the promised 'land fit for heroes' failed to materialise. The economic slump following the brief post-war boom culminated in Depression, combining with the destabilising effect of immense and tragic personal losses and the stirrings of fundamental social aspiration, to cause serious fractures in the fabric of society. The days of liberal politics drew to a close, giving rise to more polarised views and the undermining of the political elite: capital and labour were to come into increasing conflict.

In a reaction to the horrors of war, disarmament gained ground, producing the 'Ten Year Rule' which based British defence planning on an assumption that for the coming decade there would be no war. A series of international conferences, of which the Washington Naval Treaty of 1922 was the first and most influential, initiated severe cuts in armaments. Attempts to limit the sizes of the maritime powers' navies were unsuccessful because, driven by national ambitions, the most aggressive countries abandoned subterfuge and went their own way. Among the victors, Imperial Japan, whose navy had assisted the Royal Navy in the Mediterranean, rapidly expanded its new industrialised economy to create a huge military machine. Rapidly dominating the Far East, Japan established a vast sphere of economic influence across East Asia, creating a puppet state in Manchukuo and systematically dismembering the infant Chinese Republic in the Sino-Japanese War. This threatened the entire eastern hemisphere, especially British hegemony in Burma, India, Malaya and Borneo, Dutch power in what – inevitably – would become modern Indonesia, and American colonialism in the Philippines and the wider Pacific beyond.

In Britain, the political appetite for disarmament was so strong that it, almost alone among the Washington signatories, obeyed the provisions limiting warship tonnage to the letter, halting construction and leading to the scrapping of large numbers of existing ships. The Geddes-axe (so-called after the economist entrusted by Lloyd George to reduce public spending), fell savagely upon the Royal Navy. The Admiralty attempted to salvage the sacred battle fleet, but at the expense of smaller men-of-war – mainly convoy-escorts – while its neglect of anti-submarine warfare was to have a profound impact on the fortunes of the Merchant Navy twenty years later. Although the abandonment of several large cruisers provided hulls for three newfangled aircraft carriers,[3] the relinquishment of naval aviation to the Royal Air Force was another foolhardy decision Their Lordships would repent at leisure.[4] As Japanese policy revealed itself, in 1932 the Ten Year Rule was abandoned and two years later it was decided to re-arm.

However, by now Britain's commercially applied technical expertise had declined considerably, giving ground to the United States of America.[5] This was particularly true of ship construction, where conservatism prevailed and innovation failed. Great British engineering and armament firms contracted or closed, while in the manufacturing and service industries, bitter industrial strife precluded introducing new working practices. Ironically, one significant improvement, the conversion of many ships to oil-fired boilers, only contributed to problems ashore. The trans-Atlantic liners, for example, employed hundreds of firemen and trimmers and by reducing their prodigious demand for coal not only threw these men out of work, but exacerbated difficulties in the coal fields, causing a rapid and immense fall in demand. Although worst among the miners, industrial unrest was to characterise the decade. The striking of transport workers in 1923, the refusal of London's and Liverpool's dockers to work cargo, the Seamen's Strike of 1925 and the General Strike of 1926, all inhibited the smooth flow and profitability of trade, impacting upon merchant shipping. But other influential factors also took effect: natural causes such as ice closing the Danube in December 1921; a severe earthquake in Japan in 1923; a hurricane in the ports of the southern United States; a typhoon across the Eastern Sea disrupting shipping in Russian Tartary and Japan in 1926, and the freezing of the coal ports of South Wales in 1929, combined with a series of fluctuating world grain harvests to disrupt the flow of commerce.[6] There were military impediments too: the Turks laid mines outside Izmir; the French occupied the Ruhr coalfields in 1923; and in 1936 the Spanish Civil War broke out, all adding to the general air of uncertainty. In the Far East the Japanese occupation of Manchuria and the establishment of Manchukuo in 1931 and their unprovoked military aggression that led to the second Sino-Japanese War in 1937, proved to be the opening moves of the Second World War. To mitigate these influences, the governments of the maritime powers introduced protectionist policies, but without success.

Amid this turmoil there were opportunities; among other London-Greek shipowners, British-flagged ships owned by the firm of S.G. Embiricos 'carried war supplies including cavalry saddles for the Greek government free from England in 1922' during the Greco-Turkish War. The London-Greek firms of Counties Ship Management and London and Overseas Freighters chartered tramps to the USSR on long 'Sovfract Charters', but such openings were risky and relatively rare.

Occasional freight-rate rises gave grounds for hope, only to be dashed by over capacity because the world's tonnage had grown by a third during the war, while the volume of world trade had not increased at all. In 1929 half of the world's commerce comprised just eight commodities: 120 million tons of coal and coke, 44 million tons of grain, 30 million tons of iron ore, 20 million tons of sawn timber, 8 million tons of pulp and paper and 3 million tons of cotton. Coal and iron ore tended to be carried over short distances, 100 million tons of coal going across the North Sea and the greater proportion of iron ore going south from Scandinavia to Central Europe, or from South to

North America. In all this the world's pre-war premier carrier, the British Mercantile Marine, was the inevitable loser. Faced with falling returns on investment, some British shipowners sold-out; others retrenched, surviving during these lean years 'by paring costs to the bone and generally treating their usually quiescent crews extremely badly in the matter of pay and conditions'. The year 1919 saw the end of the independence of the 'senior' British ship-owning family when the Brocklebank family, along with the Bates family, sold their shares to Cunard chaired, naturally, by Sir Percy Bates. On the eve of the slump of 1921 Brocklebank had inaugurated a bimonthly service from Calcutta and Colombo to the United States and onwards to Britain. What was worse it had optimistically built a class of four ships which proved too large. The slump of 1921 had compelled Brocklebank to lay them up where they attracted crippling charges. The *Mathura* was moored as a floating hotel in Rothesay Bay, but this expedient was expensive and they were unsaleable as there was no market for redundant tonnage. Drastic action was forced onto the ships' managers and all four, *Mathura*, *Mangalore*, *Magdapur* and *Manipur* were shortened by having their central hold removed. Thus reduced in tonnage, they returned to viable service.

Curious trading patterns emerged: in 1932 several trans-Atlantic liners bore some thousands of passengers returning to their original homelands for lack of opportunity in the United States owing to the Depression, and on 6 December 1933 the Repeal of the Prohibition Act provided a much-needed revival in freights of Scotch whisky to New York. But such oddities were not long term solutions. Companies changed ownership either fully, or in part. In April 1935 the Anchor Line (Henderson Bros) Ltd went into liquidation and was purchased by a syndicate that placed Lord Runciman in its chair. Likewise Brocklebank, bought into by Cunard in 1919 but some of whose shares had been held by Anchor with which it had connections, was fully acquired by Cunard in 1940. Many other shipping companies, large and small, either vanished or, retaining their old liveries, were subsumed by the grandees heading the major consortia.

To exacerbate matters, the two great Imperial Dominions, Canada and Australia, both established 'national' shipping companies and the Canberra government reserved the Australian coastal trade for its own bottoms. And if this were not bad enough, Britain's orders for standard merchantmen from American yards during the war's crisis had wakened memories to the decline of the American merchant fleet during the Civil War, fostering a new attitude to shipping in the United States. In what was, to all intents and purposes a modern version of the old English Navigation Acts, a Federal Statute passed in 1920 declared:

> It is necessary for the national defense and for the proper growth of its foreign and domestic commerce that the United States shall have a merchant marine of the best equipped and most suitable types of vessels sufficient to carry the greater portion of its commerce and serve as a naval or military auxiliary in time of war or national emergency, ultimately to be owned and operated privately … and it is declared to be the policy of the United States to … develop and encourage the maintenance of such a merchant marine … and in the administration of the shipping laws keep always in view this purpose and object as the primary end to be attained.

Specifically, only American ships could carry cargoes coastally between United States ports, known as 'cabotage'. This Merchant Marine Act, better known as 'the Jones Act', formally recognised certain traditional rights of American seamen, allowing them to sue owners, masters or crew members for negligence, if injured. This protectionism raised prices, encouraged high costs in building and running ships and, in the very long term, priced the American merchant marine out of existence. In the short term, however, it bore heavily upon the British. Not only was hitherto British domination of certain routes brought to an end, but some American owners eager to avoid the constraints of the Jones Act 'flagged-out', registering their ships abroad under what would later be called 'flags-of-convenience', a long-established but hitherto minority practice.[7] Registration in the Liberian capital Monrovia, or in Panama, evaded the costly inspections and regulations imposed by the traditional maritime states, to which low wage rates and all but nominal taxes were an additional bonus to low running expenses. The full impact this would have upon British shipping did not become clear until the practice blossomed after 1945.

These then were the altered post-war conditions governing world trade in which the British Merchant Navy now found itself attempting to recover from the attrition of armed conflict. While hindsight indicates that the decline of British shipping began at this time, it was not immediately obvious. Indeed, there were some astute enough to take advantage of the Jones Act. Frederick Lewis – who had engineered the ousting of the Furness family from Furness, Withy in 1919 – by a series of skilfully planned acquisitions and mergers, was able to continue to exploit the American market despite these obstructions.[8] He established the Furness Bermuda Line, enhanced the Prince Line round-the-world service (run jointly with Silver Line), the New York–Rio de la Plata service which was augmented by the withdrawal of Lamport & Holt's ships for reasons that will presently appear, and the purchase of C.T. Bowring's Red Cross Line, which ran between the Eastern Seaboard and Newfoundland (then a colony separate from Canada). All these enterprises were run from New York, so that by 1938, fifteen British-flagged vessels were based in the city and backed by a network of offices and stevedoring companies throughout the United States and Canada. This arrangement, unique at the time and hardly replicated since, did not overtly flout the Jones Act but was an adroit manipulation of remaining opportunities, not least because of the Furness hold on Bermuda where, in co-operation with the island's Colonial government, the company had created an exclusive enclave of hotels and golf courses. This 'mid-ocean playground' not only attracted the plutocracy created by the American industrial revolution – the Fricks, Carnegies, Rockefellers, Morgans, *et al* – but took full advantage of Bermuda's freedom from the Prohibition Act of 1919. In 1921 Furness bought two Australian coastal passenger liners, the *Fort Victoria* and *Fort St George*, which picked up the rich and thirsty and ran them down to Bermuda, also carrying abundant fresh water in their tanks to top-up Bermudan hotels. It was these two vessels that initially formed the Furness Bermuda Line but the *Fort Victoria* was sunk after a collision in New York's Ambrose Channel in 1929 and in 1931 the *Bermuda*, purpose built for this new market in 1928, caught fire in Hamilton Harbour. There were no passengers aboard and she was towed back to Harland & Wolff's Belfast yard where, almost rebuilt, on 26 November 1932 she

Many images of passenger liners produced for publicity grossly exaggerated their size and power as this Cunard liner shows as she unrealistically dwarfs a lightvessel. (© Courtesy of The British Mercantile Marine Memorial Collection)

caught fire again. Declared a total loss and sold for scrap, she broke adrift under tow and ran ashore on the Scottish coast.

Lewis and his board then built two highly specialised liners, the *Monarch of Bermuda* built on the River Tyne and the *Queen of Bermuda*, built at Barrow-in-Furness. Powered by turbo-electric plant at a cost in excess of $6 million they entered service in 1931 and 1933 respectively. These two vessels provided 700 first-class passengers with accommodation of a luxury not exceeded in the major trans-Atlantic liners. Although constrained by the size of Hamilton Harbour, they were cleverly designed not to look inferior to the Atlantic giants that berthed next to the Furness, Withy passenger terminal at Pier 95, Manhattan, and were soon known as 'the Millionaires' ships'.[9] Service in these luxury liners was eagerly sought. Their crews were paid a 'United States Cost of Living Bonus,' receiving double the pay of their peers else-where, while the stewards received extraordinary levels of gratuities, circumstances that engendered a feeling of being among the elite, even – perhaps especially – when compared with the trans-Atlantic liners of Cunard and White Star.

Meanwhile the company attracted a steady revenue stream free from the vagar-ies of economic fluctuations affecting general cargo freight-rates. Furthermore, Lewis hedged his operation by developing Furness North Pacific Line from Europe to the west coast of the United States and Canada. Thus, in Vancouver, Furness, Withy stevedores unloaded thousands of cases of whisky from Glasgow not far from the American border. Lewis also backed a local timber merchant, H.R. MacMillan, in his plans for the export of timber to Europe and the United States, thereby securing the chartering, stevedoring, insurance and other services for this enterprise. He also sought trading opportunities with eastern European countries and Soviet Russia which resulted for several years in a steady stream of cargoes of timber and grain.

Smaller companies were also optimistic, among them Prince Line's partner, Silver Line. This had been formed in 1925 in spite of the poor conditions, from four small private firms which, between them, owned six ships. These had been built in the depressed shipbuilding town of Sunderland on the River Wear by Sir James Laing & Co. and would take advantage of the high level of trade then enjoyed by the United States, establishing a round-the-world service. The original ships were sent to the Pacific, picking up cargoes between America and the Far East. At this time a fully 'westernised' Japan was contemplating the domination of eastern Asia but devoid of resources, was importing at an extraordinary rate. Using the British Trade Facilities Act, Silver Line therefore added a further seven vessels, the first of which, the *Silverpalm*, entered service in December 1929, not long after the Wall Street Crash. The company's board consequently wrapped up the round-the-world service and sent all of their ships into the Pacific, establishing a Pacific–British India service, calling at principal ports only. By the end of the following year the board had negotiated a deal with the Java-Bengal Line run jointly by two Dutch companies and to which each of the three partners contributed seven ships. This new service was known as the Silver-Java-Pacific Line and left the newer of the firm's fleet to inaugurate another route running between the American ports on the Gulf of Mexico, India and the Persian Gulf, laying-up older tonnage. Clever use of broking agents enabled the company to survive the worst, and in 1932 it extended its services from the west coast of the United States to the Gulf of Mexico through the Panama Canal, and then to South Africa, India, the Straits Settlements of Malaya, the Dutch East Indies, the Philippines and back across the Pacific to the American West Coast. The success of this led to two developments: the addition of Canadian west coast ports and the integration of Silver Line services with the round-the-world service run by the Prince Line, mentioned earlier. This accommodation benefited both companies, reducing competition, enabling them to employ the maximum number of ships and allowing them to run light when insufficient cargo offered. This preserved all of them for the upturn of which the first signs were showing, though perhaps not in the most desirable way.

In 1933 the Japanese decreed that foreign shipping companies were precluded from carrying cargoes to Japanese ports, thereby encouraging the expansion of the already considerable Japanese merchant fleet. The Prince and Silver Line boards revised their schedules accordingly, but by 1934 increased demand for cargo and passenger tonnage from the Gulf of Mexico to South Africa compensated for this. This proved popular and in October 1935 Captain W.J. Irvine of the *Silverbeech*, a bachelor himself, assisted in the birth of twin girls, both of whom were named in honour of their birthplace. Further expansion through the Mediterranean was disrupted by the unprovoked Italian occupation of Abyssinia (Ethiopia) in 1936, following which the Spanish Civil War broke out, compelling much shipping to proceed by way of the Cape of Good Hope. However, trading conditions were improving and Silver Line increased its capacity by chartering tonnage from the Norwegian firm of Lief Hoegh & Co.

Besides Japan, America, France, Italy and Germany, others were investing in merchant shipping, particularly Norway which, aware of the quality of her seamen and their traditional employment by British shipowners, mobilised social aspiration. Norwegians seeking modest investments began putting their savings into shipping. A number of British war-built tankers, approaching their twelve-year surveys and causing anxiety over anticipated problems with corrosion, were put on the open market. Twenty-six were sold to Norway, two dozen by the British Anglo-Saxon Petroleum Co. – better known as Shell – and two from the United Molasses Co. Many of these vessels, which the Norwegians rightly ascertained were in good condition, came with charter-back deals, and young men toured the coastal communities of Norway seeking the necessary money, between £60,000 and £80,000 per vessel, knocking on doors for hard-earned krøner. They were remarkably successful, putting up between £10,000 and £20,000 per tanker, with Anglo-Saxon providing annual loans at 5 per cent. Several of the men initiating these purchases were ship-masters and the returns they received were handsome, establishing several shipping companies which began to insinuate their way into what, hitherto, had been regarded as British preserves. One such was Captain Wilhelm Wilhelmsen who, using the profits from his tankers, began building forty-five diesel-engined cargo-liners which captured a tenth of the Australian Conference cargoes destined for north-west Europe.

Although there were exceptions,[10] few British owners evinced interest in tankers while the cash-strapped tramp-owners were unwilling or unable to raise capital for such a new venture. This general post-war enervation was psychologically understandable, but it revealed that Great Britain was vulnerable to displacement as the world's carrier and, importantly, seemed unmotivated to combat this. Moreover, there was an augmenting bureaucratic complaisance that was to bedevil matters. Little trouble was taken by the 'Board of Trade' and its successors, to keep the syllabuses of the examinations for masters and mates up to date. This was of no importance in matters of navigation, ship stability, cargo stowage and collision avoidance, where the expected standard was high and neither theory nor practice underwent any great changes other than a slow increase in electrical aids. However, when addressing a candidate's general ship knowledge, irrespective of an officer's service, he was generally quizzed on the assumption that this had been gained in a simple, low-powered tramp-ship. The state's regulating authority was equally uninspired when it came to matters such as load-line requirements. Until 1933 these discriminated against British tankers while the readiness of coal in Britain predisposed British owners to remain loyal to the coal-burning steamship – precisely the vessel masters and mates were assumed to be qualifying for.

Britain's competitors did not suffer so from the dead hand of bureaucracy. The economies available to Norwegian owners, for example, not merely in their crews but in the relative costs of imported oil against imported coal, naturally attracted them to diesel power. Last, but by no means least in a competitive world, lower profit margins than were acceptable to the British owner and his shareholders naturally played into the hands of the Norwegians. In many ways Norway in the 1920s was analogous to England in the 1700s when multiple share-owning in shipping was common and syndics gathered round enterprising masters. By this time a British ship-master had little commercial input into a ship's voyage beyond being held to account for her running costs and efficiency, having become simply a heavily burdened employee.

The shipowner, of course, had long since distanced himself from the day-to-day running of his ships; his eye was on other matters, a seat in the House of Lords perhaps, or a spread of seats on several company's boards. Such men were tempted to indulgence. Naturally there were exceptions, but these were notable enough to acquire eccentric status of their own. Men like Lawrence Holt, who would walk the dockside and board his Blue Funnel liners in a grubby mackintosh to challenge his young officers' sense of security, was a byword on the Mersey, but even he kept clear of tankers.

A few British owners invested in tankers and, as might be expected of a minority bucking the trend, they were innovative in times of trouble. In 1930 the tanker market collapsed so that within three years 15 per cent of them were laid-up, idle and empty. H.T. Schierwater of United Molasses initiated a scheme under which trading owners contributed according to their charter parties up to 18 per cent, a levy from which owners of laid-up tonnage benefited to the tune of £2.4 per ton, though this was later reduced to discourage speculative building. The major oil companies tended to buy into the scheme by chartering, and as matters improved from 1937 onwards it was phased out but it had fortuitously ensured that a number of tankers were under British control on the outbreak of war two years later.

Nevertheless, it was largely the oil companies who handled the bulk movement of crude oil from the Persian Gulf to the new refineries and terminals such as that at Shellhaven at the mouth of the Thames, opened in 1916, or the Llandarcy refinery near Swansea and fed by pipeline from Milford Haven. By the time the Germans invaded Norway in 1940, her tankers had become significant oil products carriers and in turning their fleet over to Britain, the Norwegian government benefitted the British in their hour of need, but the long term effects were less comforting.

It is impossible to quantify with any precision, but while national ambition undoubtedly encouraged the desire of others to build their own merchant fleets and abandon their traditional reliance upon British bottoms, a movement which had started some years before the First World War,[11] the acquisition of tonnage by smaller countries reflected an understated lack of confidence in the ability of British ships to deliver their products and commodities in wartime. This was entirely the fault of the British authorities to introduce convoy until spring 1917, after many months of disastrous losses, for reasons aired in the preceding volume. There was also a growing jealousy of Great Britain, particularly among the Japanese military and diplomatic corps, who perceived a weakening of British power and, significantly, her concomitant resolution. But whatever the reasons, the cumulative effects of increases in state subsidies, quotas, bilateral trade agreements, currency controls and the general protection of national fleets, all combined to impact heavily upon British merchantmen.

Notwithstanding all this, and although under duress and threat, Britain remained the world's greatest carrier in proportional terms, though her survival as such was now subject to further influential changes in pre-war trading patterns that emerged as time passed. By 1914 it had become evident that the world's grain production was shifting from the Ukraine to the American mid-west. To this increase in American agricultural efficiency, the Intervention by the Western Powers in support of the counter-revolutionaries in Russia only fuelled the xenophobia of an already suspicious Soviet government when it eventually prevailed over its enemies. Such an

immense upheaval and its consequent repression of the Russian people further interrupted traditional trades, such as the ancient traffic between Scotland and Archangel.
There were some exceptions to this isolationist tendency of the Soviet leadership,
particularly under the pragmatic Lenin,[12] but once in power Stalin slammed the
doors on emigration from the Soviet Union. Almost simultaneously, the United States
half-closed their own against what was considered an excessive influx of immigrants,
some of whom were not entirely desirable. The Italians, chief source of this concern,
increasingly took over what remained of the carriage of their own North Atlantic
passenger trade. So too did the Germans, particularly under the house-flag of Alfred
Ballin's Hamburg-Amerika Linie, finally ending a steady post-war traffic, lucrative to
companies such as Glasgow's Anchor Line. On the far side of the world, however, a
steady stream of emigration persisted in the years following the war. In addition to
first-class accommodation for up to sixty persons in their coastal steamers, the Straits
Steamship Co., of Singapore, provided room for 600 deck-passengers.

> The Chinese labourer, shepherded by his secret society, was migrating into the Malay
> States in even greater numbers than in the nineteenth century. Between 100,000
> and 200,000 arrived in Singapore every year until 1928, to find a living on the new
> rubber estates or tin fields of the Malay Peninsula ... With no roads out of the island
> and no railway, they poured on to the Straits Steamship and other coastal vessels.

Among these coastal vessels were many owned by Singaporean Chinese, flying the
British red ensign, 'chief of which was the well-established Wee Bin & Co. with
sixteen ships ...' who profited from this vast diaspora throughout South-East Asia
and, like the Khaw family's Eastern Shipping Co. was later acquired by the Straits
Steamship Co.[13]

   Back home some state protection was offered by Britain's abandonment of her free-
trade policies and extensions of wartime levies on imported luxuries in 1920 and
1921. But the Government failed to maintain state involvement with a dedicated
ministry committed to a Merchant Navy which had so recently been considered
indispensable. Instead, in 1921, abolishing the Ministry of Shipping, the supervision
of the Merchant Navy was resumed by the Mercantile Marine Department of the
Board of Trade. This also assumed the role of the Admiralty's Transport Department,
along with responsibility for trooping, the overseas carriage of Government supplies
and the maintenance of contingency war-plans for shipping. The Mercantile Marine
Department thus administered all Merchant Shipping Acts, the Coastguard Act and
continued its fiscal superintendence of the General Lighthouse Authorities while yet
being only a part of the overarching Board of Trade.

   Such a retrograde measure was disguised under evidence of optimistic post-war
expansion. Shortly after its establishment in 1909, the Port of London Authority had
begun a programme of overhauling the old private enclosed dock system, amalgamat-
ing their police forces, regulating dock labour and beginning to improve the large
new docks designed to accommodate cargo-liners serving the Empire. By 1921 the
third and last of the three Royal Docks, named after him, was opened by King George
V, and in 1922 the new authority moved into its splendidly pretentious headquar-

Coastal navigation relied on visual observations and bearings. Lighthouses, buoys and lightvessels, provided by the General Lighthouse Authorities, marked shoals and other dangers. This sketch by W.M. Birchall, drawn for the *Blue Peter* magazine, shows the Royal Sovereign lightvessel off Eastbourne. (From a Private Collection)

This sketch by Birchall shows a screw-pile lighthouse designed for erection on stable sandbanks in the Thames Estuary. This is the Chapman Light, near Canvey Island in Essex; it was run by Trinity House. The lower apex of the structure marks high-water spring tides and was a useful guide to the state of the tides for masters and pilots. (From a Private Collection)

ters on Tower Hill, next to Trinity House. Before the end of the decade the Quebec Dock had been added to the Surrey Commercial Dock complex on the south side of the Thames, and further downstream Tilbury Dock had been improved by a new entrance and a modern riverside passenger terminal served by a railway link with the capital. Despite such major projects, there were ominous rumblings. With over 11,000 employees the Port of London Authority almost immediately began to suffer labour problems. A dock strike in 1911, one of many such upheavals across the country, had led to an agreement named after the port authority's chairman, Lord Devonport, a plumber's son but a man of aggressive commercial instinct. The following year the lightermen stopped work, precipitating a second general dock strike and, after the war, a series of enquiries into dock labour were held. Other ports, particularly Liverpool, Glasgow, Hull, mirrored London's experience, but in spite of her position as the centre of the world's largest empire, London had already lost its pre-eminence as the world's leading port – to Hamburg.[14]

In the 1920s freight-rates tumbled. In 1918 coal, that staple of the tramping trades the cost of which had rocketed after the war, was freighted at £10 per ton; by 1923 this had fallen to a mere 11s. These trading conditions eroded profits and dividends, compelling shipowners to review their costs and impose economies, but fluctuating freight-rates for over a decade caused over-capacity as laid-up ships were hurriedly recommissioned. This, in turn, increased competition and automatically depressed the rising freight-rates. It was not until 1934 that the general increase in world trade that had begun the previous year, had any effect upon the profitability of shipping. In such dire condition, with insurance premiums steady, fuel costs and incidentals like port charges and light-dues fixed – more-or-less – there was only one area capable of significant change: the wage bill.

To the detriment of their ability to hang onto their pre-war level of the world's trade, the British tended to react to world trends, rather than initiate them and eventually the Government was prevailed upon to step in. Amid the international financial crisis that followed the Wall Street Crash of 1929 Baldwin's Conservative Ministry gave way to Ramsay Macdonald's. In 1931 Macdonald's cabinet divided over the question of reducing unemployment benefits. At the same time the ratings' pay in the Royal Navy was lowered below the subsistence level, provoking a mutiny in the Atlantic Fleet anchored off Invergordon and echoing Merchant-Jack's reaction to similar treatment six years earlier (see below). Meanwhile Macdonald's determination to hold on to office led to his expulsion from the Labour party to which he had contributed much and by August he headed a National Government supported by the Liberals and Conservatives. He had attempted to maintain the gold standard reintroduced in 1925 after its suspension in 1914 by Winston Churchill who, as Baldwin's Chancellor of the Exchequer, had sought thereby to underline Britain's post-war economic recovery. But the 'normal' times envisioned and desired by Churchill had not returned and this had resulted in an over-valuation which led to speculation against sterling and contributed to the effects of the global slump on the British economy in general and shipping in particular. Eventually, in September 1931, only days after his new Government was in place, Macdonald conceded devaluation was necessary. The gold standard was abandoned and the pound lost nearly $1.5 dollars in its valuation, though this actually benefited shipping. Shortly after this and following the Ottawa Conference of 1932, a protectionist policy of 'Imperial Preference' was resumed, favouring trade within the Commonwealth and Empire. In 1932 an Import Duty Act imposed a more general levy on foodstuffs and industrial raw materials, raising tariffs against imports from outside the Commonwealth, but raising imperial imports from within.

As with Silver Line, others made the best of what opportunities offered, achieving modest success, such as the extension of the Straits Steamship Co.'s services in the South China Sea. Up until the war the Norddeutscher Lloyd Line (NDL) had secured cargoes from Borneo and had run ships between Singapore and Bangkok. The German defeat prevented NDL from recovering this and into the lacuna stepped Richard Holt. Eager to recover ground lost to NDL in 1899 when Alfred Holt & Co. had been obliged to sell their own Eastern Ocean S.S. Co. to the German giant, Richard Holt persuaded H.E. Somerville of the Straits Steamship Co., to expand eastwards with backing from his own company. This increased the homeward lading of the Blue Funnel Line which, like the Ben Line – with whom Somerville had spent his early years in Leith – was already benefiting from the expanding export of tin, rubber, copra and gum pouring out of the Federated Malay States.

One curious effect of the Depression in eastern waters was a Commission of Inquiry into the effects of the Conference System. Roland Braddell, a meddling lawyer with little understanding of sea trade, alleged that the depressing effect of the economic situation on Malaya was entirely due to the shipping cartel which he thought was 'an octopus which is strangling the Colony'. Happily the Inquiry concluded otherwise, though it would be fair to say that Dutch investment in their colonial ports in Sumatra and Java had diverted some trade from Singapore.

The devaluation of the pound made the impact of the Depression upon Great Britain marginally lighter than upon other countries with over-valued currencies. Where one fifth of the entire British merchant fleet had been laid-up in the early 1920s, only 17 per cent – 3.5 million gross tons – suffered that same fate in 1932. Nevertheless, Imperial Preference badly affected companies engaged in the frozen meat trade with the Rio de la Plata, chief among them Vestey's Blue Star Line. To counter this, ships were switched to the Australian and New Zealand routes in 1933 where Vestey's participation in the Australasian Conference had only hitherto included loading-rights for return cargoes. All the companies now engaged in this traffic which, besides Blue Star, comprised Shaw, Savill & Albion, the Port Line, and the New Zealand Shipping Co. and its co-partner the Federal S.N. Co., all built fine, fast, modern new diesel-powered cargo-liners. These were collectively called 'Empire Food Ships' and they were to distinguish themselves in the Second World War.[15] So successful was Vestey that two years after inaugurating Blue Star's Australasian routes, he bought the 'goodwill and services' of F. Leyland & Co. and transferred some of his ships to Leyland-registered ownership.

But other countries went much further. Led by Italy in 1932, Germany, the Netherlands and France introduced subsidies for their tramp-ships. Eventually, and long after these maritime rivals, Parliament passed the British Shipping (Assistance) Act of 1935 which provided subsidies to tramp owners. In two years £4 million were allotted to this unprecedented assistance and simultaneously a Tramp Shipping Administration Committee was established to help fix rates internationally, rule out unfair competition and deter voyages in ballast. A range of minimum freight-rates was secured, particularly covering east-bound grain and west-bound coal, 'though some threat to the scheme's success was offered by under employed [cargo-] liners. These subsidies and limitations went some way towards helping the British tramp industry to survive'.[16]

The Shipping (Assistance) Act which followed encouraged a 'scrap-and-build' policy, making £2 million available in 1935/1936 as loans to shipowners building new tonnage provided that for every ton built, two were scrapped. It was based on a Japanese model which had already been copied by some European states. In the first year 237 companies applied for grants, chief among them Ropner & Co., the West Hartlepool based parent of two firms owning a total of almost fifty tramps, which received £118,285. Andrew Weir & Co. (the Bank Line, with a similar sized fleet) was granted £76,780; a further £43,581 went to Sir William Reardon Smith's fleet of two dozen Cardiff-registered tramps. A similar sum went to the Carlton S.S. Co. and some £23,000 to Dalgleish & Co., both of Newcastle. In the following year the number of companies applying for help rose to 426, led again by Ropner (£47,741), Weir (£65,967) and Reardon Smith (£39,212), to which Hogarth & Co. of Glasgow was now added with a grant of £45,817, to yield a fleet of forty ships by the outbreak of war. A number of lesser grants were made – a mere £12 going to F. Bowles & Son of Cardiff – but this did not save several smaller firms from bankruptcy.

The scheme was poorly supervised and proved too tempting for many tramp-owners who abused it, using £3,981,014 of public money to scrap ninety-seven vessels, but to build only fifty new ships of half the scrapped capacity. This was bad enough, but of the scrapped tramps, only *six* had been the property of the tramp companies, the remaining ninety-one having been bought from foreign firms and cynically placed under the British flag for a short period. Unsurprisingly, with a new tramp-ship costing about £125,000 of which £100,000 came from the state, many shipowners made a fortune.[17] As British owners cleaned up, the bonanzas went to foreign firms who had sold old vessels above the scrap price. Thanks to a rise in freight-rates that made it less necessary and for which provision had been built into the legislation, scrap-and-build was abandoned after twenty-two months, but it had nevertheless left about 700 tramp-ships on the British register to bear the burden thrust upon the merchant marine in the Second World War.

However, as freight-rates rose, little existing useful tonnage was modernised and few emulated the Dutch, Scandinavians and Japanese by moving into motor-ships. These conferred significant advantages: although diesel engines were more costly to install and more technically demanding than steam-plant, they were far cheaper to run; their engine rooms, without boiler spaces, used less of a hull's capacity and therefore increased freight space; all of which enabled *their* owners to cut freight-rates.[18] Thus '[t]he diesel engine became increasingly economic for speeds between 12 and 17 knots for those prepared to accept its more exacting standards of technical proficiency'. That many of these were built in British shipyards, either under licence from European engine-manufacturers or, as in the case of William Doxford's Sunderland yard, of native design, was a double irony.[19] The British shipowner tended to stick to steam and while tramp-owners clung to the reciprocating engine giving a hull speed of 9–10 knots, liner owners, both passenger and cargo, increasingly turned to the geared Parsons turbine, 'as the most cost effective method of propulsion for fast cargo vessels of the highest quality'.

The change from oil to coal followed similar lines, the tramp-owner clinging to readily available coal, while more progressive liner companies with an eye to competition, adopted oil, with its advantages of cleanliness, no small matter in passenger liners. As Captain Bone of the Anchor Line had written in 1919, 'Daily we pray for an inventor to emancipate our stokehold gangs' a prayer arising largely from the unruly and ungovernable nature of these men whose conditions of existence were inconceivably tough, but a prayer not answered until his ship was oil-fired in 1928. Bone was fortunate; coal fuelled hundreds of merchantmen on the outbreak of the Second World War. P&O's 20,000-ton, 650-passenger-carrying liners *Mooltan* and *Majola* of 1924 were coal-fired, as were the slightly smaller *Ranpura*, *Ranchi*, *Rawalpindi* and *Rajputana* built the following year. But not all here were hide-bound; the Union Steam Ship Co. of New Zealand built the world's first large diesel-driven passenger liner, the motor vessel *Aorangi* for their Australasia to Canada service in 1925. Alfred Holt & Co., some of whose ships were supplied with 'Detachable furnace fronts for oil-burning' so that conversion could be achieved in a comparatively short time, also ran trials between reciprocating and turbine propulsion. In 1923 Holts adopted their first Burmeister & Wain single long-stroke diesel in the *Medon*, and a twin-engined short-stroke diesel in the *Tantalus*, but were disappointed in the weight of these engines. Typically, the company managers sought a compromise. This was the Scott-Still engine which used water heated in the diesel-engine's cooling system to produce steam. Thus in 1924 the *Dolius* was fitted with twin two-stroke diesels each of which had four cylinders with steam acting upon the underside of each piston, and steam being used instead of compressed-air starting plant. The combination proved economical, using only 8.67 tons of oil a day and the *Eurybates* utilised the Scott-Still engine until 1951, after which she spent the remaining seven years of her life as a motor-vessel. Holts abandoned the hybrids owing to their installation expense, investing instead in motor-vessels and building the small *Centaur* for their Singapore–Australia service in 1924. She was followed by a larger class of twin-engined cargo-liner in the *Eurymedon*, *Peisander* and *Prometheus*, the similar *Phrontis* and *Alcinous*, and the single-screwed *Stentor* of 1926 which had a single, six-cylinder double-acting engine. Similar to the original *Tantalus* were the *Orestes* and *Idomeneus* of 1926 which lasted into the early 1960s and had super-charged engines.[20]

Possessing solid financial reserves, Alfred Holt & Co. were well placed to avoid recession. They could afford to build new tonnage when the shipyards' order books were empty, unlike the tramp operators to whom the scrap-and-build programme had been extended. The rise in freight-rates that ended the scheme indicated that the upturn that experience suggested inevitably followed every depression had arrived, but hopes of a new trading climate having been worked out in the wake of the 'war to end all wars' were dashed. Alas, this recovery owed much to rearmament in reaction to Japanese expansion, the emerging menace of Nazi Germany, Italian Fascism and the Spanish Civil War, and although this sharpened the markets, it began to lift the curtain on another great conflict.

Thus it was only on the very eve of the Second World War in 1939 that trade stabilised, though some had benefited from Germany's defeat when some losses were made good by taking over German ships surrendered as war reparations, particularly among the large liner operators. Cunard's *Berengaria*, formerly Alfred Ballin's *Imperator*, replaced the *Lusitania*, the Orient Line acquired the *Prinz Ludwig*, which became the *Orcades*, and White Star's *Majestic* had been the *Bismarck*. But as one liner commander parenthetically remarked: 'We did not think then of the new and more economical tonnage that Teutonic ingenuity could later build in their place'.[21] One of the unfortunate and unforeseen contributions of shipping in the immediate post-war world was the transfer of the influenza virus which travelled home in troop-ships carrying the exhausted warriors of the Western Front. This had a particularly cruel effect upon Australia where thousands died in the pandemic of 1919–1920, but public health authorities improved, every port having its quarantine station and its Port Health officers. A ship that arrived at the pilot station flying the double yellow Q-flag hoist signalling suspected contagion on board, or a similar signal indicating an 'unusual mortality among the rats,' might be anchored for a thorough examination. If necessary a vessel was quarantined, or her crew transferred ashore to a remote isolation hospital, a necessary pale within which to corral infectious disease. As Michael Grey points out:

> There was such a place once on an island in Sydney Harbour. In the London River … a huge grim building … was the sole habitation on the Kent marshes and was the place where these unfortunates were kept. It was known as the plague hospital, which was an accurate description as the bubonic plague was just one of many diseases which might have presented to Port Health well into the first half of the 20th Century.[22]

These grim facilities were regularly occupied by victims of cholera and typhus; other denizens were withheld from offending society, suffering the final, dreadful ravages of syphilis, a disease with which the maritime world had had long experience, but which was to wreak havoc among the soldiers returning from the Western Front whose infection rate to their spouses – thanks largely to complete ignorance – was horrific.[23] Even before the war soldiers' deaths from venereal disease exceeded those of seamen, slightly more in the Royal Navy compared with the much vilified merchant service, though the numbers of infected men went unrecorded. Nevertheless, 'a man who joined the Merchant Service had, in 1913–1914, about twice the chance of death (7.79) that his brothers would have had, had they joined the Navy (3.25) or the Army (2.99)'. This was due principally to a far higher rate of accidental death, though many were related to intoxication. While inoculation was available against several diseases and the exposure to tropical climes meant a number of cases of malaria, the poor living conditions for ratings in most British ships spread pneumonia and tuberculosis, the latter being four times higher in lascars than in Europeans. Even a white British merchant seaman was four times more likely to die from TB than the average British male, and three times more likely to die in an accident than a coal miner: only fishing exceeding the Merchant Navy for danger.

The onset of the slump in 1920 again brought into sharp focus the primitive conditions endured in British ships, and not only tramps. In 1921 a series of articles appeared in *The Lancet*, describing the food, accommodation and mode of existence in various ships, prompting the introduction of a Merchant Shipping Bill which failed. Some companies were ahead of the game, providing relatively airy accommodation and good food, chief among them Eagle Oil and the Blue Funnel Line, but even this otherwise exemplary employer was stingy with leave. However, to retain them, most liner companies offered their officers leave-pay, although the seamen, fire-men and stewards always signed-on and off, even on the short, regular runs on the North Atlantic 'cracks'.

Tramp-steamers had changed little since before the war, in which the end of the British-flagged sailing vessel had come, perhaps prematurely, but no less inevitably. A handful remained: the *Monkbarns*, *Kilmallie* and *William Mitchell* under the house-flag of John Stewart & Co., but by 1928 this little fleet had dwindled to the last named and that year she was sent to the breakers. Stewart's London-registered ships were the last purely British deep-water sailing vessels, although the *Garthpool*, a four-masted barque registered in Montreal and owned by Sir William Garthwaite, was the last deep-water merchant sailing vessel to fly the red ensign and she was wrecked in the Cape Verde Islands in 1930 whilst engaged in the Australian grain trade. In the home-trade the barquentine *Waterwitch* made her final voyage wearing the 'red duster' in 1936, leaving a few coastal sailers, including an ancient ketch named the *Ceres*,[24] to struggle on in the West Country and on the Irish Sea. Sprit-sailed Thames barges and river craft in eastern England remained viable, alongside fishing smacks and bawleys, but the small diesel engine coughed into life and strangled the pure sailorman's craft. The one advantage the sailing vessel had over the coal-burning steamer was that for all her primitiveness, she was usually clean.[25]

During the slump of the 1920s a widening gulf opened between coastal shipping together with the bulk-carrying tramp-steamers touched upon earlier, and the liner companies whose closed, near-monopolistic Conference Systems were swiftly revived. These lessened the effect of the greater Depression which followed the Wall-Street Crash of October 1929, but this was only partial and must not be over emphasised. The severe down-turn in the world economy left no one unscathed, and disaster utterly destroyed one conglomerate. Nevertheless, although in 1931 many liner companies reduced their officers' salaries by 10 per cent, in terms of comparative impact affecting individual seafarers, the Depression was more keenly felt in the basic 'pound-and-pint' tramps where all scales of pay and provisions were 'in accordance with the Act,' conforming to the barest minima of the Merchant Shipping Act of 1894. Even here, however, mixed fortunes were experienced as when in 1931 the Soviet government chartered 96,000 tons of shipping and twenty-two British tramps found themselves in clover until freight-rates plummeted two years later, a year in which one analyst calculated that 22 million tons of space was wasted in ballast voyages.[26]

Least affected of all ships were the newfangled oil-tankers which, despite the sales of tonnage to Norway, remained significant. While the demand for oil was affected by the global economic situation, this merely slowed a steady rise. The Royal Navy had begun conversion to oil-firing from 1905 and ashore mechanised transport was dis-placing the horse-and-cart, with private vehicle ownership increasing. In 1914 world oil production had been about 45 million tons, rising to 95 million in 1920 but, by 1937 as the world emerged from Depression, it had reached 276 million tons. The actual exported tonnage carried by sea stood at 14 million tons in 1914 and 84 mil-lion in 1937, a rise from 5 per cent of world seaborne trade, requiring global tanker capacity of 1.5 million tons (of which about half was British-owned) to 21 per cent, or 11.4 million tons (of which only a quarter was under the red ensign).[27]

In the first few years of the 1920s the British merchant fleet recovered from its war losses, partly by absorbing some of the emergency-built standard ships constructed largely in the United States. Altogether it amounted to about 7,000 deep-water vessels which made up around a third of the world's tonnage at 19.3 million tons. This number increased by some 850 hulls to 20.2 million gross registered tons on the eve of the Depression when its proportion of the world's carrying had dropped slightly to 29 per cent. However, although the imperially preferential traffic to and from the Dominions and Colonies ameliorated conditions in the regular liner traffic, the global decline in trade ensured that one third of the British merchant fleet was laid-up. As already mentioned, this idle shipping consisted predominantly of tramps which were vulnerable, since cargo-liners could replace them. With superior speed, better cargo-handling gear and an efficient worldwide agency system often better able to locate cargoes than the central exchanges used by tramp-owners, surplus cargo-liners could corner the markets. Moreover, many cargo-liners were run to the immense advantage of their owners by expedients such as was employed in the Port Line's *Port Gisborne*, eighteen of whose 'able-seamen' consisted of ex-apprentices who held second mate's certificates of competency. Elsewhere officers holding first mates' and masters' certificates shipped as seamen and it was recorded that in 1933 a shipping-master on the Clyde signed-on a ship's crew of sixty men. Thirty-three of these were certificated deck-officers obliged to take work as able-seamen or engine-room hands to avoid starvation. This left those who might reasonably have expected to occupy the berths, free to trudge the streets unemployed, seeking sustenance in the soup-kitchens provided by the maritime charities. It was said at any one time 'forty thousand merchant seamen' were near-destitute, later studies revising this upward to over 50,000.

The preference for employing officers was clear: owners had invested in their training; their loyalty was more reliable and they were a greater asset to the shipowner than the ratings, not least because the ratings had, as we shall presently see, staged a damaging strike in 1925. Masters, mates and engineers would be required when matters recovered, so their preservation was a matter of self-interest to the shipowner, and their general steadfastness was therefore to be taken advantage of. Not that individuals viewed things in this light; a significant number of deck-officers joined the Royal Naval Reserve to extract them from a painful situation and provide them with alternative and steady occupation for considerable periods, an expedient that, in the light of subsequent events, was to stand the nation in good stead.

Although consisting of numerous lines with their distinguishing funnels and house-flags, the acquisitions of influential owners during and immediately after the First World War placed about a quarter of the British merchant fleet in the hands of five consortia: P&O; Royal Mail; Cunard; Ellerman and Furness, Withy. This was much the same on the outbreak of the Second World War with the important distinction that Lord Kylsant's Royal Mail Group had failed catastrophically and had been replaced in influence by Alfred Holt & Co.'s Ocean Group, of which Richard Holt was a manager. These great private fleets consisted almost exclusively of passenger and cargo liners. Tankers were, for the reasons already explained, generally owned by the oil-producing companies, while exceptions, such as C.T. Bowring & Co. among others, which had suffered heavily during the war, were acquired by the Furness, Withy Group.

As Ronald Hope points out:

> For the … the first half of the 20th century British shipping was largely control-led by, or closely associated with dynasties of ship-owning families – Inchcapes, Ismays, Roydens, Holts, Brocklebanks, Ellermans and others in the big groups, Bibbys, Cayzers, Runcimans, Denholms, Ropners and many more in smaller but … substantial companies … [S]ome of these men wielded considerable power and dis-pensed great patronage. Liner companies like Cunard, P&O, Union-Castle, White Star and Royal Mail were household names, and in consequence of the war some personal fortunes were immense.[28]

However, wartime mergers at inflated valuations left the controlling companies 'sad-dled with a heavily watered capital structure' and this was to devastate the Royal Mail Group. The impact upon the small tramp companies of north-east England and South Wales, which were backed by the export of locally mined coal, was equally profound. In 1914 Cardiff boasted some 120 such companies; by 1939 there was barely a score, a situation echoed on the Tyne, the Wear and the Esk. While these struggled to survive, the big consortia had problems of their own, especially the Royal Mail Group, built-up from several acquired companies by Owen Philipps, later Lord Kylsant.

Philipps' father was an Anglican parish priest with Welsh connections, poor yet genteel, a baronet with strong liberal but patriotic views.[29] Imbued with a strong sense of public service, Owen and his brother John intended entering politics by means of shrewd investment. In 1889 Owen had bought the tramp-steamer *King Alfred*, from which grew the King Line. The ramifications of the brothers' enterprises were complex and one senses Owen thrived on these labyrinthine complications. Tall and prepossessing, he networked well and, his eye on a Scottish constituency, he estab-lished the Scottish Steamship Co. in 1896. The following year the brothers set up the London Maritime Investment Co. and bought into other firms, such as the Mersey S.S. Co., in which Sir William Forwood was a partner.[30] Next they took majority shares in the London and Thames Haven Petroleum Wharf Co., then acquired their first tanker in the *Mexicano*, part of Northern Transport Ltd, a Tyneside concern.

In the turmoil that swirled round a series of shipping mergers and J. Pierpont Morgan's acquisition of the White Star Line before the war, Owen Philipps had been bested by Sir Christopher Furness. However, in withdrawing from a deal won by Furness, John Philipps secured an agreement from Furness allowing the Philipps brothers to acquire the ailing Royal Mail Steam Packet Co. Competition and weak management had produced low returns until the Chairman, Admiral A.J. Chatfield, announced there would be no dividend paid in 1902. Furness hoped to acquire Royal Mail's ships to join Cunard's, Elder, Dempster's, and the Beaver Line's among others, with which he intended to meet the competition threatened by Morgan's International Mercantile Marine Corporation and his British allies, Bruce Ismay and William Pirrie. Pirrie, the shipping publication *Fairplay* asserted, had 'as much [patri-otic] sentiment as a Muscovy duck …'.[31] However, in favour of securing the Tyne Steam Shipping Co., Furness abandoned Royal Mail to the Philipps brothers, and thereby the head of a small tramp-ship firm acquired a major liner company. Since this rescued a prestigious line from the predatory clutches of American capital, avoiding the fate of White Star, Philipps secured the approbation of Government, press and public. Taking over in March 1903 Owen Philipps told his new shareholders that 'much of the competition that British-shipowners have at present to meet is not fair competition,' urging the Government 'to make it impossible for foreigners or foreign corporations to thus evade the letter and spirit of the Merchant Shipping Acts, which make it abso-lutely illegal for a foreigner to own a British ship'.[32] This was a point well made, for in giving Cunard a subvention for the construction of the *Lusitania* and *Mauretania*, the Government included a clause to prevent the ships finding their way into foreign hands, notwithstanding the fact that they might be allowed – like the *Titanic* – to retain a British ensign. In April John Philipps confidently expected to restore Royal Mail's fortunes, but he wanted to 'impress it on the directors most emphatically not to be in a hurry to pay dividends again until you are in a strong position.'[33]

Owen followed John into Parliament in 1906 and took part in an Inquiry into shipping cartels, becoming Vice Chairman of the Port of London Authority on its formation in 1909. Now rich men, financing their businesses with complex loan arrangements, they both married heiresses. Owen was attracting attention, notably when he joined forces with William Pirrie, buying into Harland & Wolff prompting one banker to remark that the Royal Mail Group and Harland & Wolff were trading 'too much on borrowed capital and too little on their own'. In January 1916, amid enormous war losses, Herbert Cayzer wrote to his father that the Clan Line would run on sound business principles, 'not like Owen Philipps's shows'. Fortunately in the short term, John Philipps' appeal for shareholders' patience was largely made redundant by the war, at the end of which the Royal Mail Group had accumulated profits of £20 million. By then, in addition to the Royal Mail Steam Packet Co., the King Line and its Scots subsidiary, Owen Philipps controlled the Pacific Steam Navigation Co., the Union-Castle, Nelson (Welsh) Shire, Glen, Lamport & Holt, and Elder, Dempster Lines, the Moss Steamship Co. and MacAndrews, the Anglo-Spanish fruit carriers which had become part of Kylsant's Royal Mail Group on 17 April 1917; in 1922 he absorbed the Glynn Line. The acquisition of MacAndrew & Co. had financed the post-war rebuilding of this company by picking up bargains in the form of former German fruit-carriers. MacAndrew & Co., with all its ships now registered in Great Britain and with limited passenger accommodation, continued its trade with Iberia for citrus fruits, raisins and liquorice. In 1924 an express service had been estab-lished to Barcelona with the *Cortes* running from Liverpool and the *Pizarro* from London, the latter one of MacAndrew's – and thus Philipps' – first motor-ships. He had also bought-up several coasting firms and amalgamated them as Coast Lines Ltd. In the boom of 1919, he added David McIver Sons & Co., Bullard King's Natal Line, and – through James Moss & Co. – he acquired J&P Hutchinson, afterwards the Moss, Hutchinson Line. Like Inchcape, Philipps snapped-up standard war-emergency ships, distributing seventy-seven throughout his fleet. With Harland & Wolff, the Royal Mail Group contributed £11.5 million to the total new stock on the London market of £384 million issued in the boom of 1919.

Philipps had a philanthropic intent to better the life of the working man. Continuing to acquire assets, he worked tirelessly for several charities. Undeterred by the slump of 1920 and – unusually – motivated by an interest in new technology, he invested in motor-ships, hence the *Pizarro*. Applying for numerous Government grants under the Trade Facilities Act of 1921, he continued to raise money through issuing new stock, benefiting from the resuscitation of the liner conferences. He also introduced a deferred rebate scheme for outward consignments, a god-send to small traders.[34] By the end of 1922, rising to the peerage as Lord Kylsant, Owen Philipps had found a further £25 million, most of it by issuing stock paying a fixed interest of 6 per cent. This produced an over-gearing with interest payments in excess of a million a year, a reliance upon borrowed money and – with freight-rates falling throughout 1923 as evidence of the emerging slump – equity of diminishing value. In the following three years some companies in his group paid no dividends.

Kylsant, 'eager to maintain his reputation as a great employer' enforced economies. Along with other shipping houses, of which the most prudent were Alfred Holt & Co.'s Ocean Group and Cayzer, Irvine's Clan Line, Lord Kylsant emphasised that only by these means could 'large numbers of steamers [be kept] in commission' and the 'resultant unemployment of vast numbers of men' be avoided.[35] Like others, Kylsant tried a variety of expedients. Several companies, including P&O and Cunard, aware that the rich were less affected by the economic gloom, sent empty passenger liners a-cruising to great advantage. Royal Mail's *Atlantis* and *Arcadian* (formerly the *Asturias* which had been sunk in the war, and salvaged afterwards) ventured north as far as Spitsbergen. Cunard's *Franconia* made that company's first circumnavigation in 1926, leaving New York on 14 January with a predominantly American passenger list. She was commanded by Captain George Washington Melson and his chief officer, James Bisset, found his 373 first-class charges could be arrogant and demanding.[36] Other liners undertook circumnavigations, Canadian Pacific's *Empress of Australia*, for example, leaving New York on 2 December 1929, and returning 137 days later on 7 April 1930.

That year the Canadian Pacific Railway Co. introduced two new liners, the *Empress of Japan* and the *Empress of Britain*, the latter launched by the then popular Prince of Wales. It was customary for a woman to launch a new ship but the break in tradition was occasioned by the Prince's rather odd new title of Master of the Merchant Navy, a further manifestation of the royal connection which was rather meaningless, though it pleased some. The *Empress of Britain* was splendidly fitted out, of 42,348 gross registered tons, built with cruising in mind and capable of carrying 1,195 first-class passengers. Under Captain R.G. Latta she sailed from Southampton at the end of May 1931, her accommodation boasting

> real apartments ... There are no inside rooms ... Inboard from this sweeping, spacious [Lounge] deck is a succession of brilliant rooms. Each decorated by a great artist. Each provides its own setting for gay social life. In her decorations, her speed, her comforts, her gaiety, she is truly a ship for the moderns ... Her lavish dedication of space to a highly restricted passenger-list is probably the most astonishing development in the ocean-going world.[37]

Clearly there were many impervious to the fiscal meltdown, because an estimated 62,500 people experienced cruising before the outbreak of the Second World War. In

contrast to Bisset's observations of her first circumnavigation in 1926, Captain Britten's
account of the *Franconia*'s world voyage of 1929 conveys something of the inherent excitement, then novel even to the wealthy. It is a breathless romp, shot through
with comments redolent of contemporary prejudice, yet full of awe for the variety of
human achievement and the beauty of the natural world, but for the less fortunate, and
especially those at sea in humbler ships, this was a gloomy and fearful period.

While the *Atlantis* and *Arcadian* cruised in the remoter waters of the globe, other
parts of Kylsant's private empire were floundering. Coast Lines was badly affected
by the miners' strike of 1926 and the General Strike called by the Trades Union
Congress to support it. While the blue-chip lines under his control – Royal Mail,
Union-Castle and Elder, Dempster – continued to pay dividends, maintaining confidence in financial circles, matters worsened elsewhere. As freight-rates declined again,
the Conference System proved brittle, several companies breaking ranks in self-interest. Kylsant was obliged to admit to the shareholders of Lamport & Holt that there
had been 'no voyage profits for some time,' but the rise in freight-rates earlier in the
year had encouraged him to believe the worst was over. Notwithstanding the miner's strike, Kylsant continued expanding, Coast Lines buying up more small firms, a
policy which continued for some time. Kylsant's optimism seemed justified when the
miners' strike collapsed that winter and on 1 January 1927 he purchased the White
Star Line – from the failing empire of J. Pierpont Morgan. This was a popular move,
the American acquisition of this prestigious British-flagged fleet, notwithstanding the
loss of the *Titanic*, never having sat comfortably with the British public. Riding the
tiger, Kylsant now mopped up those shares that his group did not own in Shaw, Savill
& Albion, along with its subsidiaries George Thompson & Co. and the Australian
Commonwealth Line.

The Australian government had established the Commonwealth Government Line
in 1915 and built five emigrant ships named after Australian bays – of which the
Jervis Bay was to become famous. Two additional large cargo-vessels were built in the
Commonwealth Dockyard at Sydney in 1924. Although it had been renamed the
Australian Commonwealth Line in 1920, the company did not prosper and in 1926
the ships, which had not yet been fully paid for, were sold to White Star. Renamed
the Aberdeen and Commonwealth Line, the ships were placed under the management of the experienced firm of George Thompson & Co. of Aberdeen which had
run into trouble in 1905 and had consequently been acquired by White Star jointly
with Shaw, Savill & Albion and run as the Aberdeen Line. The merger drew to a close
the firm that had been made famous by the clippers *Thermopylae* and *Salamis*, and the
long-ranged steamer *Aberdeen*; its ships were renamed, so that the *Diogenes* became
the *Mataroa*.[38] Unfortunately the new owners had outstanding Government loans
redeemable in ten annual instalments beginning at the end of 1928, but a further issue
of preference shares followed and a modest upturn in trading conditions hinted that
Kylsant's instinct had been correct.

By now the Royal Mail Group owned 2.6 million tons of shipping, about 15 per
cent of the entire British merchant fleet. Kylsant controlled – or had interests in –
186 companies, ten of which were shipping sub-groups (one South American), with
several shipbuilding and ship-repair facilities (including Harland & Wolff and D&W

Henderson), and the diesel-engine builders Burmeister & Wain. The Group also owned or had interests in a variety of businesses including shipping agencies, brokerages, carting, transport, coaling, oil-supply and storage firms; three collieries; property companies owning hotels, offices and land; six investment companies in which the least shareholding was 84 per cent; steel fabricators, a photographic consortium; timber, wool, phosphate, frozen meat and other commodity producers; a trade and travel publications company, and a laundry. Besides its own major shipping companies, the Royal Mail Group had minority shares of 7 per cent in the Asiatic Steam Navigation Co., 3 per cent in the Bibby Steam Ship Co., 8.5 per cent in the British Motor Ship Co. and 23 per cent in the Compagnie Maritime Belge. These concerns were spread throughout the British Empire and other areas in which British investment had been active, particularly West and South Africa, and South America. That these subsidiary interests, in one way or another, serviced the principal business of the Group is clear; so too is the fact that one man – notwithstanding the greatness of his intellect, the probity of his character or the liberality of his intentions – could not in any real sense know precisely what was going on throughout such a vast commercial enterprise.

It was said of Kylsant that only he himself understood the complex share transfers that he had arranged between his various interests, but this seems doubtful, even though all these had been effected through just one, Elder, Dempster, in which Kylsant held 31 per cent of the stock – some 566,040 ordinary one pound shares – giving him control. Of the remainder, 29 per cent were held in residual trust from Lord Pirrie's estate and itself a 98 per cent subsidiary of the Group; 9 per cent was held in two investment companies which were 100 per cent and 84 per cent subsidiaries of the Group; and 24 per cent was held by the Royal Mail Steam Packet Co. (which itself was controlled by Union-Castle, Elder, Dempster and Lamport & Holt with – to further complicate matters – its own subsidiary, the Liverpool Brazil & River Plate S.N. Co.). Finally to muddy the waters of comprehension, Union-Castle was itself controlled by Elder, Dempster and the Royal Mail S. P. Co.; and Lamport & Holt by Elder, Dempster, Royal Mail and *its* subsidiary, the Pacific Steam Navigation Co. Meanwhile the remaining holdings in the over-arching Elder, Dempster Ltd were taken by other companies or individuals associated with the Group. This Byzantine convolution had a probable book value 'in excess of £60 million by 1928'. At the apex sat what the press called 'the Colossus of the Sea'. According to Edwin Green and Michael Moss in their complex unravelling, *A Business of National Importance*:

> There was nothing illegal or theoretically wrong with this system of ownership through cross-shareholdings. Kylsant was rarely tempted to inflate the ordinary share issue through simple paper transactions, to relieve pressure on profit or loss accounts, or to improve the gearing of a company … In most cases Kylsant took great care to ensure that investments in one company were covered by assets which had been conveniently depreciated …

Rich and by now patrician, Kylsant remained a man imbued with a desire to do good. Certainly he was trusted, but this cross-shareholding amounted to a complicated game of 'pass-the-parcel' round the Group and was used to maintain dividend payments in the blue-chip companies. Its fallaciousness was both deceptive and seductive and while dividend payments could be suspended in the less conspicuous members of the Group, as freight-rates fell, the Conference System tottered and trade picked up, the cracks began to appear. While Kylsant remained cool, others grew extremely anxious, particularly Royal Mail's auditor, Harold Morland, a Quaker of principle, chairman of the Friends Provident Life Office, and a partner in Price Waterhouse. Morland had discovered matters had gone too far, that revelations would threaten the security of sterling – and perhaps something far worse. Arthur Cook, a director of Lamport & Holt, was another worried man. He voiced his concerns to Morland early in 1929, repeating them to Kylsant, who appeared unmoved. Lamport & Holt's shares began to slide and Cook circulated his anxiety to his board. 'You can't get meat and milk from the same cow,' he warned. He publicly berated Kylsant: 'You have not even condescended to discuss the matter with me but have instead simply pursued a policy of drift leading nowhere except to insolvency. I am not satisfied for this to continue.' The trustees of the debenture stock should be told, Cook insisted. There was over £1 million outstanding to shipbuilders, a debt attracting interest of some £60,000 per annum. That matters had been allowed to run on, he went on, 'is nothing short of a scandal and can only be accounted for by your many conflicting interests and entanglements'. John Philipps, now Lord St Davids and presiding as a trustee over the Group's debentures, was also alarmed. The brothers argued and St Davids began to detach himself.

Kylsant remained undeterred. Seeking to increase the Group's failing liquidity by increasing the Royal Mail's 5 per cent debentures by £2 million, Kylsant issued a prospectus on 28 June 1928 admitting that:

> Although this company in common with other[s] … has suffered from the depres-
> sion … the audited accounts … show that during the past ten years the average
> annual balance available (including profits from the Insurance Fund), after providing
> for depreciation and interest of existing debenture stocks, has been sufficient to pay
> the interest on the present issue more than five times over.

Whether or not Kylsant believed this is unclear, but it was untrue. A list of dividend payments did not expose the fact that no profits had been made since 1920. The company's court authorised the issue without vetting it, and the financial press promoted it, consequently it was over-subscribed. Now, as repayment fell due on loans under the Trade Facilities Act and for the purchase of White Star, Shaw, Savill & Albion and the Australian Commonwealth Line, Kylsant attempted to renegotiate their terms. The Treasury refused any extension and then, on 12 November 1928, the Lamport & Holt liner *Vestris* foundered in heavy weather. She was one of five liners running between New York and the Rio de la Plata by way of Barbados, Trinidad and Brazil and had on board 129 passengers and 197 crew. There was no imputation of incompetence against Captain W.J. Carey or his officers, the *Vestris* succumbing to the onslaught of heavy seas that did damage to her upperworks and shifted her cargo and bunkers so that she took on a heavy list. Her pumps were unable to cope and at 14.00 the following day when, about 300 miles off Hampton Roads, Carey was obliged to abandon her. Although many survivors were rescued from her lifeboats by other ships, with 112 lives lost, including Carey himself, public confidence in Lamport & Holt as a passenger-carrier was destroyed. The threat of claims so severely damaged the line, that Lamport & Holt's passenger services were terminated. Having sold the *Vasari*, the remaining liners *Vauban*, *Vandyck* and *Voltaire* were laid-up in the River Blackwater in Essex, though the *Voltaire* was later used as a cruise ship.[39]

This was not all; by 1934 Lamport & Holt had divested themselves of about half of their forty-one cargo-liners. Meanwhile the loss of the *Vestris*, a visible failure of part of a larger enterprise that had 'been inherently unstable in consequence of its cross-shareholdings and its high gearing almost from the time when it had acquired Elder, Dempster in 1910,' prompted an Inquiry. It was not long before the Bank of England, the Treasury and the Board of Trade were involved, joining the lending banks owed money by the Royal Mail Group. Other shipowners were sucked into the vortex, most notably Sir Frederick Lewis of Furness, Withy and Richard Holt of Ocean. Many of the shrewdest business intellects in the country were involved. In a still difficult global economic climate these men made great efforts to stem a collapse which would threaten confidence in sterling itself. Sir Horace Hamilton, Permanent Secretary of the Board of Trade, wrote to Sir Charles Hipwood, the Board's Second Secretary and until recently head of its Mercantile Marine Department, admirably summing-up the situation:

> I cannot pretend to know anything like all the facts but it looks as if Lord Kylsant's methods have been unsound for a considerable time past. His various companies have all had shares in one another's businesses, and the assets were much over-valued. As long as he could get fresh money, he could keep things going, but he has practically pawned all he had got, and three things have come upon him all at once. Firstly the Treasury are pressing him for money he owes under the Trade Facilities Act, a very considerable sum. Secondly the *Vestris* case, which has discredited … Lamport & Holt, and seriously damaged their business, while incurring a liability to cargo and passengers which may easily amount to a million pounds. Thirdly the quarrel with his brother Lord St Davids has evidently come to a head, and it looks as though the more capable brother has determined to ruin the less capable … and turn him out.

By now the enquiry under Sir William McLintock was producing its early findings. In simple terms '[t]his meant that the Royal Mail Group had liabilities of something in the region of £30 million. The scale of the group's embarrassment was without precedent, and those involved seemed to have been stunned by the enormity of the problem.' The news reached the Governor of the Bank of England at a bad moment. Montagu Norman was in the throes of an attempt to reconstruct the iron, steel and shipbuilding industries amid the prevailing global economic chaos and struck out at both Kylsant and the Government. He urged receivership and the matter rumbled on; expedient measures in appointing Voting Trustees, including shipowners, to sort out the matter culminated in the final collapse of the Group towards the end of 1930. Kylsant, unaware of having transgressed, was quietly removed and sent with his wife on a sea voyage to the Cape in February 1931 aboard the *Winchester Castle*. The ship was followed by secret orders that no instructions of Kylsant's were to be acted upon. A few viable parts of the Group were sold off immediately and Lamport & Holt went into receivership.

Returning from South Africa in May, Kylsant was arrested in the boardroom of Royal Mail House on the corner of Lime Street, overlooking Leadenhall Street and St Mary Axe. He and his chief auditor Harold Morland were tried under the Larceny Act of 1861 in a case that became a *cause célèbre* and rocked the financial and shipping world. Their prosecution for publishing false accounts failed, Morland being defended by the brilliant Q.C., Sir Patrick Hastings, but Kylsant's performance did not help his case and he was sent to prison for a year, condemned for the lesser offence of 'issuing a false prospectus' in June 1928. However, the damage done by the collapse of his Group was immense. According to one authority it 'harmed the industry, and made it possible, ultimately, for foreigners to gain control of a sizeable part of British shipping.' Moreover, it 'severely weakened the Bank of England's initiatives in remodelling British industry'.[40]

In the more immediate aftermath, beyond unscrambling the financial mess, there was other work to be done. While Kylsant languished in prison, the question of his shipping companies and the carrying trade of the nation called for swift resolution, otherwise the strong foreign competition that had aggravated the *milieu* in which Kylsant had attempted to augment his empire would only too quickly seize upon its carcase. The best fiscal brains of Great Britain inhabiting the banks and the Treasury had prevented the wholesale bankruptcy of the Royal Mail Group in its entirety; it was now up to the shipowners to save what was left.

This upheaval has to be set in context. By 1931 the worst effects of the Wall Street Crash, which had occurred on 24/25 October 1929, had been felt across the world. The ailing Inchcape wrote from his yacht *Rover* moored off the French Riviera that summer that he 'had never known such a period of depression … It has been heart-rending to see the steamers leaving London, week after week … with thousands of tons of unoccupied space, so different from the old days.' He died off Monte Carlo on Empire Day, 24 May, 1932. It was perhaps as well. For the first time since 1867 the directors of P&O could not pay even a deferred dividend and as his place was taken by his son-in-law, the Hon. Alexander Shaw, the group's credit rating dropped to £281,000, which was bad enough, but other lines fared far worse. In the financial year 1932–3 Ben Line Steamers made just £30.

By 1919, Ben Line's owners, the Thomson family, having stubbornly stuck to the principle of each of their ships standing as an individual financial unit devoted to satisfying its 1/64th shareholders, found the company short of capital and unable to replace old or lost tonnage. 'The overdraft at the bank was in fact so formidable that the partners were obliged to pledge their personal fortunes against it' and were led to form a limited liability company, The Ben Line Steamers Ltd. Although Ben Line did not get some of their ships back from Government charter until long after the Armistice, they nevertheless recovered by carrying soya beans from Manchurian and Russian Tartary ports like Dalny (Dairen) and Vladivostock to European destinations.[41] In 1921 Henry Murray Thomson withdrew from the Ben Line board, buying two ships with which to trade to the Far East, later increasing his fleet to four vessels. Ben Line meanwhile, having bought and sold second-hand tonnage after 1918, turned to building anew and in 1921 completed the 5,818-ton *Benreoch*, followed by the *Benarty*, *Benvenue* and *Benmohr*, abandoning the clipper bow and bowsprit that had given their ships the soubriquet of 'Leith Yachts'. In 1924 the firm sold the *Reval*, the last steamer of its Baltic subsidiary, The Petrograd Steamers Ltd, afterwards buying out the remaining private shareholder. In 1929 the Ben Line board added the *Bencruachan* to their own fleet by building to the account of this subsidiary, though Petrograd Steamers were finally wound up when, in 1941, a second war compelled rationalisation. Thanks to their Russian contacts, in 1931 the *Benavon*, *Benlawers*, the *Bendoran* and the *Benledi* were sold to an entity called The Far Eastern Fishing Trust, an offshoot of the Soviet government which converted them into mobile canning factories to process the produce of the Kamchatka crab and salmon fisheries. This co-operation with a politically isolated government enabled the board to maintain a profitable if erratic trade in carrying the canned fish-meat from Russian Tartary to Europe, principally in the *Benmacdhui* and the *Benwyvis*. By such prudent measures, the Thomson board had avoided the fiscal horrors of Kylsant and that £30 represented survival.

The political upheaval occasioned by devaluation dislocated official involvement with the rescue of the Royal Mail Group, leading to complications, but this essentially boiled down to a moratorium on repayment of the loans under the Trade Facilities Act. A pressing problem was that of White Star which was affected by the falling demand for British passenger liners on the North Atlantic, and which had affected others. Having laid down the first of two huge new liners at John Brown & Co.'s Clydebank yard, Cunard found the first stalled by the Depression. In February 1932 the Cunard Chairman, Sir Percy Bates, approached Macdonald's Government for help. Only a state grant of £3 million enabled the construction of Job No.534 to continue. A further subvention of £5 million was promised to Bates and his Board for the second ship – the future *Queen Elizabeth* – on condition that Cunard and White Star merged, and with the subsequent agreement a further grant of £1.5 million guaranteed the combined companies additional working capital; the merger took place in 1934.

After the amalgamation, the two White Star liners *Georgic* and *Britannic* retained their White Star characteristics and on 24 September 1935, watched by a huge crowd, Job No.534 was launched by George V's consort Queen Mary, after whom the great ship was named. Once it had absorbed the White Star Line, Bates divested Cunard of the Anchor Line, selling its holdings to Runciman, and the Anchor-Donaldson Line became Donaldson Atlantic.

With these negotiations in train, another element of the Royal Mail rescue was completed. Two new companies were formed, one operating to South America, the second to West Africa. These new entities would issue shares to the existing companies for the purchase of their fleets and all other assets would be transferred to the new operators, leaving all liabilities 'to be met by income notes issued to the credi-

Ship No.534 on the stocks at John Brown & Co.'s Clydebank yard. On launching King
George V's consort, Queen Mary, conferred her own name on the new ship. Having captured
the Blue Riband, after war broke out the *Queen Mary* was soon trooping. Drawn by Frank H.
Mason for the Seven Seas Club. (© Courtesy of the Seven Seas Club)

tors' upon which the moratorium had been placed. In due course, in the spring of
1932, the first new entity was registered as Royal Mail Lines Ltd, its board chaired
by Frederick Lewis of Furness, Withy, now ennobled 'for public services' as Lord
Essendon. It consisted of the forty-three ships of Royal Mail, its subsidiary Meat
Transports, the MacIver fleet and the Nelson Line, with its four large and fine motor
vessels, the *Highland Chieftan*, *Highland Brigade*, *Highland Princess* and the *Highland
Monarch*, all built for the refrigerated meat trade with South America.[42]

The second new entity, Elder, Dempster Lines Ltd, was similarly constituted under
the chairmanship of Richard Holt, soon afterwards knighted. This absorbed the sixty-
five vessels of the African S.S. Co., the British and African S.N. Co., the Imperial
Direct Line, the Elder Line 'and Elder, Dempster's only steamer, the *Milverton*'. Both
Lewis and Holt were experienced, enjoying the confidence of the Treasury and the
Bank of England. In no fewer than twenty-eight meetings of share and debenture
holders, held in a week in March, their leadership was endorsed and in August both
boards had been recruited and their first meetings held.

Excepted from these arrangements were many other businesses especially the shipbuilding firms, including Harland & Wolff, and several shipping lines. These comprised
Union-Castle, which remained the most viable and self-contained part of the Group,
and the ships of the Glen Line, the P.S.N.C. and MacAndrews. Like the White Star
fleet, they all operated outside the two areas of interest covered by the new operating
companies, but matters now moved apace. In 1933 the Voting Trust was wound up and
the Cunard-White Star amalgamation was concluded the following year. At the same
time the Liverpool, Brazil & River Plate S.N. Co., was converted into a new Lamport
& Holt Line; James Moss and the Moss Line were liquidated and Moss Hutchinson &
Co. established and sold to the General Steam Navigation Co., itself a part of the P&O

Group. In 1935 Richard Holt bought the Glen Line with which came Jenkins' old Welsh Shire Line, and both were absorbed into the Ocean Group, retaining their red and black funnels alongside their former, blue-funnelled competitors. MacAndrews were acquired by the United Baltic Corporation on behalf of Andrew Weir & Co.[43] Shaw, Savill & Albion, having absorbed the Aberdeen & Commonwealth Line, in 1933 shared ownership with P&O. Both the Aberdeen & Commonwealth ships and Shaw, Savill & Albion were acquired by Lord Essendon's Furness, Withy Group which cemented its hold on the latter by ordering five refrigerated cargo-liners, besides building the world's largest motor-vessel, the *Dominion Monarch*.

As matters settled down the remnant entities were wound-up; others were reconstituted, particularly in the coastal shipping division where Coast Lines became a public company, having cleared profits of £360,000 in 1934, the highest since 1921. In 1937, as the various shipbuilding companies were resettled, Harland & Wolff was reconstituted to eventually become a public company in 1944.

This brief but convoluted summary does little justice to the rescue effort; it makes no mention of the subsidiary businesses whose liquidation or sale had to be dealt with, nor of the insurance companies and trust funds whose affairs required resolution; it ignores the banks involved and the complex fiduciary duties imposed upon individuals. These have been better dealt with by Messrs Green and Moss, and lie beyond the scope of this history. Kylsant died in 1937, his brother Lord St Davids a year later. Theirs had been a sorry story and while Kylsant's wisdom must be called into question, his motives cannot be harshly judged, for his attempts to mitigate the effects of economic disaster on the poor were as laudable as they proved misguided. Kylsant's anxiety to maintain employment at the Queen's Island yard of Harland & Wolff during a time when Ulster was subject to the divisive consequences of Irish Home Rule, were as well intentioned as his desire for a sustainable future for the poor of East London and while his personal wealth may have been immense, he never forgot the principals of his upbringing.

In the aftermath of his fall the efforts of Essendon, Holt, and those others involved in the rescue of the Royal Mail Group – Montagu Norman at the Bank of England, Sir Arthur Maxwell, the industrious Sir William McClintock, Arthur Cook, the Duke of Abercorn, the Runcimans and many others – were patient and constructive. Recovering from what R.H. Thornton called 'the crazy edifice' created by Kylsant was a tortuous business. Of more than passing interest, is the activity of Sir Richard Holt who, on New Year's Day, 1936 called on Alan Tod, the Liverpool agent of the merchant bank of Baring Brothers. He wished his family shipping business to take control of Elder, Dempster Lines, to move its operations towards imperial markets, away from the Far East where Japanese military aggression had appalled the West. Besides property, a wharf and a shipbuilding and repair-yard in Hong Kong, Alfred Holt & Co. owned lighters and wharfage at Pootung, Shanghai. They were, as has been observed, hand-in-glove with feeder services provided by Swire's China Navigation Co. and, with the new acquisition of Glen Line, Jardine, Matheson's Indo-China S.N. Co. Holt's anxiety over their Far East business was augmented because, following the imperial Japanese forces, came its camp-followers: Japanese business, including its shipping companies.

Tod instigated a review of Holt's affairs, revealing the largest private fleet in the world, governed by conservative business procedures and prudent financial policies. Even the style of office practices impressed, 'the partners sit[ting] on a dais in the general office … in personal contact with all their employees,' and quite different from the remote, patrician owners elsewhere. The subsequent negotiations were complicated, involving other players and several banks. They took six months and ended with the formation of a holding company and the liquidation of some of the lines listed, but Holt secured a cushion in Elder, Dempster against the exposure of the Blue Funnel and Glen Lines in the Far East, while Barings 'earned a lasting connection with [the] Ocean Steam Ship Co.' Meanwhile Richard Holt and his fellow managers of the Blue Funnel Line and new owners of the Glen Line had begun to replace the latter's ageing tonnage with the first of the splendid *Glenearn*-class of fast, twin-screw motor-vessels.

Delay in the final settlement of the Kylsant affair had been caused by the formidable Sir Vernon Thomson, a director of the Union-Castle Line which Thomson wished to detach from the *débâcle* and which was under threat from the Clan Line board. In due course Thomson got his way and by 1938 the independence of a publicly subscribed Union-Castle Line was secured. As a final act the Pacific Steam Navigation Co. was purchased by the Furness, Withy-controlled Royal Mail Lines Ltd.

Despite the difficult trading conditions the upheaval among liner companies had enabled many shipowners to prosper on a modest scale during the inter-war period. The predatory instinct that had led to Kylsant overreaching himself had not prevented other magnates from continuing their own acquisition policy whenever possible. When Lord Inverforth left the Ministry of Shipping to return to the board of his old company in 1921, he had already initiated a joint project with the Danish East Asiatic Company which had, two years earlier, founded the United Baltic Corporation. Thereafter the fortunes of Andrew Weir & Co. bear closer examination, especially as they were among a minority of owners interested in oil transportation. Following the acquisition of a few tankers, Weirs increased their stake in the carriage of bulk oils by founding the British-Mexican Petroleum Co. Ltd in 1920 with the twin-screw motor-tanker *Invercorrie* to meet the rising use of oil-fuels The new tankers, including seven built from wartime prefabricated sections made redundant by the peace, were mostly steamers and carried oil in cylindrical steel tanks. A French subsidiary company was set up in 1921 to handle oil-bunkering in West Africa; another subsidiary, the Lago Shipping Co. Ltd owned trunk-deck steamers which transported oil from Lake Maracaibo in Venezuela down to the ocean terminal at Aruba. This 'Mosquito Fleet' was to grow to twenty-five specially constructed twin-screw steamers, all built in Belfast and all of which were sold in 1936 to American and Venezuelan owners.

However, the company's main business was in general and bulk dry cargoes. In the mid-1920s Inverforth invested in twenty-one Belfast-built motor cargo-vessels, most of which were twin-screw. The first, *Inverbank*, entered service in May 1924, the last, the *Springbank*, only two years later. This was a remarkable achievement by Harland &

Wolff which was, as we have seen, operating under some difficulties, and demonstrated Inverforth's considerable faith in the new oil engines which were still an innovation. At this time the Bank Line's various sub-companies were running main-line cargo services between India, Burma and Ceylon, and the west coast of the United States (The American-Indian Line) with a separate Bombay American Line running from Bombay to New York and Philadelphia. Integrated branch line services widened this network with intermediate stops at Aden and Port Sudan if space allowed and cargo offered. Ships also ran between Calcutta and the Rio de la Plata, serving Montevideo, Buenos Aires, Rosario and Bahia Blanca. An Indian African Line took passengers and cargoes between Calcutta, Rangoon and Colombo south west to Beira in Portuguese Mozambique, then onwards to Delagoa Bay, Durban, East London, Port Elizabeth, Mossel Bay and Capetown. An Indian Chilean Line ran from the same ports in India and Burma by way of Singapore to the west coast of South America. Services were also provided by the American and Oriental Line between New York, the Malay Straits Settlements, Hong Kong, Manila and Japan; and by the Oriental African Line from Hong Kong, Bangkok and Singapore, to Mauritius, Delagoa Bay and South African ports to Capetown. Further regular sailings were advertised leaving 'the U.K. and Continent' for Basra and Bushire (Bassoura) with an onward river service from Basra up the Tigris to Baghdad; and sailings from Australia to Chile, Java and Peru. These consisted of only a few ships which were switched as freights dictated.

The Bank Line board now decided to reduce their tanker-tonnage, selling the principal British-Mexican interest to the Anglo-American Oil Company, to concentrate entirely on general cargo, along with modest passenger-carrying. To this end in the late 1920s new and second-hand tonnage was acquired. In 1933 they took over Bullard, King's Natal Line running between Calcutta, Rangoon and Colombo, and South Africa, which has been mentioned for its participation in the carriage of indentured labourers, or coolies. This service was initiated by the *Surat* as the India-Natal Line and the following year three cargo-passenger liners of 7,250 tons entered service. These smart white hulled motor-vessels – the *Inchanga*, *Isipingo* and *Incomati* – had been built to carry seventy first and second-class passengers along with up to 500 'native passengers'.

On the eve of war, besides the five former Natal Line ships, the Bank Line proper consisted of forty-three general cargo steamships and motor-vessels the names of most of which ended in the suffix '-*bank*'. Although a few were standard War-Emergency ships, most had been built in the 1920s and 1930s. Similarly named and otherwise indistinguishable from the others were five general cargo vessels owned by the Inver Transport & Trading Co. Prefixed '*Inver-*' there were also seven modern tankers, all German-built in 1938, which were initially under the ensign of the Irish Free State but in September 1939 Inverforth switched them to the British flag. By the outbreak of war in 1939 Lord Inverforth's empire had acquired other interests, chiefly the United Baltic Corporation. Consequent upon his links with the Danish East Asiatic Co. and its subsidiary Russian East Asiatic Co. from which Inverforth had acquired two ships, the *Libau* and *Riga*, sailings were extended from London's East India Docks to Danzig, Libau (Liepaja), Riga, Reval (Tallin) and later with more ships to Memel (Klaipeda) 'if inducement offered'. In 1922 the refrigerated facilities at Hay's Wharf shifted the company's Thames-side base, enabling weekly sailings to be maintained through the Kiel Canal until interrupted by winter ice. Prior to the war additional calls were made at Danzig (Gdynia) and Neufahrwasser (Nowy Port) while British terminals were opened for the carriage of butter to Newcastle and Hull, warehouses were acquired in many cities, and passengers were also catered for. From 1923 until 1939 inexpensive and popular holiday round-trips of eleven or twelve days were offered for £12. While most of the company's ships carried considerable numbers of passengers, from 1935 the 4,916-ton *Baltrover* could carry up to 200 and the ships acquired a name for smartness and promptness.

Over time the company acquired new or second-hand tonnage, for example in 1924 the *Suntemple* was bought from the Sun Shipping Co. She had been built in 1909 as the *Berbice* for Kylsant's Royal Mail Steam Packet Co, a twin-screw steamer which had been converted to oil firing. She became the *Baltara* but was wrecked on 11 January 1929 when on passage from Libau to Danzig, grounding off the entrance to the Weichsee River. A 'tremendous sea' was running and she became a total loss but fortunately her forty-three passengers and forty-strong crew were saved. Other changes included the sale of the original *Baltannic* to the Danes in 1925 to run on the Faeroe to Denmark service as the *Tjaldur*, though the vessel resumed British registry for the duration of the Second World War under the management of the Ministry of War Transport, as did a number of the Danish East Asiatic Company's ships, nine of which were lost in the war. In 1926 purchases included the EAC's *Banka*, renamed the *Baltrader* and the *Akabo* from the British and African Steam Navigation Co, a subsidiary of Elder, Dempster & Co. Ltd. The *Akabo*, which carried up to 150 passengers, was renamed *Baltonia* and served until broken-up in 1936. There was an increasing demand for passenger accommodation and in 1929 the Swedish Lloyd liner *Patricia* joined the fleet as *Baltavia*. She had had a chequered history since her building as the *Mongolia* in 1901 for the Danish East Asia Co.'s Russian subsidiary and she ran to Danzig until her breaking up in 1935. Other acquisitions followed.

Similar arrangements were going-on elsewhere, particularly in the Indian Seas under the house-flag of the British India Steam Navigation Co., part of Inchcape's consortium. The Australasian United Steam Navigation Co. formed in 1886 by British India and the Queensland Shipping Co., secured control of the Eastern and Australasian Steam Navigation Co. in 1919 and brought this into the now enormous P&O Group. British India's innovative use of redundant trooping tonnage for educational cruises was begun in the 1920s. Both the *Neuralia* and *Nevasa* were used for this purpose before resuming trooping for the Indian government in the early 1930s. At this time, British India's fleet listed sixty-six passenger liners of medium tonnage, sixty cargo-vessels, one small passenger ship and one hulk. These ships ran passenger and cargo outwards from London, Middlesbrough and Antwerp on a fortnightly basis to Calcutta and three-weekly to Karachi and Bombay, but its main-stay were the branch services. The Calcutta and East African routes were served by the large 'M'-class of cargo-passenger steamers.[44] Coastal services were run from Bombay to Karachi and the Kathiawar coast, to the Persian Gulf, Seychelles, East and South Africa. Similar services were also run between Burmese ports, Ceylon, India and East Africa; between Calcutta and Rangoon, Penang, Port Swettenham, Singapore,

China, the Persian Gulf, Australia, New Zealand and Mauritius; between Colombo and Tuticorin; between Madras, Negapatam, Port Swettenham and Singapore; from Rangoon to Mergui, Madras and the Coromandel coast; and from Singapore to Bangkok. It is scarcely surprising that B.I.'s black funnels with their two white bands dominated the Indian seas. This had been secured by Inchcape with the Victoria Point Agreement, precipitated by Inchcape's concern over the expansion of Holt's triumphs in the Far East. From its inception the Ocean S.S. Co., as dominant member of the Holt group of companies, had seen itself as a serious competitor to P&O and had, to the satisfaction of its founder, succeeded in spite of having no mail subsidy. By this time Ocean's interests and connections with Butterfield & Swire in China, and Mansfield & Co. and the Straits S.S. Co. in Malaysian waters – where the Holt share dominated fiscally but never operationally – had become too powerful for Inchcape to dislodge or ignore. As the coastal services of the Straits S.S. Co. penetrated Burmese waters in the mid-1920s, thereby overlapping B.I.'s operational area, and the powerful Holt-Swire alliance in Chinese waters steadily expanded, Inchcape summoned all parties to confer. On the one side P&O and B.I., and on the other Holt & Co., Straits Steamship and the China Navigation Co., defined three mutual areas of interest: 'The Indian', from Aden to the southern tip of Burma then called Victoria Point; 'the Straits,' from there to Bangkok but including Sumatra, Borneo and the southern Philippines; and 'the China' area which embraced the northern Philippines, the entire coast of China, Japan and Russian Tartary as far as the Arctic circle. A complex set of 'service agreements' were formulated such that the P&O and B.I. interest was preserved in the 'Indian' area, competition was restricted in 'the Straits' area to Holt's Blue Funnel Liners and the ships of the China Navigation Co. with the Straits S.S. Co. providing coastal feeder services and having wider access to the 'China' area. P&O and B.I. would meanwhile confine their branch-line services to an agreed limit. Similar provisions were made for the 'China' area in respect of the liner companies where predominance would be with the Holt-Swire faction, corresponding to that of P&O and B.I. in the 'Indian'. The Agreement, applying to the coastal and branch line traffic of the participants, was signed on 21 May 1925. As a mutually acceptable and pragmatic resolution to the problem of British competition on these coasts it proved enduring, long out-living the devastation to the local economies caused by the Depression and the Second World War. It was of enormous benefit to those same economies and all their many and varied participants when trade improved again, providing stability and steady costs, enabling the entire area to prosper.

Prior to the signing of the agreement, B.I.'s *Mulbera* [45] under Captain Walter Steadman, embarked the Duke and Duchess of York at Marseilles on 5 December 1924 and carried the royal pair to Mombasa for a tour of Tanganyika, Uganda and Kenya. On the 22nd the Royal Party disembarked at Kilindini, where 'a crowd of thousands of Africans, Arabs, Somalis and Indians greeted the visitors with hoarse cheering'. Expressing her appreciation to Inchcape, the Duchess – afterwards Queen Elizabeth, consort of George VI and later still the Queen Mother, wrote: 'The Captain and officers were so helpful, and my husband, having been in the Navy, was much struck by the way the ship was run, and by the discipline and punctuality maintained on board.' [46] On the outward passage they had met the P&O liner *Caledonia* at Port Said. She too was carrying royalty, Prince and Princess Arthur of Connaught and Strathearn, who were on their way to India. The Yorks returned home aboard P&O's *Maloja*.

By 1932 the main P&O fleet consisted of twenty-five large passenger liners, eighteen cargo and cargo-passenger-liners, all of which were variously employed on services from Britain outwards to Australia, the Far East, and the Indian sub-continent (Bombay and Karachi). It will be appreciated that these two major components of the greater P&O Group carried an immense traffic in people, cargo and mails across a major portion of the world which was also of importance to the British Commonwealth and Empire. In this sense it was P&O, running to India, the Far East and Australasia, and not Cunard on the Western Ocean, which became symbolic of British imperial pretensions. Nevertheless, the warp and weft of imperial communications was complex; as British India's M-class ran down the east coast of Africa from Mogadishu to Durban, Union-Castle's *Llanstephan Castle* and *Llandovery Castle* came round the Cape from the westwards. This cut two days off the voyage time but cost £57 – for a first-class passenger in 1937 – a £9 premium for the privilege. Competition between the two companies was 'more congenial than cut-throat and tickets … were interchangeable for passage to ports common to both'.[47]

Until the introduction of the long-haul airliner all but the shortest of overseas travel was by ship. The experience of being a passenger aboard a liner was therefore common to many people of all classes, from the impecunious emigrant or wretched private soldier on an overseas posting, to the film-star, diva or rich industrialist. It has been all but forgotten a half-century later so it is, perhaps, not out-of-place to admit one view of his fellow passengers by an observant fellow-traveller. In 1921 Cecil Lewis made a passage to China and had this to say of his shipmates:

> The first few days … were a time of getting acquainted … But, Port Said left behind, the clammy heat of the Red Sea began to shorten the temper and warm the blood. Definite cliques began to form, bridge fours, and dancing partners, while the warm nights and warmer days discouraged our energetic walking of the deck and prepared the way for those interminable conversations, leaning over the side, watching the swirl past of the water and the rising of the moon. Aden, with its magnificent and barren peaks, where the buzzards soared interminably on still wings, released us from the oppressive damp; but the temperature itself rose still higher. Partners were now definitely set. At least one love affair was well alight, and other fires were laid ready to go off at a touch. It was a beautiful example of temperature on temperament. Drinking rose steadily in volume and violence, for there was nothing to do day or night. Idleness and the maddening propinquity so worked on vows of chastity or fidelity that, by the time the ship was half way across the Indian Ocean on her ten day course (*sic*) to Colombo, morals were at a discount and scandal could not keep pace with the rapidity of developments. Couples came together brazenly, violently, and as rapidly flew apart, hearts were broken, men rowed and threatened to throw themselves overboard, girls burst into floods of tears when offered cups of tea. A few married couples, mostly English, old hands and used to the scene, looked on tolerantly and retained their integrity; but the rest of the ship was all to hell and rather enjoying its dissolution.[48]

A cadet's view was less tolerant: 'The ship is riddled with gossip of an unusually spiteful and nasty nature, and the whole ship seems in a state of upheaval with petty jealousies and malicious talk.' Such descriptions might stand for most voyages made east of Suez before the rise of air travel in the mid-1960s, an irony since Lewis was both a First World War flying ace and a post-war pioneer of commercial aviation.

Among the passengers carried out to the far flung possessions of the British Empire by ship were large numbers of the industrial poor, encouraged by campaigns intended to resettle them in better conditions. In aftermath of the First World War the British sought to redefine their relationship with their Empire, aware of the growing independence movement in India and the increasing self-sufficiency of the new, semi-independent 'Dominions' of Australia and Canada. Britain was overcrowded, overburdened by impoverished inhabitants of its industrial cities for whose abject penury there seemed no solution other than a disguised form of transportation. Trumpeted as providing unprecedented opportunity, but taking up those utterly unable to defend themselves, the authorities began to ship children in the hands of the Voluntary Societies – the orphaned, abandoned or illegitimate – to the Antipodes, a curious reprise on the carriage of convicts of the previous century. Beyond these hapless children whose fates already rested upon the charity of others, assisted-passages were encouraged, as a P&O Branch Line poster of the 1920s explained 'if nominated by Friends in Australia and approved by [the] Australian Government'. The passage cost £16 10s, less than half the full one-class price at a time when, on the eve of the Wall Street Crash, this company's credit balance stood at just over £1 million.

Some small indication of the upheavals and changes caused in company boardrooms by the economic conditions in these twenty tumultuous years is given in the fore-going. At one end of the spectrum the traditional tramp-owner had clung to the wreckage of the bulk-carrying trade, steadfastly refusing to adopt new methods and, in fairness, in some cases unable to do so. At the other, the liner companies had, largely by circumstantial means, consolidated and rationalised British liner tonnage. While other nations had done proportionately better with state subsidies and protectionism, the British merchant fleet had at least survived the turmoil. On the eve of war in 1939 it consisted of 17,891,000 gross registered tons, with a further 3,111,000 tons owned in Canada and Australia. Although much of its tramp-tonnage was worn-out and overly reliant upon standard-built ships from the previous conflict, its liner-fleet was in better shape. What remained less certain was the quality of its manpower and this was brought to the nation's attention in 1925 in the most unfortunate of ways.

A dock-workers' strike in 1889 had been the first serious manifestation of 'the labour movement' and was to many regarded as a threat to the natural order of things and seen by those remote from the stews of industrial conurbations as a direct attack on the fundamental heart of the state which stood at the summit of its imperial aggrandisement. That this pinnacle had been reached thanks as much to the sweat and labour of toiling masses in the factories of the 'Mother Country' or the plantations of the colonies as to the acumen of their masters, was not taken into much account by the political class. Less notice was taken of the saltwater estrangement induced by the sea life of those who linked the outputs of the two ends of the process. On the contrary, it was felt that sufficient progress was being made in matters of public health and education to justify a sense of national progress and well-being, against which the attitude of the dockers was characterised as base.

However, the aspirations of working people were unlocked by progress, not suppressed by it. If change was possible, then why delay it? Was it not for the good of all? While the Fabian movement, established in 1884, argued that the betterment of the disadvantaged tended to improve the moral quality of the whole, after the Bolshevik revolution in Russia in 1917 such stirrings were seen by the ruling elite as downright dangerous and a direct threat to national stability. But then, as now, extreme disparities in wealth and conditions tended to destabilise society, and when the worst effects of the global slump resulted in tumbling freight-rates, disturbance was inevitable.

Following the first slump in 1920 the leader of the Seamen's Union, Havelock Wilson, had accepted a radical cut in pay amounting to one-third of the ratings' wages. Moreover he showed no interest in Mr Sexton's proposed Bill introduced the following year for ameliorating the conditions of seafarers. A former seafarer, Wilson was by this time not only the leader of the National Sailors' and Firemen's Union, but a sitting Liberal MP. He was popularly held to have 'sold-out' to the shipowners during settlement of the industrial disputes of 1912, and he certainly regarded his position not as a mediator acting according to the expressed wishes of his members, but as a pragmatic problem solver, a man with whom the shipowners could do business and whose decision was – at least in his own opinion – the best deal he could cut on behalf of his members. In truth his position was difficult; although widely vilified for submitting to the shipowners whose position he perfectly understood, Wilson was actually attempting to preserve jobs. What his members wished him to do – reduce the personal wealth of individual shipowners and suspend dividend payments to shareholders in order to mitigate their own sufferings – though not impossible, was pie-in-the sky. It was quickly pointed out that the market affected share-prices while personal wealth was, of course, inviolate. Nevertheless, the seafarers' plight was dire. An able-seaman's wage at the end of the war was £14.5 and in a succession of cuts between May 1921 and May 1923, it dropped to £9. There were at this time about 200,000 seafarers employed in the British Merchant Navy, a reduction from the pre-war peak of 245,619. Of these, a considerable proportion was made up of officers, but the grand statistic also includes 56,000 who were lascars and 15,000 of 'foreign – mainly European – nationality'. For the seaman, fireman and steward life was grim. As a chaplain from the Missions to Seamen wrote in 1930:

> The sailor's life is perilous at best. His liability to death from violence and to accident is fourfold that of the ordinary man; his mortality from disease is said to exceed the average by 48.8 per cent ... Some ship-owners have always dealt fairly by their men; today it would be easy to name a number who take far seeing and generous action for their comfort. Some, indeed many, ships' officers have learned how to rule by virtue of character and efficiency rather than by force and are the centre of a fine God-fearing influence which pervades the whole ship. But now and again – even in the present – there are ship-owners who risk all for profit, or masters and mates who are harsh to their crews ... [T]he sailor looks for further improvement ... with the great body of the nation's workers who are looking to a fuller adjustment of life.[49]

Ratings were paid overtime, though work earning this extra money was at the discretion of a ship's senior officers, and it was often circumvented, essential tasks being undertaken by apprentices to whom no overtime was paid. Although, as Ronald Hope points out: 'Since they did not have the same expenses, ratings were financially better off than junior officers', the rate of pay at £9 per month for able-seamen and a little more – ten shillings – for firemen, was barely adequate. The Cooks' and Stewards' Union resisted Wilson's high-handed action which arose from an insoluble problem: organising seafarers in the sense that other working men were increasingly organised, was impossible. Dispersed across the globe and further fragmented on board ship by the quality of the prevailing regime of a master and his officers, and by the divisive nature of their respective departments, each with their cultural baggage, made seeking consensus a non-starter. Considered *en masse*, they were the least tractable of men.

Unlike the days of sailing vessels when the blue-water sailorman had usually been an unmarried loner, sufficient numbers of seafarers in the steamers now making-up the Merchant Navy had families to support, so reduced pay caused real hardship, £9 being insufficient to maintain a family in the 1920s. Existence became contingent upon a seafarer's wife drawing social benefit, or Poor Law relief. In ships having non-European crews the situation was no less severe, though the level of poverty among dependants is less easy to determine. Nevertheless: 'Lascars received 30 rupees a month, the equivalent of 45s., and their living conditions in many ships were abominable,' a fact Mr Sexton, MP for St Helen's, had sought to address.

The signs of economic recovery of 1924/5 proved illusory, but early in the year Wilson negotiated a partial restitution of £1, bringing an able-seaman's wage to £10 a month. Although an improvement, it brought Wilson little favour, and resentment flared that August when, without reference to his widely scattered members, Wilson *offered* the shipowners a further 10 per cent cut. The move gained Lord Inchcape's approval; he praised Wilson for his understanding of economics, claiming that he had 'done better for his men than any other leader'. Once they heard the news 'his men' thought otherwise and walked off their ships in droves in the ports of Australia, New Zealand and South Africa where their distress and their exploitation by the capitalists of London, Liverpool and Glasgow found a ready sympathy. It is a measure of the prevailing racial attitudes that from New Zealand the striking seamen claimed that not only were they engaged in a perilous occupation, but that they were the lowest paid 'white workers' in the world, a claim 'that gave rise to strong racial antagonisms'.

Interviewed by journalists in Western Australia one articulate steward deposed that of the £8.25 of his monthly wage, he made a weekly allotment of £1.50 to his wife. As this was paid at fourteen-day intervals:

> in order that my wife may live for the first fortnight [of a voyage] I draw an advance of £3. The voyages to Australia and back usually take three and a half months ... [for which] I would receive in wages £28 17s 6d [£2.855]. First of all there is the £3 in advance; then there are seven allotments of £3 per fortnight ... £1 must be paid for unemployment and national health insurance. That is compulsory ... It is impossible for a man to avoid some small expenditure; such things as tobacco and other incidentals. Put that down as £1 for the trip ... Now without expending one

half-penny on myself for clothing and enjoyment I would have between £2 and
£3 to draw when I was paid off in London. [At this point his union's officers] will
be waiting to claim another £1 for union dues. As a rule a ship [is] … about three
weeks in London, and for two weeks of that time I am unemployed …

It was therefore necessary for:

The majority of the lower paid men on British vessels [when in their home ports,
to] go on the dole right away. They are compelled to do this: it is the only possible
way they have of living until they sign on a vessel again. I may say that several of the
men on British ships today receive Poor Law relief. The wages today is not sufficient
to purchase the requirements for themselves or their families.[50]

This last admission was altogether shameful and provoked the Anglican Dean of
Melbourne, The Reverend J. S. Hart, to state that it was 'nonsense' to say that the shipping industry could not sustain higher wages.

If it can stand 'luxury ships' and pay good dividends on a heavily watered capital, it
can do simple justice to its employees. Ship-owners are not looked upon as a very
poverty-stricken class, and nowadays [thanks to the Conference System] they have
abolished competition, and, having a monopoly, can make their charges sufficient
to cover all fair expenses. If they are prevented from amassing fortunes, who cares?[51]

It was, of course, obvious that *they* did. And while they were content to earn merit by
bequeathing their art collections to the nation, few except the misguided Kylsant and
a brace of patriarchal houses like the Holts and the Booths, saw much wrong in with-
holding any charity. Setting aside any envy induced by contemplating the owners'
contrasting situation, Hart was right to make the point he did. Not for the last time
shareholders would be afforded rights superior to those who were also a part of the
wealth-generating process.

Certainly the majority of the seafarers' claims were justified. The shipowner
allowed them little in the way of amenable living conditions if he could avoid it. Even
in first-class trans-Atlantic liners the numbers of stewards and 'hotel-staff' meant that
their accommodation was spare and so overcrowded that it was colloquially known
as 'the glory-hole'. Essentially the extremity to which these men had been reduced
was a matter of bread-and-butter combined with natural justice. With a wage below
the subsistence level and the absolute necessity of claiming Poor Law relief, the moral
sense of many was outraged. They knew, the leader writer of the *Southern Daily Echo*
wrote in Southampton on 2 September, 'that the miners were successful in resisting
a reduction [in pay], and no other body of workers in the transport industry had had
their pay reduced'.

The situation in which the British seafarer and his family now found themselves was
dreadful, while the undemocratic action of their leader was reprehensible, but their
strike was to prove self-defeating. At home rumours of subversion and communist-
inspired plots raised the 'Red Spectre', of which much was made in the newspapers,

though the reality of communist affiliations in the short-lived strike-committee in London should have surprised no one. All thoughts of the men acclaimed so lately as unsung war heroes was forgotten while the shipowners moved swiftly, stopping all cash allotments paid directly to seamen's wives if their husbands were serving on ships detained by the strike. Ideas of brotherly love and revolution were equally quickly dispelled as The Trades Union Congress steadfastly refused to support the seamen, declaring their strike unofficial and therefore a 'wild-cat' action. This led to the rapid ending of the strike in British ports, though it lasted longer in those of South Africa and Australasia where the impact was more diverse after the arrival of ships in late August. Here the seamen and firemen 'declared that they would not sail again. For the next sixty to one hundred days British ships were immobilised'.[52] The seafarers' cause soon exhausted its early popularity, despite its appeal to the colonial populace who had initially welcomed the striking seamen into many homes, but such hospitality grew thin. Most of the idle ships were cargo-liners whose refrigerated holds carried to Britain the produce of her colonies. With supplies of chilled fruit and frozen mutton stalled, food prices rose at home – and therefore directly exacerbated the impoverishment of the poor in general and the seafarers' families in particular – while it grievously affected the colonial economies, rapidly eroding their markets and the one safeguard they had against the world trade situation. The seamen lucky enough to have found friends ashore soon found them cooling. They drifted back to their ships where they remained idle, yet expected to be fed. To this the cooks often objected, creating fissures in their unity while masters, mates and engineers fumed.

Solidarity was thus soon under threat: subsistence always taking priority over principle, and men grew quickly desperate. In ports where loaded ships lay idle, crews of strike-breakers were quietly mustered with cash inducements and marched aboard. Where this was not possible, more extreme measures were often taken. Masters unused to an unseemly flowering of democracy, most of them hard-bitten commanders brought-up under sail on a diet of 'belaying-pin soup', were infuriated by this disobedience. Without obedience to their lawful commands they considered the Articles of Agreement broken, the premise upon which the shipowners had moved to stop allotments. They, in turn, stopped food allowances. Many called upon the loyalty of their mates, engineers and apprentices to get their ships to sea, relying on the men coming to their senses once the ship's course was laid for home. In Durban the master of the *Sophocles* locked his ratings in their mess room, let go the moorings and headed for the open sea where a refusal to work on the part of his crew would constitute mutiny. However, in this case the crew proved united and intractable, and by calling the master's bluff they compelled him to return to port.

Others were more successful. A short stop for a consignment of frozen meat detained the *Port Curtis* at Cairns for ten weeks and a plan was hatched to escape. A police raid removed the crew in the early hours and Captain G.W. Hearn, his officers, engineers, a handful of stewards and a local pilot got the ship to sea. With the pilot on the bridge and the chief engineer in the engine room, Hearn led the stoking-party at the boilers. On the passage to Brisbane, the *Port Curtis* met the *Port Hardy* which had escaped from Townsville, whereupon coal and water were exchanged. Strike-breaking took other forms. On 8 October the Union-Castle liner *Arundel*

Castle arrived in Southampton from Capetown with the first mails for a month. She also bore a cargo of chilled oranges, £800,000 worth of gold and 160 passengers, including a clergyman, an opera diva and some undergraduates bound for British universities who thought it a lark to sign-on as members of the ship's crew. Such resilience and a demoralising reaction from the better-off, gradually eroded the resolution of hard-liners like the crew of the *Sophocles*. With international trade stagnant, the shipowners did not need to shift their ground and the Government itself could do nothing beyond encouraging the shaky economy to do what it could to carry on. To this end exports were loaded aboard foreign-flag vessels, resulting in further long-term damage to the reputation of British ships to carry even their own country's products, meanwhile shaking confidence in the already faltering markets for British manufactures. Foreign ships also brought news of the privations to which the strikers' families were reduced at home where rising food prices only sharpened their plight.

Abroad, feelings remained high. On 7 November the *Port Victor* arrived in Brisbane from New York with a crew signed-on at the lower wage, black-legs in the eyes of the striking seamen in the port. A number of these, including deserters from the *Port Sydney* and *Port Auckland*, armed with iron bars, stormed aboard the *Port Victor* and it was not until three of them had been shot and wounded by one of the ship's officers, that the attack was beaten off, leaving a dozen of the loyalists injured. Without support from the Trades Union Congress the Seamen's Strike was bound to collapse: the men drifted back to work 'under protest'. The strike petered out, ending in South Africa by mid-October and lingering on in Australia until Christmas Eve. The men who had participated usually found themselves unable to sign-on again and joined the increasing number of unemployed. The losses were calculated, one estimate of lost freight charges in *The Times* reckoned about £2 million, but the total was more complex: depreciation, port charges, pay for the officers and those not on strike, freight lost permanently to foreign carriers, all contributed to the losses to the shipowners, but there were damages inflicted upon the economies of Great Britain and the three colonies. For the owners it was a matter of principle that labour bent to the needs of capital; for the broken seafarers there was a similar recognition. This cultural legacy of polarisation would await its own outcome. What was certain was that neither side would forget, not even unto the second or third generation. The more immediate consequence of the Seamen's Strike of 1925 was that it hardened the attitude of the British public, stiffening the Government's resolve to break the General Strike that in seeking to back the miners' demands for betterment, broke out in April of the following year. There was reaction too among others more intimately connected with shipping itself.

The social upheaval that followed the slaughter on the Western Front had given greater impetus to the attempts by the mercantile marine to better itself that had been a theme of aspiration in the pre-war years. To this internal ambition were added the circumstances of Captain Fryatt's execution by the Germans as a *franc tireur*. This brutality and the post-war approbation of the state conferred a formal uniform by Order in Council upon what was widely regarded as 'the Fourth Service,' to which George V added his own declaration that privately owned fleets under the red ensign constituted a Merchant Navy. Although much of this gloss was swiftly dimmed by the

A Seven Seas Club magazine caricature showing; second from the left, Air Chief Marshal Sir Frederick Bowhill, a master-mariner under sail; third from left, Captain Taprell-Dorling, better known as the author 'Taffrail'; the small, round-faced figure in the centre is W.H. Coombs, the mercantile marine's champion. (© Courtesy of the Seven Seas Club)

economic decline that followed, the King's assertion was welcomed by many masters, mates and engineers whose attempts to unite and raise their social status had begun in the previous century with the founding of the Imperial Merchant Service Guild and the Mercantile Marine Service Association. Whilst stopping short of being trade unions, their desire to improve conditions was no less serious. Several other institutions were established, perhaps most remarkable of which was the Seven Seas Club of 1922 set up by several ex-*Conway* officers. The club was intended to provide a refuge for the officers of merchant ships in the London Docks where they could enjoy a quiet drink, write letters, read the newspapers and find 'extremely cheap, clean lodging for the night, right in the middle of London'. That it was necessary for these men to undertake the acquisition of somewhere other than their immediate places of work, speaks for itself. In 1934, the club purchased a worn-out topsail schooner, the *Friendship*, renamed her the *Seven Seas* and moored her on the Victoria Embankment adjacent to Charing Cross station. Despite the opposition of the Greater London Council, which objected to the *Seven Seas'* prime position, the club throve, attracting many members whose contributions to the club's magazine is eloquent of the eclectic intellectual interests of its membership.[53]

One club member was moved by the sea-officers' plight and the causes of the Seamen's Strike. In 1925 Captain W.H. Coombs arranged for a book he had written to be published at his own expense by J.D. Potter, the Admiralty chart agent. Signed copies of *The Nation's Key Men* were sent worldwide, for Coombs had produced a polemical work dedicated to his:

> Brethren of the Sea – the Officers of the British Mercantile Marine, to whom the British Public, the Statesmen, the Politicians, the Shipowners, the Marine Superintendents, the Board of Trade, the Lawyers and the Underwriters give great praise with their lips, while assisting (in most cases unconsciously, but in others I fear deliberately) to perpetrate an absurd, unprofitable and unpatriotic injustice – this book is affectionately dedicated ... in the fervent hope that it may in some measure materially assist in obtaining for you even a PART of that recognition and consideration so long overdue.

Coombs' objective was:

> ... to draw attention to the unsatisfactory state of affairs existing to-day among the Key-Men of Empire – the Officer personnel of the British Mercantile Marine, and to indicate a practical method of reform. It ... deals with a subject of the utmost national importance. Britain depends on her Mercantile Marine – a fact proclaimed almost daily by prominent men ... It was in the knowledge of the British Empire upon the ... Mercantile Marine, that Germany launched her intensive submarine campaign upon our Merchant ships.

Coombs adduces a remark – quoted elsewhere in this series – made by 'An American Ambassador' that 'the British Mercantile Marine has constituted one of the greatest civilising forces in history,' adding Lloyd George's description of 'the Merchant Service as the Jugular Vein of the British Empire.' His chief concern was that the shipowners' cynical disinterest in the pay and conditions of their officers would drive these imperial 'Key-Men' into the arms of 'Trade Unionism', a spectre to be avoided if at all possible: 'In view of the present-day menace of Communism.' Writing in a period of extreme depression in shipping with the ratings on the eve of their strike, Coombs felt acutely the predicament of the committed officer who was denied not only professional status or of any protection from the ravages of global recession, but a decent salary and conditions when fortunate to find himself employed. There were 'notable exceptions ... firms to whom all honour is due' but the generality of 'Officers will be found to be disconsolate men, unhappy men, and in some cases bitter men, men who are almost driven to despair by the helplessness of their own position, their sorrows shared by those patient ladies – their wives.' That this occurred in even prestigious companies is evinced by the decision of Hans De Mierre, whom we met earlier. After war service in the Royal Naval Reserve, De Mierre returned to Cunard where – as an Extra-Master-Mariner – he was Junior First Officer, married and on low pay. Despite an intense love of the sea he was obliged to give it up in 1920, telling his father when the latter complained of the amount he was paying in income tax that even as Commodore in the Cunard Line his pay would not be half as much. In due course he resigned, his connections in passenger ships giving him an *entrée* in New York where he began a career in business and industry.[54]

De Mierre was fortunate, but the loss of such talent was a serious one to the shipping industry. Fundamental to this sense of victimisation felt by the officers was the recognition of their own vital role in keeping the nation supplied with food and raw materials which, if abandoned in favour of strike action, would hit the least well-off first, which included their own families. 'The discipline and training of the sea,' Coombs said, 'produces an attitude of mind which deplores the futile waste of effort and the suffering occasioned by the folly of strikes.' Because of this 'lack of desire to strike … the position of the Merchant Officer is that of a defenceless man. In England to-day, if a vital industry is threatened, it is protected by … the Safeguarding of Industries Act.' This protection was uniquely denied the merchant service officer, not because the vital nature of his work was not appreciated in the abstract sense, but because an incontrovertible excuse to do so was offered by the fact that British shipping functioned in a competitive world.

While admitting 'the present abnormal and prolonged depression in world trade,' Coombs was savage in his attack on the real cause of the officers' low morale as 'the "good business methods" of the Shipowner … as a business man.' These were 'the prime cause of trouble' as Coombs explained: the shipowner claims that:

> he should avail himself of the obvious advantage which the excess of supply over demand gives him. A reasonable excuse … were it not for the fact that … the Shipowner has been shrewd enough to take care that the supply has always exceeded the demand as far as Merchant Officers are concerned.

To this Coombs adds the connivance of others ostensibly devoted to the welfare of the British Mercantile Marine Officer, and in particular castigates 'the lack of uniformity in the recruiting and training of cadets', many of whom were leaving the service and, most important, the Government's 'failure to keep legislation relative to the Merchant Service up to date'.

The shipowners' acumen and their appreciation of the existence of a global market-place had led them to circumvent the worst strictures of the Depression by their invention of flags-of-convenience mentioned above. These, in the period 1920–1930, were those of Panama and Liberia and while largely subscribed to by Americans, British owners took advantage in their turn of the lowering freight-rates and dropping standards that were an inevitable consequence of what was effectively a form of deregulation, made possible to some extent by the flooding of the charter-markets by a huge surplus of shipping resulting from the mass building programmes of the late war.

Coombs was well aware of the responsibilities of a ship's master. His singular and individual exposure to the vicissitudes of circumstances are eloquently enshrined in the formulation of Marine Insurance policies, for the master is deemed alone '... under God.' He is pitched against nature, a hostage to the competence of his officers and the uncompromising nature of economics. In a world where time is money, delay is anathema to his employers, though it may be that prudence, insofar as natural obstacles are concerned, dictates it. If he commands a passenger ship, he has to maintain a cordial and congenial atmosphere at all times, while in any ship crew-morale and discipline will produce problems, if not properly attended to. He must also so be mindful of his cargo, for far from remaining supine in his ship's holds, differing cargoes confront him with such diverse distractions as spontaneous combustion, tainting, shifting, wetting or deterioration. There is, of course, no place aboard his ship to which he may retreat for a moment's recreation from these manifold sources of anxiety, and consequently there are few moments when he is not preoccupied by one worry or another.

While many tough old masters lived to a ripe old age, the work often killed, or contributed to early death. Captain Sir Edgar Britten, whose tenure of command of the new *Queen Mary* in 1936 not only saw her take back the Blue Riband but must be regarded as the plum job in the entire merchant fleet, did not live to retire. He suffered a stroke in his cabin and died days later. On 31 October 1937 his remains were taken to sea in the tug-tender *Calshot* and buried at sea off the Needles. He had been much thought of, a quiet, unassuming man whose equable temper commanded respect from all who met him. Another knighted Cunard commander, Captain Sir James Charles of the *Aquitania*, also died in his cabin a few moments after berthing his ship at Southampton on his last voyage before retirement.[55] These conspicuous and well-publicised deaths of men at the pinnacle of their professions may stand as eloquent memorials to the thousands of others, Coombs's unhappy and bitter men, who felt their lives had been wasted without recognition by the society they served.

A master's work may be eased and made tolerable by competent officers, particularly his chief mate, whose principal duty is to supervise the daily running of the ship, her stability and the care of the cargo. He and his colleagues, the numbers of whom vary according to the size and purpose of the ship and the generosity of her owners, have little authority in law other than the loose binding of the Articles of Agreement signed between the master, as owners' representative, and the crew. There are penalties just as there are misdemeanours but they are light and usually confined to the fining of a day's pay, known as 'logging' since the procedure has by law to be entered verbatim in a ship's official log book.

In 1925 the stringency of the vocational certificate of competency so disparagingly and colloquially called a 'ticket' was such that only 44 per cent of examinees passed for master, first or second mate. Nor did the holding of a certificate guarantee a position at the certified rank, especially during hard times as we have had cause to note. Coombs cites the case of a junior watch-keeping officer in P&O who was a master-mariner, held a commission as lieutenant in the RNR and had fought as such at Jutland and the Falklands, thereafter serving as a navigator in submarines. He was also a Fellow of the Royal Geographical, Astronomical and Meteorological Societies, but all these achievements gained him less than £20 per month. His employer was, as we have had cause to observe, no ordinary shipping company, bound by the coarse economics of the market; it received a large state subsidy. This anonymous officer's predicament echoes that of De Mierre and was clearly a commonplace.

So much for pay; conditions were equally poor, particularly in tramp-ships, though liner companies were often little better. Describing a 'nightmare' week in Chittagong, Coombs himself recalled:

> The heat on shore was terrible, but nothing comparable to that on a ship with iron decks. My cabin was about 7 feet square, with one small porthole. There was no fan in it, and steam pipes ran outside the door to winches which were clattering night and day … One worked twelve hours continuously superintending the stowage of cargo in the holds, and it was impossible to obtain a night's rest in comfort.

Coombs contrasted this with fifty ex-German ships:

> I found on each, Officers' accommodation infinitely superior to anything I have seen in British ships … aboard Dutch and Danish ships [I] have found the same consideration given to this important (and not very costly) detail in the smooth and profitable running of a ship.

In the brief post-war boom the company for whom Coombs then worked, paid its shareholders large dividends.

Under such a punishing regime, local shore leave was often impossible, and it was common for a ship to be moved in port, requiring the presence of all hands, not just the cargo-watch. If in a home port an officer might occasionally be allowed his wife on board, though his cabin possessed nothing more louche than a high, single bunk – and a settee. Should she be willing to endure the landscape of a British port, she *might* be allowed to mess free. But while officers, caught by the economic necessities of survival, must perforce endure low pay and poor conditions, it was the subject of leave that most plagued them. They were legally entitled to a fortnight a year, though these days were not continuous and, significantly:

> if Officers demand what is their right in the way of leave, it is indicated to them by many firms that they can have their leave, but must not complain or be surprised if they fail to obtain employment again. As a result, unemployment being so sadly rife … [there are] Officers who in the last three years have not spent as much as one week in their own homes!

This was a common complaint, especially among young married officers. There were a few exceptions, as the case of the young P. Fyrth shows in 1931. A junior British India officer, Fyrth 'spent three and a half years in Indian and Persian Gulf waters to earn myself seven months leave on full pay, a rarity in the merchant ships of those days'.

Although the Articles of Agreement were originally intended to protect the seafarers' interests they are a good example of how Government legislation lagged behind the needs of changing circumstances and ceased to function as conceived, for they gave the signatories no real continuity of employment. Nor, even in liner companies, when a separate contract of employment was offered to the individual officer, did this extend longer than the two-year period of the Articles. Personal considera- tion *was* given by some companies, though this lay outside any formal, documented agreement. Coombs selects as exemplars Holts, the Booth Line, the Prince Line, and Elders & Fyffe's banana-carriers, but of these, as pencilled annotations in my copy of Coombs' book show, Holt's refused their officers cabin fans, the leave clause was rescinded in the Depression and, as Third Officer William Moore stated, they threat- ened dismissal if an officer demanded leave owed to him.[56]

The three grades of foreign-going certification for sea-going deck-officers remained, plus the qualification for Extra-Master intending a career ashore as surveyors, exam- iners and other officials of the Board of Trade or the certification societies such as Lloyd's. Cargo-liners, tankers and large passenger liners commonly carried third, fourth and even fifth and sixth 'mates', though in such companies they were usu- ally denominated 'officers', and doubled the number of deck-officers on watch. Many first-class liner companies, particularly those with mail contracts, insisted on all their deck-officers being master-mariners, a consequence of which was the slow promotion complained of by De Mierre. Officers' salaries were mutually agreed by the National Maritime Board between the Shipping Federation and the service associations, against whom Coombs inveighed as betraying the trust of those who relied upon them. In August 1925 the scales for deck-officers in a cargo-liner of 9,000 tons gross running a scheduled service worldwide provided £20 per month for a first mate with a Mate's certificate, rising to £22 after three years' service; with a Master's certificate a first mate would be paid £21 rising a further £2 after three years. A second mate holding a cer- tificate of his rating earned £15 per month irrespective of his time in the rank, though he earned a pound more if he held a superior certificate. Third mates, irrespective of qualifications and including those who held none at all, received a flat rate of £11.5 per month, fourth mates being paid a pound less. First mates in tankers received 10 per cent more than their brethren in cargo-ships, other deck-officers 7.5 per cent more. All deck-officers had their food and usually their bedding found, but had to provide items like soap along with expensive things like 'company-livery' (uniforms), sextants, nauti- cal tables and binoculars. In contrast young radio officers did not have to supply these items, being employed by the Marconi Co. and thereby 'hired-out' to individual ships whose owners undertook to supply necessities such as soap. The engineers received similar salaries to the equivalent rank of mate.

There were no agreed scales for masters, though a salary of £24–28 per month was the average in a general cargo-liner. The master stood between the owner and the whole crew, and being the person with whom the crew agreed the Articles, was seen as the owners' creature; either the fount of all grievances the owner thrust upon them, or the withholder of all favours, legitimate or otherwise, they considered their due. In contrast, his own perception of himself was more likely to be that of the pig- in-the-middle.

Such remuneration for ship's staff was poor, 'an absurd, parsimonious and unwar- ranted pittance' which, given the hours worked – an absolute minimum of 56 per week and usually a good deal more with subsidiary duties outside those of actual watch-keeping – and the long duration of a voyage, contrasts unfavourably with, for example, the pilotage fee for conducting a vessel up the Hughli to Calcutta. This work, as in all cases of pilotage being advisory, is carried out by a master-mariner and in no way relieves the ship's own master of full responsibility for his ship. But for conducting a vessel through about 120 miles of admittedly intricate and shifting channels threading through complex sandbanks, the pilot was paid the equivalent of the master's salary for a month. Although he had to make several disbursements for his boatmen, cutter and manservant, this still left the pilot a handsome fee to pocket, comparable with Coombs' own monthly salary when he served the Imperial Customs of China. Such fees and pilotage were mandatory, and apparently cheerfully borne by the shipowner, since they were paid by all vessels and therefore non-competitive.

Additional to all this there were some 3,000 apprentices at sea, 'frequently [used as] sweated labour, often working as seamen, sometimes receiving 1s [one shilling, or 5p], sometimes 30s. a month, and sixpence an hour overtime'.

The usual argument mustered to combat accusations of the shipowners' parsimony was that the food – which varied between excellent in many liners to execrable in most tramps – was free in lieu of pay. Unfortunately this did not help the officers pay the living expenses of their wives and families in an age when women of their class did not work as they do now. There were also incidental expenses, travelling and the cost of laundry, the last often dictated by an owner's standards or the filth produced by his cargo. Moreover the fortnight's leave the end of a year's service earned was, as we have observed, not only a gamble with future employment but had to be taken 'either wholly or in part as will best suit the convenience of the Owner and ship'. The Shipping Federation's capitalisation in this sentence is significant.

The reference to hours worked was no exaggeration, particularly in port when in cargo-liners there could be two gangs of dock labour working each hatch day-and-night and often two mates were required, the reason why several officers were appointed to such ships. In contrast, particularly in the Home and Near-Continental Trades:

> There were many 'two-mate' ships in which the chief and second officers kept alternate watches. Sometimes they were expected to chip [rust], scrape and paint holds or sew canvas. When down the holds at sea, they left a whistle with the man at the wheel and, if another vessel hove in sight, the helmsman blew the whistle and the officer came to the bridge. When such ships reached port, although worn out by lack of sleep, the officers had to keep cargo watches.[57]

The Depression had two effects upon the employment policy of shipowners in respect of their officers, enabling them to cheaply purchase the services of mates with master's certificates – many of whom had sailed in command – in any rank, thus notionally improving the safe conduct of their ships. They could also employ uncertificated deck-officers where the regulations allowed, so that many ships, particularly tramps, bore third – and sometimes second – mates with no formal qualifications. These men, usually long-in-the-tooth, often had a familial or social attachment to the owner. Having served their time as apprentices, though they might have failed or never have sat for any certificate of competence, they had gained through long experience sufficient knowledge to carry out the minimum duties and stand the

8–12 watch when the master was on call. Such men not only came cheap, they were bid-
dable and bound by a loyalty uninspired by anything other than the instinct for survival.

Despite the fact that the officer corps of the British Mercantile Marine was actually open to any qualified – and to these unqualified – males, admittance to it was
seen on the one hand as entry into the middle-class, but on the other to the ranks
of what were generically lumped together as 'Merchant Seamen'. Mrs Nancy Astor
may have achieved immortality as the first British female MP, but her parliamentary
proposal that as potential carriers of venereal disease all 'Merchant Seamen' paying
off ships in British ports should wear yellow arm-bands, earned her distinction of
a different sort among those she sought to stigmatise. However, no matter whether
one descended the gangway of a white hulled P&O liner, or scrambled ashore from
a grimy tramp under the coal staithes of Cardiff, the public perception of the British
merchant seaman veered from mild contempt to complete disinterest.

Of course, and especially in 1925, the plight of middle-class officers cut little ice
when compared with the widespread poverty in Britain but, despite class pretensions,
these were men whose places of work only occasionally touched their native shores and
then did so in insalubrious locations, 'districts which are studiously avoided by all those
other than those unfortunates who are compelled to live in the slums which disgrace
our Dockland, or by those whose business takes them there.' As for the individual:

> The strange person who elects to go to sea for his livelihood … [possesses motives
> so] incalculable as to repel close study. The Merchant Service Officer is usually a
> man of retiring ways, a man who does his job, grabs with avidity any leave that's
> going, and gets as quickly as he can to his fireside with his relations …

It was not, however, all bad. Among many shipping companies there were, of course, a
handful of notable exceptions. The Prince Line paid its officers:

> a good salary, and there was an excellent scheme in which Captains and Officers
> received a commission on freights, on the understanding that Officers paid damage
> claims to cargo due to bad stowage. This scheme worked well because the officers
> felt they had every incentive to work … in the interests of the ships.

Alfred Holt & Co.'s Blue Funnel Line has also already been mentioned but it was for
many years a conspicuous exception to the general rule of poor pay and conditions,
conspicuous because its management were imbued with a paternal duty towards their
employees and in particular their masters, mates and officers-in-embryo (largely due
to a heritage of Unitarian Christianity). A third officer of a Blue Funnel cargo-liner
in 1925 commanded a monthly salary of £21, above the Shipping Federation rate,
though he was paid no overtime. As a general rule at this time:

> all hands in a [Blue Funnel] ship can rely upon being relieved upon their arrival in
> a home port and getting from eight to ten day's leave absolutely clear of the ship,
> at the end of each voyage, which is usually from three to six months … Officers in
> ships which serve on the Pacific coast, and are therefore away from England for a

period of eighteen months, can rely upon six weeks' leave on their return to this country. Alfred Holt's ships are held in as great esteem by Underwriters and [cargo] Shippers as any other ships trading to the Far East, as they are so well found, and are known to be well run … Alfred Holt and Co is an extremely profitable and prosperous concern.

Despite the outlay over and above the minima of others, Blue Funnel liners were all in commission while the ships of others were laid-up, idle. Moreover their 'scheme of training … calls for great commendation' their midshipmen not being abused as cheap labour and proper care being taken of them by the provision of instruction at sea. During the war, aware that sail-training was under threat, Lawrence Holt had introduced a department dedicated to training and in 1916 a young man named Frank Wilkes became the first Blue Funnel midshipman. In March 1925 the company's requirements for entry and conditions of service speak for themselves. Applicants were required to have had a good education to that of Oxford or Cambridge Senior Local Examination, 'or the new School Leaving Certificate' in England and Wales, and to have passed the Intermediate Examination in Scotland. 'Boys between 15 and 17 still at school are preferred' and a 'good knowledge of algebra, geometry and trigonometry is essential.' An upper age limit of seventeen was imposed, 'unless the applicant has had previous nautical experience. Young men who came from the *Worcester* or *Conway* with the requisite certificates need only serve for three years, otherwise a midshipman's term of service was four years; no premium was required, allowing the company to select across the social spectrum, and a lad would be paid £6 for his first year, £12 for his second, £18 for his third and £24 for his fourth and final year. 'A sum of £10, in addition, will be paid on satisfactory completion of indentures, at the absolute discretion of the Owners.

A midshipman was to provide himself with a reefer suit comprising a double-breasted, brass-buttoned jacket, a waistcoat and trousers, a bridge-coat, boots, tropical whites, a set of dungaree working clothes and a uniform cap. The company would supply a set of brass-buttons bearing the company house-flag but the boy's parents had to fork out for a copy of Norie's *Nautical Tables*, Fletcher's *Seamanship*, a text book on trigonometry, *Gill's Nautical Astronomy* 'and, after the first year, a Sextant and Binoculars'. The midshipmen's accommodation, or half-deck, could comprise 'four boys … berthed together' and all bedding, towels, etc.,' were supplied by the company. Leave of absence was 'granted at the discretion of the Master abroad and the Owners at home'. On a Blue Funnel liner's arrival in Liverpool a lorry collected all the midshipmen's gear and they were conducted to 'the Company's hostel near Liverpool, where they come under the instruction of a [retired] Commander RN, and thus get naval disciplinary training … in navigation and seamanship.' However, as elsewhere, once out of their apprenticeships Holt's midshipmen were expected to go elsewhere for the sea-time necessary to qualify for the intermediate certificates and return to the fold as master-mariners, the dynamic Lawrence Holt, among others, continuing to favour officers holding square-rig certificates until well into the 1920s. Even when they did apply for employment they found that the company did not 'rely upon an officer's Board of Trade qualifications,' and they were obliged to submit to an examination 'before their own Captains and Superintendents,' important because the company continued not to insure their ships, a policy that in general paid-off. This was buttressed by very tight control of their vessels' navigation. They were governed by comprehensive company standing orders, strict passage routes and the putting up of a bond by every master upon which interest was paid if he kept out of trouble, but from which a mulct was deducted if he did not. Moreover, Holt's demanded an absolute loyalty so strict that one officer, Mr G.L. Hoare, third mate of the *Asphalion*, who revealed their scales of pay, 'was axed during the Depression' because 'Messrs A.H. expressed themselves as dissatisfied with this publicity.'

Despite, or perhaps because of, the depressing state of affairs the shipping industry was in at this time, training was a hotly debated subject, particularly the necessity of a background in sail long after steam-power had thrust change upon it. In 1925, 'the present state of things' was blamed on the 'lack of initiative, lack of foresight, in fact lack of anything except the immediate needs of thirty years ago'. Captain Hamilton Blair went on:

> An officer in sail was valued according to his general knowledge of practical seamanship and his running of his watch, but never as a smart navigator. In my experience as a young sailing ship officer I, personally, had to overcome many of the old prejudices [on the part of the master] before being allowed to take the most ordinary of observations [of the sun for latitude]. Such training certainly did not prepare one for the quick, accurate, and continually changing methods adopted in the modern steam ship. We must look further ahead than our predecessors did, and see that the boy of today is trained to meet the demands of the future ... [W]hen applying for a cadetship ... [a boy] should be made to show that he has passed an examination which proves he has received a sound education and has reached a reasonable standard ...

Touching upon the subject of premiums, Blair doubted that their abolition accounted for a 'lowering of the social standard,' adding: 'I am afraid that a Cardiff tramp does not offer much inducement to a better class boy'. Addressing education and the 'physical, intellectual, aesthetic and moral' standards of the generality of masters then at sea, Blair dismisses ideas that any such qualities were at that time deficient. 'The ship master has proved himself, both in peace and war, to be a rather exceptional being. Though trained in sail he has adapted himself, in most cases, to modern methods and appliances. In my experience I have not yet met any ship master in ... a predicament through lack of early education'. Intellect, he goes on to argue, 'comprehends the means by which the powers of the understanding are to be developed and improved'. If it is aesthetic education that is lacking, is this because the ship-master 'fails to see beauty in a coal tip' or in 'the scheme of artistic colouring in the design of a Cardiff tramp's funnel'? Hamilton Blair admits the high intellectual accomplishments of the scientists he had met on an Antarctic Expedition in which he had taken part, but 'found him to be very much the "specialist". All his efforts were concentrated on his own particular branch of science, and for the other things of life he cared little.' He went on:

I do not wish to convey the impression that I see no reason for any change in the educational standard of the Merchant Service personnel. The responsibilities of the liner captain of today demand a higher technical training, as well as a higher intellectual standard, than was necessary previously. But I still maintain that the present day ship master can carry on his duties quite successfully on the education of thirty years ago. The whole world requires a higher standard of education, this being by no means a special want of the Merchant Service.

The wastage in young officers and apprentices is by no means a modern problem. The sea has always shown herself to be an exacting mistress, and as a profession it is quite unlike any other walk of life. There is, and always has been, the boy who, carried away by some book of sea adventure, sees himself a daring captain. He goes to sea and finds there little real adventure. His captain is a quiet sensible type of man who seldom looks his way. The rust he had only seen on pictures of ships means endless chipping and scraping … Then there is seasickness and homesickness, no movies, no football, the grumbling of the married men, the wild talk of the young and [morally] irresponsible officer. The cases quoted [in other correspondence] of boys leaving the sea are not convincing. Beginning as they do with the Medallist, I would like to say that I go very little on the type of boy who wins the medal. Nature has her wonderful method of distribution, and shares out her gifts with a certain discrimination. Over and over again we find the medallist, as a boy, has grown up into a very mediocre type of man. I personally know of four medallists who remained but the proverbial 'dog-watch' at sea. The fame they won at School quite unsuited them for the different kind of competition they found at sea.

[As for] the various positions which certificated ex-merchant service officers seek refuge in … In this little village alone we have a policeman who is a graduate of one of the Universities, a publican who was a captain in the Army, an ex-Naval Officer who drives a bus. Fleet Street is full of briefless barristers. Victoria Street is full of expensively trained engineers, who find the greatest difficulty making both ends meet. The Merchant Service is not the only profession where hard conditions exist, and I might add that it will never improve its status so long as its personnel suffers from that inferiority complex which it undoubtedly shows.

He concludes with a side-swipe at the Board of Trade's examinations which were 'at present … quite out of date … This matter is one which requires a special discussion of its own'.[58] Hamilton Blair's opinion on these matters is of some moment because he was then on the teaching staff at Pangbourne Nautical College, established on the demise of Devitt & Moore's sail-training ships during the late war.[59]

The inferiority complex referred to by Hamilton Blair was often no more than an attitude of self-deprecation, even by men whose authority and responsibility at sea were as impressive as their experiences. In his letter from Buenos Aires covering his annual subscription to the Honourable Company of Master-Mariners in 1928, Captain Bennett Lawson of the *Maid of Lemnos* recalled 'the days when a Shipmaster was considered a little bit of a "blackguard", and certainly uncouth! Of course,' he went on, 'we are living in totally different times, when a higher standard of education, *should* produce better men'. Writing from his home in North Wales, Captain Dominy

Founder's Day 1933. The shipowner Lawrence Holt inspects the cadets at Pangbourne College, established by Devitt & Moore on the demise of their Ocean Sea Training Scheme. (Courtesy of Pangbourne College)

of the P.S.N.C. was an Extra-Master in sail who had first gone to sea in 1884 in the ship *Orinsay*, belonging to James Sheppard & Co., remaining in her until finishing his apprenticeship in 1889. After obtaining his Second Mate's certificate he returned to the same owner's *Earnock* engaged, as had been his previous ship had, in the Australian grain trade. Gaining the requisite sea-time he sat for his First Mate's certificate in August 1891 then spent a year in the tramp steamers *Herden* and *Lynton*, passing for master in February 1893. The following month, despite being a master-mariner, he was appointed 5th Officer of the Royal Mail Steam Packet Co.'s *Atrato* and served in her for a year, rising to 4th Officer, before transferring to the P.S.N.C. He remained with this company and was appointed to command as master in 1906. Having been commissioned into the Royal Naval Reserve in February 1899, he retired in April 1914 and the outbreak of war that August found him commanding the P.S.N.C.'s *Junin*, 'homeward bound from the west coast of South America. On our arrival home we were sent to the Falkland Islands with stores, etc. and on our return we were sent for one year to the Dardanelles/Salonika.' Thereafter followed a year running between France and America, a year shuttling between Glasgow and Boulogne or Dunkerque, and finally 'another year convoying and after the Armistice to North Russia ... finishing up with a voyage for the Wheat Commission ending July 28th 1919.'

For these services Dominy received the C.B.E., modestly adding that: 'My experience has been somewhat wide but for any special experience or knowledge I suppose I can only claim for the Magellan Straits and the Patagonian Canals (Smyth Channel, etc).' His career is typical of his generation of liner commander, the tone of his letter perfectly understating his not inconsiderable achievements. True, service in the Reserve from which he had retired might have brought him closer to the heat of battle, but his cabotage of the Patagonian channels would have required a high standard of navigation and cool nerve, a perfect example of that quality so eloquently adumbrated by Hamilton Blair.

The continual post-1918 references made to the vital nature of the mercantile marine in wartime by those espousing its cause, added nothing to it. The sad fact was, and perhaps it was a very product of its essential democratic nature, that the supply of officers and masters usually met demand – even in wartime. Although crises were to occur later in the century, this was not the case during the post-1921 slump, nor during the more serious Depression that followed. While officers could be, and were, dismissed for petty reasons, often being treated like blue-collar workers by the white-collar clerks in their owners' offices, their powers of redress were zero. Coombs' call for fair treatment might have suited the playing fields of Eton; it did not suit any ex-Etonians who might have graduated to Leadenhall Street, St Mary Axe, or St Helen's Place, still less did it suit a harder breed of men over whom Eton cast no spell at all. It mattered not whether they had clawed their way up to the bridge from the hard half-deck of a Cardiff tramp where their entire four years of apprenticeship had been exploited as cheap labour by a mate whose own bed had been denied a single rose, or whether they came from the Spartan but privileged cadetship aboard HMS *Worcester* and a rather more languid existence in the Peninsular & Oriental Steam Navigation Co.'s mail steamers. The profession was racked upon the unforgiving machinery of a global construct in which only those who facilitated its real movement actually had any hope of material benefit. Every other player, from the poorest housewife shopping for food to the richest shipping tycoon, was bound in mutual interest to see the cheapest bargain driven in this delicate business of fetching and carrying. To seek some charitable concession from the former was as impossible as it was to seek it from the latter. However patrician his personal lifestyle, the typical shipowner might insist on the *droits de seigneur*, but he usually had little or no sense of *noblesse oblige*.

To some extent the British shipowner was constrained in his ability to be philanthropic, even if he intended it, as did Kylsant among a few others. After centuries of protection under the Navigation Acts, British shipping now not only enjoyed no favours from its own Government, it struggled against the odds set up by the governments of other nations, nations wishing to protect their own commerce. Thus while foreign ships could trade on the British coast, British ships could not trade upon many a foreign coast. The shipowner was also bound by the common ties of his fraternity to abide by the decisions on pay reached by his collective representatives in the form of the Shipping Federation. This institution, Coombs points out, 'is able to drive very hard bargains indeed through the medium of an unofficial body known as the National Maritime Board ... constituted under the auspices of the Ministry of Shipping during the war ...'. The weakness of the National Maritime Board lay in its failure to adequately represent the real interests of those it purported to, the officers' side being in the imperfect hands of the Imperial Merchant Service Guild and the Mercantile Marine Service Association, both of which only stood for some 6,500 officers. There was besides, the Marine Engineers' Association which represented a lesser number of engineers. None of these was a trade union and none had any power of sanction, generally riding the tide generated by the more militant ratings' unions.

One reformer, willing to take the initiative, existed within the very heart of the shipowners. His name was Robert Burton-Chadwick and he had been born into a ship-owning family in Birkenhead. Sent to sea in sail as a sickly sixteen-year-old,

Above: Frank H. Mason's painting of a P&O liner leaving the Thames and passing a humble sprit-rigged Thames sailing barge, also shows one of the cradles of future master-mariners, HMS *Worcester* at Greenhithe. Among its alumni was Admiral Togo. (From a Private Collection)

Right: Under training about 1938: Officer cadets from HMS *Worcester* pulling a 32' ex-naval cutter. The *Worcester* lies in the background, beyond the old tea-clipper *Cutty Sark*. (From a Private Collection)

Burton-Chadwick recovered his health and so took to the life that he remained in sailing vessels until qualifying as Extra-Master. He then served P&O as a junior officer joining the family firm in 1897, becoming a partner in 1903. In due course his firm was absorbed by Inverforth's group and during the war Burton-Chadwick served as Director of Overseas Transport to the Ministry of Munitions, entering Parliament as the member for Barrow-in-Furness in 1918. Knighted in 1920, he was returned again as the member for Wallasey in 1922, being appointed Parliamentary Secretary to the Board of Trade in Baldwin's Conservative Government, becoming a baronet in 1935.

Whilst member for Wallasey he wrote:

> During the impressionable years of my youth I imbibed a profound admiration for
> the British Merchant Service, and particularly for the British Officer. I have always
> had a kind of haunting consciousness that the Master-Mariner has never held that
> status in the national life to which he is entitled. There are many reasons to account
> for it. His was a commercial service, and he was ground between the millstones
> of commercial interest. The diversified nature of his calling has always made col-
> lective action difficult. There was none of the fostering care of an august Board of
> Admiralty, none of the social advantage that comes to him who wears a sword and
> epaulettes, but notwithstanding all these drawbacks he gave a loyal single-minded
> service to his ship that has always inspired one with great respect.

There was, on the face of it, no real comparison with the naval service; a master-mariner, like all the officers in the mercantile marine, was a direct employee of a shipping
company. But war moved him onto a different plane: his ship was armed, it was often
requisitioned by the state and, if not, his commercial business was one of national
importance. The state, which regulated his actions and granted him his certificate
of competency, not only governed his life but demanded from him a portion of his
service, as we have repeatedly seen in this history.

Discontent permeated the Merchant Navy and was felt even amongst its bright-
est luminaries. On the eve of his retirement from command of the White Star Line's
RMS *Majestic* in 1922, Captain Sir Bertram Hayes wrote:

> Seeing that such a fuss had been made of us while the war was in progress, some of
> us thought that when it was over the Merchant Service would receive the recogni-
> tion everybody said it deserved, and that in the future it would take its part in the
> national life of the country, but apparently it has again faded into the background of
> people's thoughts and I suppose it will need another national emergency to bring
> it back …

From this disillusion among a large number of influential masters whom the war had
brought closer together and, in many cases, left in contact with each other, a number
of informal confederations came into being. On 2 March 1921 Burton-Chadwick
spoke at the annual dinner of the Liverpool ship-masters and formally articulated an
idea which had been simmering for some time: the formation of 'an efficient central
society of a beneficent and sensible character as distinct from other societies which
are necessarily of a belligerent character,' by which was meant something akin to the
livery companies of the City of London. Burton-Chadwick's reference to 'belligerent
societies' did not go down well with staunch supporters of the Imperial Merchant
Service Guild and the Mercantile Marine Service Association which, although they
were frequently at odds, had been formed with intention of improving conditions
at sea for masters, mates and engineers. Although the membership of neither would
admit to their being trade unions, they combined the work of seeking better pay
and conditions with the more elevated intentions of raising status and seeking pro-

fessional standing. However, by speaking directly to ship-masters, Burton-Chadwick had mobilised a strong sentiment and he was charged to return to London and discover the proper means by which a guild of ship-masters might be appreciated. It was at the annual dinner of the Chamber of Shipping in London, that the American Ambassador, Mr J. W. Davis, made the speech quoted earlier in this work: 'I deem it no exaggeration to say that whether in war or in peace the British Mercantile Marine has rendered more service to more men of more nations than any other human agency.'

Such an encomium from such a source spurred Burton-Chadwick on, becoming his mantra. He mobilised Sir Acton Blake, the Deputy Master of Trinity House, Sir Bertram Hayes representing the White Star Line, Sir Franke Notley of P&O, Captain R.J. Noal of Shaw, Savill & Albion, Sir Walter Baynham of the Orient Line, Sir James Charles of Cunard, Sir Charles Down of the Royal Mail Line, Sir Thomas Seagrave of Frank Strick & Co. and Captain A.E. Dunn of the New Zealand Shipping Co., with legal assistance from Captain R.F. Hayward, a Barrister-at-Law. A debate was fomented in which Coombs was prominent and of which Lord Inchcape, Lord Kylsant and Lawrence Holt, among a few other members of the Chamber of Shipping and the Shipping Federation, approved. In due course, through the medium of the City Chamberlain, the matter was laid before the Privy Council, by which time Burton-Chadwick had joined Gladstone's Government. On 8 July 1925 a meeting finalised the constitution of the proposed company, establishing its distinction from the existing maritime institutions and, eleven months later, it was incorporated, the first Livery Company to be established since that of the Fan-Makers in the reign of Queen Anne. The Prince of Wales was pleased to accept the nomination as its first Master, whereupon King George V bestowed the courtesy title of 'Honourable' – rather than 'Worshipful' – in recognition of the special nature of the company and the importance of seamanship and navigation. Its initial membership of one hundred included a large proportion of masters commanding ships at sea, besides marine superintendents, the principals of several nautical colleges, harbour masters and ex-seafaring port executives, several marine lawyers and Lloyd's underwriters with masters' certificates, and surveyors and examiners of the Board of Trade.

Initially, at a rent of £175 per annum The Honourable Company of Master Mariners occupied premises at India House in Leadenhall Street, a remnant of another now defunct Honourable Company, thanks to the generosity of Sir Philip Devitt of Devitt & Moore. This was at the heart of London's shipping, close to the offices of numerous liner companies, Lloyd's, Trinity House and the Chamber of Shipping. Meetings were held elsewhere, principally in Liverpool and Glasgow and the Honourable Company participated in such important events as the International Conference on Safety of Life at Sea held in London in 1929. Burton-Chadwick had relinquished his post at the Board of Trade in 1928 to devote his attention fully to the company and lived long enough to see it acquire its Head Quarters Ship in 1947, the redundant sloop-of-war, HMS *Wellington*. She remains moored at Temple Stairs not far from where, a few years earlier, the schooner *Seven Seas* lay.[60]

The Company made recommendations on the training of officers, retaining a traditional and increasingly out of date faith in training under sail but recommending shipping companies insist on 'a satisfactory standard of general education' before accepting applicants as cadets or apprentices, underwriting the best practice of the first-class firms. Moreover the company commended the absolute necessity of the apprentice's indenture containing 'an obligation on the part of the ship-owner to teach or cause the apprentice to be taught the business of an *officer* as practised in steamships'. Thus, at last, the core evil of the historical apprenticeship system was rooted out. The argument against sail-training may be summarised by the argument that 'you don't need to know how to ride a horse to drive a motor car' and the recommendations failed on this division of opinion. Nevertheless, although the wording was omitted from the common form of indenture, the spirit of the educational recommendation began to permeate the generality of shipping companies, though individual mates would set it at nought if the work of the ship demanded pre-eminence.

The assumption of City livery by the Master-Mariners was, in a sense, a retrograde move, though their motives for doing so cannot be criticised. Those of them that had served or were serving as masters had in any case always occupied that ambivalent middle-ground as both owner's-agent and state-servant, the latter brought into sharp focus by war. Taking livery conferred upon them a long-desired dignity and recognition, but by this very process it detached the aspiring and active among them from a more holistic improvement of the greater Merchant Navy, isolating in particular the officers upon whom they so relied. Earlier attempts to combine in the British Merchant Service League of 1919 had not lasted long, the League enjoying an existence of a mere two years, but it was at this point that Coombs resigned from his post in the Imperial Chinese Customs Service to found the Navigators and General Insurance Co. Coombs had been touched by the case of a young man whose career had been ruined by the suspension of his certificate of competency in ambiguous circumstances; he wished to offer to other officers a decent insurance policy against this eventuality.[61] This in turn had prompted the publication of *The Nation's Key Men* and the book's success gradually drew Coombs into representing the officers of the Merchant Service. In 1928 he was behind the formation of the Officers' (Merchant Navy) Federation which enabled British and Commonwealth officers' organisations to combine resources and objectives, adding weight to their espoused aims. Four years later he formed The Watch Ashore, a much-needed self-help organisation for officers' wives.

In 1933 Coombs 'mounted a demonstration on the Thames' and presented a petition of 23,000 signatures to Parliament. This complained that mercantile officers enjoyed 'no legal or customary rights to periods of leave … no fixed hours of duty, and that they enjoyed no pension rights'. There was also no control over the entry of apprentices or cadets. There was sufficient support for Coombs to 'force through some reforms'. A 'Merchant Navy Officers' Pension Fund was established and the Officers' Federation was admitted to the National Maritime Board. Finally, in 1935 a Central Board for the Training of Officers for the Merchant Navy (which later became the Merchant Navy Training Board) was set up to encourage the standard and proper education of young officers. At this time Coombs also realised that his insurance company could not double as a trade association and established the Navigator and Engineer Officers' Union. The following year, 1936, this absorbed the Mercantile Marine Service Association and the Imperial Service Guild. By now several liner companies, chief among them the New Zealand Shipping Co., the British India Steam Navigation Co. and Brocklebank & Co. were using cargo-liners as school-ships. A cadet spent his day learning seamanship on deck, undergoing formal instruction in navigation, meteorology, general ship knowledge, ship stability and other subjects germane to the *curriculae* of the Board of Trade examinations for competency. Nevertheless, whilst other boys intending to become officers could take advantage of the quasi-public schools *Conway* and *Worcester*, and the less prestigious and dubiously useful T.S. *Mercury* on the Hamble – run largely by the tyrannical wife of the cricketer C.B. Fry – the vast majority of boys going to sea as would-be officers continued to do so with no induction whatsoever. As for those urchins joining a ship as deck- or galley boy, few in real terms had had the benefit of the training available from The Marine Society, which continued its long tradition of training boys for the sea services aboard the *Warspite* on the Thames.

However, once a lad had secured a berth, some opportunity was provided for self-improvement by The Seafarers Education Service set up by Albert Mansbridge, the founder of the Workers' Educational Association. In 1919 Mansbridge had begun to provide ship-board libraries, displacing the unpopular and neglected tractarian books supplied by the seamen's missions. Encouraged by Lawrence Holt, the first S.E.S. library was put aboard the Blue Funnel liner *Aeneas* in 1922. Mansbridge's initiative was in time to become one of the great institutions which by the 1950s had transformed the British Merchant Navy. Thanks to Mansbridge and his energetic and highly motivated successor, Ronald Hope, this institution eventually provided a College of the Sea by which seafarers of any rank could gain access to proper education, both basic and higher, through correspondence courses supervised by voluntary academics, most of whom were otherwise employed by universities and technical colleges.

Nevertheless, throughout this inter-war period, the life of a merchant ship's officer, particularly in the junior ranks, was best described as 'drab'. The glories of status were largely illusory, though exceptions of course existed. These were, however, often relative to local conditions so that a mate in a specialised cable-ship on a long deploy-ment, or a junior officer in a B.I. liner on the East African service could enjoy the benefits of rank and responsibility which evaporated when and if his ship entered a British port. The fate of his wife, if he was married, was quite otherwise. Her iso-lation was all but complete, unless she lived embedded in a maritime community which, for most officers, was unusual. It was for this reason that Coombs established The Watch Ashore, but even this did not compensate a young woman, perhaps eco-nomically burdened by children, from a lonely existence. Even if her husband was employed on a vessel calling regularly at a British port, unless it was within reason-able and affordable travelling distance of her home, her chances of actually seeing him were poor. Moreover, when she was able to join him the proscriptions against wives sleeping aboard mentioned earlier often added to the financial burden of their meeting, forcing her to seek lodgings ashore in the grim environs of the docks. Not that there was much room in an officer's cabin for co-habitation. The Board of Trade ensured a minimum of 'Certified space for One Seaman' which the shipowner rarely exceeded and which was lit with a single porthole through which, in the tropics, a piece of cardboard was shoved to scoop in fresh air from the breeze caused by the ship's progress. Furnishings were equally parsimonious: a single-bunk mounted atop of a chest of drawers, a wash-basin at this date often emptying into a bucket in a cabinet below, no running water – let alone hot, even in a steamship – a slender wardrobe, and a hard settee, or daybed. Senior officers warranted a tiny desk and an upright chair, but only the master was supplied with an arm-chair for the use of the company's agents, port officials and perhaps the odd guest. Such were the usual provisions in tramps and many cargo-liners. Electric fans, or a system of air blown through 'punkah-louvres' could ameliorate the fiercest tropical heat a little, and perhaps a central heating system was available in some vessels built in the late 1930s for higher latitudes, but many officers' cabins were without heat at all, even when frozen in the ports of Canada, North China, Manchuria or Russia.

Crew accommodation was universally Spartan in British ships and in large liners employing so-called 'native' crews, such as comprised Brocklebank's P&O's and B.I.'s lascars, or the Glen Line's Chinese, the difference between officers' and crew's quarters was most marked. In many tramps the ratings, even the firemen, were still 'herded' under the forecastle in a steel space tiered with steel bunks. While the officers at least messed in a saloon, the ratings were expected to eat at a pine-table set between the bunks. Just as the officers provided their sextants, tables, and so forth, the rating was expected to turn up after signing-on with his eating irons, mess kids and enamelled steel mug, his soap and towel, his deck-knife and 'donkey's breakfast', a palliasse of straw for a mattress, upon which he turned-in under blankets without the benefit of any sheets. Portholes, if provided under the wet forecastle of a steamer, were almost never opened for fear of a soaking, and ventilation was therefore unknown. The firemen had no distinct changing room, so they brought coal dust and sweaty grime into their accommodation from which few cleaned themselves before rolling exhausted into their bunks. It was difficult to keep such a space from becoming squalid, mephitic, infested with cockroaches and rats, particularly if the ship had recently carried grain. Such a space was 'a conglomeration of smells, coal fumes, hot oil, foul air, human sweat and urine'. Sanitary arrangements were deplorable and often his shipmates contributed to the squalor. One rating reminisced that during one night in port a messmate back from a spree ashore pissed into a bucket. 'The bucket was for washing-up plates and mugs, but also for slushing down the lavatory and bathing [washing] in'. While the narrator was clearly outraged, it is perhaps not entirely surprising that many regarded such a class of men as incorrigible, if not degenerate. Such was certainly a view prevailing ashore in an age which utterly failed to comprehend tension and stress, and the effect of long periods of apparently unremitting physical effort. Heating in the forecastle was provided from a coal bogie-stove. Here too, in heavy weather any clothes that were washed (*dhobied* it was called by seamen), or had been soaked by work on deck, had to be dried. Even in fine weather some masters, believing their ships to be 'cracks', forbade the hanging up of washing on deck. In port, to save money, power generators were shut down and after dark accommodation was lit by 'bulkhead dynamos', or 'oil *battis*', as paraffin lamps were variously and colloquially known.

Deck-officers shared a common bathroom, as did the engineers; the ratings' arrangements were even more communal, often exposed on deck, with ill-fitting doors, and washing facilities were sparse and insufficient, particularly in passenger liners where large numbers of stewards were employed. Such squalor contrasted vividly with the advertised luxury of passengers' state rooms. The apprentices lived in separate accommodation usually known as the 'half-deck,' which was rarely any better than the crews' quarters though the smaller number of youths inhabiting it and the greater imposition of routine and discipline impressed upon them by their senior member, usually made them marginally more congenial than a ship's forecastle.

And the work was incessant. Day-workers, comprised of stewards, cooks and bakers, the boatswain, carpenter (who was conventionally a time-served shipwright and the tradesman who fixed everything not covered by the engineers), some junior engineers and apprentices, and on a large ships many of the seamen, turned out at 05.30 to start work at 06.00. The usual pre-breakfast routine required the decks to be washed down. On a liner this meant holystoning, or scraping the decks with halved coconut shells, to bring out the whiteness of scoured teak so beloved by chief officers. On the bridge either the standby quarter-master or the apprentices polished brass, a job that they did elsewhere during the hours that followed. Stewards and cooks meanwhile prepared food and, after breakfast, the serious and endless routines of servicing cargo gear, engine-room maintenance and maintaining steel went on. Rust was chipped to expose bare steel which was coated successively with boiled-linseed oil, primer, undercoat and finally gloss paint. Some amelioration of this occurred in heavy weather, but idleness was insupportable, so there were a legion of internal tasks to be addressed below. When and where opportunity served, the cleaning and painting of holds or tanks was undertaken, many cargo-liners carrying deep-tanks for quantities of vegetable oil, latex and other liquid cargoes. Bilge pumping systems were tested and wooden dunnage was stacked, ready for use to keep consignments of general cargo away from steel surfaces and thus free from condensation. Other stronger timbers were used as 'toms' – rammed home to prevent cargo shifting in bad weather. Often labour-intensive preparation had to be given to a hold prior to the carriage of a specific cargo, or to its cleaning afterwards, which could be a nauseating job in the case of, for instance, grain. Such tasks customarily required the watch-keepers to turn-to in their watches-below, known as a 'field-day,' adding to their fatigue.[62]

Meanwhile the watch on the bridge, the engine and boiler rooms went on at sea, while in port the decks had to be supervised whenever cargo was worked, the winches supplied with steam or power, and a security watch-on-deck maintained when it was not. Most of this work was hard and tedious, entirely lacking the stimulus and physical excitement of handling sail even in the toughest old wind-jammer. What it did have in common with the life of the old 'sailorman' was danger. Industrial injuries and the sheer wearing-out of many men being a feature of the life at sea, as mentioned earlier. Cases of infectious disease had to be declared by a master whose initial diagnosis might rely upon the medical expertise of his young third mate, and no owner appreciated his ship quarantined in an outer anchorage for weeks when the earning of freight was so difficult.

Food in tramp-ships was notorious for its monotony, if not its badness. No tramp carried refrigerated storage, though some cargo-vessels had a large ice-box for perishable stores. Most foodstuffs were much as they had been in sailing vessels with some minor improvements. Fresh bread was baked where possible, but only on alternate days, the seafarer falling back on the old staple of hard-tack – or ship's biscuit. A small ration of butter went with this and, if he was really fortunate, a large tin of jam or marmalade would be issued to the mess. Up until 1938 a rating was entitled to a pound tin of condensed milk every three weeks, one-and-a-quarter pounds of sugar, of which about a quarter was retained by the steward for cooking with, and a little tea which proved less than the civilian war-ration.

Strangely the life found its advocates, such as the relentlessly philosophical William McFee, a marine engineer whose affection for the life aboard tramps provided him with ample material for becoming a popular novelist and a serious commentator. Such a romantic perception nevertheless required an act of will, and failed to come easily to most. While John Masefield, a victim of chronic seasickness, gave up the sea after that 'proverbial dog-watch' mentioned by Hamilton Blair and took to maritime eulogy, a better remembered poet, Eugene O'Neill, remarked of his own time in tramp-steamers: 'The life was incredibly hard, and I enjoyed every minute of it.' But he did not stay at sea either.

The principle difference between a tramp and a liner of the most modest pretensions, besides the regularity of the cargo-liner's schedule, was the grub. Aboard most liners of all classes the food ranged from good to excellent. Many had refrigerating plant for their frozen or chilled cargoes and these powered additional storage for ship's stores. Non-European crews had their own cooks and ate according to their ethnic background or religion, but here too provision was usually more than adequate so that, in relative terms, a lascar aboard a B.I. liner was comparatively better-off than his British-born counterpart on that Cardiff tramp.[63] Owners, masters and mates might adopt a racially superior attitude to their ethnically different subordinates, but it was in no one's interest to antagonise them and in many ships, despite the disparity in living conditions, the relationship between the ruled and the rulers was one of easy toleration on both sides, as will be seen in a subsequent chapter. That this bordered on condescension on one part and enforced obligation on the other may be one way of looking at it, but in the temper of the times it possessed the practical virtue of functioning. Many officers learned to speak the *lingua franca* of their ratings or the ports they visited regularly: a common form of Hindustani on the Indian coast, Malay in the great archipelago, and occasionally a little Mandarin or Cantonese on the China coast. Elsewhere in other trades mates picked up Spanish or, thanks to a good education, already had French; a few learned a smattering of Afrikaans. Some, brought up in specialised trades, such as the long-established links between the east coast of Scotland and the White Sea, knew Russian and, when all else failed, they could shout in English.

Elevated above this prosaic tapestry the grand affairs of Empire went on; Royal Dukes and their Duchesses made visits conveyed by crack liners, but the 'Abdication Crisis' that brought the Duke of York to the throne provoked a flurry of activity as Indian princes attended his Coronation as King George VI. The Anchor liner *Tuscania* carried the Nawab of Bhopal, the Sultan of Makalla, the Maharajah of Jaipur and the twelve-year-old Princess Dawn of Rampur, along with their suites and servants; her sister-ship the *California* bore the Maharao of Kutch, the Maharajah Kumar of Dharampur, the Maharajam of Sirmur, the Maharajah of Jhalawar, the Rajah of Tehri Gawal and the distinguished author, jurist and president of the Hindu association, Sir

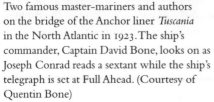

Two famous master-mariners and authors on the bridge of the Anchor liner *Tuscania* in the North Atlantic in 1923. The ship's commander, Captain David Bone, looks on as Joseph Conrad reads a sextant while the ship's telegraph is set at Full Ahead. (Courtesy of Quentin Bone)

Kenneth Shoesmith's gouache of an anonymous tramp-steamer in a North Atlantic gale represents the losses of such humble ships in war and peace. (Courtesy of Trinity House)

Hari Singh Gour. The *California* later picked up American passengers in Glasgow and took them to Tilbury where the liner acted as an hotel, allowing her passengers to enjoy London *en fête* for the Coronation, the price including seats on the procession route and a dinner and dance that evening. The *Tuscania* for her part took 600 school children 'who had been successful in the ballot for tickets' in a competition arranged by Glasgow Corporation, on a cruise through the Hebrides and out to St Kilda. Such scenes were replicated in other grand liners, the Union-Castle ships bringing dignitaries from South Africa, with British India and P&O playing their part. Many of the first-class liner companies sent ships to lie at anchor with the Home Fleet in Review Order at Spithead. Five were chartered by the Admiralty to convey foreign ambassadors, diplomats, members of Parliament and guests of the British Government when the new King carried out the Coronation Fleet Review on 20 May 1937. Led by the Trinity House Yacht *Patricia*, the Royal Yacht *Victoria and Albert*, followed by the Admiralty Yacht *Enchantress* and the five chartered liners, steamed up and down the assembled ships whose crews lined the rails and whose mastheads flew bright streams of bunting, from private standards to commercial house-flags. The warships of eighteen other nations were present, among them flying the swastika, the German 'armoured-ship' *Admiral Graf Spee*.

Prestigious though such occasions were, only the wealthiest liner companies could afford to take ships out of commercial service to lie at anchor, though many sold accommodation and acted as grand-stands to wealthy passengers. For most merchant seafarers 1937 was recalled not so much for its Coronation, but for the upturn in trade and employment prospects. Ship-board conditions improved gradually as the economic prospect encouraged owners to build new tonnage, but this was necessarily slow. Pay had picked up to its pre-slump levels by 1937 and with a rise of about a third in real terms from their 1914 value, combined with a reduction in working hours to give a sense of general improvement, but the majority of ships – particularly among the 740 tramps – remained old or ageing on the outbreak of war again in 1939.

Nevertheless the uplift in trade in 1938 brought many tramps much-needed cargoes and that year Britain exported 38 million tons of coal – about half the highest level of 1913. With long ballast passages in prospect, tramps would often carry extra bunkers in a hold, requiring the tedious labour of working it into the ship's bunkers as they emptied. Coal cargoes were also loaded from ports outside Britain; coal picked up at Durban gained an unenviable reputation for spontaneous combustion and a tramp entering port with a suppressed fire in her hold was not uncommon. Grain, held with heavy shifting boards and temporary hoppers, was a clean cargo, but residue contaminated by bilge-water would germinate and cause a revolting stench. India exported manganese ore, tea – the sweepings of which the crew enjoyed – and jute sacks, or 'gunnies'; salt was loaded in places as diverse as Spain and the Red Sea port of Massawa, but phosphate rock came from more exotic places, Nauru in the Gilbert Islands being an example where it was necessary to moor in very deep water. Such cargoes were discharged in Australia for processing with sulphur to produce a super-phosphate fertiliser, a by-product of which was choking fumes of sulphuric acid. Another cargo with a disturbing effect was copper pyrites which, loaded in Morphou Bay, Cyprus, 'had a sulphur content which clogged the nose and irritated the throat'. A bulk-cargo would often carry its own life forms: grain encouraged rats; while bagged figs from Izmir, from which 'streamed hordes of maggots in endless procession,' produced a plague only exceeded by the too-frequent and endemic infestations of cockroaches. Other side effects were more beneficial. In the days of case oil, the empty tins which had contained petrol or kerosene provided 'the standard, all-purpose bucket' in many areas of the world. Recalling the many commodities he had carried, Denis Chadwick wrote: 'Of unusual cargoes that come to mind, I particularly remember the 50 tons of dog's excrement which we took from Antwerp to the Middle East for fertiliser, and the hold-ful of slaughterhouse bones we loaded in Beirut.'

As the world emerged from the grip of economic depression, a few prescient souls recognised this was contingent upon a gearing for war. In October 1938 the Deputy Master of Trinity House, Captain Arthur Morrell, addressed the Annual Dinner of the Seven Seas Club. The shadow of the Munich crisis lay over the land, leading to 'a great number of cancellations' for the dinner at which Morrell reflected on the state of the Merchant Navy. He was, he said:

> amazed at the loyalty shown ... to their employers ... when one remembered ...
> the disabilities and hardships under which the Merchant service existed – disabilities

which were only now being ameliorated. Everyone at present was heartily sick of the word 'war,' but one could not refrain from realising the value of the mercantile marine … In 1914 we owned some 8,600 vessels of a total tonnage of 19.25 millions; today that had fallen to 6,900 vessels of 17.5 million tons. In the meantime foreign shipping had grown by 12.5 million tons. One had to remember that while the number of ships had decreased … the ships were bigger, so that any similar loss of numbers in any future war as happened in the last would be much more serious in its effect. When it came to personnel the figures were even more disturbing. In 1914 the Merchant Service amounted to about 170,000; today it was only about 100,000. That … gave us cause for very grave consideration … The Merchant Service had been going through a bad time lately, mainly due to the subsidising by foreign governments of their mer- cantile marines; subsidies that were undoubtedly of an economic nature. However, be that as it may, the Merchant Service would be called upon to fulfil a duty which would be of paramount importance to the well-being and welfare of this country. Should that need ever arise, the men who manned the ships would live up to the great traditions of the Merchant Service which had been set by their predecessors.[64]

Fortunately war was still some eleven months away and when it came: 'We were not quite unprepared for action … and certainly we were not as ill-briefed for hostilities as in 1914. The Admiralty's interest in us …' wrote Captain David Bone, 'had not been allowed to fade entirely …', its chief manifestation being the appointment of Naval Liaison Officers:

> to unusual duty in the great seaports … of the United Kingdom … [T]hey are chiefly remembered by the merchantmen as welcome visitors … Through them matters of joint interest were communicated to some higher naval authority and by them we were encouraged to express our views on points of seafaring. I recall a long discussion and some good papers … [and the] 'Star and Scatter' diagrams provided for emergency dispersal of a convoy under heavy attack – that we had to memorise in 1940 – were curiously reminiscent of the plans I heard argued with the N.L.O. appointed to the Clyde. We got along very well together, but this association did not last for long. It seems likely that the Geddes axe fell with swift decision upon such an ornamental if useful branch of the Naval Service. It was discontinued in 1922. Subsequently, our acquaintanceship was remote, if not quite forgotten.

There followed fifteen years of neglect until a stirring in Whitehall consequent upon events during the Spanish Civil War reinvigorated matters (see Chapter Two). The First Sea Lord, Admiral Lord Chatfield, had presided over a series of meetings which sought to draw the Admiralty and Board of Trade closer to the various shipowners' bodies and indeed, to individual companies whose boards were known to possess talent and a proactive disposition. In the autumn of 1937 a series of Merchant Navy Defence Courses were instituted, for:

> the Merchant Navy had again become an interest of the Admiralty. All masters and officers were brought into the scheme of instruction as a necessity for continued

employment at sea. Ship-owners too were advised to put the ships in order against the requirement of convoy practice. We were warned in time.

Attending classes at the Royal Naval Volunteer Reserve headquarter in Glasgow's Whitefield Road over a period of twelve months between voyages, David Bone completed his course of instruction full of profound misgivings. The instructor, Lieutenant Commander R.A. Cassidi 'was lucid and fluent' and, having had experience of convoy work in the First World War, was familiar with the men who now sat before him. However:

> International Law as it affected the merchant seaman was the subject of the first lecture and it seemed curious to learn that there was still an insistence on our non combatant status. Many who sat to listen had been shot at on sight on the high and international seas [in the previous war] and put up embarrassing questions … that were not answered. It was not known with certainty, the lecturer went on, that the enemy would resort to 'sink at sight' when hostilities were opened. In the strict ruling of International Law, we could only defend our ships when directly attacked. Procedure then was to turn the ship's stern towards the enemy and emit smoke. Our guns would be so fitted that they could only be trained on a sternward bearing, and fire must not be opened except upon the direct order of the Master or – in his absence – of the next senior officer. It seemed incredible that the lessons of the last war had been so soon forgotten. But there was a derisive grin on the speaker's face as he noted the ill reception of such a *pronunciamento* … he hoped he had our assurance that Counsel's opinion on the matters of ship defence would be given due attention.

By the time Bone had finished the full programme of lectures and drills the country was on the brink of war. The Admiralty's Department for Defensively Armed Merchant Ships was mobilised by the end of 1938 and he found it:

> strange to be back again, alongside what I think was the same Vickers 4-inch gun at which I learned a little in 1917 … It seemed odd that the course should open with a text on International Law and end on a note that envisaged a breach of it. We were told that the Germans would possibly use poison gas from the air against us and an exhibit of the garb in which we might have to navigate and fight, worn by a stalwart navy rating, was paraded in front of us … A startling apparition! I wondered how we could be expected to stand up in such encumbrances when quick seamanlike duty was to be undertaken. The class looked on gravely.

Trials of the kit, they were told, had not been entirely successful: 'In the minutiae of arrangements the claims of Father Neptune had been overlooked. It was found impossible to combat sea-sickness in a gas mask!'

There were other muddles and confusions. Initially the Government did not consider itself responsible for the supply of gas masks, steel helmets and sand bags, but it was found almost impossible for private firms to purchase these. The corn bags supplied in their place were too heavy to be manipulated round a ship's wheelhouse.

Anti-gas measures were resolved when the Shipping Federation took the initiative, but the Board of Trade's lectures for officers on air-raid precautions were undone by the failure of any of the instructors to have any knowledge of ships. By the spring of 1939 matters were better ordered and many ships returning to British ports were fitted with A-frames over their bows for the streaming of paravanes when in coastal waters where minefields were likely to be encountered. Sand bags, steel helmets and gas masks were supplied and companies formulated plans for defence, particularly in the region of a ship's bridge which, it was assumed, would be vulnerable to aerial strafing. Some companies built 'bullet-proof structures' on each wing of the bridge which, fitted with telephones and voice-pipes, would enable the ship to be conned. Orders were laid down that the master and radio officer would station themselves in the starboard wing, the navigating officer would occupy the port box. 'The theory of abandoning the wheelhouse in favour of protected control points was tested in the North Sea,' but was not adopted, since no suitable command post could be devised. Better success was achieved with arrangements for standardising radio procedures for ships in convoy.

But, amid the gathering storm clouds, shipowners had other matters to fret over. The revival of bulk freight-rates in 1937 showed a downward tendency again in 1939, the year of a good European harvest. Despite the earlier help, shipowners were not in a position to be ordering new tonnage, even the liner companies were feeling the pressure of competition of heavy state-subsidised foreign lines, many operating with efficient new vessels built under their own, better implemented scrap-and-build schemes. Another drafted Shipping (Assistance) Act was laid before Parliament and although not passed before the German invasion of Poland in late August, nevertheless enabled the ordering of some hundred new ships, but half would be sunk by the enemy within months and the redeeming effect of the rest upon the larger merchant fleet was to be small.

Despite the economic turbulence of the preceding years, on the eve of war British trade was still enormous: the export value of wool, cotton and other textiles was £92 million; machinery exports stood at £58 million, motor vehicles at £45 million, iron and steel at £42 million, coal at £37 million and chemicals at £22 million. The bulk of the merchant fleet consisting of liners of one sort or another amounted to 1,170 ships owned by sixty-eight companies and grossing 8,744,469 tons. A further 129 companies of different sizes[65] owned 739 tramps of over 3,000 tons, grossing 3,449,401 tons. In addition there were hundreds of short-sea traders and coasters, among them the coastal passenger steamers of Coast Lines Ltd, the cross-Channel ferries of the railway companies, the short-sea cargo-vessels of the General Steam Navigation Co., the little 'puffers' of the Clyde, the yellow-hulled coasters of Fred. Everard of Greenhithe and the sprit-sailed barges of the Thames.

Although smaller than the fleet of 1914 which had borne half the world's trade, the British merchant fleet now carried only a quarter, but the ships of 1939 consisted of over half the world's large passenger liners (which would prove invaluable for trooping), over half of its refrigerated capacity, and there were also a considerable number of tankers and whale factory ships capable of conversion to carrying other oils, all of which amounted to a quarter of the world's total tonnage of tankers.

The General Steam Navigation Co.'s *Halcyon* of 1924 was typical of coastal- and short-sea passenger services required beyond the cross-Channel ferries run by the railway companies. Painting by Jack Spurling. (Courtesy of Trinity House)

The Southern Railway Co. cross-Channel steam-packet *Worthing* lies in Newhaven at sunset in 1928. Similar steamers maintained services from Harwich, Dover, Folkestone and Newhaven to the Netherlands, Belgium and France. Artist unknown. (© Courtesy of The British Mercantile Marine Memorial Collection)

NOTES

1. The League of Nations, *inter alia*, supervised the territories of the Middle East mandated to France and Britain, gave material assistance to the settlement of refugees from the USSR (Russia) and Turkey and arbitrated in border disputes between the USSR and Poland, and Italy and Greece. But it proved impotent to check Japanese aggression in Manchuria, Italian aggression in Abyssinia, or German aggression in Czechoslovakia. Japan and Germany walked-out in 1933, Italy followed four years later and the USSR was expelled in 1939 after invading Finland. The League's remaining functions were taken over by the United Nations in 1946.

2. Correspondence with George Swaine, August 2009.

3. These were *Furious*, completed before the end of the war, *Courageous* and *Glorious*, all converted from shallow-draught hulls built for the Baltic under plans by Admiral Sir John Fisher. Japan and the USA both scrapped capital-ship programmes, converting the hulls to aircraft-carriers.

4. A British naval aviation mission to Japan under Captain Sir William Semphill RN was influential in establishing the highly proficient Japanese naval air arm.

5. The USA owed its commanding lead in engineering to President Roosevelt's New Deal which saw the construction of many huge hydro-electric and other power schemes with concomitant improvements in plant layout, unit weight, and in turbine manufacture by Westinghouse, among others. These gave the United States its advantage in ship construction and aircraft manufacture in the Second World War which remains unchallenged, although the USSR with its centrally controlled economy, tried in vain to better it for fifty years. The United Kingdom's intellectual lead in matters such as radar, computers, jet engines, etc., was soon swallowed by the American colossus. Britain had already lost her overall economic supremacy prior to the First World War, overtaken by America and Germany in steel production and by the latter in the manufacture of chemicals.

6. To take as an example the situation in 1930, when a good harvest in Europe reduced the demand for imported grain, compelling many tramp owners to send their ships to the Ukraine. This over-capacity in empty tonnage in the Black Sea forced the freight-rate down and led to congestion. In the Argentine the harvest failed, although a number of tramps lay in the River Plate waiting for cargoes that failed and for which there was no market. When the later maize crop proved good, the European surplus was still obstructing the import-market. Tramps could not be diverted to assist elsewhere, since underemployed cargo-liners filled the gap – particularly in the Far East. A glimmer of hope came from offers of charters by the Soviet Union, but the Russians had a reputation for slow payment and – relying upon their desperation for business – used British tramps to undercut the actual market-rate. This lack of homeward cargoes was exacerbated by a consequential drop in outward exports of coal, thanks to the lack of demand for bunker coal for idle international shipping. It is clear from the foregoing that the complex inter-relationships of shipping and national economies was intimate and that the bulk-carrying capacity of the British merchant fleet lay at the whim of many influences over which it, as a service industry, had no control whatsoever.

   Even in 1937, when a general improvement was under-way, the American grain harvest was poor, falling short of the expectations which had led many tramp-owners to send their ships thither. In the event many were obliged to load scrap for which there was an insatiable demand in a militarised Japan at war with China. On the other side of the coin, the Sino-Japanese War reduced the timber trade between Shanghai and North America and by this time many countries had become self-sufficient in coal, further reducing the carriage of this in British bottoms.

7. See *Britannia's Realm*, Chapter Two, for an early (late eighteenth-century) example of British-owned ships belonging to the Ostend Company flying the Austrian flag, Ostend then being a Hapsburg possession. In the first decade of the twentieth century ageing British sailing vessels were registered under the Norwegian flag to take advantage of less stringent hull-survey regulations and efficient, cheap crews. See also *More Days, More Dollars*, Chapter Two.

8. Christopher Furness whose enlightened business sense was mentioned in the previous volume, died in 1912. A man of immense wealth his social conscience was not sufficient, it was said, to prevent his having bought the Harrogate Hotel in order to sack the head waiter and whose fraught relationship with his son Marmaduke was believed to have inspired Kipling to write *Captain's Courageous*. On his death he employed 50,000 men in what was declared in his obituary as 'a great Imperial asset'. 'Kit' Furness appointed his nephew Stephen to succeed him, but he was killed shortly afterwards in an accident, leaving Marmaduke in the hands of Furness's godson, Frederick

Lewis. Seeing he had a liability on his hands, with the help of Barclays' Bank, Lewis engineered a buy-out of their shipping interests from the Furness family for £10 million, leaving the collieries and steel-mills with Furness. During the 1920s Marmaduke, now a Viscount, set about working through his inheritance, his valet reputedly ironing his shoe-laces while his wife allegedly attended to the needs of the Prince of Wales. He seems, however, to have left about £5 million to his son Christopher on his death in 1940. Unfortunately Christopher died that year, killed with the Welsh Guards at Arras in circumstances that won him a posthumous Victoria Cross.

9. Although Furness, Withy sold their Bermudian hotels to pay for new tonnage after the Second World War, they maintained the New York–Bermuda service until the advent of the jet-airliner, withdrawing in 1966.

10. Two tankers sold by Anglo-Saxon were bought by the Hadley Shipping Co., notable as remaining in existence at the time of writing (see Chapter Six). Incorporated in 1926, Hadley was established in 1912, when two directors of Houlder Bros, Maurice Houlder and Walter Warwick, joined forces with Sydney Kaye, active in the South American meat trade, to form the Immingham Agency Co. Houlder Bros were by this time part of the Furness, Withy empire and benefited from a practice established by Christopher Furness whereby in return for a small shareholding (in this case 10 per cent), senior managers and directors were permitted to operate their own businesses or fleets, provided excessive time was not taken from their Furness, Withy responsibilities, and that they channelled their insurance, stevedoring, agency and chartering requirements through Furness, Withy. Other minority British tanker owners were comparatively rare in the tramping sector, one being Billmeir & Co.'s Stanhope Steamship Co. which owned three tankers in 1939, as against sixteen general-cargo vessels. Significantly, however, they were somewhat vintage, the *Stanbridge* having been built in 1917, the *Stanmount* in 1914 and the *Stanfield* in 1892. However, the *Stanfield* was broken-up in 1939 and the *Stanbridge* was sold to the Germans just prior to the outbreak of war. Andrew Weir's Bank Line subsidiary Inver Tankers also owned a small tanker fleet.

11. Wilhelmsen's brother Halfdan had begun operating cargo-liners as early as 1910 while the Italian government had insisted the valuable Italy–New York route was increasingly in the hands of Italian shipping companies, so much so that two vessels building for Furness, Withy's Prince Line had to be sold on the stocks to become Italian ships.

12. With the new Bolshevik government in need of hard currency, Frederick Lewis smoothed the way for a resumption of the Russian timber trade in which he was involved. Among other ventures, Lewis helped form a company with the Soviet government, the Russo-British Grain Export Co. Ltd. The intention was to revive the former Ukrainian export of grain which had declined before the war but ceased with the entry of the Ottoman Empire on the side of the Central Powers. Considerable benefits accrued to Furness, Withy as a result, but after the death of the 'arch-pragmatist' Lenin, Stalin took a hard-line approach to economics and the agreement collapsed. Nonetheless, a residual link remained with the USSR and her eastern European satellite states with Furness, Withy acting as agents, chartering brokers and agents until the 1970s. I am indebted to George Swaine for this and other details concerning the operation of Furness, Withy.

13. See Tregonning, K.G., *Home Port Singapore*, p36. For the acquisition of the Eastern Shipping Co. see *More Days, More Dollars*, Chapter Four. The shrewd Straits S.S. Co.'s board, which was composed of several Chinese and British businessmen under the chairmanship of H.E. Somerville, made a number of other acquisitions or secured controlling interest in a number of other Chinese-owned, Singapore-registered short-sea and coastal companies until the Depression struck Far Eastern waters in 1931. These included Soon Seck Ltd's two steamers, the *Ban Whatt Hin* and *Sri Muar*, owned by eight Chinese shippers who employed them conveying their rubber and other plantation produce from Malacca to the entrepôt of Singapore (purchased in 1923 though soon afterwards closed down); the Sabah S.S. Co. of Sandakan, who ran coastal services in British North Borneo with three modest vessels, the *Kinabalu*, *Kalamantan* and *Klias*; and The Sarawak S.S. Co., which maintained a service from the state capital of Sarawak at Kuching to Singapore, in which Somerville secured a controlling influence in 1931. When Americans and Europeans stopped buying, the effects of the Depression bit deeply in the area. Malay rubber and tin, Borneo timber and sago from Sarawak became worthless. Trade almost entirely ceased. The Straits S.S. Co. anchored their ships off Singapore, placed them in the charge of Chief Officer Tilley, who had to maintain them in working order, and waited. No staff members were sacked, but all took a drop in pay. Under such circumstances, other less capitalised concerns were exposed to takeover and two caught the eyes of the Straits S.S. Co. board. Possessing attractive assets and based at Muar, south of Malacca, the Hua

Khiow S.S. Co. owned the new-built 280-ton coaster *Hua Tong* and the smaller *Najam*. Somerville bought the company in April 1932 and in October made his last purchase before retirement, the Ho Hong S.S. Co. This had been established by a redoubtable Chinese migrant named Wee Bin and established a trade with Bali. This non-Muslin island raised pigs and the massive influx of pork-loving Chinese migrants flooding into the Malay States offered rich rewards to anyone who could satisfy this burgeoning new market. Wee Bin and his successors had, by 1890, set up regular sailings linking British North Borneo and Peninsular Malaya with the Dutch East Indies. Moreover, to feed this market and enable their fellow-countrymen to seek a better life in Singapore and the Straits Settlements, Wee Bin & Co.'s ship sailed south on alternate days from Amoy, Swatow and Hong Kong. By the 1930s the Ho Hong S.S. Co., was but part of a large commercial empire which, by this time had passed out of the hands of the male descendants of Wee Bin through the Lim family, Wee Bin's son-in-law. The Ho Hong name appeared on oil and rice mills, a Portland cement firm and a bank, but the close credit interlinking of an enterprise with few reserves was vulnerable to collapse as the world economy fell-in. The bank, being unusual among Singapore banks in having foreign-exchange dealings, failed when Japan invaded Manchuria and Great Britain abandoned the gold-standard. The death of the world trade's therefore devastated an over-extended coastal shipping firm and the Ho Hong Line passed to the Straits S.S. Co. As it was a well-established British-flagged Chinese company its composition is worth a moment's attention. At the time of its purchase in 1932, it owned three old and largely worn-out ocean-going steamers plying with migrants, general cargo and Chinese delicacies between South China, Singapore and Rangoon, taking rice to China. One of these was the former Glen liner *Glenfruin* of 1888 which had in 1897 become the *Kalgoorlie*, used for transporting 'Diggers' from Sydney to the goldfields of Western Australia, after which, in 1911 she had become a coal hulk, stripped of her engines. Her Scots-built hull remaining sound, she was purchased by Ho Hong during the shipping boom of 1919 when almost anything that could float was brought into use (see *More Days, More Dollars*, Chapter Six). Re-engined and renamed the *Hong Hwa*, she was in use until scrapped in Japan in 1933. The other large steamers were the *Hong Kheng* and *Hong Peng*, commanded and officered by Britons, with Chinese crews. There were also a dozen small coasters and an auxiliary launch which carried small parcels of cargo and produce between Singapore and the distant kampongs throughout the archipelago, much to the irritation of the Dutch colonial authorities. These acquisitions extended the Straits S.S. Co.'s services considerably, particularly after the reconstruction with newer tonnage of the Ho Hong Line with its loading berth at Rangoon, stretching the constraints of the Victoria Point Agreement.

14. The date Hamburg's superseded London as the world's leading port was actually 1912.
15. These were: Federal S.N.Co.'s *Dorset* and *Durham*; Savill & Albion's *Waiwera*, *Waipawa*, *Wairangi*, *Waimarama* and *Waiotura*; and, laid down for the New Zealand Shipping Co., but delivered to P&O and managed by Federal S.N. Co., whose livery they wore, and the *Essex*, *Sussex* and *Suffolk* – all three larger versions of *Dorset* and *Durham*.
16. See Hope, R., *A New History of British Shipping*, p367.
17. The Burrell Collection in Glasgow is the one example of a personal fortune from shipping.
18. Where a steamship burnt 1000 tons of fuel, a motor-vessel burned only 280 tons, making the fuel cost £340 less at 1930's prices. Although a motor-vessel used twice as much lubricant, she required only eight men against twenty-one in a steamer, reducing the wages in proportion. See *A New History of British Shipping*, p371.
19. In a sense the Doxford diesel-engine, which gained a reputation for breaking-down, was a triple irony for although its development was among the earliest, its first installation in 1921 was in a Swedish ship, the *Yngaren*.
20. Other innovations were adopted in these years besides oil-firing and diesel-engines. Wireless, introduced to passenger liners before 1914 had become widespread during the war years and radio direction-finding equipment was fitted in merchant ships after the peace. In 1919 Cunard's *Aquitania* became the first British merchantman to be fitted with a gyro compass. By 1931 some 850 merchant ships were using the Sperry gyro-compass worldwide. Support for navigation was by now offered worldwide by lighthouses, lightvessels, buoys and beacons. The power of major lights covered ranges of twenty-five miles and buoys, using oil-gas and acetylene powering coded flasher-units efficiently marked sandbanks many miles offshore. Fog signals had also reached a high state of development and the war had advanced some of this technology, including the buoying of sea-channels swept clear of mines.
21. Bone, D., *Merchantmen Rearmed*, p5.

22. See *Lloyd's List*, 26 June 2009.

23. See Quétel, C., *History of Syphilis*, Chapter 8.

24. The *Ceres* had been built at Salcombe in 1811. She had carried military stores to Wellington's army before resuming normal trading and was registered in Bude in 1826. Her rig was altered in 1865 and she was lengthened by 15ft, enabling her to carry 84 tons of cargo. In 1912 she had an auxiliary diesel-engine fitted 'which enabled her to keep close to the shore, and so avoid the fate of several coasting vessels sunk by Submarines off the North Cornish Coast during the Great War'. She passed her Board of Trade survey in 1933 and was still working three years later, the oldest vessel on the British register.

25. The cleanliness of a deep-water sailing vessel is remarked upon in almost all of the memoirs written by men who began their careers under sail and graduated to the command of large liners. While in bad weather the seamen's accommodation could be foul enough, this was remedied as soon as the vessel reached better weather and nothing compared with the filth produced by coaling a steamer. As for the world of the coasting craft, this was immortalised by the short-stories of W.W. Jacobs (1863–1943) who was born in Wapping where his father was the manager of the South Devon Wharf. Published in periodicals such as *The Strand Magazine*, Jacobs's yarns are redolent with the vast array of characters that inhabited the coasting craft and the waterfront and contain marvellous vignettes of a long forgotten way of life on the Thames.

26. See Thomas, P.N., *British Ocean Tramps*, Vol. One, *Builders and Cargoes*, p 135 *et seq.*

27. Figures from Ronald Hope's *A New History of British Shipping*, p369.

28. See Hope, R., *A New History of British Shipping*, p 363. Dr Hope might have added Bates, Currie, Ismay, Pirrie and Weir to his list of surnames, most of whom were closely interlinked through complex arrangements as the final chapters of the previous volume demonstrated.

29. Of the Rev. Sir James Philipps's six sons three became peers, one a major general and a knight. The sixth and youngest son Lawrence founded the Court Line in 1905, while of his five daughters, one became an assistant director at the Ministry of Food during the First World War.

30. For references to Forwood see *Masters Under God* and *More Days, More Dollars*.

31. See *More Days, More Dollars*, Chapter Three.

32. *Fairplay*, 19 March 1903, quoted Green and Moss, *A Business of National Importance*, p19.

33. John Philipps addressing the Annual General Meeting of the Royal Mail Steam Packet Co. Ltd, 29 April 1903, *ibid*, p21

34. For a full explanation of the Conference System and deferred rebate schemes, see Vol. Three in this series, *Masters Under God*, Chapter Five.

35. Kylsant's acquisition of Harland & Wolff in the wake of Pirrie's death was to avoid widespread unemployment in Belfast. Work had formerly been guaranteed by J. Pierpont Morgan's, International Mercantile Marine Corporation and this was about to be abrogated as the IMM disintegrated (see *More Days, More Dollars*).

36. 'All, young or old, had the self-confidence of wealthy people, which in some cases amounted an arrogant attitude – the belief that money can buy anything.' Bisset, *Commodore*, p164 *et seq.*

37. The Canadian Pacific Railway Co.'s publicity brochure of 1931 describing the *Empress of Britain*. Among the 'great artists' who had contributed to her Art Deco interior were Sir John Lavery RA, W. Heath Robinson, Sir Charles Allom, Edmund Dulac and Frank Brangwyn RA.

38. When the Aberdeen Line, as a subsidiary of White Star, took control of the Australian Commonwealth Line its own vessels took the White Star House-flag and became known as the Aberdeen White Star Line. The former Aberdeen Line's house-flag was retained by the ships coming under the banner of the Aberdeen & Commonwealth Line.

39. Two years earlier on 25 October 1927 Lamport & Holt's *Rossetti* had gone to the assistance of the Italian liner *Principessa Mafalda* off the coast of Brazil and assisted in the rescue of her passengers and crew. Captain W. Denson had been awarded a gold medal by the Italian Chamber of Commerce.

40. See Hope, *A New History of British Shipping*, p 365. For a detailed account of this sorry affair, see Green, E., and Moss, M., *A Business of National Importance, The Royal Mail Shipping Group, 1902–1937*.

41. At this time Vladivostock was in the hands of Admiral Kolchak's counter-revolutionary White Russians. See *More Days, More Dollars*, Chapter Six, Chapter Note 10, for details of an incident involving the *Benledi*, Captain James Struth.

42. In 1929 the Nelson Line had sold three steam-vessels to Messrs Kaye and Co., already shipowners in another field, when the want of a direct service to Jamaica to convey both passengers and bananas was answered by the formation of The Jamaica Direct Fruit Line. More ships were added

and operated on behalf of the Jamaica Banana Producers Association. The vessels called at Plymouth and Rotterdam and each carried about 10 million bananas.

43. This change coincided with the outbreak of the Spanish Civil War and while lying in Barcelona in 1936 the *Pinto* was lucky not to be hit by a shell.

44. Strictly speaking they were not a class, varying in tonnage between 7,300 and 9,100 grt, but were 'classed' by name for the purpose, such simulacrum being a useful business identity. They were *Madura, Malda, Mandala, Manela, Manora, Mantola, Margha, Mashobra, Masula, Matiana, Merkara, Modasa, Morvada, Melbera* and *Mundra*.

45. In 1926 the *Mulbera's* Fifth Engineer was The Hon Victoria Drummond, God-daughter of Queen Victoria and the Merchant Navy's first female engineer. She also served with Alfred Holt's Blue Funnel Line but was never passed for Chief Engineer as the Board of Trade deemed it inappropriate for a woman to act in that capacity, persistently and deliberately failing her in her examinations on *thirty-seven* occasions. The redoubtable lady distinguished herself in the Second World War when she remained alone in the engine room of the *Bonita*, though sprayed with hot oil maintaining full speed when the vessel was under air attack. She obtained a Liberian certificate and served successfully as chief engineer in Chinese-owned ships sailing from Hong Kong until her retirement in 1962. She died in 1978.

46. HRH The Duke of York, afterwards King George VI served in the Royal Navy and fought at Jutland. He had previously travelled aboard the P.S.N.C. liner *Oropesa* when, with his elder brother, HRH The Prince of Wales, he had made a tour of South America.

47. See Kohler, P.C., *Sea Safari, British India S.N. Co. African Ships and Services*, p119.

48. See Lewis, C., *Sagittarius Rising*, p189. The ship in which Lewis was a passenger was the Italian Lloyd Triestino liner *Innsbruck*.

49. Gollock, G.A., *At the Sign of the Flying Angel*, p26.

50. *Westralian Worker*, 2 October 1925, quoted by Hirson, B., and Vivian, L., *Strike Across the Empire*, p3.

51. *Ibid*, 6 November, quoted by Hirson and Vivian, p3.

52. See Hirson Vivian, p2. The authors point out that: 'In South Africa the strike undoubtedly started the rift in the all-white labour Party and distanced it from the National Party, its partner in the government.' They also relate that the leading South African communist, S.P. Bunting, complained at a plenary session of the Sixth Congress of the Communist International held in 1928 that there had been no support from European communists – a sure indication of the remote plight of the isolated seafarer.

53. The *Seven Seas* was damaged beyond repair by a German near miss in the Blitz of 1940 but the Club exists today though largely as a dining-club dedicated to 'the fellowship of the sea' and raising funds for charity. Sadly, its present membership includes few ex-merchant officers and none serving at sea. In the 1930s through to the early 1950s its membership was composed of many well-known merchant sea-officers and included members of the Royal Navy, among whom may be numbered Burton-Chadwick, Captain Taprell-Dorling DSO RN, better known as the author 'Taffrail'; another author, Sir Lewis Ritchie whose pen-name was 'Bartimeus'; Rear Admiral McCoy, a distinguished destroyer commander; Admiral Sir Henry Moore; Vice-Admiral F.W. Caulfield; Air Vice Marshall Sir Frederick Bowhill, sometime C.-in-C. of Coastal Command, who had begun his career at sea under sail and held a master-mariner's certificate; the reforming Captain W.H. Coombs; Commander Kerans who extricated HMS *Amethyst* from the Yangtze-Kiang in 1949; the writer, poet and Parliamentarian, A.P. Herbert; the sometime Poet-Laureate John Masefield; the broadcaster Richard Baker, who held a commission in the RNVR, and the yachtsmen H.R. Illingworth and Sir Alex Rose. It also boasted a number of well-known marine artists, among them Kenneth Shoesmith – who had himself been to sea and produced numerous posters, particularly for the Royal Mail Line; Jack Spurling, Frank H. Mason and Montagu Dawson, all of whom contributed to the magazine and to the menus of the Club's formal annual dinners. Of the less illustrious, an example was T.E. Hight, a Cunard, White Star officer who served in small naval craft with a commission in the RNVR in both wars during which he lost an eye and had to give up the sea professionally. Nevertheless, with three friends, Lieutenant Commander Hight purchased the redundant Padstow lifeboat and sailed to the United States and back in 1954.

54. For twelve years De Mierre was Managing Director of the General Motors factory in Bombay, spending the last four years of his career as an executive director of the Opel factory in Germany.

55. Captain Sir James Charles was said to be so large of girth that the ship's shell doors had to be cut away to permit the dignified passage of his corpse.

56. Captain W.J. Moore's typescript *Memoirs of a Rocky* – meaning an officer in the Royal Naval

Reserve – is in the Imperial War Museum. He was to command a convoy escort in the Second World War and earn the DSC before returning to Alfred Holt's employ after the war.

57. Hope, R., *A New History of British Shipping*, p375.

58. I am indebted to Captain Peter Adams for sending me Hamilton Blair's letter which was among papers found aboard the HQS *Wellington*.

59. For full details, see *More Days, More Dollars*.

60. The Honourable Company had sought to acquire the former British four-masted barque *Archibald Russell* which, having arrived in Hull with a cargo of grain under Gustav Erikson's house-flag in August 1939 had been requisitioned when Finland entered the war as an Axis ally. She was used as a store-ship for the Ministry of Food and moved to Goole, where the former master of Devitt & Moore's *Medway*, the sixty-eight-year-old Captain David Williams, took charge of her. Williams encouraged the idea of her returning to the red ensign as a training-ship and in 1946 she was taken to the Tyne for repair, but she was in a sorry state. Austerity Britain had no appetite for such frivolities; strapped for cash the Attlee Government sent the beautiful non-magnetic Royal Research Ship *Research*, which had been laid-up in the River Dart in 1939, to the scrapyard and the *Archibald Russell* was returned to Erikson in March 1947, but he died that August and she was put up for sale. With no one willing to take her on she was sent to be broken-up. She had been the last large sailing vessel built on the Clyde for British owners (Hardie & Co.) and the neglect she had suffered during the war had rendered her unsuitable for conversion as the Honourable Company had wished. Instead they purchased HMS *Wellington* for £2,000.

61. There had been a number of local attempts to do this, some of which were successful, but this piecemeal approach robbed the profession of an overall standard and a common protection. There is a painting by J. Fannen dated 1889 of a steam-vessel wearing the blue ensign and an Admiralty trooping number which also flies the flag of the British Shipmasters' and Officers' Protection Society of Sunderland, an interesting comment on a vessel in Government service.

62. To take a single example of one such practice employed for the carriage of bulk sugar: The 'spar-ceiling', or permanent wooden lattice intended to keep most cargoes off the ship's steel shell plating, had to be removed and stored, and all interstices, angle-irons and lodgements in which the sticky sugar might settle and consolidate on a long voyage, had to be blanked off by the application of sheets of heavy brown paper, glued into place. After the cargo had been discharged, the paper had to be removed, the whole space hosed down, dried and the spar-ceiling replaced. Work such as the cleaning and waxing of deep-tanks prior to loading latex, or the construction of shifting boards and building of wooden hoppers for the carriage of bulk cargoes of grain were often under-taken by shore-labour – in the case of tank-preparation in Singapore, by Chinese women.

63. There were a number of charitable institutions dedicated to the needs of native ratings and the Christian Missions catered for them without proselytising. Liverpool had a Chinese Seamens' Welfare Centre which was established during the First World War but closed during the Second. After 1945 a Chinese Seamen's Pool was set up in Liverpool.

64. Quoted from *Lloyd's List* in *The Seven Seas Magazine*, Vol. 14, No.56, December 1938.

65. The sizes of tramp operators' fleets are of passing interest. Thirty owned only one ship; two dozen owned two; sixteen owned three, nine owned four and fifty owned five or more vessels. The largest was Ropner & Co. with fifty, followed by Hain -- part of the P&O Group – with thirty-one. Other prominent tramp owners were: Runciman with twenty-one; J&C Harrison with nineteen; Reardon Smith, sixteen; Common Bros, fifteen; Hogarth, twenty-one; Larrinaga, twelve; Watts, Watts, fourteen; Turnbull Scott, twelve.

TWO

'JUST A JOB THAT HAD TO BE DONE'

Seafaring in Hard Times, 1921–1938

Among the German merchantmen interned in neutral ports at the beginning of the First World War was the Hansa Line's *Imkenturn*, a single-screw steam-vessel of 5,004 gross tons, built in 1909. She sat out hostilities in Surabaya in the Dutch East Indies, during which her crew had tended her upper-works, decks, cargo-gear, and topsides; they had not, of course, been able to clean her underwater body which was fouled by weed and crustacea. In August 1919 she was taken over by the British Shipping Controller as part of Germany's war reparations, dry-docked in Singapore, granted temporary papers and sent home. On arrival at Leith in December she was again docked, surveyed and repaired, chiefly upon her bottom where a species of barnacle had colonised large areas of the underwater shell-plating, a discharge from which had caused corrosive pitting. Where this proliferated the plates were replaced. In less infested areas the plate was drilled out and a rivet passed through the hole and hammered tight, the Lloyd's surveyor content that the hull 'was as sound as she could be made'. Having had £36,000 spent on her, she was refloated in January 1920, classified to Lloyd's A1 100 standard and sold for £86,000 to the Hain Steamship Co. of St Ives to supplement their war losses. She was renamed *Trevessa*.

On 2 January 1923, under the command of Captain Cecil Foster, she left Liverpool for Sydney, Cape Breton Island. Manned by a standard crew for a tramp-ship of her tonnage, Captain Foster had three mates, a wireless operator and five apprentices; four engineer officers; a chief, assistant and mess-room stewards and two cooks; a boatswain, carpenter, seven able-seamen and a donkeyman, greaser and firemen, all of whom were British. She had a further fourteen engine-room ratings comprising a second donkeyman who was Singaporean, and Swedish, Burmese, Arab, West African, Indian and Cape Verdean firemen – in short a typical polyglot mixture. Foster was thirty-six years of age, but one of his able-seamen, Michael Scully was sixty-two and his first mate, James Stewart Smith, was forty-one. The apprentices were in their teens.

The *Trevessa* had no cargo and was in ballast. It proved a rough passage, Foster writing afterwards that:

> we passed right through a hurricane which was then travelling across the North Atlantic, encountering fierce winds and high seas as we approached the middle of the storm, in the centre high seas rumbling in all directions with no wind, and overhead a small patch of blue sky, and we then passed out on the other side into a shrieking blizzard. The ship could not keep on her course and fell away a couple of points, but she plodded steadily on until ... we had cleared the worst of the storm and she was able to carry on on her proper course.

At Sydney they began loading for Australia and New Zealand but ice threatened to close the port, freezing the cargo-gear, so they shifted to Louisburg where loading resumed, the cargo having been carried thither by rail. Despite freezing weather and heavy snow, further cargo was taken in at St John's and New York, after which the *Trevessa* proceeded to Auckland by way of the Panama Canal, making a 'splendid passage' across the Pacific. The discharge of the *Trevessa's* cargo took in several ports in New Zealand from where they made their way to Melbourne and finally Sydney, New South Wales. On Sunday 29 April 1924 the *Trevessa* lay at Port Pirie at the head of Spencer's Gulf, loading zinc concentrates from the Broken Hill mines. This had a stowage factor of some seventeen to 20 cubic ft per ton and was generally regarded as impervious to water.

> When shipped the concentrates are a very heavy dust of the consistency of half-set cement, more solid than mud ... and usually have five to ten per cent water in them, the moisture being sufficient to keep the mass semi-solid ... The concentrates loaded in the *Trevessa* were the property of the British Metal Corporation, to whom they had been sold by the Board of Trade, and were shipped by authority of the Corporation, the ship being chartered by the Zinc Producers of Melbourne ... Like all cargoes taken in at Port Pirie, that of the *Trevessa* was loaded under the supervision of Captain Mars, Lloyds' Register surveyor there ...

Prior to loading, Mars had discovered a couple of rivets in No.1 Hold weeping and had had these hardened-up; he ensured that the limber boards that covered the ship's bilges were 'chinsed' so that the zinc 'slime' did not clog the pump-roses. The method of loading was standard and had proved satisfactory. According to Foster, only one previous consignment had caused trouble. The *Port Auckland* had encountered heavy weather and in the violent seas her hull had buckled, forcing her to turn back for repairs. The *Trevessa* was not to be so fortunate.

There was one other complication to Port Pirie, there was insufficient water to load alongside so that only a partial cargo could be taken before the ship had to move off to an anchorage and finish loading from lighters. The judgement as to how much could be taken alongside depended largely upon the state of the tides and Foster and his chief officer calculated accordingly. They decided that only two days need be spent at anchor and on 14 May the *Trevessa* lay loaded to her marks. The following day the vessel weighed anchor and began her passage towards Antwerp via Fremantle and Durban. The *Trevessa* took in coal at Fremantle and at 06.00 on 25 May she departed, heading west.

In order to lessen the effect of the prevailing westerly headwinds, Foster laid a course to the north-west, into more clement weather. His ship was deeply laden and would make better speed, but he encountered strong winds which sometimes blew at gale force and occasionally rose to fierce squalls. What made matters worse was a dispro-portionately heavy sea, caused by stronger winds to the westwards adding a heavy groundswell. However, neither Foster nor his chief officer was anxious until Friday 1 June when the seas were such that Foster reduced speed to ease the ship and avoid unnecessary damage. All went well until Sunday when: 'A huge sea crashed aboard' over the port side, sweeping the boat deck, tearing Nos 2 and 4 Lifeboats from their chocks and bursting into the chief engineer's cabin. Foster hove-to. At 22.00 the sea remained high but the wind appeared to have dropped and Foster and Chief Mate Stewart Smith were on the bridge when Able-Seaman Scully reported hearing water forward. Foster ordered Second Officer Richard Hall to sound the hold-wells with the carpenter while he told Chief Engineer Robson to start the pumps. From the bridge the *Trevessa* seemed to be coping well, her bow rising to the onrushing seas but when Foster himself went forward to the crew's forecastle, he felt the ship 'was not lifting as she should'. However, no water was found in the wells, the pumps were not picking any up and all ventilator and hatch-covers were secure. Inside the forecastle there was con-trary evidence. By placing his ear to the deck Foster could hear what had caused Scully's anxiety. Immediately the fore-peak was opened up and, hearing the noise of water quite distinctly, Foster ordered the chief and second engineers below to knock the heads off several rivets in the collision bulkhead to allow the water that was clearly in No.1 Hold to drain into the forepeak-well from where it could be pumped out. He then went back on deck to order the carpenter to knock out the hatch wedges and open a corner of No.1 Hatch so that they could see what was happening below but, to his alarm, he discovered the forward well deck was now washed by the seas coming over the rail.

Meanwhile Robson and his second, David Mordecai, had begun chiselling the heads off the rivets. In the rusty space which would have been rising and falling with sickening effect and illuminated only by the lamps the two engineers carried, this was a Herculean labour but they were not at it for long. Looking up, Robson noticed that a portion of the bulkhead itself, 'about the size of a dinner-plate' was bulging and water was squirting through a crack high enough up and with sufficient force to reveal the hold was full. The whole bulkhead was in imminent danger of collapse and both men scrambled up on deck. It was 00.45 and Foster now knew he had no chance of saving his ship.

He had already ordered Hall to turn the ship but as she filled forward her feed-water system began to play up, the engine was stopped and the engine room abandoned, though all auxiliaries were left running. Fortunately Foster's wartime experiences of having been torpedoed twice within sixteen hours in two different ships had encour-aged him to give some thought to his boats, even in peace-time. Moreover, with twelve deaths among the thirty-one survivors, he had acquired basic survival skills and these were about to stand him in good stead as he gave orders for the starboard boats to be prepared for lowering. It is clear from his modest account that his officers and men were professional to a man and he is high in praise of them. 'The behaviour of all was wonderful, and it is a privilege such as is accorded to few to see what men can do in cold blood to combat a situation with all the odds against them.'

The wireless operator had transmitted a distress message with the *Trevessa's* position and while his chief and third officers were busy on the boat-deck, Foster and Hall made preparations for a boat-voyage, collecting a sextant and charts, but no chronometer, while the crew were issued with life jackets. Able-Seaman Gordon Lister also provided a sextant, which suggests he was a qualified officer fallen on hard times, or a former apprentice. When Captain Foster was satisfied that all necessary precautions had been taken, he instructed Able-Seaman J. M'Green to: 'Leave the helm amidships and take your place in the boat'. He then gave the order to abandon ship.

Only a sailor can realise the difficulties to be overcome in swinging boats out under such circumstances, with a heavy sea running, the ship tumbling about, a gale blowing, and in the dark, with the constant danger that the boats would take charge, *i.e.* become unmanageable. Every man had to act quickly and use every ounce of his strength to hold the boats [off the side] as the ship rolled. One mistake would cause the boat to be smashed … The crew right through were magnificent. The boats were dropped successfully into the water with the few [men] in them who had been ordered in to unhook and fend them off … the others waiting for the order to them to enter. When this was given they took their places … either by jumping … when they were almost level with the rail on top of a sea, or by sliding down man-ropes which had been rigged on the ship's side, and letting go as the boats rose towards them. The boats were kept alongside while I collected a few of the ship's papers, all the men's discharge books, and a few things which afterwards proved most valuable … for instance clothes … About half an hour elapsed from the time the boats were ordered out … [O]ne of the firemen, Joseph Abrahim, fell into the water between the boat and the ship's side, but was got safely into the chief officer's boat. The seas were very high – we estimated them to be from 20 to 30 feet – and the force of the wind was 7 to 9 Beaufort scale … Lifebelts had been issued to all hands, but some did not put them on, so as not to be hampered in the heavy work of swinging out the boats … M. Scully, A.B., [later at the formal Enquiry] summed up his reason for not wearing a lifebelt very clearly: – 'When I went into that lifeboat I didn't want no life jacket. I wanted to be loose and help to assist all I could. You want to be active … If I were to get into the water I would go without a belt, because it would be no use to me. Who is to pick you up? What is the good of going down with a life belt round your neck? It is nonsense … If the boat would not save me, the ruddy lifebelt would not save me' – an opinion shared by many of the older A.B.'s. During the voyage in the boats the life belts were used for the men to lie on to keep them out of the water … The boats kept near the ship … for as long as she remained afloat … As she disappeared there was a murmur all round, 'She's gone' … for a while it produced a rather depressing effect …

Captain Foster's account, prepared from his report for the later Board of Trade Inquiry is quoted at length for its detail. Foster behaved with meticulous precision, making his decision in good time, delegating essential tasks to his officers and ensuring he had everything with him necessary to make a long voyage, even though he hoped that the signal transmitted by Wireless Operator Lamont would bring aid within a few hours. He had ensured that the boats were fit for purpose, had ample supplies of water, biscuit and condensed milk on board, and had brought extra clothes – which saved the lives of scantily clad firemen who had been on watch in the boiler room at the time of the sinking – and the ship's and crew's paperwork, without which he would have run into commercial and bureaucratic problems. His account is also of interest for an analysis of the morale of his crew and, bearing in mind the war of attrition that was to come, the difficulties of launching lifeboats in heavy weather without the presence of an enemy.

No ships were to rescue them, though two of their own company's vessels, the *Trevean* and the *Tregenna* would search the ocean for several days. They were about to embark on a three-week voyage. Both Foster and Stewart Smith were sparing in their doling out of rations, no water being issued until the third day, and the single complaint received about this was soon mollified by Foster explaining that they had to take into account the fact that they might be a long time in the boats. Thereafter the crew's behaviour was 'magnificent'.

The *Trevessa* had sunk 1,600 miles from Fremantle and 1,728 miles from Mauritius, but the slant of the wind gave them a fair chance of reaching the latter with the added advantages that the further north they got, the likelier the chance of rain providing fresh water and the warmer the weather. The nearest islands of St Paul's and Amsterdam were inhospitable, with heavy seas, cold weather and little chance of rescue; returning eastwards was too hazardous, while heading for northern Australia or the Dutch East Indies meant a long passage in tropical waters with a remote and dangerous landing. The charts were in the mate's boat and without a chronometer both boats would have to rely on 'Parallel Sailing', that is making for the latitude of their destination and then running along it, for which both boats were equipped with a small magnetic compass. Having obtained the latitude of Rodriguez, Foster decided to make for it.

Their voyage told constantly on the gear and they had to resort to improvised and ingenious repairs. Cold, cramp, sea-sickness from the unusual motion, constant wetness and fatigue began to take their toll as day succeeded day. Allchin the cook foolishly drank sea-water and others would make the same mistake, but Foster refused them more than their ration of fresh. They had plenty of cigarettes and these gave them what Foster called a degree of contentment. For a few days the boats kept company. Able-Seamen M'Green and Scully were cheery and kept morale up, while Chief Steward James was assiduous in handling the stores.

On 9 June difficulties experienced in keeping together persuaded Foster and Stewart Smith to proceed independently for the Mascarene Islands. With a greater spread between boats, if one was picked up it could direct assistance to the other. Before parting company they exchanged all navigational data they could muster. Foster's No.1 Boat had a larger sail than the chief officer's, so that morning they gave three cheers and parted company. Some rain fell that day and eased their thirst a little, but by now all were haggard and drawn, a few had developed saltwater boils and all suffered from constant chafing. Foster had in his boat three men who had been unwell while on board the ship, one was M'Green who suffered 'from a discharging hip bone,' an affliction that cleared up during the boat voyage, but broke out again soon after landing. Several men were to die in Foster's boat: Jacob Ali an 'Indian fireman' and Mussim Nagi an 'Arab fireman'. Ali had drunk sea-water and had aggravated haemorrhoids. 'Until the illness overtook him,' Foster recalled, 'he was one of the most willing workers, and showed wonderful spirits' but he was fifty-seven and this told against him. 'From close personal observation,' Foster wrote, 'I was soon able to determine the capabilities of those round me, and in what way each could be called upon to give of his best. The more able ... soon showed up prominently; no one was spared, and every one responded willingly when called upon'.

In Foster's boat the chief and third engineers, Norman Robson and Thomas Fair 'helped tremendously by the calm, matter-of-fact way in which they took the whole position, and in the way they made various suggestions. The sound practical support they gave me was incalculable'. Third Officer Arthur Tippett and Able-Seaman Michael Scully were both capable small-boat men and upon

whom I could always depend to take the tiller in bad weather. Mr Tippett, being a certificated officer, was not only able to take the tiller and handle the boat, but could steer a course as well by day as by night, keeping the sun at the angle required by day, and by the same method during the night, using the stars ... Of course, with the sun travelling round as the day wore on, the angle in relation to the boat's course kept on changing, and this ... had to be allowed for, which entailed considerable skill and knowledge. At night, too ... with flying clouds, as was the case on most nights, we would frequently have to change the star by which we steered. Owing to this, Mr Tippett was usually called upon to steer during the night, and Scully during the day.

Steering in these conditions was difficult owing to an inclination 'to sink into a semi-comatose state' and routines had to be worked out to keep the helmsman awake. This catalepsy increased as the voyage went on and they grew weaker. Foster and Scully maintained one watch with a third hand, Robson, Tippett and another the second, while all maintained a lookout and baled. The firemen were huddled amidships and the seamen forward, ready to handle the lug-sail. Foster mentions others who helped materially, among them Donald Lamont, the Wireless Operator, Able-Seaman Gordon Lister who was 'most restless ... continually offering his services ...' and his faithful chief steward, Robert James, from whose implicit faith in him Foster derived 'great encouragement'. Foster concludes:

I could not have chosen a crew that could have given me better or more loyal support than those who went through this severe test with me ... I used to wonder at the time, and have often wondered since, which was the harder, to be one of the crew who had merely to struggle along day after day, relying absolutely on those who were using their skill and knowledge to bring the boat to safety; or to be one of those who had the responsibility of bringing the men through? This is a problem I have not yet solved. The various difficulties and adversities we met with were tackled and overcome each as they arose, I will not say cheerfully, for it was just a grim struggle. Every accident was met and countered before another could put us in a worse plight, and each man was called upon to to give his last ounce in the way in which he was most capable. Those who were stronger or more skilful always rose to the occasion when called upon, and never have a hint that they thought they might be doing more than those who were not so well equipped.

Driven by sheer necessity each man discovered a well of reserve, though the privations were horrible, not least the slime forming in the mouth for which some remedy was found by sucking small lumps of coal or buttons. They discussed how the ship had sunk, without coming to any conclusion and most mornings, when the wind fell light, they got out the oars, to some benefit both in progress and morale. They ran sea-water over their heads and took primitive and satisfactory 'baths'; they massaged their feet in storm oil; they swore at each other when the least contact proved agonising, and when they could they caught rain water, for which Foster's rubber-lined Mackintosh came in useful. Then, late on the eleventh day they found the south-east trades and the wind freshened so that on the fourteenth day they broached and, had not everyone begun baling, might have capsized. However, they had reached the latitude of Mauritius and now set a westerly course.

It was on the seventeenth day that they began their greatest trial with heavy seas and strong squalls. At 03.00 the now hallucinating fireman Jacob Ali died and was buried, his fellow Indian, Tom Patchoo, performing burial rites. Mussim Nagi expired the following morning to the distress of his brother, who was also in the boat and whose morale was badly affected. They now endured continual bad weather with water constantly coming into the boat and soaking them. It was at this point that two or three of the white seamen began to play up. One drank some of the compass spirit and storm oil, another claimed that during the war he had drunk sea-water without ill effect. Both activities threatened Foster's authority but the former was severely ill and had to be 'forced' to 'keep-going', coercion that saved his life. 'If these facts were not put on record,' Foster wrote, revealing much of the purpose of his account was for the benefit of those among his colleagues who might one day have to endure similar privations, 'this narrative would be incomplete, but it speaks volumes for the loyalty and discipline of the crew that this is all the fault I have to find.'

On 26 June a heavy sea crashed over the stern damaging the rudder head, so they began steering by oar while repairs were made. That afternoon they sighted Rodriguez, lying to the ENE of Mauritius. Rounding the north point about midnight they ran in towards a light on the Eastern Telegraph Co.'s station and, passing the Government Steamer *Secunder* anchored off Port Mathurin, made for the beach, crossing the reef with the help of a fisherman to land at the Telegraph Company's jetty. Not a man could walk as Foster now doled out the last of the water, but with help from of a clergyman, a magistrate and a doctor besides the Telegraph Company's staff and the Rodriguans, Foster's men were ready to move four days after landing.

Meanwhile Chief Officer Stewart Smith's boat had been undergoing its own ordeal. The sea had destroyed all means of keeping a log, severely hampering navigation. Joseph Abrahim died on the 18th and John Ali the following day, both in consequence of drinking sea-water. On the 22nd William Barton the Assistant Cook died; Able-Seaman Thomas M'Gee followed him next day when Stewart Smith thought they should sight Rodriguez. On the 24th, with a heavy sea running and all hands in a greatly weakened condition Second Engineer David Mordecai stood up to reach his rain-catching tin and was pitched over-board. At the tiller Stewart Smith ordered the sail doused and the oars shipped but, although Mordecai was seen several times, they were unable to approach and eventually lost sight of him. It was a bad day: before sunset Apprentice Henry Sparks also lay dead.

About 16.00 on the 28th they sighted the Peak of Mauritius, twenty-five days after abandoning the *Trevessa*. Sadly, before they could reach it, Joe Baptiste the Donkeyman died that night. An attempt to anchor offshore and await daylight was abandoned owing to a heavy, breaking surf and eventually at daylight they found a gap in the reefs and made the Baie du Cap. Few could walk properly but help arrived and those needing it were carried to an estate hospital where the cook, William Allchin who had drunk sea-water, expired.

Foster's No.1 Boat had covered 1,556 miles to Rodriguez in twenty-two days nineteen hours; Stewart Smith's No.3 Boat had made 1,747 miles to Mauritius in twenty-four days, twenty hours. Thanks to the proximity of the Eastern Telegraph Co.'s terminal Foster was able to signal the fate of his ship and boat's crew and thanks to Lord Inchcape's 'kindness and thoughtfulness' all messages to friends and relatives were paid for by the parent company. Soon afterwards HM Cruiser *Colombo*, Captain Wolfe-Murray RN, arrived and Foster initiated a search for No.3 Boat but this was halted on the 29th when news of its arrival at Mauritius reached them by way of a Clan Line steamer then at Port Louis. In due course all were reunited on Mauritius by the Royal Navy and to a tremendous reception from the inhabitants. Amid Allchin's funeral and several services of thanksgiving, Foster had the sobering duty of accounting for events and an Inquiry was set up under the presidency of the local magistrate assisted by Captain Murdoch MacDonald, the local marine surveyor, and Captain George Owens, master of the *Goorkha*, a Union-Castle liner in Port Louis. The findings were that 'a serious leak' caused water to get into No.1 Hold, that the pumps were in good order but that 'the nature of the cargo prevented the water finding its way to the pumps'.

Most of the *Trevessa*'s crew sailed home aboard the *Goorkha*; some of the Indian firemen awaited the next B.I. steamer heading for Colombo, dispersing thereafter to Rangoon and Aden. At Durban, Norman Robson presented Foster with a gold cigarette case during which ceremony neither man could speak properly, so overcome were they, and when the *Goorkha* entered the Thames on 23 August they were overwhelmed at the reception, with ships dressed over-all and a reception and presentations awaiting them from several organisations, including one by the Joint Seafarers' Council chaired by Havelock Wilson. Other representatives included directors and the marine superintendent of the Hain S.S. Co., the Imperial Merchant Service Guild, the United Kingdom Pilots' Association and the Secretary of the Seaman's and Fireman's Union. A full Board of Trade Inquiry, held at the Royal Courts of Justice, began on 15 November. This was chaired by the Wreck Commissioner, W.H. Disney, with Captain D. Davies, a Younger Brother of Trinity House, and Messrs J. McLaren and A. Younger sitting as Assessors. It found nothing different from the preliminary hearing in Port Louis, concluding that the ship sprang a leak in heavy weather but did not allude to the possibly decayed state of her plating owing to the corrosion attributed to the crustaceans in Surabaya. Instead it contented itself with 'its members' admiration of the fine seamanship and resolution' of Foster, his officers and crew, and expressed its condolences to relatives of the eleven men who lost their lives. The remaining crew were finally paid-off and on 24 January 1924 Foster and Stewart Smith were received by King George V and Queen Mary at Buckingham Palace.

> The King asked many questions and showed that he had a thorough practical knowledge of the difficulties and dangers we had to contend with in seamanship and navigation, and also of the physical hardships we had to endure through our cramped position and lack of food, and congratulated us very heartily on our success in coming through.

Scarcely ever before had an exploit by the mercantile service generated so much august approbation. Both Foster and Stewart Smith received gifts from the Board of Trade and Silver Medals from Lloyd's.[1] Though by no means the longest small-boat voyage made by British seafarers after losing their ship, nor the most extreme example of endurance or privation, the *Trevessa* was no Government expedition ship with a selected crew lost in extraordinary circumstances, nor had she been sunk by enemy action.[2] She was a simple tramp-steamer pottering about her lawful occasions, when catastrophic hull failure occurred in a short space of time, the consequence of which redounded to the credit of Captain Cecil Foster and his typically polyglot crew.

On 28 September 1927 Mr Harrold, the Registrar of the General Register and Record Office of Shipping and Seamen then based on Tower Hill close to Trinity House and the Headquarters of the Port of London Authority, wrote to Captain L. A. Brooke-Smith RNR at the Meteorological Office at the Air Ministry in the Kingsway. Mr Harrold gave Brooke-Smith an abstract of the 'number of Masters and Mates employed during the year 1925 on trading vessels of 500 tons net and over registered in the British Islands'. It makes indicative reading: there were eleven sailing vessels in the home trade and five still deep-sea, employing forty-nine masters and mates; the 261 home-trade steamers and three home-trade motor-vessels bore a total of 787 masters and mates; foreign-going motor-vessels, of which there were 126, carried 521 masters and mates with 12,282 in 3,142 foreign-going steam-vessels. Given Morrell's foregoing rough totals of 8,600 ships in 1914 and 6,900 in 1938, a sum of 3,142 ships in actual use, places the extent of the slump in context.

For those who found employment, matters went on much as before. At sea they had work, accommodation, food and pay, perhaps not much of the last, but better by far than walking the streets on that desperate business of seeking employment that Conrad had found so demeaning. But the seafaring world was full of contrasts. A young mate's life on the Indian coast seems idyllic. The Malabar and Coromandel littoral of southern India often consist of miles of beach, fringed by palms. Here and there stood 'a house and a flagstaff. Sometimes there was a small river or inlet,' recalled Mr P. Fyrth, a junior B.I. officer.

As we steamed along a mile or so off the coast we would see our own identification signal on the flagstaff and would slow down to receive the news: 'Five hundred bags of copra to load' or 'one thousand bales of coir and two hundred bags of coconuts for you'. Then we would anchor near the shore and small sailing craft or even canoes holding a dozen bags of cargo in addition to the paddling crews would come alongside for us to load up.

It was a far cry from the rigours of doubling the Horn under sail. Most young officers had little interest in sail, or regretted its passing. Conditions and opportunities were so very different in liners, with status and regular schedules conferring a new quality to seafaring, while the new technology demanded new skills. While the Honourable Company of Master Mariners debated the desirability of continuing sail-training and Lawrence Holt retained his 'almost mystical regard' for former sailing-ship apprentices, the steamship man had to master the handling and stowage of cargo which became increasingly sophisticated, and nothing altered the tempering a man's character received when exposed to the sea's indifferent malice.[3]

The Belgians, Germans and Scandinavian countries retained sailing cadet ships for their mercantile marines and of the last the Danes maintained a former German five-masted barque, the *København*, which was posted missing in 1928. The barque's disappearance has never been explained, but two other sailing vessels, the Finnish four-masted barques *Hougomont* and *Ponape* were later believed to have been in her vicinity off Tristan da Cunha making 13 knots in strong winds and thick weather with ice in the offing. Since the *København*'s position was unknown, the Blue Funnel liner *Deucalion* and P&O's *Beltana* assisted in the search of the southern Indian Ocean for her and her cadets. With his regard for sail-training, Lawrence Holt ordered the *Deucalion*, then at Capetown, to search along the *København*'s assumed course, and to verify no survivors had landed on remote Gough Island. The landing, made by the *Deucalion*'s bridge-boat under her chief officer, remained indelible in the memory of her second officer, Geoffrey Drake, who manned one of the oars.

The west coast was the weather coast where any flotsam, or any survivors, would be most likely to make a landfall. But a landfall is one thing and a landing something else. When we opened the west coast a feeling of helplessness struck us: cliffs from a few hundred to over a thousand feet high rose steeply, and sometimes sheerly, from the sea, a sea which hurled itself in unceasing breakers at the base of the cliffs. There was nowhere a beach worth the name: nowhere a boat could have landed. We blew our steam whistle constantly as we steamed slowly southward, and we watched the foreshore closely through binoculars. All the life we saw was seals and albatrosses. No trace of human visitation was evident ... Avoiding the off-lying stacks we rounded the southern-most point and headed up for the hoped-for landing place. Gough is a mountain peak ... rising sheer from a great depth ... Everywhere its cliffs are quite awe-inspiring, with hanging valleys from which water falls the last hundred feet to the sea. But just north of Archway Rock ... there opens a glen at sea level ... At its mouth there is a little beach of stones and boulders where we knew a landing had been made by the Scottish Antarctic Expedition of 1903 ... so we lowered our boat

... and pulled shoreward under the Mate's command ... There was no sign of recent human activity. Up the green glen we could see the pinnacle of Hag's Tooth, a 2,000 foot peak of rock, and beyond that, nothing ... [4]

This extra effort so moved King Christian X of Denmark, that he wrote a personal letter of thanks to Holt, but the loss of the *Københaven* led to Denmark selling her other deep-water sail-training ship, the *Viking* (though the private and much smaller *Georg Stage*, later Alan Villers's *Joseph Conrad*, was retained) and the disaster brought to a head the debate about training under sail. [5] Those in favour argued that well-found steam-vessels inexplicably went missing, that of Furness, Withy's *Asiatic Prince* in the same year, being a case in point, while the *Trevessa*'s sudden foundering added to it. The loss of the *Asiatic Prince* with all hands was as mysterious as that of the *Københaven*, though less notice was taken of it at the time (see Chapter Five).

Nevertheless the argument was sustained for some time because there were for many years masters and mates who had served in sail, even after the Second World War, but these were 'wind-jammer men'. One, Captain Wilfred Dowman, having commanded two sailing vessels – *Cambrian* and *Dovenby* – and been driven into steam as fourth officer in the Orient Line's *Osterley*, had then taken the chief officer's berth in the *Port Jackson*, mentioned in the last volume. While in her he had met and married a Courtald heiress and they had settled in Falmouth where they acquired a brigantine, the *Lady of Avenel*, as a static training-ship. In 1922, the Dowmans bought the former *Cutty Sark* from Portuguese owners, and moored her in Falmouth. On Dowman's death in 1938, his widow Catharine presented the old tea-clipper to the Thames Nautical Training College, better known as the *Worcester*, and she was moved to Greenhithe. However, for most the tea-clipper had long passed into history, though in the 1920s there yet remained a few relics from this earlier era. Captain Alexander Jenkyns had served his apprenticeship in the *Samuel Plimsoll* and had been the last British master of the clipper *Thermopylae* before her sale to foreign owners.

Shortly after the end of the Great War he left Mauritius in a small steamer called the *Taiwan* bound for China. When she was four days out her propeller dropped off ... and left her helpless ... Captain Jenkyns tried to get his officers to rig a yard, but they couldn't ... So the former apprentice of the *Samuel Plimsoll* ... showed them how it was done and a cargo-boom soon went aloft as a yard, upon which was spread every scrap of canvas in the shape of awnings that could be mustered. Not daring to test her to windward, the skipper took advantage of the southerly breeze blowing and set a course for the nearest land to the north, the Seychelles. The prospect at best was a dismal one, for there were many coolies on board to be fed and watered. But so well was this unhandy steamer handled that she covered six hundred and eighty miles in less than three weeks, and during one patch of heavy monsoon weather logged a hundred and twenty sea miles in twenty four hours ... She reached the Seychelles and eventually got a new propeller and completed her voyage. [6]

By 1927 Jenkyns was seventy years old but still working, returning to the Far East where he was master of the steamer *Hang Cheong* on the Yangtze-Kiang.

Despite the presence of a Royal Naval squadron based at Hong Kong and with its units more generally showing the flag on 'the China Station' with a regular presence at Shanghai, Wei Hai Wei and other Treaty Ports, shipping on the Chinese coast ran a constant risk of piracy. The most common form of this was for Triad members to board among the passengers and either to attack the bridge and engine room, taking over the ship and carrying her into one of the quiet anchorages along the southern coast, Bias Bay being particularly favoured. Here fellow passengers, targeted for their wealth, were kidnapped and ransomed. This was particularly easy since the regulation of the numerous deck-passengers was in the hands of compradors, or *Chinchews*, who 'sold' deck space to provide their income.

In these Chinese-owned companies whose ships, registered in Hong Kong, Shanghai or Singapore, flew the red ensign, the *Chinchew* was superior to the British master. His control over the cargo gave him immense influence and it was he, not the master, who decided not only when the ship sailed, but where the cargo was stowed. As has been hinted in earlier volumes, service as a European in such ships represented the last refuge for the drunk and dysfunctional, or the man whose ticket had perhaps been suspended previously under suspicious circumstances. Since the employment of a master of British nationality was necessary, but the *Chinchew* was the owner's real on board agent, the history of his ship's master's certificate of competency was of little interest to a Chinese shipowner. Occasionally, however, the practice backfired; inexpert cargo stowage and excessive overloading with both cargo and deck-passengers undoubtedly contributed to losses among small coastal steamers in bad weather, a subject returned to later. Catering was contracted out to *Cha'tzes* who had adopted the old title once reserved for the esteemed tea-tasters of the coast. While many of these men may have been scrupulous in their dealings, others were in the pay of the Triads while most deck-passengers embarked under the 'protection' of their secret societies. All these circumstances abetted the pirates who, having abducted their quarry, would disappear ashore pending the successful outcome of negotiations.

The major all-British carriers on the coast were the ships of Butterfield & Swire's China Navigation Co., still colloquially known as 'beancakers' among seafarers and as 'Taikoo' among the Chinese. Attempts made in the post-war years to stamp out the anarchic practice governing passenger embarkation failed in the face of Chinese intransigence and unionisation of the *Cha'tzes*, even though the penalties for piracy were severe and public executions by beheading were common. China Navigation's ships were boycotted at Canton and the company was obliged to lose face by backing down. There thus prevailed a state of siege aboard the passenger ships plying along the coast because the very real threat of seizure had to be countered. The approaches to bridge and engine room were secured by steel grilles, a rack of Lee Enfields was carried on the bridge and the master and officers were issued with side-arms. Professional anti-piracy guards of White Russians, British ex-servicemen, or Sikhs seconded from the Hong Kong police were also carried. Similar precautions were taken in the ships of other companies, such as the Singapore-owned Ho Hong Line where the bridge was 'wired off' and whose officers 'rather ostentatiously' practised their pistol shooting in full view of the passengers.

However, even these precautions proved inadequate as the central government of the Chinese Republic lost control of so vast a country and power was seized by rival war-lords who kept their localities in a state of permanent civil war. Such a fluid state of affairs empowered local bandits, pirates, Triad gangs and ne'er-do-wells to make hay whenever they could and by the end of the 1920s this state of lawlessness reached a critical state. Whereas kidnapping did not seriously damage confidence in the shipping company, which was to some extent accepted as a fatalistic act to which the rich exposed themselves by travelling, and from which redemption by ransom was common, more determined attacks for the seizure of large sums of money was a different matter.

Despite their almost fortified state, there were occasions when even the best protected vessels, those of Butterfield & Swire, suffered badly. In October 1923 the *Sunning* was attacked, some $20,000 were stolen and the ship's master, chief officer and one of the armed guards were wounded. Two years later, in December 1925 the master of the *Tungchow* was severely wounded when his ship was off Wei Hai Wei and $40,000 was taken out of her. The following August whilst at Wanhsien on the Upper Yangtze-Kiang, the river steamers *Wanhsien* and *Wantung* were both robbed and in the consequent fire-fight one chief engineer was killed. On 15 November 1926, during the *Sunning*'s passage from Amoy to Hong Kong, pirates badly wounded the chief engineer, looted $200,000 and set the ship on fire; she was seriously burned before the flames were extinguished. Almost exactly a year later the passengers aboard another of Butterfield & Swire's river steamers, the *Siangtan*, were confronted with pirates in their midst. The *Siangtan* was seventeen miles below Ichang on the Yangtze when the piracy occurred, the passengers and crew were robbed and the master was held to ransom. In the following May the *Te-an*, on a passage to Hong Kong from Hoihow, suffered when a passenger was murdered and robbed of $4,000. Six months later the *Shasi*, also on the Yangtze below Hankow, had her passengers and crew robbed; two passengers were wounded and a *Cha'tze* was killed. With their ability to safely carry cash and valuable cargo in doubt, companies like Butterfield & Swire claimed the territoriality of their vessels entitled them to Government assistance and to this end armed guards comprising either a detachment of naval ratings or marines were assigned to various coasting passenger vessels of British registry.

In 1930 the Admiralty, irritated by this drain and diversion of manpower, attempted to secure payment for this extraneous service, a levy challenged by the shipowners who claimed a right of protection. Meanwhile, men-of-war on the China station had been active, two destroyers retaking the British, Hong Kong-registered Chinese-owned steamer *Hai Ching* off Chilang Point, on the south coast of China on 8 December 1929. The next outrage to affect coastal passenger ships of the China Navigation Co. occurred in November 1931, when the *Hanyang*, on a voyage between Shanghai and Amoy had her cargo looted. Such robberies were by now seriously damaging to the company's reputation, particularly when the cargo itself was plundered, and the piracies were no longer confined to the southern coast, but were occurring further and further north. In 1932 the dispute over the funding of naval armed guards reached Appeal in the House of Lords and, to the shipowners' disappointment, the Law Lords found for the Government. However, Their Lordships were soon embroiled in a real crisis which entailed rather more that the deployment of a handful of blue-jackets or marines when, on 29 March 1933 the *Nanchang* was lying in Pan Shan Bay at the head of the Gulf of Liaotung awaiting a pilot to proceed into Newchwang.

The port of Newchwang lay on the eastern side of the of the Liaotung Peninsula, forming part of the new Japanese state of Manchukuo. The last member of the Q'ing dynasty, the deposed Emperor Pu Yi, had been installed as the puppet ruler, propped up by Imperial Japanese forces. Although the indigenous Chinese were held in thrall by the hated security police, the *Kempei Tai*, the vast, flat, open countryside, seamed by wide, tidal rivers, proved ungovernable, ensuring that a state of virtual anarchy prevailed beyond the confines of the towns. The small Treaty Port of Newchwang had enjoyed a period of prosperity but the Japanese occupation had reduced trade, the commercial ex-patriate communities – chiefly British and German – had declined, and only the previous year an English couple had been abducted when riding beyond the outskirts of the town's mud rampart. Mr Corkran and Mrs Pawley 'had spent several weary and embarrassing weeks tied together by the wrist, and had been released by the bandits only after the payment of a considerable ransom'.

Nevertheless, when he had anchored the *Nanchang* on the Pan-shan Bar late the previous evening, Captain Robinson had entertained no apprehensions. Piracy was unknown in this area and he was far more concerned about obtaining a pilot, for he had nineteen miles of tricky navigation through one of the several silt-clogged estuaries that characterise the shores of the gulf. The *Nanchang* was in company with several other coasting steamers but while sampans dropped pilots off to most of these at daylight, there was no one available for the *Nanchang*. Her sister-ship, the *Chekiang*, signalled that her pilot requested Robinson weigh the *Nanchang's* anchor and follow. The short notice was insufficient for steam to be raised and Robinson was obliged to watch the *Chekiang* disappear into the vast distance and await the return of the pilot boat at the next high-water.

> The weather was typical of the short spring in north-east Asia. There was an early morning bite in the air, for the coastal ice had only recently broken up and the river was still dotted with floes from the upper reaches. The sun shone golden across the water; the low coastline, unrelieved by hills or woodland, was visible beyond the Bar, and to the north-west the reed-fringed shallows of Pan-shan Bay were dotted with fishing junks of every shape and size. South eastwards, the distant hills of the Liaotung Peninsula rose out of the quiet sea. To all outward appearance things seemed much as before the Japanese occupation …

However, matters were far from normal. Among the fishing junks working in the bay were two moving towards the solitary, anchored British ship. At 11.00 and without raising any suspicion among the Chinese crew working on deck, nor the third mate on anchor watch, these ran alongside. Grapnels caught on the ship's rail and a moment later a group of men, some dressed in the remnants of military uniform but all armed with a variety of weapons, Mauser pistols, rusty rifles and smooth-bores of uncertain antiquity, appeared on deck, firing indiscriminately into the air. Ricochets superficially wounded two of the crew as the pirates stormed into the accommodation, having reassured the astonished ratings that they entertained no malice towards fellow Chinese, only towards the hated foreign-devils. Of those in the accommodation, only Captain Robinson and Chief Engineer Jeffrey succeeded in escaping. The other off-duty officers were scrambling for their Winchester rifles when, following a hail of bullets, the pirates seized Chief Officer Clifford Johnson, Second Officer W.E. Hargrave, Second Engineer A.D. Blue and Third Engineer F.L. Pears. As Blue wrote afterwards: 'One minute we were in the saloon, the next down in the dark hold of a junk'. A number of the crew were beaten by way of interrogating them about the presence of more foreign-devils while the officers' and crews' accommodation was pillaged.

> Woollen garments were much prized by people who normally have to content themselves with padded cotton coats and trousers, and the officers' wardrobes were thoroughly ransacked. Money, watches, and other valuables were also taken, together with all forms of tobacco and such foodstuffs as could be found.[7]

Then, amid a fusillade of shots to deter pursuit, the pirates withdrew to their junks and made off. Meanwhile Captain Robinson had reached his ship's wireless room and immediately ordered steam-up and the transmission of a distress message which took too long to reach Butterfield & Swire's agent, Burton, to be of any use to the *Nanchang*. Burton nevertheless sent warning cables to the masters of the *Te an* and *Luchow* at Dairen, and the *Newchwang* and *Nanning*, then in the Gulf of Po Hai.

The ship's Chinese crew had not betrayed the presence of any further *fan-kwei* and Robinson now got the *Nanchang* under weigh but his attempt to follow the junks as they made off for the estuary of the Shwangtaitze River was frustrated by the extensive shallows and he was obliged to call off his futile pursuit. Acquiring replacement officers, Robinson made his call at Newchwang and continued his voyage, leaving his abducted officers to the best endeavours of the diplomatic process which was rapidly aroused following the arrival of the news in Hong Kong and London. However, this was not easy, because the British Consul had been withdrawn from Newchwang with the Japanese occupation and Great Britain did not recognise the regime of Pu Yi, still less the Japanese police and army who were the *de facto* authorities. The Guomindang government of China had moved their capital from Peking to Nanking but there remained a British Military Attaché and several assistants in Peking and one of the latter, Captain J.V. Davidson-Houston, was sent by Japanese steamer from Tientsin to Dairen and then by train to Newchwang. Here he gathered the handful of resident Britons involved with the English-language press, trade and the railway, and made contact with both the local Japanese army and police commanders, and the collaborating Chinese general.

At this juncture HM Sloop *Cornflower*, Commander Hammill, arrived 'to remind the authorities, both Japanese and Manchurian, that England was still interested in the preservation of law and order'. She also carried an intelligence officer and matters appeared to move forward when one of the *Nanchang*'s officers, Third Engineer Pears, walked into Newchwang. He had brought a letter demanding money and arms ostensibly to throw out the invading Japanese but this apparently propitious start to negotiations was frustrated by a number of factors, not least the divided nature of the local power structure, the complexities of negotiating with a pirate band through tortuous intermediaries, the desire of the Japanese to assert their 'reconstructing' authority by attacking the pirates (which might result in the 'unfortunate' deaths of the hostages), and the blank refusal of Butterfield & Swire to pay ransom.

Soon after the pirates had sent Pears with their demands to Newchwang, Johnson, Hargrave and Blue managed to escape one night when the junk in which they were confined was left by the tide. They had only the vaguest notion of where the land lay and having walked for hours through thick mud into which they sank occasionally as far as their thighs, they realised there was no end to the mud flats. They were exhausted and the tide was coming in. Retracing their footsteps with the greatest of difficulty, they scrambled back aboard the pirate junk as the waters swirled about their legs. Seeing their muddy state the pirates guessed what had happened, the prisoners realising their plight was dire. Although they received millet and hot water twice a day and were not malnourished, the space in which they were confined was infested with cockroaches and lice, freezing at night, dark, hot and oppressive by day. By the time a week had passed, the daytime temperature began to rise rapidly. The junk, along with others, lay hidden up a narrow creek lined with reeds up to 15ft tall. On 11 April the junk was taken over by a new group of rebels, a fact that further confused Davidson-Houston's negotiations. Objects of curiosity, contempt and derision, the three men were regularly humiliated, even urged to copulate with local peasant women for their captors' amusement. When they refused they were offered males, but this was more easily resisted. Generally, however, they were not seriously ill-treated, since the pirates' objective was ransom. Although eaten alive by lice and, as the weather warmed up, mosquitoes, they became inured to the face-losing humiliations of having their hair, ears and 'long' noses pulled, manifestations of a rough curiosity rather than brutality.

In due course a correspondence was established with their would-be rescuers, but although Japanese aircraft regularly flew overhead, the junks lay concealed by the towering reeds, now fully grown in the hot summer weather of June and July. The junks were frequently moved and almost set on fire when the dry under-growth of last-year's vegetation was ignited by a cooking-fire. After over five months the patient diplomacy of Davidson-Houston and his colleagues, working with the Japanese, found the captives exchanged on 3 September for a far smaller sum than had been demanded, some $20,000 – about £1,000 at contemporary rates. The actual exchange was effected by a Japanese army officer, Captain Obata, who, in entering the pirates' lair 'in command of very unreliable Manchurian troops, was,' in Davidson-Houston's words, 'a very brave man'. The money advanced by Obata consisted of a sum from British funds for 'expenses', the balance coming from the Japanese. The kidnappers were left in no doubt that this was not ransom money, rather a sum of the acceptable 'squeeze' that allowed face to be saved all round. Their captors left their unwilling guests with cheerful valedictions that they were to: 'Please join us next year, and together we will kidnap others.'

A few hours after boarding an armoured train Johnson, Hargrave and Blue arrived in Newchwang to be welcomed by immense crowds and the press-corps. Endless photographs were taken, largely for propaganda purposes, the Japanese being keen to demonstrate their civilising mission in Manchukuo and to offset the rumours that were then beginning to circulate over their treatment of the subjugated Chinese. Finally the British officers 'went to Grant's house for late breakfast, bath and hair-cut. Grant was our Newch[w]ang agent, and he made us more than welcome,' Blue concluded. Although the ordeal of the three British officers had ended, a number of awkward questions remained unanswered. Captain Robinson had received no acknowledgement of his original radio signal sent at noon on 29 March, but Burton had received intimation that the *Nanchang's* failure to arrive was rather more complex than a failure to raise steam. It was afterwards thought that the delay was deliberate, engineered by the Japanese radio operators at the Dairen shore-station, not to obstruct a distress message for its own sake, but as part of a general non-co-operation policy with British shipping. Burton had had extreme difficulty in getting the Japanese radio station at Dairen to send his warning signals to the masters of the other ships, and in arousing Japanese interest in the piracy of the *Nanchang* herself. This had been achieved only with the personal arrival of Davidson-Houston in uniform.

The Japanese attitude to British ships was partly in petty revenge for the failure of the British Government to recognise Manchukuo (which was done only by Nazi Germany and Fascist Italy), and partly to discourage British coastal traffic itself. This was an extension of the reservation of Japanese cabotage to their own vessels on their home coasts. In the full throes of imperial expansion, Japan's jealousy of her sphere of influence excluded all others, particularly the British who were seen partly as their western counterpart – an island monarchy with an empire, washed by a benign warm-water current and blessed by military good fortune – and partly as having too much of the world under her own domination, a point of view frequently expressed in these inter-war years by the Japanese and one which had been aired to Davidson-Houston during his enforced stay in Newchwang.

The *Nanchang*, having been built in 1922, survived the war and was broken-up in 1950. As far as her officers were concerned, Robinson and Jeffery had retired before the outbreak of war in 1939, Johnson rose to command and retired in 1960. By this time Hargrave was in command of a Butterfield & Swire ship and Blue was a chief engineer.[8] Notwithstanding the arrival of HM Destroyer *Whitshed* in Newchwang to back-up Davidson-Houston during his protracted negotiations, and despite further naval activity along the coast, piracy persisted in Chinese waters.

On 17 June 1934 the passengers and crew of the *Shuntien* were robbed and the third officer wounded after she had left Tientsin bound for Shanghai. Off the estuary of the Huang-Ho – the Yellow River – several of the passengers, revealing themselves as pirates, seized the ship. They then looted her before abducting about twenty passengers, including the naval lieutenants J.D. Luce of HMS *Osiris* (a future First Sea Lord), and P.L. Field of HMS *Oswald*, and two of the *Shuntien's* deck-officers. The pirates and their hostages then boarded several junks that by previous arrangement were soon on the scene, and the *Shuntien* was suffered to proceed on her voyage. The master promptly broadcast news of the incident and Japanese, American and British warships were alerted. The aircraft-carrier HMS *Eagle*, escorted by two destroyers left Wei Hai Wei and doubled the Shantung Peninsula at high speed. On 20 June the Admiralty issued a communiqué, announcing that 'as a result of a naval action' the British naval and mercantile officers were safe on board HM Destroyer *Whitshed*.

In January 1935 the *Tungchow* was raided a second time when pirates, who had boarded as passengers at Shanghai waited until she was on her way to Tientsin before killing a White Russian guard and wounding one of the ship's officers. The *Tungchow* was ordered into Hing Hai Bay where the pirates escaped with their loot, but the

$2,000 they lifted were unsigned and proved valueless. Nevertheless, the murder roused the authorities, both British and Chinese, to offer considerable rewards for the names of the leaders of the gang. After the outbreak of the Second World War, on 1 December 1939, the river-steamer *Wulin* had her cargo looted when the vessel was in the Yangtze delta at the cost of a Russian guard's life. It was not to be the end of piracy in the China Seas, but the outbreak of war changed the complexion of affairs and ended what, for many, was a pleasant enough life. Captain Elwyn Jacob recalled his inter-war years with the Asiatic Petroleum Co.'s tankers on the Yangtze-Kiang. This included 'snipe shooting on the Yangtze delta, summers in Cheefoo and winter skiing in Japan.'

Wild-fowling was possible further south where, though not entirely extirpated, piracy was rare in the placid waters of Sumatra, Malaya and Borneo where the expanded fleet of the Straits Steamship Co. plied their trade. The development of the Malay Peninsula by British interests had begun with tin, initially worked by Chinese immigrant labour but later by tin-dredges. By 1930 the rubber production introduced at the turn of the century was immense in value but, while short lengths of road and railway joined the rubber estates and tin-producing areas with the small ports dotted between Singapore and Penang, neither road nor railway ran longitudinally down the sparsely populated peninsula. Even on Singapore island itself, outside the environs of the thriving port-city, nature was largely undisturbed a century after Stamford Raffles had raised the Union flag. Everything went by sea, and most was carried by the fleet of the Straits Steamship Co. managed from its headquarters in Ocean Building close to the landing steps at Collyer Quay.

The close association of this company under its parent, Mansfield & Co, with Alfred Holt's Ocean S.S. Co. in Liverpool was betrayed not only by the name of its head office but by the funnel colours of its ships. These small vessels bore the distinctive black and blue of Holt's ocean-going liners, with the lower third white, so there was no mistaking the connection with a *Semprong Kapal Blau* of the larger line. As noted in Chapter One, by the 1930s the Straits S.S. Co.'s services were extensive, and although only a handful of its ships grossed over 1,000 tons, it shifted an immense amount of cargo and is, perhaps, the finest example of a fleet providing the feeder traffic that made Singapore the great *entrepôt* that it was. The little ships linked a thousand small *kampongs* (villages) and modest ports with the outside world. Except for a few hours when crossing the Strait of Malacca from Penang to Belawan, or on the run from Singapore to Sandakan in North Borneo, its ships were never out of sight of land, but the complexities of littoral cabotage or the pilotage in the constantly silting rivers of the hinterland still required the specialised skills related in an earlier volume.[9]

The Straits S.S. Co. was a firm of wide ethnic diversity. Its board was Sino-British, its shore-side technical and managerial staff comprised Britons, Eurasians and Chinese, its shore-labour Chinese and Malays, its sea-staff Britons, Chinese and Malays. On the mainland not far from its insular northern hub, Penang – itself an *entrepôt* of importance if lesser magnitude than Singapore – the company built a shipyard at Sungei Nyok. Here were built the little '75-tonners' that were the backbone of the entire operation. The first two of these were designed by Alfred Holt's naval architect in Liverpool and built on the Clyde. They were, however, not riveted, but bolted together so that they could be knocked down, shipped-out and reassembled at Sungei Nyok. With engines installed and the hulls fitted out their capacity was of 74 net tons for cargo, with space for 200 deck passengers. These, the *Rengam* of 1924 and the *Rompin* of 1925, were fitted with the new diesel engines. They were followed by six similar though steam-powered craft all designed and built at Sungei Nyok. In 1927 three very economical and successful 75-tonners were built at the Taikoo yard in Hong Kong and later, after the worst effects of the Depression had begun to recede, an advanced motor-powered 75-tonner was built at Sungei Nyok. This, the *Rantau*, established the breed, her diesel operating at 40 per cent the cost of the steamers; she drew only 7.3ft yet could carry 208 tons of deadweight cargo on a measured net tonnage of a mere 66.4 tons.[10]

Where a full master-mariner's certificate was required for larger vessels, hence the British masters and mates manning them, careful design of these coasters – unique to Malaysian waters – kept their net registered measurement below 75 tons so that they fell within the limits imposed by the Straits Settlements Merchant Shipping Ordinance of 1912 governing the qualifications for their masters. This followed an earlier ruling of 1882 which had set the tonnage limit to 50 tons, being amended upwards to 75 tons in 1922, allowing them to be commanded by a competent and experienced Malay *serang* capable of passing the 'fairly straight forward tests' set by the Straits authorities. This was a major advance, enabling the Straits S.S. Co. to develop its ships and services and while the amounts of cargo might seem trivial, if the numbers of ports called at, and the numbers of voyages made are taken into consideration, in a year a 75-tonner regularly lifted as much cargo as one of the 8,000-ton Blue Funnel liners it fed. Thus, in terms of public benefit, the two were of equal utility.[11]

Generally these little vessels plied their vital trade without mishap, the exception occurring on the night of Sunday 23 October 1933 off Pulau Pisang when a sudden high wind as occasionally blows up in the vicinity of Singapore was of sufficient persistence to raise an equally high sea in which the *Tronoh* was overwhelmed. Such a wind was known as a *sumatra* after the island whence it generally comes. R.S. (later Sir Stewart) MacTier wrote in his diary two days afterwards that:

> out of the 55 crew and passengers on board, 33 are missing and inevitably drowned. It is a disaster – a fine new ship of 220 tons [her gross, not her net tonnage] and only 60 miles from Singapore. Salek, the captain, the *chinchew* and another *chinchew* I know well, Tan Mah Siang, are all missing. All the engine room crowd are gone and all the senior Malays. The Malays may well say that this area is haunted by evil spirits – it has a terrible name among the fishermen. The ship went down within a mile of the lighthouse [on Pulau Pisang]. Seven of the survivors were picked up by the *Rantau* after 36 hours in the water and fourteen more were rescued by the lighthouse keeper.[12]

These last had been spotted at the lighthouse by one of the company's trainee managers, W.I.L. Legg, who as a member of the Singapore Flying Club made a search from his de Havilland Moth, while Captain Ali Bin Osman of the *Rantau* had had previous experience of saving life at sea. There was no suggestion that Captain Salek had been persuaded by his *chinchew* to overload the *Tronoh*, though both were permitted legitimate perquisites, but in ordering a modified design for a new 75-tonner in 1945 from Holt's naval architects, the *Tronoh* had not been forgotten. The Straits S.S. Co. board required their projected new ship to have sufficient stability to 'satisfy the worst service condition, say leaving Muar with considerable shelter deck cargo and little or no cargo in the holds, maximum number of deck passengers with *barang* (luggage) and a bad *sumatra* thrown in'.

The Straits S.S. Co.'s fleet comprised some fifty vessels of varying size, larger vessels being employed on the Malay Peninsula's east coast and the Bangkok route which, like the longer run up to Sandakan and Tawau on the east coast of British North Borneo (Sabah) was exposed to the north-east monsoon.[13] Nevertheless, the largest ship, the *Kedah*, was on a scheduled service in the Strait of Malacca which encompassed Penang and Belawan, a port newly developed by the Dutch on the east coast of Sumatra. It was said that one could set one's watch by the *Kedah*'s departure and arrival times in Singapore Road and she regularly exceeded her specified design speed of 18 knots. Built at Barrow-in-Furness by Vickers she grossed 2,499 tons, had first-class accommodation for eighty-eight, could carry 960 deck-passengers, and had space for 1,700 tons of cargo in three holds.[14] She left her own assigned anchorage off Singapore bound for Penang at exactly 11.30 on Thursday morning and made a fast passage northwards, through the shallow Kra Channel, her stern wave rolling ashore, rising 'higher and higher, to break behind her, until she seemed on the point of surf-riding,' to anchor off Fort Cornwallis, Georgetown, at 08.30 precisely. Her passenger list preceded her by telegraph, appearing in the morning editions of *The Straits Times*. When Penang enjoyed a Race Week the *Kedah* carried the well-heeled Singaporean punters and many of the participating thoroughbreds.

From Penang the *Kedah* crossed the Strait to Belawan over the weekend, returning to Penang and then Singapore. Under the command of Captain R.J. Work she was a

It was said that one could set that one could set one's watch by the departure time of the Straits Steam Ship Co.'s *Kedah* from Singapore Road at 11.30 on a Thursday morning. The *Kedah* was one of many ships providing coastal services in eastern waters by this company. (From a Private Collection)

popular ship, her passengers enjoying airy accommodation unsurpassed by any other coastal passenger steamer.[15] Her only disadvantage was her coal consumption, over 50 tons a day being required to maintain her high speed, for Work frequently pushed her in excess of 20 knots. Later MacTier devised a scheme to install diesel power, which would have cut operating costs in half, but it would also have reduced her speed to 15 knots and while her freight and passenger fares rarely covered her operating costs, it was her passengers who were paramount in the eyes of the Straits board. Loss of speed meant loss of prestige, so MacTier's plan was scrapped. One significant commodity in her holds was the carriage of bagged Australian flour which was discharged at Penang into the company's coasters and the wooden sailing barges, or *tongkangs*. These in turn distributed along the coasts of Province Wellesley, peninsular Thailand to the north, and the Sumatran littoral to the west. The *Kedah* loaded this at Singapore, whither it was carried by the Blue Funnel Line – chiefly in the *Centaur, Charon* and *Gorgon*.

By the mid-1930s, in addition to tin and rubber, palm oil was being exported from Malaya and the Straits S.S. Co. built 75-tonners with tanks for the bulk transport of this which was transferred into the deep-tanks of the ocean-going cargo-liners at Singapore. As was the practice on the China coast, all this freight was in the charge of the influential *chinchew*. Although the *chinchew* lost his autonomous status in Straits S.S. Co. ships towards the end of the 1930s, the position remained highly sought-after. The rapid turn-around, even in Singapore but more so in the small ports, combined with the variety of items, commodities and consignees, made his work arduous, though he was assisted with a small staff of *cranis*, or tally clerks. Nevertheless the *chinchew* was often required to work all night preparing manifests as his vessel ran between one port and the next. The variety of cargoes handled was staggering. Outward from Britain and Europe came all manner of machinery from spare parts for tin-dredges to motor cars for the estate proprietors and vehicles for their plantations; outwards too came rubber tyres, gin, whisky and other liquors together with beer brewed in Singapore; fuel oil, cigarettes, clothes, books, cosmetics; pigs in rattan baskets from Bali or Hong Kong, Chinese foodstuffs, rice-wine and *samsu*, dried-fish, fish frozen in ice-boxes, chickens, Australian flour, old newspapers and mail. Homeward from the coasts they loaded tobacco at Belawan, along with pineapples for canning, coffee and copra, though these commodities could as easily have come from Penang, or from Borneo or Sarawak where timber, sawn and rough – even uncut logs – were also picked up, along with bags of sago and birds' nests. Bundles of long doubled rattans, manila hemp, gum dammar, several kinds of fruit including mangoes and of which the foul-smelling but delicious-tasting durian was perhaps the most exotic. Live animals might also feature on the *chinchew's* manifest. Live cattle for *halal* slaughter, race-horses and gun-dogs for the European males, a rare poodle or decorative spaniel for the females; occasionally a Sumatran tiger destined for the Hamburg zoo, or an elephant for Regent's Park – it was arguably the most diverse lading taken up anywhere in the world.

No *chinchew* employed by the Straits S.S. Co. was permitted to gain a hold over a master, not least because in 1896 the company had acquired the assets of Tan Kim Tian Steamship Co. thought to have been the first locally owned steamer operator when it acquired the *Rangoon* from B.I. in 1871. Lee Cheng Yan, one of the original directors of the Straits S.S. Co., had joined the Tan Kim Tian board when it was in difficulties operating five coasting steamers between Singapore and Java,[16] but this failed to save the company after it lost the steamer *Celestial*, a disaster attributed by *The Straits Times* of 21 February 1896 to the fact that 'the *chinchew* is in certain matters the permanent authority and the master is his instrument. The *chinchew* will consult with officers occasionally, but otherwise they must do what they are allotted, and must sail when his order is given'. The loss of the *Celestial* brought down the company which fell into the hands of the Straits S.S. Co.

A later Shipping Commission enquiring into the practice of employing *chinchews* had nevertheless concluded that their employment was indispensable.

> [S]hippers and passengers are mainly Chinese, and European officers are naturally ignorant of the Chinese language and Chinese usages … the *chinchew* looks … after his employer's interests even to pressing ship-masters to carry excess cargo and passengers. Trouble mostly arises in small vessels, the masters of which are too much afraid of owners to dare to interfere with a *chinchew*'s usurpation of power.

Nevertheless, even in the vessels of the Straits S.S. Co., the *chinchew* not only controlled the freighting, he dispensed patronage and was in charge of the Chinese coolies who loaded and discharged it. With no facilities to handle cargo at the small ports, the craft had to be self-sufficient, in derricks, winches and labour. The cargo-gear was looked after by the Malay seamen under their *serang*, or boatswain. A good *serang*, such as Ali bin Osman of the *Rantau* who had been coached by Captain J.M. Daly, successively master of the *Malacca* and *Ipoh*, could earn promotion once he had passed the Local Steam Vessel examination. The masters, mates, chief and second engineers were generally British or Eurasian. They were often charismatic characters, for it took a certain stamp of man to settle in this demanding trade. Constantly on the move, the masters of these little ships needed a wealth of local knowledge and although, in conformity with the practice of Alfred Holt & Co., the company laid down courses between headlands, islands and so forth, navigation in shallow rivers and estuaries bordered by constantly growing mangroves meant a master and his mates had to be alert in the execution of their duties. There were neither tugs nor pilots, and all hinged on expertise, both on the bridge and in maintaining power below. When the coaster did stop for cargo, the cargo-gear had to work flawlessly, for time was money and the comings-and-goings of the big liners at Singapore were demanding. Captain F.W. Chamberlin who had been Work's chief officer in the *Kedah*, married his daughter, rose to be the company's Marine Superintendent, a post that 'was to be helping the finest lot of captains one could ever hope for. There was always a wonderful spirit'.

One feature of these small vessels was the juxtaposition of Muslim Malay seamen, pork-loving Chinese firemen and stewards, and a handful of Europeans; there had to be three galleys, each catering for the disparate diets of these diverse groups. An atmosphere of concord nevertheless prevailed and they were well known as settled and happy ships. Most of the Malays came from *kampongs* near Malacca where employment in the Straits S.S. Co. became a father-to-son tradition, while the Singaporean Chinese, were predominantly Cantonese, with Hailams as cooks and stewards, though Singapore itself tends to be populated by Hokkiens.

The Chinese diaspora and lack of cheap land transport ensured that a steady stream of deck-passengers crowded the company's ships. These people not only provided labour for the expanding rice, coffee, rubber and palm-oil plantations, and manned the tin-producing areas, but created a market for pigs, as we have noted, and Chinese produce, particularly vegetables and delicacies at festivals such as the Chinese New Year. At such times additional passenger traffic was created but these were by no means divided simply into Europeans travelling first-class and the 'venturesome' Chinese on deck. As Professor Tregonning points out:

> a most astonishing number [of people] were found lying on their rattan mats or squat-ting in groups on the decks of Straits ships … possibly no other line in the world could match the assortment. It might have a Burmese woman next to an Iban timber-cutter; an Anglo-Burmese railway official next to a Brunei fisherman; a Bhuddist monk from Thailand next to a Muslin hadji; Sikhs; Malays; dapper Vietnamese; a half-naked Dyak; and a Dusun policeman; a Murut and a Suluk; a Javanese and an Achinese; Muslims returning from Mecca, a Nepalese seller of precious stones, a Tamil rubber tapper, an Arab coming from his shop in Tunis, and above all, Chinese.

Given the numbers of this diverse humanity it is remarkable that trouble so very rarely erupted. On the occasion it did, however, it could end tragically, as was the case aboard the *Klang*, running between Singapore and Port Swettenham in the autumn of 1925. The *Klang* had not yet cleared the line of deep-water merchantmen in Keppel Harbour when a report that one of his 400 passengers had run *amok* reached Captain MacDonald on his bridge. He was a cheerful Gaelic-speaking Scot, 'notable, it seems, for his bulk, blue eyes, and a long beard hanging from rosy cheeks …'. Putting the ship about, he shoved his revolver in one pocket and cartridges in another with the obvious intention of over-awing the *amok* without injury, then left the bridge to the chief officer. The *amok*, a Malay armed with a long knife known as a *parang*, had already killed and wounded several fellow passengers. MacDonald approached him but: 'With one violent slash, the Malay almost disembowelled him'.

In his capacity as Mansfield's agent, W.I.L. Legg had been calling on a Blue Funnel liner in the anchorage when he saw the *Klang* returning with signals for police and medical assistance flying above her bridge. He ordered his launch alongside immediately.

> The signal had been seen by Fort Canning [the signal station], and simultaneously with our arrival Inspector Bostock of the Marine Police came alongside in a police launch. On gaining the deck we were horrified to find dead and wounded strewn everywhere. There were no signs of crew or passengers. Those who had avoided the *amok* had barricaded themselves in cabins or on the after boat deck. On gaining the lower passenger deck, we were confronted by the *amok*, only a few feet distant. He approached us in a most threatening manner, brandishing a 12-inch double-edged knife. I called to Inspector Bostock to shoot the man in the legs, and so bring him down. He tried but not low enough. The *amok* received two shots, one in the groin and the other in the thigh. He fell to the deck and we were able to disarm him with-out difficulty.[17]

A few minutes later they found MacDonald, bleeding profusely and mortally wounded. They tried binding his belly with sheets ripped from his bed but he died as they did so. Meanwhile his wife, as was her custom, had driven to the western end of the island to watch the *Klang* clear Keppel Harbour but then inexplicably turn back. By the time she reached the *Klang* she was a widow. As Bostock took the *amok* ashore to land on Johnston's Pier he struggled to escape and died in the attempt; he had killed or mortally wounded nine people and seriously wounded sixteen more. H.M. Tomlinson recalled in his history of the Straits S.S.Co., *Malay Waters*: 'Only an unusually strong, kindly and courageous man would have resorted to pacification in an *amok*. That shipmaster's blue eyes and other befriending characteristics are remembered only because he came to a strange and untimely end.'

A few months later, in April 1926 the company lost the *Penang*, six hours out of Singapore on her way to Port Dickson, between Port Swettenham and Malacca. Just after sunset on the evening of the 22nd, fire broke out in the cargo which comprised, among other inflammable items, 2,900 cans of kerosene, 500 drums of oil fuel and thirty-eight large jars of *samsu*, a Chinese spirituous liquor. The fire grew rapidly, defying the efforts of the crew to subdue it and the master ordered the boats launched. Only two were now clear of the flames and one was lowered too quickly, one end dropping and pitching people into the sea. Rafts were thrown overboard and all escaped except eight of the Chinese crew who died in a fire thought to have been caused by a carelessly discarded cigarette butt. The *Penang* herself sank the following morning.

Other incidents occurred from time to time. The company's insistence that its masters followed prescribed courses was not necessarily a guarantee of safety, as when a steeple-rock was discovered on one of the company's safe-tracks. In February 1929 the *Darvel* grounded as she left Sandakan at night when, with no lights to guide her in what was thought to have been a blinding rain squall, her quartermaster failed to hear her master's order to alter course. The *Darvel* ploughed doggedly over several hundred yards of silt and fetched up with her bow among nipa palms and monkeys gambolling on her boat-deck. A more serious loss was that of the *Kinabalu* which in September 1940 struck the Batu Mandi Rocks which extend from Tanjong Ajah north of Jesselton (Kota Kinabalu). Heavy tropical rain on a poorly lit, featureless coast could make these coastal passages hazardous. Ironically the Straits S.S. Co. had lost another ship on the same reef.[18] Having struck, the *Kinabalu* rolled onto her side so that most of her officers were cast into the sea, though the vessel stayed wedged on the reef. Peter Edge, a government officer on his way to Lahat Datu, was thrown overboard and swam all the following day until he reached shore where he was eventually rescued. The master, Captain R. Atkinson, and Chief Engineer Hiley also struggled ashore, and all but three unfortunate deck-passengers and a child who must also have been cast into the water, were found safe aboard the wreck.

In the days before generous pensions these coastal companies provided employment for ageing masters like Captain Jenkyns. One such firm, founded and run until 1931 by the government of Sarawak when it was acquired by the Straits S.S. Co., was the Sarawak S.S. Co. For some time it had been run on the rajah's behalf by E. Parnell, nephew of the Irish Nationalist. The Depression badly affected the fortunes of Sarawak and the company was rescued by Somerville, retaining a separate identity within the group. For many years the master of the fleet's premier ship, the *Vyner Brooke* (named after the third rajah), was Captain A.C. Benfield who had spent fifteen years in sail before going into steamers in 1911. He joined the Sarawak S.S. Co. in 1920 and commanded a succession of the rajah's ships. The *Vyner Brooke* was built in Leith in 1927 and had a suite of staterooms for the rajah, besides having first-class accommodation for thirty-five passengers. Her arrival and departure at Kuching were major events and on the last occasion, before his retirement to Singapore in 1940, Benfield took the *Vyner Brooke* downstream to the strains of the Constabulary Band, turned out by Rajah Vyner Brooke in his honour.

Writing of her time as the wife of a colonial official at Sandakan in the 1930s, Agnes Keith said of such men:

> Perhaps the real reason for liking a Borneo steamer is in the generous proportions of the captain's heart ... The captains of these coast steamers carry personal messages, books, magazines, news, dogs, servants, children, radios and flower gardens from one isolated out station to another. This time our captain had been entrusted with a bouquet of orchids from the garden of the Resident's wife, to be carried for a two days trip to the District Officer's wife, for her dinner party.[19]

But there were drawbacks, as Keith admits: 'cockroaches ... frolic in the tiny cabins' a 'single bath to accommodate all ... indefinite arrivals and departures from ports' and 'the boisterous motion with which the boat wallows through the sea'. Nevertheless: 'Our cabin was small, but the door stood open and let in the horizon of the Sulu Sea, than which I think there is no sweeter, softer, bluer stretch of water in the world'. To which a manager of the British Borneo Timber Co. adds:

> I doubt whether the world today can visualize what the ships and men really meant to Borneo. They were always ready to carry out a small favour in the very true spirit and in an emergency were eager and ready to give every assistance. They contributed greatly ... without any spectacular gushing but giving devoted and faithful service ... [20]

The attractions of working in such small ships appealed to Captain R. Storrar Boyd, who served as master of thirteen coasting vessels having joined the Straits S.S. Co. from Blue Funnel in 1924.

> I liked all the runs ... but I am slightly partial to the West Siam run. It involved difficult navigation, lack of good charts (sometimes I had to make my own ...), bad monsoon weather and lots of rocks about. But the social life was very pleasant and passengers a nice friendly lot. Also we sometimes carried Chinese theatrical troupes, travelling round the coast to the isolated tin centres, and they were many a time willing to give performances on board as we steamed along, much to the delight of passengers and crew.[21]

To the social life and the professional demands and satisfaction of complicated cabotage, men like Boyd appreciated the beauty of the coastline from Penang northwards past the Langkawi Islands, to Phuket – still sometimes referred to as Junkseylon – and through the Mergui archipelago to Moulmein. It was, Professor Tregonning, remarks, of exquisite and timeless beauty. 'Old Bhuddist temples and ancient shrines on prominent bluffs, golden in the late afternoon sun, would pass close by and always there were graceful palms lining the beaches, tranquil islands and a blue sea.' Although Boyd came home to serve on the Dundee Harbour Trust, others were utterly seduced. Many, like Captain Benfield, lived out their days in the east.

Such coastal services as prospered round these coasts had equivalents elsewhere. The Irrawaddy Flotilla and British India's East Africa service are mentioned elsewhere. The complex feeder, short-sea and coastal traffic that, though dominated by B.I., nevertheless included many other companies, both small and large – such as the Asiatic S.N. Co. which was acquired by B.I. in 1935 – covered the waters of the Persian Gulf, the Indian sub-continent and the Arakan coast of Burma as far as Victoria Point. Just as some overlap occurred north of this promontory with the steamers of Straits S.S. Co.'s Ho Hong subsidiary, the Asiatic ships ran down the Malacca Strait while monopolising traffic with the Andaman Islands.

Similar coastal runs were by now thriving along the coast of West and South Africa, Australia and Chile, where the steamers of the Pacific S.N.Co. threaded their way through islands of a different kind as far south as Patagonia. There were Canadian Pacific subsidiary fleets operating out of Vancouver and serving the isolated communities spreading up that beautiful coast; and on the Great Lakes and the Bay of Fundy, while others, such as Bowring's Red Cross ships, linked Newfoundland, Nova Scotia and the eastern United States. All had grown to service the great imperial *entrepôts*, of which Bombay, Calcutta, Singapore and Hong Kong were the greatest, bringing parcels of produce for loading into the ocean cargo-liners and distributing the manufactured goods and luxuries that they, in turn, had discharged. To this were added the passenger and mail facilities, and the not inconsiderable benefits of news, gossip, cultural and personal services that connected isolated communities with the outside world. Of them all, however, the inter-island, riverine services run by Sino-British enterprise in the Far East are the most extraordinary; a hotch-potch of inter-related interests, borne in a variety of small and medium-sized ships, inter-racial in character with all the cultural complications that such diversities might be expected to bring, yet – for the most part – remarkably harmonious in their apparently chaotic disparity.

Although the Straits S.S. Co. served principally Alfred Holt's Blue Funnel and Glen liners, the combination of all these small coastal firms was to feed the cargo-liners of all the major European lines that were associated with the Far East Homeward Conference. An increasingly important British player in this was the Ben Line of Leith which in the 1920s acquired new tonnage, initially buying up Dutch ships from the Holland-Amerika Lijn which gave them the largest ships in their fleet and whose disposal of ageing vessels to the Soviet Russian government's Far Eastern Fishing Trust featured in the previous chapter. The company also found freights by shipping 'battle-field scrap' to the Far East where, with Japan on the march, there was a demand for steel.

Before it acquired a name for imperialist brutality, Japan was widely admired in the West for her rapid modernisation, industrialisation and the part she had had played in the First World War. In the 1920s, as the military elite formulated their plans for rapid

imperialist expansion throughout South-East Asia, there was an insatiable demand in
Japan for raw materials for armaments, the country having no deposits of iron ore.
This provided freights for many ships which would otherwise have been laid-up, until
the Japanese restrictions on foreign shipping imposed in 1933.[22] One unexpected side
effect of this was to provide help when, about noon on Saturday 1 September 1923, the
Tokyo –Yokohama area was devastated by the Great Kanto earthquake and soon many
of the wooden buildings of both cities were ablaze. A number of British ships were
among those in the bay and, once the alarm had been raised by the master of a Dutch
vessel, boats were lowered to go to the assistance of thousands of people congregating
along the shore. Among those in Yokohama was the *Bengloe*, Captain McCorquodale,
who sent a boat under Chief Officer J.P. Drummond with two cadets and two seamen
to render assistance. By the evening McCorquodale's people were tending 500 refugees
and he requested help in feeding them from the *Benreoch*, anchored further out, and to
which some were transferred. Other vessels assisted, among them the Blue Funnel liner
Lycaon, but the master of the *Philoctetes*, having narrowly avoided colliding with another
vessel in the chaos, took his ship to sea, clear of danger, for which he was later criticised.
His decision was, as we shall shortly observe, in accordance with his owners' standing
orders and the *Lycaon* would probably have done the same had her main boilers not
been blown down while she worked cargo. The earthquake and the subsequent fires
and devastation caused the deaths of 142,000 people.

   Like other companies the Ben Line had its share of mishaps. In the early 1920s a
flooded engine room in the *Bengloe* – bought after the war and renamed – was caused
by a defective injection valve. The water extinguished the boilers despite the diligence
of Third Engineer A.E. Cooper who repeatedly dived into 10ft of water to free the
valve, while the deck crew got a collision mat over the side to stem the ingress of water.
Remaining immobilised the *Bengloe* began to suffer from worsening weather and rolled
appallingly until Cayzer, Irvine's *Clan Monroe* arrived on the scene and took her in
tow to Aden. A few years later in 1925, when homeward bound from China by way
of the Panama Canal, the *Benalder* under Captain J.H. Cole, a master who had distinguished himself in the late war and been awarded the DSC, caught fire in one of her
lower bunkers. Chief Engineer Hughes and Second Engineer Goldie both entered the
space with hoses but were overcome by fumes and it was Cole who extricated them,
earning a Lloyd's Silver Medal. He was a man without apparent fear, being awarded
for other acts of humanity at risk to his own life. Less fortunate was Chief Engineer
Grimwood, who was swept overboard from the deck of the *Benarty* in a China Sea
typhoon in 1931. At the time the ship was commanded by Captain J.P. Drummond, the
promoted chief officer of McCorquodale's *Bengloe*. This was a difficult year for shipping
in general, but the Ben Line in particular as the company almost lost the *Benmohr* on
Prawle Point, South Devon, when she was on her way from Avonmouth to Leith. Her
master, Captain George McMillan, was a legendary figure in the company. A tough,
uncompromising seaman of the old school, he became well known for his ability as
a swimmer. On her transit of the Suez Canal his ship had sheered her stern into the
bank. As she ran down the Red Sea the noises from under her stern and in her shaft
tunnel were disturbing so, in the Gulf of Aden, McMillan stopped the ship and dived
overboard to inspect the damage. He had done likewise elsewhere, even recovering

a lost anchor at Port Swettenham by diving for it, but the case of the *Benmohr* was to test him further. It was initially feared that the vessel had driven so hard upon Prawle Point that she was a total loss. Having got his crew ashore McMillan remained on board until worsening weather persuaded him that she could not be got off. However, in due course, with a salvage tug to assist and after a month aground, McMillan succeeded in refloating the *Benmohr*. Another Ben liner to strand in the inter-war years was the brand new *Benwyvis*, which took the ground off the Frisian island of Terschelling when on passage from Hamburg to Antwerp. Time and money saved her and her damage proved less than that sustained by the *Benlawers* in December 1934 when in the North Pacific on her way towards Japan. She was commanded by the unlucky Drummond when on the 19th she encountered an unstable wave of exceptional height which broke over the ship.[23] Her foremast and forward deck-winches were destroyed, her mainmast was bent, her port-side accommodation was wrecked, her galleys flooded and no food was available for two days as Drummond struggled back to Victoria, British Columbia, where in dry dock it was found that fathoms of her steel-wire cargo-runners, stripped from her winches, had wound round her propeller.

In 1919 the Ben Line had owned eleven steamers with a combined tonnage of 64,500 gross tons. Twenty years later, on the eve of another war, the fleet consisted of twenty vessels grossing 146,000 tons, a remarkable achievement amid the economic chaos of the time. Capital had been hard to find, freights were sometimes as elusive in any quantity, but the Ben Line had survived like many other firms and, at the same time, managed to expand its tonnage. At sea the chief dangers were still fire and fog. The two fires that swept through Furness, Withy's *Bermuda* in 1931 were mentioned in the previous chapter, and in 1933 P&O had sold the *Khiva* after a devastating fire, while fire had consumed the New Zealand Shipping Co.'s *Paparoa* which sank off St Helena in March 1926. Fog was a particular hazard on the North Atlantic run and resulted in collisions and groundings of varying seriousness. In 1922 the P&O steamer *Egypt* sank off Ushant in dense fog after a collision with a French vessel. Ninety-six souls perished,

W.M. Birchall's sketch of a wallowing ketch being passed by a 'raised quarterdeck' coastal steamer shows that coastal waters in the 1920s remained the last province of British commercial sail. (From a Private Collection)

twelve passengers and eighty-four of her crew, while £1,054,000 in gold and silver
went down with her but was later salvaged by Italians after seven seasons' work. The
Anchor Line's *Transylvania*, groping her way towards Cherbourg after a cruise from
New York in March 1929, struck a rock ten-miles west of her destination. Jettisoning
500 tons of oil she was refloated and, after completing her passage, was dry-docked in
Glasgow, but it was the following summer before repairs were complete and she was
fit to resume work. Whilst thus detained, a grand ball was held on board to raise funds
for the RNLI and this was such a success that a second was held the following year.
Collisions occurred in fog, and in clear weather when miscalculations were made. The
White Star Line liner *Britannic*, popularly known as 'Old Reliable' struck and sank
the Nantucket lightvessel on 15 May 1934. Of the eleven men of the United States
Lighthouse Service then on board, seven were killed in the accident.

As in the case of the *København*, British ships assisted in search and rescue attempts
and the *Transylvania* took part in several of these. With the Baltic-America liner
Estonia, she had stood by the foundering *Herrenwijk* in hurricane-force winds in
November 1928, pumping oil while a gallant attempt by a boat from the *Estonia*
saved a handful of the German ship's crew. She and the Cunarder *Carmania* searched
in vain for the American aeroplane *Old Glory* in September 1927 and in June 1930
she and the *American Merchant* both transmitted radio bearings to assist the Australian
Kingsford-Smith, the disorientated pilot of the aeroplane *Southern Cross*, to locate his
position and land safely. Similarly, the Brocklebank cargo-liner *Mahsud* helped to save
seventy-two passengers and seventy-seven crew from the blazing French liner *Georges
Philippar* which caught fire off Cape Guardafui on 16 May 1932. Her master, Captain
R. Kershaw, was afterwards decorated by the French. There were also the cases when
ships went to the assistance of a civil population, as with the Japanese earthquake
of 1923. On 3 February 1931, the Federal Steam Navigation Co.'s *Devon* arrived at
Napier, on New Zealand's North Island, almost immediately after a devastating earthquake had struck the town. The *Devon* provided the first aid from outside, her large
number of trainee cadets helping while the ship herself provided the only immediate
source of potable water for Napier's citizens.

The most dangerous meteorological phenomenon that could endanger even a
powerful modern steam-vessel was the tropical revolving storm, known in Chinese
waters as a typhoon. In 1937 an exceptionally ferocious typhoon struck Hong Kong
where scores of deep-water cargo-ships lay moored to buoys loading cargo from
junks and sampans. The small-fry scuttled behind the breakwaters of the typhoon
shelters but the merchantmen, alerted by the storm-warning hoisted above the signal
station at Kowloon, had to use their engines at slow speed to avoid breaking adrift.
The typhoon struck late in the season, in September, and many vessels were in trouble.
British India's 1923-built *Talma* – the company's first passenger-cargo-vessel to exceed
a gross tonnage of 10,000 tons – was blown ashore. The Ho Hong Line's *Hong Peng*
was alongside at the Taikoo Dockyard, her engines opened up for survey. Powerless
and flung against the quay, her plates sprang, she opened up, and sank. Another Ho
Hong liner, the *Hong Siang*, had just embarked his passengers when she broke adrift.
Her master, Captain D.M. Cole, already having steam-up, decided to make for the
open sea, but first had to turn the ship round. As he put the helm over and called for

full speed, the wind struck the *Hong Siang*'s superstructure. Blowing at 100 knots, it's force heeled the *Hong Siang* onto her beam ends, to the terror of 800 passengers who were convinced for several long moments that she was capsizing. Cole succeeded in bringing his ship round and, avoiding collision with other struggling vessels, cleared the port and sheltered under the lee of the islands in the estuary of the Pearl River. Elsewhere the Japanese liner *Asama Maru* was driven ashore to become a total loss, numerous sampans and junks were wrecked, and one coaster was left high and dry on Stonecutter's Island. The *Talma* was got off and later resumed her voyage, while the *Hong Peng* was refloated and returned to service, but such occurrences, though rare in such extreme form, were not unusual. Nor were they confined to Chinese waters. The onslaught of a hurricane in the Atlantic has already been recounted in the outward voyage of the *Trevessa* and tropical revolving storms afflicted ships elsewhere. The Bay of Bengal and the southern Indian Ocean were renowned for the damage that a cyclone could inflict while the West Indian hurricane gave its name to any wind blowing at a speed in excess of 65 knots – or Force 12 on the Beaufort scale.

Such winds as Cole experienced were far in excess of this, but one of the most remarkable survivals of a ship beset by a tropical revolving storm of the most extreme violence was that of the Blue Funnel liner *Phemius* in 1932. She was commanded by a highly competent master, Captain D.L.C. Evans, a Welshman born aboard his father's barque off the coast of Chile, in honour of which he was christened 'Chile'. Like his colleagues, Evans had been obliged to put up a bond of £200 against his safe management of his ship's voyage. This was Holt's policy as their ships carried their own insurance; if a master conducted his voyages safely and profitably, he received an annual return on his bond. If he failed in some way, as judged by the company's managers, he forfeited a part of it in proportion to his offence.

The *Phemius* was a powerful, oil-fired cargo-liner of 7,615 gross registered tons, outward bound to the Far East by way of the Panama Canal and the Pacific. Having passed the Windward Passage between Haiti and Cuba, she was heading for Colon when, at noon on 4 November – very late in the season – with the wind fresh and the sea moderate, she received a weather report giving notice of a hurricane of small intensity to the east and moving WNW. That afternoon Evans altered course to increase his distance from the track of the hurricane and during the night the barometer rose, as might have been expected.

It was not until 06.00 the following morning that the first indications of danger appeared. The barometer began to fall rapidly and, alerted by his chief officer, at 07.00 Evans altered course to due south 'to give all reefs to the westward a wide berth'. Weather reports from Colon indicated fine conditions and Evans decided that, in view of the ship's position and the reports now reaching the radio room of other vessels within 150 miles being hove-to in heavy seas, he would do the same. 'My barometer continuing to fall puzzled me … The ship hove-to without taking a drop of water on board'.

Evans was puzzled by the conflicting evidence of the reported position and predicted track of the hurricane, with the evidence of the prevailing conditions. He knew that the revolving nature of the storm meant that he had to avoid the quadrant where, even by heaving-to, his ship would be driven inexorably into the centre of the storm. He also knew that while a storm-path usually ran a little north of due westwards on a curve, they occasionally behaved in unpredictable ways, veering in other directions. At noon, with his '[b]arometer falling continuously, wind increasing, sea rising ... I began to realise [that the] storm was not in position given or it had recurved'. Two hours later the 'wind was of hurricane force with terrific squalls'. The ship could not now be held on a steady heading and fell off the wind which had now 'reached indescribable violence, and owing to flying spray visibility was nil'. This complete lack of visibility deprived Evans of any possibility of handling his ship as she was scoured by the spray and wind. The canvas bridge dodgers were torn away and the wheelhouse windows blew-in. Then at 15.00:

> Wind further increased to such a terrific force as to be beyond human conception. I had reduced speed at noon and now put engines on 'slow' – as no power could cope with this terrific wind-force. At this time during a few moments lull saw some wreckage close alongside and saw some dark objects flying in the air. These proved to be our No.2 hatch covers. Ordered pumps to be put on No.2 Hold at once.

Reports came in that No.6 hatch was stripped and the chief officer was sent aft with a working party consisting of the third officer and some of the midshipmen and 'what could be done, was done'. Nevertheless these men were confined aft for many hours owing to the wind strength. Thus far the *Phemius* had taken no heavy water aboard, the damage had all been done by the wind. This forced the tarpaulins over the steel coamings of the five hatches with such force that they were 'carried away as if by a knife; the pieces remaining in the cleats and wedges afterwards proving this'. All this time the ship yawed and rolled, the wind swinging from right astern to just abaft the port beam.

At about 18.00 the chief officer regained the bridge and Evans handed over to him as he wished to see how matters stood in the engine room.

> After considerable difficulty I got down, and found the engineers doing all they possibly could. I ... pointed out that at all costs the pumps had to be kept going on No.2 and 6 holds. Whilst I was going down the engine-room a steam pipe burst in the stoke-hold ... Main steam started to go back, fumes and smoke came back into the engine-room. Undoubtedly these men were doing their utmost under most difficult circumstances. I left the engine room with a feeling of confidence ... On reaching the deck I was caught in choking smoke ... Then on looking up and around ... I discovered that the funnel had gone. I managed to reach the bridge ... As it was then approaching 8 p.m., the funnel must have disappeared about 7.30 p.m ... I now again left the chief officer in charge and went down to the saloon ... I found the saloon awash and all the rooms on the starboard side flooded, undoubtedly a pitiful state of affairs. I noticed that words of encouragement were needed here, and that was done with good effect. The chief engineer did everything in his power down below but conditions were so bad that every effort produced no results. I then returned to the bridge and tried to estimate the force of the wind. By putting my arm out ... the force of the spray striking the hand was agony, and for some minutes after remained numbed as if after a severe electric shock. My estimate was that the force of the wind was 200 miles an hour ... [21.00] Steam failed, fires

blew out with the back-draught and oil ran out through the furnace doors. Ship in total darkness. After this notes were taken … with the aid of electric torches … dictated mostly by myself and the chief officer scribbled on wireless forms which were then stowed away in one of the electric switch boxes in wheel-house. These notes were written by the third officer … The constant almost solid sheet of spray, but no heavy water continued to blow over the open hatches throughout the night, and I estimated that ten tons an hour went down the open No.2 hatch and five tons an hour own the Nos 1 and 6 hatches. We were now without fresh water.

At about 02.00 on 6 November the hurricane's centre passed over the *Phemius*. The wind dropped dramatically but there was a very high, confused sea. Nevertheless, the instant the wind eased, parties of Chinese seamen under the mates drew new tarpaulins over the three exposed hatches in the two hours lull before the wind increased to Force 12 and the ship was again assailed by wind and sea. Having rigged an emergency radio aerial in place of that lost with the funnel, and 'After due consideration,' Evans transmitted a distress signal at 09.30 which was intercepted by the *Ariguani*, a banana-carrier owned by Elders & Fyffes. He now knew that the ship was being carried along by the hurricane but hoped that it would pass over them quickly. 'I want to say this,' he wrote in his report to Alfred Holt & Co., 'that every message I sent out from first to last was well considered, calm and deliberate'. On his own admission Evans never 'gave up hope or allowed myself to be disheartened – although realising to the full our very serious position'. Throughout the 6th the engineers toiled to raise steam by any means possible, but not even the donkey boiler would respond. By noon all efforts had failed and with burning oil running out of the furnace doors, the engineers were obliged to play fire-extinguishers on this to avoid a serious fire. They were all by now 'feeling the need of food and water'. With the ship rolling down on her starboard side, a permanent list, and her pumps out of action, their 'position was now very serious.'

Then at 16.00 the *Phemius* again passed through the hurricane's centre with a high spiky sea rising all around her. Again her crew turned out along the decks to secure the hatches until an hour later the: 'Gale increasing again and so through the night, barometer showing signs of rising only to fall again, and by midnight hurricane again increased to a fury, and continues unabated.'

At daylight next morning, the 7th, Evans recorded:

Nos 2 and 5 hatches again stripped … Short lull again [at 08.00], secured Nos 2 and 6 hatches, but before 9 a.m. wind again blowing with violence. Rolling heavier and shipping heavy lee water, but so far no large volume entering hatches. All attempts at sending out further wireless messages fail, wireless room wet and set earthing from excessive water. This gave me further concern as I fully realised the anxiety of all concerned. Barometer again falling, ship rolling and lurching. Starboard gangway carried away, dragging rails with it, by lee water. Very dangerous rolls these. Braked [steering] quadrant. I now realised that I had an excellent chief officer, ready and anxious to carry out any order. I was, of course, closely observing the rest of the officers and crew, and at varying times made it my business to be amongst them to keep up their spirits.

At noon the conditions were unchanged with a 'tremendous sea' running. At 13.00 Evans realised they were passing over a reef as the 'sea was dangerously high'. With the wind now from the SSE and 'blowing with terrific violence' and the ship lying with her head to the ENE, the heavily listing starboard side was now exposed to the weather. By now the wind had eased a little, allowing the sea to build to a terrific height. During the last lull oil had been taken forward into the crew's forecastle latrines from where Midshipman Hay was ordered to trickle it out through one of the lavatory pans and to 'keep going at all costs'.

They were struck by a heavy sea which, Evans estimated, carried over 100 tons below into No.2 hold. He was continually telling his crew that little water was going below, a white-lie that was now causing him great anxiety. He managed to get a cast of the lead of sixty fathoms and although the wind carried the lead line out from the leadsman, distorting the reading, he estimated to put them over the Serrana bank – though it later proved to be the Serranilla Bank. Despite his misgivings about keeping his crew informed of the true gravity of their situation, Evans nevertheless ordered everyone to don their lifebelts.

I must repeat and report on the sterling qualities of my chief officer. He was cool, calm, and fearless … [and] I want to say how I appreciate and will always remember his confidence in myself. This was the true test, for I realised that if anything was going to happen it would happen quickly. It will be realised that the desire for water and food was very much felt and showed itself but in a quiet manner amongst the crew. All possible were now stationed pouring oil and I call attention to the splendid conduct of the … midshipmen … The difficulties of carrying along five-gallon drums of crude oil to the forward latrines were terrible, and although the crew, led and assisted by the chief officer to get things going, worked fairly well, I must with pleasure state that the three boys mentioned and the third mate in this case and subsequently, are deserving of the highest praise I can give them. As for myself I frequently went along to give all encouragement possible … All through the night the pouring of oil was carried out and although suffering from bruises exhaustion, hunger and thirst the work was carried out without ceasing. The engineers carried on amidships and all worked hard. The second officer superintended the after latrines oil supply. The effect of the oil was almost beyond belief, towering seas tearing along direct for our exposed (listed) side crumpled up within ten feet of the ship's side, and although we could not entirely escape them, they landed on board in heavy volumes of dead water. Without question, and in this report I make no random statements, the ship would have foundered had the pouring of oil not been carried on continuously.

There was by that evening over 6ft of water in the engine and boiler rooms as, yet again, the *Phemius* passed through the hurricane's eye. A little fresh water was obtained from an after tank during the lull, an action in which the surgeon helped. He too earned Evans's approbation as he strove to assist the wireless operator as well as attending the cuts and gashes among the crew. 'His helpful willingness is certainly worth reporting,' remarked Evans. 'His loss in belongings was the greatest among the officers, for almost everything he possessed was destroyed.'

Throughout the ordeal the *Phemius's* Chinese crew:

> worked fairly well, but some of the time they were terror-stricken. However, when lulls came along they worked well and with a will, but the only ones I could mention (commend) were the lamp-trimmer and second and third stewards. The second steward particularly so.

At dawn on the 8th the darker colour of the sea revealed the *Phemius* was again in deep water which afforded Evans 'much relief'. The barometer rose again, only to fall and by 14.00 the storm-centre passed them again. At every lull efforts were made to exclude the sea from the damaged hatches and by now the ship was being stripped to effect this. The awning spars and the awnings themselves were being pressed into service. Evans found the several passages of the hurricane's eye over the *Phemius* depressing, even distressing.

> The ship was overwhelmed with all kind of birds, also insects, both large and small, each time we reached the centre. Large birds of the Heron species landed on the ship in such large numbers that I considered it possible that they added to our danger – as we had a dangerous enough list without adding to it. I do not wish to dwell on this but must mention things as they then were and be done with it. The decks, bridge, etc., were crowded with small birds and it was almost impossible to walk with[out] crunching them under our feet. They landed fearlessly on our bodies wherever they could. Added to this was the oppressive heat, and the dead silence of the centre of a storm, with a depressing barometer. These were moments to test the nerves of any man! I patiently waited for the blast that I knew had to come from an opposite quadrant and was glad when it came, carrying with it to destruction all those birds and insects. During these times I had seen sharks but kept that to myself – later when [the] weather moderated they were of course seen by all.

Food and fresh water continued to be a problem as, during the afternoon they were once again assailed by the wind. Evans wished to preserve the frozen stores, knowing that once opened the refrigerators would rapidly warm up and everything would be spoiled, so water and biscuits were used from the lifeboats that mercifully still lay lashed in their chocks.

By dawn on the 9th the wind was beginning to moderate and the wireless operator and surgeon managed to rig an emergency aerial. The wireless room was dried out with blow-lamps and the consequent distress signal produced numerous offers of assistance which could not be picked up by the operator, but were heard on the private wireless of the second mate. At noon they obtained an observation showing they had been carried 209-miles slightly north of due west and although the wind had dropped to no more than a fresh breeze the sea and swell remained violent. The third mate dived into the store room wearing lifebelt and lifeline, extracting some tins found washing about, sufficient to prepare hot food.

Even now Evans's anxieties were not over, for the waterlogged *Phemius* continued to roll violently.

with very heavy pounding on the starboard quarter. This rolling and pounding continued throughout the night (of the 9th/10th). I was now more concerned over the motion of the ship than when she was in the storm – the lee lurches were dangerous owing to cargo on [the] starboard side absorbing more water. I again gave orders to [the] chief engineer … [to get the pumps working]. But no results.

By mid-forenoon on 10 November help was on hand. The salvage-tug *Killerig* arrived and lay-to, lowering a boat with fifteen men in it. Evans ordered his chief officer to allow no one but the salvage master on board and at 11.15 Captain Tooker met Evans with the remark: 'Captain I congratulate you.' When Evans asked what 'the good old ship looked like?' Tooker was candid: 'You look pitiful.' Pitiful or not Evans was obliged to conclude a Lloyd's Open Salvage Agreement and, after a short argument as to whether Evans would allow Tooker's men on board, arrangements for a tow to Kingston, Jamaica, were concluded. Water and food were supplied by the *Killerig* and the tow proceeded.

Meanwhile and in spite of their exhaustion, the *Phemius's* engineers continued to attempt to raise steam on the donkey-boiler. A dummy funnel was made from a ventilator but Tooker objected to the use of oil which continued to run out of the furnaces owing to the list and endangered his salvage. After working all night, at 10.30 on the 11th, sufficient steam pressure was raised to operate the steering gear and thereby ease the strain on the tug. The *Killerig* arrived at Kingston with the listing and funnelless *Phemius* in tow on the following afternoon. Having anchored the tow, she went alongside to supply steam in order to pump the Blue Funnel liner dry. Her survival owed much to the courage and persistence of her crew, led by a master imbued with quiet confidence, but also to the massive scantlings of Holt's ships, making them immensely strong. The ordeal of Evans and his crew was something of a *cause célèbre* and was used by his principal owner, Lawrence Holt, to inspire the cadets at Pangbourne Nautical College on Founder's Day, 2 June 1933 with what was widely regarded as 'an epic of the sea'. Holt held up the example of Evans and his crew to the assembled cadets emphasising, with a characteristic shrewdness,

> that even the Scottish steward at the very crisis of anxiety did not fail to neglect the responsibility entrusted [to him]. Officers and men were worn out, at the limit of their endurance. They needed some stimulant, and bottles of beer were forthcoming; but not casually. The steward – though the ship might sink and everyone with her – carefully made a note of how much would be owed him on each bottle consumed.[24]

Such virtue, if virtue it be, was countered by Lawrence Holt's decision to mulct Evans of his entire bond. While Lloyd's presented Evans with a silver medal and the Lord Mayor of Liverpool gave a reception in his honour, Lawrence Holt ruled otherwise. 'He will be required to forfeit his insurance deposit of £200 to us on the ground that he failed to exercise due forethought and prudence thereby bringing his ship into manifest hazard and causing the company a heavy loss.' Such were the penalties of serving in a 'crack' liner company! However, Evans was to have a distinguished war career (see Chapter 4) and on his retirement in 1944 Lawrence Holt – a man of ruthless probity – reimbursed the £200.

The mid-1930s winters in the North Atlantic were bad. On 15 November 1933 the British tramp *Saxilby* foundered in appalling weather. The following winter of 1934/35 was even worse. A succession of hurricane-force gales raged, raising huge seas and making trans-Atlantic crossings in the largest liners unpleasant, and proving fatal to vulnerable, low-powered, deeply laden tramp-steamers. In early October the *Millpool*, a coal-burning tramp was bound from Danzig to Montreal with a cargo of rye when she ran into trouble in mid-ocean. On the 2nd she sent out a distress signal saying her after hatch was stove and she had three men injured. The message was intercepted by two ships, the Cunard cargo-passenger liner *Ascania* and Canadian Pacific's cargo-liner *Beaverhill*. Captain James Bisset in the *Ascania* had the greatest difficulty laying a safe course towards the casualty's position.

> Now hurricane [force] squalls were sweeping over the *Ascania* at intervals of about fifteen minutes, reducing visibility to half a mile. Between the squalls, in driving spindrift, the visibility was not above three miles. The seas were forty feet high from trough to crest, and short between the crests … It seemed impossible that a little old steamer, such as the *Millpool*, with her hatch stove in could live in the trough of such a sea.[25]

In the early hours of 3 October Bisset intercepted the predicted line of drift the estimated the *Millpool* would take and, at considerable risk, turned the *Ascania* into the wind and sea to steam slowly to windward in the hope that he might locate her. To windward of him, closer to the last reported dead-reckoning position transmitted by the *Millpool's* master, the *Beaverhill* lay hove-to searching the surrounding sea. They had both been in touch with the wounded vessel's radio operator at 22.50 the previous evening; he had reported that he did not 'know how things were on deck now but the wireless room is flooded and I am wet and cold – hope to see you soon.' Daylight brought more help; the British ships *Beaverford*, *Hazelwood* and the *Millpool's* sister *Wearpool*, and the German *Bockenheim* were all in the vicinity as the weather gradually moderated and visibility improved. Bisset summed up the tragedy thus: 'No trace of the *Millpool* was ever found. She and her complement of twenty-three men had vanished.'

Bisset cleared the *Ascania* out of Montreal on her next voyage on 23 November, not quite the last vessel to leave the St Lawrence before the ice closed in that year. Completing her loading was another British tramp, the *Usworth*. The *Ascania* had a difficult passage down the St Lawrence and was passing Quebec next morning in dense fog when she fouled the anchor cable of the *Beaverbrae* and while attempting to get clear, the Donaldson liner *Salaria* 'loomed out of the fog and scraped across the *Ascania's* stern'. In due course the *Ascania* reached London, was discharged, dry-docked and loaded for her next voyage, leaving the Surrey Dock on the Thames at noon on 7 December 'with a light cargo and not many passengers … bound for Halifax and New York'. The ship took on mails and passengers at Southampton and Le Havre and headed west. By Thursday 13th, the *Ascania* was 1,300 miles into her passage and pitching heavily into a westerly gale which had been blowing since the 11th and was now increasing in violence. Bisset, tired after three days with little sleep, was compelled to reduce speed as 'the wind hissed and tore at the seas, whipping their crests to spindrift, which obscured visibility and streamed in dense gusts of spray over the bridge'.

That midnight, with the *Ascania* 'labouring and straining heavily, and shipping water fore and aft,' Bisset wrote up his night orders and was about to turn in when his duty wireless officer reported a ship in trouble. He had intercepted an 'all-ships' signal from the Belgian cargo-vessel *Jean Jadot*, Captain S. Gonthier, of Antwerp. Gonthier's operator had himself heard a faint distress message from the British tramp *Usworth* and the Belgian master announced that he was proceeding to her assistance. Gonthier's call for reinforcement was implicit, consequently Bisset headed the *Ascania* for the *Usworth's* last-known position.

The *Usworth*, Captain J.J. Reid, had been the last vessel in the icing St Lawrence, leaving Montreal early on 7 December laden with 5,600 tons of Canadian wheat. Although classed A1 at Lloyd's she was an ageing vessel of 3,535 gross registered tons, fitted with rod-and-chain steering-gear and owned by the Dalgleish Shipping Co. of Newcastle-upon-Tyne. She was manned 'according to the Act,' which meant she was a 'pound-and-a-pint ship' with no frills and her crew worked watch-and-watch, a minimum twelve-hour day. Besides Reid there were twenty-five souls on board, a chief and second mate, one wireless operator, a boatswain, a carpenter, four seamen and four apprentices, a cook, a steward, three engineers and eight Afghan firemen.

On 11 December she had shipped a damaging sea and Reid decided to heave-to and ride out the gale but, in turning head-to-sea, the rod-and-chain steering-gear carried away. The crew made a gallant attempt to steer by rigging wire tackles onto the steering quadrant and leading the wire-falls to the poop winch, but the following morning the wires parted leaving the *Usworth* helpless, lying in the trough of a heavy sea. Reid transmitted the distress signal to which Gonthier responded, the *Jean Jadot* arriving on scene an hour later. The *Usworth's* crew meanwhile were attempting to re-rig their jury steering-gear but this achieved nothing, until a slight lull in the weather enabled Gonthier, in an act of highly commendable seamanship, to get a line across to the *Usworth's* stern. With the *Usworth's* engines reversed to assist, Gonthier commenced a stern-tow and laid a course for the Azores, 700 miles away. Then, as darkness fell and the weather again deteriorated, the tow parted and Reid's crew made another attempt to rig jury steering. This was completed next morning and, with the *Jean Jadot* standing-by, Reid set an easterly course in deteriorating weather. Nevertheless, the *Usworth* proceeded under her own steam and ingenuity for twenty-five miles until the strength of the wind increased to hurricane-force. Reid put his helm down and left it so that the *Usworth* lay hove-to as 'darkness fell, and the gale increased phenomenally'. Two hours before midnight three huge seas struck the *Usworth*, throwing her on her beam ends whereupon her cargo shifted and she lay with a port list of 25°.

The seas now broke over her, tore away her wireless aerial, smashed and buckled her after hatch coamings and part of her bridge superstructure, distorted hatch-beams and tore two derrick-booms from their stowed positions so that they swung wildly about. All her lifeboats were destroyed, their davits being bent like wire. The mates, seamen and apprentices, rigged a tarpaulin over the gaping hold and Reid ordered all hands below to begin shifting the wheat in the 'tween decks back to starboard, an expedient that, desperate though it sounds, had saved many ships. All but two of the firemen responded, but despite pumping and shovelling, little could be done to save the *Usworth*. It was now that Reid transmitted a full 'SOS' signal just as Gonthier lost sight of the *Usworth* in the darkness and appalling visibility. He accordingly re-transmitted the signal intercepted in the *Ascania* and Bisset altered her course to assist.

A stream of signals passed between the three masters that night of 13/14 December, initiating an ordeal that was to last many hours but began at dawn when both the *Jean Jadot* and *Ascania* were watching the wallowing *Usworth*. Her plight was all too clear. Bisset could see a handful of men huddled on her steeply canting deck in the lee of the funnel, and Reid's signals told of their exhaustion. Knowing the ship was lost, evacuation was now the only option. Bisset immediately began pumping oil to reduce the effect of the sea while Gonthier attempted to get a line across to the *Usworth* so that a lowered boat might be pulled across to her. This failed. As *Ascania's* log recorded, there was a: 'Strong gale with frequent heavy squalls. High steep sea and very heavy swell. Mainly cloudy and clear.'

Reid was increasingly desperate; his ship was foundering under his feet, his men were 'done-in' and the tone of his signals was extremely anxious. To Bisset he said 'can you possibly man a boat and get my crew off?' But both Bisset and Gonthier had their own worries, not the least of which was avoiding colliding with one another and the *Usworth* as they manoeuvred in difficult conditions in ships not designed for such close-quarter operations in the open ocean, all with differing rates of drift. Bisset moreover had a ship full of 800 people and neither master wished to end up a second casualty. All they had effectively succeeded in doing was covering the *Usworth's* decks with a slick of oil as they strove to mitigate the effects of the seas upon her, an irony not lost on Bisset. James Bisset had not only written the then standard handbook on lifeboats, but he had recently published an article on the use of oil at sea. He was called upon to put both theories into practice that day, and ordered a boat prepared for launching, but it was the gallant Belgian who made the first move. At noon there was a moderation in the weather and Gonthier lowered and manned a boat under Second Officer Leblanc, with Fourth Officer Lambert and eight seamen. With great skill and no little difficulty Leblanc worked the boat under the lee of the *Usworth's* amidships superstructure and fourteen of her crew jumped into it. Reid and a dozen others held back, for fear of swamping Leblanc's boat, two of the Afghan firemen refusing outright, preferring to die aboard their ship.

Meanwhile one of the *Ascania's* lifeboats had been prepared, with mattresses lashed along her gun-whales as fenders. Bisset had called for volunteers to man her and all his officers and seamen, along with several catering staff stepped forward. In the event Bisset selected Third Officer E.J.R. Pollitt, 'a young and keen officer, who was a Lieutenant in the Royal Naval Reserve', who picked his own ten-man crew from among the fittest able-seamen. When all was ready a squall severely reduced visibility and Bisset was obliged to manoeuvre to avoid the *Jean Jadot*, then herself trying to recover her own boat, but in due course he brought the *Ascania* to within 100ft of the *Usworth* and ordered the boat away. Pollitt and his crew were lowered directly from the boat deck but Bisset found that the *Ascania's* drift to leeward was too strong for the boat to sheer off and as she worked forward he feared his plunging stem would destroy the lifeboat. Fortunately, as he rang full astern on the engine-room telegraphs, a wave coming round the ship's bow carried the boat clear at the last minute, and a relieved Bisset watched her pulled across to the stricken *Usworth*. There were about three hours of daylight left.

It was at this point that Bisset received a message from Gonthier that his own lifeboat had capsized. All but two of the *Usworth*'s crew, Apprentice Brey and Fireman Waris Khan, had been lost and Gonthier had also lost Fourth Officer Lambert and Able-Seaman de Jongh. The oil had been ineffective in sufficiently quelling the breaking seas and had besides added to the plight of the men flung into the water by choking and befouling them. This news only increased Bisset's anxiety for his own people. He could see the *Usworth* was very low in the water, her sluggish motion testimony to her lack of buoyancy. He manoeuvred *Ascania* to keep his own boat in sight alongside the *Usworth*, level with her funnel where her tilting deck was already awash.

Pollitt skilfully 'back-watered' stern-first into the wreck's side, whereupon three of the *Usworth*'s survivors decided to jump into the oily water and chance being hauled into the boat, but they reckoned without the oil and the 4-knot drift of their ship. They were swept helplessly along the *Usworth*'s side and irretrievably lost under her stern, despite attempts to throw lines and life-buoys to them. It was clear that Pollitt would have to lie alongside and this he judiciously achieved, the mattress fenders materially assisting.

> As the boat surged up level with the … deck, the nine men there … joined hands and jumped into her. They fell exhausted into the bottom of the lifeboat. One of them, an Afghan weighing eighteen stone, jumped onto the legs of A.B. Seaman K. Campbell … breaking [his] thigh. Without a moment's delay, Pollitt shoved off from the side of the wreck. All but eight of his oars were now broken, and one of his men crippled. But, by great good fortune, the boat was flung clear of the wreck's side.[26]

Bisset now brought the *Ascania* close to windward of the lifeboat which still lay in the heavy slick, which Bisset was convinced saved her from sharing the fate of the Belgian boat. Now, using the *Ascania*'s greater windage to advantage, he allowed her to drift down on her lifeboat. Meanwhile willing hands had opened the shell door in B-deck and thrown out lifeboat boarding ladders, but the lifeboat was still ranging vertically 20ft up-and-down the *Ascania*'s side.

> The big Afghan fireman, jumping for a ladder, missed his hold, and fell between the ship's side and the boat. With great difficulty, four of our seamen hoisted him into the boat again, all of them in imminent danger of being crushed. Bowlines were then lowered, and most of the men hoisted up in them. A few climbed up the ladders, and Pollitt was the last to leave the boat. He had accomplished an heroic and remarkable rescue.

Bisset abandoned the by now badly damaged boat and resumed his voyage, setting course for Halifax. He and his crew were later to be showered with honours, medals from several humane societies, commendations and sums of money from the owners of the *Usworth*, and the Cunard board. Worst of all on arrival in Canada and, later, New York, they were to be swept up in a distastefully over-dramatising frenzy of journalists and broadcasters. Bisset and, especially Pollitt dismissed all attempts to turn them into heroic figures, the latter simply maintaining that 'it was just a job that had to be done, and one which any others in the Merchant Service, irrespective of flag, would have been only too pleased to do in like circumstances'.

The *Usworth* was not the only British tramp to be lost in the North Atlantic that terrible winter, for the *Blairgowrie* shared her fate, suffering a similar catastrophic failure in her steering gear on 26 November 1935. When her first distress message was transmitted it was already late afternoon and within half an hour a second told that her forward hatches had been smashed in and whatever followed must have soon been over. A year earlier the tramping oil-tanker *La Crescenta* had been posted-missing on a passage from California to Japan. It was thought that she was over-loaded and under-manned and her loss, plus those of the *Millpool*, *Usworth* and *Blairgowrie* which had cost the lives of ninety-seven British seamen, caused the seafarers' organisations to point out the large sums of insurance recovered by their owners. 'There was,' according to Alan Villiers, 'considerable disquiet and the matter was aired in the House of Commons'. In May 1935 a Board of Trade Inquiry was convened under Lord Merrivale, a former president of the High Court of Admiralty. Among its conclusions were two salient facts: the *Millpool*, which had been built in 1906, was of such an age that her condition probably contributed to her loss. The case of *La Crescenta* was far more serious. She had been overloaded 'in conscious disregard of the law'. Lord Merrivale considered Captain N.S. Upstill to have been a competent master-mariner who had been obliged to overload his ship by 441 tons on her departure from Port San Luis on 24 November 1934 on the express orders of her managing owners.

> Moreover, the ship leaked notoriously. The pathetic letters which the captain had written to his wife were read out in court, in so far as they showed what the conditions had been like aboard – how he had been virtually commanded to overload, how he had had to go down into the ship's tanks himself to help clean out the filthy, heavy sludge, so poorly was she manned, how he had helped fix leaky rivets, and to keep the junior officers' bridge watches for them while they also worked. Why he had done these things was only too clear. If he had not, someone else would, and jobs were much, much more scarce than mariners.[27]

All that was ever found of *La Crescenta*, was an enormous slick of crude oil in the estimated position of her loss, a position that could be located with reasonable accuracy placing the assumption beyond all reasonable doubt by an exchange of wireless signals between *La Crescenta* and another British tanker, the *Athelviscount*. The owners were ordered to pay £3,400 towards the Inquiry's costs 'and Lord Merrivale left no doubt as to what he thought of them'.

It was not only tramps that were overwhelmed by the sea. The well-found *Vardulia*, owned by the Glaswegian firm of Donaldson Bros had been acquired by them in 1929. She was then twelve years old and had been built as a cattle-carrier but when she departed from West Hartlepool on 12 October 1935 she was loaded with a general cargo and a quantity of coal, properly loaded with shifting boards. There was no question as to her under-manning or of doubts as to her condition, but when well into her Western Ocean passage she reported being in 'a whole gale' and requested the positions of other ships receiving her message. This was usually an indication that a ship was in trouble and preliminary to her distress. Next morning, Saturday 19 October, a signal giving the same position requested immediate assistance owing to a dangerous list. It was followed by the cryptic: 'Now abandoning ship'. Nothing further was heard; the *Vardulia* was lost with all hands.

Fortunately, not all events had such tragic outcomes. The British tramp *Kingswood*, owned by Joseph Constantine of Middlesbrough was lying in Port Pirie, in South Australia's Spencer Gulf on 3 January 1937, when her donkey-boiler exploded, severely damaging the ship. She was patched-up and towed home to the Tyne for repairs by the Dutch, Smit-owned tug *Ganges*. The Dutch had, not long before, towed a floating dry dock to Wellington, the longest ever tow and that of the *Kingswood* is considered a close second.

For most boys going to sea at this time little had changed, though they were aware of the difficulties they might encounter later if trading conditions did not improve. But sixteen-year-old boys do not think much of the future, when a four-year apprenticeship stretches ahead of them. Adventure and the sea stories of Percy Westerman and others were the lure and the variety of ports they might visit in their four-year 'time' could be staggering. During his apprenticeship in tramp-steamers, William Mutimer ventured as far a-field as Port Pirie on Australia's Spencer Gulf and Igarka, which was not only in Siberia, it was 400 miles up the Yenisei River – a far cry from his native Surbiton.[28] Having been a passenger in a Cunarder on several occasions and admired her deck-officers, George Radford's mother thought the mercantile marine an eminently suitable life for her son.

> My family were business people and the intellectual side of life was never too prominent – even the facts and pitfalls of life were carefully avoided. Before leaving home my mother told me that my father would have a word with me before I left – I remember the words quite well: 'Well, son, I suppose your mother has told you everything. Don't forget to look after your feet, you know the trouble I have with mine. Always cut your toe-nails square and your finger-nails round'.[29]

But Radford did not join the Cunard Line, instead, in August 1929, he joined the *British Progress*, a 10,000-ton deadweight tanker of the British Petroleum Co., Captain Ralph Thoburn, owned by the Anglo-Persian Oil Co. He thereby embarked upon four years of tolerable, managed misery, living:

> aft in the poop-space in the same alleyway as the refrigerator and engine-room access, where the incessant main engine clatter was punctured from time to time by thuds and bangs from chunks of meat flung out of the refrigerator ... [T]o earn some extra money we undertook to wash officers' clothes. Ten shillings a month was the charge, which was only five bob each. It could not have given us much more than an extra pound a month, but a pound note was worth something in those days – we could buy from, the captain (through the steward) half a pound

of Capstan fine cut tobacco for four shillings, which with care we could make last four weeks ... It was always hot in our cabin, especially east of Suez ... There we would be busy studying, ironing clothes, writing letters or sleeping. Sleep was our greatest desire – or maybe it was food. There was little to choose between them ... Study was helped by an encouraging second officer, 'a real character who was a tubby, jovial snuff addict ... His periodic sneezes could be heard all over the ship. He gave great help and encouragement to us with our studies ... Mr Wilson ... prided himself on his navigation'. And, even in these difficult years there was a 'professional' third officer, 'a Mr Jones ... from North Wales. He was middle-aged, tall and cadaverous ... He was without doubt a very thorough seaman. Claiming my awe and admiration in spite of the tobacco juice he squirted around to our disgust. He taught us to sew canvas properly, rope awnings and other skills not found in our text books. After our evening meal in the dining saloon he would often enthral us with stories of his days in sailing ships ...

Although claiming that his apprenticeship 'were the happiest days of my life' his later service as a junior officer soured his attitude.

During the time about which I write, a good shipping company would expect their officers to serve continuously for at least one year before applying for leave. The normal length of time away was two years [the length of the standard Board of Trade Articles of Agreement], by which time one could expect a spell at home of two months on pay.

Radford admitted that:

It would be fair to say that for many like myself, tied to the tanker life with its constant and gruelling demands over such long periods – often years – it deprived some people of a basic aspect of the business of living, sometimes with irreparable harm in later life.

When he finished his time, Radford's family circumstances had declined owing to the Depression and he felt constrained to earn some money before sitting for his Second Mate's Certificate. Having walked the Swansea Docks for weeks he bribed a ship's bosun with a pint of beer and was tipped off to report to the Shipping Office where he secured a berth as quartermaster on Elders & Fyffes banana carrier *Matina*, then outward bound for Jamaica. His completed indentures qualified him as an able-seaman and the bonus of being quartermaster added ten shillings a month to his wage of £8, removing him from the drudgery on deck to bridge duties at the helm.

After the four years in oil tankers she seemed like a large yacht to me with her white hull and buff funnel and steaming at fourteen knots. There were twelve passengers and apart from our tricks at the wheel the quartermaster's duties were confined to the boat-deck and the comforts of the passengers. I found the changed life rather pleasant ...

In due course, however, having qualified for second mate, Radford returned to British Petroleum and was appointed third officer of the *British Lord*, Captain Cunningham, at the end of March 1934. After two years during which he served in the *British General*, again under Thoburn, Radford was accepted by the Royal Naval Reserve before joining the *British Officer*, commanded by Captain Watkin Watkin-Thomas, who was:

> a rare character, whose Welsh accent and unpredictable ways can never be forgotten ... He chain smoked ... was never known to visit the bridge unless his presence was really needed, nevertheless he insisted on being kept informed by voice-pipe. He was much over-weight and drank his gin from a small wine-glass; entertaining only when there were passengers aboard ... The engineer officers had little cause to be fond of Watkin-Thomas due to his intense displeasure whenever thick smoke was emitted from the funnel ... As I recall the *British Officer* was a fairly unhappy ship.

Watkin-Thomas's paranoia about smoke probably originated from his experiences in the recent war. At all events he took the matter seriously and on one occasion when, heading eastwards through the Strait of Gibraltar with a following wind by night, dense back smoke billowed over the bridge and lay in a pall across the deck forward of the wheelhouse. A disturbed Watkin-Thomas climbed laboriously from his cabin, stopped the engines and ordered Radford to hoist the 'Not-under-Command' lights. He then instructed Radford to make a log entry to the effect that the *British Officer* was stopped 'due to impaired visibility'.

Like many other officers who held RNR commissions, Radford was called-up into the navy during the war, joining men like W.J. Moore of the Blue Funnel Line who became commanding officer of HM Frigate *Whimbrel*, and Hedley Kett, who, having begun his sea-going career in reefers and wing-collar aboard Glover Bros tramp *Shakespear*, rose to command a submarine. Interestingly Radford himself, after a varied war, ended as Commanding Officer of HM Corvette *Genista* with the rank of lieutenant commander but had yet to pass for master-mariner. They, like others of their age, despite their being at sea in the worst years of the Depression, found that their youth and the RNR preserved them from its worst impact.

Even as the world emerged from Depression, life remained uncertain for many. Victor Making, an Extra-Master-Mariner and Lieutenant in the RNR had gone to sea in sail 1902 and had been castaway on a remote island after his ship had caught fire. During the war he had served in the Royal Navy. His wife had been killed when the P&O liner *Majola*, in which she was a passenger, was blown-up off Dover by a mine. By 1920, the widowed Making had been promoted to master of the Red Star line's *Pennland*. Mentioned in the previous volume, this company was beneficially owned in the United States but had ships under the Stars and Stripes, the Belgian *tricolore* and the red ensign. They specialised in the carriage of live cattle, but also provided a passenger service and – like others upon occasion – ocean cruises. Captain Making's career ended abruptly, on Christmas Eve, 1934.

> We docked in Antwerp, our homeport, that afternoon, and after wishing us a Merry Christmas the company's officials informed us that most of the officers were to be

discharged at once, as the ships were being laid up to be sold. For some time the fear of being stranded 'on the beach' was allayed by the news that a British syndicate was trying to buy ... [the company] and would retain us in the positions we then held. Eventually, however, for reasons that gave rise to questions in Parliament and to comments in the Press, it was prevented from doing so, and the Red Star Line was taken over by the Bernstein Line of Hamburg. On February 20th, 1935, those of us who still remained on board watched the British ensign hauled down and a German flag run up in its place; and a few minutes later we walked down the gangway, involuntary recruits for the army of the unemployed. What made matters worse was that the prospects of finding employment in another company were not very bright. One of the officers, a man of about 40 years of age, married, with one child, who for some years had been First Officer of a 16,000-ton Red Star liner, was eventually obliged to take a job as quartermaster. Another, an older man with a family, who had served as First Officer on the 27,000 ton S.S. *Belgenland*, was unable to get another ship and finally found work in a London office. After a while he had to give that up on account of his health.[30]

Not all careers were so blighted and on some the fates smiled; one such was Malcolm Bruce Glasier, who was born in Derbyshire in 1903, the son of an architect and journalist who was also a social evangelist and who succeeded Kier Hardie as chairman of the Independent Labour Party in 1900. Glasier's mother was no less politically active; a Cambridge Classics graduate, she interested herself in improving the working conditions of women, joining the Fabian Society where she met her future husband. Glasier's grandfather, however, had been master in sail and his parents moved about the country, inducing a restlessness in their son who, aged fourteen, ran away to sea in June 1917 and served on several steamers. Accepting their son's inclination, his parents arranged for Glasier to serve his time as an apprentice with John Stewart & Co. of Billiter Street, London, owners of sailing vessels.

One of these, the full-rigged ship *Monkbarns* had put into Rio de Janeiro with her crew in a state of mutiny and flying signals for assistance. Captain Donaldson [who was 'well over 70 years of age'] and his officers had been carrying small arms for self-defence. On arrival at Rio de Janeiro on 25 June 1918, Donaldson anchored under the guns of HMS *Armadale Castle*, an Armed Merchant Cruiser (AMC) and former Union-Castle liner, receiving the man-of-war's boarding party with relief. In due course the mutineers were tried aboard the *Armadale Castle* by a Naval Court and sentenced to terms of imprisonment in British gaols, to which end they were confined aboard the warship. Having cabled Billiter Street, Donaldson awaited new crew members, transhipping his cargo to the *Highland Rover* in the interim. His replacements consisted of ten apprentices, one of whom was Glasier, and on 18 September, the ballasted *Monkbarns* weighed for Western Australia to load a full cargo of jarrah wood, a red hard-wood derived from the eucalyptus, which she carried to Capetown, losing a man overboard on the passage. Loading maize at the Cape she sailed for Cork, arriving on 4 June 1919; she then went to the Rio de la Plata in ballast, carried a cargo of linseed to Bristol before loading coal from Cardiff to Las Palmas and a long passage in ballast to Newcastle, New South Wales, during which she encountered heavy weather and suffered a partial dismasting. With the wreckage to her fore and main topgallant masts and yards cleared away she made her destination, loaded coal for Iquique and proceeded thither. On 25 May 1921, having loaded saltpetre – potassium nitrate – she departed for Falmouth where she received orders to discharge at Bruges where she offloaded what must be then have been a poorly freighted cargo at a time of impending slump. The *Monkbarns* was now laid-up and Glasier, like the rest of the crew, was discharged, unable to complete his time. However, thanks to his parents' connections, young Glasier corresponded with Lawrence Holt, in consequence of which he was able to complete his apprenticeship in various Blue Funnel liners, obtaining his Second Mate's certificate in January 1923. Though Holt had befriended Glasier, he was not prepared to continue his employment as an officer without a Master's certificate, preferably in sail. In the meanwhile Glasier's old ship had been towed round to Birkenhead, refitted and loaded with rock salt for New South Wales. The *Monkbarns* sailed on 8 March 1923 under a new master, Captain Davies, who had spent forty years at sea, thirty of which had been in command. Glasier signed-on as third mate.

While running her easting down in a strong gale on 9 May, Davies was obliged to heave-to. The *Monkbarns* shipped heavy seas which flooded part of her after accommodation and damaged her boats. The cargo shifted and one of the apprentices, Cyril Sybon, was lost from a yard as the ship listed until her lee rail was under water and the crew went below to shovel it up to the weather side. Three days later a moderation in the weather allowed Davies to head for Capetown where he arrived on 16 May. Her cargo restowed, the *Monkbarns* left on 23 June to resume her voyage. Once again heavy weather caused havoc. On the night of 15 June green seas swept the main deck, injuring the chief mate and eight seamen. A few days later a halliard block carried away, killing Second Mate Samuel Hales and smashing the hand of Apprentice Sam Wallis, but the *Monkbarns* arrived in Sydney after a thirty-nine-day passage from the Cape.

Having discharged her cargo of salt in Sydney and Newcastle, the *Monkbarns* loaded coal for Iquique, where the crew discharged it into lighters; she then loaded saltpetre for Melbourne, arriving on 7 July 1924, and made a short ballast passage to Newcastle to load coal again. By this time Glasier had accrued sufficient sea-time to sit his next examination. Coming home to pass his First Mate's Certificate of Competency in sail and steam, he did secure a third mate's berth with Blue Funnel, finally passing for Master on 25 June 1928. By now Glasier was married and the following year he determined to enter the Trinity House pilotage service for the London River, so was obliged to ship in a coaster to obtain the requisite experience on the Thames. However, having kept his eye on the young man, Lawrence Holt offered Glasier a position as Assistant Marine Superintendent in Birkenhead where Holts had extensive facilities and from where the outward-bound Blue Funnel liners departed for the Far East. Here Glasier prospered and in 1939 he was sent to London as the third superintendent in the company's Marine Department. Glasier was a tough, no-nonsense character and became embroiled with the difficult dock-labour and stevedoring affairs in the Port of London. He and his wife purchased a house in Ilford as war broke out, placing additional demands on Glasier's talents. In 1940 Holt's Marine Department assumed responsibility for Elder, Dempster's ships when they lay in the London docks and that year Glasier was co-opted to assist Lawrence Holt and Kurt Hahn in the establishment of the Outward Bound Sea School at Aberdovey, mentioned in detail elsewhere. Finally, in 1943, as Aberdovey acquired a training ketch, the *Garibaldi*, Glasier was appointed Holt's Chief Marine Superintendent in London.[31]

He had already done sterling wartime service attached to the Ministry of War Transport (MoWT), assuming an active role when occasion demanded, such as the grounding of the *Meriones* in January 1941 when he worked in concert with that doyen of the Royal National Lifeboat Institution, Coxswain Henry Blogg of Cromer, in the most appalling weather. After the war Glasier was made a CBE in the 1949 Birthday Honours. The Glasier family's politics acquainted him with Britain's post-war Prime Minister, Clement Attlee, and when Attlee's son Martin expressed a desire to go to sea it was natural that he signed indentures with Alfred Holt & Co. Attlee himself, along with his wife, boarded and enjoyed tea aboard Glen liners in London's King George V Dock on several occasions, a distinction unique among British prime ministers.[32]

Such opportunities affected the very few. For the vast majority of merchant seafarers fortune's smile was wan. For a number employed in a handful of tramps, just as the economic situation slowly improved, the spectre of war – increasingly edging into the public consciousness – became a reality.[33] On 18 July 1936 the right-wing army officers stationed in Spanish Morocco began a fascist revolt against the democratically elected socialist Popular Front Republican government of President Azana. The revolt spread, turning into a civil war which the rebels won three years later with support from Fascist Italy and Nazi Germany. During the war Spain became a battleground for the competing ideologies of the left and right. Under General Franco the fascist rebels, dignifying their cause as 'Nationalist', soon secured the entire Portuguese frontier which, with the declaration of Cadiz for the Nationalists, provided a vital supply route. In June 1937 Franco's forces seized the Basque port of Bilbao and, assisted by armed intervention from Germany and Italy during 1938, caused the Republicans to totter. Although Madrid withstood a long siege that year, the Nationalists broke through in Catalunya. Over-powered, riven by internal factions, and deprived of Soviet aid, the Spanish Republic collapsed. Barcelona fell on 26 January 1939, Valencia and Madrid capitulated on 28 March. The British and French policies of encouraging non-intervention had proved a complete failure, while Italian and German support had secured Nationalist victory. While the sympathy of international socialists and communists had led to the formation of the voluntary 'International Brigades', this was not the only involvement of outsiders in this dreadful conflict.

The outbreak of the Spanish Civil War, contemporaneous with Mussolini's aggressive intervention in Abyssinia (Ethiopia), made the Mediterranean an area of extreme sensitivity. For Britain, just beginning to recover from the weary years of the Depression, the maintenance of her normal trade added to the protection of her communications with India and the Far East, ended the Royal Navy's banyan days in the Middle Sea. Showing the flag became more than the mere exercise of imperial prerogative. On the outbreak of the war in Spain the main protection of British interests in Iberia was the job of the British Mediterranean Fleet's destroyers, led by Rear Admiral James Somerville. Somerville was responsible for safeguarding all manner of British activities, ranging from protecting shipping to wandering poets, interdicting gun-running and enforcing international law.[34] In these complex tasks he proved exemplary, despite his distaste for the Republicans, largely owing to their communist taint and their 'predilection for murdering their [right-wing] officers'.

The early successes of the Nationalists provoked Madrid into declaring rebel-held ports in a state of blockade and to seek to interfere with the international port of Tangier, whose status the Nationalists were suspected of abusing. This was a breach of International Law and rapidly drew the international maritime community into the struggle. Somerville, flying his flag in HM Cruiser *Galatea*, was anchored of Majorca on 18 August 1936 in company with the German *Panzerschiff* the *Deutschland* and the Italian destroyer *Lanzerotto Malocello*. When reports that a Republican attack on the port of Palma was imminent, the three foreign men-of-war put to sea. HMS *Galatea* led, the German and Italian 'maintaining very good station' astern; 'just clear of territorial waters … the "international squadron" patrolled at 10 knots …'.[35]

Somerville also formally protested over the unlawful stopping of British merchant-men outside territorial waters. On 16 August the *Marklyn* had been thus victimised and on the 23rd the small Gibraltar-registered *Gibel Zerjon* was detained. Somerville's note concluded that the British navy:

> Fully recognises the difficult task with which the warships of the Spanish Government are faced but he desires it to be most clearly understood that this affords no pretext for illegal acts … any recurrence will immediately be resisted by the ships of His Britannic Majesty, who will not hesitate to open fire if necessary in order to protect ships under the British Flag from illegal interference.[36]

The *Marklyn* was a Cardiff-registered tramp, built as a standard-ship in 1920 and one of many which carried Welsh coal to Spain, returning with iron ore and pyrites. Many of the iron-ore mines in the Basque country had been owned by British companies based in Wales and the mines near Huelva on the Bay of Cadiz remained in British hands, being owned by Rio Tinto Ltd.

Despite the early Republican blockade – largely of Cadiz – and their interdic-tion of shipping, Madrid soon lost control of the sea.[37] Republican merchantmen were sunk by the Nationalists, one being shelled to destruction in the North Sea, which led to increased shipment of Spanish cargoes in British ships. This situation led to a conflict of interest; on the one hand the British Government was anxious to pursue and to encourage in others a policy of non-intervention. On the other hand, despite widespread detestation of the Republicans for their increasing reliance upon the communists, the Madrid government remained the legitimate democratic power and British shipowners, scenting profit, maintained their right to trade and to call upon the protection of the Royal Navy to do so. Such was then the authority of the British navy that the Republicans formed shipping companies in Britain, covered by the red ensign.

While British enterprise could be relied upon to continue normal trade, the acqui-sition of arms was another matter, something that British owners were less eager to become embroiled in, for the carrying of contraband cargoes carried the high risk associated with interdiction. The Spanish government, however, had no such scruples, seeing in the protection of the British flag a way of circumventing what was increas-ingly a Nationalist blockade aided if not implemented by Franco's Fascist and Nazi *de facto* allies. The Prosper Steamship Co., Howard Tenens Ltd, and the Burlington S.S. Co.

were among half a dozen firms established in this way. Another device used by Madrid was the establishment at the Spanish embassy in London of the Mid-Atlantic Co. Ltd. Run by 'a Basque Nationalist and a socialist,' this company chartered-in tonnage which, with the formal firms, was 'founded to purchase arms abroad, but later used for making commercial profits for the communists'. This subverting of the Republican cause by the extreme left caught the British Government between a hammer and an anvil.[38]

Along with specially formed Anglo-Spanish companies, cargoes for Republican Spain were also carried by beneficially Greek-owned concerns, but the wearing of the red ensign made them British in law. While the British Government expressly forbade the export of arms to either side, in the early stages of the war this did not prevent British ships from carrying cargoes of munitions to Spain from other countries. While the Commons seethed with indignation that 148 foreign ships were being transferred to the British register to obtain the protection of the Royal Navy, it paid little attention to the fact that the British flag was being insulted by a rebel – and therefore unlawful – faction.[39] Later that year Parliament prohibited the carriage of arms in British ships with the Merchant Shipping (Carriage of Munitions to Spain) Act. However, some British-owned ships, such as the *Yorkgate*, captured by the Nationalist cruiser *Canarias* on 4 March 1937 laden with over 450 tons of arms and ammunition consigned to the Basque government, evaded this proscription by flying the Estonian flag. This was in fact the *Yorkgate*'s fourth voyage carrying war material to Spain, and her triumphant prize-crew were directed to take her into Pasajes. However, she was intercepted by the Republican destroyer *José Luís Diez* and four armed trawlers, one of which was sunk with all hands in the struggle, and, having been carried into Bermeo, discharged her cargo to her consignees.

By this time, however, it was the Nationalist blockade that was effective, many Spanish warships defecting to the right. More incidents involving British merchant ships ensued. On 12 January 1937 the *Bramhill* of Newport was stopped by the Nationalist trawler *Larache* off Cape Tarifa after the firing of a shot. Hearing her distress call, HM Cruiser *Sussex* soon arrived from Gibraltar and ordered the *Larache* to desist from her intended action. This was complied with but the captain of the *Sussex*, maintaining an even-handed policy, ordered the *Bramhill*'s manifest inspected for contraband. The ship had left Barcelona, called at Tarragona and was homeward bound with a general cargo after bunkering at Gibraltar via Bilbao.

The *Hillfern* left Malaga on 7 February after a heavy bombing raid but in the midst of the battle for the port. Soon after getting clear the ship was stopped by the Nationalist cruisers *Canarias* and *Almirante Cervera* which came under fire from Republican batteries at Torremolinos. The *Hillfern*'s distress signal was intercepted by HM Destroyer *Brazen* whose appearance caused the *Canarias* and *Almirante Cervera* to sheer off. On 23 March the *Menin Ridge*, passing the Straits of Gibraltar with a cargo of Welsh coal for Oran, was signalled to stop by a Nationalist armed trawler. Under the threat of shelling Captain Powell was ordered to reveal his destination.

> I disregarded both orders [he wrote] and maintained my course and speed. He
> fired a warning shot, but shortly afterwards a French destroyer came along and the

trawler turned back. I reported the matter to the Admiralty at Gibraltar and shortly afterwards HMS *Garland* caught us up and was given particulars of the incident. Our position at the time was … outside Territorial Waters.

Complaints from the Nationalists that British ships were running munitions into Republican ports specifically named the *Stanholme* and *Springwear*. The accusations compelled the British naval authorities to detain and inspect the two ships to maintain the policy of transparency. Nothing was found in either vessel, though the *Stanholme* was owned by the Stanhope S.S. Co., of which more later. On 28 March the *Magdalena*, owned by Abraham Lensen of London, while on passage from Tunisia to Bayonne with minerals, was fired on and stopped twenty miles off Santander. The Nationalist boarding-party found no contraband and allowed Captain James Thompson to continue his voyage. Two days later the *Thorpehall*, bound from Valencia to Bilbao by way of Gibraltar for bunkers, was ordered to stop by the Nationalist *cañonero* (sloop) *Eduardo Dato*. Captain Joseph Andrews ignored the order and turned about for Gibraltar. Next morning, escorted by HM Destroyer *Gipsy*, the *Thorpehall* continued her voyage unmolested. The *Thorpehall*'s owners were the Westcliffe Steamship Co. Ltd, a company set up not by Spaniards, but by two Greeks – Messrs Pandelis and Katepodis – who held all but two of the company's shares. The balance of two were held by the company secretary, a British national named Gordon Till, and the purpose of the firm was to take advantage of the British flag in a trading venture with the legitimate Spanish government.

After Malaga fell, the Nationalist offensive stalled at the gates of Madrid. At sea, however, the Nationalists had the upper hand and the *Andra*, a Panamanian-flagged vessel on charter to a Cardiff company, was shelled and sunk in fog when approaching Bilbao on 5 April 1937. Her assailant had been the cruiser *Almirante Cervera* which, with the armed trawler *Galerna*, next day encountered the *Thorpehall*. A shot was fired across the tramp's bows and Andrews transmitted a distress signal which was immediately picked up by three British destroyers, *Blanche*, *Brazen* and *Beagle*. The *Blanche* had on board the British consul from Bilbao and on closing the Spanish cruiser he demanded to know what the Nationalist cruiser was doing. The captain of the *Almirante Cervera* claimed the *Thorpehall* as a legitimate prize, so the ships' companies of *Blanche* and *Beagle* went to action stations while *Brazen* approached the *Thorpehall* with the obvious intention of recovering her. At this bold approach the rebel Spaniards yielded and withdrew, *Brazen* seeing Andrews's ship safely to the three-mile limit from where she proceeded into Bilbao. It was this same day, 6 April, that Franco – aware of such commercial legerdemain as was evidenced by the Westcliffe S.S. Co. – declared the Basque coast under close blockade.

This immediately prompted the Board of Trade to inform all British ships of the situation. Those with cargoes consigned to the Basque ports of Santander, Santoña and Bilbao were ordered to await developments off St Jean de Luz, beyond the French border. Within a few days several lay at anchor. One was the *Hamsterley* of Newcastle, Captain Still, the remaining three were all Welsh tramps and were all commanded by masters named Jones. Angell's Cardiff-registered *Marie Llewellyn* was under Captain David J. Jones, the Guardian Line's *Macgregor*'s master was Captain Owen Jones and another Captain Jones was master of Stone and Rolfe's Llanelli-registered *Sarastone*. All four had cargoes of foodstuffs, though the *Marie Llewellyn*'s lading of potatoes for Santander was said to conceal a quantity of arms. The predominance of potatoes in the *Marie Llewellyn* and grain in the other two Welsh vessels encouraged the press to label the former's master 'Potato' Jones and the latter's 'Corn Cob' Jones, though these nicknames are thought to have originated from the Royal Navy, to differentiate among the many Captain Joneses commanding these Welsh tramp-ships. Not to be left out, the *Sarastone*'s master was labelled 'Ham and Egg' Jones.[40]

These were joined by the *Seven Seas Spray*, Captain William H. Roberts, who had been diverted from entering Bilbao by HMS *Blanche* and the appearance of the *Almirante Cervera*. On 11 April the *Macgregor* sailed for Bayonne to await further orders from her owners, where she was joined by the *Leadgate* of Newcastle, in ballast but seeking to load a cargo of iron ore. Meanwhile naval forces in the southern Bay of Biscay were being augmented by several nations, most notably the British who now had the battleship *Royal Oak* and the battle-cruiser *Hood* off St Jean de Luz. This show of overwhelming force was clearly designed to place the situation beyond provocation, as might have been construed by the dash of the destroyers. Next day the British prime minister, Stanley Baldwin, announced the presence of the *Hood* – herself a well-known and iconic symbol of British naval sea power – and while 'warning British shipping that, in view of conditions at present prevailing at Bilbao, they should not, for practical reasons, and in view of the risks against which it is at present impossible to protect them, go into that area ...'. Baldwin added: 'His Majesty's Government cannot recognise or concede belligerent rights and they (sic) cannot tolerate any interference with British shipping at sea'.

The imposed immobility of the ships at St Jean de Luz was not to be tolerated, at least by 'Potato' Jones whose cargo of spuds was spoiling in the *Marie Llewellyn*'s holds. With public interest focussed on the beleaguered ships and British pride inflamed by this interference of their trade, the press found in David John Jones the bluff, no-nonsense spokesman for their frustration. Declaring his contempt for the Spanish Nationalist navy, 'Potato' Jones displeased both the Royal Navy and His Majesty's Government, but not the public. Pressed for their intentions, most shipowners issued statements that they would act only on the advice of the naval authorities. Convoy escort was refused but the Royal Navy was willing to provide protection while the ships lay outside Spanish waters. Many ship-masters, however, were less tractable and wished to continue with their voyages. Still of the *Hamsterley* was one, his ship being fitted with radio; 'Corn Cob' Jones was reported to be of the same opinion, though his owners denied it; 'Potato' Jones, whose *Marie Llewellyn* was not fitted with wireless, demurred.

On the morning of 15 April Lensen's *Magdalena* arrived – after dodging on and off in bad weather – and with her the news that the Sunderland-registered tramp *Brinkburn* had left Bilbao the previous day laden with a cargo of iron ore. Other ships had left too and, although the Nationalists were more interested in supplies of arms and food arriving, it began to get abroad that the efficacy of the Nationalist blockade was being vastly exaggerated. That afternoon the *Sarastone* was ordered to Bayonne by the French to have her cargo examined and she weighed and proceeded north. Shortly afterwards she was followed by the *Marie Llewellyn*. 'Potato' Jones had received neither orders nor permission from the French authorities but, after following in his namesake's wake for a while, the *Marie Llewellyn* was observed to head into the heavy south-westerly swell, the residue of a strong gale. Was he hove-to or heading for Bilbao?

It was widely thought that 'Potato' Jones had wished to break the blockade, but he was dissuaded by a patrolling British destroyer and the *Marie Llewellyn* returned to St Jean de Luz next day, reportedly 'a crestfallen ship'. But *The Times* reporter did not find her crew downcast when he boarded 'over bulwarks thoughtfully coated with fresh paint for the convenience of visitors'. Indeed, he detected 'an air of mystery' about the ship, her usually loquacious master uncharacteristically silent, while 'her mate's description of the night's escapade was a nod and the words, "not so bad" '. 'Potato' Jones's own explanation of his movements was an anxiety to replenish his fresh water at Bayonne, an attempt defeated by the heavy swell still running on the bar there after the recent bad weather.

In fact the *Marie Llewellyn* had been in danger of falling foul of the Spanish battleship *España* which she had sighted in the distance as HMS *Brazen* warned her that once inside Spanish territorial waters in defiance of the British Government's instructions, she would be beyond the Royal Navy's help. A few days later the *Marie Llewellyn*, her cargo ruined, headed for the Mediterranean and Alicante where a cargo of fruit could be loaded for Avonmouth. In the meantime her spoiled spuds had to be dumped. The notion that Jones managed to trans-ship a consignment of arms to small craft off the coast on the night of 15/16 April is unlikely, but like all myths has an enduring quality.

While David Jones was making his name known worldwide, the Chamber of Shipping in London was taking a longer view, recommending the wording of charter parties made clear the difficulties of trade with Spain but which essentially guaranteed payment of freight to the shipowner whatever happened to the ship or her cargo. All vessels were insured against war risks and, after many arguments, the owners finally agreed to pay their crews a war bonus of 50 per cent of their wages when within twenty-four hours of the declared war zone. Bonuses were now also offered to the ships languishing off St Jean de Luz by a Basque government then coping with a starving population. Rumours of a minefield were dismissed and, as proof, the case of the *Thorpehall* was cited, Andrews having coasted westwards towards Gijon after leaving Bilbao before his owners got cold feet and ordered the ship to La Pallice. On 19 April, the day the *Thorpehall* left Gijon, the *Sarastone* arrived at Bordeaux, whither she had been summoned by the French to have her cargo examined. The combined official Anglo-French policy of non-intervention which gave the French powers to so instruct British merchantmen was one thing, but the increasing solidarity of the working classes over the plight of the Basques in particular and the Republican cause in general, persuaded the French dockers to stop unloading her cargo of ruined foodstuffs when it was clear that the non-intervention control officers were really in search of her putative cargo of arms. Eventually the trade union relented, the spoiled cargo was offloaded and, no arms being found, she was released.

None of these ships had traded profitably but 'Potato' Jones's failure, conspicuous as it was, had persuaded all parties, including the Spanish Nationalists, the British

Government, Board of Trade and Chamber of Shipping, and the Royal Navy on the spot, that the blockade of Bilbao had been successful. The starving Basques knew it for a fact but this was not a *fait accompli* for Alfred Pope, principal partner in the Veronica Steamship Co., the owners of the *Seven Seas Spray*. Pope sent his partner Thomas McEwen to St Jean de Luz to confer with her master, Captain Roberts.

At 22.00 on Monday 19 April Roberts got his ship under weigh and, ignoring the signals from the shore to stop, put to sea without lights. A passing man-of-war, generally thought to have been a patrolling Nationalist vessel, failed to spot the tramp-ship as she stood to the west. Ten miles off the Basque coast a vigilant British destroyer called up to the darkened ship with the traditional: 'What ship? Where Bound?' Roberts replied 'Bilbao' which called forth an official warning over his intentions and a private wishing of good luck.

As the *Seven Seas Spray* stood in towards Bilbao she was met by Basque patrol craft and, with aircraft overhead and a rapidly growing crowd gathering along the port approaches, the steamship berthed to public acclamation. Roberts – a Cornishman – stood on the bridge, his daughter and McEwen beside him, while the hungry population – misunderstanding the ship's largely Welsh origins – cried out '¡*Viva los Marineros Ingles! ¡Viva Libertad!*'

While the Basque government dined McEwen, Roberts (who wore his uniform for the occasion) and his daughter Florence (who had refused to stay at St Jean), Pope told reporters that he knew it could be done and that:

> Franco's blockade is nothing but boast and tommy rot. A British steamer has opened the way for shipping. I hope that the *'Spray* has blazed a trail and shown the rest of the vessels at St Jean de Luz the way to Bilbao … My partner and captain did the trick … We were determined to get in and we got in. We hope that other people will get in as well. We have been trading to Spain for a long time … General Franco is not going to keep a single one of our ships from going about its lawful occasions …

Roberts telegraphed the *Western Mail*, emphasising the warmth of his reception and 'the great ovation all along both sides of the river from all the people and children'. He also complimented the others aboard the *Seven Seas Spray*. 'My daughter was not the only lady on board, as Mrs B. Docker wife of the Chief Engineer, was also on board. I had the loyal co-operation of officers, engineers and crew, and the ladies entered into the venture with zest.'

While the British Government was officially embarrassed, largely by the absence of the declared minefield, Franco fulminated, promising vengeance and a tightening of the noose. On the day following Roberts' breaking of the blockade 'Corn Cob' Jones arrived back at St Jean de Luz from Bayonne. The *Hamsterley* was still at anchor and they were joined by Captain Prance in the *Stanbrook*, one of Stanhope's steamers whose owner, the charismatic Jack Billmeir, was committed to breaking the blockade. As a go-getting capitalist, Billmeir was disliked by many seafarers for flirting with dangerous and profitable assignments for his ships, but he was not lacking in personal courage. He had begun his career with the acquisition of two second-hand coasters, establishing the Stanhope Shipping Co. shortly before the outbreak of the

Spanish Civil War. He was soon buying-up ageing tonnage in order to circumvent the difficulties of insuring ships for blockade-running and while he undoubtedly ran arms and other essential *matériel* to the Republicans, he also supplied petroleum, losing one of his ships, the *Stanburgh*, when she was loading the volatile spirit at Sété in southern France in 1938. Whatever his reputation, Billmeir seems to have had little difficulty recruiting masters, mates, engineers and crew for his daring enterprise, though doubtless his cash inducements, in contrast to the long, lean years of unemployment, played their part.

Stealing a march on the opposition, 'Corn Cob' Jones boarded the *Hood* and requested a consultation with Vice Admiral Blake. It was privately and unofficially agreed that on the morning of St George's Day, 23 April, HMS *Hood*, that symbol of British naval puissance, would be cruising off Bilbao. Jones returned to his ship by way of the *Stanbrooke* and *Hamsterley* and so, having consulted with their masters, on the evening of the 22nd, the three tramps weighed and proceeded west.

News of their departure was quickly passed to the Nationalists who sent the *Almirante Cervera* and the armed trawler *Galerna* to intercept them. On the morning of the 23rd the three groups converged on the approaches to Bilbao, ten miles off-shore, beyond the limits of Spanish territorial waters. The first British merchantman to turn towards the coast was the *Macgregor*, a move which provoked the *Almirante Cervera* to fire a shot across her bow. Astern of the humble tramp-ship loomed the *Hood*, accompanied by the destroyer *Firedrake*, both with their guns trained on the Spanish warships. Blake warned the Nationalist commander against interfering with British shipping or face the consequences and signalled Jones to proceed at his discretion. The *Macgregor* ploughed on, but was tailed by *Galerna*; Blake sent the *Firedrake* inshore to escort the tramp to the three-mile limit and, when *Galerna's* commander fired across the *Macgregor's* bows, the destroyer's captain repeated Blake's warning. At this point the shore batteries at Bilbao opened fire on the *Galerna*, which withdrew rapidly northwards, allowing the *Macgregor* to enter Bilbao. The other two ships followed without incident, and in the succeeding days others arrived, mostly loaded with foodstuffs. The *Stesso* of Newcastle and *Thurston* of West Hartlepool arrived from La Pallice on the 25th; the same day the food-laden *Jenny* of London and the coal-carrying *Oakgrove* arrived at Santander after being fired on by the Nationalists and supported by a British destroyer. Next day the *Sheaf Garth* came into Bilbao; it was the same day that the Condor Legion bombed Guernica.

Bilbao was also attacked from the air that day, the *Hamsterley* suffering some damage, though no casualties. The news of the idle ships at St Jean de Luz had already evoked widespread sympathy for the starving Basques and prompted trade union, churches, the International League of Friends, private individuals and other organisations to muster to their support. Co-ordinated by a committee, these worthies sought a vessel to take to northern Spain the aid which the British people were subscribing in considerable quantities to northern Spain. In due course the Dalgliesh SS Co.'s *Backworth* was chartered and loaded at Immingham. With volunteering for the International Brigades increasing, many wished to join the ship, but all were refused. Only her crew and the mandatory control officer from the Non-Intervention Committee took passage under the command of Captain Russell. Loaded with food and medical stores, the *Backworth* sailed on the same day that the *Macgregor* led her two consorts into Bilbao, 23 April – St George's Day.

With the *Royal Oak* and HM Destroyer *Fury* patrolling offshore, and the Spanish battleship *España* off Santander, the *Backworth* approached the coast. In a 'rain swept ocean' approaching the three-mile limit, Russell was warned that he would be bombed or fired upon if he was caught, then asked what his intentions were. 'We intend to proceed,' he called back through his megaphone, whereupon the gun crews on *Fury*'s upper deck cheered. '*Backworth*', Russell wirelessed the press in London through Nationalist attempts to jam him, 'had never travelled so fast, belching black smoke over bay, took Pilot aboard [at] seven, now entering harbour, behaviour of crew magnificent ...'.

This success contrasted with a diversion off Santander where the ore-laden *Consett* had been turned away by HMS *Royal Oak* in the presence of the *España*, to head instead for St Jean de Luz. However, more British ships arrived at Bilbao in the succeeding days, covered by *Royal Oak*. On the morning of 29 April the *Portelet*, *Marvia*, *Thorpehall* and *Sheaf Field* entered the port without interception. Although Bilbao was bombed shortly afterwards, damaging shore installation, none of the ships was hit. The *Consett*, meanwhile, made another attempt to enter Santander, from which she was again dissuaded by a shelling from the *España*. That day a sister-ship, the *Knitsley*, attempting to enter Castro Urdiales – which lay between Bilbao and Santander – was fired at by the Nationalist torpedo-boat *Velasco*. At this time a Republican air attack was mounted upon the *España* in the distance and the *Velasco* withdrew to her assistance as the Spanish battleship was sinking after striking a mine, allowing the *Knitsley* to escape.

As the tide of war ebbed and flowed round the Basque ports – Bermeo falling to an Italian force, only to be surrounded by Republicans – British masters anchored off Gijon, Bermeo, Santander and Bilbao judged to a nicety the moments to move. However, the successes of the Nationalists persuaded others that they might be caught so, on 5 May, Captain Still's *Hamsterley* headed seawards with refugees on board. He was chased and shelled as he steamed towards the distant silhouette of the *Royal Oak*. Other refugees left on Basque vessels pursued by the *Almirante Cervera*, which claimed the right to sink them. When this was signalled to the British battleship, the *Royal Oak* responded by throwing an escort of destroyers about the Basque ships and stationing herself between the rebel Spaniard and her quarry.

The food shortage in the Basque ports now affected British ships delayed by offloading cargo. Those who had spare food on board often left what they had for the besieged population, but increasingly departing ships bore refugees and in time the audacity of the British merchantmen, though it saved many from starvation for the time being, was not to go unavenged. The Nationalist forces invading Basque territory drove the hostile population towards the ports where crowds of rootless refugees exacerbated the food problem and encouraged the chartering of ships by the Basque government to evacuate them. Numerous British vessels were involved, while the Royal Navy attempted to maintain the freedom of navigation on the high seas amid the increasingly harsh blockade imposed by the Nationalists. On 23 May the *Oakgrove*, anchored just within the port of Bilbao, was showered with bomb splinters.

Assistant Steward Robert Blackburn was severely wounded and a seaman was slightly hurt. On the 19th five vessels had left Santander for France, full of refugees. These were the *Kenfig Pool*, *Hillfern*, *African Trader*, *Surreybrook* and *Latymer*.

The evacuation of the population became acute when on 19 June Bilbao fell to the Nationalists. On 22 June the *Marion Moller*, carrying 2,000 frightened people, was stopped by the Nationalist vessel *Cuidad de Palma*. The master summoned the aid of HM Destroyer *Boadicea* which warned the *Cuidad de Palma* from interfering and the *Marion Moller* made for St Jean de Luz, only to be initially turned away by the French until, eventually, she landed her refugees at Pauillac on the Gironde. Such incidents became common in the succeeding weeks as the Nationalists triumphed. One of the last ships to leave was Alfred Pope's *Seabank* which carried the assets of the Bank of Bilbao and those of several British merchant banks in the city. Loaded with gold, securities, deed-boxes, jewellery and cash, the *Seabank* hovered off La Pallice for a week, making a rendezvous with the Basque steamer *Axpe Mendi* to transfer her valuable lading. On 25 June the two ships were ordered into La Pallice by the French who lent weight to the argument with force. The action followed an injunction laid by the British and Republican banks in Bilbao, presumably hostile to the independent pretensions of the Basque authorities. Registering protest with the British consul, the *Seabank*'s master was informed that his ship was not under arrest and she would be freed after discharge of her cargo. Once again the French dockers refused to comply with their orders out of sympathy with the Basques, and it took intervention by the trade unions on the promise of the retention of the valuables in bond, pending a judicial decision. The *Seabank* left La Pallice for Santander on 24 August 1937.

These events dislocated the normal intercourse of trade so that ships like the tramp *Gwenthills*, arriving off Castro Urdiales on 30 June to load iron ore, was informed by the patrolling British destroyer *Boreas* that the port had been taken over by the Nationalists. She consequently headed for St Jean de Luz, undergoing a brief shelling outside territorial waters by a Nationalist gun-vessel. By July ships of several countries were either lying off St Jean, or steaming at slow speed just outside the three-mile limit, seeking opportunities to dodge the Nationalist blockaders. Under charter to the Basque government, some carried food and sought to embark refugees. On 4 July the Frenchman *Tregastel* 'misjudged her opportunity and was captured by the *Almirante Cervera*. Four shells were fired across her bow before the steamer submitted and was escorted into the Nationalist held Bilbao'.[41] Two days later the British-flagged short-sea trader *Gordonia*, making for Santander, was apprehended by a gun-boat and the *Almirante Cerevera*. Only the summary intervention of HM Destroyers *Bulldog* and *Escapade* prevented her capture and she escaped to Bayonne to await orders.

Many of the British masters, motivated by both their obligations under their charter parties, a humanitarian objection to the Nationalist tactics, and a pig-headed defiance not to be shoved around, made gallant efforts to evacuate the increasingly desperate populace. Whether imagined or not, a kinship between the Welsh tramp-ship owners, masters and crews and the wretched Basque refugees proved a powerful force in all this. A committee for Spanish relief had been set up in Cardiff, among whose patrons were David Lloyd George, Professor H.A. Marquand, the Archbishop of Wales and the shipowner Lord Glanely. Glanely had chartered his two oldest vessels, the steamships *Molton* and *Pilton*, to the Basques. Under the command of Captain R.H. Stears the former crossed the three-mile limit at 05.45 on 14 July heading for Santander. With the battleship HMS *Royal Oak* lying impotently in the offing, she was rapidly intercepted by the *Almirante Cervera* and, after several shots were fired across her bow, the *Molton* was carried into Bilbao under the escort of the *Galerna*. Simultaneously with the *Molton*'s capture Billmeir's *Stanhope* was leaving laden with refugees, and that afternoon a steamer called the *Kellwyn* arrived off Santander. She was in fact the renamed *Marie Llewellyn*, commanded by 'Potato' Jones, who, on receiving a warning of the morning's events from the *Royal Oak*, altered course for Gijon and brought out 800 refugees. Attempts by other ships, notably Pope's *Kenfig Pool*, the Nailsea S.S. Co.'s *Nailsea Vale*, Westcliff Shipping's *Thorpebay* and Thameside Shipping Co.'s *Marvia* were thwarted. On 17th the *Sarastone* succeeded in dodging under the Republican coastal batteries to reach Gijon, but the *Candleston Castle* was arrested and carried into Coruña.

William Patton, chief engineer aboard Glanely's *Pilton* approaching Santander at this time with a cargo of coal, salt-fish and 200 motorbikes, describes the scene:

> Ahead was a long line of British ships riding on the three-mile limit: we steamed up to them, then stopped engines. Between the ships and the shore, Franco's cruiser the *Almirante Cervera*, moved about waiting for the chance to pounce upon any ship that got within [territorial waters] … The distant rumble of gunfire could be heard coming from over the range of mountains where Franco's army, after capturing Bilbao, was pressing on to Santander.[42]

Since the Spanish cruiser was covering Santander, Gijon and Aviles, the *Pilton* and two other vessels made a dash for their destination when the blockader was out of sight. Having arrived, however, Patton and his shipmates were soon 'aware that we were in a doomed town'. A mud-hopper was loading rotten potatoes from the *Backworth*, discharging her ruined cargo close by, prior to taking them to sea and dumping them. Those for whom the cargo had been intended scrabbled among the filth of the wharves, spending hours sifting for grain which had spilled from the grabs that had discharged a recent arrival. Orphaned and feral children begged for food at the foot of the gangway. The town itself was full of refugees and wounded Republican soldiers. In the hope of evacuation: 'Thousands … found their way down to the waterfront, sheltering as best they could in railway trucks and open sheds. At night the quayside was lit by innumerable small fires around which destitute families clustered for warmth …'.

As those ships that got into port discharged, 'carpenters were … engaged to fit wooden ladders into the ships' holds, and the refugees were herded down there like so many head of cattle.' Disrupted by air raids, it took two weeks for the *Pilton* to be unloaded as the rumble of gunfire amid the hills grew ever closer. Worst of all, Patton describes how:

> The Government [Republican] warships in the harbour did not fire on the bomb-ers that came over killing women and children, nor did they go out and try to break

the blockade; it was said that the commanders of the two opposing fleets were brothers-in-law. At sea, the blockade was strangle-tight, ships went out, but none came in.

For the crews of these tramps the recent humiliations of the Depression gave their sympathy and solidarity with the beaten Basques a political edge: Patton was appalled amid the desperation of the dispossessed that 'over the whole scene the painted ladies smiled wickedly down from their balconies, ready to welcome the oncoming conquerors' while the fascist opinions of an elderly ex-patriate English lady plumbed depths of cruelty that disturbed him.[43] He also inveighed against the rank profiteering of some 'ship-mongers':

> On one occasion thousands of refugees waited all day on the landing-stage to board a British steamer that would have taken them away from all the bloodshed, hunger and cruelty of the civil war. As they were lining up to board the ship the sirens sounded. The refugees became panic-stricken, and a mob cry of fear went up as they rushed away from the ship towards the town, dragging their children after them. The ship could not wait for their return, and hundreds missed their passage to safety. Two British ships, having discharged their cargoes, lay idle at the buoys waiting for the human freight market to rise before helping in the evacuation of the town. The Spanish Government chartered ships at £100 a day, small ships that had been rusting on the scrap heap only a few months ago. But this was not good enough for the ship-mongers, and not until the freight [rate] rose to £200 a day did they move.

Despite this, the vessels alongside working cargo were often used as air-raid shelters, particularly by the dock workers. Just before the Nationalists marched into Santander, the *Pilton* embarked:

> a silent procession ... [of] old men and women, sad-faced children clasping their dolls and toy planes, and girls whose faces lit up when they stepped on the deck, glad enough no doubt to escape from the horrors of the Civil War. No men of military age were allowed to come on the ship. Relatives and friends who had come to see them off were barricaded behind hastily erected fences on the quayside. Now and again a man would break through ... for a last embrace of his wife and children. For the rest, the men stood silently by ...

The *Pilton* took her 2,500 refugees to St Nazaire, passing the *Almirante Cervera* and, beyond the three-mile limit, the waiting merchantmen and watching British men-of-war. She was not molested, 'but the refugees were plainly alarmed at the sight of Franco's warship, and the name *Cervera* was on everyone's lips'. By this time the *Pilton* was rolling and pitching in the Biscay swell and her wretched human cargo lined the bulwarks to retch and vomit: 'Truly a most remarkable state of affairs'. Later, 'exhausted by the trials of the day [the refugees] lay down in utter despair'.

During the passage to St Nazaire, Patton was heatedly blamed for the condition of the *Pilton* while the master was subjected to threats of assault by 'the more ignorant and aggressive of the women' and decided to make for La Pallice where he was refused entry by the authorities. Again the *Pilton* put to sea but by now a more disciplined spirit prevailed and she was cleaned up as the weather improved into a fine, moonlit night. As a group of young Spanish girls sang, standing close to the warm funnel, Patton anticipated with them a better day, but within hours the night was disturbed by cries of 'Fire!' After a small fire in the forward hold had been extinguished the cry went up that the women were trying to takeover the engine room. Patton discovered his machinery spaces secure, but three firemen armed with the shovels of their trade escorted three sheepish young male stowaways out of the shaft-tunnel. Having 'no right on the ship … they were roughly handled by the women …'. Next, in this eventful night, a woman was brought to bed with a child who was born an orphan, his father having been killed in the fighting. Silent crowds greeted the *Pilton* as she arrived next day at St Nazaire, apprehensive of the arrivals bringing in typhoid. Nevertheless: 'The French people were really good to these unfortunate victims of a civil war in which the majority had no part'. As he parted from one of the fiercely Communist nurses that had accompanied the refugees – a woman who 'might have been beautiful in happier days' – she turned to Patton 'with fire in her voice, and said presciently, "Why don't you English come in [to the war against Fascism] now? You can't escape it, it's your turn next".'

Not all the vessels putting to sea with refugees were unmolested. On 22 July Captain 'Corn Cob' Jones's *Macgregor* was fired on by the *Almirante Cervera* within the three-mile limit. With 2,000 terrified people on board Jones pressed on for international waters and the comforting silhouette of the destroyer HMS *Kempenfelt*. Two days later the *Backworth* finally left Santander while the *African Trader*, owned by the African and Continental Steamship & Trading Co. of London, had an encounter with the Spanish cruiser *Baleares*, escaping arrest under the guns of the *Royal Oak*. After retiring to St Jean, she subsequently sneaked into Gijon, along with the *Marion Moller* which bore urgently needed medical supplies and anti-gas serum which had been specially requested, but the *Mirupanu* was caught, arrested and ordered to Ferrol for cargo-examination.

On 27 July the *Sarastone* and *Tuskar Rock* left Gijon full of refugees while in the week that followed, two British-flagged tramp-steamers and one tanker, the *Bobie*, *Marvia* and *Valletta*, broke the blockade inwards. As July turned to August, the ripples of the peninsular crisis spread. The French, despite a broad sympathy with fellow Republicans, decreed that no further refugees could be accepted without prior arrangement, thus throwing a barrier of bureaucracy and health-control across the bows of any vessel attempting to arrive speculatively off a French port of refuge. The British Board of Trade was asked to inform British masters of this restriction. Meanwhile the British Government, entering into secret negotiations with Generalissimo Franco to preserve supplies of iron ore, secured an agreement that allowed 60 per cent of exports to be sent to Britain. Franco's only stricture was to forbid entry to any ship that had previously traded to a Republican port. This accommodation infuriated Hitler and Mussolini, whose aid to Franco's cause had been overt and influential, but the diversion of revenue into Franco's needy coffers was worth more than the temporary discomfiture of Berlin and Rome.

Interdiction went on at sea: on 11 August the *Caper* was arrested and sent in to Ribadeo but on the 16th the *Nailsea Vale* and *Bramhill* escaped from Aviles and Gijon respectively with almost 6,000 refugees. Then, on 25 August Santander finally fell to Nationalist forces, while Santoña was taken by the Italians. Four ships either owned or on charter to Alfred Pope and then chartered to the Basque government were seized, the *Seabank* and *Kenfig Pool* at Santander, the *Seven Seas Spray* and *Bobie* at Santoña. Arrangements were made with the Italians for the latter pair to leave with refugees, but this was overruled by Franco. After disembarking these forlorn and wretched people, the *Bobie* was then allowed to sail – with seven stowaways on board – but Captain Roberts and his ship, notorious to the Nationalists for being the first to break their blockade of Bilbao, was prevented from leaving. On 27 August bombing raids on Gijon persuaded the masters of the *African Trader* and Billmeir's *Stanwood* and *Stanbridge* to get clear. The *Stanbridge* suffered damage forward, being unable to weigh her anchor, but on 11 September she was able to depart. In the meantime the *African Trader*, which had also received severe bomb damage forward, had got clear of the port but was taking in water. Captain Bullock requested assistance and the destroyers *Fearless* and *Foresight* stood by her as she wallowed her way across the Bay of Biscay to be beached by Bullock near La Pallice (she was later repaired).

The Nationalist advance shortened the patrol line of their most potent cruiser, the *Almirante Cervera*, not only reducing the numbers of Republican-held ports, but increasing the effectiveness of the blockade. British masters found it impossible to penetrate the cordon and the task of evacuation was now well-nigh impossible. Although on 2 September the *Seabank* and *Kenfig Pool* were released from Santander, they came out empty of people. As the tide of the war turned in Franco's favour it appeared that some sought to transfer their traffic to the winning side and Jack Billmeir's reputation for opportunism fostered the belief that he was not above dealing with both sides. In the aftermath, the victorious Franco banned Billmeir's ships from trading with Spain but at the time, although Billmeir's thirty-seven tramps of the Stanhope S.S. Co. had been engaged in trade with the legitimate government of Spain, the circumstances surrounding the capture of the *Stanwold* at 22.00 on the 8 September were suspicious enough to alert the Royal Navy to the possibility of collusion either by her owner or her master. Approaching Ribadella on the Costa Verde, east of Gijon, she received a warning from the patrolling British battleship, HMS *Resolution*. Just inside the three-mile limit a torpedo-boat had been observed lying-to and as the *Stanwold* approached she was immediately intercepted, a shot was fired across her bow and the British tramp was observed to alter course in apparent conformity to the torpedo-boat's directions. On inquiry, the *Stanwold* signalled by radio to the *Resolution* that: 'I am captured.'

The seizure of British ships was now concerning London and, after repeated protests and diplomatic pressure the *Molton* and the *Candleston Castle*, both taken in mid-July, were released on 10 September. But that day the *Hillfern* was shelled thirty-five miles from Gijon by an armed trawler and later strafed by aircraft. Another of Billmeir's steamers, the *Stanmore*, making for Ribadella to pick up refugees, was also turned away after an air attack on 15th, but on 3 October, the Veronica S.S. Co.'s *Bobie* loaded with food from Antwerp to Aviles was intercepted and carried into Ribadeo.

The ship was actually owned by a relative of Pope's partner Thomas McEwen, W.H. McEwen of Parkstone, Dorset, who had registered her in Gibraltar and manned her with non-Britons. She flew the red ensign, however, and had been chartered to Alfred Pope who, in turn, had chartered her to the Republican government. The Nationalists sent her to Ferrol where she arrived three days later.

Equally complex was the ownership of the *Yorkbrook* which was last encountered under the Estonian flag. By October 1937 her ownership was wholly in the hands of Claude Angel of Cardiff, who had chartered her to the Republicans to carry refugees from Gijon to Bordeaux, but she was arrested approaching Gijon on 5 October. That day saw the capture of another British ship, the *Dover Abbey* of London. Captain A.E. Jackson's vessel was bound from Antwerp to Gijon with a cargo of dried peas and maize when, outside territorial waters but also out of sight of any British men-of-war, the *Dover Abbey* fell foul of the Nationalist patrols. As the fighting round Gijon drew closer on 20 October, an armed Nationalist trawler captured Billmeir's *Stangrove* after she had left Gijon with 600 refugees and was beyond territorial waters. In the offing lay the persuasive bulk of the *Almirante Cervera*, but so too was HM Cruiser *Southampton*, which secured her release under protest from the captain of the Spanish cruiser. Next day Gijon and Aviles fell to Franco and his allies and the civil war in northern Spain ground to an end; during November the remaining seven ships held by the victors were released.

The issue of opportunist owners making use of the Royal Navy's protection of the red ensign of Great Britain and her colonies and overseas possessions rumbled on for some time. Of the seven released by Franco – the *Seven Seas Spray, Stanwold, Bobie, Caper, Dover Abbey, Mirupanu* and *Yorkbrook* – the *Dover Abbey*'s crew of nineteen included six non-Britons, the *Bobie* had a French master, the only Briton on the *Caper* was her master and the *Mirapanu* was entirely foreign-manned. While 'foreigners' had long been carried in British merchantmen, the muddled ownership of ships wearing the red ensign troubled the Admiralty and embarrassed the British Government, for most had borne non-intervention control officers, a fact that gave them a legitimacy that could be conceived as spurious. Such was the perceived protection of the Royal Navy and such the extremity of the terrorised population whose situation demanded international shipping did its best to relieve their sufferings, that temporary certificates of British registry had been issued, largely by British consuls abroad.[44]

Notwithstanding this irregularity, nor indeed the rank-profiteering of the 'ship-mongers', nor their own war bonuses, merchant seamen ran considerable risks in entering Spanish ports. Some lost their lives and others were wounded, including Captain Cossintine, the sole Briton aboard the *Caper*, while the ship was detained at Ferrol. A row broke out between the crew and the six armed soldiers guarding the ship. Three of the former – a Dutchman and two Russians – were shot dead and Cossintine was wounded in the chest.

The collapse of the Republican cause in the north did not end the war, nor the involvement of other nations. Portugal dismissed British observers from her border and France, as part of her attempt to limit the influx of refugees already mentioned, closed the Pyrennean crossings. As for the maintenance of a seaward international non-intervention patrol in the Mediterranean, this soon dissolved. Here the task had been allocated to the German *Kreigsmarine* and Italian *Regia Marina* where it bore a marked contrast to the attitude of the Royal Navy. Many British naval officers, opposed to the influence of the growing Communist faction within the Republican movement, nevertheless sympathised with the plight of the Basque people. The on-the-spot attitude of British naval commanders was therefore pragmatic and largely humanitarian, as evinced by the conduct of the British 'non-intervention' squadron. Elsewhere however, suspecting British owners of supplying arms to the Republicans, the Royal Navy had attempted to prevent this, stopping a number of British ships thought to be gun-running. The *African Mariner*, for example, making for Barcelona from the Soviet Russian ports of Odessa and Novorossisk, was stopped in the eastern Mediterranean in November 1936 by HM Destroyer *Greyhound*. Escorted to Valletta her cargo of ammonium sulphate, salt-fish and Ukranian wheat was searched, but no arms were found and she resumed her voyage.

But at midnight on the 19 April 1937, only hours after the successful arrival of the *Seven Seas Spray* at Bilbao, the non-intervention policy had acquired sharper teeth. Just as the British – given responsibility for the north coast of Spain – enforced the policy of non-intervention with a humanitarian cast, Guernica was bombed. By the end of June the mask was cast aside and Germany and Italy both withdrew from their supposedly impartial patrols on the Mediterranean coast of Spain and soon, whilst Nationalist warships were responsible for a number of attacks on international shipping, including the bombing of the *St Quentin* of Newport, Monmouthshire, at Valencia, Italian submarines were acquiring some useful experience in torpedoing merchantmen that ought to have been a louder warning than it was. On 2 September the tanker *Woodford* was sunk while in international waters approaching Valencia from the Romanian port of Constanza. She too was somewhat spuriously British-flagged, for the vessel's crew was largely Greek, with an Hungarian radio operator and a Romanian cook, the only Briton on board being a control officer. Although only one man was killed, eight others were injured, a small casualty list for a vessel laden with 10,000 tons of petroleum.

In December the *Bramhill* was shelled in Burriana, north of Valencia, but escaped serious damage and it was here that similar superficial wounds were inflicted on Claude Angel's *Seabank Spray* on 16 January 1938. This ship was, in fact, the *Seven Seas Spray*, renamed in honour of the Seabank Hotel in Porthcawl where Angel lived. That month the *Thorpeness* was bombed at Tarragona with the loss of seven men, after the *Thorpehaven* the second of Thamesside Shipping Co.'s vessels to be sunk in the war, and on 31 January the British *Endymion* was torpedoed and sunk by an Italian submarine. Eleven of her company were lost, including the master and his wife, circumstances which increased British ire, despite the prompt response of Republican vessels which rescued the remainder. Angel's *Bramden* was bombed at Sagunto on 25 February and although three men suffered splinter wounds the bomb failed to explode. More deaths occurred when Billmeir's *Stanwell*, Captain David Jones, was attacked at Tarragona on 15 March; two of her crew and the Danish non-intervention officer were killed, and the *Hillfern*, another of Angel's ships, was again attacked and damaged on 17 April, this time at Cartagena. Heavily committed to Spain, Angel's and Billmeir's vessels were constantly in the firing line and on the 25th the former's *Fredavore* and the latter's *Stanland* were damaged in air attacks on Valencia. They were not alone, another Welsh tramp, Stone and Rolfe's *Isadora* and the Blue Star passenger-cargo liner *Celtic Star* were also hit and although all suffered, none was rendered useless. Barcelona was attacked on 12 May and the *Zelo* and *African Mariner* were hit, a crew member of each being wounded. Angel's *Yorkbrook* was again in the news when she was present during an air attack on Valencia without serious consequences.

During the final days of May and the first of June the Barry Shipping Co.'s *St Winfred* was discharging foodstuffs at Alicante when she was the target of a series of bombing raids. She was severely damaged and after being towed to Marseilles, where she was declared a constructive total loss, was sold to Italian owners who repaired her and renamed her *Capo Vita*. During the attacks, five members of her crew including two boys were killed, deaths that persuaded her owner's managing director to pull all his vessels out of the Spanish trade. Air attacks over several days also caught the *Penthames* in Valencia. Captain Cochrane deposed that his ship had been the victim of German aircraft whose markings had been clearly visible and on Friday 20 May one caused 'an enormous hole' which destroyed a portion of the accommodation and wounded two officers and a Chinese boy rating. On the 25th the *Thorpehall* was sunk in the outer anchorage and, after sustaining a determined series of assaults, the *Penthames* sank at her berth on the 31st. Two days previously the *Jeanne M.*, discharging coal and general cargo at Barcelona had also been hit by splinters and a near miss. Having escaped destruction at Valencia in April, the *Isadora* was severely battered by bombing on Castellon on 9 June and sank next day. Her crew were evacuated by the Royal Navy shortly before the collapse of the Republicans there and the ship herself was raised, repaired and put under the Nationalist flag as the *Castillo Frias*.

By this time the Nationalists had severed the Spanish Republic, making support for them increasingly complex. Cargoes destined for the legitimate government were discharged in Oran or Marseilles, and trans-shipped – usually in British bottoms at considerable profit – into the shrinking remnant of democratic Spain. The profiteering of British shipping at this time has to be set against the long years of laid-up ships and unemployed seafarers. Increased costs in war-risk insurance and crew war bonuses were adequately covered by the prevalent freight-rates and the former encouraged the use of old tonnage, underwriters being unwilling to insure new ships in a war zone. British tramps were chartered to organisations outside the United Kingdom anxious to ship foodstuffs to Spain, many of which loaded their cargoes in Antwerp and Rotterdam and, to pay for them and maintain a balance of payments in the accounts of the Spanish Republic, brought home traditional cargoes of fruit or shipped commercial ladings of phosphates from Sfax. They also carried wood pulp from Sweden, needed for the packing of exports of fruit. Others, encouraged by Republican subsidies, ventured east to the Black Sea ports of the Soviet Union to pick up cargoes that the Russians were willing to supply but not to ship.

Two new ships, the *Melrose Abbey* and *Margam Abbey* were lucky to escape unscathed during 16–18 March when the Italian *Regia Aeronautica* bombed Barcelona.[45] These air attacks prompted a number of the British masters to lodge formal protests with the various British consuls for forwarding to the Foreign Office. Several of these were veterans of the Civil War but their proceedings had little effect.[46] A bombing raid on 15 June damaged the *Macgregor*, but without serious loss. The following day, however, an air raid killed Seaman Edgar Marquet of the *Seabank Spray*. While British ships suffered as collateral damage in such attacks, a quite deliberate strike was made on the *Sunion*, lying at anchor a mile off Valencia on 22 June. Hit by two incendiary bombs the African & Continental Co.'s steamer was set on fire and sank, but not before her crew and her German non-intervention officer had been rescued. Later that day the *African Trader* arrived off Valencia under the escort of HM Destroyer *Imogen* which had come to her assistance after she had been threatened by a Nationalist seaplane.

Alicante was bombed on 27 June; during the raid the *Lalcham*, *Bramden* and *Stanwold* were superficially scarred, but the *Farnham* was sunk. Valencia was hit again the same day and the tanker *Arlon* of London, laden with aviation spirit, was set ablaze by a sustained attack. According to her second mate 'forty bombs [were] dropped in a straight line along the wharf, fifteen falling on the wharf-side, one hitting us flush and another falling between us and the dock …'. A Roumanian crew member was killed and a second man injured. The ship was towed out to sea and sunk. A bomb fell between the *African Trader* and the *Yorkbrook* lying alongside each other in Valencia on 10 July, the splinters killing the latter's Belgian non-intervention officer and twelve days later the *Dellwyn* and *Bramhill* were caught-up in a Nationalist attack on Gandia. The *Bramhill* escaped, but in the following days the *Dellwyn* was repeatedly bombed and strafed until, on 27th, evacuated by her crew, she received a direct hit and was sunk within sight of a British warship. Later raised, she too joined the Nationalists' new merchant fleet as the *Castillo Montesa*. The 28th saw another Nationalist bombing of Valencia which caught 'Potato' Jones's *Kellwyn*, ex-*Marie Llewellyn*, discharging sugar and coffee. The raid killed her Chinese cook and Danish non-intervention officer, her mate and three other able-seamen sustaining wounds. Such air attacks were being made by Franco's Nationalists but more effectively by the *Luftwaffe* and *Regia Aeronautica* of his allies. Franco's response was to counter-claim that 'Britain has an easy remedy to stop the bombing of her merchant vessels … [by] prohibiting the use of the British flag to protect the undignified contraband traffic in arms to the Republican zone'.

At the time about 140 British bottoms were engaged in an entirely legal trade with the remaining Republican enclaves, carrying mainly foodstuffs to Spain and clearing outwards with cargoes of fruit. Claims – in some detail – listing British ships engaged in gun-running, were unsubstantiated and included the *Isadora*, *Bramhill*, *Kellwyn*, *Stanburgh* and *Dover Abbey*. In the meanwhile the Royal Navy stopped and examined any vessels that were suspected of carrying arms. While the possibility of British merchantmen cannot be ruled out – and indeed is, in a few instances, likely – most of those employed made sufficient profit from the high freight-rates to obviate the need to run the greater risks of placing themselves beyond the law.[47]

Nevertheless Franco's propagandising of British support for his enemy sanctioned attacks on British ships whether in port or off the Catalunyan coast. The *Hillfern*'s radio operator, R.A. Amery, was killed and the British non-intervention officer aboard the Cardiff-registered *Fredavore* wounded on 15 August. Other ships were near missed or slightly damaged, superficial wounds being sustained by Captain Johns and the Dutch chief engineer of the *Bobie* in an attack on Barcelona which also implicated the *Seabank Spray*. This city was now under a sustained air assault and three days later, on 16 September, the *Bobie* was hit and her Greek cook, M. Athanasy, wounded; the *Seabank Spray* and the Estonian-flagged *Lake Hallwil* were also struck, while Billmeir's *Stanlake* took a bomb full on her poop. On 3 October a bomb detonated deep in the half-discharged cargo of wheat in the *African Mariner*. Much of the energy was absorbed, but one bulkhead was blown-out, though no one was hurt. Nor were there any casualties next day when the *Hillfern*, *Lake Hallwil*, *Thorpebay* and the tanker *Gothic* were all damaged. None of the ships was rendered unseaworthy until late in the evening of the 9th, when Captain Thomas Parker's *Bramhill* – discharging a cargo of beans and beef – was bombed by a Nationalist seaplane and set alight. Having burst in the mates' accommodation, much of the explosive force was expended in the vessel's coal-bunkers and no one was hurt as the crew were sheltering ashore at the time of the raid. The shock of the bomb combined with two near misses to pepper the shell plating and fracture steam pipess. This knocked out the derrick winches, further delaying her discharge. On the 19th the *Lake Hallwil* and the *African Explorer* were severely hit, the blast blowing a hole in the side of the latter as she discharged wheat, wounding three of her crew. The *Candleston Castle* suffered slight damage at Barcelona on 12 November, her third engineer and a fireman being injured, while the *Kenfig Pool* and *Bramhill* also endured an air attack at Barcelona on 23rd. The *Transit* and *African Mariner* were among four British ships slightly damaged there on 5 December and the *Transit* was sprayed with bomb splinters again on 4 January 1939.

The much-battered *Transit* had been Lord Glanely's *Molton*, taken off Santander in July 1937. She had been sold to the Continental Transit Co. of London after her release in the following September and renamed. She was lying in Valencia discharging coal trans-shipped from Oran on 10 October 1938 when a bomb wrought considerable damage along her upper deck and superstructure, though it left her hull intact allowing her to continue trading.

Elsewhere the *Yorkbrook* received a shaking at Almeria in early November and the *African Explorer* was compelled to make for Marseilles for repairs after an air raid on Cartagena. At Valencia four ships, were hit after a bombing on 28 December. These represent a good cross-section of the intermediate tramp-steamers engaged in trans-shipping cargoes into Republican ports from French North Africa and Marseilles. They were all owned or managed by firms chartering to the Republican government. The *Stanhope* was one of Billmeir's ships, Pope's Veronica S.S. Co. had chartered the *Bobie* from William McEwen, the *Kaolack*, like the *Hillfern* and the *Bramwell*, belonged to Claude Angel and the *Cemenco*, like the *Transit*, was owned by the Continental Transit Co. of London though managed by David Barnett. Another of Barnett's ships, the *Emerald Wings*, was bombed at Valencia on 28 December and three of her crew suffered injuries. A further raid on that port on 14 January caused bomb splinters to strike the *Bellwyn*.

The war was now nearly over and the rebel Nationalist Falange victorious as Franco's forces ground out the last vestiges of resistance in Catalunya. Tarragona was taken on 15 January and Barcelona invested by the 20th. The *Seabank Spray* took a direct hit in her cargo of coal there on the 21st, but the ship remained seaworthy. The *African Mariner* was less fortunate the next day as she disgorged a welcome cargo of meat and wheat, her midships structure sustaining a thumping in one attack and four Greek sailors being killed in a second. That day the *Yorkbrook* was bombed and her side blown out below the waterline causing her to sink in her berth, while the London-registered *Huntress* and *Dover Abbey* were also peppered with holes, none of which affected their watertight integrity. These two ships were hit again in the following two days, as were the *Seabank Spray*, *Thorpebay* and Angel's solitary tanker, the *Miocene*, which was sunk as a consequence, though later raised and repaired by the victors. On the 25th, the day before Barcelona fell, these battered veterans left the doomed city and steamed to Marseilles.

After the Nationalist triumph at Barcelona, British shipping all but withdrew from the scene as Republican resistance crumbled. The *Emerald Wings* was hit again at Cartagena on 5 February in a bombing raid which killed two of her crew, and again on the 10th, while her sister-ship, the misnamed *Lucky*, was sunk at her berth nearby. Of Barnett's other ships, the *Atlantic Guide* was slightly damaged in an air attack on Valencia on the 9th and a further attack there on the 26th hit the *Transeas*. By now Barnett was almost alone in sending his ships into the dwindling number of Republican ports, although when the Nationalists declared the entire coast of southern Spain forbidden to navigation, it caught a handful of other tramps by surprise.

At 21.32 on 10 March 1939 the master of the steamer *Bellwyn* transmitted an all-ships (CQ) message stating that his ship was in international waters twenty-three miles to the NNW of Cape San Antonio, Ibiza, and was under orders from a Nationalist warship to make for Palma, Majorca. The *Bellwyn*, on her way to Almeria to load fruit and in company with the *Stangate*, also reported the 'Steamer *Stangate* under escort, proceeding Palma ...' thereafter the message was jammed. At 22.24 the *Bellwyn* made a second transmission, declaring that she had 'refused to submit [and was] now left alone'. However, hoping the signal would be intercepted by a British man-of-war, she added: 'Please rescue steamer *Stangate* ...'.

The message was picked up by HM Destroyers *Intrepid* and *Impulsive* which headed towards the Balearics and upon demanding the release of the British vessel, secured this without further ado. The *Stangate* was then taken under escort for Gibraltar. As Valencia fell on 29 March, the *Atlantic Guide* was approaching the port, unaware of the critical situation ashore when she was strafed from the air. She withdrew some hours later, having embarked a number of refugees. As Madrid capitulated at the end of March the *African Trader* and *Stanbrook* left Alicante laden with nearly 3,000 refugees. This was the last withdrawal of people, for the Republicans' own ships of the Mid-Atlantic Co. had refused to help, claiming they had not been paid, while a formal Republican appeal to London to evacuate 10,000 refugees to Oran or Marseilles was impossible. In Hugh Thomas's phrase, the British Government 'had neither the desire nor the means to help on so large a scale'. HMS *Galatea* took off a handful of Republican leaders, but refused passage to 300 'armed communists'. In the end the Royal Navy embarked about 650 persons, a small proportion of the estimated 20,000 at Alicante alone. It was the end: Almeria, Alicante and Cartagena – the last remnants of democratic government in Spain for a generation – fell to the rebels next day and on 1 April the Spanish Civil War was over.

A total of twenty-seven British merchantmen were lost in the conflict,[48] out of a total overall of about 140 carrying cargoes to and from Spain, about the same as the number of the dead. Whilst their owners and crews had undoubtedly profited from their engagement, the ships had filled the vacancy left by the Nationalist capture of many Spanish merchantmen, most of which had withdrawn from their native waters to engage in international tramping. As for the elderly, battered British tramp-steamers, most were to be lost to the enemy in the greater world war that was now only months away.

During the civil war the part played by these vessels was an embarrassment to the British Government, which was 'almost distracted' by its plight. Noting that most damage was caused by air attacks in port beyond the protection of the Royal Navy, 'the subtle vocabulary of R.A. Butler, Parliamentary Under-Secretary at the Foreign Office, was taxed to explain why the government would not permit the export of anti-aircraft guns to Republican Spain, nor the merchant ships to carry their own arms.'[49] Pleas for effective action had come from all sides of both Houses and attempts to establish a neutral port – Almeria – foundered. Most humiliating was the sinking of the *Dellwyn* on 27 July 1938, for it had taken place within sight of a British warship. Even the American ambassador in London lamented this event, remarking that it was 'the first time in history'. And in Spain too, there was astonishment. Indalecio Prieto y Tuerno, a socialist minister in the Republican government, asked:

> Who would have thought it possible, we who, in our study of international rela-
> tions, have come across mention of the arrogance and pride of England, who would
> not tolerate the least harm to its material interests, nor an attack on the lives of one
> of its subjects? Yet here, in our cemeteries, are the bodies of English sailors who have
> paid with their lives for the confidence they had in the protection of their Empire.

British hesitation was not on account of Franco's powers, but because of his backers, Mussolini and Hitler. German aircraft and Italian submarines had played a significant part in the Nationalist victory and Prime Minister Chamberlain, damned by history for his policies of appeasement, was desperate to avoid another war with the carnage of the last augmented by air raids on a civilian population. While Chamberlain had ago-nised over this dreadful spectre, General von Reichenau was cheerfully claiming that 'two years of real war experience have been of more use to our immature *Wehrmacht* … than a whole ten years of peaceful training …'. In response Chamberlain's Foreign Secretary, Lord Halifax, had suggested Britain:

> should draft an appeal to the contending sides to stop the war. Such an appeal
> would, of course, be based on grounds of humanity, Christianity and so forth … it
> would not be likely to succeed, but it would strengthen the moral position of His
> Majesty's Government.

It was a poor enough conclusion; while the Royal Navy had done its best, its support had been politically constrained and the participation of British merchant ships had little moral foundation, whatever the political sympathies of their crews. While Von Reichenau was embracing the lessons of the war for Germany, seeing in the Spanish Civil War a dress rehearsal for the Armageddon to come, the prescient British mer-chant Jack might also have glimpsed the future. It was, for him, to be bleak.

The first whisperings of impending catastrophe came with the Munich crisis; a year later they were more urgent. On 28 August 1939, sixty-five-year-old Captain David Bone was preparing to leave the Anchor Line berth alongside Pier 45, Manhattan. Keen

to have his ship ready for every eventuality, Bone and his agent scoured New York for
thick paper to blackout his ship's portholes. He eventually found a supplier who had just
done the same thing for the Norddeutscher Lloyd liner *Bremen*, then the fastest ship on
the North Atlantic, which lay alongside Pier 88. The *Transylvania* sailed the following
morning and four days out, at 07.00 ship's time the ship's senior radio officer brought
Bone the signal he had been anticipating. It informed him that a state of war existed
between Great Britain and Germany and instructed him to open a sealed envelope –
Envelope Z – that had been handed to him by the Waterguard of HM Customs prior
to the Munich affair, but some of the contents of which he had already guessed. Having
attended the requisite courses and served in the previous war, there were no surprises
for Bone when he, like 2,000 other British masters all over the globe, learning that 'a
state of war' existed between Great Britain and Germany, noted the declared danger
zones and passed instructions to his officers in accordance with the Admiralty's contingent orders. Bone, steaming eastwards, altered his course far to the northwards, posted
additional lookouts and steered a zig-zag course.

Far away in the Irish Sea, on a passage to Glasgow from Tilbury, the *Clan Alpine*
'passed a German ship … the *Hugo Stinnes*, and she had … a great bow wave and
smoke was pouring out of her funnels and she was trying to get back to Germany or
some other neutral port', recalled Apprentice Joseph Wharton. When the *Clan Alpine*
berthed in Glasgow 'that fateful Sunday morning … we heard the Prime Minister on
the radio and that was it.'[50]

Aboard the *Transylvania* later that day Captain Bone heard the news of the sinking of the *Athenia* and, as his ship ran down towards Oronsay, they came across an
empty lifeboat. Bone circled it cautiously, then turned the *Transylvania* for the Mull of
Kintyre and the Clyde beyond.[51]

NOTES

1. Foster's lifeboat was purchased by the Eastern Telegraph Co., who brought it to Britain and
   exhibited it at the British Empire Exhibition at Wembley.
2. One can compare Foster's achievement with Shackleton's boat voyage in the *James Caird* after the loss
   of *Endurance* in the Antarctic ice – which ranks for me as the most extraordinary of such survival stories
   – or with that of Lieutenant William Bligh of HM Armed Transport *Bounty*, though readers of this
   series will recall other remarkable voyages in small boats to which the coming war was to add yet more.
3. Despite the revolution in naval warships in the nineteenth century and increasing specialisation,
   the Royal Navy retained small training brigs in the belief that young men benefited from the
   experience, to which has to be added the moral connection with the great age of the sailing navy.
   However, when HM Brig *Eurydice* was 'knocked-down' and overwhelmed with the loss of all but
   two hands of 330 in a ferocious channel squall in March 1878 the Admiralty realised the game was
   not worth the candle and naval sail-training was abandoned.
4. My thanks to Captain Joshua Garner for Geoffrey Drake's moving account of *A Landing on Gough*
   which he wrote when chief officer in the static training-ship HMS *Conway*.
5. Today Denmark maintains the full-rigged ships *Georg Stage* (II), belonging to the Georg Stage
   Foundation, and the *Danmark*, owned by the Ministry of Trade, Shipping and Industry.
6. Frank Oliver, *The Blue Peter*, Vol 7, No.66, September 1927.
7. Readers may recall the attempts by the East India Company and later William Jardine and James
   Matheson, among others, to import woollen garments into North China, this being a plentiful
   export from Britain and one which would have been of immense benefit to the Chinese of North
   China. It was the refusal of the Chinese to entertain extensive trafficking along their coast, let

alone the import of woollens, that turned Jardine, Matheson and many others to their ruthless exploitation of the Chinese weakness for opium.

8. In 1987 the late A.D. Blue produced a PhD thesis for the University of Strathclyde entitled *British Shipping in China, 1836–1914*.

9. See *More Days, More Dollars*, Chapter Three, which also includes an account of the genesis of the Straits S.S. Co. Ltd.

10. The first six 75-tonners actually built at Sungei Nyok were the *Ampang. Gemas, Tapah, Tronoh, Jarak* and *Klias*. Those built at Butterfield & Swire's Taikoo shipyard at Hong Kong were the *Malacca, Jeram* and *Jerantut*. They were followed by many more culminating in the *Rhu* of 1940 and the *Resang* of 1941. Diesel-engined with cellular double-bottom and electrical deck-machinery these were cargo-liners in miniature, capable of lifting 305 and 315 tons respectively, on net tonnages of 74 and 75. A third vessel, the *Renong*, was on the slipway when the Japanese invaded and was still there when the war ended four years later. Owing to post-war steel shortages she was not finally launched until 1948. All building was supervised by H.E. Ward, a Eurasian who had suffered a spinal injury when falling into Penang dry dock and used his long hospitalisation to self-educate himself in marine engineering and naval architecture. He was working for the Eastern Shipping Co., the original owners of Sungei Nyok when the Straits S.S. Co. took over and was retained while the yard was modernised. The yard also repaired the fleet's ships.

11. After the Second World War the limiting tonnage of a Local Master's certificate was raised to 100 net tons. The fact that a *British* officer could earn qualifying foreign-going sea-time for his certificates in theses waters where a local certificate was allowed albeit for small tonnage, rankled with officers operating larger ships in home waters but where they were limited in their ability to earn qualifying sea-time and were for many years denied any 'time' at all towards a foreign-going certificate, even though the conditions they operated in were admittedly more hazardous than those in the east.

12. Quoted by K.G. Tregonning, *Home Port Singapore*, p84 *et seq.*

13. The abortive early attempts of Alfred Holt & Co. to trade with North Borneo with the East India Ocean S.S. Co. had given way to the German Norddeutscher Lloyd Linie, which acquired the Blue Funnel ships on the service. The Imperial German Navy had made an unprecedented appearance off Kudat in the north in March 1914 when Admiral Graf Von Spee anchored there in SMS *Scharnhorst*, flagship of the German Pacific squadron. However, the war ended German colonial ambitions and British investors, who had founded the British North Borneo Chartered Company in 1881, gained increasing economic power over a sparsely populated region covered with rain-forest. The company was originally led by Alfred Dent and his brother, whose partnership of Dent Bros stemmed from the Dent & Co. of Hong Kong and opium notoriety (see *Masters Under God*, Chapter Two) in the early 1840s. Alfred Dent was a friend of William Mackinnon, founder of the British India S.S.Co. and exploiter and pioneer in Uganda and Kenya (See *More Days, More Dollars*, Chapter Three). Interested in government, Dent eschewed the owning of a line of steamers, writing to Mackinnon that 'there are prospects of improving trade but I doubt whether the company could work a line to the same advantage as is done by private enterprise. The moment we own a steamer of our own, we are troubled with Captains, Mates, Engineers, and the many thousand difficulties that beset owners of vessels'.

14. Reckoned at 40 cubic ft per ton, which was the standard 'space-ton' used in trades where space rather than weight was generally the ruling factor in allocating cargo capacity and varied significantly from the measured ton of 100 cubic ft used to calculate gross and net tonnage, or the avoirdupois ton of 2,240 pounds used to measure deadweight tonnage – that which actually submerged a vessel's hull. Ships loading cargoes governed by their capacity, rather than their load-bearing ability – that is to say feathers rather than lead – were rarely loaded 'down to their marks'.

15. The *Kedah* was so much admired that one passenger, Robert Dollar the owner of the American President Line, persuaded Vickers to build a copy. Work was hard to come by and the news was kept from Holts in Liverpool and the Straits S.S. Co. at Singapore, though it later leaked out. The vessel was named *Mayon*.

16. These were the *Flevo, Zweena, Penang, Giang Seng*, and *Giang Ann*. Among these the *Flevo* was sold on, for in 1904 she was Captain Frank Hendry's first command when then owned by Teo Tao Lye & Son. See *More Days, More Dollars*, Chapter Three.

17. W.I.L. Legg to Tregonning, 10 May 1965, quoted by the latter in *Home Port Singapore*, p96.

18. This was the *Poh Ann* in 1914. See Tregonning, p119 *et seq.*

19. See Keith, A., *Land Below the Wind*, Little, Brown & Co., Boston, 1939, p215 *et seq.*

20. H. Parnell to K.G. Tregonning, 3 October 1964, quoted *Home Port Singapore*, p110.

21. Quoted by Tregonning, p 148. Even as late as the 1960s I recall a home-made chart – to which we were expected to add details – being used by Blue Funnel on the west coast of Borneo when loading logs at Bohihan Island. The master-copy was held by the company's agent at Singapore and picked up when bound for the isolated logging headquarters.

22. One effect of the Depression was to almost entirely kill-off the once thriving business of the pier-head ship-portrait painter who had supplied cheap images of their ships to many masters, mates, etc. It lingered longest in Japan where artists like Shimidzu continued catering for a relatively comfortably off clientele until 1933. The naïve paintings with which some of these volumes have been illustrated re-emerged in a more elevated art-form, beyond the pockets of most mariners.

23. See *More Days, More Dollars*, Chapter Three, and Chapter Six of this volume.

24. Captain Evans's report to Alfred Holt & Co. is found in several places, viz, Appendix IV in Malcolm Falkus's *The Blue Funnel Legend*, Ronald Hope's *The Seaman's World*, and E. Keble Chatterton's *Valiant Sailormen*. Keble Chatterton personally heard Holt deliver himself of his 1933 address and records the yarn of the Scottish steward. The tale enjoyed a wider telling in Richard Hughes's novel based on the ship's ordeal, *In Hazard*. Hughes interviewed the principles, including Midshipman Hay who won wide acclamation for his persistence in pumping oil out through the forward lavatories. *In Hazard* was compulsory reading for Blue Funnel midshipmen in later years.

25. See Bisset, *Commodore*, p231. Seamen speak of a hurricane *force* wind as being above Force 12 on the Beaufort Scale, that is, in excess of 65 knots. It does not mean or imply that the meteorological disturbance causing such a wind was a tropical revolving hurricane.

26. Bisset records nine men being saved but gives only eight names: Captain J.J. Reid, Chief Engineer J. Ellerington, Third Engineer K. Gray, Apprentice H. Bottomley, Carpenter J. Rourke, Able-Seaman F. Andrews, Firemen Said Rasul and Rizwan Ullah.

27. Villiers, A., *Posted Missing*, p209.

28. William Mutimer's account of his war experiences, Part One, *The Journal of the Honourable Company of Master Mariners*, Vol XVIII, spring 1993, No.213.

29. See Radford, G., *Captain Radford's Diary*, p1.

30. See Making, V. L., *In Sail and Steam*, Introduction.

31. It was usual in liner companies to select bright young officers early in their careers for superintendents' posts. To give them authority they were commonly given a single voyage in command, after which they adopted the courtesy title of 'Captain'. Glasier became known as Captain but it appears that in his outstanding case the practice was waived.

32. I am indebted to Captain Brian McManus for information on Glasier's life. Glasier stood high in Lawrence Holt's esteem and Holt himself was an *eminence grise* during and after the war. As a cousin of Sir Stafford Cripps – who was successively British ambassador to Moscow (1940), an emissary to the Indian Nationalists and in 1942 Minister for Aircraft Production – Lawrence Holt had the ear of Government and was an indispensable source of information about merchant shipping and the reality of conditions in the ports. In 1947, at the height of an exchange-rate crisis, Holt entertained Attlee to lunch at his country home on the Lleyn Peninsula, during the course of which 'Holt unsuccessfully attempted to persuade Attlee of the merits of Gladstonian free-trade'. In 1949 the new Blue Funnel liner *Hector* was launched from Harland & Wolff's Belfast yard by Mrs Attlee. Lawrence Holt had commissioned John Mansbridge, son of the founder of the Seafarers' Education Service, to paint a mural for the officers' lounge and the features of the Attlees appeared as the two principal characters. Attlee's son Martin, who succeeded his father in the Earldom, was born in August 1927 and died in July 1991. According to his Obituary in *The Times*, 29 July 1991, when Princess Elizabeth dined at 10 Downing Street after the war, Martin Attlee, at home on leave from the Blue Funnel Line, entertained her with stories of his experiences in the China seas.

33. Seafarers other than those employed in tramps were caught-up in the Spanish Civil War. Companies like MacAndrews, with their long association with Spain, and Yeoward Bros operated on its fringes but without undue interruption of their shipping. It was, therefore, tramp-shipping that bore the brunt of these attacks.

34. The extreme variety of the Royal Navy's tasks is exemplified by the rescue from a Spanish beach by a British destroyer of the poet Laurie Lee as recounted in his autobiographical account, *As I Walked Out One Midsummer Morning*.

35. Somerville's *Report of Proceedings*, 21 August 1936.

36. Somerville's note to the Senior Spanish naval officers at Cartagena and Malaga, HMS *Galatea*, 24 August 1936, See *The Somerville Papers*, p20. On the 20th the Spanish government cruiser *Libertad*

stopped a German merchantman, the *Kamerun* and on 29 May 1937 the *Deutschland* – later renamed *Lützow* – was bombed by Republican aircraft while anchored off Ibiza. Thirty-one German sailors were killed and seventy-eight wounded. Two days later the *Admiral Scheer* and four destroyers bombarded Almeria as a reprisal, killing nineteen and reducing thirty-five buildings to rubble.

37. Not least because, realising they were more likely to sympathise with the rebels, President Azana had allowed all naval officers who wished to, to retire on full pay. Elsewhere mutiny affected the exercise of the government's sea power, which consequently rapidly withered.

38. See Hugh Thomas, *The Spanish Civil War*, Penguin, Third Edition, 1977, pp 821, 827 and 914. The Spanish also formed one company in Marseilles.

39. To the 148 foreign vessels transferred to the British flag must be added a further fifty-one which were granted temporary certificates. As P.N. Thomas points out in his *British Ocean Tramps*, Vol. One, *Builders & Cargoes*, p138: 'The largest number belonged to The Netherlands (45), USA (26) and France (19).'

40. Prior to this notoriety Captain David John Jones had been known by his colleagues as 'Swansea' Jones. At this time, assuming the character of a folk-hero, he was also known to the Americans as 'Casey' Jones and to the Spanish Republicans as '*el Patatero*'. Jones was in fact a part-owner of his ship, being a shareholder in the Dillwyn S.S. Co. and had been retired from the sea for some time before the Spanish Civil War. So infuriated was Franco by the blockade-runners that he placed a price upon the head of 'Potato' Jones.

41. See P.M. Heaton's comprehensive *Welsh Blockade Runners in the Spanish Civil War*, p56, to whom I am indebted for most of the details in this section.

42. Excerpt from Patton's *The Scrap Log of an Engineer*, quoted by Heaton, p58.

43. This charming creature told them of the fate of a local lighthouse-keeper whose post lay close to an old royal palace used as a prison. From here, 'as reprisals prisoners were dispatched over the cliffs from time to time'. The keeper asked to be relieved, being unable to stand the shrieks of women being hurled to their deaths below. 'His plea was ignored and three nights later the light went out … the lighthouse keeper had committed suicide'.

44. There were other influences at work and the cost of second-hand tramp tonnage doubled between 1930 and 1937. A 7,500-ton deadweight steamer would cost between £90,000 and £105,000, whereas in 1930 the cost had been between £36,500 and £39,750.

45. Franco, true to his promise not to freight a vessel which had been in a Republican port, refused entry to the *Melrose Abbey* when she attempted to pick up a cargo from Valencia at the beginning of the Second World War. She was swiftly replaced by the *Tintern Abbey* which had been left unregistered at her moorings immediately after building, her older sisters earning handsome profits while she awaited her own opportunities in the wings – a good example of a shipowner's cunning, in this case that of Frederick Jones & Co. of Cardiff.

46. Noting protest was formal procedure undertaken by a master before a consular officer to register a circumstance that might affect the profitability of his ship's voyage but which was beyond his control. Usually in connection with heavy weather, protest limited insurance claims against his ship, pleading damage by Act of God. In times of war an air attack constituted 'an unavoidable accident' for the purpose of protest. In this case the masters were Nesbitt of the tanker *Gothic*, Lewis of the *Stanburn*, Davies of the *Stanbrook*, Lamb of the *Sea Glory*, Jones of the *Alex*, Still of the *Hamsterley* and the unknown master of the *Kenfig Pool*.

47. The possibility of private trading remains the most likely source of consignments of arms under the British flag, but the volume of such shipments must have been relatively small. Accounts of the spy-ridden ports also makes the landing of large shipments unlikely and even a small one dangerous. The trans-Pyrenean route was far harder to police.

48. Among the lost ships omitted from the main text are the Stag Line's *Euphorbia* of North Shields, and Billmeir's *Stancroft*.

49. See Hugh Thomas, *The Spanish Civil War*, p827

50. Audio archive, 13242, Imperial War Museum, quoted Hewitt, N., *Coastal Convoys, 1939–1945*, p44.

51. The *Transylvania* was taken up as an AMC and much to Bone's disgust he was retired – though not for long. His ship was sunk in August 1940. The *Bremen*, which the Royal Navy attempted to intercept on her homeward passage, escaped by heading for Murmansk, then a port friendly to Nazi Germany. She later made a passage back to Germany by way of the Norwegian leads.

THREE

'WE ARE A SEAFARING RACE'

The Merchant Navy in the Second World War, 1939-1945

On the afternoon of 1 September 1939, the *Franconia* lay alongside the Cunard berth on Manhattan's waterfront preparing to sail for Boston and Liverpool. Captain James Bisset was disturbed by news of the German invasion of Poland followed by a coded message from Cunard. A few hours later the *Franconia* was invaded by workmen with paint-pots and brushes, departure was postponed to the next day and some of *Franconia's* passengers 'cancelled their bookings, and could scarcely be blamed for doing that'. Bisset mustered his crew and told them war was liable to be declared while they were on passage and they would be required to work incessantly until the ship was prepared for wartime routines at sea.

> Not one of my crew of 400 deserted, or showed any signs of funk. Tons of sand and thousands of bags, were hoisted on board and stacked at various places. The crew set to work with a will, filling the sandbags and placing them in positions on board to protect vulnerable parts of the ship – such as the wheelhouse and chart-rooms, the steering gear, the entrances to the engine-room, crews' (sic) quarters and passengers' quarters, and deck-gear – against air-attack or gunfire. These precautions were defensive only. We had no guns mounted in the ship. All glass portholes were painted black. All openings onto the deck were screened with curtains or doors. While all this was being done by the crew, the gangs of painters from on shore were slapping 'battleship-grey' over the *Franconia's* formerly immaculate 'cruise-ship white' …

The pilot's valedictory 'bon voyage' as he disembarked off the Ambrose lightvessel 'was much more serious than usual' and early on Sunday 3 September, when the *Franconia* was off Nantucket, Bisset heard Prime Minister Neville Chamberlain's announcement that, having protested in vain against the German invasion of Poland, Great Britain was at war with Germany. The *Franconia* arrived at Boston at 15.30 where Bisset found additional passengers had booked and that he was to proceed to the nearest British port, Halifax, Nova Scotia. The *Franconia* was now under Admiralty orders and sailed from Boston with 330 passengers two and a half hours later. As the sun set her navigation lights remained unlit, extra lookouts were posted and Bisset ordered a zig-zag course that veered at variable angles either side of a median rhumb-line.

Having served through the First World War, during part of which as a naval reservist he had commanded a destroyer, Bisset knew that along with the other Cunard White Star liners, his ship was likely to be requisitioned on her arrival at Liverpool and his first priority was to get her home safely. Although he and his ship's company had had sufficient warning to put the *Franconia* on a basic war footing, Bisset had no idea that on 21 August the Germans had ordered the commerce-raider *Admiral Graf Spee* to take up her assigned 'waiting station' and that her supply-ship *Altmark* was on her way to America to load a full cargo of diesel. Two days earlier fourteen U-boats had left Wilhelmshaven, followed by several others, including *U-30*. A second *Panzerschiff*, the *Deutschland*, and her supply-ship *Westerwald*, were also at sea and, on 25 August, the German radio station at Norddeich broadcast a long-range instruction to all German merchant shipping warning them of the probability of war. On the 27th they were ordered to head for home or, if this was impossible within four days, to make for a friendly or neutral port. By this time the *Deutschland* lay off Cape Farewell, the southern point of Greenland, ready to strike southwards at trans-Atlantic shipping. According to Hitler's first War Directive, the *Kriegsmarine* was 'to operate against Merchant Shipping with England as the focal point … [while] the Luftwaffe is to take measures to dislocate English imports …'.

In London on 26 August orders were issued that would affect the movements of the entire British merchant fleet for the foreseeable future. The Cabinet Committee responsible for 'Defence Preparedness,' in consultation with the Foreign Office and the Board of Trade, formally authorised the Admiralty to 'adopt compulsory control of movements of merchant shipping … [in] Baltic, Dutch, Danish or Mediterranean ports, and should include the routeing of ships in the Atlantic'. This was transmitted as Navigation Order No.1, 1939, and would in due course result in the Naval Control of Shipping (NCS) over a wider area and reliant upon a large number of Naval Control Service Officers, or NCSOs. Already appointed in every British and Commonwealth port and soon to appear in many neutral and American ports, these were usually older or retired naval captains, commanders or senior naval reservists with a working knowledge of mercantile shipping and commercial port operation. They acted as the link between the distant Admiralty and the individual ship-master and it was from them that a master obtained his basic instructions, confidential orders, codebooks and a two-volume general guide as to self-defence, described by Stephen Roskill as 'the first ripple in the tide of printed material which was to arrive in an ever increasing flood in the cabins and safes of Ship Masters'. It would be, as the system matured, the duty of the NCSOs to pass on convoy orders and they would become the point-of-supply for practical items such as zig-zag clocks, fog-buoys and other special 'convoy stores'. These elderly men performed a vital and largely unsung task and were the catalyst in transforming a myriad of privately trading vessels into a Merchant Navy. Other matters were set in motion on 26 August; the Admiralty notified all owners whose ships had been earmarked for Government service, whether as AMCs, Boarding Vessels, Hospital-ships, transports or troopers, that their vessels were requisitioned, and secondly, the plan for defensively arming all British merchantmen was implemented.

Everywhere in those last days of peace, owners were warning their masters of the dangers of war but business went on as usual, for the nation's commerce had to continue. While the officers in the Admiralty Trade Division mustered the merchantmen suitable as naval auxiliaries, transports and so forth, the Government's fear of air raids was such that orders were issued for the evacuation of children. Some of these went by sea, the excursion steamers of the General Steam Navigation Co. being summoned to embark them from Gravesend, Tilbury and Dagenham. Between 1 and 3 September eight of the company's ships – the *Royal Eagle*, *Crested Eagle*, *Golden Eagle*, *Laguna Belle*, *Royal Daffodil*, *Royal Sovereign*, *Queen of the Channel* and *Medway Queen* carried 19,578 children to the East Anglian ports of Felixstowe, Lowestoft and Great Yarmouth. Captain Johnson, bound to Tilbury in the *Royal Daffodil* after delivering evacuees, obtained his outward clearance certificate from the Lowestoft Custom House 'two hours after the declaration of war.' Undertaken at short notice this operation was judged by the Minister of Health as 'a very remarkable achievement'. General Steam's main fleet was composed entirely of coasters and short-sea traders, many of which were in danger of seizure. The chairman, Robert Kelso, who 'had had the misfortune to be held a prisoner of war in 1914–18', was anxious that none of his ships should be caught in German ports and interned. Kelso succeeded in successfully extricating all of them before hostilities began.

Meanwhile, as the grey-painted *Franconia* was making for a landfall off Malin Head, the enemy had already sunk the first British merchantman of the war, the Donaldson liner *Athenia* which had taken her departure from the same headland only a few hours earlier. In defiance of orders to act 'in accordance with international rules,' by which was meant the London Protocol of 1936, the Prize Regulations of which required a U-boat commander to stop and remove the crew of an enemy merchant ship 'to a place of safety' before sinking her, the commander of *U-30* had torpedoed the *Athenia*.[1]

The ageing Donaldson liner *Athenia*, Captain James Cook, had left her home port of the Clyde and called at Liverpool and Belfast to embark the last of her passengers. These included over 300 American citizens anxious to escape the increasingly brittle atmosphere of Europe. There were also some Jewish refugees fleeing Nazi persecution and a number of children being evacuated from British cities in response to the fear of air raids following the evidence of the Spanish Civil War. John C. Coullie, an American passenger, wrote: 'We took on an awful lot of people …'. In fact, of the 1,417 persons aboard the *Athenia*, 1,102 were passengers. Shortly after the ship sailed they were notified that a state of war existed between Great Britain and Germany, but Cook assured his passengers that, under the Prize Regulations, the *Athenia* was safe from submarine attack. Nevertheless, he took the precautions of darkening ship and zig-zagging in accordance with the Admiralty's instructions. At 19.43, just as the gong sounded for the third sitting for dinner, a torpedo struck the liner, exploding in way

Engineers – from the war memorial on the Pier-head, Liverpool. (The Author)

Fireman and Trimmer – from the war memorial on the Pier-head, Liverpool. (The Author)

of the watertight bulkhead separating the engine and boiler rooms. The consequences were catastrophic. Although the *Athenia* took some hours to sink and many of her passengers and crew were saved by a number of ships, both mercantile and naval, her sinking was widely regarded as an outrage.

Although it was intended that the *Athenia* would be converted to an AMC when she reached Montreal, there was no substance in Kapitänleutnant Fritz Julius Lemp's later defence that he thought that she was an AMC. However, the disobedience of Lemp, in torpedoing the *Athenia* without warning, had one effect directly benefi-cial to the British. Its abrupt brutality within hours of Chamberlain declaring war, convinced the Admiralty that Germany had embarked on unrestricted submarine warfare.[2] The response, imperfect though it was, was to implement convoy in home waters and the North Atlantic immediately.[3] It was in stark contrast to the arguments advanced against this measure in 1914 but its effect was marred by two major flaws. The first was the Admiralty's assumption that the greater threat to British shipping lay, not in the U-boat, but in the enemy's surface-raiders, the disguised *Hilfskreuzers* and the *Panzerschiffs*. Secondly, it was believed that the U-boat was effectively neu-tralised by 'Asdic', then the name for sonar, fitted in the smaller warships of the Royal and French Navies. This second error was the worse for several reasons, not the least of which was that it was mounted in too few convoy escorts; this was in turn compounded by their being too few escorts, while those that were available lacked expertise in hunting submarines. Anti-submarine warfare had been scandal-ously neglected between the wars, having been relegated as a speciality to which less-able officers were sent. Those exercises that had been carried out had been, on the evidence of naval officers involved, lacking in rigour with frequent fiddling of their results – what the submarine commander Alastair Mars recalled as 'flogging the log'. No anti-submarine tactics to speak of, let alone co-ordinated measures for a convoy escort group to take when their charges came under attack, had been worked out properly.

Battle experience against U-boats in the North Atlantic during the first years of the war brought many naval officers close to despair. 'We were good for picking up survivors,' one confessed, 'but not much else.' It was therefore left to the men of what was immediately transformed from a theoretical into a very real 'Merchant Navy' to accept a high level of attrition. This seemed, in the bitter winter of 1942/43, to be culminating in Germany's favour until the dramatic triumphs of the Allied naval forces in May of 1943 turned the tide.

At the beginning of the war a few U-boat commanders had observed the Prize Regulations; there had been some fraternising, with German crews handing out tobacco to British seamen in their lifeboats and submarine commanders giving courses and distances to the nearest ports to the masters of the ships they had just sunk. One of these had been Lemp, perhaps touched by anxiety over the sinking of the *Athenia*, who was scrupulous in his despatch of the steel-laden *Blairlogie* of Glasgow on 11 September 1939, giving Captain Daniel McAlpine gin and cigarettes. He was sinking his next capture, the *Fanad Head* of Belfast, with her cargo of grain when he was attacked by aircraft from the carrier HMS *Ark Royal*. On the 8th and 13th Kapitänleutnant Otto Schuart of *U-29* had sunk the tanker *Regent Tiger* and the tug *Neptunia*, giving the tug's crew brandy and cigarettes. On the 14th he stopped the tanker *British Influence* and ordered Captain I.H. McMichael and his crew into the boats, firing flares to attract the attention of a Norwegian vessel to them before he sank the tanker. As the U-boat drew away the two crews gave each other three cheers in an apparently spontaneous outburst of goodwill. Reports of any such conviviality disturbed officers at the Admiralty's Trade Division; some recalled the Jeremiah who, in 1913, had unjustly claimed that if the Germans used submarines against British merchant seamen, they would either refuse to sail, or would submit. It was not easy for naval officers to comprehend that a merchant ship-master's responsibility to his owners was to look after their ship and to his crew to preserve their lives – particularly if his vessel had no means of self-defence. Old animosities and misunderstandings seemed about to resurface. Although the action of Captain W.H. Poole of the Cunarder *Bosnia*, in turning away from *U-47* when ordered to stop, gave Kapitänleutnant Gunther Prien an excuse to open fire, it seemed that perhaps, after all, with the exception of the sinking of the *Athenia*, the Germans *were* adhering to the Prize Regulations.

Captain James Gair of the Hall Bros' two-year-old tramp *Royal Sceptre* was homeward from Rosario with grain when, on 5 September and 300-miles north-west of Cape Finisterre, he was ordered to stop by Kapitänleutnant Herbert Schultze in *U-48*. Calculating he might outrun the U-boat in the rough sea, Gair sent out the SSSS signal indicating he was being attacked by a submarine and increased speed. Intercepting Gair's signal, Schultze opened fire, killing Gair and wounding others. Chief Officer Hartley stopped the ship and ordered her abandoned. Closing the *Royal*

Sceptre as her boats pulled away, Schultze observed her radio officer still on board. Giving an assurance that he would not sink her until the man had been rescued, he directed one of the ship's lifeboats to return and told Hartley that he would send help. That done and his prize sunk, Schultze resumed his patrol, later encountering Lamport & Holt's outward-bound liner *Browning* and firing a shot across her bow to stop her. Extracting a promise from the *Browning's* master that he would not broadcast *U-48's* position, Schultze indicated the whereabouts of the *Royal Sceptre's* boats. Hartley and his company were picked up and the promise was honoured. Three days later Schultze intercepted the Cardiff tramp *Winkleigh*. Captain Thomas Georgeson ordered the transmission of an SSSS signal and then stopped and abandoned his ship. Georgeson was brought aboard *U-48*, where he was greeted by Schultze 'very cordially and said he was sorry he would have to sink my ship … He gave me four loaves of bread; then he brought a bottle of Schnapps up, and taking out a packet of cigarettes, offered me one and put the remainder … in my hand.' Seven hours later Georgeson and his crew were picked up by a Dutch vessel.

Captain Thomas Prince of the Ropner tramp *Firby* received similar treatment from Schultze on 11 September as *U-48* headed home by way of Rockall. Prince had attempted to run and Schultze had opened fire, wounding several men. Prince abandoned ship and was summoned on board while Schultze's medics attended the wounded in the *Firby's* lifeboats. Prince was given a drink and asked for his master's certificate and his ship's manifest. In exchange Schultze 'gave him four rolls of bandages and six loaves of bread for the wounded'. Prince was also informed that Schultze 'would send … an SOS … to Churchill' – a promise he kept and which Churchill later admitted in the Commons – and, after a dreadful night in the boats, the *Firby's* survivors were picked up by HM Destroyer *Fearless*.

Other examples of similar conduct by U-boat commanders were reported to the Trade Division. On 7 September Captain James Barnetson had been taken aboard *U-33* from the *Olivegrove*, laden with a cargo of Cuban sugar. Kapitänleutnant von Dresky asked him 'Why does Mr Chamberlain want to make war on us?'[4] Barnetson was given a course to steer for the Fastnet Rock, almost 300 miles away and later Von Dresky fired flares to direct an American ship to the position of Barnetson's boats. When Kapitänleutnant Rollman in *U-34* intercepted and seized the Common Bros' tramp *Pukkastan*, Captain J. S. Thomson reported him as 'very courteous and anxious that everybody was off the ship before sinking her'. After the propaganda 'gift' of Lemp's atrocity of sinking the *Athenia* without warning these reports were far from welcome in London, an opinion reinforced by the vain search of several neutral ships in the position reported by the *Royal Sceptre*. Then, on 24 September, off the Fastnet Rock, Kapitänleutnant Habekost in command of *U-31* had sunk the Newcastle tramp *Hazelside*. Eleven men, including Captain C.H. Davis had been killed, too many to suggest that any attempt to observe the Prize Regulations had been made. Two days later, under prompting from the Ministry of Information, the British press weighed in, *The Times* citing the examples of the *Athenia*, *Royal Sceptre* and *Hazelside*, thundering that they had been the victims of 'a foul act of piracy on the high seas …'.

However, a few days later the *Browning* arrived at Bahia Blanca in Brazil, where Hartley and his shipmates told a different story, weakening Britain's position in the eyes of the outside world, particularly in the United States. Embarrassingly, Admiralty analysis of the first thirty interceptions of British merchantmen had already – on the 21 September – led to the conclusion that contrary to the assumptions made after the *Athenia's* sinking, the Prize Regulations were generally being observed. And to compound this, in the naval staff's eyes, the non-combatant merchant seamen involved were displaying 'a somewhat excessive enthusiasm' for the conduct of the enemy. This general assumption was flawed; none of the vessels involved had had the means to do more than the Germans demanded and most had transmitted the SSSS signal that the Admiralty required of them in the Emergency War Orders issued to every master, though some, still at sea homeward bound, had yet to receive them. A contrary spirit was not long in manifesting itself. The Brocklebank passenger-cargo liner *Manaar* had been among the first British merchantmen to be armed with a stern-gun for self-defence and she left Liverpool on 2 September, bound for Calcutta and Rangoon by way of the Suez Canal with a general cargo under Captain Campbell Shaw. By morning twilight on the 6th she was off Cape Roca, steaming south on a straight course but without lights. Campbell and his Chief Officer were on the bridge when a shot plunged into the sea ahead of them, raising a column of water. Campbell ordered maximum speed and rang the alarm bells so that his gun's crew closed-up aft.

The attacking U-boat, *U-38*, emerged from the semi-darkness her deck gun blazing. The previous day her commander, Kapitänleutnant H. Liebe, had stopped and released the French steamer *Pluvoise* whose master had transmitted the SSSS signal. German U-boat commanders were under orders not to harm French merchantmen and the French master's action provoked Dönitz to reissue his non-provocation order: the enemy was Britain. Liebe approached the *Manaar* expecting an easy success when, to his astonishment, she opened fire. Her first shot fell short; her second was closer and *U-38's* gun-crew responded with rapid fire, hitting the *Manaar* six times. A shell 'burst on the port side of the bridge,' the main aerial was carried away and with escape impossible, Campbell stopped engines and ordered the *Manaar* abandoned. The boats were lowered under fire, several of the crew being killed. In the confusion one of her radio officers, named Turner, and two lascars, one seriously wounded, were left on board.[5] As one of the boats turned to recover them, Liebe's torpedo hit the *Manaar* amidships. Almost as soon as Turner and one of the lascars boarded the lifeboat a second torpedo hit the ship. Half an hour later, as the boats pulled away, a third broke the *Manaar's* back.

With his victim in her death throes Liebe made off, leaving the men in the *Manaar's* lifeboats to fend for themselves. They drifted apart but Shaw and twenty-nine men were picked up by a Dutch vessel, sixteen in another lifeboat were rescued by a Portuguese ship and the remaining seventeen by an Italian vessel. All were landed at Lisbon, but Shaw had lost seven men and by his defiant action he had given Dönitz the excuse he needed to counter British claims over the piratical sinking of the *Athenia*. A fortnight later the British Ministry of Information, in the wake of the first German air raids, broadcast inaccurately that 'a British merchantman had engaged and driven off a German U-boat'. A few days later Churchill publicly announced what the *Manaar* had demonstrated and that he was intending to arm British merchantmen. This, combined with an Admiralty order to British masters to make every effort to ram surfaced U-boats and Campbell's action, enabled Dönitz to claim that

British merchant ships were not conforming to the passive role expected of non-combatant civilian-manned vessels, but were armed and acting aggressively on the state's instructions. This edged him closer to persuading Berlin to lift their curb on unrestricted submarine warfare.

Arming ships like the *Manaar* had been planned by June 1939. All those that had been stiffened were ordered to be fitted with stern-guns either at home or in Commonwealth ports where stocks of guns had been held and as the ships became available. The *Blackheath*, a tramp-steamer owned by Watts, Watts & Co., arrived in Liverpool from Vancouver whereupon:

> an army of painters immediately descended on the ship and proceeded to paint every-thing in sight a battleship grey. These hurriedly-recruited paint brush warriors could not tackle the yard-arm and top-mast. Many of them had never set foot on a ship before. So yours truly had to do the job since I was able to shin up guy ropes, etc. At the same time another army of workers set about strengthening the poop deck preparatory to mounting a 4-inch gun. It never ceased to amaze me how, in a few days, hundreds upon hundreds of merchant vessels were treated in the same way. An incredible feat.[6]

With the guns came the men of the Defensively Armed Merchant Ships Organisation, colloquially known as DEMS, which provided a nucleus of a gun-crew to every armed merchantman. This handful of naval ratings was placed under the ship's gun-nery officer, usually the third mate, with members of the ship's crew making up the numbers to serve the gun and pass the ammunition. As in the First World War the non-combatant status of merchant shipping meant that guns could be fitted only for self-defence, hence the appearance on the stern of vessels of guns of some antiquity, most of which were those that had survived the previous war and of which over 1,000 had been in storage ever since. Their origins were exotic; not a few were Japanese and dated from the 1890s, and many had been stored in equally odd locations, some in the sands of India. Most were of 4.7-inch calibre, larger liners receiving a 6-inch gun, the usual weapon reserved for fitting in some numbers in AMCs. Smaller ships received 12-pounders while others, particularly those operating on the East Coast convoys, were fitted with lighter weapons, such as Hotchkiss and other machine guns. While most DEMS gunners came from the Royal Navy, a few were drawn from specialised territorial units such as the Honourable Artillery Company. They were all signed-on as supernumerary deck-hands in order to put them under the master's – civilian – authority and thereby avoid problems in neutral ports. Being 'elderly and generally of settled disposition they were notable for good conduct, but on occasion there are venial faults that come under the consideration of the ship's master,' explains Captain Bone. 'In that event, a DEMS rating can elect to have his case taken up under the Merchant Shipping Act and no entry is made in his service record.' Later, when more sophisticated guns such as Oerlikon and Bofors mountings were available, and mer-chant ships had forsaken any pretence at bearing only defensive armament to be fired over the stern at a pursuing submarine but were armed for air defence and combined operations, the Maritime AA Regiment – later the Maritime Regiment of Royal Artillery – was formed.[7]

The presence of these men and their gun stiffened morale among merchant seamen which, by late 1942, was at a low ebb following heavy losses in the Atlantic and the disaster of Convoy PQ17. To enable a ship's crew to support the DEMS gunners, over 100,000 officer and ratings had been sent on gunnery courses by the war's end. Training facilities were set up in most major ports with mobile units provided by converted buses. Retired from the Admiralty Board for his sympathetic attitude to the Invergordon mutineers, Admiral Sir Frederick Dreyer had volunteered for convoy service and had initially been appointed Commodore, 2nd Class, RNR. In April 1941 he was appointed Inspector of Merchant Navy Gunnery and enthusiastically oversaw the training of these men, visiting ships and generally improving matters, for they had not always gone smoothly. In spite of having DEMS gunners, during a practice shoot in the Gulf of Aden aboard the *Empress of Australia* on her way to Bombay as a troop-ship, the recoil of the stern-gun was inadequately absorbed by the gun's mechanism. The resulting recoil destroyed the ship's hospital upon which the weapon was mounted and she entered Bombay with a pile of humiliating wreckage on her poop.

The defensive measure of gathering ships in convoy was war-winning. It had its detractors and its disadvantages, but these were outweighed by experience. It placed much greater demands upon personnel than peace-time passage-making, not simply because of the difficulties of station-keeping in close company and stoking old ships with inferior fuel, of receiving and sending signals with inadequate staff and of combating excoriating tiredness, but because of considerably increased levels of bureaucracy and organisational effort. This affected everyone; whether they were a master and his second mate working out the routeing instructions and familiarising themselves with the zig-zag patterns, the signal-book and special orders for night steaming; the mate anxious about the unusual cargo and the strength of the deck lashings; the third mate fretting over his signals, the apprentices over the lifeboat stores, the able-seamen over additional – and tiring – lookout duties; or the firemen piling the boiler ashes and clinker on deck along with the galley boy and his refuse (for such evidence of their progress could not be thrown over-board in daylight for fear of betraying the convoy's presence). And all had to conform strictly to the blackout. No chink of light must be seen, not even the soft red glow of a surreptitiously drawn cigarette.

The ordinary daily routines in convoy added to the crews' duties, falling mostly upon the officers on the bridge watching for the commodore's signals, and the engineers below who had constantly to adjust engine revolutions to accommodate the demands of station-keeping. Most Commodores at the beginning of the war had been relatively senior admirals with a penchant for signalling, and the illusion that they commanded 'a fleet' must have warmed many an old heart. That these gallant old gentlemen and the wayward mariners they now commanded soon worked out a common method, was to the credit of both parties. That it actually functioned is attested to in numerous convoy reports submitted by Commodores, of which the most complimentary was that on Convoy SC130 which arrived in the Mersey on 24 May 1943 at the turning point of the Battle of the Atlantic. It was the last North Atlantic convoy to 'be seriously menaced' and had begun in some disorder amid the fogs of the Grand Banks off Newfoundland. Notwithstanding this inauspicious start when ships assembling from all quarters of the globe were taking station and getting the measure of each other, by the time it approached the Liverpool Bar it was capable of manoeuvring 'with the precision of a battle-fleet'.

Much of the preparedness of individual ships depended upon the calibre and quality of her master and his officers, but much also depended upon that of the NCSOs, most particularly those despatching convoys from British ports, and those sending them from the assembly ports of North America: Halifax, Nova Scotia; St John's, Newfoundland; and finally and climactically, New York. These, their staffs and boats' crews did unsung service, often defusing difficult situations, assessing morale and generally attending to the material and psychological readiness of the crews about to undertake an ordeal that would hazard their lives. While most convoys made their way across the Atlantic unmolested, no one knew which those would be and, to take one simple example of the strain that convoy duty imposed and without resorting to the psycho-babble of trauma and stress, it was not unusual for watch officers to suffer a temporary blindness from simply staring into the darkness as they strove to determine the distance of their own ship from that next ahead in order to increase or decrease their own engine revolutions and keep proper station. Second Mate Ronald McBrearty was among those who experienced this.

> One morning, about 2 o'clock, I suddenly realised that I wasn't seeing anything, no blacker than black shapes, no blue stern light, nothing at all. I blew down the voice-pipe to the Captain's bed-room and he came on the bridge immediately. After explaining my symptoms I was sent below to rest. Before the watch was over I had recovered and was able to hand over in the normal manner.[9]

The transformation effected to the appearance of Bisset's *Franconia* in New York was to be replicated in the coming weeks aboard almost every British merchantman across the world except those on branch line services which escaped for a while the rigours of war. Grey paint, sand-bagging, guns, a handful of DEMS ratings and the assembly of convoys were the outward signs of the British state's mustering of its merchant fleet.

While initially many shipping companies strove to maintain normal services, for Britain had to continue trading to pay for the war, the Admiralty requisitioned many large passenger liners from the outset. As in the First World War a number were converted as AMCs and served as convoy escorts, on blockade duty in the Norwegian Sea, or as Ocean Boarding Vessels to enforce the blockade of Germany. These were essentially thereafter naval ships and their history properly belongs to that of the Royal Navy. As in the First World War, those merchant seafarers indispensable to the running of such ships taken up by the Admiralty signed T124 Articles and were thereby temporarily converted into naval personnel subject to the rigour of the King's Regulations and Admiralty Instructions as they applied to every British man-of-war. The arrangement allowed the ratings to continue to receive the higher rate of pay prevailing in the Merchant Service, while the officers retained any pension rights and seniority that might pertain to their civilian employment. The ratings' higher pay rankled with the naval men but few of a liner's deckhands were transferred in this way. 'For the most part, the men transferred to the Navy were victualling and

stokehold ratings, neither of whom are renowned for attachment to a ship's disciplinary regulation'. One odd reciprocal event occurred in the early months of the war
when a temporary lack of naval ratings' accommodation occurred in Glasgow. It was
suggested that raw, 'Hostilities Only' men should be placed on board trans-Atlantic
liners where, as extra lookouts and gun-crews, they could acquire their sea-legs before
receiving their final training and posting to HM Fleet.

When the former Aberdeen and Commonwealth liner *Jervis Bay* immolated herself in defence of Convoy HX84 she did so as HMS *Jervis Bay* under the command
of Captain Fogarty Fegen RN, though a large proportion of Fegen's crew were the
ship's peacetime complement. A similar situation obtained aboard the P&O liner
Rawalpindi under Captain Kennedy RN which engaged and was destroyed by the
German battle-ships *Scharnhorst* and *Gneisenau* on 27 November 1939. Besides the
AMCs and Ocean Boarding Vessels a number of other merchantmen were requisitioned for special service, as will presently be seen.

Shortly after the First World War the Admiralty had determined that in any future
conflict the Royal Navy would be some seventy-five cruisers short of requirements. As
a result it was decided to stiffen some fifty new merchant ships in order to facilitate the
fitting of armament if required. The Treasury expressed misgivings, arguing the expense
of this and putting forward the argument that a large number of ships had been stiffened
for the late war. Most of these were either too old to consider useful for future hostilities
or had had their stiffening removed. The Admiralty was acid in its response:

> The Treasury remarks are based on insufficient knowledge of the purpose of the
> scheme which aims at protecting our Mercantile Marine in the most economical
> way. It is suggested that the Treasury be informed … that if they are not prepared
> to sanction this expenditure they are in fact turning down the Admiralty convoy
> scheme … in time of war which scheme depends on these armed escort ships. It
> cannot be stated too often that the U.K. relies on the maintenance of the Mercantile
> Marine for her food supplies and existence … [10]

By 1936 forty-five liners built after 1921 had been stiffened for use as AMCs. They
comprised five Aberdeen & Commonwealth ships, including the *Jervis Bay*; three
Bibby liners, six from the Anchor Line and its subsidiaries; one each from Canadian
Pacific, Furness, Withy, Leyland, Lamport & Holt, Union Castle and Union Steam
Ship Co. of New Zealand; two each from Blue Funnel, Royal Mail, Houlder Bros,
and Port Line; five from Cunard White Star, and twelve from P&O. Almost sixty such
liners had been requisitioned, converted and commissioned by the end of 1939. Like
the obsolete *R*-class battleships they were to sit in the centre of North Atlantic convoys and cover the entire passage – which the low-endurance anti-submarine escorts
could not do – in case their convoy was attacked by a commerce-raider. They were
to prove gallant but largely ineffective, the *Jervis Bay*'s defence of Convoy HX84, brilliant though it was, did not prevent the *Admiral Scheer* from destroying several vessels,
as we shall see. Once the true menace proved to be the U-boat and not the big-gun
raider, they were a liability and redundant, being either returned to their owners or
employed as troopers, hospital- or depot-ships.

Among the most useful non-naval ships taken up from the mercantile marine were a number of vessels converted as auxiliary anti-aircraft ships. These were divided into two classes, coastal and sea-going. The former included short-sea traders and the popular excursion paddle-steamers of the General Steam Navigation Co., among others. Lightly scantlinged they could not bear heavy weapons and although they shot down few aircraft they were extremely useful in East Coast convoys – the significance of which will appear presently – by the sheer barrage they put up, deterring attacks and making up a little for Fighter Command's lack of aircraft to cover this vital route. The sea-going variety was of a different calibre, initially dignified by the classification of 'anti-aircraft cruisers' until the term was required for the *Dido*-class of light-cruiser specially armed for anti-aircraft defence. They comprised three Bank Line vessels, the *Alynbank*, *Foylebank* and *Springbank*, MacAndrews' *Pozarica* and *Palomares*, the Canadian National Railway's steamer *Prince Robert*, the Isle of Man Steam Packet Co.'s *Tynwald* and the Belfast S.S. Co.'s *Ulster Queen*. Fitted with proper gunnery control systems and modern 4-inch high-angle mountings, neither of which was fitted to AMCs, they were to earn a reputation for battle-worthiness, particularly in support of Russian convoys. Like the AMCs their usefulness diminished as more suitable warships – specifically the *Didos* – became available and those that survived ended the war fulfilling other functions with equal distinction. The *Alynbank*'s end is described later, while the *Ulster Queen* and *Palomares* were converted into Fighter Direction ships to serve at D-Day.

A few Special Service Vessels were fitted out in emulation of the Decoy, or Q-ships, of the First World War, but they were decommissioned in 1941 through lack of success.[11] The impracticability of the large AMCs stopping and searching neutral shipping by lowering oared pulling-boats in the Norwegian Sea, led to the taking-up of a number of passenger-cargo liners as Ocean Boarding Vessels.[12] Having lower freeboard these were better able to carry out this task than the high-sided AMCs, and included the Booth liner *Hilary*, Elders & Fyffes fruit-carriers *Cavina* and *Ariguani*, Ellerman & Papayanni's *Corinthian*, Blue Funnel's *Maron*, the B.I. liners *Chakla*, *Chakdina* and *Chantala*, and Lamport & Holt's *Voltaire*. Several smaller, short-sea ferries were also utilised, and both types were later converted for other purposes as the need for boarding vessels diminished. This was because the neutral countries, particularly Norway and Denmark, were overrun by Germany, or the neutral shipping of countries like Sweden became increasingly vulnerable to attacks by U-boats and tended to seek the shelter of British, and later Allied, convoys. Again, the demand for these vessels fell off after 1941 and they were either converted to other purposes such as depot-ships, barrage-balloon vessels or auxiliary anti-aircraft ships, while others were simply returned to their owners and the carrying trade for which they had been built.

Advantage was taken of merchant ships in convoy by fitting a few with aircraft catapults capable of rocketing off a Mark 1 Hurricane, redundant for front-line service but putatively useful for shooting down long-range German reconnaissance aircraft, particularly the Fw200 Condor. Such 'Cam-ships' – or Catapult Armed Merchantmen – were a limited success. More successful were Merchant Aircraft carriers, or MAC-ships, which had a flight deck fitted over a mercantile hull. With a handful of Swordfish anti-submarine biplanes and a small air-crew and maintenance team embarked, they were otherwise merchantmen. Carrying a full cargo, they were the oddest hybrids of this extemporised fleet. Most MAC-ships were state-built vessels constructed under the War Emergency programme. They were, however, allocated to shipping companies to manage and to man on behalf of the MoWT. Besides these, several merchantmen building when war broke out were taken over and their hulls used to provide the basis for proper light-aircraft carriers, capable of carrying not just a handful of anti-submarine Swordfish, but a flight of fighters as well. The value of air patrols over a convoy to keep U-boats at a distance had been observed towards the end of the First World War by junior officers, but little notice had been taken of this by the naval staff. The presence of these 'escort-carriers' in a convoy was to prove decisive, particularly on Russian convoys after the *débâcle* of PQ17, but they were fully commissioned naval ships.

As in 1914–1918, a large number of small merchantmen, trawlers and drifters were requisitioned for a variety of tasks. Chief among these were the smaller fishing vessels converted to the highly dangerous task of mine-sweeping, and the deep-water trawlers armed and fitted for anti-submarine escort duties. These filled the gap until the purpose-built and barely adequate Flower-class corvettes were available. A number of fast cargo-liners became military transports and later Landing Craft Infantry. Among the former the *Glenartney*, attached to the Fleet Train that operated out of Manus in the Admiralty Islands replenishing the warships of the British Pacific Fleet was notable for the fastest transfer of stores and ammunition. Perhaps the oddest mercantile conversions also occurred not at the beginning, but towards the end of the war. They too were in the Pacific and the ships were also owned by Alfred Holt & Co. Initially requisitioned as mine-layers, in 1944 the two Blue Funnel liners *Agamemnon* and *Menestheus* were converted to 'Amenities ships' to support the British Pacific Fleet.[13] The latter was fitted with a brewery and at the end of the war the Admiralty attempted to buy her, but Alfred Holt & Co. were unmoved and required their ship returned.

The military success of the Western Allies in mounting several invasions from the sea relied entirely upon infantry assault-ships capable of conveying the invading troops to within yards of the beach from which they could be launched in small landing craft. These were supplied in the European and the Indian Ocean theatres by the conversion of suitable British merchant ships. The possible requirement for such vessels arose from studies undertaken by an inter-services group set up in 1938 by the British Chiefs of Staff but were ignored in the disastrous Norwegian campaign. Later the versatility of the cargo-liners had become appreciated and indeed larger liners were requisitioned for the purpose. However, it was the fast, 18-knot *Glenearn*-class that provided the template and she and her sisters *Glengyle* and *Glenroy* were converted to convey and land a commando of 550 men. These were beefed-up considerably in the light of operational experience, able to carry larger numbers of troops and the *Glengyle*, for example, took part in the raid on Bardia, the evacuations of Greece and Crete, where she and the Anchor liner *Cameronia* embarked 6,000 Argyll and Sutherland Highlanders. A few days later she was landing troops at the Litani River in Syria before assisting in the resupply of Malta, the Dieppe raid and the landings at Diego Suarez in the taking of Madagascar in May 1942. That November she landed American troops at Oran as part of Operation TORCH, which was followed by Operation HUSKY, and landings at Salerno and Anzio. She was finally refitted in conformity with other Landing Craft Infantry (Large) and was sent east, to land the first garrison troops at Hong Kong within three weeks of the Japanese surrender.

As the German U-boats' attrition of merchant shipping in the North Atlantic increased, the actual losses of merchant seamen and the effect this was having upon morale persuaded the authorities to improve the recovery of survivors. There was by the autumn of 1940 a justifiable sense among merchant seafarers that the Royal Navy was failing in its duty to protect them adequately. Convoy escorts, when present, were largely ineffective against U-boats and the diversion of these small warships to the business of rescuing survivors from torpedoed merchant ships when they should have been counter-attacking U-boats, was having a correspondingly bad effect elsewhere. It was therefore decided to fit out a number of small short-sea traders as Ocean Rescue Ships and equip them with recovery nets, modest medical facilities, emergency clothing and facilities for feeding and accommodating men who were suffering from exposure, trauma and wounds. Attempts to incorporate them into the Royal Navy failed and they were put under the blue ensign as auxiliaries and manned by mercantile crews. Basic in the extreme, they were in fact a microcosm of the best and worst of the Merchant Navy.

> The Rescue Ship organisation [based on Greenock] was perhaps a typically British compromise, compounded of complete incompatibles, which emerged as a highly efficient measure. It owed much of its success to the fact that it was composed of small-ship men, most of whom had the greatest of gifts, a sense of humour, and of men who had served together, or belonged to the same company. It was also fortunate in having as its shore organiser an extremely keen and able officer who made it his business to see that it did work. In addition to the regular deck hands and firemen, the crews occasionally included in their number a sprinkling of 'Billy' boys from Glasgow and a few ex-convicts. Yet there never was any question about their behaviour at sea; one and all carried out their duties magnificently, often under the most dangerous and arduous conditions. By contrast, in harbour, when tensions were relaxed, anything could happen, and on one occasion in Halifax a free fight broke out after a Christmas party, and the Mounties had to be called in to restore order.[14]

Nevertheless, their manning was comprehensive, as George Russell points out, for their own peace-time crews were

> augmented as necessary to Foreign-Going levels but many other additional personnel were required. Three Navigating Officers and an extra Rescue Officer were carried, Nine ABs were required to man the rescue boat and rescue station, there were six Radio Officers, three each for normal radio traffic and three for HF/DF watch-keeping. Each ship had a Sick Bay equipped as an Operating Theatre which was staffed by an RN Surgeon and one or two Sick Bay Attendants. The bridge had two RN signalmen to handle the large amount of convoy signalling and up to sixteen gunners were carried. The normal peacetime crew of thirty Officers and men therefore became a wartime complement of nearly seventy, the extra personnel in the *Copeland*

being largely accommodated in thirteen excellent two-berth passenger cabins. Also in the *Copeland* the Operating Theatre/Sick Bay was in the former Passenger Lounge directly under the bridge [on the] port side, while survivors were berthed in the large space under the bridge deck which in peacetime was used for cargo and cattle in stalls. The rescue station was on the main deck immediately forward of the bridge with the top half of the cargo doors removed to provide ready access overside.

George Russell had joined the service by default. Reporting to Donaldson's offices for another ship he:

> was horrified to be told there was no likelihood of this … Donaldson's had only seven ships left out of twenty-one, with another three managed for the MoWT. They were therefore quite unable to offer me further employment and that was that. In this situation I readily accepted a post as Chief Officer of the Clyde Shipping Company's *Copeland,* one of twelve such coastal passenger steamers then operating as Ocean Rescue Ships … [15]

The rescue of survivors was accomplished by a number of basic techniques, as Russell explains:

> by launching and recovery of her own rescue boat (oar propelled to begin with but later fitted with engines), and also by taking men direct from life-boats and life-rafts or from the water itself in circumstances often of the greatest difficulty. Various equipment was developed and fitted as experience was gained but the principal item was a simple scrambling net, hung overside and from log booms which enabled survivors to be 'swept up' from the water. The ships were defensively and heavily armed for their size; being frequently alone and stopped astern of a convoy they had to adequately defend themselves.

Despite their rag-bag composition the Ocean Rescue Ships were commanded by some outstanding masters whose seamanship proved of the highest order and all of whom were decorated for distinguished service. They included the Shetland ferry *St Sunniva*, Captain McGowan, which was lost with all hands in January 1943 and was thought to have capsized in heavy weather off Nova Scotia owing to an accretion of ice; and the *Toward*, Captain Hudson, which was torpedoed on the night of 7 February 1943 as she rejoined eastbound Convoy SC118 after transferring her surgeon to the *Celtic Star* and having withdrawn both him and a seamen injured from falling from a mast. The loss of life was heavy. Two Rescue Ships which served with distinction were the *Zamalek*, Captain O.C. Morris, and *Zaafaran*, Captain C.K.McGowan, of the Pharaonic Mail Line of Alexandria. These, together with the Clyde Shipping Co.'s *Rathlin*, Captain A. Banning, formed part of Convoy PQ17 in July 1942, when the *Zaafaran* was lost, McGowan afterwards transferring to the *St Sunniva*. The London & North East Railway Co.'s steamer *Stockport*, Captain T.E. Fea, was also lost with all sixty-four of her crew and ninety-one survivors on 24 February 1943, and MacAndrews' *Pinto*, commanded by an Australian, Captain L.S. Boggs, was sunk while recovering survivors in September 1944. At the end of this year a number of Castle-class corvettes then being built, having been superseded by better anti-submarine frigates, were converted to Rescue Ships, but proved less successful owing to their lack of the slab-sides of the little merchantmen that facilitated easier recovery from the sea.[16]

By the time Russell joined the *Copeland* in June 1943 she had:

completed two-and-a-half years as a Rescue Ship with fifty convoys, having made round trips to Halifax, Gibraltar, Reykjavik and one to North Russia in the roughly handled PQ 18 convoy. At the beginning of the Rescue Ship service and like the few available escorts, convoys were accompanied only to the point of dispersal in the Western Approaches. The escorts and Rescue Ship (when there was one), then transferred and returned home with an inward convoy. Later as the escort situation improved the Rescue Ships remained with the convoys until about halfway across, then refuelled in Iceland and returned with a homeward convoy ... In the PQ 18 convoy in September 1942 which lost five ships, the *Copeland* picked up 214 survivors. Her most recent act of rescue was in the voyage before I joined her, when in an outward Halifax convoy she picked up the twenty surviving crew of Andrew Weir's *Aymeric*, torpedoed and sunk by a U-Boat on 17 May 1943. For the remainder of the war ... each voyage of the *Copeland* was little more than routine. There were frequent transfers of sick seamen from ships in convoy to our Sick Bay, and much of our sea time was spent in following astern of the (by now almost standard) escort-carrier when flying-off and flying-on, in case an aircraft had to ditch. At the beginning of November 1943 we were allocated to a North Russian convoy and issued with special Arctic clothing, such as we would have given our eye-teeth for on the *Empire Redshank* two years earlier. This gear comprised the thickest 'Long Johns' and singlets made of Arran wool, together with long stockings and sweaters of similar material. On top of all this was a leather jacket with lambswool lining and a canvas coat, again wool lined, plus a canvas cap with ear flaps. On this North Russian trip we left Glasgow on 8 November 1943 and Loch Ewe four days later in a convoy of about twenty ships, of which about half each were American and British. I recall nothing of note about this trip and as we had no cargo to work in Kola, we were only there five days before we set off in a small return convoy, which suffered severely from the weather but got us back to Glasgow on 10 December in time to enjoy both Christmas and New Year at home. We sailed again on 2 January 1944, making a round trip to Gibraltar before another Arctic voyage to Kola and this convoy, which sailed from Loch Ewe on 20 February, comprised over forty ships (about thirty being American Liberty-ships) and enjoyed the luxury of a cruiser and escort-carrier as close escort in addition to several destroyers, corvettes and frigates. U-Boats certainly gained contact with this convoy but were kept down and one or two [were] sunk by aircraft from the escort-carrier, which were constantly in the air. Despite this a U-Boat managed to torpedo one of the destroyers, *Mahratta*, which blew up and sank with heavy loss of life. When manoeuvring into the anchorage at Kola Inlet on 28 February the Russian pilot and our Captain Armour had either a disagreement or a misunderstanding (I never knew which), resulting in the

Copeland colliding with a ship at anchor and smashing up two of our life-boats, still then in the swung-out position. This necessitated our remaining in port to have the boats repaired, which cost us a quick return in the next convoy sailing two days later. Our stay in Kola was a rather long and drab five weeks ...

These small ships, which had no business being in the North Atlantic, were in service early in 1941 and they made one important additional contribution to winning the Battle of the Atlantic. Being manned by radio officers, they were fitted with radio direction finding apparatus and therefore added an additional cross-bearing to those obtained by the escorts when intercepting the injudicious 'chatter' the German U-boat commanders indulged in when surfaced and stalking convoys by day. This increased the accuracy of fixes and enabled the battle to be taken to the enemy. Not a few U-boats were surprised on the surface by the sudden approach of a British or Canadian – or later American – frigate speeding towards them.

Besides the specialised tasks undertaken by the fast and versatile *Glenearn*-class, the most consistently useful merchantmen taken up from trade were those large liners used as troop-ships. At the beginning of the war Cunard-White Star's *Queen Mary*, was laid-up on arrival at New York near the French liner *Normandie*, kept there by the threat of German capital ships at sea. Equally concern was felt in high places for the fate of her half-sister, the brand new *Queen Elizabeth*. A sitting duck for the much-feared air raids that were thought to be imminent, she lay at the Clydebank yard of her builders, John Brown & Co., and although no air raids had yet occurred, it was clearly only a matter of time.

Terrible though they were, Germany's air raids were not as catastrophic as had been feared, but the apprehension felt about the possible fate of the *Queen Elizabeth* was

A publicity watercolour of the Cunard liner *Queen Elizabeth*. She began her life trooping and made her maiden voyage with passengers after the war. Such ships were displaced by the trans-Atlantic jet air-liner. (From a Private Collection)

not without foundation. In the event it was not the Clyde that first felt the enemy's violence, but another marine target. With France fallen, the first indication of the coming *Blitz* was an air raid on the docks of Swansea on 10 July 1940, but by this time the great bird had flown. As she neared completion the *Queen Elizabeth* was painted grey and the news was leaked that she was to leave Clydebank for a passage to Southampton. Here she would enter the large graving dock for final fitting-out and in late February a crew of 500 were signed-on under Captain J.C. Townley. Once her destination was widely known, she left her berth with a Southampton pilot already embarked and moved slowly downstream to anchor off Gourock. Here Townley mustered his crew and told them their real destination. After the most perfunctory of sea trials, Brown's handed her over and on 2 March she slipped to sea. Five days later she berthed in New York, alongside the *Queen Mary*, the *Normandie* and the new *Mauretania*, which had enjoyed a brief conversion to an AMC but had been considered too good a target and restored to her owners. On 20 March the *Queen Mary* sailed for Sydney via Trinidad and Capetown; she was followed by the *Mauretania*, which proceeded by way of the Panama Canal, and the *Queen Elizabeth*. At Sydney these and other liners were converted for trooping.

Meanwhile others had been busy. On her arrival in Liverpool on 12 September 1939, the *Franconia* had been stripped of her interior furbishments and the work of fitting her for the carriage of 3,000 troops was carried out. Her crew was reduced, largely by paying off many of the now redundant stewards and stewardesses and she had a 6-inch gun on her stern, manned by the Honourable Artillery Company. On 25 September the *Franconia* sailed for Southampton where 1,300 soldiers were embarked for Malta and on the 28th she left in company with the Royal Mail liner *Alcantara*, Canadian Pacific's *Empress of Australia* and the Union-Castle liner *Athlone Castle*. From Gibraltar the convoy, minus the *Athlone Castle*, proceeded to Malta and then Marseilles carrying 700 Polish airmen who had escaped the German occupation of their homeland and were making for Paris. Bisset brought *Franconia* home alone via Gibraltar.

The *Franconia*'s next trooping task was part of the disastrous Franco-British expedition to Norway in April 1940. Bisset embarked a 'Dock Battalion' of the Royal Army Service Corps intended to handle military supplies but they were not required and, having carried these men to Norway and landed them by means of a Mersey ferry – the presence of which in these northern waters astonished Bisset – he was ordered to bring them home again.

On 10 May Guderian's Panzers rolled across the Netherlands and Belgium, the coalition National Government led by Winston Churchill took over from the ailing administration of Chamberlain in which Churchill had served as First Lord of the Admiralty, and Royal Marines landed in Iceland. The island was a dominion of Denmark but as the Germans had marched into Copenhagen a month earlier the British Occupation was necessary to protect shipping in the North Atlantic. Had Dönitz's U-boats had an operational base in Iceland the outcome would have been very different. That same day Bisset's *Franconia*, and the *Lancastria*, Captain Rudolph Sharp, sailed from King George V Dock, Glasgow. The *Lancastria* had been cruising shortly before the outbreak of war and she had received the same treatment as the *Franconia* upon her arrival in New York from the Bahamas. The two Cunarders rounded Cloch Point, with some 3,400 troops, two dozen army nurses and army stores for the permanent garrison of Iceland. Escorted by two destroyers they arrived at Reykjavik on the 17th.

As Narvik fell in the far distant north and the Allied operation in Norway collapsed, the Germans drove into northern France. Alongside their French allies, the British Expeditionary Force fell back under the onslaught and in the days that followed every conceivable type of vessel assisted in the withdrawal of troops from the beaches of Dunkirk. From Thames sailing-barges to cross-Channel ferries, the red ensign proved a welcome sight to exhausted men. The withdrawal, Operation DYNAMO, was controlled from Dover from where the ferries in particular ran a shuttle service under shell fire and air attack. Altogether, some 220,000 British, and 112,000 Belgian and French troops were safely carried across the Strait of Dover, though without their equipment which had been abandoned in the face of the German advance.

Having disembarked their troops in Reykjavik, the *Franconia* and *Lancastria* returned to the Clyde in expectation of assisting with the evacuation of the British Expeditionary Force from France, which began on 26 May. However, by 24th it had become clear that the Allied forces in northern Norway could serve no useful purpose and the decision had been made to withdraw them, despite their capture of Narvik. Several liners were mustered for this, the two Cunarders were joined by their White Star sister *Georgic*, Furness, Withy's slower 19-knot *Monarch of Bermuda* and two Polish liners, the *Batory* and *Sobieski*. A second group consisted of the Orient liners *Oronsay*, *Ormonde* and *Orama*, the Blue Star Line's *Arandora Star* and three Irish Sea ferries.

By 10 June the first group was safely anchored at Gourock, having avoided the sortie made by a heavy squadron of the *Kriegsmarine* in which the carrier *Glorious* was sunk. Here they learned that Italy had declared war on Britain and France. Behind them, off Narvik, the *Orama* had been sunk by the heavy cruiser *Admiral Hipper*, which also sank the *Oil Pioneer*. And while the *Scharnhorst* had suffered the hospital ship *Atlantis* to proceed, Lamport & Holt's *Vandyck*, serving as an Armed Boarding Vessel, was bombed and sunk. Seven of her crew were killed and the remainder captured and imprisoned.

By this time, after ten months of war, no fewer than 228 British merchant ships had been lost, most to submarines and mines, a few to aircraft and a mere handful to the dreaded commerce-raiders. Fortunately the movement of troops, which besides the evacuation from Dunkirk was considerable, was largely successful but the withdrawal of the remnants of the BEF was not without tragedy. In the mythologizing consequent upon Operation DYNAMO, it is often forgotten that not all British forces were brought off the beaches of northern France. A substantial number of units were driven further west and shipping was hurriedly mustered to recover them. These ships proceed from Plymouth to Brest where the situation became fluid and uncertain. When Captains Sharp and Bisset arrived off Brest they were warned off and coasted to Quiberon, where the *Franconia* was attacked by a solitary aircraft. Both she and the *Lancastria* anchored in company with several other transports, including the *Georgic*, *Arandora Star*, *Otranto*, *Strathaird*, the *Ettrick*, *Batory* and *Sobieski*, while Bisset's engineers sought to stop a leak. Sharp, meanwhile, had received orders to proceed to Charpentier Road, St Nazaire, where he began to embark British troops. Other British ships were similarly employed in Operation AERIAL and by 17 June the *Lancastria* had what was estimated to have been over 9,000 soldiers on board when she was heavily attacked by Dornier Do17 bombers. In a long sustained but successful attack the *Lancastria*, one bomb having passed down a funnel to detonate within a boiler room, caught fire and began to founder. Sharp summoned help and numerous small craft assisted. Within twenty minutes the *Lancastria* rolled over to port and sank bow first.

Those who escaped into the water found themselves swimming in boiler oil, which rapidly choked off the brave souls who sang *Roll out the barrel*. Since no one knew precisely how many soldiers had embarked in the *Lancastria* the death toll was uncertain but is thought to have exceeded 5,000. About 2,500 survived, including Sharp. Nearby the Blue Funnel liner *Teiresias* was also sunk, near misses 'cracked the ship right across the deck and down to the waterline', reported Captain J.R. Davies. Another of Holt's ships, the *Glenaffric*, under Captain W.G. Harrison entered St Nazaire:

> on an ebb tide … [and] without pilot or tugs the ship was skilfully and safely brought into the quay, where the embarkation of the remaining [4,000] troops was quickly carried out. After a trying night, during which the town was raided twice by enemy aircraft, the ship was brought out of harbour under the most adverse conditions and, the convoy [of transports] having already departed, the Master proceeded unescorted to a British port.

Harrison's conduct earned him and his crew the approbation of the War Office while Churchill suppressed the terrible loss of life in the *Lancastria*, relying on the legend of Dunkirk to prepare the British for their lonely stand against fascism.[17]

While Operation AERIAL was in progress the *Queen Mary, Mauretania, Aquitania, Andes, Empress of Japan* and *Empress of Britain* had arrived in the Clyde with Australian and New Zealand troops. This reinforcement did little to dispel the gloom. With France capitulating, Britain's isolation was stark. On 5 July a fast convoy left Greenock. It comprised the Polish liners *Batory* and *Sobieski*, the *Monarch of Bermuda*, the battleship *Revenge* and the cruiser *Bonaventure*. A week later it arrived at Halifax and discharged its precious cargo, £192 million of the British Government's gold reserves sent to Halifax for safe keeping. This marked the end of the first phase of the war at sea. Britain's sea communications, so vital to her survival, were attenuated and exposed and while her commitment to defend them was unquestionable, her ability to do so remained in doubt. Britons had been on rationing for seven months and with the loss of the BEF's equipment in France she stood in grave need of both guns and butter. Encouraged by the Neutrality Act passed by Roosevelt's Democratic government in Washington which had allowed Britain and France to buy arms from the United States, Churchill now sought greater aid from his mother's country.

While in due course Churchill would secure Lend-Lease from Roosevelt's Administration, resulting in hundreds of cargoes of armaments coming across the North Atlantic, the urgency with which the Prime Minister himself pursued the most essential requirements in the face of a threatened and imminent invasion is shown by his personal minute to his Chief of Staff, General Ismay, dated 13 July and concerning a massive shipment of arms that had just left New York.

Draw Admiralty attention to the importance of all these ships, especially the *Western Prince*. What is her speed? It would be a disaster if we lost these fifty thousand rifles. Draw attention also to the immense consequence of the convoy which is leaving New York between July 8 and 12. When will these convoys be in the danger zone? When will they arrive? Let me have a report on the measures taken.

Both Furness, Withy's *Western Prince* and her sister the *Eastern Prince* 'carried enormous quantities of arms and ammunition from America to Britain to urgently replace *matériel* lost in France' as part of a series of HX convoys. These consisted from fifty ships up to seventy-six in Convoy HX62, a number unsurpassed until two years later when the tide of war was on the turn. Although Great Britain went into debt to pay for these munitions, until Lend-Lease was arranged in the following spring, most of these first shipments of arms were paid for directly so that both the spectre of invasion and the necessity of paying for those 'fifty-thousand rifles' required the transfer of further bullion to Canada. Operation FISH was the code designation for the carriage of some £800 million across the Western Ocean, an eighth in Furness, Withy ships.

All this was set against a background of mounting losses of merchantmen, losses provoking Churchill's anxiety for the safety of the *Western Prince* and her fellows. The consequences of the fall of France were to deprive Britain of the use of Southampton as a port and the English Channel as a convoy route from that port and London. This fact was brought home in all its horror with the massacring of outward-bound convoy OA178 which left Southend on 3 July and proved to be the last deep-sea convoy to transit the Channel (see Chapter Four). In the North Atlantic the U-boat became again the deadly weapon it had proved itself in 1917, although at first it seemed that the Admiralty's fear of surface commerce-raiders had been justified, and in distant waters they remained a threat for some time. The *Admiral Graf Spee*, so admired at the pre-war Spithead Naval Review, had had a spectacular run of luck in the South Atlantic in the opening four months of hostilities, despite large Franco-British squadrons hunting her. By disguising his ship and dodging deep into the Southern Ocean to reappear off Mozambique to sink a British coastal-tanker, Kapitän sur Zee Hans Langsdorff was able to elude his pursuers for some time. Having been at sea before the declaration of war Langsdorff began his attack on British shipping off the shoulder of Brazil on 30 September 1939 with the sinking of the Booth liner *Clement*, Captain F.C.P. Harris. He sank the Newcastle tramp *Ashlea*, Captain Charles Pottinger, on the 7 October, and another Tyneside tramp, the *Newton Beech*, Captain Robison – which he had captured a few days earlier – on the 8th; he captured a cargo liner belonging to T&J Harrison of Liverpool, the *Hunstman*, Captain A. Brown, on 10 October. Having looted her of part of her valuable cargo and a good deal of her consumable stores, Langsdorff sank her on the 17th. On the 22nd he sank the Hain tramp *Trevannion*, Captain J. M. Edwards, before making his sortie into the Indian Ocean, the coastal-tanker *Africa Shell*, Captain Patrick Dove, being despatched on 15 November. Unable to sight anything on the Capetown–Australia route, Langsdorff returned to the South Atlantic, replenished from the *Altmark* into which he transferred his prisoners on the 26th and sank the large Blue Star liner *Doric Star*, Captain William Stubbs, on 2 December. The following day he sank Shaw, Savill & Albion's *Tairoa*,

Captain W.B.S. Starr, before heading west for the choke point of the Rio de la Plata. Replenishing again on the 6th he sank the Headlam tramp *Streonshalh* of Whitby, Captain J.J. Robinson, next day; she was his last victim. A week later the *Admiral Graf Spee* lay wounded in Montevideo after an action with a cruiser-squadron of the Royal Navy under Commodore Harwood, which placed the German *Panzerschiff* under blockade. On the 17th, Langsdorff left port and headed to sea. Crowds lined the coast in expectation of a resumption of the battle; instead he scuttled the *Admiral Graf Spee* within a few miles of Montevideo. A few days later, his crew interned in the Argentine, he shot himself.[18]

While the *Admiral Graf Spee* was active in the South Atlantic, the *Deutschland* under Wennecker accounted for a number of ships in a largely ineffective cruise further north. Despite these sorties, the heavy units of the *Kriegsmarine* were generally less successful than the disguised merchantmen, or *Hilfskreuzers*, of which mention will presently be made. Langsdorff's achievement would be surpassed by several competent U-boat commanders. His actions had drawn the wrath of the Royal Navy down upon him and ultimately deprived his country of a trained crew, most of which were to languish in South America until the end of the war, occasionally meeting British merchant seamen ashore in neutral Buenos Aires where, on a few occasions, games of football were played.

There was one significant occasion when a trans-Atlantic convoy was seriously mauled by a 'pocket-battle-ship' and that was HX84, which was attacked on 5 November 1940 by Kapitän sur Zee Teodor Kranke in the *Admiral Scheer*. Eastbound Convoy HX84 consisted of thirty-eight ships – among them two neutral Swedes – deployed in eight columns and was under the direction of Commodore R.H. Maltby, a retired rear admiral who was embarked in the Cardiff-registered *Cornish City*, Captain Isaac, leading the fifth column. Indistinguishable from the rest of the convoy that surrounded it was its ocean-escort, the AMC, HMS *Jervis Bay*. She was commanded by Acting Captain E.S. Fogarty-Fegen RN and among his crew of mixed regular, RNVR and T124 men were the ship's peace time chief officer, Mr G.L. Roe, Second Officer W. Hill, Third Officer N.E. Wood and Fourth Officer H.G.B. Moss. Her chief engineer, Mr J.H.G. Campbell, led the engineers, all of whom, like the deck-officers, had been commissioned 'in accordance with their rank in the ship'. Her purser, Mr E. White, was also commissioned as a Paymaster Lieutenant Commander.[19]

Once the attacking *Admiral Scheer* made her presence known at 17.10, Fogarty-Fegen hauled out of the convoy and, his guns blazing, proceeded to engage the German warship. Other ships opened fire, Second Mate McBrearty of the tramp *Lancaster Castle* thought that his was 'the first merchant ship to open fire and we managed to get quite a few 4-inch shells away but '… hits were not possible'. McBrearty described the drill:

> It was the ship's carpenter's job to pass shells out of the locker and they were then passed up to the main deck via a ladder, then up another ladder to the gun-platform [on top of the poop deck house]. The human chain passing up the ammunition was made up of apprentices plus cabin, mess-room and galley boys. The eldest could not have been more than seventeen-and-a-half and some were much younger.

As Krancke pressed his attack Commodore Maltby ordered the convoy to scatter. It was late afternoon and the wintry twilight was already dimming the eastern horizon as the ships' courses rapidly diverged and each increased to her full speed. The self-sacrifice of the *Jervis Bay* in defence of her convoy is well known, but in so doing she was only partially successful and much of what followed is forgotten. It was almost dark as the ships scattered and the *Admiral Scheer*'s gunners switched targets. Captain Barnett extricated the New Zealand Shipping Co.'s *Rangitiki* under fire but at speed, much to the relief of her seventy-five passengers. Astonishingly, although illuminated by the German searchlights after dark, Ellerman's Papayanni *Castilian*, laden with 400 tons of high explosives, avoided a shelling. In contrast her sister-ship, the *Andalusian*, was hit, though not seriously. Having briefly consulted his officers on the bridge of the *Lancaster Castle*, Captain Hugh Williams – 'a very experienced master, respected by all' – decided that 'every time we saw a gun flash we would turn our stern to it and make as much speed as possible …'.

One of Krancke's victims was the Eagle Oil Co.'s tanker *San Demetrio*, which was set on fire. Captain Waite ordered her abandoned but later a party led by Second Officer Hawkins reboarded her. Extinguishing the fire, Hawkins and Chief Engineer Pollard brought her home with most of her cargo of vital oil after a determined struggle in which initiative and extemporisation triumphed. But the losses of Convoy HX84 were not limited to the *Jervis Bay* and her people. At 18.30 star-shells illuminated the Ulsterman *Kenbane Head*. She was then hit by a full salvo from the *Admiral Scheer*'s 11-inch guns. Firing back with her stern-mounted 4-inch gun she lay over on her port side and sank. Of her forty-five men, twenty-three took to the water. Seeing her predicament, Captain Pettigrew of the Canadian Pacific cargo-liner *Beaverford* attempted to draw Krancke's fire with his two stern guns. It was a gallant act in view of the fact that while the *Beaverford* was laden with foodstuffs and timber in her 'tween-decks, her holds were full of munitions. Because of this, her station had been immediately astern of the *Cornish City* and she was followed by Brocklebank's *Maidan* which was similarly laden. Both of these vessels headed south making smoke, but as the guns of the hotly pursuing *Admiral Scheer* were laid on first one ship and then another, shells penetrated the *Maidan* and exploded in her holds, counter-mining the explosives. Captain Miller and all eighty-nine of her people were incinerated in the fire-ball.

The *Admiral Scheer* next opened fire upon the *Trewellard*, Captain Daniel, deeply laden with steel billets and pig-iron. Her crew had just sufficient time to launch three boats, saving twenty-three lives with the loss of sixteen souls as the tramp sank. Krancke now finally concentrated his main armament on the *Beaverford*, with which he had been desultorily engaged for several hours. Pettigrew had employed every ruse he and his ship were capable of, with constant alterations of course and a dogged return of fire. Illuminated by the *Admiral Scheer*'s star-shells, Krancke's guns were laid by optical range-finder and at approximately 22.45 their explosive shells found their mark. The *Beaverford* blew-up, killing all seventy-seven on board.

Owned by Smith & Co. of Cardiff the commodore's ship, the *Cornish City*, escaped. Her sister-ship the *Fresno City* was less fortunate and received the *Admiral Scheer*'s full broadside when only two miles away. Captain Lawson ordered his ship abandoned and all but one of her crew escaped with their lives, though little else. Aboard one of the two Swedish ships, the *Stureholm*, Captain Olander consulted his crew and all most gallantly agreed to turn back and to search for survivors. The following dawn the *Stureholm* picked up sixty-eight men from the *Jervis Bay* before putting back for St John's. Sadly the *Stureholm* was lost in Convoy HX93 on 12 December, torpedoed by *U-96* and took with her survivors from a British tanker. Far astern of HX84 was the Bristol City Line's *Gloucester City*, which had been part of the dispersing Convoy OB238. Her master also made a brave decision in view of the presence of a marauding raider, and shaped a course to pass through the position of the attack. After being buffeted by strong winds and heavy seas, on the morning of the 7th, when the conditions had moderated, Captain Smith came in sight of the first of seven boats spread over a wide area. Twenty-five men from the *Trewellard* and twenty-three from the *San Demetrio* were rescued; twenty from the *Kenbane Head* were also picked up, as were twenty-four from the *Fresno City*. As Krancke returned to a hero's welcome at Bergen from Grossadmiral Erich Raeder, Hawkins and Pollard struggled east with the battered *San Demetrio*, but the escaping *Vingaland*, the other Swedish ship in HX84, making the best of her way eastwards, was spotted and bombed by a FW200 Condor and sent to the bottom with the loss of six lives. Although the German High Command claimed the complete destruction of the convoy, the Admiralty made no secret of the losses of several merchant ships. Nevertheless the valorous immolation of the *Jervis Bay* and the dogged triumph of the *San Demetrio* has obscured the gallantry of others, most notably perhaps, that of Olander and his crew, and of Pettigrew of the *Beaverford*.

Although the first convoy had sailed from Gibraltar the day before war started, the convoy system was constantly evolving as the enemy threat altered, in terms of both tactics and strategy, especially as the extended areas of U-boat operations would reach westwards as far as the Caribbean and southwards to the Cape of Good Hope and beyond. German commerce-raiders operated in the Atlantic, Indian, Pacific and Southern Oceans, while after December 1941, Japanese warships fell upon British and Allied merchantmen in the Far East.

Although there would be many supplementary arrangements feeding the main ocean convoys, the principal routes established in 1939 were: homeward from Gibraltar (HG) and Sierra Leone (SL); outward across the Atlantic through the North Channel (OL) or south of Ireland (OB); and down the English Channel (OA). As well as the regular coastal traffic – chiefly coal to the power stations of the south of England – east-coast convoys distributed inward deep-water shipping to places other than Liverpool, Glasgow and the Bristol Channel ports.[20] These were run between Methil on the Firth of Forth and Southend in the Thames Estuary, and coded FN and FS. All shipping in these convoys was very vulnerable to attack by destroyers, fast torpedo-armed E-boats, aircraft, the occasional U-boat in northerly waters, and mines. Later convoy routes and designations were added, reflecting the widening of the colossal struggle and there would in due course be several hundred convoy designations. The most important of these were those across the North Atlantic. The HX series left from Halifax, Nova Scotia, though they later assembled and departed from New York. The SC series began in 1941 running from Sydney, Cape Breton Island, to Britain, but later incorporated some slower convoys running from Halifax or New York. The OA series from the

Thames to Liverpool included Atlantic-bound ships and was changed in July 1940 to signify Methil to Liverpool by way of the Pentland Firth and The Minch. These, usually after joining an OB convoy, dispersed in the North Atlantic. The OB convoys were basically outward from Liverpool. From 1941, outward convoys from Liverpool for the United States were coded ON, with those bound south towards Sierra Leone coded as OS. Some convoys, particularly later in the war, were split into Fast (F) 7 or 8 knots groups, and Slow (S) 6-knot sections. Of the other convoy routes, the most notorious were those to North Russia, initiated to assist the Soviet Union after the German invasion of July 1941. These were originally coded PQ (outwards) and QP, but after the hiatus occasioned by the withdrawal of warships required for the invasion of North Africa known as Operation TORCH, they were renamed JW and RA. Finally, there were a number of fast strategic military convoys consisting of troopers and transports operating in logistical support of a campaign in progress. These received the designation of WS and were known as 'Winston's Specials'.

Although there were local convoys elsewhere in the world, the principal routes of significance in the Battle of the Atlantic were all to the northwards of Sierra Leone. Here, at Freetown, all ships bound for the South and East Africa, the Persian Gulf, India, Australasia or the Far East would disperse from convoy and make independent passages. Similarly homeward bound they would assemble at Freetown to make up a north-bound convoy. On the far side of the Atlantic Halifax, Nova Scotia, and Sydney, Cape Breton Island, provided the assembly anchorages for ships coming up from the Caribbean, many of which arrived from the Far East and Australasia via the Panama Canal. Owing to the presence of ice in the winter, soon after the United States entered the war, New York became the western assembly port.

In the early days, although a trans-Atlantic convoy would have stationed within it an elderly *R*-class battleship or an AMC for fear of a commerce raider – as was the case with HX84 – anti-submarine escorts did not have the range to cross the Western Ocean. Instead the escort would break off once the convoy was beyond the 'danger-zone', and meet an incoming convoy. The vastly extended increased range of the U-boats after the fall of France and Norway endangered a convoy throughout its passage and this problem was eventually solved by the participation of escort groups from the Royal Canadian Navy, and later of the United States Navy. These groups would transfer their responsibilities at 'Mid-Ocean Meeting Points,' handing over east and west-bound convoys and occasionally refuelling at sea when conditions allowed. Such arrangements necessitated the most complex planning, managed insofar as the warships were concerned, by the Commander-in-Chief, Western Approaches, in Derby House, Liverpool, and his opposite numbers across the Atlantic in Halifax and New York.

Thanks to the discipline inherent in an efficient armed service the Royal Navy was eventually able to capitalise upon its experience and, with more and better-equipped convoy escorts was, with its fellow Allied Canadian and American navies together with air support from Coastal Command and the USAAF, able to dominate and eventually defeat the enemy. There was a corresponding struggle to organise merchant shipping in its vital work which also changed over time and has received scant attention from historians. British merchant shipping, supported to some extent by chartered neutral ships had several tasks to fulfil. Underlying the war effort at sea was the need to keep regular commerce going. Britain's economic life had to go on, to maintain the nation's livelihood, to feed, clothe and maintain her population. Clearly this normality was hugely disrupted by war – by enemy air raids, by the drain of manpower into the forces, and by the military demands of the nation itself – but the war actually increased the necessity to maintain a level of trade to earn the wherewithal to prosecute it.

To this has to be added the actual progress of the war and its effect upon the nation's day-to-day ability to fight it. The very success of convoy, flawed though it was, presented huge complication to port operations. Most of the ports lacked investment in modern equipment owing to the Depression and the general opposition of the trade unions to modernisation. The intransigence of dock workers took little notion of the circumstances of war and strikes over conditions continued, to the embittered astonishment of many merchant seamen whose lives had been at risk and who, while they might have joined the dockers in peace-time, deeply resented what they regarded as a privilege in war. But these disputatious disruptions were relatively minor compared with the congestion occurring in many ports when large convoys arrived with numerous ships clamouring for cargo-handling facilities. This not only strained the port itself, but often congested its hinterland's infrastructure of road and rail.

This was made even more complicated by enemy air raids which destroyed dockside cranes, graving-docks, warehouses and the homes of dock labourers, sank ships alongside, blocking berths for months, filled the docks with debris and generally disrupted a system that, in peace-time prosperity was seething with action. Much road transport was still by horse-and-cart while cargo-handling itself, with the exception of bulk cargoes such as oil, grain and ores for which special terminals or facilities were available, was by hand, sling after sling. To this disturbed normality now had to be added the imperatives of war: the additional movement of war-supplies, both inward and outward in support of forces on foreign duties: ammunition, stores, food, equipment, guns, vehicles, tanks and all those items indispensable to an army on campaign that are collectively known as *matériel*. On top of all this, the blackout restrictions prevented any cargo-work at night, delaying matters further.

Almost the only easement was in the reduction of passenger numbers – though this was by no means total – which enabled disciplined troops to move with comparable rapidity through passenger terminals, but all ships, whether humble tramps discharging phosphates, or liners embarking a Guards brigade, also needed their own replenishment of fuel, food and stores to which the movements of their crews, the regulating processes of signing-on and off, of clearing inwards and outwards and customs formalities still had to be carried out.

This dispersal of goods, loading of cargoes of exports or the inward movement of *matériel* often caused confusion, not least insofar as prioritisation was concerned. Thus, up to the point that a ship left her berth to head for her convoy assembly anchorage and thereby came under the Naval Control of Shipping, she was liable to be affected by the competing demands of her inward cargo consignees, her outward cargo shippers, her owners or their agents, the War Office in the form of transport officers, and the port authority. The state was also represented by HM Customs & Excise, the Board of Trade in its peace-time regulating capacity and the Ministry of Shipping which functioned as the Government's agent responsible for merchant shipping. Third Mate William Mutimer of J&C Harrison's tramp *Harlesden* recalled a row between his owners' marine superintendent and a Board of Trade surveyor over rust holes in a lifeboat's buoyancy tanks. The former wanted the defect overlooked in the hurry to get the ship to sea, Mutimer sided with the latter, against his company's interests but in light of what might happen to the *Harlesden*.

The revival of the Ministry of Shipping which had proved its worth in the First World War now produced mixed results. One aspect of the Ministry's work which must be accorded a success was its moderation of the obscene profits that the shipowners had enjoyed during the First World War. Within a few weeks of hostilities, a licensing system was in place and freight-rates were controlled. Early in 1941 requisitioning was enforced and all British-owned ships were taken on Government charter, with rates adjusted to allow the owners a profit of 5 per cent on the agreed value of the vessel, plus a 5 per cent allowance for depreciation. These strictures curbed excess earnings in Britain, where the controlled freight-rate was less than neutral shipping might earn, but there were neutral owners who cashed in.[21] These differentials shrank as the war progressed and neutral shipping became increasingly integrated in the overall Allied convoy system. In this first phase of the war merchant ships therefore remained largely under the management of their owners, unless directly requisitioned by the Admiralty as described earlier. Otherwise, liners continued functioning through their broking agents while most tramps were allocated by the Ministry to liner operators to avoid the fluctuating vicissitudes of the disrupted commodity exchanges. All management fees were to be at cost and devoid of profit. In order to answer other military demands the Ministry chartered ships itself. Since the management of the Ministry consisted of shipowners supported by civil servants and members of their own co-opted staff, this was effected with reasonable efficiency, but the country's overall system of transportation, complicated enough in peace-time, was ground down by the excoriations of war. Delays, disruptions and prevarications prevailed and by the summer of 1941, when Churchill had been in office as Prime Minister for a year, its effects impinged upon Whitehall.

In July the Germans invaded Russia, turning upon their former allies with whom they had carved up Poland. Despite the ideological gulf existing between Churchill and the Soviet Union, Churchill pledged British aid and ordered the diversion of much-needed *matériel* – needed to re-equip the British army which had left its guns on the beaches of Dunkirk, and the Royal Air Force after its losses in the Battle of Britain – to help the Russians. This decision added to the load on the docks and the Merchant Navy. This was eased later in the year when America entered the war and American ships joined the Russia-bound convoys in the Icelandic assembly anchorage at Hvalfjord from which they proceeded to Archangel or Murmansk, but the upsurge in the shipping of military equipment had called forth a solution from Churchill himself and this solution arose from his wilderness years of penury.

Back in 1929 Winston Churchill had been out of office and in straightened circumstances, a situation he sought to remedy by expanding his literary work. By maintaining unofficial contacts with members of the Foreign Office and the secret services he was able to monitor, cajole, admonish and warn of the dangers of German rearmament and the ambitions of the Nazi Party under Hitler, but his lack of income hampered him. Fortunately, on 17 July 1929, James Mackay, the Earl of Inchcape and

Chairman of the immense Peninsular & Oriental Shipping Group, offered Churchill two directorships in two P&O subsidiaries. Both were in firms under the over-arching Group subsidiary of William Cory & Co. specialising in transport, coal and oil bunkering. The total salary Inchcape offered was £1,000 per annum but in consequence of this Churchill came into contact with Frederick Leathers. Leathers had been born in Stepney, the son of an impoverished carpenter who died in Leathers' infancy. At the age of fifteen he had joined the Steamship Owners Coal Association which acquired coal for ship's bunkers and had been bought in 1913 by William Cory & Co., a Thames lighterage firm. Leathers' managerial abilities were outstanding and he was invited to join the Cory board, becoming joint managing director before the end of the war and securing interests in other companies either dealing in coal or shipping services. Leathers' expertise was conspicuous and during the First World War he was called upon to advise the Ministry of Shipping on port operations. In 1920 Cory & Co. were involved in a joint venture with a P&O subsidiary running the Mercantile Lighterage Co. By 1928 Leathers was deputy chairman of Cory & Co. and developed alongside the firm's coal-bunkering, a strong business in the supply of oil-fuel. Here too, he met a new director, Winston Churchill, who for eight years regularly attended monthly board meetings of the two Cory subsidiaries at which, Churchill afterward recorded, 'I gradually became aware of a very remarkable man. He presided over thirty or forty companies …'. Churchill 'soon perceived that Frederick Leathers was the central brain and controlling power of this combination. He knew everything and commanded absolute confidence.'

On the outbreak of war Leathers volunteered his services to the Ministry of Shipping but by May 1941, amid 'the stresses of the Battle of the Atlantic, and with the need for combining the management of our shipping with all the movements of our supplies by rail and road from our harried ports,' Churchill wrote afterwards, 'he came more and more into my mind. On 8 May I turned to him.' The Ministries of Shipping and Transport were amalgamated into 'one integral machine'. Leathers was made Minister of War Transport and, to give him full authority and put him out of the reach of meddling intriguers from other ministries,[22] Churchill made a special submission to the Crown 'that a peerage should be conferred upon him'. Lord Leathers took his title from Purfleet, where the Steamship Owners Coal Association had given him his start in life before turning his formidable intellect onto the multifarious problems confronting the country. His experience in the First World War helped, but so did his selection of his key men. He appointed William Currie of P&O to head the Liner Division, Basil Sanderson of Shaw, Savill & Albion to direct the Port and Transit Control Division, and Ernest Murrant of Furness, Withy to act as the Ministry's Middle East Representative and Special Advisor – a crucial task in respect of Britain's war in the Middle East, Malta and the eastern Mediterranean. In this he was assisted by others, including I.M. Hooper from the General Steam Navigation Co. who had served as a commissioned officer in the RNVR. Early in 1943 Hooper was attached to the Cairo Planning Staff preparing for the invasion of Sicily. Later he was, with one of the company's masters, Captain L.H.J. Thompson, the Director of Sea Transport's representative in Algiers and both men moved to Caserta in 1944 working on plans for Operation ANVIL, the invasion of southern France. This demonstrates both the integral importance of merchant

shipping to these military operations and the vital part of the MoWT. Among other
luminaries at the MoWT in London was the brilliant Charles Wurtzburg who had
headed Mansfields, the Blue Funnel agents in Singapore, and had run the cargo-feeding
Straits Steamship Co. In 1937 Wurtzburg, with his knowledge of cargo-liner operations, agency work and the inter-relationship of complementary shipping services, had
moved to London to become Managing Director of Glen Line.[23]

The MoWT's duties and responsibilities were vast and complex. In addition to supporting the military ambitions of the Allies, by ensuring the aircraft, guns, tanks and
vehicles arriving from America were received by the specified units expecting them,
it had to ensure a smooth flow of the necessary raw materials arriving for the munitions factories, and tend to the mundane but absolutely vital business of feeding the
people and keeping those other industries going upon which the economic life of
the nation depended. The MoWT had many divisions, of which two have been mentioned and a third, the Sea Transport Division, alluded to. One of the most important
in the matter of ensuring food was available was the Coasting and Short-Sea Division.
With the south coast ports closed to deep-water shipping and the east coast ports,
particularly London, vulnerable to air raids and difficult of access owing to the exposure of the east-coast convoy route, most deep-sea ships discharged and loaded on the
Mersey or the Clyde. A few went north-about to the ports on Scotland's east coast,
and fewer still joined east coast convoys at Methil and ventured further south, but
the risks they ran in so doing tended to dissuade the MoWT from over-use of this.[24]
Cargoes were trans-shipped into smaller coasters and short-sea cargo vessels of several
types, which also relieved the considerable congestion on the railways.

Sam Brown's grisaille of the Mersey shows the variety of shipping in the 1930s. A new,
outward-bound motor vessel is casting off her tug as she passes a small brigantine towing to
sea in the charge of a tug. A Mersey 'flat' is in the background and two ferries pass between
the shipping. (© Courtesy of The British Mercantile Marine Memorial Collection)

An important feature of such cargo was the distribution of frozen meat from Liverpool and the Firth of Clyde to London. In addition, over 200,000 tons of seed potatoes were so distributed. The cross-channel service to Ireland had to be maintained. A special problem of the [Coasting and Short-Sea] Division was the importation from Ireland of live cattle, which usually amounted to 10,000 head per week. In one period there were 24,000 a week. There was a shortage of suitable ships, and they had to be turned round with the least possible delay. These ships also supplied milk from Northern Ireland to Glasgow. Special ships were laid down for the purpose. It was the duty of the Division to be ready at a moment's notice to fulfil all requirements.[25]

British operations in the Middle East, and the Western Desert in particular, relied upon Murrant's Middle East Supply Centre in Egypt, effectively an outpost of the MoWT's Sea Transport Division. This handled all movements of troops, whether the regular reinforcements, such as WS Convoys taking soldiers to join the Eighth Army, or for special operations, such as Operations HUSKY and ANVIL. It is unnecessary to emphasise its importance in the formulation of the plans for such mighty endeavours, the complexities of which stagger the imagination of a later age, but under Sir Ralph Metcalfe the detailed schedules for Operation NEPTUNE, the maritime component of OVERLORD, better known as D-Day, were painstakingly worked out. For this, the expertise of men with mercantile experience was vital, for the first of the two great anxieties of the naval staff in overall responsibility, was the large numbers of large landing craft which had to be turned around rapidly if the momentum of attack was to be sustained sufficiently to crush the German defences before they, with much easier terrestrial communications, called-up reinforcements; and the second was the handling of the many hundreds of merchantmen which would be involved, particularly once the Mulberry Harbour was operational off Arromanches. In order to achieve this, a number of units were established at key points, known as TURCO – or Turn-Around Control, whose personnel were drawn from the MoWT.[26]

But this is to anticipate; all lay in the future as Leathers assembled his key men and their respective staffs in the Ministry of War Transport's headquarters in Berkeley Square. Ronald Hope succinctly outlines some of the demands placed upon the new Ministry and the Merchant Navy it controlled in 'the worst year of the war,' which opened just three weeks after Japan – which had spent the previous ten years securing her hold over much of eastern Asia – attacked the United States naval base at Pearl Harbor.

During 1942 Britain was trying to supply nitrates to Egypt, coal to east Africa, Arabia and Ceylon, phosphates to South Africa, Australia and New Zealand, armaments and other equipment to Russia, and food grains to East Africa, India and Ceylon. Burmese supplies of rice to India had been cut off by the Japanese invasion of that country. All these cargoes, which make heavy demands on shipping, needed to be moved at a time when ship losses were at their peak. British losses in the first quarter of 1942 were double what they had been in the last quarter of 1941 and went on rising throughout the year. A thousand British and British-controlled ships were lost in 1942 and for the first time in the war the British-controlled merchant fleet began to fall steadily. Through its control of all merchant ships the Ministry of War Transport was able to make effective use of space by loading both military and civil cargoes in the same ships, and it economised in the use of space by devising new stowage techniques. By March 1943 the Ministry had organised the transport of over a quarter of a million British troops and their equipment to North Africa alone. But there were conflicts over the use of shipping, both in European waters and in the Far East. There were many narrow squeaks and some failures. Many people throughout the world, including of course the United Kingdom, went without things to which they were accustomed. The United Kingdom was forced to run down its capital equipment because proper maintenance was impossible. In India there was starvation: severe food shortages in Southern India and famine in Bengal led in the summer of 1943 to the deaths of 1.5 million people.[27]

As soon as Leathers had made his genius felt, matters showed a marked improvement. According to Churchill, he quickly 'won the confidence of the Chiefs of Staff and of all departments at home, and established intimate and excellent relationships with the leading American in this vital sphere ...' especially Lewis Douglas of the United States Shipping Board, and later American ambassador in London. Leathers's initiative was able to make difficulties 'disappear as if by magic,' Churchill recalled.[28] This was not merely timely, it was essential. Though remaining neutral, the United States was taking measures to protect shipping in the Western Atlantic and on 1 May President Roosevelt issued a directive raising hopes in London that assistance from American merchant shipping would ease the position in the North Atlantic. This early optimism was disappointed by obstructions from the United States Navy, chiefly emanating from Fleet Admiral Ernest King, and ineffective administration in American government agencies. Leathers

> played an absolutely essential role at the highest level of Government, not so much in forming strategy as providing the capability for implementing it successfully. In general, it is realised the British Chiefs of Staff were of an extremely high calibre, particularly Alanbrooke. Even after the entry of the USA into the conflict, the inter-service squabbling and occasional Anglophobic tendencies of some members of the American administration, tended to blunt the efficiency of their 'managing' abilities. Lewis Douglas, Leathers's opposite number in the United States and his London representative, Averill Harriman, were 'deeply impressed' with British civilian control of wartime shipping and civil/military co-operation, in sharp contrast with the USA. Thus we have the paradox of overwhelming economic and manufacturing efficiency with poor strategic management in the United States, contrasted with battered, strained and inefficient manufacturing capabilities, with excellent strategic thinking and implementation in the United Kingdom.[29]

Although American assistance was about to improve dramatically owing to Lend-Lease and the more active presence of her warships in the Western Atlantic, in the months prior to Pearl Harbor the lack of hard currency in Britain prevented full advantage being taken of chartering shipping for the shortest route across the Atlantic from the United States. Even after the entry of America into the war the increased attrition in the Atlantic and the effects on shipping and supplies caused by Japanese aggression in the Far East, made heavy demands upon Leathers and his Ministry. At the end of 1942 he complained of the diversion of American resources to the Pacific theatre, particularly of merchant shipping rolling out of the new shipyards. Nor could the United States Navy provide its quota of escorts for the next Russian convoy. Despite the participation of American warships, this operation was under British naval operational control but the American navy had witnessed what appeared to be gross mismanagement by the Admiralty, resulting in the butchery of Convoy PQ17 that July, circumstances that seemed to justify Ernest King's intense dislike of the British navy.

Lord Leathers, in Washington with the British Merchant Shipping Mission, tirelessly tried to persuade the Americans of the need for a redistribution of Allied shipping resources in proportion to the requirements of the varying operational theatres, along with the supply route to Britain. While these problems were never fully resolved, the principle was accepted and matters finally improved towards the end of 1943, so that advantage could be taken of the Allied naval ascendancy secured that spring. This, although subsequently seriously threatened, was never thereafter relinquished and the consequent combined operations that culminated in D-Day therefore became possible.[30]

As touched upon earlier, merchant shipping was absolutely essential to the success of the combined operations in North Africa, Sicily and Italy, and the vital opening phase of the invasion begun on D-Day, 6 June 1944. During 1943, Leathers attended the conferences at Casablanca, Washington, Quebec and Cairo convened to determine Allied strategy. Failures in consultation over shipping at Casablanca endangered the success of subsequent operations, chiefly the invasion of Sicily, as they exceeded the carrying capacity of the available tonnage. Thereafter Leathers was taken more fully into consultation. One of his objectives at the Joint Chiefs-of-Staff meeting in Washington in January 1941 was to secure two hundred American-built standardships on bare-boat charter to overcome the scheduling difficulties arising from the then standard practice of chartering on a voyage-by-voyage basis. To facilitate this, it was pointed out that the Americans had a shortage of seamen, whereas, owing to its losses, Britain had a surplus, an argument that won over President Roosevelt. Leathers learned of this decision on the eve of his return to Britain.[31]

In September 1940 Dönitz had deployed his first wolf-pack, a small group of U-boats vectored onto a convoy to attack simultaneously; they achieved immediate success with seven ships sunk out of forty-seven and the dispersal of the convoy, HX72.[32] The rising tempo of the war in the Atlantic had been signalled a few days earlier with an attack on Convoy SC3 and then the outward and dispersed ships of OB213, raising the curtain upon what the U-boat crews would later call *Die glückliche Zeit*: the Happy Time. Amid the carnage, the *City of Benares* was torpedoed. Besides having Commodore E.J.G. Mackinnon, a retired rear admiral, and a number of adult passengers on board, the *City of Benares* was carrying a large number of children bound for Canada. So strong was the fear of aerial bombardment in Britain that the wholesale despatch of children was thought desirable and, under Government auspices and with specially recruited adults to attend them, the second shipment of evacuees had embarked in the Ellerman City liner. The first wave had left a few weeks earlier aboard the Dutch liner *Volendam* and she too had been torpedoed, though she had been kept afloat and towed into safety with no loss of life.[33] Despite this near catastrophe, the *City of Benares*, Captain L. Nicoll, was suffered to depart in convoy and when thought to be clear of the danger zone, the escort had been dismissed and the merchantmen dispersed to proceed independently to their destinations.

The previous month Captain Bone, transferred to the *Cameronia*, had sailed from the Clyde on 14 August and had proceeded independently from the start. For several voyages his ship had been carrying large numbers of German nationals, mostly Jewish refugees escaping persecution by the Nazis. On this occasion, however, she carried young children sent to Canada and the United States by anxious parents so that Bone's 'little argonauts' were not therefore embarked under any Government scheme. Bone had already carried a large consignment of bullion, belonging to the Polish government-in-exile but: 'The transport of over four hundred young children in a ship would have been a matter for grave consideration at any time, but … such an embarkation in time of war was an almost unbearable charge upon all those responsible for their safety … I would confess this voyage the most wearying and anxious of all my days at sea.' The 'seavacuees' were not amenable to discipline and, despite the presence of 'wardens', the ship's staff were at their wits end when, for the third time, Bone tried to hold a boat drill.

> It proved a long and tiresome business punctuated by tears and outcry and fits of temper. Inevitably, lifebelts were lost or mislaid and had to be replaced, children … disappeared, straggled, fidgeted on the chalked deck spaces beside the ship's out-swung life-boats: the adult passengers who were not directly connected with the seavacuees objected to long standing at stations but, as moral support, could not singly be dismissed: there was, throughout, the shouted call and counter-call from one group to another, the sudden dart from place and the shrill demand for the same standing-room on return; there was argument, near quarrel – indeed, a scrap or two developed over some points of preferment. But at length there had come some shade of attention … Even the almost despairing but indefatigable Mr Squires, the Chief Officer, had the look of one who had achieved something when at last he came to report progress. Throughout all … [t]he babies in their cots and prams were sleeping peacefully for it was summer and the day was warm.[34]

Bone's unhurried description of a practise drill leads the imagination to the horrors of a night-time torpedo strike against the *City of Benares* and the terror of evacuating such an apparently indestructibly large artefact as a passenger liner 'in a rough sea and a heavy swell'. When the torpedo hit the vessel 'The ship shuddered and the lights went out …'. In the ensuing tragedy it is incredible that anybody survived. One hundred and five survivors were rescued by HM Destroyer *Hurricane* and a further forty-two in No. 12 Boat under Fourth Officer Ronald Cooper, assisted by Miss Mary Cornish, a 'warden', were adrift for eight days before being picked up by the destroyer *Anthony*. Captain Nicoll, Commodore Mackinnon, all three of his signals staff, 121 crew and fifty-five adult passengers and seventy-seven children were killed by Kapitänleutnant Heinrich Bleichrodt's attack in *U-48*.[35]

But, tragic though it was, the *City of Benares* was not the only ship lost that night. Cooper had come across a lifeboat from the *Marina*, Captain Richard Payne, who was afterwards awarded the George Medal and Lloyd's War Medal for bravery at sea. Combined, the tonnages of both ships were but a fraction of the losses that summer and early autumn. In May thirty-one British, Allied and neutral merchantmen had been destroyed, amounting to 82,429 gross registered tons; in June this rose to sixty-one ships, grossing 282,560 tons; in July sixty-four, grossing 271,056 tons; in August fifty-six at 278,323 tons and in September sixty-two at 324,030 tons, among the largest monthly totals of the war.

The news of the sinking of the *City of Benares* reached Glasgow hours before the departure of the *City of Simla* which was due to leave for Capetown and Bombay. She too had embarked a number of evacuees who had trooped aboard with labels round their necks and were swiftly put ashore when the news was heard, leaving 167 passengers, including a number of children travelling with parents. Among these was six-year-old Maureen Cleave, who recalled the departing evacuees and the refusal of Captain Herbert Percival to countenance their carriage. Once clear of the Clyde a muster was held and life-belts were tried on, after which Mrs Cleave insisted her daughters turned-in wearing shoes, a wise precaution in the event. The *City of Simla* sailed in Convoy OB216 consisting of twenty-seven ships and which was ambushed by *U-138* when fifty-two-miles north-west of Rathlin Island on the late evening of 20 September 1940. Oberleutnant Wolfgang Lüth successfully torpedoed three ships. The *New Sevilla*, owned by Christian Salvesen & Co. of Leith and under Captain Richard Chisholm, killing the three men on watch in the engine and boiler rooms. She was a whale-factory ship being used as an oil tanker and had a huge crew of 281 souls. Lüth's second victim was the coal-laden *Boka* of Panama in which eight died, and his third the *Empire Adventure*, Captain Thomas Phinn. She had been the Italian *Andrea*, renamed after her seizure in Newcastle when Mussolini declared war, and placed by the MoWT under the management of Walter Runciman & Co. Twenty-one of her crew were lost, her survivors being rescued by the Swedish *Industria*, while other survivors from all three ships were picked up by the convoy's escorts. The *New Sevilla* and *Empire Adventure* were both damaged and taken in tow by HM Rescue tugs, but both sank before they could be brought into a safe haven.

At about 02.00 on the 21st, Lüth had made a second attack and torpedoed the *City of Simla*. Miss Cleave recalled the thump of the explosion and, in her pyjamas, dressing gown and shoes, being piggy-backed by her mother who at the same time carried her younger sister. She then descended a rope ladder to squeeze into a lifeboat holding eighty-nine people. More fascinated than frightened by the 'big waves' by which they were surrounded, they remained adrift for about eight hours, sustained by the singing, among other songs, of *It's a long way to Tipperary* accompanied by a mouth organ. They were rescued by the United Africa Co.'s *Guinean*, which loomed alongside, her crew throwing ladders, nets and lines over her side. Miss Cleave remembered her sister being hoisted up in a bowline, sustaining a blow to her head against the ship's side, while she herself scrambled up a rope ladder. They were later transferred to the destroyer *Vanquisher*, which landed them at Londonderry. Remarkably, only one member of the Ellerman liner's 182-strong crew and two passengers lost their lives.

Dönitz's offensive reached a culminating point in October, when Convoy SC7, composed of thirty-four ships, lost seventeen to a large wolf-pack.[36] It was clear to Lord Leathers at the MoWT that replacement of tonnage was a priority, so much so that victory would soon be down to the chillingly simple necessity to build, man and freight more ships than the enemy could sink. To that end more ships were required. The British merchant fleet had benefited in tonnage from a small number of captures and seizures of German and Italian ships on the high seas and in British and Commonwealth ports. Like the *Empire Adventure*, these war prizes had all been renamed, beginning with '*Empire* …' and handed over to the management of commercial companies with experience of the type of vessel and in some recompense to ships they had in turn lost to the enemy. The MoWT, retained ownership and usually loaded such ships with cargoes of war *matériel* of one sort or another.[37] While few British ships had been interned on the outbreak of war, the German invasion of the Low Countries, France, Denmark, Norway and Greece found a large number of these countries' ships in British imperial ports where most of their crews opted for exile, the major exception being France. Some French ships remained either manned by Free French after De Gaulle had raised the cross of Lorraine, or were left to British management, their crews returning home. Many Danish and Greek ships' companies elected not to return to an occupied country and were integrated into the British system, coming under the Admiralty's control, their freighting being handled by their various shipping agencies. The greatest contribution came from the Norwegian government which, in going into exile in Great Britain, ordered all Norwegian merchantmen in foreign waters or on the high seas to make for ports controlled by the British and to place themselves under British orders. The Dutch government, also arriving in London, did much the same and these countries established state agencies to attend to the requirements of the exiled merchant seafarers, both in Britain and abroad, particularly in New York. There were several significant aspects of this, perhaps the chief being the large number of tankers that thus came under British control thanks to the acumen of modest Norwegian investors mentioned earlier. A second advantage was obtained from the fact that Norwegian merchant masters and officers had had naval experience and thus integrated easily into the convoy system, while the Norwegians, Danes and Dutch had sizeable fleets of vessels engaged in distant cross trades or, as was the case with the Dutch, a virtual second merchant fleet in the Dutch East Indies. The Greek merchant fleet was large and possessed numerous tramp-ships, many of which enjoyed a close relationship with Britain, where many Greek owners registered their tonnage and were only too happy to charter their ships to the British Government. Finally, since English was the recognised international language of the sea, the masters and mates of all nations were competent in its use insofar as their professional requirements were concerned.

Despite this augmentation of the ships at his disposal, Lord Leathers was aware that he had no margin for complacency. By the end of 1940 it was clear that provision had to be made for greater state control over many more ships, hence his representations at the Washington meeting of the Joint Chiefs-of-Staff in January 1941 for 200 new bottoms. There was more to Leathers' anxiety than simply making good the losses of shipping. While the Royal Navy had yet to develop and perfect its anti-submarine tactics, it was keen to emphasise the deficiencies in its charges. There is more evidence of the difficulties experienced by convoy escort commanders and their subordinates in herding their sheep, than complaints about ineffective convoy defence, chiefly because the former was reported by means of official naval channels, while the latter were private submissions to owners. However, owing to the many shipowners with representatives in the MoWT the matter was not overlooked.

At the heart of the complaints about the poor station-keeping of merchantmen, the low speeds and indifferent firing of boilers which resulted in smoking, lay a number of factors, the chief of which was old age of many of the tramps bringing bulk cargoes across the Atlantic. Many of these were simply worn-out, some having been constructed before 1914; many more were ships built in the United States under the Emergency shipbuilding programmes of the previous World War, others had never been designed for anything other than a slow economic speed, and all had suffered from a measure of neglect owing to the Depression. Such old low-powered vessels – and it was these that caused the naval escorts such headaches – were not fitted with sophisticated engine speed control, making station-keeping extremely difficult in bad weather, especially when a vessel was 'flying light' in ballast, or only partially loaded as occurred on outward passages from Britain. Since these were not infrequently conducted in the teeth of westerly or south westerly gales, holding such vessels in any sort of order became all but impossible. As to boiler-firing in such ships, all of which were coal-fired, the anxieties of the escort commanders over the making of smoke – the most conspicuous indicator of a convoy's presence to a distant surfaced U-boat – were understandable, but the condemnations of inefficiency took little heed over the frequent poor quality of the coal supplied. The worst in quality, known as 'Natal steam coal' which was said to 'glow red then turn to ash without giving heat', actually came from the Rhodesian (Zimbabwean) mines near Wankie, a name inviting seamanlike comment.[38]

However, the problem of ageing tonnage could exacerbate smoke-making and prove expensively embarrassing. Having himself passed the official age of retirement, it fell to Captain David Bone, quondam Commodore of the Anchor Line, to nurse a number of ships which ought in all justice to have been superannuated. These were elderly liners required for trooping, the first of which was the *Nea Hellas* which had been sold to Greek owners in 1936. Bone himself had commanded her ten years earlier when she had been the *Tuscania* and she had been returned to the British flag when Greece was invaded by Axis forces. As part of a large, fast troop convoy carrying reinforcements to the 8th Army in the Western Desert, Bone found her unable to proceed without making embarrassing quantities of thick, black smoke, a fact which endeared neither Bone nor his ship to the convoy Commodore. On arrival at Freetown Chief Engineer James Spencer ordered his firemen to clear the neglected boiler-tubes. Bone paced the boat-deck high above. '[A]s I passed and re-passed the stokehold ventilators [stout Clydeside voices] gave me assurance … my shoes *crunched* upon the mounting layers of boiler-tube sediment that was being blown upward through the tall funnel from her hardening arteries'.

But fate had worse in store for the patient Bone. He was sent to Philadelphia to takeover the USS *Catlin* as a British troop-ship. She had been built in 1908 for the

Hamburg-Amerika Linie and when the United States entered the First World War, she had been in New York where her crew had sabotaged her boilers before the ship was seized. With these patched-up she served the Americans as a trooper, thereafter joining the Reserve Fleet until the Second World War brought her out of retirement to be sold to the British in their hour of desperate need under the name *George Washington*. Bone's misgivings on joining her in November 1941 were not misplaced. To his horror she was a coal-burner and he had no great love of the unruly firemen necessary to feed her crapulous Scotch boilers. He was in for worse shocks. The first of these was that the ship had a set of reconditioned water-tube boilers assigned to her and lying in the Philadelphia Navy Yard. Unfortunately the expense of acquiring and fitting them was beyond the MoWT's purse, so the idea was dropped. Nevertheless, the US Navy assisted Bone, a foreign merchant ship-master, until Sunday 7 December, when the unprovoked Japanese attack on Pearl Harbor changed everything. Anxious to disencumber themselves of the huge ship, the Americans pressed Bone to depart. His crew had been mustered and held in Nova Scotia and they were now brought south. To his horror Bone discovered the quality of his firemen. Though he never mentions it in his memoirs they were largely drawn from Barlinnie Gaol and he thought it necessary, in case of trouble, to ship a small contingent of British naval ratings from a co-operative Captain Drew whose cruiser, HMS *Manchester*, was undergoing the repair of battle damage in the American Navy Yard.

On the short passage north to New York from the Virginia Capes the recalcitrant boilers demonstrated their defects and further repair was under-taken under the local director of the MoWT, Mr Philip Rees, at a New York shipyard. The boilers were seamed with welds before the *George Washington* proceeded to Halifax where 4,110 Canadian soldiers were embarked and Bone himself was appointed convoy Commodore. With all preparations in hand and the convoy conference held, the ships were to weigh from Bedford Basin on 2 February 1942. As the *George Washington* began to move, her boilers failed and she lay immobilised for weeks, her troops being moved to other ships in succeeding convoys until, in due course, she staggered back to New York to be returned to the US Maritime Commission. Later, in the following year, Bone saw her in Bombay, trooping under the Stars and Stripes, fitted with the water-tube boilers intended for her in the first place.

This extreme example indicates the extent to which desperation drove the British in their search for tonnage.[39] The co-operation of Captain Drew is evidence of the professional co-operation that could exist between officers of the Royal Navy and the mercantile marine, but the presence of smoking or slow merchantmen in any convoy was a frustrating circumstance which caused anger to all parties, but which excited naval remonstrance most conspicuously since the merchant personnel involved were seen, largely unjustly, as part of the problem.

Leaving until the following chapter the cultural chasm which existed between the two sea services of the British Empire, the upshot of this corrosive stream of complaint and the dire situation developing in the North Atlantic persuaded Lord Leathers that it was essential to cover the losses to be anticipated from sustained and effective submarine warfare by the Germans by replacing as much as possible of the older tonnage. This was a tall order but Leathers was the man to perceive a means by which it might become reality. In the mid-1930s the United States merchant fleet had been in no better a condition than the British, despite the construction of some 2,500 standard ships in the First World War. Between 1922 and 1937 only two large bulk dry-cargo ships were built in American yards, although twenty-nine passenger-cargo liners and a number of tankers had been constructed under an earlier Merchant Marine Act of 1929. As in other maritime nations emerging from the prolonged Depression, moves to rebuild the national fleet after years of neglect led to Congress passing the Merchant Marine Act of 1936. This stated the need for 'a new, modern and efficient merchant marine' which 'should be capable of serving as naval or military in time of war or national emergency'. The consequently formed United States Maritime Commission was to be the authority under which this revival was to take place, and it was spurred by the realisation that another European war was increasingly likely to seriously disrupt global trading patterns and that, even if the USA remained in isolation, this would potentially disadvantage the growth of the American economy.

In America at this time there were only ten shipyards and forty-six slipways capable of producing a hull of the 400ft required for an ocean-going ship capable of lifting 10,000 tons. The Commission intended to implement a ten-year plan which would produce fifty standard vessels a year consisting of three types of freighter and a high-speed oil tanker. These could be tailored to individual company specifications if this did not compromise the simple standard production method. The situation in Europe accelerated the original schedule, doubling it in the summer of 1939, then doubling it again in August 1940. By this time the steam-turbine-powered 'C'-Type freighter produced by the Commission's nineteen contracted shipyards had proved their worth, one crossing the Atlantic at 17 knots. Then, in November 1940, the first of the Commission's all-welded hulls rolled down the ways with a saving of 500 tons in weight, labour, time and materials.[40]

Nevertheless, when the first British Shipping Mission visited the United States in September 1940 the bulk of the American merchant fleet, both privately owned and in the Government's reserve Fleet, remained in excess of twenty years old. The Mission was led by Cyril Thompson, managing director of the Sunderland shipbuilding firm of Joseph L. Thompson & Sons, who took with him the plans of the *Dorrington Court*, built for the Court Line in 1939. Joseph L. Thompson & Sons had, uniquely among British shipyards, utilised the lack of orders caused by the Depression to modernise their yard on the River Wear. As the economic gloom lifted they were in a position to take advantage of contracts for new ships for such customers as Furness, Withy and the Silver Line, to whom Cyril Thompson was an advisor.

Utilising the new technique of partial prefabrication and unitised construction which greatly reduced costs and sped up building time which they had pioneered, Thompsons were in the vanguard of the new developments that would shortly transform merchant ship construction. In 1935 they had built the *Embassage* for Hall Brothers of Newcastle-upon-Tyne, a 9,300-ton coal-burning bulk carrying tramp and she was followed by two dozen sister-ships. This innovative initiative on the part of Thompson had attracted the attention of Frederick Leathers even before he was raised to his new position by Churchill, and it was to this basic design that Leathers advised the then Minister of Shipping to turn when confronted with the mounting losses in the Battle of the Atlantic. A modified hull measuring 7,157 gross tons and capable of a cargo of 10,000 tons deadweight was built for the Ministry and launched as the *Empire Liberty*. Capable of 11 knots with a modest power plant of 2,500 indicated horsepower she was followed by a variety of 'types' not all of which were coal-burners and comprised tramp-replacements, smaller cargo-vessels and tankers. Unfortunately most British shipyards were, for geographical and historical reasons, crammed in between the workers' houses and the river and therefore incapable of expansion. They were also hampered by old-fashioned facilities and working methods, and already committed to the rapid construction of naval corvettes, urgently required for convoy escort duties in the Atlantic and deliberately conceived so as to make use of standard equipment and plant readily available for the building of small merchant ships. All this would be familiar to the new warships' largely RNR officers and easy to operate by the conscripted 'Hostilities-Only' ratings destined to man them. Whatever capacity was spare was devoted to repairing merchantmen and warships.

It was therefore almost inevitable that those responsible for replacing lost merchant tonnage would look across the Atlantic. Canada was one place where space was available and which was already in the throes of expanding her navy and building corvettes. Orders were placed by both the British and the Dominion Governments so that Canadian shipyards were soon turning out ships built to British standard designs, the *Parks* to be manned and managed by Canadians, with *Forts* for the British MoWT. But Canada was unable to fund enough ships, nor to expand her capacity to increase production to the level envisaged by Leathers and his colleagues. Cyril Thompson was therefore appointed to head the Shipping Mission which was required to persuade the Americans to undertake the construction of sixty ships to the account of the British MoWT.

Cyril Thompson's plans of the *Dorrington Court* did not impress the head of the United States' Maritime Commission, Admiral Land, who considered the design too 'simple and slow'. However, Land conceded that if the British wanted sixty ships they could have them from the new yards turning out welded ships. In consequence two contracts, each for thirty ships, were awarded to the yards of Todd Shipyards Inc. and Henry Kaiser, with additional equipment provided by a combination of engineering manufacturers known as Six Services Inc. A few months later, in January 1941, Land and his colleagues were confronted with their own failure to deliver sufficient ships in accordance with their own schedule. The pragmatic Land eventually abandoned the American plan for quality shipping in favour of the British emphasis on numbers, turning to Cyril Thompson's basic design. This was both proven and lent itself readily to the prefabrication and welding which Henry Kaiser was advocating. The Americans put their considerable weight behind the project and the first of the *Oceans, Ocean Vanguard*, American-built for British operation, was named by Mrs Land on 15 October 1941.

Meanwhile a simple American design was coming forward, capable of lifting 10,000 tons and making 10 knots. Land was sensitive to President Roosevelt's description of them as 'dreadful-looking objects', and christened them the 'Liberty fleet,' declaring 27 September as 'Liberty fleet Day' on which the first of them was to be launched. She was named *Patrick Henry* in honour of the Virginian lawyer who had raised his rebellious cry of 'Give me liberty, or give me death!' in 1775, a guying of the British.

The second Liberty-ship was launched the following day on the Pacific coast and building time was soon whittled down in the huge new shipyards that mass produced them. With the 30,000 components necessary for one vessel manufactured in thirty-two of the United States, assembly averaged some forty-two days – though one, the *Robert G. Peary*, was launched on 12 November 1942, just four days and fifteen and a half hours after the keel had been laid and was fitted out and ready to steam to sea three days later. Although never matching the American output, corresponding effort was being made in Canada, whither Cyril Thompson had gone to assist extending production after concluding negotiations in Washington. And although construction of various *Empire*-types of merchantmen continued in British yards, it better suited them to concentrate on warship-building, in particular the frigates which soon proved more successful convoy escorts than the earlier corvettes.[41]

A year after the launching of the *Patrick Henry*, as the Battle of the Atlantic approached its crisis, American shipyards were capable of despatching three Liberty-ships a day. That this was critical is illustrated by the fact that during 1942, by which time the Americans were fully committed to the war, the Western Allies – Britain, Canada and the United States – constructed 8 million tons of shipping at a time when the Axis were destroying 11 million tons. However, victory was achieved by the sustainability of the former effort and the ultimate failure of the latter.

With the American Liberty-ships named after home-grown heroes, those handed over by the MoWT to be run by British companies had names prefixed by *Sam* – not a reference to Uncle Sam, but deriving from the acronym for 'single accommodation-block amidships' differentiating them from the *Oceans*, *Parks* and *Forts* which had divided superstructures and misaligned Sampson posts to foil periscope-targetting. On 13 November 1941, after U-boat attacks on American warships, but three weeks before Japan struck at Pearl Harbor, Congress amended its Neutrality Act. All American war-built tonnage was fitted with proper armament. The gun-pits appearing on forecastle and bridge wings called for an increase on the British side in manpower of the DEMS organisation, a final abandonment of the long-since facile presumption that a merchantman was a non-combatant. The Liberty-ships and their Canadian half-sisters eventually saved the situation in the Atlantic, though there were a few that proved defective, not all the welding being of a standard to withstand a Western Ocean gale. They were to be followed by several more sophisticated freighters, the steam-turbine-powered Victory-ships, and the T2 tanker, but the overall organisation of this extraordinary programme was one of international co-operation. There were inevitably occasional hitches in the smooth, 'just-in-time' supply of components, so that when Canadian hulls were short of steam-plant, engines completed ahead of schedule in the United States were diverted north. Later, some American-built Liberty-ships incorporated Canadian parts. The whole programme initiated by Land and Thompson came to fruition in February 1942 when the American Maritime Commission was wound up, being replaced by the War Shipping Administration, run on lines similar to the British MoWT. Like their British allies, American shipowners became managing-agents of the United States government.

In the summer of 1941, a few short but desperate months before the full might of the United States fell in behind embattled Britain, Churchill realised the effects of this re-gearing of the nation's merchant fleet would take some time to bear fruit. In the meanwhile the psychological impact of the enemy's success, which was all that the merchant seafarer enduring intermittent attack by U-boats knew about, was eroding morale. Although many convoys reached port unscathed – an important point to remember, for the North Atlantic was not 'swarming with U-boats', as Dönitz wished – and many more were suffering losses in single numbers, whenever a wolf-pack made a determined assault, the Royal Navy remained powerless to help. These devastating attacks came at night, often in moonlight and were sudden, terrifying and effective.

One reason for this was that practised technicians like Korvettenkapitän Otto Kretschmer of *U-99*, had developed a tactic of remaining submerged until after the advanced escorts, of which the senior officer's ship was usually one, had passed overhead. He then surfaced inside the defensive cordon and, moving down between two advancing columns of passing merchantmen, torpedoed them at close range. If two or three U-boats could achieve this, it not only threw the cohesion of the convoy itself into confusion as ships hauled out of line to avoid a casualty ahead and thereby risked collision with their neighbour in an adjacent column, but it utterly confused the naval escort, the units of which dashed about to little effect. When the U-boats dived under the tail-end escort, the latter's sonar was barely effective in the collective turbulence caused by the propeller-races and wakes of the convoy. Since the junior corvettes were usually occupying these stations, it fell to them to pick up survivors, or standby severely damaged and sinking ships. Thus the enemy escaped, even when pursued by an ageing destroyer, commanded by a vengeful senior officer. In due course, counter-tactics were worked out and the resources to maximise them made available, but it took time and, for reasons more fully explained in the next chapter, morale in the Merchant Navy became a source of anxiety in high places.

This had been exacerbated by misperceptions and misunderstandings from the start of the war. Even peace-time British crews, with mixed nationalities in tramps and 'native' sailors and firemen in many cargo-liners, could be polyglot, but by the spring of 1940 this was made worse by the influx of exiled ex-patriate seamen from occupied countries. Anti-British agitators, particularly in United States ports, where anti-British sentiment could be found, and where rumours of sabotage also circulated, were able to unsettle these anxious men. Great Britain, they were assured, 'would fight to the last drop of Polish, Norwegian, Dutch and Danish blood'. Such rumours left men uncertain of their future wondering whether delayed-action bombs had been concealed in their cargo, aware that such things had occurred, albeit rarely, in the First World War. Intelligence suggested that the Nazis were investing in such ploys, especially in Lisbon, a neutral port full of intrigue where it was possible for Nazi agents to seduce British merchant seamen. Attempts were made by German agents to suborn members of the crew of the Yeoward liner *Avoceta* which called there regularly. German intelligence agents were eager to glean information about British shipping movements, but these met with only minimal success. It is difficult to judge what might be learned, since the information available to seafarers was limited, and indeed it was a political decision to keep merchant ships' crews generally ignorant of their movements, which played well with the prevailing culture of keeping men in the dark anyway. In fact this small passenger-cargo-liner – which would be sunk by *U-203* on 21 September 1941 when acting as the commodore's ship when Convoy HG73 was terribly mauled – had been instrumental in evacuating downed airmen or escaping British soldiers left behind after the evacuation of the British Expeditionary Force the previous year. These were passed by the Comète organisation rooted in the Belgian resistance which smuggled more than 800 service personnel and some civilians through France, Spain and into Portugal where, in Lisbon, they embarked in the *Avoceta*.

Until Germany turned on its ally, the Soviet Union, in the summer of 1941, and while both countries were carving up Poland between them, there existed among the naval staff and higher echelons of Government a paranoid conviction that Communist infiltrators determined to end British capitalism and her imperial pretensions were at work. These were fomenting unrest among merchant seamen intended to pro-voking stoppages, delays, wild-cat strikes and claims for higher war bonuses. There were indeed disturbances among some crews, not to mention the dockers. Delays were caused and a few ships failed to be ready to sail on time; there were sit-down strikes over minor differences and cases of desertion. Occasionally, there was deliber-ate damage to engines and machinery. Most such cases were drink-related and most occurred on the worst-manned, pound-and-pint tramps where it remained the case than a man's pay stopped the moment his ship was sunk. After years of unemploy-ment this old injustice remained, and would resist reform for some time yet, but the Government's reaction to this was crass: in British ports it sent in MI5 officers to investigate! In Canada, however, commonsense prevailed and the NCSOs of the Royal Canadian Navy at Halifax, moving among the ships assembling in Bedford Basin for the departure of their convoy, were more subtle. They made proactive efforts to win the confidence of the crews, developing relationships with regular traders and much of the smooth-running of the convoy system was entirely down to these men and their staffs. Being seamen themselves, they could distinguish anxiety and bragga-docio, detect resentment and sense the atmosphere in a poorly run ship. Confidential reports took time to take effect, but the close co-operation in Britain between the Admiralty's Trade Division and the ship-owning members of the Ministry of War Transport weeded out unsuitable masters, while the eventual establishment of the Merchant Navy Pool, which allocated men to individual ships on an 'as required' basis, generally worked. However, it is important to stress that the majority of mer-chant ships, whether or not manned by Liverpool-Irish crews or lascars, may have grumbled, but did their duty and did it without question.

Churchill was sensitive to this complicated situation and in July 1941 made refer-ence to the Merchant Navy in one of his speeches.

> We are a seafaring race,' he said, 'and we understand the call of the sea. We account you in these hard days worthy successors of a tradition of steadfast courage and high adventure and we are confident that the proud tradition of our island will be upheld wherever the ensign of a British merchantman is flown.

Nevertheless, the morale of the Merchant Navy was to vacillate in the coming years. It was severely damaged by the effect of the rumours, half-truths and plain misunderstandings that arose from the Admiralty order to scatter Convoy PQ17. The secrecy essential to the successful prosecution of war necessarily deprived even the wretched survivors of this catastrophe of an explanation – not that it would have given them much comfort – but the perception that the convoy had been deliberately deserted by its escort found fertile ground elsewhere. The severity of enemy attacks on several convoys, OG71 being the worst, led to a widespread belief that they were used as decoys to attract German interest while 'more important' convoys – particularly Winston's Specials – passed unscathed. Such perceptions arose from the fact the homeward QP convoys from Russia were routed south of the outward and heavily laden PQ series. Occasionally within sight of the ice-bound and precipitous coast of German-occupied Norway, many believed they were bait intended to lure the capital-ships of the *Kriegsmarine* from their moorings in the northern fiords to ultimate destruction by the guns of the Royal Navy's Home Fleet.

Such suspicions were not entirely unfounded. The small but potent 'fleet-in-being' held – as one German naval officer expressed it – 'like chained dogs' in northern Norway, actually chained-down major units of the British navy at Scapa Flow. Even the most amateur strategist could surmise that a westbound convoy might tempt a battle-squadron to sea in search of easy pickings. Moreover, the foxes would be among the chickens long before the hounds appeared. Such speculations gained favour as the nature of the manpower of the Merchant Navy underwent the subtle changes caused by the war itself. Shortages of merchant seamen led to the most extraordinary and extempore measures being taken. As we have noted in the case of the Ocean Rescue Ships, the Merchant Navy continued to provide a refuge for scoundrels. Low-risk criminals were occasionally released to make up numbers, especially among the firemen required for coal-burners, as Bone had discovered. The most flagrant and prejudicial of such expedient compromises was inflicted upon the master of the *Empire Archer*, Captain Maughan, who had on board Commodore Melhuish, responsible for the fifteen, mostly American, cargo ships of Convoy JW51B.

Bound for Murmansk the convoy was attacked on the morning of 31 December 1942 by Vize-Admiral Kummetz in the heavy cruiser *Admiral Hipper* with the *Panzerschiff Lützow* and six destroyers. In what became known as the Battle of the Barents Sea the convoy escort, a mixed force of five destroyers, two corvettes, one minesweeper and two anti-submarine trawlers under Captain Rupert Sherbrooke in HM Destroyer *Onslow*, brilliantly fought off the German force until it was finally driven away by the appearance of two cruisers, *Sheffield* and *Jamaica*, under Rear Admiral Burnett. As Onslow skilfully threatened Kummetz with his torpedoes in the gloom of an Arctic winter forenoon, Commodore Melhuish with equal *sang froid* manoeuvred JW51B out of harm's way thanks to a smokescreen laid by the old destroyer *Achates* which was sunk by the *Admiral Hipper* for her gallant pains.

The *Empire Archer* and her convoy ploughed on, receiving a few near misses from long range shells from the *Lützow*, but neither Maughan nor Melhuish were entirely confident in their crew. Two days earlier a group of firemen had broached a consignment of rum bound for the British minesweepers based at the Russian Naval base at Polyarnoe, near Murmansk. This had quickly led to an argument and in the ensuing violence two men were knifed. The fighting occurred simultaneously with the threatened break-adrift of a heavy railway locomotive which, among a deck cargo of eight heavy tanks, had parted some of its lashings in the prevailing heavy seas. While a party of seamen under the chief officer saw to this, Maughan and his second officer disarmed and ironed the drunken firemen. Out of desperation for seamen, £100 bonuses had been offered to inmates of Scotland's notorious Barlinnie Gaol, and a party of these had been signed-on the *Empire Archer* as firemen!

There were also individual cases of utterly unsuitable men being sent to sea, perhaps the most startling of all being that of Douglas Scott-Ford, who acted as a German spy. Douglas Scott-Ford, however, came from the Royal Navy, from which he had been dismissed in 1941 for falsifying entries in his Post Office savings book. Disaffected, Scott-Ford signed-on the *Finland*, and in Lisbon he passed information on shipping and naval defences to a German agent for money. His treachery was soon rumbled; on the *Finland's* return to Britain in August 1942 Scott-Ford was arrested and charged with treason. Found guilty at the Old Bailey he was hanged at Wandsworth prison that November.

As the toll of war reduced the numbers of older hands, and its conduct demanded increasing numbers, particularly once the Allies could go over to offensive operations, the quality of merchant seamen suffered a definite dilution. Many young men with no previous experience were sent to sea and were of indifferent mettle. If the older men grumbled, the younger were rebellious, many considering the war won once the Americans 'were in' and were resentful of being assigned to so unglamorous a task. This was mirrored in the Royal Navy, particularly in the Pacific Fleet, resulting in several mutinies which were forcibly suppressed, but the Merchant Navy had long since operated a system of looser discipline. Disaffection was usually dealt with by men well able to handle callow youth, though where the quality of masters and mates had suffered similar dilution due to war's attrition, trouble could still break out.

Ironically on the other hand, the war produced a steady improvement in seafarers' conditions, a consequence of the dawning realisation that they were in fact vital parts of the mobilised nation, and not simply feckless wastrels who got drunk at the first opportunity. State interest had in fact begun in 1938 when the Government had accepted the International Labour Conference's *Recommendations on Seamen's Welfare in Ports*, hitherto a matter left to the maritime charities, the Missions to Seamen, the British & Foreign Sailors' Society, the Apostleship of the Sea and King George's Fund for Sailors, among others. However, the Depression had seriously reduced donations and the charities often found themselves duplicating effort and effectively competing with one another both for money and in offering benefits. Movements to improve conditions at sea in merchantmen owed much to other institutions such as the National Union of Seamen and the British Social Hygiene Council, but a lack of new shipping owing to the Depression inhibited these good intentions, as did Government resistance. Matters began to change with the demand for better accommodation and facilities when war had been declared, which laid a heavy burden on the seamen's missions and sailor's homes. With a concomitant need for spiritual support, this 'must have constituted the best missionary opportunity' of the century,[42] but the state's increasing interest in social amenities necessary for the mobilisation of the population for the successful prosecution of the war led to many initiatives which would culminate in the post-war birth of the Welfare State. While the well-known Beveridge Report delivered conclusions on social security, the Graham White Committee was set up in November 1943 to review seamen's welfare in port and reported in January 1945.

In February 1940 there were modest improvements in the victualling scale, particularly in respect of fresh food and that December a Merchant Navy Reserve Pool was established and run by the Shipping Federation for the MoWT. Men completing their leave and ready to return to sea could be allocated to ships about to sail, meaning that continuous employment could now be offered, while the state could keep track of its seamen. As Professor Alston Kennerley has pointed out: 'More than in the First World war these measures in effect placed seafarers in one organisation, the closest that the Merchant Navy would ever come to being a fourth armed service.' Men wishing to go to sea for the first time – an alternative to conscription into the armed services or, later, the coal mines – were not supposed to be accepted unless they had undergone a course of training as an ordinary seaman or fireman. In desperate times this was a regulation occasionally observed in the breach, while boys well below military age could join the Merchant Navy.

Nevertheless, despite the MoWT's over-arching management, the seafarers still worked for the shipowner and pay-negotiations persisted. It was all, as Miss Behrens cogently explains:

> typical of a service which belonged neither to the world of fighting men nor to the world of civilians and in which the practices of peace and war were combined after a fashion that only the British ... with their habit of grafting the new to the old ... could ever have tried to make work.[43]

In 1943 the Central Board for the Training of Officers of the Merchant Navy set up eight years earlier was reorganised as the Merchant Navy Training Board. This was to monitor the training courses and schemes run under the auspices of the shipowners' organisation, the Shipping Federation. Concerned about his valuable sea-staff's survival if forced into their ship's lifeboats by enemy action, the patriarchal Lawrence Holt consulted Kurt Hahn, the exiled German educationalist, and in consequence the Aberdovey Sea School was established in mid-Wales in 1940 with the aim of providing training in boating skills to all ranks. The extent to which this benefited the crews of Alfred Holt & Co. may be judged by what follows in Chapter Four.

By May 1941 the merchant seaman's contribution to the war effort was made the subject of an Essential Works Order. All merchant seafarers had to register and were issued with new identity documents. Moreover, despite the war, or perhaps because of it, national mobilisation ensured that manning levels were high so that, by 1943 a routine fifty-six-hour working week was increasingly the norm at sea, better than heretofore. Corresponding improvements had been made in respect of pay. In 1939 an able-seaman's monthly pay had been £9 12s 6d, but on 15 September a 'war-risk' payment of £3 was added. In 1942 this had risen to £10, and by February 1943 – at the very height of the struggle for domination of the North Atlantic when the U-boats appeared to have the upper hand – an able-seaman's pay inclusive of war-risk payment was £24. This aroused a great deal of jealousy among naval ratings but, as will be seen in the following chapter, it was more than made up for by the more considerate treatment they received ashore by the authorities and charities. It was at this time that the old injustice of stopping pay when a ship was sunk was abolished. Now a man received his full pay, including war-risk money, until he returned to the United Kingdom and had enjoyed his survivor's leave of a fortnight added to any ordinary leave that he had accrued. A 'survivor' also received a small cash grant to purchase new clothes. This, at least, was the theory. Unfortunately, much suffering had already occurred and had burnt itself into the collective consciousness of the breed, and occasionally there were still incidents of failure to pay allotments to wives and other such errors, while officers who had lost their sextants, nautical tables, binoculars and uniforms, found the survivors' cash grant inadequate. Even among the institutions bound to help, particularly the National Union of Seamen, there were tragic failures and ensuing hardship.

Nevertheless, in 1942, Chinese seamen, following the lead of their white colleagues, became better organised. Having been excluded from the fraternal affections of their seafaring brethren's union movement, they started their own, agitating for a degree of equality with white ratings, most especially demanding they be paid the £10 war bonus given to them. They were in a strong position, for the drafting of white merchant seamen into the Royal Navy coincided with the expansion of the British merchant fleet, providing berths for Chinese ratings who thereby bore much of the brunt of the Battle of the Atlantic. In compliment to this, a needy British state had formed a Chinese Reserve Pool of Seamen which functioned in the same way as the main Reserve Pool.

All these advances in pay and conditions, though limited, were nevertheless real, growing out of pressing necessity, but importantly, they set new standards.[44] As a consequence of the far better provision of amenities aboard the Liberty-ships and other American-built tonnage, some improvements in accommodation followed in British ships, though this was not universal. Such beneficial changes were a consequence of the national need and the overall management of a proper Mercantile Navy by the MoWT derived from this. Profit to be shared among shareholders, with niggardly doles handed to the necessary evil of a crew, were no longer the underlying imperatives behind ship-owning. War made a difference, even to the extent of the state's interest in its seafarers' morale, for Welfare Officers were appointed in British ports and abroad in New York, once that great port-city had become the western convoy terminus. Many of these improvements owed a great deal to Ernest Bevin, a former dockers' leader who had been made Minister of Labour and National Service in Churchill's National Government.[45]

But if he was denied the excess profits of the previous war, the shipowner was not exempt from reasonable consideration either, not least because shipowners were at the heart of the MoWT. An equitable plan was drawn up in 1942 whereby vessels built to the Government's account could be sold to owners who had suffered losses. This Tonnage Replacement Scheme allowed owners to acquire ships at cost-less-depreciation. The cost of a lost vessel was repaid, together with a 25 per cent supplement intended to cover the increases in war-risk insurance premiums. Overall, the liner companies held their own, just able to compensate for losses and rising building costs. Tramp operators made no more than in a reasonable pre-war year, though they were not able to match the profits of 1937.

During the Second World War Great Britain lost 11 million tons of shipping representing 60 per cent of the total fleet, 2 million more than in the First World War. However, wartime building, prizes, purchases from America and finally allocation of enemy shipping by the Inter-Allied Reparations Agency restored the fleet so that compared with the overall gross tonnage in 1939, the post-war merchant fleet had declined by only 3.6 million tons. And while this represented a reduction of 21 per cent, the 7.4 million tons replacing this were mostly new. Serious though this gross loss was, most other countries had suffered worse, reflected in the stark fact that the tonnage of the world's merchant shipping had been reduced by war from 61.4 million tons to 32 million tons. The exception was the United States which had increased its fleet exponentially, with Canada adding a huge amount of tonnage to that of the British Commonwealth. Ironically therefore the British Commonwealth, along with the United States of America and Sweden were, in fact, owners of larger fleets in 1945 than they had been in 1939.

While the vast bulk of the nation's merchant ships maintained the flow of imports and exports augmented by war *matériel*, a very few played parts that proved influential in other ways, perhaps none of which equalled in its consequences the unfortunate role of the Blue Funnel liner *Automedon*. Following the fall of France the British hoped that French forces in her colonies would maintain the alliance with Britain, particularly in the Far East, where the French dominated Indo-China. Here the British were weak: although Hong Kong's commercial power was large, as a small coastal enclave her strategic position was vulnerable. The Malay Peninsula was under developed, the longitudinal railway and trunk road system barely installed, its linking causeway between Johore Bahru and Singapore island was new, and throughout the countryside there were virtually no defences in place. Singapore, like Hong Kong, was vulnerable, its naval base, city and installations protected only from the sea by which, until the eve of war, the principal supply and transit services had been provided. Borneo and Sarawak were even more exposed to an enemy and the Japanese were mustered in force in south-east China.

Acutely sensitive to the invasion of Burma and north-east India, the curious arrangements of the French capitulation with an independent government in Vichy, combined with the effects of the Royal Navy's raids on Oran and Dakar, destroyed all hopes of French resistance in the Far East. The Dutch, on the other hand, with their homeland under occupation, stood firm but, like the British, they were overstretched. In consequence of this the British Chiefs of Staff advised the War Cabinet that Britain should avoid war with Japan. In August a twenty-eight page secret document – COS (40) 302 – was prepared for transmission to the Commander-in-Chief, Far East. Marked 'To be Kept under Lock and Key' it was put aboard the *Automedon*, then loading for the Far East. A King's Messenger handed the sealed package, addressed to Air Chief Marshall Sir Robert Brooke-Popham, to the vessel's master, Captain W. B. Ewan, a man 'in his early fifties'. The 14.5-knot *Automedon* was armed with the standard stern-gun for self-defence, but was otherwise making what was, to all intents and purposes, a normal voyage, although part of her lading was intended to beef up the defences of Singapore. Amid a general cargo of mail, foodstuffs, spirits, cigarettes, steel, copper, medical supplies, machinery parts, cars and lorries, were military uniforms and some fighter aircraft, while among her three passengers were the Fergusons. Mr A.S. Ferguson, was a chief engineer in the Straits Steamship Co., of Singapore and he and his wife had been on leave in France when the country surrendered to the Germans. Escaping Paris ahead of the invaders, the Fergusons reached Bordeaux where British ships, interrupted in their working of cargo, were embarking refugees. In due course the Fergusons took passage in the *Automedon* to return home to Singapore, sailing on 24 September. The *Automedon* was in convoy as far as Freetown and then proceeded independently by way of Durban towards Penang.

At about 07.45 on 11 November – Armistice Day – the *Automedon* was off Achin Head, the northern tip of Sumatra, and within a day's run of Penang when she encountered another vessel. Second Officer Donald Stewart, who had the morning watch sighted a ship hull down on the port bow, judging by her course that she was on a track between Madras and the Sunda Strait. He nevertheless notified Captain Ewan before handing over the watch to his relief, Third Officer P.L. Whitaker. Although Ewan had received two signals about suspicious ships, the naval intelligence officer at Durban had told him no enemy was thought to exist in the Indian Ocean; consequently he had dismissed the 'alarms' as false. Meanwhile Able-Seaman Stan Hughill had relieved the wheel and was some twenty minutes into his trick when:

we spotted away over to port a rather big vessel … the Old Man was walking up and down the bridge and turns to the … mate … on watch, and says 'I think she's a Dutchman.' Next minute '*Bang!*' over the bows with a warning shot, up went the battle flag … The Old Man said to me, 'Hard a-starboard!' Next minute we were at right angles to the raider …

Stewart was shaving at 08.20 when 'a sudden blast of gunfire' drew him to his cabin port. He was 'horrified to see the ship, now flying the swastika, steaming parallel to our course and about 1,000 yards distant'. Rushing to warn Extra Second Mate T.G. Wilson, both men rushed to the bridge, accompanied by the chief officer, Mr P.F. Evans. As they joined Ewan, he ordered the chief officer to secure the safe keys in his cabin and dump the confidential books and mail. Evans had just gone below when 'all hell was let loose' as shells burst on the *Automedon*'s bridge. Concussed for several minutes, Stewart came round to find himself between the bodies of Ewan and Whitaker among the wreckage of the wheelhouse; Wilson was also dead. Knowing of Evans's mission he scrambled below and found him on the threshold of the master's cabin, severely wounded. Stewart knew that there was a secret consignment in the strongroom and that the key was in the chief officer's cabin but the whole area had been 'reduced to a shambles'.

In the *Automedon*'s engine room Fourth Engineer Sam Harper, the duty engineer, recalled that he was 'startled by a loud bang … right overhead'. Then the telegraph rang 'Standby' and he prepared for manoeuvring but there was the 'scream of steam escaping … pandemonium broke loose' and 'the Chinese scarpered for the deck. They were my firemen …'. At this point the engine room telegraph rang for 'Stop!' and Harper carried the order out just as Chief Engineer J.P. McNicol arrived, his head streaming blood. With him came the fifth and the second engineer, slightly wounded having been briefly trapped in his cabin, with news that the third was seriously hurt. McNicol returned to the deck to find out what was happening and ran into 'a squad of German marines'.

The *Automedon* had run into the German *Hilfskreuzer Atlantis*. Her commander, Kapitän sur Zee Bernhard Rogge, knowing that Blue Funnel liners passed Achin Head every day had not only decided to strike at them, but had disguised his ship as one of Holt's vessels, the *Antenor*. Rogge knew she had been requisitioned as an AMC and thereby hoped to deceive others. As the *Automedon* swung away from the *Atlantis* and the alarm bells rang, Hughill claimed that Ewan called out, 'We'll fight them!'[46] However, on Harper's evidence, Ewan must have ordered the engines stopped a second before the enemy's salvo hit the bridge. It is thought that the gun's crew ran aft and the radio officer certainly managed to transmit a short signal prefixed by the RRRR that indicated attack by a raider. The signal contained the *Automedon's* latitude but not her longitude, the shelling had seen to that.[47] Rogge scored eleven direct hits, one hitting the *Automedon's* stern destroying her gun just as the gunners manned it. Killing them all, the shell also disabled the steering gear. Soon afterwards *Automedon* came to a stop, the only sound that of escaping steam and the chatter of her crew as they assembled on deck and awaited the inevitable.

Lying on a main shipping route Rogge gave his senior boarding officer, Leutnant Mohr, just three hours to remove the *Automedon's* people and stores, and search her. Discovering Stewart, Mohr asked him to take him to the master. Learning that Ewan was dead, Stewart was ordered to conduct Mohr round the ship. According to the German report:

> the *Automedon* presented a picture of devastation. The numerous hits had riddled all the superstructures, wrecked the davits and boats, penetrated the funnel and turned the Master's and Mate's cabins into a shambles. A number of dead and wounded were lying about the deck. The Master, mangled by a direct hit, had fallen on the bridge, and the [extra] Second Mate had been killed outside the chart-house ... the death of the officers and the heavy damage to the bridge had hindered the destruction of secret material. We found all the Admiralty's instructions, course directions and secret log books; and after breaking into the Master's safe we found the Merchant Navy Code, conversion tables etc.

The German officers and men who scrambled up the *Automedon's* side from their launch were tasked to search for these confidential but routine instructions for merchant ships in order that they might profitably raid the routes the Admiralty specified. In the wrecked chartroom they had discovered the unjettisoned weighted canvas bag with the ship's confidential books and routeing instructions, but there was more – much more.

The surviving crew numbered thirty-one British, two of whom were mortally wounded, fifty-six Chinese, and the passengers, including Mr and Mrs Ferguson. Mohr ordered the crew, particularly the Chinese, to pack essential personal effects and then to assist in the transfer of stores. A large quantity of frozen meat and other foodstuffs were lowered into the raider's boats. The Germans were also informed where 500 cases of whisky were stowed, along with a large consignment of cigarettes. Meanwhile Mrs Ferguson was advised that as they would be taken as prisoners to a cold country, she should pack some warm clothes. Ferguson protested these were in a crate in the baggage room and Stewart was now approached. Aware of the contents of the 'baggage-room,' he tried to bluff the Germans by taking them to the bonded-store. Unfortunately the practice of the *Kreigsmarine* to provide their commerce raiders with mercantile officers from the German naval reserve who had a good command of English, meant they knew merchant ships and were therefore invaluable in leading boarding parties.[48] The subterfuge was quickly unmasked and it was realised that Stewart was deliberately hiding something. He was placed under close arrest, and the Germans blew off the baggage-room doors. As the German report revealed, in addition to the Fergusons' personal effects:

> In the mail-room(sic) we found a number of bags marked 'SAFE HAND. BRITISH MASTER ONLY'. This contained material surpassing our expectations – the whole of the Top Secret mail for the High Command, Far East; new code tables for the fleet; secret 'Notices to Mariners'; information about minefields and swept areas; plans and maps; a War Cabinet Report giving a summary on the defence of the Far East [COS(40)302]; Intelligence Service material; and many other documents.

It was a bonanza, the consequences of which were profound. Having transferred his prisoners and ordered the *Automedon* destroyed by scuttling charges, Rogge realised the significance of the secret papers, especially that of the Chiefs of Staff Assessment. In the previous few days he had captured two Norwegian tankers and, proceeding to a rendezvous off Kerguelen Island, he put the haul aboard the *Ole Jacob* in the charge of his prize-crew commander. The *Ole Jacob* contained a valuable cargo of aviation spirit which would net Rogge a handsome profit, while his prize-officer would reap a greater dividend when, after taking a circuitous route to Kobe, he put the secret papers in the hands of the German Naval Attaché in Tokyo. He in turn handed it over to Admiral Kondo, Chief of the Japanese Naval Staff, later stating that 'Kondo told me how valuable the information contained in the War cabinet's memorandum was to the Imperial Navy, such as the significant weakening of the British Empire's outward appearance'. This persuaded Admiral Yamamoto of the feasibility of dealing a double-blow in the Pacific, one towards the Americans at Pearl Harbor, and the other south at the Anglo-Dutch in Malaya and the East Indies. The first would neutralise the United States' Pacific Fleet, the second would destroy British power and prestige, and deliver the Dutch oil fields into their hands. That done Burma and India lay in prospect. Yamamoto wrote an appreciation of this opportunity on 7 January 1941. On Sunday 7 December naval aircraft operating from carriers attacked Pearl Harbor. Hong Kong surrendered and Singapore fell on 15 February 1942 by which time the Japanese were landing in the Dutch East Indies and Anglo-Dutch resistance finally crumpled with the defeat of the combined naval squadron under Schout by-nacht (Rear Admiral) Karel Doorman in the Java Sea on 27 February 1942.[49] In their offensive the Japanese 'gained control of the skies and seas across a quarter of the world's surface'.

British reaction to news of the loss of *Automedon* was less enthusiastic. Naval Intelligence unwisely assumed that Captain Ewan had succeeded in dumping the secret material, blithely unaware of its stowage. In consequence only the naval codes were changed as a precaution and Brooke-Popham and General Perceval in Singapore had no idea that Tokyo was reading the papers that should have been on their desks. As far as the Fergusons and their shipmates were concerned, they were kept aboard the *Atlantis* for four weeks before being transferred deep in the Southern Ocean south of Capetown into a captured Norwegian ship, the *Storstadt*, acting as tender. They then moved cautiously north and, in company with several other German blockade-runners and without sighting a single Allied warship, they slipped into Bordeaux in March 1941.[50]

Imprisonment awaited the men of *Automedon*, along with the crews of several other British ships mewed up in the *Storstadt*, including those from the *Port Wellington*, *Maimoa* and *Nowshera*. A few were lucky, among them Sam Harper who was one of those taken first to a holding camp near Bordeaux. After five weeks they were put on a train for transfer to Germany. The next day Harper and three others, the fourth and fifth engineers of the *Maimoa* and the fifth engineer of the *Nowshera*, jumped from the train, avoiding breaking any bones but heavily bruised. They began walking inland in pairs to avoid the 'heavily militarised French coast'. They were stopped by a French policeman who proved friendly, telling them where the nearby border between Occupied and Vichy France lay. Helped by a French peasant farmer and later a friendly French official – an elderly Mayoress – from whom they obtained forged French army papers, they were instructed to make for Marseilles where they successfully remained for three weeks until making contact with the Rev. Donald Caskie of the British Seaman's Mission. Caskie set them *en route* over the Pyrenees but they were arrested when on a train to Madrid and eventually found themselves confined in a Spanish labour camp where:

> You either got a boot up the arse or a smile. We slept adjacent to these two Dutch guys we'd met. You were supposed to work but with the help of the British [Naval Attaché to whom Harper had smuggled a note] who seemed to have some pull, we got out of that. We got quite friendly with these Dutch chaps who said they wanted to get back to England to become involved in the war. They gave me a letter to take back to the Dutch Government-in-exile once I returned to England. We were released ... by the British Naval Attaché who sent a[n] ... Embassy official with orders to cross the palms of the Spanish guards with silver. It was June 27, 1941, that I again set foot on British soil; seven months after being taken prisoner.[51]

Other ships played roles of significance. The *Glenearn*-class have already been mentioned, and they were joined by Anchor and Bibby liners – among others – in providing the mass transport for Allied Operations but they became, partially at least, men-of-war, inhabiting a grey area of classification, less clear than auxiliary warships hoisting the white ensign of commissioned naval ships. The principal purpose of trooping was the simple task of mass reinforcement, a job at which the *Queen Mary* and *Queen Elizabeth* excelled and which, in the preparations for the first of the great Allied invasions, Operation TORCH, they began the shuttling of large numbers of American troops across the North Atlantic. On the return voyages they were not entirely empty, carrying prisoners of war away from British soil where the slow build-up for D-Day made the presence of German and Italians undesirable. They also conveyed British merchant crews appointed by the managing companies and the Reserve Pool to the newly building Liberties and Forts being made ready in the United States and Canada.

In the case of offensive operations, in addition to fighting troops, it was necessary to provide back-up of all sorts, from the Dock Labour battalions of the Royal Army Service Corps or the sappers of the Royal Engineers, to members of the pay corps, plus essential civilians such as salvage officers, dockyard clearance divers, hull and engine surveyors, 'owner-experts' of the MoWT in addition to the Military Transport staff attached to the ship who handled the liaison between the master and the embarked military. Such was the variety of expertise in a trooper that one master remarked than his ship 'seemed to hold the nucleus for the founding of a distant colony' – which, in a sense, she did.

Most such ships assembled for these WS convoys at the Tail o' the Bank anchorage on the Clyde, off Gourock under the eye of Naval Control Headquarters at Marymount, a villa overlooking the pier. This anchorage was of considerable importance, not just as a convoy assembly point but as an 'Emergency Port'. Such was the demand for berths, and so incapacitated by bomb damage had the docks of Glasgow, Liverpool and London become, that the insistent demands of rapid turn-around of shipping demanded a radical expedient and this was found in the Clyde estuary. The wonderful shelter afforded by the surrounding hills, the lochs and the dog-leg to the south taken by the river round Cloch Point in debouching into the sea, made a safe anchorage of considerable extent. Here many ships could lie and, using their own derricks, discharge into lighters, coasters, Clyde puffers, Dutch *schuyts* and specially built tenders and other war emergency craft.

> The additional berthing facilities were required in a position where bombing, if not impossible, was at least difficult, and the vicinity of the Tail of the Bank in the Clyde was selected. This proved to be a wise selection, as after the Anchorages were established, the area was only bombed twice and the damage to shipping was nil.

The project was begun in September 1940 and while the larger coasting vessels distributed cargoes to their destinations, two railway passenger piers at Fairlie and Craigendoran were equipped to unload the barges. The following year Gourock pier was fitted with electric cranes and electric trucks and 'was continuously used until August 1945 in connection with troop embarkation and disembarkation'. In addition the jetty in Cardwell Bay was made available for the small craft used to store the many troopships which used the Emergency Port. The entire anchorage, with the offshoots of Loch Long, the Holy Loch and the Gareloch were protected by a net boom stretched across the estuary, the gate of which was opened by a boom-defence vessel. In strong winds the smaller craft found the sea conditions difficult in the estuary, which is four miles wide off Gourock, and much of the cargo-work was carried out in the Holy Loch to the west of Cloch Point. The Emergency Port handled 1,885 deep-sea ships, 2,056,830 tons of cargo and more than 6 million packages of equipment, mails and stores. Among the cargoes were munitions, tanks, military vehicles, meat, bulk grain, timber, metals, canned goods, fresh and dried fruit, and other foodstuffs, besides the fuelling, storing and victualling services necessary to turn round the ships. Despatch was officially described as 'consistently high and compared favourably with work done in any port in the country'. One advantage was that damaged ships could be attended to swiftly and without the delays inherent in working them upstream and into berths. It was here, for example, that Captain N. Rice brought the torpedoed *Orari* of the New Zealand Shipping Co. in December 1940. The *Orari* had been hit on the night of the 13th when some 450-miles west of the Fastnet Lighthouse by *U-43* (Lüth). She was homeward bound from Australia with a cargo of frozen meat in heavy seas and with equally heavy rain squalls reducing visibility. Emerging from one such squall she was confronted by a U-boat on the surface ahead of her. Rice attempted evasive action, and turned *Orari*'s head to starboard just as Lüth fired from both bow tubes. As *Orari* swung towards the quartering seas and rolled heavily to port, her bow climbing to meet an oncoming wave, her stern sinking into the preceding trough, the first of the torpedoes hit her high up on her port side. The blast counter-mined the second and its war-head inexplicably detached itself to land on *Orari*'s No.4 Hatch. The gunners on the poop got off a shot as *U-43* disappeared into the murk from which the *Orari* had emerged but a few moments earlier.

Rice now had a difficult decision to make. He knew that launching the boats under such conditions would be hazardous, but the after part of his ship was waterlogged with the seas breaking over it. Fortunately No.6 Hold was intact and, with strenuous and ceaseless efforts, the lines were cleared and pumping began, despite leaking bulkheads admitting water into the engine room. Best of all, no one had been hurt: Rice decided to bring his ship in. Patiently coaxing his vessel, assisted by the weather and the long hours of darkness at the winter solstice, he nursed the *Orari* until, rounding the Mull of Kintyre and passing Ailsa Craig, he was within sight of refuge. Here, however, he found the defensive boom closed for the night and no Clyde pilot would board *Orari* until morning. With her heavy port list and drawing 45ft aft, the *Orari* was compelled to await the opening of the gate the following morning. Anchored at last on the forenoon of the 17th she caught the eye of the visiting war artist, Arthur Burgess. Patched up in Glasgow, the *Orari* went to New York for proper repair, served in Malta convoys and survived the war.

It was at this time that Admiral Dunbar-Nasmith, then Commander-in-Chief, Western Approaches advised the First Sea Lord, Sir Dudley Pound that the convoy system was failing. Losses continued to mount steadily, and they would get far worse, but it was not the convoy system that was failing, it was the Royal Navy's inability to defend them and destroy the submarine menace. This would come in time but in the meanwhile, it was the Merchant Navy that suffered. Many shipping companies lost up to half of the ships they had at the outbreak of war, the heaviest loss of tonnage being borne by the Canadian Pacific Railway Co.

An examination of one shipping house will have to stand exemplar for them all, but the vicissitudes endured by Lord Inverforth's ships are by no means untypical. Broadly speaking Inverforth's group consisted of three subsidiaries, the Bank Line, the United Baltic Corporation – or UBC – and a smaller tanker-owning subsidiary. However, the picture is more complicated with UBC owning MacAndrews & Co. which, it will be recalled, Inverforth took over in 1935 after the collapse of Kylsant's Royal Mail Group. The demands of war spread the UBC ships far from their native Baltic, from which war debarred them, sending them worldwide. Two acted as refrigerated feeders shipping meat from the outports of New Zealand to reduce the number of calls made by the larger 'Empire food ships'. Of their own fleet UBC lost four vessels to enemy action, the *Baltrader*, *Baltanglia* and *Baltallin*, all of which were torpedoed, and the *Baltonia* which was mined. The company was also charged by the MoWT with the management of one standard-built vessel and twelve Danish East Asiatic ships[52] which, though manned by their exiled crews, temporarily adopted British registry. Of these only three survived the war.

The parent Bank Line had, meanwhile, suffered similarly. Just prior to the war the Weir board had a revival of interest in the carriage of oil with the formation of what became Inver Tankers. These ships had mixed fortunes due to instability in Nazi Germany, where money was frozen and Weirs sought to build tonnage and thereby release its German investments. The tankers' future was also threatened by the failure of an intended refinery to materialise at Dublin and consequently the seven tankers (*Inverliffey*, *Inverdargle*, *Inverlane*, *Inverlee*, *Inverilen*, *Inversuir* and *Invershannon*) spent many months laid-up in the River Fal in Cornwall. However, matters were transformed in September 1939 when the war began. Britain was desperately short of tankers and these were immediately required, so much so that they were tempting targets and all were lost to U-boats while serving as Admiralty oilers.

As mentioned above, three Bank Line vessels were requisitioned by the Government, the *Foylebank*, *Alynbank* and *Springbank* being commissioned as anti-aircraft ships, the *Springbank* later having a catapult and fighter fitted in addition. None returned to the company's service after the war. The *Springbank* was sunk after suffering severe torpedo damage from *U-201* in September 1941 when escorting Convoy HG73. The *Foylebank*'s end is described in the following chapter, but the *Alynbank* was sunk as a blockship on 9 June 1944 off Arromanches to form the eastern breakwater of Mulberry B, the artificial harbour necessary for the invasion of Occupied France. Afterwards she was raised and scrapped.

The rest of the Bank Line fleet suffered at the hands of the enemy. On 31 January 1941 the *Rowanbank* was bombed and sunk by a Fw200 Condor west of Ireland and the *Speybank* was captured off the Seychelles by the German raider *Atlantis*. A gift to the *Kriegsmarine*, she was taken to Bordeaux where she was converted into a minelayer and blockade runner. Renamed *Doggerbank* and placed under the command of Kapitänleutnant Schniewind, she left La Pallice on 21 January 1942 and by calling herself *Levernbank* deceived the light cruiser *Durban* off Capetown and then as *Inverbank* fooled the AMC HMS *Cheshire*. Schniewind laid mines off Cape Agulhas which claimed several ships, damaging more and sinking the P&O liner *Soudan*. Having refuelled the blockade-runner *Dresden* and revictualled the raider *Michel*, the *Doggerbank* proceeded to Japan by way of Batavia (Djakarta) with 177 British Merchant Navy prisoners destined for PoW camps in Japan. Loading a valuable cargo of oils and rubber in South-East Asian ports under Japanese control, she sailed for France. Now, however, her indisputably British profile betrayed her. Off the Canaries, on 3 March 1943, she was hit by three torpedoes fired from *U-43* by Oberleutnant zur See H-J. Schwantke. Only fifteen men, Schniewind included, escaped to languish in a small rubber dinghy. According to the sole survivor, Fritz Kurt, Schniewind shot four of the crew before putting himself out of his misery. Kurt was rescued by the Spanish ship *Campoamour* on 29 March.

Losses of Bank Line vessels, including the former Natal Line ships, were heavy and included the war prizes *Naimes* and *Congella*, the *Inveric*, *Gifford*, *Pindos*, *War Burman*, *Tymeric* and *Incomati*; the *Forafric*, *Tinhow* and the managed ship *Ile de Batz*; the *Birchbank*, *Cedarbank*, *Elmbank*, *Kelvinbank*, *Oakbank*, *Tielbank*, *Teesbank*, *Thornliebank*, *Thursobank* and *Trentbank*, the *Rowanbank*, *Willowbank*, *Empire Heron*, *Empire Attendant* and *Empire City*. Besides these vessels, the *Testbank* was lost at Bari in circumstances described in Chapter Four.[53]

Just prior to the war UBC's subsidiary, MacAndrews & Co. were running joint services with other companies such as the Yeoward Line to the Canaries, and short, cheap cruises at £1 per day. The practice of registering many of their ships in Spain had been ended in 1917 and shortly before the outbreak of war the company built two new motor vessels, the *Palomares* and *Pozarica*. These were intended to run a fortnightly express service from London to Malaga, Cadiz and Seville by way of Gibraltar, but the war intervened. As touched upon earlier, both of these vessels were, like the *Foylebank* and *Alynbank*, converted to anti-aircraft ships and commissioned under the white ensign. Having distinguished themselves as escorts to Convoy PQ17, the *Palomares* was badly damaged off Algiers. Refitted as a fighter direction ship for combined operations and taking part in the landing at Salerno, she was again hit when off Anzio beach. Returned to her owners after the war she served until her sale in 1959 and thereafter, run by a succession of owners, she lasted until 1973. After serving in northern waters, *Pozarica* was also sent to the Mediterranean as a convoy escort. She was hit by an aerial torpedo when approaching Bougie on 29 January 1943 and sank without loss of life. In addition to these two vessels, the government also requisitioned the *Pinto* and the *Florentino*. The latter was sunk as a blockship during the dark days of May 1940 and the *Pinto*, not requisitioned by the state until July 1943, became a Rescue Ship. Off Tory Island on the night of 8 September 1944, when attending Convoy HXF 305 consisting of ninety-seven merchantmen on passage from New York, the *Pinto* went to the assistance of the 15,720-ton tanker *Empire Heritage*. This war-prize was formerly the German *Tafelberg* and she had been struck by a torpedo from *U-482*. With a full cargo of fuel oil and 1,942 tons of deck cargo including tanks and trucks, the *Empire Heritage* was ripped open and sinking.

Captain L.S. Boggs had stopped the *Pinto* to pick up the survivors bobbing in the water when she was herself struck by a torpedo from the same U-boat. Surgeon Lieutenant P.N. Holmes was attending the survivors:

when there was a rushing sound blended into a tremendous explosive crash. The deck seemed to jump up and the whole ship to shudder. Smoke, coal and water were all around. I was flung against the rails and temporarily dazed by quantities of debris, including considerable amounts of galley coal which landed on my head and back. Much of the superstructure of the ship seemed to be crashing down … [and she] was already heeling over and beginning to sink by the stern. Water was rushing along the alleyway. I went to make sure that the hospital was clear and then went to report to the Captain. He was … shouting to the men to get over the side … [A]bout three seconds after I had spoken to the Captain the ship seemed to make a sudden drop. I was standing … up to my waist in water when I last saw the Captain. I was carried down a long way, and became jammed against the rigging … When I became free I began to rise again, and on reaching the surface, about half a minute later, the ship had gone.[54]

Boggs was lost, along with several members of his crew and survivors of the *Empire Heritage*. Captain J.C. Jamieson, twenty-four of his crew, three gunners, a signalman and twenty Distressed British Seamen, survivors of earlier sinkings being brought home, were rescued with Holmes and forty men from the *Pinto* after about two hours in the water. They were picked up by HM Trawler *Northern Wave* and landed at Londonderry. The total loss from the *Empire Heritage* was 114, including a further fifty-three Distressed British Seamen.

Of the twenty ships owned by MacAndrews in 1939 ten, including *Pinto*, *Pozarica* and *Florentino*, were lost. One, the *Churruca*, commanded by Captain Trevor Jones, was sunk at Alexandria but was afterwards raised and repaired. One hundred and four employees were killed, fourteen of the company's staff were decorated for war service, five masters receiving the MBE and two engineers the George Medal for gallantry. MacAndrews' war losses were *Calderon*, *Cervantes*, *Ciscar*, *Cortes*, *Pizarro*, *Florentino*, *Pelayo*, *Pinto*, *Ponzano* and the anti-aircraft ship *Pozarica*.

Such then, was the loss of tonnage typical of a robustly managed shipping company, but it fails to convey the losses in human terms, or the experiences of those who survived.

NOTES

1. The first merchantman interdicted in the Second World War was in fact the German tramp *Hannah Böge*, which was stopped by HM Destroyer *Somali* in accordance with the Prize Regulations but scuttled to avoid capture.

2. This was not, in fact the case. See the author's *The Real Cruel Sea*, Chapter One. The so-called Prize Regulations are not rehearsed here as their implications were detailed in the preceding volume, *More Days, More Dollars*. Suffice it to say that, insofar as U-boats were concerned, they were quite impractical, though in the early days of the war several U-boat commanders did make some effort to conform and one or two ameliorated the conditions they left their victims in. However, the embarkation of a merchantman's crew in the U-boat was an operational and a practical impossibility. Commanders of conventional surface commerce-raiders, such as Langsdorff of the *Admiral Graf Spee*, with space to confine prisoners and a supply-ship to provide more, did conform to the conventions, though other commerce-raider commanders were not so punctilious.

3. In fact an eight-ship convoy had left Gibraltar – a port under tight naval rather than commercial control – for Capetown on 2nd. Lemp's action actually confirmed the rightness of the Admiralty's caution. The first major troop convoy of eleven transports left the Clyde for Gibraltar on 5 September, the same day that the Cunard 'brig' – the nickname for that company's smaller vessels on their Mediterranean service – *Bosnia*, Captain W.H. Poole, was sunk by gunfire from *U-47*

(Prien) some 120-miles NNW of Cape Ortegal. She was homeward for Manchester from Sicily with a cargo of sulphur. One man was killed and the survivors picked up by the Norwegian tanker *Eidanger* and landed at Lisbon. On the 6th the tramp *Rio Claro*, Captain J.A. Robson, was sunk off Cape Finisterre and the *Manaar* was sunk off Lisbon as described.

The first 'Trade Convoys' set out on the 7th. These were OA1 outward from the Channel and OB1 from Liverpool. Until the fall of France the Commander-in-Chief Western Approaches, at this time Admiral Dunbar-Nasmith, was based at Plymouth. After France fell no convoys were routed through the Channel or St George's Channel and the killing ground off southern Ireland was abandoned, a circumstance forced upon the Admiralty by the absolute refusal of De Valera's Irish government to honour the agreement to allow the British use of Berehaven on the west coast of Ireland as a base. That did not prevent citizens of the Irish Free State from joining the British armed services or the British Merchant Navy, nor did it exempt Irish ships from being sunk, including lighthouse tenders of the Commissioners for Irish Lights.

Following the collapse of France the Commander-in-Chief removed his headquarters to Derby House, Liverpool, from where Dunbar-Nasmith's relief, Admiral Noble, began the direction of convoy operations which would eventually be brought to a successful conclusion by his successor, Admiral Horton.

There had been some opposition to the formation of convoys, the first of which was a belief that the Germans would not again embark on a policy of unrestricted submarine warfare on the notion that having done so in the First World War its inevitable consequence once American lives had been lost was to bring the might of the United States into the war against Germany. This argument to some extent explains the Admiralty's belief that the greatest danger to merchant shipping was the big-gun of commerce-raiders. The second reason was the opposition of the Air Staff who insisted that convoys would prove vulnerable to aerial bombing, the general anticipation of which seems to have been grossly – though quite understandably – exaggerated.

4. Despite Hitler's invasion of Poland and Great Britain's treaty obligations to her, the declaration of war by Chamberlain was widely regarded in Germany as aggressive. In his *Memoirs* Dönitz makes great play of it, though he later blames Hitler for going to war prematurely, as far as the *Kriegsmarine*'s preparations – chiefly from Dönitz's point of view, the lack of U-boats – were concerned. The German navy's war-plans as formulated by Grossadmiral Erich Raeder and his staff, known as the Z-plan, calculated that the building programme of warships, including U-boats and an aircraft carrier, the *Peter Strasser*, would be complete in 1944.

5. Isolated in their radio rooms, earphones clamped to their heads and desperately transmitting SSSS or distress signals, it became commonplace for radio officers to be left on board. Turner was made an OBE for his action and one of the lascars was also decorated.

6. *Journal of the Honourable Company of Master Mariners*, Vol. XVIII, spring 1993 No.213. Subsequently the 'battle-ship grey covering British merchantmen was replaced by a lighter grey and later still the upper spars, funnel – anything conceived to show significantly above the horizon when viewed from a U-boat's conning tower – were painted white.'

7. In 1940 the DEMS organisation consisted of about 2,000. By the end of the war it had provided some 24,000 naval gunners, the MRRA another 14,000.

9. See McBrearty, R.F., *Seafaring, 1939–1945, as I saw it*, Pentland Press, Edinburgh, 1995.

10. Admiralty Memorandum from the Director of the Trade Division dated 21 May 1920 quoted by Osborne, R., Spong, H., and Grover, T., *Armed Merchant Cruisers, 1878–1945*, p139.

11. One, the *Fidelity*, was retained under Free French command and manning. She was no more successful.

12. Strictly speaking these ships were divided into two classes, the Ocean Boarding Vessels and the Armed Boarding Vessels.

13. Furness, Withy's *Southern Prince* was another minelayer, later converted into an accommodation vessel.

14. See, Schofield, B., and Martyn, L.F., *The Rescue Ships*, p9–10.

15. Captain George Russell, *Six Years on the North Atlantic, 1939–45*, article published in the *Journal of the Honourable Company of Master Mariners*, Vol XVIII, summer 1993. No.214.

16. These were the *Empire Rest, Empire Peacemaker, Empire Comfort, Empire Lifeguard* and *Empire Shelter*. By this time the tide of the Battle of the Atlantic had turned in the Allies' favour and their total of recovered merchant seamen was nil, though the *Empire Peacemaker* recovered three 'downed' RAF aircrew. After the war some were used as troop transports for the North Sea crossing, often repatriating German PoWs. The overall numbers rescued by the twenty-three adapted

merchant-ships amounted to several thousand, the largest haul being made by the *Rathlin*, which picked up 634 men, followed by the *Zamalek* with 611, the *Perth* with 455, the *Copeland* with 433 and the *Toward* with 341.

17. Survivors of the *Lancastria* were forbidden to mention it for fear of punishment under the King's Regulations. Those missing were officially listed as 'missing in action' and presumed by their relatives to have died while crossing France in the retreat to St Nazaire. The news was broken by the New York newspapers on 26 July 1940 and soon afterwards the British press got hold of the story, but were more restrained and the matter faded from the public consciousness. The official papers relating to the tragedy remain sealed under the Official Secrets Acts until 2040.

18. For a detailed account of the cruise of the *Admiral Graf Spee* see the author's *The Battle of the River Plate*, Pen & Sword, 2008.

19. Wood and Moss survived, Wood being awarded the DSO. Fogarty-Fegen was posthumously awarded the Victoria Cross.

20. The Bristol Channel ports were Milford Haven, Swansea, Barry, Penarth, Cardiff, Newport, Avonmouth and Bristol, with coastal traffic also using Watchet and Appeldore.

21. One of these was the Norwegian, E.D. Naess, whose vessels were registered in Panama. Naess had made $1 million available to the British Government in 1940 when the country was suffering a foreign-exchange crisis and before Lend-Lease was established. However, the following year Naess paid his shareholders a 25 per cent dividend while putting large sums in reserve. As an example of the difference in freight-rates, that for neutral ships in the Rio de la Plata meat trade was £2.75, while for British ships it was £1.625; elsewhere other rates were similar in disproportion. See Naess, E.D. *Autobiography of a Shipping Man*, Lloyd's of London, Colchester, 1977. Greek owners also enjoyed a bonanza and this accounts for the post-war emergence of several wealthy Greek shipowners. However, by the time the war ended only about one tenth of the world's shipping was operated by neutrals, whereas the United States' fleet had grown by 370 per cent.

22. The Ministry of Shipping had been under intermittent attack from the Ministry of Supply which seemed incapable of quantifying the precise amounts of raw materials and imports it required for the output of the commodities for which it was responsible, and from the Ministry of Food which was unable to state precisely what stocks of foodstuffs were actually in the country – usually by under-estimation. What was worse the Minister concerned did not have Churchill's confidence.

23. In conformity with tradition in Alfred Holt & Co.'s shipping group which expected its managers – it was a private company at this time and had no directors – either to be members of the Holt family, or have first-class degrees. Wurtzburg's was in Classics and he was an alumnus of Emmanuel College, Cambridge. Besides his commercial career, Wurtzburg was a public servant of some standing, having served on the Straits Settlements Legislative Council.

24. The loss of large, deep-water cargo-vessels on the east coast was largely unnecessary, but a case in point was the Blue Funnel liner *Meriones*, Captain Peard, mentioned in Chapter Two. On a voyage from London to Australia by way of Hull she ran aground on the Haisborough Sand on 22 January 1941. The chief officer had been maintaining station on the ship ahead and, in taking avoiding action in a strong tide, the ship touched this notorious shoal. Although partially unloaded under the supervision of the company's marine superintendent from London, Captain M.B.Glasier, the *Meriones* was bombed by German aircraft and set on fire before she could be refloated.

25. See Hancock, H.E., *Semper Fidelis*, p94.

26. In 1943 the MoWT had organised the transport of no fewer than 250,000 service personnel and their equipment to North Africa alone.

27. See Hope R., *A New History of British Shipping*, p387, and Behrens, C., *Merchant Shipping and the Demands of War*, p343.

28. The talents and personal expertises of shipowners, like people in other walks of life, are often tangential to their main business. When Sir John Reeves Ellerman died in July 1933 he left a personal fortune of £40 million. He was succeeded by his son who shared his name, but there the similarity ended. John Ellerman II was a withdrawn, philanthropic, scholarly man who shunned publicity and insisted on having the boat deck of one of his ships boarded up when he made his annual voyage to South Africa. The reclusive second Ellerman had a passionate interest in rodents, having a species named after him, and became an acknowledged world expert on the genus.

29. Correspondence with George Swaine, to whom I am extremely grateful for his insightful advice in this matter and, more generally, on ship-owning in the twentieth century.

30. At the end of May 1943, after a period of unparalleled success, Dönitz withdrew his U-boats from

the Atlantic in the face of the Allies' successful counter-attack. He was to reopen the campaign that autumn and the U-boats remained a potent threat, sinking many British and Allied merchantmen, but they never regained the initiative and suffered a relentless harrowing until the end.

31. Lord Leathers later attended the conferences at Yalta and Potsdam, but the agendas were political and he was frustrated in failing to achieve any of his objectives as regards transport. Leathers returned to public life with Churchill's ministry in 1951, being appointed to oversee transport, power and fuel. This was not a success and he retired in 1953 to resume his business career. He was an underwriting member of Lloyd's and a member of several City institutions, being created Viscount in 1954. He died in west London in March 1965 in his 82nd year. He deserves to be better remembered for his major contribution to victory, but his oblivion is symptomatic of the disregard of history for merchant shipping.

32. The seven vessels torpedoed from Convoy HX72 were the *Blairangus*, *Canonesa*, *Baron Blythswood*, *Dalcairn*, *Elmbank*, and the tankers *Invershannon* and *Torinia*.

33. The *Volendam* had been carrying 230 'mostly working class children' aged between six and sixteen.

34. See Bone, D., *Merchantmen Rearmed*, p70. Bone's unassuming but evocative memoirs are classics of sea literature.

35. For a full description of the torpedoing of the *City of Benares*, see the author's *The Real Cruel Sea*, p175 *et seq*.

36. The seventeen vessels lost from Convoy SC7 were the British ships *Assyrian*, *Beatus*, *Clintonia*, *Fiscus*, *Creekirk*, *Empire Brigade*, *Empire Miniver*, *Languedoc*, *Scoresby* and *Sedgepool*, the Dutch ships *Boekelo* and *Soesterberg*, the Greek vessels *Nirotos* and *Thalia*, the Norwegian *Snefjeld* and the Swedes *Convallaria* and *Gunborg*. The monthly total for October 1940 was sixty-three ships grossing 301,892 tons.

37. This did not necessarily mean a military cargo. It could, for example, consist of steel intended to manufacture tanks or warships, but the cargo consisted of freight loaded on Government account.

38. After the publication of *The Real Cruel Sea* in 2004, I received a letter from a former fireman who was indignant over the frequently iterated allegations of inefficiency caused by bad boiler-firing in *naval* histories. The subject caused endless strife aboard many ships as masters and mates complained as a result of receiving signals to 'Make less smoke!' from the Senior Officer of the escort, and the engineers tried to justify and explain the problem. It is not too strong a point to make, but such embedding of a technical misunderstanding in naval history soured many a merchant seaman's memories and went a long way to explain why they turned their M.N. badges upside down and wore them as N.W. which they claimed meant 'Not Wanted'. The consequent embitterment, which arose from many other, but similar, causes, ran very deep.

39. This is not perhaps the most extreme example. Most of the much-vaunted fifty destroyer escorts of First World War vintage that were secured from the United States Navy by the Royal Navy to augment the available convoy escorts for the North Atlantic proved similarly defective and needed extensive remedial work done in British yards before they were fit for commission as HM Ships.

40. It was far easier to train welders than riveters and although women became members of the wartime riveting teams in British shipyards, armies of women welders would be employed in the green-field shipyards of America.

41. This is something of an over-simplification. A considerable number of differing classes of *Empire* tonnage was built in British yards during the war, some 360 of which were for deep-sea service. These included tramps, cargo-liners and refrigerated ships, Merchant aircraft-carriers (MAC-ships), smaller general cargo vessels, seven types of tanker, colliers, tugs and small service vessels such as dredgers, hoppers and water-carriers and specialised heavy-lift ships. Several of these were sent to Russia to assist with the discharging of tanks and heavy vehicles sent to the Red Army from Britain when it was found difficult to turn the ships around owing to lack of working equipment in Archangel and Murmansk due to bomb damage and a lack of labour owing to conscription into the Soviet army.

42. Alston Kennerley, *British Government Intervention in Seaman's Welfare, 1938–1948*, Congress of the International Commission for Maritime History, Montreal, 1995. My thanks to Professor Kennerley for access to his work.

43. See Behrens, C., *Merchant Shipping and the Demands of War*, p174.

44. The MoWT authorised the Seafarers' Education Service mentioned in Chapter One to extend the issue of libraries to vessels owned by the Government.

45. The trade unions took advantage of the facts that both the control of merchant shipping was in London, as were the representatives of exiled seafarers. In 1944 they drew up an International Seafarers Charter which formed the basis for the agenda of the International Labour Conference

at Seattle in 1946. There was, however, no international ratification of any such charter, only 'some minor advances'.

46. Stan Hughill, had served in sail and later became the bosun at the Outward Bound Sea School at Aberdovey. He was an accomplished artist and collector of sea-shanties upon which he became an authority, publishing several books and articles on the subject, besides becoming a familiar Merseyside personality, well known for singing shanties. His account does not quite square with that recorded by Captain Stephen Roskill in *A Merchant Fleet at War*, p65 *et seq*.

47. The *Automedon*'s RRRR signal had been intercepted by another Blue Funnel liner, the *Helenus*, Captain P.W. Savery, who was suspicious at the lack of a longitude, and she relayed it to Colombo wireless station. This traffic was picked up aboard the *Atlantis* and, thanks to the captured codebooks, interpreted. It was revealed that the *Helenus* was not far away but by the time Rogge was alerted it was dark and the ships had passed each other at a distance. In due course Enigma decrypts allowed HM Cruiser *Devonshire* to engage and sink *Atlantis* while the U-boat she was refuelling at the time submerged. Outgunned, Rogge ordered his ship destroyed and abandoned and after the cruiser had disappeared, *U-126* returned, embarked some of the *Atlantis*'s crew and towed her lifeboats towards the supply-ship *Python*. This rendezvous was interrupted three days later by HMS *Dorsetshire* which sank the *Python* before moving away, knowing that a U-boat was in the vicinity. More U-boats and Italian submarines arrived and the *Atlantis*'s lifeboats were towed into St Nazaire. Gross Admiral Erich Raeder invited Rogge and his crew to a grand reception in Berlin where awards were doled out. Rogge was afterwards one of only three Germans decorated by Emperor Hirohito, the others being Göring and Rommel.

48. The use of reservist officers familiar with British mercantile practice by the *Kriegsmarine* in their commerce-raiders was pioneered during the First World War. The most extreme example of this was aboard the *Komet* (see Chapter Four) where one of her officers had actually sailed under the red ensign as a mate in an Elder, Dempster cargo-liner.

49. Fought north-east of Surabaya the Allies (the Dutch cruisers *De Ruyter* and *Java*; the British cruisers *Exeter* and *Perth* and the American cruiser *Houston* accompanied by two Dutch, three British and four American destroyers) under Doorman were overwhelmed by Admiral Takagi. *Perth* and *Houston* escaped only to meet nemesis in the Sunda Strait on the night of 28 February/1 March when they encountered a squadron under Kurita.

50. The Fergusons were separated in Bordeaux, he to go north to Marlag Milag Nord and she to a camp in the Black Forest, each took one of the crates removed from the *Automedon* with them. He took one full of their crockery, she took her warm clothes. From the Black Forest Mrs Ferguson wrote to her husband requesting that he send her the crockery since their camp had very little and the Germans obliged. Later the camp was properly supplied by the Red Cross and Mrs Ferguson repacked her crockery. She was repatriated through the same institution in 1943 and two years later she was reunited with her husband. On the eve of their departure for Singapore she received notice that a crate had arrived for them from Germany. It was sent after them and, as Professor Tregonning relates in *Home Port Singapore*, p227, he used the crockery it contained when interviewing the Fergusons in 1965.

51. Sam Harper's account appears with some comments by Hughill on the internet (www.merchant-navyofficers.com/automedon) whose webmaster makes the comment, 'there seems very little sympathy for the crews of the ships which the German Commerce raiders sank … [there are] numerous sites on the net with regards … [to U-boats] but nothing at all on [their victims]. You begin to ask yourself what did they die for?' Stephen Roskill relates an expanded version of Harper's escape in *A Merchant Fleet at War*, p72 *et seq*.

52. The DEAC vessels were: *Afrika*, *Amerika*, *Bintang*, *Boringia*, *Chile*, *Danmark*, *Malaya*, *Peru*, *Siam*, *Erria*, *Kina* and *Panama*. The last three survived and, since there was already a *Siam* on the British registry, the Danish vessel of that name was temporarily renamed *Siam II*.

53. To set the war losses of the Bank Line in context, the firm had lost five vessels in the inter-war period. These comprised the *Orteric*, wrecked in December 1922; *Haleric*, wrecked April 1933; *Laganbank*, wrecked January 1938; *Luceric*, lost in the Hughli in July 1938; *Lindenbank*, stranded and later sank, May 1939.

54. Schofield and Martyn, *The Rescue Ships*, p147.

FOUR

'SO RARELY MENTIONED IN THE HEADLINES'

The Merchant Seaman's War, 1939–1945

Unless they were already members of the naval reserve, seafarers were exempt from military call-up, being in a 'reserved occupation' essential to the prosecution of the war effort. The degree to which their work was affected by convoy have been alluded earlier[1] but, although such unglamorous problems have received scant attention, the fact that hundreds of ships served in convoy without mishap, is a mute but eloquent testimony to how well masters, mates, engineers and others adapted to their new conditions. Fortunately many had had experience in the previous war; unfortunately, however, that experience had often been gained in those same ships which now they were taking into a second war.

The advanced age of much shipping did not help their crews readjust to their new environment. Losses of power and steering gear such as disabled the *Blairgowrie* and *Usworth* in peacetime continued to plague old tramps, and even well-found ships could be caught-out in poor weather with visibility reduced to a few yards in windless fog or blinding snow. While measures such as the highly effective fog-buoy – a wooden scoop towed astern which threw up a column of water by which the next ship astern might steer – worked reasonably well, it was of less use in confined waters. With ill-suited vessels jockeying for position, collision was a serious danger from the very beginning, one of the earliest occurring to the Harrison liner *Chancellor* which left Halifax on 2 December 1939, the second ship in the third column of Convoy HXF11, following the commodore in Furness, Withy's *Newfoundland*. HXF11 was a fast, 11-knot convoy, but at 19.00 that night it ran into dense fog. The Commodore blew his siren to signal a general reduction of speed, but this was not fully understood aboard the *Chancellor* and it seems that Captain W.B. Wilford failed to conform sufficiently. At 19.42 the stern of the *Newfoundland* loomed close ahead and the *Chancellor*'s head was swung to starboard. After she was clear and slowed down, it was put over to port to resume station. At that moment the lookout on the forecastle head rang the bell for a ship to starboard. Nothing could be seen from the bridge but the engines were stopped a second or two before the bow of the tanker *Athelchief* broke through the fog and struck the *Chancellor* in way of No.2 Hold, opening her hull to the sea. There was little Wilford could do but stop engines and abandon ship, an order he passed at 20.20. In the calm conditions the boats were launched without incident as the *Chancellor* slowed to a stop. By great good fortune the lifeboats lay in the grain of the Pacific Steam Navigation Co.'s liner *Oropesa*, Captain Dunn, which had been designated the convoy's rescue ship, and two hours later all the *Chancellor*'s crew were safely aboard and the *Oropesa* hastened after the convoy. By the following day the fog had cleared and a south-easterly gale was blowing. Shortly after midnight on the 4th the *Oropesa* encountered the outward-bound *Manchester Regiment* and struck her just abaft the bridge, flooding No.3 Hold, the engine room and stokehold. Nine men were lost from the *Manchester Regiment* as they abandoned ship in conditions very different from what had prevailed earlier. Picking up sixty-one survivors Captain Dunn put the *Oropesa* about for Halifax, following the damaged *Athelchief* back into the port they had so recently left. Meanwhile on the 3rd a salvage tug from Halifax had reached the *Chancellor* with a view to salvaging her, and although a line was secured aboard, she soon afterwards foundered. At the subsequent Inquiry the *Chancellor* was held entirely to blame.

Later on, merchant ships were forbidden to stop and rescue survivors, leaving the task to the trawlers or corvettes acting as 'tail-end Charlies' with consequences we have already examined. The case of the *Chancellor* demonstrates that even in war time the civil processes of obeying the rules governing the conduct of ships at sea prevailed and the Harrison Line were, like other firms, to lose ships to what were called 'marine causes' rather than the malice of the enemy, even when some of those marine causes were directly attributable to the war itself. Harrisons were to lose twenty-seven ships to enemy action and a further three due to marine causes, the *Barrister*, *Magician* and *Politician*.[2] The best known of these was the last. The *Politician* was a relatively new, steam-turbine-powered 8,000-ton goal-poster built in 1935, which came to grief in February 1941. The ship left Liverpool bound for Jamaica and New Orleans with a commercial cargo of cotton goods, general merchandise, military stores for British forces in the West Indies – and 22,000 cases of whisky. This was only a part cargo and she rode at a relatively light draught, well trimmed by the stern. Captain B. Worthington had been ordered to proceed independently and was to pass through the Minch before turning west into the Atlantic, taking him well clear of the convoy routes and the then common hunting grounds of the U-boats. The *Politician* therefore made her way north with a following gale, in heavy seas and blinding rain squalls. On her way through the North Channel, she had encountered an incoming convoy which had necessitated some smart manoeuvring in the dark, which may have had some bearing upon what followed. At 07.40 on the morning of Wednesday 5 February Chief Officer R.A. Swain suddenly and quite unexpectedly saw the loom of land on his starboard bow. He ordered the helm hard a-port and went astern. Steam turbines do not give good stern-power and take some time about it, so the *Politician* continued before the gale, the helm order turning her away from what turned out to be the island of Hartamul, drove her towards the island of Eriskay. A moment later she ran hard aground, her light bow riding over the rocks of Rohinish Point upon which she impaled herself in the way of the stokehold, engine room and the after holds, Nos 4 and 5. The crew was all rescued and although attempts were made to lighten and salvage her, the weather prevented it and in due course the *Politician* broke her back. Later she was partially salved and scrapped but her chief claim to notoriety lay in the fact that the islanders of Eriskay considered the consignment of whisky a 'gift from God'. The subsequent shenanegins inspired the author Compton Mackezie's novel *Whisky Galore* and belong properly to folklore, but the example of the *Politician* demonstrates the difficulties of navigating in confined, tidal waters in pre-radar days during bad weather.[3]

But the *Politician* was outward bound, theoretically still in sight of land – 'in bearings' in nautical parlance – a situation much better than a convoy coming in from the Atlantic in bad weather and seeking a landfall. This was the plight of another of Harrison's ships, the *Barrister*, as late as 1943 when all convoy escorts had been equipped with radar. The *Barrister* was returning to Liverpool having delivered a consignment of military stores to Algiers in the wake of Operation TORCH, the Allied Invasion of Vichy French North Africa. She joined a large homeward convoy of fifty-five ships at Gibraltar and from the moment of departure on 27 December 1942 the weather was vile. Convoy MKS4 took a wide sweep into the North Atlantic and on 3 January orders were received to divide it. One section would approach the Irish Sea from the south and the *Barrister's* would proceed by way of the North Channel so that by the small hours of 4th the *Barrister* was heading for a landfall in the vicinity of Malin Head. She remained in company with a number of merchant ships and warships, one of which was an escort aircraft-carrier and it was known that most men-of-war were by now fitted with a highly secret but brilliant new device which was able to penetrate fog and rain. Although Captain H. Collins and his officers were anxious about the dangers of making a landfall on dead-reckoning positions alone, they had great confidence in the new equipment and, for them, maintaining station on the escort-carrier, assumed priority and reassured them. However, the weather continued boisterous and only indistinct shapes could occasionally be discerned through the murk of a winter dawn. With a heavy swell, under overcast skies and a persistent drizzle, Third Officer J. Bean could see very little when he took over the watch with Cadet Cubbin, who recalled that:

Suddenly, out of the mist, and becoming more distinct with each leaden second, loomed the black silhouette of an enormous rocky crag … At its base clouds of white spume rose high in the air as the Atlantic swells swept in. It could not have been more than half a mile away …

The Third Officer reacted swiftly:

The helm was put over but it was too late. As the elderly Captain Collins reached the bridge the ship struck and 'he leaned on the rail and stared ahead at the broken water in utter disbelief … Incongruously, a steward vigorously sounded the first gong for breakfast.' The ship was vibrating madly under full astern power, and the wash was sweeping forward, but the bow, held fast by the rocks did not budge. The stern of the ship, on the other hand, was undulating ominously to the swell. There was a crack like a rifle shot from somewhere below the bridge. Then another, quickly followed by a rattle like a burst of machine-gun fire. The rivets holding the ship's members together were bursting under the strain. Sadly, Captain Collins rang 'Stop' on the telegraph and went to the engine-room voice-pipe. He spoke to the Chief Engineer [Ernest Mossman] … 'Shut down, Chief, and bring your men up from there. Abandon ship!'[4]

The *Barrister* broke her back having run aground on Inishshark, an island off the Connemara coast, miles from their intended track and a sad indictment of the navigation of the entire convoy. The error must have been apparent elsewhere for as the crew of the *Barrister* took to their boats one of the escorts, the Canadian corvette *Kitchener*, lay rolling offshore. Soon afterwards HMS *Landguard* appeared on the scene and her commanding officer was incensed that although the confidential books had been destroyed by Second Officer Harold Skelly there were some additional secret papers in the master's safe. According to Graeme Cubbin's account it is clear that Captain Collins was badly shaken by what had happened and the difficulties of crossing the fissure that fractured the *Barrister*'s deck in order to get to the boats had driven all thought of secret papers from his mind. The *Landguard*'s commander instructed Skelly to retrieve the papers and, although at first unwilling to go, after awaiting a moderation in the heavy surf through which they had been lucky in working the boats, an attempt to board the wreck was made on the following forenoon. At dawn on the 5th, armed with gelignite, Skelly, the *Landguard*'s gunnery officer and a party of ratings, made for the forward section of the *Barrister*. That was all that was left of her, the after part having broken away, to disappear into deep water. Clambering aboard by way of the port anchor they found the accommodation wrecked, but both safe and, incredibly, the safe keys remained, along with Collins's sextant. Retrieving what they had come for and returning to the *Landguard*, Skelly was now ordered to land and formally report the wreck to the Irish Receiver of Wreck. He took with him Third Officer Bean and Cadet Eric Parry and they landed courtesy of a local fishing boat which came alongside. While Collins, who was clearly at sixty-three years of age badly affected by the loss of his ship, and the remainder of the crew reached Liverpool aboard the *Landguard*, Skelly and his small party found themselves taken to the adjacent island of Inishbofin. Here they stayed several days, objects of curiosity and some hostility from the islanders.[5] Eventually they reached the mainland and signed over the wreck afterwards making their way to Dublin and from there to Liverpool. Captain Collins retired in 1950, though he never served at sea after the loss of the *Barrister*. He sold the retrieved sextant to Harold Skelly, who rose to command in the line.

There were other causes of loss, icing and defective welding accounted for a few ships, but the sheer power of the ocean to cause a ship to founder was, although rare, an ever-present possibility. The French cargo-liner *Ville de Tamatave* had been owned by the Nouvelle Compagnie Havraise Péninsulaire de Navigation and had been built in 1931 for a service between France, French North Africa and the Indian Ocean. Upon the fall of France she had not returned home, but had come under the aegis of the

British Ministry of Shipping who had placed her management with Alfred Holt & Co. Although she wore the red ensign of Great Britain, she retained her French crew under Capitaine G. Dault with the exception of her two radio officers who were British. A well-found vessel, she was selected as the commodore's ship for the west-bound convoy ONS160 which sailed on 12 January 1943. The climax of the long battle for the domination of the North Atlantic was approaching and it was one of the worst winters within living memory for cold, high winds and heavy seas. The privations endured without the intervention of the enemy were appalling and twelve days out, when roughly 500-miles east of Cape Race, the senior officer of the escort reported the ships under his wing had been badly scattered by the weather. All of the merchantmen were battered and many were damaged, but the *Ville de Tamatave* was lost with all hands. There were no details, beyond a report that she had been seen on her beam ends.

The weather and the cruel sea – in that phrase borrowed by Nicholas Monsarrat with telling effect from Captain Gilbert Roberts at the Anti-submarine Tactical School in Liverpool – was an old and acknowledged enemy.[6] It was the sudden shock of a torpedo-strike that most seamen feared. The hunting methods adopted by the German U-boats invariably resulted in attacks between the hours of 22.00 and 04.00. Time after time the casualty figures for British merchantmen show the ominous number three: the duty engineer, fireman and greaser. And while such high-octane fuels as aviation spirit exploded and burned with a ferocious and searing heat, there cannot have been much to choose between it and super-heated steam. Perhaps the most dangerous cargo was a heavy ore, which took a ship down to her marks but did not fill her, so that any breach in her hull allowed water to pour in. In such circumstances a ship foundered quickly and many cases are recorded where the number of *survivors* was also three: the helmsman, lookout and the officer-of-the-watch. Eye-witness accounts speak of ships still forging ahead at full speed and driving downwards to the abyssal plain four miles below the surface. Indeed, unless they were loaded with inflammable spirit, an oil tanker laden with a low grade, lighter-than-water oil had, with her strong longitudinal framing, a better chance of surviving than almost any other build of ship if she had the misfortune to be torpedoed. Among those that did so were Houlder Bros' *Imperial Transport*, the Eagle Oil Company's famous *San Demetrio* mentioned earlier, and the bomb-damaged *Ohio* which ran a much needed cargo of oil into Valletta Harbour as part of Operation PEDESTAL.

Ironically, owing to her survival, the story of the tanker *Ensis* was almost unknown until recently, when an account, written by her junior radio officer came to light. The *Ensis* belonged to the Anglo-Saxon Oil Co., better known as Shell, and had been built in 1937. She was capable of carrying over 9,000 deadweight tons and the description of the torpedo-strike against her is particularly vivid. On Sunday 8 June 1941 the *Ensis* was steaming west, into a heavy Atlantic swell which she was riding well, with a strong wind on her starboard beam after her convoy had been dispersed beyond the 'danger-zone'. The *Ensis* was in ballast, her tanks largely empty as a watery sun attempted to break through the cloud and the Third Radio Officer made his way aft along the flying bridge towards the smoke room where he hoped to spend a quiet half-hour enjoying a read and a smoke before starting his radio watch. It was, of course, only here that smoking was permissible.

On entering the smoke-room I took up a position by the starboard bulkhead, and reclined on the settee. I noticed that the clock wanted four minutes to 11.30 a.m. also that seated in places about the smoke-room were one of the British sailor-gunners [a DEMS rating], and two officers absorbed in books. I had barely opened my book, when a terrific ear-splitting, explosion occurred. I was lifted bodily as if by giant hands from my position on the settee, and literally hurled across the room, to be brought up sharp by the port bulkhead, the impact sickened me, and left me breathless. The starboard door, which is made of a two-inch thickness of very stout oak, had been torn from its moorings, and flung along the after deck in many pieces. Two … panelled lockers had been virtually torn to shreds and the after deck itself was cracked and littered with glass, china and steel. A soldier and officer were picking themselves up from beneath a smashed bookcase, and our sailor was doing likewise from beneath an easy chair. The two big electric fans … were nowhere to be seen and the two radiators were blown to bits. The porthole frames made of a composition of brass and some other metal equally heavy, had been torn from their sockets (one of which it transpired later had struck one of the soldiers a violent blow on the jaw, needless to say breaking it) in point of fact the whole place was a shambles. All this I noticed in seconds – nerve-wracking, terrifying seconds I will never forget. It seemed to me that I lay there for hours, trying to gather my scattered senses' actually it could only have been a few brief moments, before I deemed it advisable to drag my bruised and aching body to a standing position. The others had made their feet and were scrambling through the port-side door. I did likewise. I stepped out into the fresh air, and made my way along the deck to the wireless-room for standby. At this stage I had the feeling that my lungs were about to burst oweing(sic) to the over abundance of cordite contained in them from the exploded torpedo. The wireless-cabin had been badly damaged, and our main valve transmitter had been rendered useless. We were able to get the receiver going and our senior radio officer, a splendid fellow, proceeded to send out our distress call on the emergency transmitter, not much use in a case like this, when it is remembered that we were over two thousand miles from the nearest point of land, and this transmitter possesses only a comparatively small wave range.

While the gunners ran aft and fired ineffectively 'at the submerged U-boat,' the *Ensis*'s master gave the order to abandon ship.

I made my way to the life-boat, pandemonium had broken loose amongst our Chinese crew, who were running everywhere, shouting and gesticulating frantically. However, in a very short time we restored them to something like sane human beings. We contrived to get them to their allotted life-boat, whence we gave the order to lower the boats. Panic again broke loose when the lowering ropes of the starboard after life-boat snapped and the boat itself dropped into the sea and drifted away. These were terrible moments and I pray God I am never called on to relive them … If you can imagine yourself aboard a ship apparently sinking quickly, by this time the *Ensis* was heeled over badly and her starboard lower deck was completely submerged in water – and you have forty or fifty wild-eyed, panic-stricken

Chinese to handle – coupled with the fact that you are alone in the middle of a mighty ocean, except of course … that somewhere in the vicinity lies an enemy submarine, who[se] commander may decide to put more torpedoes into your ship, you will get a rough idea of our feelings … I feel I must … lend praise to my gallant and courageous colleagues, whose remarkable calm and snappy orders did so much to tide us over this unhappy turn of events … In something like twenty minutes following the impact of the torpedo, which incidentally struck us slightly forward of the engine-room on our starboard flank, we were well clear of the ship and pulling on the oars for our very lives. A few minutes later we were due for another shock, and this to my mind was the most terrifying part of the whole proceedings, and I think I can truthfully say that it was this threatened danger only that scared me proper … After having rowed some considerable distance from the ship the navigating officer gave the order to rest oars, after having done so we looked back at our ship … suddenly and without warning (I think we had all forgot about the U-boat) the U-boat's periscope portruded(sic) from the water only a few yards from our small craft, and was greeted by glances set well back, too far back in pale faces, eyes which only a moment before had shone with hope and defiance. I thought of home so far away, these moments which might have been my last I was determined to spend with my beloved wife, and a further glance told me that the thoughts of my pals were trending on similar lines to my own – we had become resigned to die. A strange and ghostly silence had descended on our little craft … It was as much as I could do to take another look at the sub. but what I saw served to relieve my feelings … for the sub. was heading away from us in the direction of the *Ensis*. She … [went] around the stern, and then crashed two more torpedoes into the port side amidships. Two bright orange flashed leapt up seemingly to the sky, and our good ship shook convulsively and began to settle on her port beam … She seemed certain to sink[.T]he U-boat commander thought so too, for he surfaced and cruised full speed ahead disappearing over the horizon.[7]

In the euphoria of survival the writer praises the U-boat commander in allowing them time to abandon ship before administering the *coup de grâce*. The U-boat commander was Kapitänleutnant Engelbert Endrass of *U-46*, one of seven U-boats sent out to attack shipping in mid-Atlantic after covering the *Bismarck*'s last and fatal sortie. The survivors' enthusiasm for the 'wonderful and most complimentary behaviour' of Endrass waned as the day wore on. The seas were running high, the Chinese in the boat were desperately sea-sick and efforts to sail to keep close to the ship were defeated by a rising wind. Driven to keep pulling at the oars their will and energy were soon sapped. Towards evening the chief engineer, with uncommon good sense, suggested that as the *Ensis* had not sunk, they might as well spend the night on board where hot food and drink could be obtained. They might also reinstate their main transmitter in order to contact Land's End Radio. If they were to have to make a long boat voyage they would be foolish not to better provision the boats. The chief engineer, second mate, the first radio officer, second engineer and two of the DEMS gunners had scrambled back on board where they were joined by the master and chief officer. The boats were stocked with extra food and blankets and then lay off where, helped by a moderation of the wind overnight, those left in them snatched a little sleep. It was observed that there was an:

> absolute lack of fighting spirit shown by the Chinese. They seemed resolved to lay down and die, and nothing we could do (we tried coaxing, then threats, we even ordered our naval gunners to draw their revolvers and shoot a few of them, if they did not show a willing … spirit) could bring them to realize we not beaten yet. They simply lay about the boat hindering us in our work, they refused to pull an oar or to help bale out the water in the life-boat … I tried to find sympathy in my heart for them but could not. A man who won't make some [effort] … deserves to die, and if I had my way, I would have put a bullet into every one of them who refused to pull an oar, without the slightest compunction. Here we were, arms and legs aching horribly, hands blistered and bleeding, pulling a bunch of utterly useless Chinese about the Atlantic, contempt would not explain my feelings for them … I would ask my readers to forgive this sudden and rude outburst, but I would point out that such were my feelings at the time.

Dawn brought a rapidly freshening wind and it was quickly resolved that they had little hope of survival in such circumstances. The seduction of a hot drink aboard the *Ensis* proved overwhelming and, already suffering from lack of nourishment – no water was issued on grounds of conservation – they struggled alongside and secured the boats to the lee side of the ship. Once aboard, fed and watered, morale rose rapidly; the gunners went aft to man their gun and keep a sharp lookout; others worked as directed to re-establish some command over the ship.

> The ship was in a terrible state, the decks literally torn to shreds, the bridge was shattered, steering smashed, the centre-castle had a huge gaping hole in it, and was taking tons of water inboard, rivets bolts (sic) were scattered everywhere, cabin doors were blown off, with the exception of the engine-room, where only the slightest damage had been done, the ship was a veritable wreck …

But after some hours of work on the main transmitter the senior radio officer announced that he was in contact with Land's End, news that transformed them 'into men filled with zest and endeavour, and a will to win yet …' but the master again ordered them to abandon ship as he was convinced that the transmission would have been monitored and that U-boats would return for a final kill. Boarding the boats they pulled away and lay at a safe distance. The hours passed, the promised rescue failed to materialize; again spirits sank and remained depressed until the afternoon, when a smudge of smoke was seen and within an hour two corvettes lay wallowing alongside. The senior officer ordered the survivors aboard but now, with anti-submarine protection, the *Ensis*'s master decided they should try and save the ship. The corvette commander was derisory but grudgingly agreed. Reboarding the *Ensis* the engine was started – she was a motor-vessel – and course shaped for St John's, Newfoundland, 1,100 miles distant.

At ten past four (on Monday 9 June) the engines began to rev and the good old *Ensis* staggered and lurched forward. The tension at this moment was terrific as we all realized the mighty dangerous task we had set ourselves. We knew there would be no time to sleep, and regardless of rank it would mean every man giving of his best and then some, if the success of getting our little more than skeleton of a ship to port was to be achieved. Everybody worked like the devil, including the Chinese ...

Groaning and creaking ominously, the *Ensis* moved slowly north-west, all hands in expectation of her breaking her back and the strain thereof showing on every face.

By the end of four unforgettable days we had covered 500 miles. The corvette had kept close at hand, in case we should break in two, and kept a ceaseless lookout for U-boats. We had engineers posted day and night at our most dangerous points ... to give the alarm ... On our sixth and seventh day following the torpedoing ... we were slowly feeling our way through ice-fields and invariably in thick fog ... A great feeling of triumph and pride swept over our boys when at 1 a.m. on the 15th June the lights of St John's shone dimly on the ... horizon ... [A]t 7.15 a.m. we staggered into St John's harbour and dropped anchor ...

The ordeal of the *Ensis* and her crew set alongside those of the *San Demetrio* and *Ohio* lacks some of the heroics that have accrued to these well-known epics, but it is a tale – told frankly and without undue embellishment – of a job well done. The *Ensis* was saved to carry oil again. On 4 April the following year she was 'slightly damaged' by 20mm shellfire from *U-572* (Hirsacker), and on 29 February 1944, when operating in the Mediterranean off the Syrian coast she was again torpedoed and damaged, this time by *U-407* (Korndörfer). Nevertheless, she survived the war, thanks to the determination of the crew that manned her in June 1941.[8]

For the most part trans-Atlantic trooping in fast liners was without incident; most of the ships engaged were simply too fast for the U-boats and by the time such mass movements were under way the threat of the surface raider had been eliminated. Most of the grand liners so employed shuttled back and forth, and pre-eminent among them were the *Queen Mary*, which had made her first such voyage of 7 August 1942, and the *Queen Elizabeth*, which joined her a month later, making ten voyages before the end of the year. These two ships carried immense numbers of men, on one occasion in July 1943 as many as 15,740 boarded the *Queen Mary* for a voyage from New York to Gourock. With her crew of 943, the total of 16,683 souls under the care of Captain James Bisset was the greatest number ever embarked in a single ship on an ocean crossing accomplished in four days, twenty hours and forty-two minutes at a speed of 28.73 knots. Before settling down on this shuttle the two huge liners, along with their Cunard-White Star sisters the *Aquitania* and *Mauretania*, the requisitioned French liner *Île de France* and the chartered Dutch liner *Nieuw Amsterdam*, 'had already done a prodigious amount of steaming between Australia, New Zealand or India and the Middle East, and from the west coast of America to the Antipodes,'[9] carrying 'thousands of troops of many nationalities safely to their destinations. Many other liners were engaged at one time or another on the trans-Atlantic run, among them Canadian

Pacific's *Empress of Scotland* and the Royal Mail liner *Andes*. Although their speed and voyages individually routed by the Admiralty were their best defence against attack, the possibility of a lucky torpedo or a concentrated air attack in the Western Approaches could not be ruled out. Consequently they were seen clear of the American or Canadian coasts, where a U-boat might be lurking, and met inwards around the 12th Meridian West by a fast anti-aircraft cruiser and up to six destroyers. By the autumn of 1942, the two *Queens* had established their regular shuttle of single-ship, 'operational convoys' and between July and December that year 194,850 American troops had been safely conveyed across the Western Ocean to Britain.[10] Despite the Admiralty's anxieties these operations were to be marred by only one incident, and one in which the Royal Navy had a part. Commanded by Captain Illingworth, the *Queen Mary* had Canadian troops on board and was bound from New York to Gourock, on the Clyde. She had met her inward escort of HM Cruiser *Curacoa* and four destroyers and was approaching the North Western Approaches, zig-zagging at 28 knots. The precise details of what occurred on 2 October are confused, various accounts differ, but the outcome was indisputable: the *Queen Mary* rammed and cut the *Curacoa* in two. The visibility was good, though squally, with a fresh north-westerly wind throwing up a rough sea, both ships were zig-zagging but the precision of the timed turns somehow became desynchronized. Several times prior to the actual collision, the *Curacoa* had passed so close under the *Queen Mary*'s sharp and towering bow that she had disappeared from the view of the officers on the liner's bridge. As Sir James Bisset describes: 'It was a horrifying moment for those on the bridge and decks of the *Queen Mary* when they saw the halves of the *Curacao* (sic) rolling over and over, one along each side of the giant ship, to disappear in the turbulence of her wake.' Some rafts were thrown over from the liner but she was forbidden to stop, though the damage forced her to reduce speed to 20 knots as the four escorting destroyers rescued the handful of survivors. Of the *Curacoa*'s complement of 410, 338 lives were lost but, as Bisset comments, the heavy loss of life would have been far worse 'if the cruiser's ammunition had exploded under the bows of the *Queen Mary*'. The liner was patched-up at her builders and sent to Boston for proper repairs. Meanwhile the case was heard in the High Court of Admiralty and all blame was attributed to HMS *Curacoa*. Not content with this, the Admiralty appealed and the case went before the House of Lords where the blame was adjusted, the *Queen Mary* shouldering one third.

Liners engaged in trooping from Canada carried on their outward voyages Canadian service personnel going on leave or others bound for duties abroad, as well as Merchant Naval crews being sent to join the new ships being acquired in America and later to join those being built in the United States and Canada under the Emergency War Building Programmes. Prior to joining the Ocean Rescue ship *Copeland*, as described in the preceding chapter, the young George Russell, had been one of these.

On 20 January 1941 signed on as 3rd Officer of the steamship *Braddock* at the Shipping Office in Glasgow. The name of the ship was quite unknown to myself or any of the other Donaldson personnel being engaged, but four days later as a complete crew we embarked as passengers on the Orient liner *Orontes* at the Tail of the

Bank anchorage. That same evening, *Orontes* departed the Clyde as an independent sailing, crammed with 3,200 RAF, military and naval personnel and reached Halifax safely and without incident eight days later. Here we were bundled into a train and made our way by various railroads and numerous stops in American towns and cities to the US Gulf port of Mobile, in Alabama, where at last we found the *Braddock*. This old steamer turned out to be one of a hundred American laid-up ships, built at the end of the First World War, which the Ministry … had purchased for service under the Red Ensign. Most had been laid-up for twenty years or so, the *Braddock* certainly for ten years, and we found her completely mothballed, yet it took the local labour only three weeks to prepare her for sea. This was remarkably done by untrained labour, many of whom had hardly seen never mind been aboard a ship. We had the odd mistake like trying to fit the starboard sidelight on the port side and vice versa, but otherwise everything worked as it should have done when we finally got to sea. Like all of her kind the *Braddock* was a three-island ship with five hatches, ten derricks and the old counter stem. She was 6,615 tons gross and 411ft overall length. However, unlike her British counterparts fitted with 'up and down' engines and coal fired boilers, the *Braddock* was turbine driven and oil fired! We got away from Mobile in the last week of February 1941 and loaded in Tampa a full cargo of cotton, and then steamed up to Halifax to join a homeward convoy, but were delayed there three weeks undergoing boiler repairs. We sailed from Halifax in Convoy HX 119 with the AMC *Aurania* (another ex Cunard liner) as Ocean Escort. This was an uneventful crossing which ended at Oban, where we joined a coastal convoy going north-about to Methil Roads, thence to Hull for discharge. The *Braddock* remained in Hull for nearly four weeks having various wartime equipment and armament fitted (the Neutrality Laws did not allow this to be undertaken in the United States, which was not then at war). Also at this time the *Braddock* had her name changed to conform to Ministry (MoWT) nomenclature at the time, and became the *Empire Redshank*.

At the start of our next trip on 24 May 1941, it was with heavy hearts that we locked out of Hull docks into the Humber, having just heard on the BBC that Britain's mighty battle-cruiser, *HMS Hood,* had been sunk in the Atlantic in an action with the *Bismarck*. We were bound for the States in ballast, initially in a very slow coastal convoy around the north of Scotland, and during this passage were elated to hear the BBC now announce that the *Bismarck* had been sunk. Our coastal convoy put in first to Loch Ewe in Wester Ross, which had become a vast convoy assembly anchorage, and from there to Oban where we joined an outward ocean convoy and finished up in Baltimore. We loaded there and at Hampton Roads, mostly Lend-Lease cargo comprising all kinds of military stores, vehicles and equipment and returned home in the by now customary Halifax convoy, this time with the AMC *Ranpura* (ex-P&O) liner as Ocean Escort. The Lend-Lease cargo was all discharged in Swansea.

On our next trip back to the States we left Swansea in ballast on 24 August 1941, joining a coastal convoy in Milford Haven and the ocean convoy in Belfast Lough. After another uneventful crossing we were directed to load in New Orleans and soon after entering the Gulf of Mexico ran into a hurricane. It was the classic textbook Tropical Revolving Storm with the wind and sea gradually increasing with torrential rain until we reached the eye of the storm when everything suddenly ceased, the sky and sea turned yellow, then, wham, the fiercest wind and sea from the opposite direction. In due course as the storm passed and the weather improved we ran into an area of muddy brown water strewn with broken trees, vegetation and dead livestock. This proved to be the great Mississippi spewing out the devastation caused by the hurricane but very soon led us to pick up the pilot for the 80-mile passage up the river to New Orleans Whilst in the river, however, our orders were changed to load instead at Houston and Beaumont, and somewhat disappointed therefore, had to turn around without even getting alongside in New Orleans.

As we shall presently see, the *Empire Redshank* was bound for Russia.

There were many very young men at war in the Merchant Navy, boys who were actually under military age. Most were galley- or deck-boys, cadets or apprentices and a few were radio officers, such as David Craig who went to sea aged fifteen. Among the galley boys was Joseph Brooks, who had been sent from his east-end of London home to an orphanage because his father could not afford to keep him. Brooks escaped this fate, being recruited into the Merchant Navy at the age of fourteen.[11] Such youth did not absolve a few from appalling consequences; the fourteen-year-old Reginald Earnshaw was killed when his ship, the Newcastle tramp *North Devon* was attacked by aircraft off Sheringham on 5 July 1941. Others assumed heavy responsibilities, particularly the young mates who, receiving accelerated promotion, found themselves in charge of lonely lifeboats while some found themselves caught in odd situations and acted with considerable initiative and courage. When the Harrison liner *Dalesman* was sunk at Suda Bay, Crete, on 14 May 1941, her survivors were co-opted by the army and, in anticipation of the imminent German invasion from Greece, formed into unarmed anti-paratroop patrols. Among these was a seventeen-year-old cadet named John Dobson. When General Freyberg evacuated Crete Dobson was among those left behind to fall into the hands of the pursuing Germans. While being marched into captivity Dobson decided to grab one of the guard's machine guns and, turning it on the Germans, made good his escape. Soon afterwards he joined a group of New Zealand soldiers as they trudged south, over the mountains during which he suffered from a grumbling appendix. The party reached Khora Sfakion where they boarded an abandoned tank landing craft and, while the Kiwis could start the engine, they turned to Dobson to navigate the vessel to Egypt. Despite having been on his first voyage to sea, Dobson accomplished this, although they arrived within five miles of the front line. In due course, his appendix removed, Dobson was shipped home where he was interviewed in Liverpool by Admiral Sir Percy Noble, then Commander-in-Chief, Western Approaches. On 4 August 1942 Dobson was gazetted with a BEM, Civil Division, though he never subsequently served at sea as he suffered from post-traumatic stress.

For damaging long-term strain, however, the most unusual ordeal must surely have been that of eighteen-year-old Peter Johnson, a junior radio officer aboard the Blue Funnel liner *Memnon*. Lawrence Holt's practice of training his people in small-boat sailing at Aberdovey paid-off on several occasions. Those deck-officers who came from the *Conway* and the *Worcester*, were highly proficient boat-handlers and entry into the Blue Funnel Line from the *Conway* was as natural as was joining any of the several companies in the P&O Group by cadets from the *Worcester*. But Holt's wisdom attempted – not entirely successfully, as will be observed – to enable all ranks in Blue Funnel liners to make themselves useful in a lifeboat. It also greatly improved the co-operation of the otherwise fatalistic Chinese ratings, for whom Holt had a special affection. Thus the passages made by lifeboats from Blue Funnel and Glen Line vessels contrast well with the rather bumbling efforts of the crew of the *Ensis*, those of the *Memnon* and *Rhexenor* being notable. That of the *Memnon* was consequential for a handful of her crew, but Blue Funnel men were not the only people to distinguish themselves in this way. The voyages of the *Anglo-Saxon*'s jolly-boat and No.7 Boat of the Anchor liner *Britannia* are also of interest.

In early July 1940, the Vichy authorities issued an order to all French submarines and aircraft to sink British merchant shipping. On 9 July the Blue Funnel liner *Memnon*, homeward bound from the Far East, was anchored off São Vincente, Cape Verde Islands, when her radio operators intercepted this operational order, transmitted *en clair* in French from Dakar. The *Memnon*'s junior radio officer, Peter Le Q. Johnson, spoke fluent French and it was quickly realised that the order from the Vichy authorities was in reprisal for the Royal Navy's pre-emptive raids on Oran and Dakar in the previous week. Captain J.G. Phillips was therefore appraised in good time and later that day, at about 18.00, by which time the *Memnon* was fifty miles clear of the islands, his vigilant lookouts spotted torpedo tracks, which fortunately passed astern.

Following her turn-around, that November the *Memnon*, together with a number of other cargo-liners – including the Glen Liner *Breconshire* which was fully commissioned as a Military Transport – were loaded with military stores and essential supplies and proceeded to Alexandria by way of Capetown prior to taking part in a major operation to reinforce Malta. Having executed this duty and returned to Alexandria, the *Memnon*, now commanded by Captain J.P. Williams, was released from transport duties and headed home the way she had come. At Freetown, however, she was not attached to a convoy, but routed independently and she sailed for Liverpool on 8 March 1941. By the afternoon of the 11th she was about 200-miles west of Cape Blanco, zig-zagging at 15 knots. This did not save her from a torpedo fired from *U-106* (Oesten) which had been deployed with some other Type IX U-boats to target an area hitherto relatively safe for British shipping. On the bridge Williams ordered a SSSS signal transmitted with the ship's position; he also ordered the boats lowered immediately as the ship appeared to be settling fast. Four of the six boats were launched successfully, and all the mustered hands scrambled into them as the *Memnon* sank, before two of the boats were discovered to have been damaged and leaked badly, so their men clambered into the others. Captain Williams had secured some basic navigational equipment and joined Fourth Officer Eric Casson on No.1 lifeboat. As they pulled clear Casson recalled:

> The ship lay with her poop submerged. Only the tops of her sampson posts and the standing derricks on them showed above water. Just then the two Radio-Officers were seen on the boat deck. They had stayed behind, sending out the distress call

as long as possible, and had then left the radio-room to find all the boats had gone. No.1 was the only boat in a position to rescue them, No.5 having gone astern of the ship to pick up some men on a raft …

The two radio officers were George Whalley and Peter Johnson, who later recalled his horror as he 'saw my bloody lifeboat pulling across the after well deck!'[12] The two men were ordered to jump into the sea which they did, Whalley being 'in great danger of being dragged down No.6 hatch, when an uprush swept him clear. We were very fortunate in being able to reach and rescue them both,' Casson continued.

> Then a movement was seen in the ship. A bulkhead had collapsed, her bows lifted higher and higher, and when her deck reached an angle of forty-five degrees she began to slide under. The end was terrible and violent. The rush of water forced oil, air, fumes, etc. in a great red cloud out of the funnel. The force must have been enormous. As the funnel was disappearing it collapsed at the base, reared in the air and fell. The rest of the ship quickly followed, the truck of the foremast barely missing No.4 boat (which had just floated off the poop). As the ship vanished the surface of the sea became very confused, and No.4 boat was practically swamped. Mr Whalley was picked up in the very nick of time – just as this surge of water reached our boat. The U-boat had meanwhile surfaced and closed first No.5 boat, then No.4 and then ourselves. She appeared to be about 700 – 800 tons, and was armed with a 3-inch gun forward and a machine-gun aft. The men in the conning tower shouted and pointed. We pulled in the direction indicated and sighted a Chinese member of the crew hanging on to wreckage. He was picked up.

Whalley's distress message had been acknowledged by a Spanish ship and the two boats streamed sea anchors and settled to await her appearance. Besides Williams and Casson, in No.1 Boat there were twenty-two men; forty-four more were in No.5 Boat under Chief Officer R.J. McCarthy and Second Officer L.R.H. Hill, and the rough seas prevented them being evened out. Baling had to be carried out continuously until the boats dry planking 'took-up' as they wallowed under a full-moon. 'The night seemed interminable. Though the boat rode well … cold spray drenched us all. Flares were burnt every three hours, and threw a lurid light on to an unforgettable scene. We could see No.5 boat as a dark silhouette, tossing on the moonlit waters.'

Next morning men and stores were shared and on the 13th Williams and McCarthy gave up their wait for the Spaniard and resolved to make a landing near Dakar, 400 miles away, and then run on to reach British territory at Bathurst in Gambia. After a day of uneven progress Williams, whose boat sailed better, decided to press on ahead. Progress was slow with worsening weather requiring No.1 Boat to be hove-to for some hours. Williams conserved rations and this and the constant baling made demands on his men. At 09.00 on the 19th, a week after leaving the ship, they sighted land which Williams recognised. They were ignored by a coastal steamer and Williams pressed on until on the 21st, with the water all but gone and no one able 'to go on another day' they approached the small fishing village of Yoff. That evening they were ashore in the military hospital 'where they received food and rest'. Here they were joined by the boatswain and steward from McCarthy's boat who explained what had happened to No.5 Boat.

Perversely McCarthy's boat had made good progress, arriving off Port Louis on the 21st where she encountered the Chargeurs Réunis steamer *Kilisi* whose master proved friendly. Advsing McCarthy not to head for Dakar but try and make Bathurst, he reprovisioned the lifeboat and took out of her the boatswain and steward who were in a bad way. McCarthy had lost one man on the passage but otherwise reached Bathurst, a passage of 600 miles made in thirteen days. Both crews behaved admirably, except for an assistant steward in McCarthy's boat whose stoppage of rations 'quickly reduced him to order'. In addition to the man who died in McCarthy's boat, three Chinese had been lost with the *Memnon*. The Elder, Dempster Line's agent in Bathurst looked after the survivors from No.5 Boat and Mr Justice Gray of the Supreme Court in Gambia wrote to Lawrence Holt of his admiration for the exploit. 'Reading between the lines … one can find another story – of fine seamanship, pluck and endurance, which were well worthy of the best traditions of a very fine service.'

McCarthy's men were soon on their way home but in Dakar matters were not so straight forward. Having landed safely, Captain Williams and the older men were quickly released by the French. The younger fell foul of the Vichy French who were not sympathetic to British survivors, not least because of the alleged betrayal of Oran and Dakar. Fourth Officer Eric Casson, George Whalley, and Peter Johnson were among those who found themselves imprisoned in Koulikoro where the camp's Senior British Officer was Lieutenant Crabb of the Fleet Air Arm, who had been shot down over Dakar. Here a rather dejected Casson found that the *Memnon*'s chief engineer, Mr A. Jackson 'was goodness itself and helped me philosophise on our position'. In due course, as was the Vichy authorities' practice, the three were released and sent to Freetown, Sierra Leone, marching across the border into the Gambia where: 'Two Englishmen were awaiting us … We passed through a native village, and cheered loudly when we saw a tiny Union Jack'. At Bathurst they embarked in HM Destroyer *Highlander* and Casson wrote: 'I am free. A few feet away, streaming grandly in the breeze, is her White Ensign. Free! It is wonderful!'[13] But it was not to prove wonderful, for Freetown was packed with over 1,000 survivors all trying to obtain berths in homeward-bound ships.

Casson was fortunate, leaving Freetown aboard a troop-ship after a few days, but with so many seeking a homeward passage, the others found it impossible until they learned volunteers were sought to man a war-prize named *Criton* which had been captured from the Vichy French and seemed to offer the *Memnon*'s two radio officers what they were seeking. She was placed under the command of Captain C.T. Dobeson, late master of the torpedoed tramp *Wray Castle*, and her crew was made up by a number of British mates, engineers and seamen, some West African firemen and, as 'sparkies', Whalley and Johnson who described her as:

> an appalling vessel. Cockroaches of enormous size roamed freely around … The engines were of doubtful ability with a hopefully estimated speed of seven knots. The radio equipment was sound and the emergency transmitting and receiving sets were in the chart room. The Bridge equipment was dubious. The so-called signalling lamp was home-made – by the Chief Engineer. It consisted of a large Capstan

tobacco tin in which an ordinary electric lamp bulb of about forty-five watts had been fitted. Thus it was totally useless in daylight. For defence there were four moveable tripod mounted Lewis guns and also two hand held stripped Lewis guns.

After her capture the *Criton* had not been subject to due process through a prize court and should therefore have born a naval prize-crew but only an officer, Sub-Lieutenant Stretton, was present. However, with Stretton aboard, Dobeson's signature on her Certificate of Registry and a white ensign at her foremasthead, she wore the red ensign at her stern when she proceeded upstream to Pepel to load a full cargo of iron ore. Returning to Freetown to await convoy, another radio officer, Ronald Carter, joined. Dobeson had openly expressed the opinion that *Criton* was unfit to sail in convoy, being unable to make the required speed. Unfit himself, he found himself in a ship whose

> cargo was almost as dangerous as petrol. If a torpedo strikes a ship loaded with petrol she promptly moves upwards; with iron ore she generally breaks her back and goes straight down. On top of the obvious psychological effect that these facts must have had on Captain Dobeson he also had to cope with an unknown crew suffering from 'survivor jitters' plus native firemen, a terrific panic risk in an emergency, who the Chief Engineer, N. Clear, had told him were useless. However, the Naval authorities said she had to sail …

The *Criton* duly left Freetown in a twenty-two-ship convoy escorted by the AMC HMS *Esperance Bay* and HM Cruiser *Shropshire*. By night-fall the *Criton's* firemen were having difficulty maintaining steam pressure, but she kept up with the convoy until its speed increased next morning, whereupon she straggled astern. The *Esperance Bay's* powerful signal projector began chiding her. Dobeson shouted at Peter Johnson to respond 'with my high powered Capstan Tobacco Tin Signalling Unit which, of course, she could not see.' Realising the *Criton* was a lame-duck the *Esperance Bay* ordered Dobeson to return to Freetown. Dobeson 'went berserk,' demanding an escort. 'He raved through a megaphone that all he had told Naval authorities in Freetown had now come to pass and he was now expected to creep back totally undefended.' The *Esperance Bay's* commander's response was unhelpful. ' "No escort I'm afraid. You'd better run along now. Good luck!" '

The *Criton* turned south and next morning was being followed by a strange ship. Dobeson ordered Whalley to transmit a 'Suspicious Vessel' message which was immediately acknowledged by Freetown radio station. Standing in the wireless room door watching the strange vessel approaching on the port quarter, Johnson noticed a flash from her fore deck, whereupon a shell screamed overhead. Turning to Whalley, he said:

'Quickly, tell Freetown we are being shelled.' Whalley paused, did nothing, and only commented 'We have no orders to do so'. He was of course right … A moment later the wireless room telephone rang again and was answered by Johnson. A voice said 'The Captain says do not transmit'.[14]

The *Criton* was stopped and the warship revealed herself as Vichy French. Dobeson was ordered to proceed to Conakry. Chief Officer Chalmers, a Ben Line officer, remonstrated, and the result of the delay in obeying was a burst of machine-gun fire over the bridge. Dobeson immediately ordered the ship abandoned. As Third Officer Christie's port lifeboat was lowered into the water, the assembling firemen panicked and ran across the deck where they infected those mustering by the starboard lifeboat, which was lowered on Second Officer Newman's orders. Dobeson, the last man to leave the ship, was found to be speechless with shock and Newman had not got his boat clear before the French resumed fire. In due course the French rounded up both boats and took everybody on board.

The prisoners were interned in a camp near Conakry where they endured intern-ment for eighteen months until being released when the Allies invaded North Africa. For the first weeks they all remained together then the fit Europeans were separated from the West African firemen and transferred to Timbuctoo. A few sick were left behind in hospital at Conakry and earned, through misconduct, the disapprobation of the French who had them moved eastwards to Kan Kan as soon as they were fit. The exception to this was Sub-lieutenant Stretton, who was 'quickly sent to Koulikor to join Crabb'. The ambiguities surrounding the *Criton* were sufficient to ensure that the men who had volunteered to take her home were compromised in the eyes of the Vichy French. Other survivors from torpedoed British merchantmen arrived, stayed for a few weeks and were then released. Then, about two months prior to the release of all PoWs in French hands, the camp at Timbuctoo was closed and the *Criton's* crew members were dispatched south to join those at Kan Kan.

Among the British left in the hospital at Conakry was Peter Johnson, an engineer named Allan Taylor and eight ratings. Though only eighteen, Johnson's command of French and his honest character commended him as camp leader and he was to endure months of responsibility, several of his charges making life extremely difficult for him, not least because they were:

> well cared for and slackly guarded, the guard generally being of two natives who spent most of the time asleep in a chair. Those were ideal escape conditions. They were also conditions which common sense suggested should not be abused. One afternoon, one of the seamen, K. Wallace, walked out of the hospital and was brought back by the police the worse for liquor. The Commissioner of Police firmly told us that if there was another similar incident he would have us all sent up country, the implication being Timbuctoo.

Several escape plans were hatched and attempts were made, but Johnson's insistence that they all escaped together or not at all, found them condemned to weeks of idle-ness and speculation. Johnson was approached by one furtive French officer who wished to join the Free French by way of Freetown, but tentative plans to leave – with all ten of the Britons – came to nothing. Wallace made an attempt to escape and got drunk and although Johnson skilfully played the civilian and military off against each other, the man's conduct provoked their move to Kan Kan. Although conditions were better, the '[f]ood was bad and medical attention vague ... We had traumatic rows with the French from time to time, some being most amusing and some distinctly potentially dangerous …'. Frequent searches for hidden radios and a slow disintegration in the French sense of certainty as the tide of war turned against Vichy, divided loyalties and discipline became increasingly brittle.

> All through the last quarter of 1942 the camp at Kan Kan steadily increased in numbers. Frenchmen, who were suspected of being pro-British, joined us. They complained to the French authorities that they now had no servants to sweep their quarters and that the British native firemen should be told to act as their servants.

Johnson protested to the camp commandant in writing as to 'your treatment of the coloured British subjects and in view of your threat to fire at or upon these people I hereby inform you that I absolutely and positively refuse to accept any responsibility whatsoever as to the consequences.' As Chief Engineer Clear deposed after the war.

> Just before the camp was closed down and we were released, tension was running high with the French Authorities who ordered my native firemen to perform menial duties for pro-British French Europeans who had just been interned with us. Peter refused to allow this. The whole camp was lined up, now numbering over 100 men and the guards ordered to open fire. This the European Sergeant of the guard refused to do. Peter informed the French Commanding Officer that he would take no responsibility as to what would happen if his guards did open fire. He was immediately personally attacked by the French Native Sergeant. At once the camp, almost to a man, moved to his assistance. Peter, quickly realising a potential riot with disastrous results, ordered everyone to 'Stand back!' The potential riot quelled, Peter and the French Lieutenant retired to the Lieutenant's quarters to discuss matters. It is of course questionable if the guards would have opened fire but [such] after-thought is always easy. At the time it was generally thought that Peter's quick action and firm order very commendable, and at great personal risk.

Johnson now learned that their release was imminent.

> Suddenly I realised I was not dreaming. I was no longer going to have to cope with being shut in like a caged animal pacing up and down the compound everlastingly gazed at from sentries outside with rifles; men who would kill me if I went outside the palisade … There would be no more cases of malaria to treat. No more worry about the less strong who suddenly broke into tears the cause of which they could not explain. No more incessant roll-calls by the guards and, perhaps mostly of all, no more need to have to keep outwardly unmoved no matter what the crisis … The reaction to the news caused terrific excitement; in some cases almost hysteria. Others said not a word. The guards were removed from sentry duty but remained with us until the last evening when they suddenly quietly vanished.

Two days later a lorry arrived to take them to Kan Kan railway station.

I … turned from outside the camp and looked into it; a view I had rarely seen except under guard. The buildings stood out in the moonlight. There was silence save for the noise of crickets and bull frogs … I turned and went with them and climbed aboard the last lorry to leave – the others had already gone … So the men of the *Criton* were free at last but even then release was saddened. Four days after arriving in Sierra Leone a young cabin boy named Hyland died of black-water fever. After the war I met his parents in Melbourne. They told me that their other son aged seventeen was also lost in the Maritime service.

The confinement of the *Criton's* crew, arising out of the confusion of the ship's status caused her crew months of unnecessary misery. Clear concludes their ordeal.

After we were released Peter returned home on a Blue Funnel ship which sailed to the U.K. from Freetown, via the West Indies, New York and finally to Liverpool. The full report he wrote about this camp so he tells me, and I have NO reason to doubt his word, was sighted by British Military Intelligence in the West Indies, American Security in New York and finally confiscated on board by a British Lieutenant from MI5 before he left the ship in Liverpool. In addition the Lieutenant informed him that he was to write no more reports AND that included even writing one for his own employers … I am just one who will never forget what one very young Officer accomplished often at great physical cost to himself and there are many who would agree with me.[15]

While the ordeal of the *Criton's* crew bore no resemblance to the horrors of imprisonment by the Japanese, Johnson's conduct was meritorious and displayed a mature rectitude for a junior radio officer three years short of his majority. The confidence placed in him by his fellow prisoners is no less noteworthy. Not all came home from the Vichy camps; two war graves lie yet at Timbucktoo, both marked with the initials 'M.N.' enclosed by a loop of rope. They are the last resting places of Chief Engineer William Souter, who died aged sixty, and Able-Seaman John Graham, aged twenty-three, who were both from the Cardiff tramp *Allende*, Captain T.J. Williamson, torpedoed off the Liberian coast on 17 March 1942 by *U-68* (Merten). Six men were killed in the attack and Williamson and his crew of thirty with two DEMS gunners landed at Taba on the Côte d'Ivoire, to be interned initially at Bobo Dinlassu.

As Clear states, Johnson was lent on to keep quiet, while the post-war sum of compensation paid by the French was absorbed by the Labour Government of Clement Attlee, never reaching those for whom it was intended – such are the workings of diplomacy.

Less than a fortnight after the sinking of the *Memnon*, at 07.45 on 25 March, the German *Hilfskreuzer Thor*, Kapitän sur Zee Otto Kähler, encountered the Anchor liner *Britannia*. Independently routed outwards from Liverpool for Bombay with 484 souls on board, she was 750-miles west of Freetown when seen. It was standard practice for independent ships to turn away from any other vessel but on this occasion it availed the *Britannia* nothing, for the *Thor* opened fire with telling effect. The

Britannia's master increased to maximum speed and dropped smoke flares to confuse the enemy while her radio officers broadcast their fate. Her gunners went into action, firing ineffectively before a shell from the *Thor* killed or wounded them and put their weapon out of action. By 09.00 the *Thor*, making 17 knots, was gaining, easily exceeding the *Britannia's* stately 14, her shells repeatedly hitting their target, igniting the superstructure, killing and maiming crew and passengers, and damaging the lifeboats in complete defiance of the Prize Regulations. The *Britannia* was stopped and her boats began to descend her high sides. As they were lowered the *Thor* continued to fire – 159 rounds in all – closing the range to point-blank. The *Britannia's* surgeon, Dr Nancy Miller, calmly attended to the wounded and dying and was the last person into No. 3 Boat as it surged wildly alongside. With the boats clear of her prize the *Thor* sank the *Britannia* and then simply steamed away, Kähler arguing he had intelligence of a British warship in the area.[16] The *Britannia's* master and fourteen officers, eighty-nine lascar ratings and a dozen passengers were dead; others in the boats were wounded, though some were fortunate to be in the devoted care of Dr Miller.

By a coincidence the *Britannia's* radio signal was intercepted by the AMC HMS *Cilicia*, herself a former Anchor liner. Furthermore, her medical officer, Dr Thomas Miller, was father to the *Britannia's* surgeon and his anxiety may be imagined. At 06.30 on the morning of the 28th the *Cilicia* hove in sight of a small vessel which was stopped and a boat was lowered to search her for war contraband. The vessel was a Spanish steamer, the *Bachi*, and she had on board sixty-three survivors of the *Britannia's* No. 3 Boat. The boarding officer brought them all back, and among the last to board was Dr Nancy Miller, who was later made an MBE. HMS *Cilicia* proceeded to Freetown where all those she had picked up were landed, to augment the numbers awaiting passage home and encountered by the *Memnon's* survivors when they arrived.

The *Britannia's* No. 7 Boat was less fortunate; certified for fifty-six people, she had eighty-two on board, sixty-four lascars and eighteen Britons, all in the charge of Third Officer W. McVicar. Out of sight of the other boats amid the heaving waters of the ocean, McVicar confronted a difficult decision. Aware that it would be impossible to sail to windward, the shorter distance to the African coast, McVicar boldly resolved to carry the trade-wind west, a decision made slightly easier because he had aboard an RNR officer and a regular Royal Naval officer, Sub-lieutenant I. McIntosh, both of whom were passengers but both of whom could handle a boat. In addition to being grossly overcrowded and therefore under-stored, No. 7 Boat was riddled with splinter damage from the *Thor's* shells, so patches – or tingles – were extemporized from tin lids caulked with torn up blankets applied by Sub-lieutenant McIntosh who hung over the side, his legs held by others. Between them, the three officers devised a rough chart so that navigation was relatively straightforward. There remained the problem of victualling so many mouths on sixteen gallons of water, forty-eight tins of condensed milk and two of ship's biscuit on a passage which, they estimated, would last twenty-four days. Having picked up the south-east trade they made a passage under 'extremes of heat and cold, drought and rain, hope and disappointment' during which more than half the boat's occupants died, including the unknown RNR officer. On the twenty-third day they made a landfall on the Brazilian coast near São Luis, having covered the remarkable distance of 1,535 miles. Out of the original eighty-two who had scrambled aboard the lifeboat, 'thirty-eight emaciated survivors, one of whom was told he managed to combine in one body "half the deficiency diseases in the medical dictionary," crawled to land'. Afterwards, McIntosh remarked of McVicar, 'You can imagine how valuable it was to have a quiet, undemonstrative, reliable seaman as one's companion in such circumstances'.[17]

This was a period when the German commerce-raiders continued to enjoy their run of success in the wider oceans beyond the convoy system, thereby exposing the weakness of the British counter-measure supposedly provided by AMCs. Kähler's *Thor* successfully fought off the AMCs HMS *Alcantara* and *Caernarvon Castle* and on 4 April 1941 sank the former Lamport & Holt liner HMS *Voltaire* with the loss of seventy-two lives, an action which decided the Admiralty to dispense with large passenger ships as cruisers.[18] A few weeks after these events the German battleship *Bismarck* sank HMS *Hood* and, during the summer of 1941, several other German *Hilfskreuzers* were active, including the *Kormoran*. The German strategy of surface commerce-raiding, although it undoubtedly had its successes, was ultimately unsuccessful, 'the final climax to the long and romantic era of ocean raiding'.[19] But, overstretched as it was, the British navy's arm was long. While several *Hilfskreuzers* survived to reach Axis ports as distant as Japan, others were destroyed, *Pinguin* by HMS *Cornwall* in May, the *Kormoran* and HMAS *Sydney* had their mutually destructive encounter in November, and the *Atlantis* was sunk by HMS *Devonshire* three days later.[20]

Among the many boat voyages made by merchant seamen those undertaken by the survivors from the *Anglo-Saxon* and the *Rhexenor* rank among the notable. A 5,600-ton cargo-vessel owned by the Nitrate Producers' S.S.Co. managed, like her four sisters, by Lawther, Latta & Co. of Billiter Street, London, the *Anglo-Saxon* ran between Britain and British Colombia, and from there to Western Australia. In August 1940 she was outward bound from Newport, Monmouthshire, towards Bahia Blanca with a full cargo of coal. As was then the practice she had been in convoy until this reached 17° West when it had dispersed and its constituent ships made their own way towards their destinations. At 20.20 on the 21st the *Anglo-Saxon* was about 810-miles west of the Canary Islands when she suddenly came under shell fire from the German *Hilfskreuzer Widder* which rapidly closed the range from one mile to a mere three cables. In the pitch-black night the former Hamburg-Amerika ship had approached unobserved and the *Anglo-Saxon* was taken completely by surprise. The *Widder* shelled and strafed her at point-blank range. As the alarm bells rang Captain Flynn emerged from his cabin, his confidential books ready for dumping, to be cut down by machine-gun bullets. Seaman-Gunner Richard Penny was wounded before he reached the stern-gun which, with the poop on which it was mounted, had been the first target of the *Widder*'s heavy guns.

There is no doubt that the *Widder*'s attack was disproportionately vicious. With the *Anglo-Saxon*'s boat-deck under a withering fire, Chief Officer C.B. Denny was unable to launch the boats and instead managed to lower the ship's jolly-boat which lay on chocks on the lower bridge-deck. This, although a substantial craft used for odd jobs in port, was not fitted out as a lifeboat; it was simply the only means of escape. Denny and Able-Seaman Widdicombe raised her from her chocks, swung her out over the side and began to lower her. As they did so a few men on the main deck jumped in and the boat hit the water, dragging astern on her falls and painter as the *Anglo-Saxon* still forged ahead. Denny and Widdicombe then slid down the rope-falls, searing their hands. More men tumbled in as, cast-off, the boat fell astern along the sinking *Anglo-Saxon's* side as she continued to move forward. Fending off, the survivors were suddenly confronted by the threshing propeller passing them. Then they lay exposed. The dark, looming hull of the *Widder*, illuminated intermittently by her gun-flashes, passed within a hundred feet before they shipped the oars and pulled rapidly away. Astern, survivors' life-jacket lights bobbed; a searchlight beam swept over them, followed by the chatter of machine-gun fire. Beyond the flash of an explosion as the *Anglo-Saxon's* ammunition magazine detonated, the dark shape of the *Widder* faded away to the east. It was all over.

At daylight, Denny took stock. With him were Second Radio Officer R.H. Pilcher, Gunner Penny, Third Engineer L. Hawkes, Second Cook L. Morgan, and two able-seamen, Robert Tapscott and Wilbert Widdicombe. Denny, his own hands badly burned from his descent into the boat, did his best for his men but Penny was severely wounded in the right hip and wrist. Pilcher had had one foot reduced to a bloody pulp; Morgan had a deep wound in his right ankle and a badly contused hand. Tapscott had received three minor shrapnel wounds and one rather more serious, which had burned but not broken the skin in his groin; he had also broken a tooth, exposing the nerve. As for provisions, the jolly-boat contained a half-full barricoe of water, some ship's biscuit and a few tins of mutton and condensed milk, both of which induced thirst.

Denny decided to make for the West Indies, so sail was hoisted and some encouragement was derived from the fact that the jolly-boat was known to sail rather better than the lifeboats, but under the hot sun, thirst and physical deterioration set in early. Pilcher's foot began to putrefy and they all became constipated. During the second night a dark shape appeared and circled them. They dropped the sail, fearing it was the *Widder*, but it vanished and on Saturday 24 August Denny was able to note that the crew were 'cheerful' after a little water and biscuit. Later they had mutton and joked about their predicament, but the stench of Pilcher's rotting foot had now been joined by that of Morgan's wound. Nevertheless, largely due to Denny's leadership, they remained cheerful for a few days, 'trusting in God's will and British determination' to make a landfall until overwhelmed by thirst. For a while a fair wind allowed them to skim along at 5 knots but with so little water, their throats began to swell and their tongues grew dry. Denny was wracked by cramp and nausea and on Tuesday 27th Pilcher died, which had a bad effect upon Denny. The others, occasionally cooling off over the side, now became subject to mood swings, veering from black despair to ridiculous optimism. One or two drank sea-water; Widdicombe and Tapscott fell to arguing and Hawkes was obliged to intervene as a failing Denny attempted to mediate. On 2 September Denny made a last entry in the log as the others fell to arguing about his successor in command. Morgan's mind was wandering and Penny was in a poor way. Hawkes, on his first voyage to sea, thought his status as an engineer placed him in charge, but Widdicombe protested himself as best qualified, not least because he could navigate. A tall, truculent twenty-one-year-old former *Conway* boy, Widdicombe had opted out of his cadetship in the Union-Castle Line and shipped as a seaman. Tapscott came from a seafaring family of Cardiff pilots and had been at sea since he was fifteen. Both had knocked about the globe, serving in ships supplying the Republicans during the Spanish Civil War, both had been in action and they cordially disliked each other.

That evening a depressed Penny slipped over the side when taking his trick at the helm and next morning, their thirteenth, the rudder carried away. Although a steering oar was shipped in its place, it was the last straw for Denny. He asked if anyone else would join him and Hawkes agreed; after a little while Denny gave his signet ring to Widdicombe and asked that he give it to his mother. After instructing them to 'keep going west' Denny shook hands with Hawkes and the two of them went over the side, leaving the boat to sail on. Those left aboard tried to pray, but were unable to take their eyes off Hawkes's mop of fair hair that could be seen for some time, bobbing astern on the rising swells.

Widdicombe took over and wrote up the log: 'Chief Mate and Third Engineer go over the side. No water.' They were now very weak, badly sunburnt and dangerously de-hydrated, their skin cracking, their tongues swollen and their breath foul. Every action took time and immense effort. Having drunk sea-water, Morgan was losing his reason and struggled with an enraged Widdicombe who threw the empty barricoe of water over-board. On the evening of 9 September Morgan became quite calm, rose to his feet and announced that he would take a walk down the street for a drink. He stepped over the side, leaving Widdicome to write: 'Cook goes mad; dies. Only two of us left.' Tapscott and Widdicombe were now in extremity. They tried drinking their own urine, only to discover that what little they produced tasted foul. When the wind fell, the consequent despair turned their rambling thoughts to suicide. Both went into the water but fell to arguing, which so annoyed them that they both clambered back into the boat. The only fluid left in the boat was the compass spirit which damped the card's oscillations, so they drank the raw alcohol and collapsed in the boat's bottom, to be awakened hours later by failing rain. Suddenly galvanized, they filled the boat's buoyancy tank, but their cramped stomachs rejected what they swallowed and they were racked by vomiting.

After the 12th the rain became regular; they began to re-hydrate, to sleep better. Sharing the remaining biscuits they got the boat sailing again, their morale rising. By the 20th they thought themselves near land, but four days later the biscuits and water had gone; no land had appeared. That night it rained again. The following morning they picked up clumps of passing sea-weed and began to eat it. Day followed day; one morning they woke as the boat ran aground, but the sudden appearance of a fluke alongside told a different story. They fished unsuccessfully. A ship passed them. Four days later the wind rose and they tried to keep the boat's stern to the breaking seas as they tumbled in over the jolly-boat's transom. The gale persisted for two days and three nights at the end of which they were chewing anything: small crabs caught on the sea-weed; Pilcher's tobacco pouch. They grew hysterical, then subdued, demented. All they could do was keep the boat heading west in a blur of semi-consciousness. Their burnt skin was disfigured by lesions and boils; their lips were blistered, their faces a peeling red. On 27 October they fell into a violent argument over the steering: they began to fight until exhaustion forced them to collapse.

Later Tapscott tried to apologise; Widdicombe sulked. They caught a fish and shared it, seeing what they thought to be land. Tapscott crawled forward and navigated Widdicombe at the steering oar through a gap in a reef. A few minutes later they drove ashore on a sandy beach. They clambered out of the boat and collapsed in its shadow. They had survived a passage of 2,275 miles. They were found on the morning of 31 October in Alabaster Bay, Eleuthera Island in the Bahamas, by two islanders, Mr and Mrs Johnson. In Nassau hospital they were diagnosed as suffering from pellagra, insomnia and deranged nervous systems but the less emotional and stolid Tapscott plunged into deep melancholia, while the mercurial Widdicome recovered rapidly. After eight days the doctors deemed them ready to meet visitors and they found the Duke and Duchess of Windsor at their bedsides.[21]

Early in 1941 Widdicombe was discharged. He was sent to New York where he signed-on Furness, Withy's *Siamese Prince* which was making an independent passage. Captain Edgar Litchfield took a northerly route and was 180 miles to the north-west of St Kilda when the ship was struck by a torpedo from *U-69* (Metzler). Eight passengers and all hands, including Widdicombe, were killed. Tapscott survived the war in the Canadian Army, and in 1947 gave evidence before a British Military Court in Hamburg against the *Widder*'s commander. Korvettenkapitän Hellmuth von Ruckteschell was charged with firing on British seamen clinging to rafts, not making provision for the safety of the crews of the ships he sank, and continuing to shell ships that had obeyed the orders he issued to them by radio. Von Ruckteschell denied machine-gunning his victims; suggestions that survivors exaggerated the circumstances of the enemy's attack owing to the stress of the moment may have had some truth,[22] but what remains incontrovertible are the facts that there was no 'place of safety' to the 'non-combatant' seaman other than the dubious refuge of his lifeboat and that, according to the Prize Regulations, any act that prevented him gaining access to this was a war crime. In addition to the ruthlessness he had shown against the *Anglo-Saxon*, Von Ruckteschell had acted similarly when attacking the Harrison liner *Davisian*, Captain T. Pearce, in July 1940, though only one man had been killed; and again, when in command of the raider *Michel*, in the sinking of the *Empire Dawn* in September 1942. While the youthful Tapscott was undoubtedly affected by his subsequent ordeal in the jolly-boat,[23] Captain William Scott gave evidence against Von Ruckteschell. The *Empire Dawn* had been attacked at night without warning and twenty-two of the ship's company of forty-four had been killed. Von Ruckteschell was acquitted of firing on the *Anglo-Saxon*'s survivors, but guilty of not providing for their safety. He was also guilty of continuing to fire on the *Davisian* and the *Empire Dawn* after their masters had signalled they were abandoning ship. His ten years' imprisonment was reduced to seven, but Von Ruckteschell died shortly before his release.

In February 1943 Alfred Holt's 8,000-ton *Rhexenor* was on a commercial passage between Freetown and St John, New Brunswick, fully laden with cocoa – an unusual circumstance for one of Holt's cargo-liners. Besides Captain L. Eccles and his sixty-seven strong crew, she carried three passengers. Eccles had been sunk three years earlier, when chief officer in the *Protesilaus* which had been mined off Swansea. By the morning of 3 February the *Rhexenor*, proceeding independently, was torpedoed under her port-bridge wing. She began to settle by the head, so Eccles rang 'finished with engines' on her telegraph, the signal for the evacuation of the engine room. As the radio officers transmitted the submarine attack signal, the ship's name and position, the mates manned the boats. Nos 2 and 4 Boats had been destroyed and No.1 Boat, the master's, was held at the davit heads while a chronometer, charts and the portable radio were put in it. Meanwhile Nos 3 and 5 on the starboard side and No.6 on the port side were lowered, the officers all wearing 'soft hats and raincoats' to disguise their rank. Eccles and Chief Officer M. J. Case placed their own sextants in their lifeboats as a U-boat surfaced on the port bow. Eccles formed the opinion that she was about to shell the ship and ordered the last boat away.

This was *U-217*, and Kapitänleutnant K. Reichenbach-Klinke fired twenty shells into the *Rhexenor*, igniting her. After two hours she turned onto her port side and sank. Now *U-217* approached No.1 Boat, seeking the master and chief engineer, but no one betrayed them both sitting in their raincoats. The U-boat called No.5 Boat alongside. Fourth Officer C. W. Allen denied knowing where the master was and suggested he had gone down with the ship. This did not placate Reichenbach-Klinke who ordered Allen aboard and up to the conning tower:

> where the Captain said he would take me round each of the life-boats, and if I
> pointed out the Master I would be allowed back into my boat. Otherwise I must
> go with them to Germany. And so, with a machine gun trained on me, I was taken
> round all the life-boats, and at each one of them I answered 'No'. Horrified at the
> thought of going to Germany, particularly in a U-boat, I was then ordered below.

U-217 motored away, leaving Eccles and his people adrift in mid-ocean. Eccles ordered the Third Mate to replace Allen in No.5 Boat and evened out the numbers so that each boat, all of which were adequately provisioned, had an equal chance. As they lay in the grain of the north-east trade-wind they headed for Antigua, some 1,200 miles away.

Captain Eccles with nineteen men in No.1 Boat made good progress, losing sight of the others after two days. With an initial average of seventy miles a day and what appeared to be a steady trade-wind, he estimated the passage was going to take them three weeks and arranged rations and water accordingly. On the fourteenth day the second cook died 'more from lack of spirit than any other cause, since the rations were ample to sustain life'. At noon on 20 February No.1 Boat made her landfall at Guadeloupe where they 'landed on a sandy beach over the swell without mishap'. Later they were taken to Martinique and reached New York 'by devious stages,' being repatriated in British ships, Eccles himself serving as Staff Captain on the *Prometheus*.

Case, in No.4 Boat with fourteen men, made similar progress, though contact was swiftly lost with the others. On the fifth day a rising sea persuaded him to heave-to and ride out the strong wind with a sea anchor. The boat's violent motion destroyed the upper rudder gudgeon, but repairs were made 'with the boat's resources'. On the 9th, after a week, heavy rain allowed them to top-up, but the deluge of chilling water depressed them. With small tots of rum and an issue of extra rations, Case improved morale and late on the afternoon of the 20th he could not believe his eyes 'but there it was,' the island of Antigua right ahead. They lay-to during the night and next morning a fishing boat towed them into St John's, the crew landing 'in good health except a bit groggy on the legs'. The second officer, Mr W.M. Thomas, was in command of another seventeen of the *Rhexenor's* crew in No. 3 Boat. It was this that remained in touch with Eccles and No. 1 Boat for two days as they headed west, making steady progress and on the twenty-first day two aircraft flew overhead and dropped water containers and cigarettes. They signaled that rescue was at hand and late that evening they were taken on board a vessel named the *Conqueror*, landed at St Thomas and were eventually repatriated by way of New York. No. 5 Boat seems to have endured the worst weather. Third Officer S.A.G. Covell had his sextant with him and had set his watch by the chronometer in Case's boat. For the first few hours Covell and Case kept company and outran the others. 'When daylight came there was no trace of any boats.' Covell settled his crew down and organised watches. By the third day, 5 February, the wind had freshened.

> Hove to all day, Heavy sea running and high squally wind. The crew at this stage were very wet due to repeated rain squalls and spray. We managed to collect a considerable amount of rainwater … [It was] was tainted by the dye from the sail, but it was drinkable. At this stage Corby, A.B., complained of not feeling well. I think he caught a chill, in fact all hands were shivering due to exposure to the elements. The 7th dawned fine and clear, with light airs. Mr. Ward 5th Engineer, flipped a fish out with his hand, and we cooked it in the boat. It was a welcome change, and I think that fishing lines put in the boats, would be a great asset. Fresh water can be obtained from the flesh of the fish also. During the afternoon a strong wind came from the S.W. and we made good way till 8 p.m. when storm clouds gathered. I decided to shorten canvas, which was just as well. Rarely have I seen such strong squalls and torrential rain. These conditions prevailed all night. A fair quantity of rain water was caught.

The following morning was 'dull and wet' until a breeze sprang up:

> and off we went once more, with breaks showing in the clouds which gave us poor drowned creatures some hope of the sun. Everyone was shivering intensely, due to exposure, and not being able to have dry gear. I am very doubtful if Corby will pull through. [Next day the resourceful Covell] tried a new experiment … Having several surplus cans of rainwater, I heated this by means of old wood burnt in the bailing bucket, which had fallen to pieces … I added some cooking chocolate and condensed milk, and the resulting mixture was very palatable and sustaining. This, and the use of massage oil, did much to improve our condition. A small stove would be very useful.

Hitherto, alone among the boats they seem not to have found the trade-wind but on the 9th and 'long over-due' it came away from the north-east, true and steady with a clearing of the weather. 'The spirits of the crew rose with the wind, and I estimate the speed to be four knots.' There was one exception, Able-Seaman Corby who was 'sinking fast'. By 11 February Covell was able to note that:

> The crew seems to have settled down now, and are more at home in the boat. Their lack of knowledge of small boat sailing was very noticeable, and I have had a full

time job teaching them. The help rendered to me by the 5th Engineer was invaluable, he being very quick to pick up the fundamental rules of boat sailing.

Next day, still carrying along with a fair wind, Covell worried about the accuracy of his longitude. He could still observe latitude and reckoned to make land in about a week. On the 13th he wrote:

> If this holds, it will not be long before we are consuming the iced drinks which continually float before our eyes and form the big part of our conversation. At 4.15 pm. Corby A.B. passed away. His death was witnessed by myself and Rogers (Carpenter). The Carpenter said a last prayer for the dead, and he was committed to the deep. It cast quite a gloom over our little band, but we have to look ahead …

With a failing wind, Covell worried about the water. 'The milk tablets go down well,' he recorded. 'They are good to chew during the night, and keep the thirst quenched a certain amount'. He discovered the Vitamin C tablets had a similar effect, but the boat's lack of progress frustrated him. It was now the 15th.

> We have just finished our evening meal and are now lying back prior to going to sleep. The only men moving about are the watch keepers. The water ration is 6 ozs per day, and 10 ozs on Sunday, four biscuits per man with pemmican spread on it. I served prunes or raisins in the morning. This fruit when chewed did to some extent alleviate the thirst between meals. The health of the crew is fairly good, except for the usual weakness around the legs, and tempers are inclined to be short, but the conduct of the crew is excellent.

A breeze picked up and for several days they ran on. An observed latitude on the 19th persuaded Covell that he should alter course 'in order to make southing and counteract set which is experienced here', and the following day, with rain in the offing, he increased the rations in anticipation of making the land.

> We are very thin now, and resemble a bag of bones, but we are all still in good spirits. A cake of salt water soap would come in very handy for washing, as we are all very dirty. S. Tate (Fireman) developed a septic hand as a result of rope burns. The arm commenced to swell so I decided to open the hand with a razor. The operation was satisfactory and he is now quite well again.

On the 21st it seemed at first that their privations were near an end.

> Called this morning to hear the glad cry of 'Land'. The island was bearing S.W. from us and the wind having come round from that direction, we could not make any headway towards the land. Three planes flew over us, but did not see us, in spite of my signals. The smoke flares were very poor and would not be visible to a ship any distance away … We pulled all night, and daylight found us quite close to land, but the men were very tired, so I tried sailing again, but wind and current being adverse, it was of no avail. In the cool

of the evening I again got the oars out, putting Tate, the man with the bad hand, at the tiller. We pulled continually till 2 am. when I let go the anchor in two fathoms of water. The coast being steep to, I decided to wait till daylight before landing. After twenty days in a boat, eleven hours continuous pulling is a feat worthy of mention.

When dawn broke, we found ourselves lying off rock-bound coast, with slight surf. I decided to beach boat, as, if we had gone looking for a sandy beach we stood the chance of being swept out to sea by the swift current which ran between this group of islands. I headed the boat on to the beach, keeping my stern on to the slight swell by means of my kedge anchor. I held her there while the crew got ashore and then allowed her to swing on to the beach, where she lay quietly, enabling us to remove such food as we required. O'Connel and Tate then climbed the hill behind us, and there contacted some natives, who directed them to the village. The natives came down to us, giving us some hot coffee which tasted very good indeed. We experienced some difficulty in walking, due to the motion of the boat and the continuous sitting posture ... About 2 p.m. a boat took us all round to the native village, where we were given hot coffee and porridge. I cannot say enough about the kindness of these simple people, who had not been spoilt by the invasion of so called Western civilisation.

We attended a thanksgiving service for our safe deliverance, and then the Commissioner of the B.W.I. came and took us to Tortola, where we obtained hot baths, and so to bed.[24]

This Pepysian end to Covell's ordeal does not end the story of the *Rhexenor*'s people; there remained the unfortunate but honourable Allen, mewed-up in *U-217*. Allen was among a handful of British merchant seamen who were captured in this way and subjected to a miserable and uncertain journey into captivity. Reichenbach-Klinke's war patrol was ending and he had been heading home when he encountered the *Rhexenor*, a small advantage for Allen, who was berthed in the forward torpedo space with the ratings. For some ten days the U-boat remained surfaced, undertaking practise dives twice daily and replenishing from outward-bound U-boats on the way. On one such occasion, which coincided with Allen's twenty-first birthday, he was given a drink, otherwise he was allowed the run of the submarine, except for the engine room. Many evenings he sat and 'talked and argued on many subjects' with the 'Captain and Chief Engineer'.

I was continually told I was very foolish not to have identified the Master of the *Rhexenor*, and it was obviously a sore point that the submarine was returning home after a three month voyage with only one ship sunk, and proof of that evidence in the form of a Fourth Mate instead of a Master. The Captain explained his tactics in sinking the *Rhexenor* and showed me his charts. He had followed our ship for sufficient time to work out which zig-zag we were using (there was a copy of the official British zig-zag book on board, also the signal books, etc!), and then knowing the mean course, had surfaced and got ahead of us. He had then waited in exactly the right spot to torpedo the *Rhexenor* at daybreak. I should say that all the crew were really quite reasonable, except for the First Lieutenant who was the Gestapo representative and at all times wore a white pullover with the German eagle and swastika emblazoned across it. At every opportunity he was as rude as possible, and although it was obvious that the Captain and the rest of the crew disapproved of his manner, not one of them ever dared to cross him.

On 20 February the distant crump of depth-charges drew nearer and Allen was told they had been detected by an Allied warship.

[W]e remained submerged and stopped for what seemed like an age. Everyone on duty was ordered to lie down to conserve oxygen. During the next day the depth-charges were exploding very near. The noise was deafening and the submarine was badly shaken. Later this day the air became so poor we could only breathe by taking great gulps at each breath. The following night I was told that there was no option but to surface and make a get-away if possible in the dark. By this time the tension in the submarine was almost unbelievable, and something I shall never forget. However she then surfaced and made her escape. On February 23rd we arrived at Brest, where lined up on the quay was a reception party with brass band playing and a line of young women along the front, each with a bouquet of flowers. As *U-217* came alongside I was ordered below, so as not to see the ensuing ceremony. Soon each member of the crew came below with a flower in his buttonhole and a lipstick smear on his cheek. They all seemed well pleased with their reception. And so I commenced my time as a prisoner-of-war.[25]

There were many other boat voyages, all of which demonstrated human strengths and weaknesses. The caprice of fate could mean liberty for some and incarceration for others. When the *Sithonia* was sunk by *U-201* (Schnee) in July 1942, Captain Charles Brown and twenty-one of her crew made an eighteen-day voyage in their lifeboat only to fall into the hands of the Vichy French at Timris, Senegal. They were interned. The chief officer's boat, having made good 850 miles, fell in with a Spanish fishing-vessel which took aboard all twenty-six men and landed them at Las Palmas. The *Sithonia*'s owner, Henry Thomson, it will be recalled, had broken away from the family firm of Ben Line Steamers and established his own small firm. The losses of the *Sithonia* and the *Orfor* to *U-105* (Nissen) in December 1942, constituted half of his fleet, a by no means unusual proportion even among the grandest.

Among these survivors' ordeals, two rate mention as epics. The Ben Line's *Benlomond* was torpedoed by *U-172* (Emmermann) while on a voyage in ballast from Port Said by way of Capetown to the American coastal convoy rendezvous of Paramaribo before moving on to New York to await a trans-Atlantic convoy. By 23 November 1942 she was 750-miles east of the Amazon estuary when, shortly before noon, Emmermann struck. The *Benlomond* sank rapidly. Two officers struggling to launch a lifeboat were swept off the boat deck and Captain John Maul, forty-four crew – mostly Chinese – and eight DEMS gunners were all killed, leaving a sole survivor, Second Steward Poon Lim.

Poon was almost drowned but had managed to don his life jacket, the buoyancy in which brought him back to the surface where he grabbed a piece of wood, worried about sharks. After some time he spotted a life raft and made for it, sighting another raft and hearing some distant cries for help. However, the rafts drifted apart and the cries soon died away. Soon afterwards the conning tower of the U-boat loomed close and he called to men cleaning her gun on the casing, but they waved him away dismissively and the U-boat vanished. Poon was now quite alone, but he reckoned he had sufficient water and food for about fifty days and considered he would be picked up in the area which was also frequently deluged by rain. He did indeed see many ships, but not one stopped to recover him. Poon proved a man of singular self-discipline, severely rationing himself to a meagre portion of biscuit, chocolate, pemmican, lime-juice, evaporated milk and water. He also proved resourceful, stranding the life raft's life-line and making a fishing line, fabricating a hook out of a nail he patiently extracted from the raft's structure and bending it in his teeth. He baited it with a little wet ship's biscuit which was left to dry before attempting to catch anything, and when he caught a small fish, he used it as bait for larger quarry. He also managed to grab seagulls when they landed on his raft, and once when one alighted on his shoulder. Using the pemmican tin as a knife, he butchered the gulls but he suffered dreadfully from sunburn, though this was slightly mitigated by a covering of fuel oil. He lived thus for three months and it was not until the one hundredth day that the rain stopped, preventing him from topping-up his water. Twenty days later it rained again and an aeroplane overflew him, rocking its wings in recognition. Poon's spirits lifted, but successive flights by the Brazilian Air Force were unable to locate him and by the one hundred and thirtieth day he was almost done for. Three days later a Brazilian fisherman discovered Poon lying inert upon his raft only ten miles off Salinas. He was picked up and landed at Belém and, once ashore, he astonished his rescuer by eating hot peppers by the handful.

He continued to amaze the medical staff at the Beneficienza Portuguese Hospital, for apart form malnutrition, he had only a slight stomach disorder and in little over a fortnight Poon was able to report the loss of the *Benlomond* to the British consul at Pará. Much later he was decorated with the MBE by King George VI at Buckingham Palace. Although his 133 days on his raft were the record – if that is the right word – for survival alone, two lascars actually existed for 135 days after the *Fort Longueuil* was torpedoed in the Indian Ocean off the Chagos Archipelago on 19 September 1943. Seamen Mohamed Aftab and Thakur Miah drifted 3,400 miles, only to land on an island in the former Dutch East Indies and to fall into the hands of the occupying Japanese.

Better documented were the experiences of those merchant seamen who fell into the hands of the Germans. Typical of these was Third Mate William Mutimer of the *Harlesden*. She had left the Clyde under sealed orders to be opened after dispersion of her convoy half way across the Atlantic and the voyage proceeded smoothly in good weather until Saturday 22nd February 1941 when about 500-miles east of Newfoundland and bound for Halifax, Mutimer was on the forenoon watch when he learned that the wireless office had picked up a series of messages: 'Suspicious vessel sighted.' 'Suspicious vessel closing.' 'Shelled.' As he wrote afterwards, 'That one laconic word was the last.' He was enjoying a cat-nap that afternoon when, about 15.00, he:

> was awakened by a shattering explosion and staggered up to find a panic party rushing along the alleyway past my cabin. My tin hat had disappeared. On

going out on deck I saw the disturbed water to port and astern where a bomb
had exploded, and, looking up, saw an aircraft rounding to descend on us again.
I rushed up to the bridge to discover the Second Mate lying face down on the
bridge with what appeared to be a serious head wound. By this time the Captain
was in the wheelhouse (which was protected by concrete blocks) giving continuous
change-of-course orders to the helmsman in order to dodge the bombs and vicious
machine-gun fire. Another bomb dropped which was a near miss. By this time our
gunner was mounting our Hotchkiss machine gun. The plane made several more
sweeps firing at the bridge, and on one occasion it dropped a weighted wallet on
No.2 hatch. It had a long red ribbon on it and I rushed down to pick it up. The
skipper shouted from the bridge to throw it overboard, and, without thinking, I
did as ordered, so that what it contained we'll never know. Some thought it was an
instruction to steer a course to the enemy vessel. Throughout this confused time I
was worrying about the Second Mate and how I could help him, so I went below to
… see if I could find anybody to assist in rendering first aid. (We had no doctor on
board but both the cook and steward were well grounded in first aid). The response
I got initially was 'We are not all heroes you know.' Eventually a young Swedish
seaman volunteered to help me, and while lifting the Second Mate by the shoulders
I heard the clatter of the aircraft's machine-gun again. The seaman ran for the shelter
of the wheelhouse. I continued to drag the Second Mate towards the wheelhouse.
That's when I felt like an iron bar hit me with an almighty force in the right upper
arm. I had earlier sustained a whiplash wound across my right foot which I had not
regarded as of any consequence. But now I knew my right humerus had been shattered and I was bleeding profusely. I went below to seek help and by that time the
plane had left, having succeeded in knocking out all the Deck Officers leaving only
the Captain to keep watch.

   It was clear that the aircraft must have been sent off from a vessel at sea, and a
formidable one at that. The cook managed to put a good splint on my arm and stem
the flow of blood. The steward gave me a mixture which contained morphine and
mercifully the worst of the excruciating pain left me. Thus I was left with nothing
else I could do other than lie on the settee in my cabin and hope that help would
come from Newfoundland.

At about 21.00 the *Harlesden* came under shell fire from her starboard quarter. The
cacophony seemed endless and when at last Mutimer ventured out on deck, he found
himself alone and standing in the full beam of a searchlight. 'I looked around and saw
that most of the funnel had disappeared and deck houses were burning fiercely on the
starboard side.' Still worried about Second Mate David Souter, 'who was a friend and
a very nice man,' Mutimer found him unconscious in his cabin, then sat down on a
hatch-coaming telling himself that:

   it was the end, and then I saw that the port life-boat was being lowered. Despite
   my condition I ran towards it and clambered in when it reached the height of the
   bulwarks. As soon as the boat touched the water it was apparent that the ship was
   still moving ahead at a few knots because the sea was breaking over the bow of the

life-boat. There was a great danger of us being swamped, but the lowering tackle was released and the life-boat shot away from the ship's side. It was obvious that debris from the ship had cut the life-boats' painter.

Meanwhile men were still on the rope ladder leading down to the life-boat, and those on the ship's deck were yelling to us to bring the life-boat back, an impossible task. I shouted to the Bosun to take the tiller and ordered all who could to start rowing. We picked up some men from a raft they had managed to launch. The first to enter the life-boat was our elderly Chief Engineer who immediately told me how badly I had handled the life-boat. I simply said, 'Shut up, Chief. Grab an oar, there are lives to be saved.' He did exactly as he was told without a further word. I knew by shouts around for help that there were a number of men in the water. Most of us had lifejackets on with a small electric lamp which when the top was turned would glow red …

For some time they picked up survivors, six in all, as the *Harlesden*, almost on her beam ends, suddenly appeared to right herself, the bow rose in the air and then sank rapidly. Of the forty-one men aboard, seven went down with her.

It was an awesome sad sight. It was not only my ship but also my home which disappeared beneath the waves of the Atlantic Ocean. I thought of those who must have gone down with the ship. I thought also of my £14 sextant and navigation books etc., and of my workbook with all its painstaking notes. Suddenly I felt very lonely in a life-boat in the middle of the ocean.

They were not long left alone, however, for a light was seen, high above them and a guttural voice ordered them alongside where rope ladders and scrambling nets hung down the steel sides 'of a large ship'. Mutimer called up that he had wounded in the boat and received help, with ropes lowered. One of the DEMS gunners put the bowline over Mutimer's head and he was hoisted upwards, his legs hitting the ship's side and prompting him to ask that no one touched his right arm. This request was respected and he found himself hurried below:

into what looked like an operating theatre. I was told to lie on the table and had my splint taken off. The Surgeon Officer asked me who had put it on and I told him it was our ships' cook. He remarked in perfect English that a very good job had been done. I was then strapped to the table, a wet wad was placed over my mouth and I was told to breathe deeply. Suddenly a much wetter wad was slapped on my mouth and firm fingers pinched my nose. I began to cough and choke and thought to myself, 'after all this they intend to choke me to death'. After what seemed an eternity of choking and struggling, I noticed that nothing worried me anymore and I knew that the anaesthetic was taking effect.

This was Mutimer's introduction to the battle-cruiser *Gneisenau*.

He woke in company with 'our First Mate with one foot in plaster and our Second Wireless Officer whom I learned had a very deep flesh wound on his left buttock. It was little wonder that he had been grumbling and cursing while pulling an oar in the life-boat!' Also present was Captain Parry 'whose face was black and blue' after being knocked unconscious for a while by debris falling on him from the bridge. They spent 'a miserable five days in the bowels of the German battleship'. A rubbed bed-sore at the base of Mutimer's spine turned gangrenous and he received several doses of morphine. Nevertheless, the food 'was just awful' and it was with considerable relief that in due course he was trussed in a stretcher and taken up on deck. The sky was grey, 'but looked beautiful to me,' however, Mutimer's joy was short-lived. He was lowered over the side into a waiting motor-boat and had the opportunity to look round.

> [S]igns of German might seemed to be everywhere. Two big battle-cruisers, *Gneisenau* and *Scharnhorst*, and two large supply ships the *Ermland* and the *Altmark*, also a number of U-boats. It was an awe-inspiring sight and I asked myself, 'Where the Hell is the British Navy?'

He and his colleagues were taken aboard the *Ermland* where he was 'laid on a clean bunk with clean sheets and blankets' in an airy compartment.

> Compared to the *Gneisenau* it was heavenly. A good meal was soon provided for us, as was lime juice cordial. It was good old English Rose's Lime Juice, what a surprise! We learned that practically all the food on this ship was British NAAFI stores captured at Dunkirk. My companions were our Second Radio Officer and the First Mate. Captain Parry had fully recovered.

Along with survivors from the two battle-cruisers' prizes, Mutimer spent about a month aboard the *Ermland*, appearing to cruise in mid-Atalntic at slow speed.

> Every second day or so the ship's surgeon … would operate on my arm without anaesthetic in an attempt to combat the gangrene which was clearly suppurating continuously. The pain was dreadful but the surgeon said that he could not keep giving me general anaesthetics because I was too weak. He was also a very kind and caring medic who did all he could to deal with my surgical and medical needs. The same applied to the two sick-bay orderlies who were also careful and knowledgeable nurses. I still have a photo of one of them Willi Krebs. It is true to say we became friends. There were two occasions of 'action stations' when the orderlies would rush in and close the portholes. Nothing happened … [but] I have to confess that in my helpless position I was glad that we were not attacked by our own countrymen.

On 24th March 1941 the *Ermland* reached La Rochelle in the Bay of Biscay and Mutimer was hospitalised. Here he continued to receive treatment, sustained for a little while by 'our First Mate and our Second Sparks whose wounds had not quite healed. I was very sorry when they left, but by that time I had managed to learn enough German to get by for my immediate needs'. Mutimer was in great pain and he also suffered from 'thirst and lack of attention'. His wounds had putrified and were suppurating constantly. Eventually the soldier in the next bed to me took pity on me and brought me a bottle of lemonade from the hospital canteen each day which he paid for himself. I had no money. I had become a mere skeleton of a man with stinking gangrenous wounds. I was urgently in need of the best medical and nursing care.

Mutimer's life, if not his arm, was saved by a German Red Cross nurse. She dressed his wounds properly, placed water cushions beneath him washed the lice out of his hair, and 'washed where she could … She also brought me an occasional cup of real coffee, and red wine with an egg yolk whisked in it …'. But Mutimer's arm was beyond saving. In due course he was taken to an operating theatre. 'I was then made to face the wall for about 15 unhappy minutes'. On coming around from the operation he was told things looked promising. However:

all the bone was badly infected. Many operations were carried out and even disarticulation at the shoulder did not end it all. A number of openings were made in the shoulder flesh and rubber tubes inserted to drain the infection. I remember on one occasion coming to and feeling a knife cut into me. I shouted, 'I'm awake. You are hurting me.' I felt the ether being sprayed through the mask on my face, and out I went struggling.

He was nevertheless growing progressively weaker and was losing the will to live. It was clear he needed blood but no one knew his blood group. He was given a small injection of the:

universal blood group O. In about an hour I was asked how I felt and I was minded to say, 'Bloody awful!' but in deference to their kindness and care I said, 'just the same.' Even then I said to myself, 'All these people going to such lengths to save my life when one of their countrymen had done his best to kill me.' The sad paradox of war! Within a short time I was again wheeled into the operating theatre and laid alongside a young German orderly. A direct man-to-man blood transfusion ensued and this was repeated twice.

Mutimer was still making little progress, largely due to his inability to eat anything. In due course 'his' nurse asked him what he would like to eat, whereupon he responded with a request for ' "Real chipped potatoes, fried egg and bacon, fried bread and fried tomatoes." 'Then I managed a laugh. She looked me straight in the eye, and said but one word, "*Ja!*" Shortly after this had been spirited up, Mutimer's fortunes changed and he celebrated his 22nd birthday on a rising tide of expectation.

The final act of my dear friend and saviour, the Sister, was to wean me off morphine. For weeks and months, first on the battleship then the supply ship and the hospital I had been injected with morphine regularly. It appeared that the Germans had no other effective pain-killer. There was no doubt that I had become an addict and would sometimes shout out for the drug if it was not given to me when I expected it. The addiction had become more stressful than the pain brought on by my wounds, bad though they often were … Finally, the big moment came: 'Will you manage without an injection tonight? I will give you two tablets.' Gloomily I accepted, and fortunately for me the good Sister had won. I had no more morphine.

On 8 August 1941, Mutimer left hospital and had an unpleasant interrogation before being taken to a prison camp under construction by French Sengalese troops for their own occupation. Here he found further friendship among these fellow prisoners.

> One morning there was a bang on the window of the hut. It flew open and some white French bread landed on my bunk along with some fruit and a few cigarettes … Every day whilst I was a lone prisoner in this camp, a similar incident occurred. On the day before I left we managed a short chat and when I told him I would be leaving the next day he said how sorry he would be to see me go. These incidents made a very deep impression on me, and taught me a sharp lesson. As an arrogant young sailor I had not always adopted a friendly attitude to many of those deemed by a lot of the white fraternity to be 'bloody wogs'.
>
>   The German Major who was in charge of this camp was quite a chatty friendly elderly man who set about finding me some reasonable clothes since all I had was my trousers, vest, shoes and … great coat. He found me a Royal Marine Light Infantry tropical jacket and trousers. I managed to fit my one stripe Merchant Navy epaulettes on to the jacket and the end result was rather pleasing. At last I looked a little more respectable.

A few days later, 15 August, an *Obergefreiter*, or lance-corporal, was introduced to Mutimer. He was to escort the young third mate into Bordeaux and then across France to a prison camp in northern Germany. Here, he hoped to meet up with 'fellow seaman and particularly old shipmates'. Alone among the *Harlesden's* survivors, Mutimer had not been registered with the International Red Cross as a PoW and his mother had received four dozen letters of condolence. 'When it was learned that I was alive she received five letters … [saying] "Glad to hear etc., etc." '[26]

Until February 1942 British mercantile Prisoners of War in German hands were held captive in a variety of places. At this time, however, two camps were established at Westertimke, near Bremen. *Marlag* – or *Marine Lager* – was intended for naval personnel; *Milag* – meaning *Marine Internierten Lager* was for mercantile seafarers which, at its peak of 3,500, were predominantly British and included a number of unfortunate passengers,[27] all but a handful of whom had been captured by commerce–raiders. These, taken in the early months of the war, were denied access to formal communications through neutral Switzerland and the International Red Cross owing to the German desire to conceal the successes of their commerce-raiders. Both camps were under Kommandant Schuur with *Milag* itself commanded by Kapitän Prusch. With their racial prejudices, the Germans interned the so-called 'native' ratings in the *Inder Lager*, which accommodated several groups of which there were a number of Chinese, but a majority of Indian lascars. Here a British officer,

Chief Officer Herbert Jones of the Harrison liner *Dalesman* – taken after his ship was sunk in the evacuation of Crete – voluntarily acted as 'Confidence Officer'. These were men of probity acceptable to both the prisoners and the camp authorities. Jones's knowledge of Hindustani proved invaluable and in this capacity he appears to have done everything possible for the betterment of his fellow inmates.

> Several hundred Lascar crewmen had been kept imprisoned for a year or more in a separate camp several miles from *Milag*. They received scant consideration from their Nazi captors, and their misery was compounded by their inability to communicate with their families, or shipping companies, particularly regarding the allotment of money to their folk at home. The Germans claimed they had no censor who understood Hindustani.[28]

They were, however, moved to join the others in *Milag* in early 1943 where the common circumstances eroded racial differences.

Conditions at this bleak prison camp were poor. Many survivors arrived in the clothes in which they had abandoned ship and were issued with uncleaned ex-*Wehrmacht* uniforms. Internal camp administration was in the hands of a German-approved committee led by the Confidence Officer, Captain Lewis, a veteran of the Spanish Civil War, who was replaced in 1943 by Captain Notman. The committee's main concerns were the receipt and issue of Red Cross parcels, health, sanitation, the hospital and food. With poor victuals, Red Cross food parcels became crucial to survival, particularly in the winter cold. The camp was afflicted by typhus, tuberculosis, cancer and cardiac-arrest and thirty-six bodies are known to have been buried in the Christian cemetery, and a further fourteen occupy the second, or 'Indian'.[29] The hospital was staffed by three medical officers, a British Army doctor, a Royal Naval surgeon and the ship's doctor, Karl Sperber, from the Blue Funnel liner *Automedon*. As Peter Elphick points out:

> Sperber's Czech medical qualifications may not have been acceptable to the British Medical Association, but it was highly valued in *Milag*. He was very much respected, not least for having overcome an, outbreak of typhus in a previous camp with the minimum of facilities and medicines. At *Milag*, using very basic methods, he had some success against diphtheria. Sperber was a Jew and hence not popular with the Germans, and towards the end of 1942 was taken away to a concentration camp, but he managed to survive the war.

Among the internees were captives from the vessels who failed to escape the German blockade of Swedish ports in Operations PERFORMANCE and BRIDFORD, accounts of which follow later. The largest contingent was the crew of the Orient Line's *Orama* which had been sunk by the *Admiral Hipper* off Norway on 9 June 1940. Fortunately the *Orama* had not been carrying troops at the time but under the T124 arrangements her peace-time dance-band had been retained on board as sick-berth attendants, stewards and gun-layers. Under their leader, Neil Block, they formed the Orama Band, providing concerts and backing for the amateur dramatics of three theatrical companies. These were inspired by Henry Mollison, a Shakespearean actor who had been a passenger on a ship captured by the commerce-raider *Thor*. Other groups and ensembles were set up, including a predominantly Welsh choir. Complex leagues and tournaments in almost every sport were formed, buoying-up morale and keeping the prisoners as fit as was possible on their meagre diet. The most extraordinary ingenuity was manifested in providing modest equipment, backed by a sophisticated bartering system.

Most remarkable were the study groups organized by the senior officers, allowing instruction to be given to those younger men who intended continuing their careers at sea after the war. Captain T.W. Morris initiated this, giving classes to the apprentices 'to keep them out of trouble'. In due course, through the good offices of the Red Cross in Geneva and the co-operation of the Board of Trade, examination papers were forwarded and sat under German invigilation. 'In April 1944 over a hundred [candidates] … took these … the papers being returned to London via Geneva, and the pass rate turned out to be over 75 per cent'.[30] Among the tutors was Second Officer Donald Stewart of the *Automedon*, a Master-Mariner who made an outstanding contribution, building a deviascope, essential instrument for candidates seeking to pass for Master. Stewart also constructed a section of the working deck of a cargo-liner, complete with mast, heavy-lift derrick, hatch and winches, by which prospective mates demonstrated their knowledge of cargo-rigs and stresses. After the war Stewart was Mentioned in Despatches and commanded Blue Funnel liners.[31]

As Arthur Bird wrote:

> Let it be said of our merchant seamen that the nature of their calling, and the life and conditions at sea in those days, bred men of resource, tolerance and adaptability, ideally suited to making the best of captivity. When considering these aspects of life in *Milag*, it should be remembered that rank had little significance. Masters, Mates and Engineers did not have the same authority over their crews as did officers and N.C.O.s in the other services. It is therefore to the greater credit of those men, both officers and ratings, who by their natural abilities became the initiators and leaders of the many healthy activities that were developed.[32]

Among the more remarkable of achievements of men mewed-up in Milag Nord was that of Stan Hughill, the quartermaster at *Automedon's* wheel at the moment of her capture by Rogge in *Atlantis*. A veteran of Cape Horn, he took up a lively interest in the shanties of his formative years, turning this to good use in his later life. He also developed a considerable skill as an artist, his painting of the Risen Christ decorating the camp chapel.[33] Hughill, as Arthur Bird recalled, was also active in the theatrical shows.

> While the normal run of productions depended upon enthusiastic teamwork, Stan Hughill, who had a touch of the 'Treasure Island' romantic about him, distinguished himself by writing and producing two plays for which he also painted the scenery and made the costumes. He also acted in one of them.

Possession of a foreign-going master-mariner's certificate qualified its holder to command a British ship of any size or class, voyaging anywhere on the world's oceans but, as this cartoon by the former radio officer Norman Mansbridge demonstrates, distinctions existed between vessels. The pipe-smoker on the left wears the relaxed rig of a cargo-liner master; his haughty companion the 'Number Tens' of a passenger carrier's commander. (Courtesy of The Marine Society)

Books and sports equipment were forwarded from several of the shipowners whose personnel languished in *Milag*, by way of the Red Cross and the Order of St John of Jerusalem. Not everyone developed intellectual tastes. Others turned to more frivolous forms of entertainment, an adaptation of ship-board 'horse-racing' allowed a totaliser system to be set up and a proportion of the winnings was set aside for charity, so much so that after the war a cheque for £1,391 was sent to the International Red Cross. Forms of trade were established, and particularly adept at this were the Egyptian seamen from the Société Misr de Navigation Maritime's *Zamzam*. Although registered in Alexandria and technically neutral, the *Zamzam* had been another of the *Atlantis*'s victims, mistaken by Rogge for a Bibby liner, which, in fact, she had once been.[34] Her men acquired a formidable reputation for their trading abilities and distinguished themselves by so successfully bribing their guards that when repatriated in 1944, they traveled in some style on the railways through Germany and Austria.

Despite these attempts to ameliorate conditions, the camp diet was inadequate and the location of the camp exposed it to the bitter cold winds off the North Sea. Resistance to the Germans found expression in the secret manufacture of radio sets, eagerly undertaken by the several radio officers in captivity. Discovery of these was severely punished and searches were conducted regularly. The resourceful Dr Sperber hid one in the bedding of an Indian patient adorned with the label 'Infectious', which deterred close examination, and played upon the Nazi susceptibility to racial contamination. German methods also concealed from their eyes a map of Europe regular updated from BBC bulletins by a radio officer named Warner. It was on the back of one of the hut doors which, when opened by the guards, was always thrown violently open, to crash back upon the adjacent wall. Possession of this information increased the psychological burden borne by the inmates who lived in fear of being bombed by their own side.

A number of exchanges of prisoners took place by way of Sweden, men like the wounded Mutimer, who was repatriated in October 1943, and certain 'protected personnel' such as padres and some of the civilian passengers. They were taken to Rostock, on the Baltic, put aboard a ferry to Trebourg in Sweden and from there carried to Gothenburg. Here a cartel in the shape of the Canadian Pacific liner *Empress of Russia* awaited them, to be escorted clear of the Skagerrak by a German destroyer.

The camp boasted an escape committee and several tunnels through which a score of men escaped, only to be recaptured, returned to the camp and appropriately punished. The only successful escape by a Briton was that of Third Officer Arthur Bird of the *Australind*, one of Trinder Anderson's vessels. In the beginning of his own account of his escapade, Bird writes tellingly that his ship was homeward bound after 'thirteen months out of Bristol'. During that time the *Australind* had:

> shipped war materials to Egypt by the long haul round the Cape, salt from the pans near Suez to Calcutta and oriental foodstuffs from India and Burma across the world to a string of West Indian islands. Then on to the States to load general cargo for Australia, and now, laden with zinc-ore, honey and dried fruits, she was nearing the Galapagos Islands at her stately nine knots, heading for Panama ...

It was a typical voyage except that it was August 1941 and in anticipation of action once she cleared the Panama Canal and shaped her course for the main convoy rendezvous at Halifax, the boats and guns were being given the once-over. On the afternoon of the 14th the *Australind* was shelled without warning by a ship that had, until a few moments ago, flown the then neutral flag of Japan, an image of which was also painted on her topsides which bore the name *Ryoko Maru*. She was in fact the *Komet*, commanded by Konteradmiral Essen, and the Japanese flag had been replaced by the swastika, a large one draped over the painted rising sun. 'The young' Captain Stevens was killed on his own bridge and the upperworks of his ship were quickly reduced to a shambles. The usual boarding procedure was followed; the wounded were removed first, then the remainder, the last being Chief Officer Ronald Willoughby. For Boatswain A. Jesson it was a case of *dejá vu*: he had been captured in the previous war by the *Möwe*. After further captures of the Dutchman *Kota Nopan* – loaded with tin which was carefully looted by the Germans – and British India's *Devon*, the *Komet* made a rendezvous with the *Atlantis* and the supply ship *Munsterland*. Bird and his fellow prisoners were joined by men from Lamport & Holt's *Balzac* and Watts, Watts & Co.'s *Tottenham*, and the Egyptian *Zamzam* who all eventually arrived at *Milag*.

An admirer of all things Scandinavian, Bird was engaged to a Norwegian and his escape was greatly facilitated by his ability to speak passable German, Norwegian and Swedish. Nevertheless, he had an almost unbelievable run of luck. Reaching Harburg, a small port on the south bank of the Elbe near Hamburg, he was helped by the men of a Swedish ship running iron ore into the Reich. In Stockholm the Norwegian Resistance arranged for him to be reunited with his fiancée and the British Embassy enabled them to marry in some style. After working for the British Embassy as a courier, meeting aircraft flown regularly between Leuchars in Scotland and Arlanda near Stockholm by air crews from the British Overseas Airways Corporation, Bird and his bride were themselves flown to Britain.[35]

After weeks of fear and uncertainty, the inmates of Milag spent their last hours as PoWs in the No Man's Land between the retreating Germans and the advancing Allies, 'frantically digging trenches and dug-outs'. The camp was liberated at noon on 27 April 1945. Cadet William Errington, formerly of B.I.'s *Devon*, seized and sunk, like Bird's *Australind*, by Essen's *Komet* on 19 August 1941, had been attempting to doze when a fellow inmate woke him.

> I was out of my bunk like a shot … We ran like hell over to the wire. What a terrific sensation. A couple of blokes were standing by the [watch-]tower, both had on tin helmets. It was a beautiful sight. I was too full for words. After all these years I could only stand and gape at them. One of them, a Sergeant, said, in a strong Scots accent. 'Hello there. Is this *Milag* Prison Camp?' Someone managed to gibber a reply. Then an officer came up and told one of the men to cut a way through the wire. He asked us … if there was anything we needed … and the only thing … was water. That, he said, was impossible. They hadn't got any. In the meantime the Sergeant had cut his way through to us and the first thing we did was to shake hands with the first free British men we had seen for four years. He gave me a hip flask and I had my first drink of rum … it was very appropriate that it should be the first drink I should have in freedom.

While preparing for his solitary escape-bid Bird had kept his own counsel, conduct mistaken for collaboration. Unequivocal collaboration had been entered into by a few of *Milag*'s inmates, all of whom joined the British *Freikorps* of the Waffen SS. John Amery, a virulent anti-communist and the wayward son of a British War Cabinet minister, Leopold Amery, had run guns across the Pyrenees to supply Franco's army during the Spanish Civil War. Caught-up with fascist politics, at the end of 1942 Amery was persuaded by a like-minded Frenchman that it was essential that Britain joined Germany against the Soviet-Union, otherwise Germany would lose the war and the USSR become over-powerful. Conceiving the idea of a Legion of St George, Avery toured the prison camps and raised a force of thirty men from the thousands of British prisoners. The most committed of these from *Milag* was Able-Seaman Alfred Minchin who, recruited in May 1943, returned to the camp several times resplendent in SS uniform to suborn others. He was successful in only two cases and that only after some heavy-handed persuasion from the German guards. Herbert Rowlands was a greaser from the *Orama*, and Ronald Voysey (born Barker in Australia) had been a cabin boy on the tanker *British Advocate*. The final member of this traitorous quartet was Kenneth Berry who had been aboard the Admiralty oiler *Cymbeline* as a boy of fourteen when the ship was sunk by the *Widder* on 2 September 1940. Owing to his extreme youth, after landing at Bordeaux, Berry was permitted to live in Paris in the care of a paroled

British female resident but in 1943, when seventeen, he was interned. Interviewed by John Amery and fed an abundance of propaganda, the wretched youth agreed to join the corps. After the war all four were charged with 'assisting the enemy,' Minchin being sentenced to seven years hard labour, Rowlands and Voysey received two-year terms and Berry only nine months. Amery, whose brother Julian had fought with the partisans behind enemy lines in Albania, was arraigned on eight charges of treason before Sir Travers Humphreys on 28 November 1945 at the Old Bailey. He pleaded guilty and was hanged by Albert Pierrepoint at Wandsworth Prison on 19 December.

Bird's repatriation with his bride was enabled by the special aircraft making flights between Leuchars and Stockholm. These had several purposes, one of which was to maintain communications with the neutral government of Sweden, an important conduit between London and Berlin. The situation of the Swedes was complex; officially neutral, there was considerable sympathy with Germany in its war with Britain, and Stockholm bristled with German agents. German troops passed between the Fatherland and Occupied Norway by way of Malmö, yet the Germans sank neutral Swedish shipping which consequently took shelter in Allied convoys. Most important to Germany was the flow of Swedish iron ore, while Sweden managed a lucrative trade in ball-bearings and other components of especially hardened steel, in the production of which the Swedes were accomplished specialists.

TOTALS OF BRITISH SHIPPING.

BRITISH VESSELS AT SEA	1345
OTHER BRITISH VESSELS AFLOAT including	
Great Lakes, Coasting Vessels, Railway Services, etc.	226 1771 vessels afloat.
BRITISH VESSELS IN HARBOUR :—	
Ports in the British Isles	287
„ „ Western Europe	43
„ „ Scandinavia & the Baltic	5
„ „ Mediterranean	41
„ „ India	62
„ „ China, Japan & East Indies	59
„ „ Australia & New Zealand	41
„ „ Africa	30
„ „ Canada, U.S.A.(E.Coast) & West Indies	83
„ „ „ , U.S.A.(W.Coast)	14
„ „ S. America (East & West Coasts)	40 705 vessels in harbour.
GRAND TOTAL	2476

NOTES ABOUT SHIPPING.

Ships are plotted in their actual positions as nearly as the scale of the Chart will allow. ⬥ = Ships of 3000-10,000 tons Gross. ⬦ = Ships of over 10,000 tons Gross. The figures in circles indicate the number of British Ships in harbour grouped in areas on the 24ᵗʰ November 1937. The figures in brackets against the names of Ports indicate the number of British Ships at those Ports on the 24ᵗʰ November 1937.

NOTES ABOUT COMMODITIES.

Separate details are not shown of imports which are less than 5% of the total. For classification of imports by commodities see separate list accompanying this Chart.

(© National Maritime Museum, Greenwich)

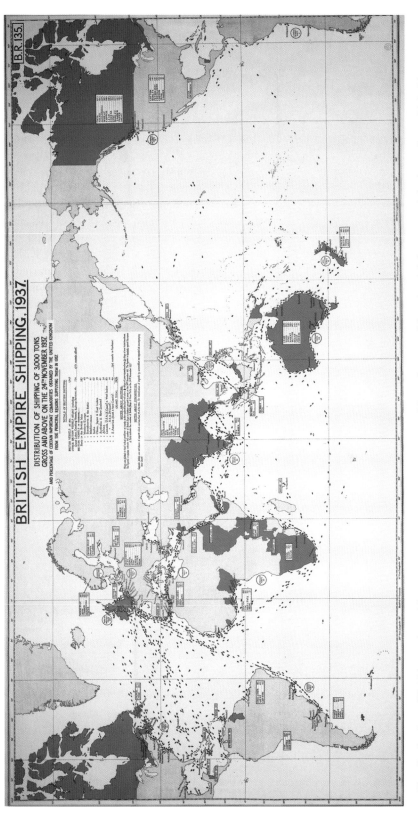

1. The distribution of British merchant ships over 3,000 gross tons at noon on 28 November 1937. Note the global extent and the intervals at which ships are extended along the imperial trade routes and on certain coasts, not all of which are coloured red. (© National Maritime Museum, Greenwich)

2. Imperial servant: The British India Steam Navigation Co.'s elegant cargo/passenger-liner *Golconda* of 1919, with her open decks suitable for deck passengers. (© Courtesy of The British Mercantile Marine Memorial Collection)

3. Imperial workhorse: Cayzer, Irvine's Clan liner, *Clan Matheson* of 1919 in a heavy sea. She has heavy-lift derricks at both masts and retains the counter-stern of a sailing-vessel in this atmospheric painting by Gordon Ellis. (© Courtesy of The British Mercantile Marine Memorial Collection)

4. The *Sithonia* was bought by Henry Murray Thomson, a third-generation member of the Thomson family of Leith, when in 1920 he broke away from the family firm, Ben Line. The *Sithonia* is shown off the Japanese coast with Mount Fuji in the background. She is flying her 'numbers' above her bridge, with Thomson's house-flag at her main masthead, the Japanese ensign as a courtesy flag at the fore. Sunk during the Second World War, her crew made two long lifeboat voyages. From a painting by the Japanese artist H. Shimidzu. (© Courtesy of The British Mercantile Marine Memorial Collection)

5. The Peninsular & Oriental Steam Navigation Co.'s *Mooltan* of 1923, one of many liners maintaining communications between Great Britain, India and Australia. She flies the blue ensign, denoting her commander and several of her officers are officers of the Royal Naval Reserve. Painting by Jack Spurling. (From a Private Collection)

6. British India's *Tairea*, one of three *T*-class liners maintaining services in the Indian Ocean and the China Seas after the acquisition of the Apcar Line. She saw active service at Madagascar in 1942 and the Sicily landings the following year. She was broken-up in 1952. Painting by Jack Spurling. (From a Private Collection)

7. Lamport & Holt's *Voltaire* leaving New York for South America. After the disastrous loss of the *Vestris* she was switched to cruising and in the Second World War was requisitioned and converted to an Armed Merchant Cruiser. She was sunk in action with the German commerce-raider *Thor* on 9 April 1941. Painting by J.M. Browne. (© Courtesy of the Honourable Company of Master Mariners)

8. One of a vast fleet owned by Furness, Withy, the *Chinese Prince* of 1931 was owned by the subsidiary Prince Line. She is shown here in a watercolour by the Japanese artist P. Shimidzu off Mount Fujiyama, Japan. She was sunk on 12 June 1941 by Korvettenkapitän Erich Topp in *U-552* with the loss of 45 men. *U-552* was responsible for sinking three of the company's ships. (© Courtesy of The British Mercantile Marine Memorial Collection)

9. With a fall off of regular passenger traffic during the Depression, many passenger liners switched to catering for the rich by offering world cruises. It was customary to repaint the ships white as this attractive image of Cunard's *Carinthia* by Kenneth Shoesmith shows. (© Courtesy of The British Mercantile Marine Memorial Collection)

10. Shaw, Savill & Albion's *Dominion Monarch* embarks her pilot off Sydney Head from the cruising pilot-cutter *Captain Cook's* pulling boat. The cutter was coal-fired to support the local mining industry. The painting by Malcolm Armstrong hangs in the London headquarters of the International Maritime Organsiation, a UN Agency, and was presented by the International Maritime Pilots' Association. (© Courtesy of Malcolm Armstrong and the IMO)

11. The conspicuity of coal-fired steamers which so worried the naval authorities on the outbreak of war is demonstrated in this atmospheric watercolour by the talented Gordon Ellis, showing the laden Harrison liner *Wanderer*, having picked up her tugs after a voyage to the West Indies, passing Dumbarton Rock on her way up a glassy Clyde. (© Courtesy of The British Mercantile Marine Memorial Collection)

12. An anonymous 'raised-quarter-decked' coaster owned by Monroe Brothers of Glasgow crosses Mount's Bay towards the Lizard on a breezy morning, a reminder that pre-war, much cargo was carried round the British coast by those salt-caked coasters immortalised by John Masefield. Another of Gordon Ellis's minor masterpieces. (From a Private Collection)

13. The Donaldson liner *Letitia* was a sister-ship to the *Athenia*, the first ship to be sunk in 1939. During the war the *Letitia* served as an AMC, troop and hospital ship. Later she was commanded by the *Athenia*'s last master, Captain James Cook. Remaining under Donaldson's management, she was later chartered by the New Zealand government, renamed *Captain Cook*, and carried thousands of emigrants to New Zealand. Painting by Odin Rosenvinge. (© Courtesy of The British Mercantile Marine Memorial Collection)

14. The flying of a defaced blue ensign and the wearing of the distinctive Blue Riband on her white hull denotes a Government-chartered troopship. The Bibby Line specialised in this and the *Devonshire*'s commissioning in 1939 was timely. Painting by James S. Mann. (© Courtesy of Sir Michael Bibby)

15. Many liners were used as assault-ships for Allied landing operations. Here, the Bibby liner *Derbyshire* is shown in a painting by James S. Mann fitted with landing craft, anti-aircraft armament and, above her bridge concealed in a grotesque tower, radar. (© Courtesy of Sir Michael Bibby)

16. Standing under a ventilation shaft in the ferocious glow of a boiler fire a fireman slices and rakes in the stokehold of a merchant ship. These were the intractable men who showed little liking for discipline, but in wartime few escaped if their ship was torpedoed in her engine room. If they did, they had little chance of survival dressed for the heat of the boiler room. Painting by Henry Marvell Carr. (© National Maritime Museum, Greenwich)

17. Even though the perils of sail were long gone, seafaring remained a dangerous way of life. Whether working in the holds, the tanks or aloft, an able-bodied seaman still required skills unknown to his brother ashore. Here a gang of seamen are painting a mast from bosun's chairs. Note the size of the tackle on the heavy-lift derrick behind the mast. Painting by an unknown merchant seaman. (© Courtesy of The Marine Society)

18. With a dummy funnel, a canvas screen to resemble a deck-house, and her real funnel painted white, the war-built tanker *Empire Emerald* is seen here in convoy disguised as a tramp-steamer. Watercolour by Lieutenant D.W. Lambie RNVR. (© Courtesy of Peter Lambie)

19. Ellerman's City cargo-liner the *City of Pretoria* of 1947 is an example of the post-war tonnage built to replace losses. Smart but conventional, such ships operated worldwide, providing cargo-space and passenger accommodation. Gouache on grey paper by W. McDowell. (© Courtesy of The British Mercantile Marine Memorial Collection)

20. Although owned by the Hain S.S. Co. of St Ives, Cornwall, the tramp-ship *Tregenna* of 1949 was part of the vast P&O conglomerate. Painting by Arthur Burgess. (© Courtesy of The British Mercantile Marine Memorial Collection)

21. The owners of the *Baron Gareloch*, built in 1958 and seen here in the Clyde Estuary, were known throughout the Merchant Navy as 'Hungry' Hogarths. Painting by Leslie Wilcox. (From a Private Collection)

22. Although built for the Booth Line's South America service in 1955, the immaculate cargo-liner *Hubert* ended her days under the red ensign in eastern waters, running between Malaysia, Singapore, Indonesia, New Guinea and Australia as the Austasia Line's *Australasia*. Watercolour by Walter Thomas. (© Courtesy of The British Mercantile Marine Memorial Collection)

23. Set against the heather-covered hills of Scotland, Norman Wilkinson's painting depicts the Union-Castle Line's *Pretoria Castle* of 1960. With her distinctive lavender-coloured hull, she was the largest liner built for the Cape mail service. With a speed of 22 knots and a stop at either Madeira or Las Palmas, she made the passage in eleven days carrying 822 passengers. (From a Private Collection)

24. Sister-ship to the ill-fated *Dara*, the *Dwarka* had also been subjected to a terrorist outrage when the cabin of the Interior Minister of Muscat and Oman, then a passenger, was wrecked by a plastic explosive. The Minister was dragged clear by another passenger. The Omani rebels, under their exiled leader Ghaleb bin Taleb, began campaigning for independence against the hereditary Sultan who was protected by a treaty with the British. (© Courtesy of the artist, Robert Lloyd)

25. Under a lowering sky the tanker *British Reliance* carries 16,800 tons of crude oil to Britain from the Persian Gulf. She was built in 1950, four years before her owners changed their name from the Anglo-Persian Oil Co., to British Petroleum. Not much bigger than the T2 standard war-built tanker, such ships were soon out of date with the arrival of far larger vessels. (© Courtesy of the artist, Robert Lloyd)

26. By building the 20-knot *Benloyal* in 1959 the Ben Line rattled the complacency of their chief competitors on the Far East service, Alfred Holt & Co., provoking a building programme by both companies of fast cargo-liners that were soon superseded by container-ships. The ship is seen at Hong Kong. (© Courtesy of the artist, Robert Lloyd)

27. Shown here outward bound in a heavy Biscay sea, Alfred Holt's Blue Funnel liner *Antenor*, though only capable of 16 knots, was one of a large and versatile class of cargo-liner. Able to carry chilled, liquid and dry cargoes, her array of derricks, including a heavy-lift capability of 70 tons, meant hard work for her crew. Holts built to a standard higher than Lloyd's. (© Courtesy of the artist, Robert Lloyd)

28. Although Swire's China Navigation Co. owed its fortunes to Holt's Blue Funnel Line, it has outlasted its progenitor. Driven from the China coast in 1949, the company developed new cargo-services based largely in the south-east Pacific with ships like the *Kweilin* of 1962 whose names reflected Swire's origins. (© Courtesy of the artist, James Pottinger)

29. One of the last pure passenger liners, P&O's *Canberra* of 1961 was designed to take advantage of the Assisted Passage Scheme for 'Ten Pound Poms,' Britons wishing to emigrate under a subsidised scheme of £10 per passenger. She enjoyed a chequered career as emigration declined and the jet airliner took off, but as 'the Great White Whale' achieved fame in the Falklands Campaign of 1982. Later she cruised, being scrapped in 1997. (© Courtesy of the artist, Robert Lloyd)

Germany was not the only market for ball-bearings: Great Britain was in desperate need of them and to maintain a supply, the special flights between Leuchars and Stockholm were established, the acquiring agency in the Swedish capital being a trade mission at the British Embassy. This was naturally an important centre of diplomacy and espionage, the British Naval Attaché, Captain Henry Denham, becoming an important player in this game of cat-and-mouse. While ball-bearings and agents – some from Norway – were flown out, others were flown in, among them luminaries of the artistic world, such as the distinguished conductor, Sir Malcolm Sergeant. Several of the flights were 'lost' while flying over the high latitudes of the Norwegian Arctic and the supply of Swedish ball-bearings imported by air was limited.

Considerable consignments of precision-engineered ball-bearings and associated steel had been ordered on the outbreak of war. As hostilities developed these became increasingly urgently needed, chiefly for aircraft production where few moving components could function without them. This, of course, was equally true of other machinery, so much so that it was necessary to establish a Controller of Bearings in the Ministry of Supply to allocate these essentials components. Unfortunately, the German invasion of Denmark and Norway in the spring of 1940 closed the Baltic to British shipping and ended the export of ball-bearings to Britain in Norwegian ships, a number of which were on charter to Britain, loaded and ready to sail. In due course five of these whose masters had determined to escape Nazi domination made contact with London. A break-out was organised, code-named Operation RUBBLE, and in late January 1941, supported by the Royal Navy and Coastal Command, all five ships reached Kirkwall.[36] The British determined to extricate another ten chartered Norwegian vessels still lying loaded in neutral Swedish ports. The key players in this were the banker Sir Charles Hambro, who established a Scandinavian Section of the Special Operations Executive in Stockholm; Sir William Waring, who, with his wife had escaped from Norway where he had held a commercial post in the Oslo Legation; Sir George Binney, a former Arctic explorer who worked in the Iron and Steel Control Section of the Ministry of Supply and had been appointed a temporary Assistant Commercial Attaché in Stockholm, and Captains Eccles and Lees of the Admiralty's Operations Division.

The chances of success were compromised by the concentration of German naval forces in the Kattegat and Skaggerak, the commitment of British naval forces to the new Allied convoys to the Soviet Union, and by the necessity of the Swedish government not to be seen to favour Britain resulting in constant objections to any movement of the Norwegian ships. Despite a series of set-backs, Operation PERFORMANCE began, but the British naval cover was weak and the escaping ships, which left just after midnight on 1 April 1942, with their disparate speeds, became strung out. One vessel was sunk within seven miles of Gothenburg, a slow 12,000-ton whale factory ship was attacked and was scuttled and a third ran aground, to be destroyed by gun-fire. Two more were attacked by the *Luftwaffe* while running the gauntlet of the Skagerrak and it was only when the first five were abeam of Kristiansand that British Mosquitoes arrived to engage German aircraft attacking them. This, however, did not reassure either the *Lionel* or the *Dicto*, which turned back for Gothenburg. By the time the remainder were within 180 miles of Scotland, there was still no sign of the Royal Navy's destroyers and an eighth ship was bombed and sunk. Only two of the ten actually reached a safe haven, resulting in several prisoners being added, as noted, to the inmates of *Milag* camp.

Nevertheless, there remained the cargoes of the *Lionel* and *Dicto* which, although the Swedes had now boomed them in, were a tantalising temptation to Binney. As the year wore on, excepting the influential disaster of PQ17, Malta was saved from starvation; Operation TORCH saw Allied troops land in Vichy French North Africa and Rommel's hitherto victorious Afrika Korps was stopped in its tracks by Montgomery's Eighth Army at El Alamein. Once it became clear that Britain was not going to be defeated by Germany, the Swedish government began to shift its stance, following public opinion already much in sympathy with the situation of Great Britain and her powerful new ally, the United States of America. Despite these triumphs, the shortage of ball-bearings in Britain had passed from being chronic to acute.[37]

The possibility of trans-shipping into destroyers the ball-bearings aboard the *Lional* and *Dicto* was quashed by a Swedish decree forbidding the entry of belligerent war-ships into Swedish waters unless in distress. Having secured an undertaking that the Swedes would release these Norwegian but British-chartered ships, British diplo-macy was countered by that of the Swedes who considered it necessary to inform the German embassy of their decision. Thus the minute the vessels left Swedish waters they would be ambushed, and an increase in German naval units in the Kattegat emphasised this. The failure of Operation CABARET, an attempt to break-out the *Lionel* and *Dicto* by British forces, did not deter Binney, who had taken part as an observer. On 22 April 1943 he presented a new plan to the influential Leathers at the MoWT in Berkeley Square, the upshot of which was a decision to modify a number of fast gunboats under construction for the Turkish navy for the carriage of cargoes of 40 tons of ball-bearings. The craft were registered in London, owned by King George VI and on bare-boat charters to the MoWT, who placed them under the management of Ellerman's Wilson Line. Both the conversions and the operational plans were complex, relying on a number of things: shallow draught to cross mine-fields, meticulous navigational plans that placed the craft exactly in the right place to run the Skagerrak during the long winter nights, and upon new diesel engines of indeterminate reliability. These blockade-runners were to be armed with Oerlikon and Vickers guns against air and surface attack, and fitted with expensive and sophis-ticated gyro compasses. Lastly they would rely upon crews of equal unproven mettle, because these fast cargo-craft were to be manned by the Merchant Navy and fly the red ensign. They would use smaller ports and the *Lionel*, commanded by a Briton, would act as mother-ship while they were briefly in Swedish waters.

With conversion in hand the selection of crews was made in Hull by Binney who was gazetted a temporary Commander RNVR and put in charge of Operation BRIDFORD. Based in Hull, where Ellerman's Wilson Line had its head office, the company's marine superintendent and an official from the MoWT joined Binney on the selection and vetting panel. To act as masters and mates a number of Ellerman's Wilson Line's chief and second officers, with their familiarity with the Baltic, were recruited on undertakings of secrecy. Their crews, also sworn to silence, were drawn

A poster of Ellerman's Hull-based Wilson Line. Known for its green hulls and its ship names ending in 'o' the line traded with the Baltic, its advertised services integrated with Ellerman's other companies, the Pappayanni and City Lines. Ownership was in the hands of John Reeves Ellerman. In the Second World War German propaganda suggested that his initials, embroidered on the house-flag, signified 'Jews Rule England'. (From a Private Collection)

largely from the Wilson Line and the fishing trawlers for which Hull was well known and made up a score of officers and ratings. The pay was good – £541 per annum for a master, mates around £30 a month, chief engineers around £35, second engineers £28, greasers £15, able-seamen £14, cooks and stewards £17.5. In addition all were paid the standard War Risk Money plus a bonus for every successful trip. Five gunboats were prepared: the *Hopewell* was commanded by David Stokes, the *Nonsuch* by Herbert Jackson, the *Gay Corsair* by Robert Tanton, the *Gay Viking* by Harold Whitfield and the *Master Standfast* by Godfrey Goodman.

Since a British merchantman was permitted defensive armament these craft also bore a member of the armed services to handle the gunnery – their equivalent in law of a DEMS detachment. In fact these were all provided by Special Operations Executive and led by a 'chief officer' each of whom was gazetted with an RNVR commission, irrespective of any previous rank held.[38] A small shore-base was set up in the Albert Dock in Hull where Lieutenant Commander Edward Thomas RNVR and his team of mechanics undertook the maintenance of the triple sixteen-cylinder

The *Hopewell*, one of the fast, armed motor-boats manned by Ellerman's Wilson Line used to run the German blockade and carry much-needed Swedish ball-bearings for the British war effort under the red ensign. Specially drawn by John Morris.

Davey Paxman Ricardo diesel engines fitted in each boat and which were supposed to give cruising speeds of 20, and a maximum of 25 knots. Prior to making a run the craft were moved to the Coastal Forces base at Immingham from where their departure could be better concealed. A small maintenance team and a meteorologist were flown over to Sweden to take post aboard the *Dicto*. Finally, plans were laid for the operation to begin on moonless nights after the onset of autumn darkness.

Working-up trials proved lengthy and the last two boats were not handed over until late August, by which time the *Lionel* and the *Dicto* had quietly moved fifty-miles north, from Gothenburg to Lysekil, where Waring, his wife and a cipher clerk from Stockholm established themselves in a local hotel to deal with cargoes in collusion with the Wilson Line's agents. Operationally the vessels were loosely held – thanks to Binney's rank in the RNVR – to be linked to the Commander-in-Chief at The Nore, whence emanated intelligence briefs on German naval dispositions in the Skagerrak and Kattegat. On the eve of the first run to Sweden Lord Leathers sent an encouraging message, clearly indicating the necessity for the obtaining of ball-bearings prior to the much desired opening of a Second Front in Europe.

> You are about to embark on an enterprise which will bring lasting honour to the Red Ensign under which you sail. The Prime Minister has told the country that we never call on the officers and men of the Merchant navy in vain … Your task is great, but success will add mightily to the preparation for our great onslaught for victory … I pray God to watch over you in your adventure and confidently rely on your skill, your courage and your resolution, under His providence, to bring it to a resounding success.

But bad weather and an intelligence leak delayed matters and it was not until 25 October, with Binney embarked in *Hopewell* and Leathers's last, succinct message – 'Go to it!' – ringing in their ears that they slipped down the Humber and into dense fog. Somewhere on the Dogger Bank they were detected by hostile fisher-men who warned of British gun-boats being at sea and soon afterwards the *Gay Viking* developed engine trouble and dropped astern. Later the remaining four boats were half-heartedly attacked by aircraft when running parallel with the Danish coast. Binney broke radio silence to request air support, but the message was not received at Wick. After reversing course for some hours and throwing the enemy off, they resumed their passage. Now, as they approached the position from which to make the final dash to Lysekil under the cover of darkness, all four boats successively developed engine trouble; Binney had no option but to abort the mission.

On arrival back at Hull there was no sign of *Gay Viking*. An anxious Binney was relieved when, the following day, Whitfield brought her home laden with ball-bear-ings. Unable to communicate with Binney and assuming he had simply been left behind, Whitfield had pressed on, to find the *Gay Viking* the only arrival. Circled by a Heinkel HeIII Whitfield had hoisted the swastika and dodged observation by other patrolling aircraft until nightfall, when he cranked up his diesels to full power and tore through the darkness. At 04.40 on 28 October Hallö Island light came in sight and the *Gay Viking* passed the litter of rocks, reefs, islets and islands of the *skargard* that lie several miles off the Swedish mainland, into quieter and neutral waters. At daylight the *Gay Viking* approached Lysekil, her powerful if unreliable diesels throt-tled back, an enormous red ensign flying above her open bridge and her merchant crew lining the deck, naval fashion. A large number of the local populace turned out to watch, including the German consul. Waring organised a sauna and breakfast at the Statshotel, after which the *Gay Viking* moved a few miles to Brofjord where the *Lionel* and *Dicto* lay at anchor. Having loaded her cargo and embarked some Norwegian passengers, *Gay Viking* returned to Lysekil before leaving on the evening of the 29th. Although the Germans knew of her presence in Swedish waters, the swift turn-around of the *Gay Viking* was probably what saved her from intercep-tion. On her safe arrival in Hull, Leathers reported the 'successful start' that had been made in securing a 'small quantity of ball-bearings and other special cargo'. Churchill responded: 'Good'.

In the subsequent operations of this small squadron much was to go awry. The diesel plant proved largely unsuitable and, as one master reported: 'rarely did we return to base with three engines working.' The *Gay Corsair* and *Nonsuch* had seri-ous engine defects from the start, then Goodman of the *Master Standfast* injured himself and was replaced by George Holdsworth, the senior mate promoted out of the *Gay Corsair*. Thus he was in command when the *Master Standfast* and *Hopewell* – with Binney on board – made a second attempt, leaving Hull the evening of the *Gay Viking*'s return, 31 October. Unfortunately the two craft lost touch with one another during a complicated run inside Danish waters, undertaken to avoid German patrols. The *Hopewell* arrived at Lysekil early on the morning of 2 November but there was no sign of Holdsworth's *Master Standfast*. It was five days before the *Hopewell* moved to Brofjord and began loading from the *Lionel* and *Dicto* and the only news of Holdsworth had come from Denmark by way of the Swedish navy. The *Master Standfast* had been escorted into Frederickshaven by a German armed trawler and ambulances had met them.

In due course, after engine repairs and a moderation in the weather, the loaded *Hopewell* sailed for Hull but was turned back by heavy seas and a failure in one of the gear boxes. With iron nerve, Stokes drove through a narrow gap in the *skargard* at considerable hazard, to arrive at Lysekil where she had to wait for a gearbox to be flown from Leuchars to Gothenburg along with Lieutenant Commander Thomas. Stokes took the *Hopewell* to Gothenburg under escort of a Swedish warship, only to be fired upon by a fort. However, his little ship received a hero's welcome as she moved along the Gota Canal to the shipyard at Hote where the repairs were under-taken. Finally, on 30 November, Stokes left Lysekil and headed for home; the forecast was poor but the *Hopewell* escaped detection when passing a German destroyer off Kristiansand. Shortly thereafter the centre engine failed, reducing her speed to 15 knots. A few minutes after she received air cover from a brace of Beaufighters, her port engine failed and her rolling progress was reduced to a crawl. The star-board engine gave out as she passed through the locks into the Albert Dock on the morning of 2 December and she was dragged to her berth where her 40 tons of ball-bearings justified everything.

The trials of the flotilla continued, an operation began that evening by *Nonsuch*, *Gay Viking* and *Gay Corsair* being aborted after they ran into dense fog and then, on heading back up river in blind conditions, *Gay Viking* and *Nonsuch* ran heavily aground, shedding propellers and leaving *Gay Corsair* to make a passage alone, begin-ning on 4 December. Cramped conditions on board the little vessels had brought on bouts of influenza and scabies, but strenuous efforts to ready the damaged craft for another attempt went on round the clock. Meanwhile, after a contretemps with a British fighter, Robert Tanton arrived at Lysekil on the morning of the 6th. Having loaded at Brofjord, Tanton set off for home, enjoying a Christmas dinner of bacon sandwiches before making the Humber. In his absence, at 18.00 on the 23rd, Binney had left Immingham in the *Hopewell*, with *Gay Viking* and *Nonsuch*. They bore small consignments of cargo for the Swedish Air Force but heavy weather, which was a problem in that it would delay their arrival time at the entrance to the Skagerrak and expose them to disclosure, turned them back. To make matters worse, the *Nonsuch's* centre-engine crank-shaft shattered yet again.

Despite this apparently unreliable shambles of engine failure, groundings, bad weather and worse luck, the remaining boats had already paid their way. The MoWT's audit showed that between 1 July to the end of the year the air route of 157 flights had carried 110 tons of freight and 181 passengers at a risk of 370 aircrew. Four aircraft had been shot down and twenty-three souls killed or captured. Operation BRIDFORD had returned only four successful voyages at a risk of eighty lives and nineteen passengers. One vessel and twenty men had been lost or imprisoned, but altogether 120 tons of cargo had been carried. The slender advantage was encourag-ing to desperate men and Binney was already engaged in a further mission, having left the Humber on 26 December in *Hopewell* with *Gay Viking*. Late in the evening of the 27th, after a frustrating passage hampered by the weather and a consequent trim-ming of speed, the *Hopewell* suffered a further series of engine and steering failures. Hailing Whitfield, Binney offered the option of *Gay Viking* heading on alone, but Whitfield loyally decided to stick by the *Hopewell*. Equally determined, Binney and

Stokes decided to press on after the steering had been botched-up and the fuel-lines cleared. A brush with the enemy off Kristiansand failed to develop into an action and both arrived at Lysekil, though the *Hopewell*'s plant was all but useless, with thirty-two broken valve springs and a damaged starboard gearbox. They were confined to port not merely by the *Hopewell*'s defects but by a prolonged period of bad weather. Apart from the extreme and wearing discomfort of attempting a passage in heavy weather, the timing of the run to ensure maximum chances of making it with a cargo relied upon a degree of precision which in turn was impossible without at least moderate sea conditions. There was no point in risking losing the cargo, while letting it fall into enemy hands was even worse. On the other hand, delay attracted the attention of German agents and informers, one such even boarding the *Hopewell* disguised as a curious Swedish naval officer. In due course the change of attitude of the Swedish government and the good offices of Denham and others in Stockholm, enabled Swedish patrols to be set up to deter any attempt by the Germans to limpet-mine either the ships or the blockade-runners.

In moderating weather at 15.00 on 16 January 1944, the *Gay Viking* made her departure with Binney and eight Norwegians on board, leaving the *Hopewell* to complete repairs. Clear of the coast *Gay Viking*'s gyro-compass played up and then, almost home and approaching the boom guarding the Humber's mouth in darkness and a thick mist, she collided with a small coaster, the *River Trent*. The *Gay Viking*, shorn of her bow, reached Hull with her cargo intact but now *hors de combat*. The following day, 19 January, *Gay Corsair* made a passage and came home with the *Hopewell*, both full of ball-bearings. On 15 February the *Nonsuch* redeemed herself by making the fastest round voyage, returning fully laden on the 20th. In early March Binney, once more in the *Hopewell* and in company with the *Gay Corsair*, set off on what was to prove the last passages made in Operation BRIDFORD. Needless to say the *Hopewell*'s engines let her down; Binney transferred to the *Gay Corsair* and made a successful round trip which ended on 18 March 1944. With the Vernal Equinox upon them, this was to be the end of the flotilla's runs but, in addition to 347 tons of ball-bearings, other vital equipment had been brought out of Sweden: roller bearings, special steels and tungsten wire, electrical parts and small manufacturing plant – against a further 64 tons delivered by air. Matters had been brought to a conclusion of sorts. As Lord Leathers was informed by Andrew Duncan, President of the Board of Trade, Operation BRIDFORD gave the British 'a substantial part of the equipment for a vital new ball-bearing factory which we are putting up, and which should enable us to maintain our own supply of ball-bearings. There is no need for me to exaggerate the importance of this'.

With the conclusion of the operation, the masters were awarded the OBE, Military Division, as were three of the chief engineers. Nine other officers received the MBE, nineteen crew members either the BEM or Commendations, but the little vessels' achievements remained cloaked in secrecy which was maintained rather better than was usual on British waterfronts. In announcing the awards, the citation in *The London Gazette* merely mentioned they were 'For gallantry and initiative in hazardous circumstances'. Binney, of course, received the DSO, his fellow 'chief officers', the DSC. Captain Holdsforth of the *Master Standfast* died of his wounds in April 1944, just short of his 36th birthday, leaving a widow and baby. He was the sole casualty in the only real interdiction made on the gun-boats during the operation, having encountered a German patrol vessel, the *V-1606*, in the early hours of 2 November. In accordance with his orders, Holdsworth had attempted to run, but the *V-1606* pursued and, in the beam of her searchlight, is thought to have picked out the streaming red ensign, upon which she promptly opened fire. Shells struck the bridge and deck house and Holdsworth, Chief Officer Reynolds-Brown and Mr Jardine, the mate, were all wounded. The withering fire prevented the crew from detonating the scuttling charges or abandoning the *Master Standfast* at speed. '[A]fter some hesitation,' they stopped to surrender. With Holdsworth retained at Frederickshaven Hospital, the others were interned at *Milag Nord*.

It was not quite the end of the flotilla's history. Three of the gun-boats' crews transferred into three small tankers specially built and intended for Operation NEPTUNE, the important maritime component of OVERLORD, or D-Day, then imminent. Jackson and *Nonsuch*'s crew were turned over into the *Chant 43*, Whitfield and the *Gay Viking*'s men joined the *Chant 44*, and Stokes and the *Hopewell*'s to *Chant 45*. Robert Tanton and the *Gay Corsair*'s complement took over the dry-cargo coaster *Empire Factor*. Once the beach-head had been established and the Mulberry Harbour at Arromanches was being supplied with fuel by way of PLUTO – the pipeline under the ocean – the *Chants* were laid-up and their crews returned to Hull, rejoining the *Nonsuch*, *Gay Viking* and *Hopewell* (the *Gay Corsair* having gone to the Royal Navy in the interim). These three then resumed their covert runs, carrying agents and equipment to the resistances in Norway, Denmark, Belgium and the Netherlands, encouraging sabotage behind the lines of the German *Wehrmacht* as it was assailed in front by the Allied Armies. For this operation, code-named MOONSHINE, changes were made in the organisation of the flotilla, Stokes took over the *Gay Viking*, Whitfield the *Nonsuch* and Jackson the *Hopewell*. Operating under the auspices of Special Operations Executive – though no longer under Binney who had had a heart-attack – they remained hampered by engine failures, bad weather and fog, and also by increased enemy activity in coastal waters, so that little of promise was fulfilled. Nevertheless, having transferring their operational base to Aberdeen, where the fog was less of a problem, they made a run across to Lysekil in January 1945, dropping off agents aboard a Danish fishing boat manned by the resistance. From Lysekil a Swedish warship escorted them south to Gothenburg whence the *Lionel* and *Dicto* had been moved, and the flotilla secured alongside the Norwegian ships flying their large red ensigns to the cheers of on-lookers. Here each loaded over 30 tons of strategic materials before being escorted north again, this time to Hunnebostrand.

They began their homeward run on the late evening of 5 February and had passed The Skaw into the Skagerrak when mist and then fog closed in. The *Gay Viking* and *Hopewell*, having lost touch with *Nonsuch*, acting as leader, in the poor visibility, were now beset by another catastrophic equipment failure. It was clear to Stokes in *Gay Viking* following Jackson in *Hopewell* that they were not on the correct course. In fact they were approaching the Danish coast and should have altered course some time previously. At this point Jackson admitted his vessel's gyro had malfunctioned, asking Stokes to take the lead but as Stokes did so and altered onto the correct course in the fog, his consort suddenly appeared out of the murky darkness. The two collided and at 20 knots the *Hopewell* drove her sharp bow into the *Gay Viking's* engine compartment. She was abandoned and her scuttling charges detonated, then in disregard of his orders, Jackson picked up all of the *Gay Viking's* crew while two unidentified craft circled them suspiciously.

With his own vessel damaged, Jackson had no option but to make for a Swedish port and at daylight the *Hopewell* was struggling along at reduced speed. Enemy and neutral coastal shipping lay within sight but no pursuit appeared until they were only a few miles outside Swedish waters. A rapidly approaching German destroyer failed to catch them before they had reached sanctuary and the *Hopewell* limped south, back to Lysekil. Here they received help and while the *Hopewell* was undergoing repairs, some of the *Gay Viking's* survivors were flown home. Here they discovered that all the trouble had been caused by *Nonsuch* making an emergency alteration of course after detecting an echo on her radar. Although a signal had been flashed by masked lamp, in the prevailing conditions it had not been seen, hence the following two craft, *Hopewell* and *Gay Viking*, standing-on oblivious to their leader's diversion. A few weeks later, after the *Hopewell* had returned to the Humber, the blockade-runners made a final passage to the River Dart where they were laid-up and paid-off. The 'ball-bearing run' and its ancillary activities were over and, with the onset of peace, most of the officers and men of the mercantile gun-boats returned to the red-and-black funnelled and green-hulled short sea traders of Ellerman's Wilson Line on their lawful occasions in the Baltic.

That the majority of trans-Atlantic convoys made their voyages undetected and unmolested[39] attests to the success of the convoy system, but it in no way mitigates the horrors and privations inflicted by the battle *for* the Atlantic that raged for so long. The psychological stress and anticipation of attack and the prospect of imminent death that overshadowed every convoy were rarely absent until the effectiveness of the counter-measures of the Allied navies had become well enough proven to reduce apprehension. In this matter there were no guarantees. If it was the sinking of the Donaldson liner *Athenia* that lifted the curtain of war for the British nation within hours of its declaration, it did not fall simultaneously with the German surrender, as will presently be seen. And there was good reason for anxiety, though the fact of the matter was that the last act of the German enemy at sea was the sinking of a British merchantman, the *Avondale Park*, not in the vast wastes of the North Atlantic, but in the Firth of Forth on 7 May 1945, only hours before Grossadmiral Dönitz, Hitler's successor as *Führer*, finally surrendered, a brief account of which is rendered later.

The Battle of the Atlantic was part of the western arm of the titanic pincers, the other of which was the Russian Red Army's assault from the east, by which Nazi Germany was defeated. Without victory at sea in the Western Ocean nothing else could have been achieved against 'Fortress Europe'. But this is only part of the picture; the success of the convoy system across this ocean, while it comprised the 'guns and butter' of American aid, also included an export trade, and an import traffic that was drawn from all corners of the globe. Moreover, in the many and varied tasks to which British and Allied merchantmen were assigned and which included the military supply convoys to Malta and North Russia as well as the combined operations on the beaches of North Africa, Madagascar, Syria, Sicily, Italy and France, the contribution made by merchant ships and merchant seamen proved vital. If, then, the majority of convoys saw the safe and timely arrival of their charges, there was a handful that did not. Four in particular merit attention: Convoys OA178 and OA177G, OG71 and PQ17.

Convoy OA178 consisted of fifty-three laden vessels as it assembled off Southend-on-Sea, weighing on 3 July 1940. Though France had fallen to the German advance, only a single Flower-class corvette, HMS *Clarkia*, was present as escort as German aircraft were observed high overhead. Some hours later, in an extended single column the line of ships threaded their way through the Gull Stream, inside the Goodwin Sands. Unmolested during the night, aircraft were seen the following morning and Captain Rogerson of the *Hartlepool*, a tramp owned by J&C Harrison of London, considered the convoy to be 'parading' provocatively. Rogerson was on the bridge by 07.00 on the 4th, when:

> the mate pointed out … the Isle of Wight, which appeared to me to be rather far away. I commented that we must be south of our course. After breakfast I took double-altitude positions with the 2nd Officer and after obtaining the result I remarked to him 'Good Heavens! We should be able to see Cap [de] la Hague and Alderney.' With that I went out of the Chart-Room door and without the need for binoculars I saw the whole of … the French coast and also the Channel Islands …

Even so, it was 13.00 before a flight of Ju87 Stuka dive-bombers of *Stukageschwader 2* attacked 'one after the other, diving almost vertically with a frightful whistling noise'. Captain Jenkins of Radcliffe & Evan Thomas's Cardiff tramp *Flimston* estimated they descended to 300ft before releasing their bombs, to hit four vessels. For two hours, in sixes, the Stukas fell upon the hapless ships, inadequately defended by the *Clarkia* whose anti-aircraft gunnery was pathetic. Chief Officer J.D. Holm of the *Deucalion*, formerly owned by the Koninklijke Nederlandsche Stoomboot Maatschappij NV (the Dutch Royal Netherlands S.S. Co.), estimated the Stukas' descent to a mere 100ft.[40] 'The first bomb hit us while the Captain and I were on the bridge and there were about eight direct hits after that … when the fifth or sixth bomb hit us the whole deck was opened right up and the winches were blown away.' With the master and carpenter badly wounded and the ship sinking under him, Holm ordered her abandoned.

The DEMS gunner attached to Reardon Smith's tramp *Dallas City*, Captain Norman Shalton, fought back, but eventually a Stuka dropped a fatal stick of bombs. One fell through the engine-room skylight, another down the funnel and a third penetrated the hatch covering of No.3 Hold. All exploded, lifting the ship bodily out of the water, stopping her and igniting fires. Fortunately only two men had been injured but the blazing *Dallas City* veered widely as she lost way, colliding with the following vessel, the *Flimston* herself damaged from near misses. The two ships were locked together for some time, before Captain Jenkins extricated the *Flimston* and headed for Portland. Having lost his starboard lifeboats, Shalton lowered those on the port side, staying on the *Dallas City*'s deck until 'about 17.00,' during which time 'there were a number of terrifying explosions from the engine and boiler room. The fumes from the cargo [of ammonium sulphate] were getting very bad and flames were starting to come through Number 3 Hatch.'

Meanwhile the tanker *Antonio*, owned by the New Egypt & Levant Shipping Co. of Alexandria which registered some of its ships under the British flag, had been damaged by near misses and strafed. Her propeller shaft and rudder had been affected and she was obliged to reduce speed and could be steered only with some difficulty. As Third Officer Peter Webster recalled, 'It was a time of great fear and tension. I personally suffered damage to my ear from the sound of the explosions and noise of the Ack Ack gun, which I was in charge of …'. Steaming her erratic course, the *Antonio* rescued the survivors from the *Deucalion* and the *Dallas City*, and with these sixty-seven extra men on board she too headed north, dropping anchor off Portland shortly before midnight. This course of action was in conformity with the commodore's signal, but Portland, despite being a naval port, was poorly provided for with air defence. In view of this the large artifical harbour boasted the auxiliary anti-aircraft ship HMS *Foylebank*, and she too became a target in *Stukageschwader 2*'s offensive against Convoy OA178. Attacked by twenty-six Stukas before many of her crew even reached their action stations, the carnage was bloody. Even the ship's surgeon lieutenant was incapacitated, and 'was sat on a bollard with his guts in his hands …'. With shore-craft crowding alongside to help and 176 of her crew dead or mortally wounded, the *Foylebank* gave up the ghost. Close by the three cargo-vessels now found themselves trapped. They too received the enthusiastic attention of *Stukageschwader 2*.

With Portland ruled out as a haven of refuge, Convoy OA178 was now ordered to resume its passage and with darkness coming on, the *Luftwaffe* withdrew, only to be replaced by the *Kriegsmarine*. Two flotilla's of what the Germans called *Schnellboots* – or S-boots – and the British called E-boats, left Boulogne before dark and thundered down Channel in hot pursuit, catching up with the remains of the convoy shortly before midnight as it approached Start Point and rushing in for the kill. Crest Shipping's tramp *Elmcrest*, zig-zagging at her best speed of 5.5 knots, dodged the first torpedo, but was struck by the second. Captain William Clibborn ordered his ship abandoned as Leutnant sur Zee Götz Freiherr von Mirbach circled his victim in *S-20*. Clibborn's formal report to the Admiralty makes chilling reading:

> In less than a quarter of an hour from being hit, I was just going down on to one of the rafts on the port side, when a second torpedo hit the ship on the starboard side in the engine room. His torpedo had passed under the starboard life-boat, which was just pulling away from the ship, and this caused the boat to capsize. Sixteen of these men were drowned.[41]

The *Elmcrest* was sundered and sank in seconds. A few moments later S-26 (Fimmen) fired a torpedo into the tanker *British Corporal*. Captain R.R. Williamson reported that:

> A torpedo struck us on the starboard side in way of the after-peak. There was a dull explosion, no flame, but a great column of water shot up and covered everyone in soot and oil. There were pieces of metal flying all over the for'ard deck. It went right through the after end, took away the rudder and had blown a hole through

the counter exposing a number of steam-pipes. The after boat had completely disappeared and various ventilators and the accommodation were damaged. The 4.7-inch [stern-gun] had gone over the side … there was no list on the ship but she seemed to settle aft. The Chief Engineer reported the engine-room was flooding.

As the crew mustered to abandon ship and the second engineer and cook were found to be missing, a second torpedo exploded in the boiler room, causing a catastrophic explosion.

By this time, S-26 had torpedoed the tramp *Hartlepool* despite Captain Rogerson's gallant attempt to out-manoeuvre his assailant. Again the ship's propeller was blown off and the explosion caused a fire, igniting the improvised cordite locker for the stern gun. As the crew prepared to abandon ship, the *Hartlepool* was machine-gunned, the only casualty being the chief officer's nose, which was grazed by a passing bullet. Despite this, Rogerson was reluctant to leave his ship. Only on the insistent order of a naval patrol craft which arrived on the scene, did he do so, much to his regret. In fact he had no need, for the following day she was picked up by tugs from Portland, towed inshore and beached near Weymouth. The *British Corporal's* survivors had laid a course for the coast and were later picked up by the same naval patrol boat. In due course the *British Corporal* was also salved and towed into port where her two missing crew members were found dead.

Rather late in the day the destroyer *Broke*, Commander B.G. Scurfield, arrived to reinforce the escort. Scurfield reported that he found Convoy OA178 'in some confusion,' but the remaining ships proceeded to the west and, having reached the dispersal point, continued on their respective voyages. Many had suffered casualties and, in addition to those sunk or rendered *hors de combat*, eleven had been damaged.

The attack on OA178 had been preceded a few days earlier on 2 July by a similar, though cumulatively less damaging, air attack by Stukas on Convoy OA177G. The loss from this convoy of thirty-three vessels was only one ship, the Blue Funnel liner *Aeneas*, commanded by Captain D.L.C. Evans, late of the *Phemius*. Evans was leading ship in the fifth column and serving as Vice Commodore. There had been exchange of fire with Royal Naval motor torpedo boats off Dungeness, without ill effect to either side, and during the night, off the Isle of Wight, the commodore ordered two complete reversals of course to delay the convoy's passage down-Channel. This was assumed to have been because the convoy would be well ahead of its planned position for the arrival of expected air cover at dawn. However, when this materialised, it did not remain overhead for long and this conjunction of delay and short-lived support, proved fatal to the *Aeneas*. At 07.50 a Stuka pounced on her out of the sun and before any gun could be laid upon it. The dive-bomber screamed down and dropped a near miss alongside *Aeneas* that shook the ship from stem to stern, although the machine gun fire which accompanied the attack did no harm. Evans reported that 'the whole ship's company, European and Chinese, took this attack quite calmly, carrying out their duties as if nothing had happened'. Continuing to 'amble along at 7 knots' for most of the day, the convoy was approaching Start Point at 16.15 when the *Aeneas* was subject to another dive-bombing. A hail of bullets struck the sea 'like a shoal of flying fish diving together' and were followed by bombs, the first of which struck the

Aeneas on her port side, the second penetrated the after cross-bunker and blew out the starboard side of the ship with a 'terrific' explosion, and the third was a near miss. 'The whole ship shivered and trembled violently. She took a sudden list of about 15° to starboard, and I felt instinctively that the poor old ship had been punished too severely.' The attack was over in less than a minute and before any of the guns had been manned *Aeneas* had been mortally wounded, though she was to take some time to sink. The engines slowed down for lack of steam and no one answered calls to the engine room: clearly the damage below had proved fatal to the firemen, the duty engineer and the greasers on watch. Chief Officer H.H. Large ordered the starboard boats lowered and he and Chief Engineer O. Shanklin went round the ship checking for casualties and managed to haul a Chinese trimmer out of the bunker-hatch. The crew showed 'no excitement whatever' and as they manned the lifeboats another Stuka fell on the ship and dropped a stick of near misses, which destroyed the port boats on the high side of the ship. The *Aeneas* was now on fire and Evans, 'realising our helplessness to do anything to save the ship', walked round her himself before concluding that 'it was advisable to leave …'.

The convoy meanwhile had passed out of sight and Evans found himself with the majority of his officers in one boat which had been damaged by machine-gun fire and leaked badly. They had not long to bail, for HM Destroyer *Witherington* arrived soon afterwards, having turned back from her post as escort, to search for survivors. Just as they were leaving the scene a man was observed on the *Aeneas*'s deck. The destroyer lowered a whaler and plucked Steward Galloway to safety. He had been in his cabin and the explosion had stunned him so that he had not heard the shouts of Large, Shanklin or Evans as they searched the vessel. Evans and his crew were landed at Plymouth where they received 'every care and solicitude'. Of the ship's company of 120, eighteen were missing, most of them from the engine room or stokehold. One man died in hospital shortly afterwards. Next day, learning that the *Aeneas* was still afloat, Evans called for volunteers to attempt her salvage but was dissuaded from proceeding further by the naval authorities: 'at this very moment enemy planes are bombing your ship,' he was told. After he had reached London, Evans learned that the *Aeneas* had sunk.

These two attacks on convoys prompted Churchill to enquire about the safety of the Channel route and it was decided that in future the Channel was closed to all but coastal convoys supplying the power stations or engaged on other essential work. From now on, all deep-water sailings from the Thames Estuary would be routed north, by way of Methil although the demand for coal meant that the coastal convoys continued to pass through the Strait of Dover. Until Hitler's attack on Russia on 21 June 1941 diverted German resources, they were to be pressed intensely with July and August 1940 subjecting the coastal colliers to multiple evils. Besides the Stukas and deadly E-boats, the heavy guns soon installed in the cliffs of the Pas de Calais – though they never actually hit a passing coaster – nevertheless posed a constant threat, playing a subtle psychological role in what the Germans called *kanalkampf*, or Channel war. Before their redeployment eastwards, some counter-measures were achieved against the Stukas by deploying barrage balloons and kites, kits of which arrived at the dockside and were installed in selected coasters while a series of small

merchantmen became commissioned ships and formed a Mobile Balloon Barrage
Flotilla. The Stukas were, of course, replaced by other aircraft and a special corps
of the DEMS organisation was formed, known as the Channel A.A. Guard, which
shipped aboard coasters as required, mounting their Lewis guns on the rails of their
assigned vessel with special clips. They departed with their weapons when the vessel
berthed, to travel overland by rail and board a ship in the next convoy. Many of these
men were Canadians from the Royal Canadian Volunteer Reserve who fitted-in
well and were more amenable to the relaxed ways of the coasting merchant marine.
The air attacks over the Channel convoys were the opening phase in what would
become the Battle of Britain and fighter support was often summoned to assist.
According to a Hurricane pilot, John Ellacombe, the vulnerability of these convoys
was clear, but so too was their value. His squadron, No.151, flew numerous patrols
that summer of 1940:

> up and down, up and down, one end to the other, watching these poor wretched
> ships ploughing along. We were told that a convoy of ships was the equivalent of
> about 1,000 trains so that they were absolutely essential to get the goods from one
> part of the country to the other.

As far as the Ministry of Shipping was concerned, the westwards (CW) and eastwards
(CE) Channel convoys maintained 'a precarious but quite invaluable stream of supplies'.

Further up the east coast, from the Thames north towards Methil in what became
known as 'E-boat alley' to aircraft and the menacing E-boats that lay in wait for the
attenuated convoys there was an added danger of German mines sown in the convoys'
grain. The acoustic and magnetic versions were particularly feared and the changes
of polarity, and bi-polar nature of the latter, often negated the effects of degaussing.
Some amelioration from acoustic mines was achieved by the use of pneumatic scal-
ing hammers which would detonate acoustic mines prior to the passing of a ship, but
delayed fuses equally frustrated this and the game of advance and counter-measure
– though it brought satisfaction to those engaged in it – cost the lives of many merchant seamen. The Royal Navy did its best to provide escorts; in time the worn-out
First World War V- & W-class destroyers were augmented by the new Hunt-class, but
all too often these were knocked out by bomb-blasts, leaving the convoys exposed.
This excoriating conflict of air attacks by day and E-boat ambushes by night had a
bad effect on morale. In his Survivor's Report consequent upon the bombing of his
coastal steamer on 25 July during the passage of CW8, Captain G.W. Thompson is
clear where the blame lay.

> The master wishes to bring to the notice of the Authorities that there is great dis-
> satisfaction amongst the crews owing to the very slight protection which is given
> to convoys and he foresees the time arriving when the crew will just refuse to take
> the ships to sea. In the present case there were only two [armed and commissioned
> HM] trawlers to escort a convoy of twenty-one ships stretching for about six or
> seven miles.[42]

It would appear that the matter of morale was already causing anxiety within the Ministry for in September one of its officials, C.W. Eakins, shipped with the commodore of CW11. The latter was Lieutenant Commander Newman RNR, known as Non-stop Newman on account of his perennial desire to get into port and enjoy a pint of beer. Both men joined the coaster *Polgarth* whose master told him that his ship's crew was 'scratch' and 'that the deck hands were very raw; indeed some of them had no experience on deck before'. Eakins discovered that this was because:

> The regular crew of the ship [had] refused to sail on the convoy and left the ship at Blyth. Every member of the crew to whom I spoke told me that he would not sail in the convoy again. Their general attitude was that they would be prepared to sail if the cargo carried by the ships of the convoy was of vital importance to the national effort, but they would not sail if the ships were merely carrying cargoes of household coal which can be sent by other routes. I found it very difficult to find an answer to this complaint, if, indeed, there is an answer … [43]

During the convoy's passage it was attacked by Ju88 dive-bombers, less intimidating aircraft than the Stukas but little less formidable to the convoy below. They made for the new Hunt-class destroyer *Atherstone*, crippling her. Despite this Eakins discovered that 'the fear of shelling from the French coast … seems to be the dominant factor in creating the crew's dislike of this convoy [route]'.

Although the attacks on the convoys in both the English Channel and the North Sea were to continue with little less ferocity, particularly on the part of the *Kriegsmarine*, the crisis was passing, for the Battle of Britain drew the *Luftwaffe* over the English mainland and, by the end of June 1941, Hitler's invasion of the Soviet Union drew off the *Stukageschwaders*. Nevertheless, this remission was not particularly noticeable to the victims; the vile weapon of the mine in all three of its manifestations remained a problem, the guns of the Pas de Calais maintained an active intimidation, and the E-boats, occasionally reinforced by sorties of German destroyers, kept the threat alive. Moreover, from time to time, they struck with ferocious effect. An unpleasant feature of the conflict was the German habit of machine-gunning the decks of torpedoed merchant-ships as they swept past in their E-boats. These would lie, engines stopped and often secured to the navigational buoys marking the swept channels and maintained by Trinity House. Such attacks came 'out of no-where' as a convoy passed. When counter-attacked by any escorting destroyer, the E-boats slipped away over the minefields where, owing to her greater draught, the destroyer could not follow. The *Luftwaffe*'s air crews were equally cavalier in their disregard of The Hague Convention. In an attack off Aberdeen in November the Muir S.S.Co.'s tramp *Creemuir* was hit by an aerial torpedo and, as her thirteen survivors struggled in the water, they witnessed the fate of the enemy's next victim. Bound from London to Philadelphia in ballast, Hain's *Trebartha* was hit and caught fire. 'In very little time it became a raging inferno. The men took to the boats and the enemy came back and machine-gunned them, being guided by the light of the burning ship which lit the whole scene quite plainly'. The intensity of the fire was tremendous, sufficient to melt the heavy glass in her portholes. Behind one of these the chief wireless operator was trapped.

We tried to get the hoses to bear, but the water supply failed. We could hear him shouting, his cries gradually growing fainter. He was under the table and the bulkheads had collapsed on top of him, we tried to get him out another way but it was impossible.

The burning *Trebartha* drifted ashore, breaking her back two weeks later.

Incredibly, the intimidating strafings induced more terror and anger than fatalities. Only four men, including the poor chief wireless operator died in the *Trebartha*, but it was a very one-sided fight. Occasionally, and much to the Ministry of Information's delight as it sought some light in the gloom, a vessel fought back with a measure of success. The outstanding example of this was that of the *Highlander*, owned by the Aberdeen, Newcastle and Hull S.S. Co., which was attacked by Heinkel He115 seaplanes off the north-east coast of Scotland when on passage from Aberdeen towards Leith.

She was a coastwise vessel of small tonnage and about twelve knots speed, carrying passengers and cargo on the regular schedule she had maintained for many years. She was lightly armed with one Lewis gun and a Holman projector – the latter, an early form of rocket entanglement – and her weapons were served by her own seamen … She carried no special naval ratings for gunnery duties, but her men had been trained and exercised at DEMS establishments on shore at her way ports.

The Lewis gun was aft, set in a wooden, sand-bagged gun-pit, manned by Able-Seaman George Anderson and Second Steward Lawrence Halcrow, and both men must have reached it as the strafing aircraft flew the length of the ship having dropped her torpedo. The second mate had thrown the *Highlander's* helm over just in time to avoid the torpedo as the long, high-latitude twilight gave Anderson and Halcrow a glimpse of their attacker. Captain William Gifford described the action between his gunners and the enemy aircraft.

This is to report that at 11.45 p.m. (1st August 1940) vessel was attacked by enemy aircraft with machine gun fire and one aerial torpedo which missed vessel passing close under stern. Fire was opened by ship's machine gun and Holman projector …

The He115 circled the *Highlander* and then made a second attack from the port side 'at 00.10 a.m. (2nd August)'.

The bomb from the Holman Projector struck the machine head on, and this, together with the fire from the Lewis gun, caused the plane to sheer (probably having wounded the pilot) so that his tail caught our midships port boat. He was almost level with the deck then, the port wing fell on the deck, the rest of the machine carried on, carrying away the after cranes and flattening the Holman gun, and then it fell into the sea just astern and caught fire … Life-boats Nos 4 and 5 were smashed, Wireless Aerial put out of action, Holman Projector also put out of action and William Birnie, A.B., and Bert Whyman, Fireman, who were operating the same received facial injuries.

These two men were taken below 'where they were looked after by the stewardess'. Even now the enemy had not finished with the *Highlander*.

> [A]t 00.30 a.m. this day, vessel was again attacked by enemy aircraft, and two aerial torpedoes were seen in close vicinity which again passed close astern, ship's course being altered to avoid same. Aircraft also opened fire at close range and gunfire was returned from ship's machine gun and kept up until 00.50 a.m. when Aircraft was hit and crashed into sea about 100 yards astern of ship. On both occasions Geo. Anderson, A.B. and Lawrence Halcrow, 2nd Steward, were operating machine gun.[44]

Once safely berthed in Leith and with the injured Birnie and Whyman transferred to hospital, the *Highlander* was visited by the war artist Muirhead Bone, brother of the Anchor Line's Commodore, Sir David, who drew both the mangled ship and Anderson and Halcrow in their gun-pit. Both Gifford and Anderson, who laid the Lewis gun, were decorated. The presence of a stewardess – who may well have been married to one of the male crew – on this small coastal passenger ship reminds us that the railway was not then the only way of making a long journey, and that companies like the Aberdeen, Leith & Hull S.S. Co. could co-exist alongside the larger conglomerate, Coast Lines.

Despite the destruction in coastal waters, some ships survived, one of the most remarkable being the Eagle Oil Co.'s oil tanker *San Roberto* which was too slow and too old for ocean convoys and shuttled regularly between the refinery at Grangemouth and London. The *San Roberto*'s large bridge and generous accommodation ensured that Captain Cyril Allison was always joined by the convoy Commodore and his staff. An institution on the east coast, the *San Roberto* survived the war after carrying an estimated one million tons of oil cargo, for which Allison collected an OBE having repeatedly traversed what was probably the most consistently dangerous of all the convoy-routes. Short in comparison with the great tracks across the North Atlantic, it was indisputably nasty, lying as it did within the range of aircraft and German destroyers throughout its length, within reach of E-boats for about half, and subject to long-range guns when it reached the Strait of Dover. Mines could be dropped anywhere and encountered anytime and, towards the end of the war, it was subject to U-boat attacks. Even without the enemy the strong tides could kick-up a rough sea when opposed to a fresh breeze and when opposed to a gale could make life very disagreeable. Fog was an ever-present danger and the buoys left on station were often too few to provide adequate guidance in those pre-radar years, but a strong gale could bring with it wrack and rain that reduced visibility as effectively as a pea-souper. The southward-bound, coal-laden Convoy FS559 which left Methil for Southend on 4 August 1941 consisted of forty-seven ships, strung out over some seven miles of sea. Early on the morning of the 6th the convoy was approaching The Would, the channel lying between the shoulder of Norfolk and a large shallow offshore shoal known as the Haisborough Sand. The area had claimed the lives of ships and seamen for centuries and was littered with the wrecks of colliers and coasters owing to the lack of seamarks. With the Haisborough Lighthouse and North Haisborough buoy dimmed, and little visibility owing to the drizzle and gale-driven spume this occasion would prove no different. The leading escort missed the alter-course position, realised that the distance had been overrun and turned to drop back through the convoy to see if the second escort had spotted the vital buoy. The reassuring sighting came too late; the senior officer rushed off to the head of the convoy and the alter-course was signalled. Unfortunately, as the leading ships of the convoy, turned late but safely into The Would, the last seven merchantmen and HM Trawler *Agate* steamed doggedly onto the Haisborough Sand to become total losses. As tail-end Charlie the *Agate* was never seen again: 'She must have struck and been rolled over and broken up'. The wrecked British coasters were the *Aberhill*, *Afon Towy*, *Betty Hindley*, *Deerwood* and *Oxshott*; the French lost the *Gallois* and the Estonians the *Taara*. Thirty-seven men were drowned in the disaster but, despite the conditions, the remarkable Coxswain Henry Blogg of the Cromer lifeboat put to sea and rescued 137 men.

In the event the anxieties over the morale of the generality of men manning these ships proved unfounded. There were a number of incidents of refusal to sail which, as Eakins realised, were not entirely unreasonable. A few days after the disastrous passage of Convoy FS559 the Admiralty Press Office despatched the popular travel writer Major Owen Rutter to accompany Convoy FN505 and produce an account of an east-coast convoy. Unfortunately from our present point of view the master of the *Bury*, to which Rutter and Commodore Mills RNR were assigned, demurred and instead they shipped aboard an ancient Polish collier, the *Kronan* whose master was a Captain Drydeck, a most remarkable man. Drydeck had escaped Poland in his ship just ahead of the Germans, he had repeated the performance at Bergen and had almost been caught in Dakar, but had steamed through the boom and escaped. His equally remarkable wife, having herself escaped through Slovakia, reached London by way of Budapest and Paris to become the *Kronan*'s purser. The rest of the crew were equally mixed: Poles, Norwegians, British, with British DEMS gunners. While Rutter's experience amid such an eccentric company made good copy and played-up the Allied cause, it did not expose the mood of British seamen. Like most propagandists, howsoever mild, Rutter was obliged to produce an upbeat narrative. Later he worked up his notes into a history of convoy, but for the record, despite the hard-bitten nature of the coasting crews, they stood their ground and proved their worth. Even Eakins had discovered that they were prepared to do their duty in the national interest: coal for power stations was fair enough; coal for commercial profit by coal merchants was not. But there were others in these convoys, the larger, ocean-going vessels such as the *Creemuir* and the *Trebartha*, whose passages were not regular and for whom the coast was an unfamiliar environment. Like the *Meriones* aground on the Haisborough in January (see Chapter Three, Note 24), the 9,275-deadweight ton tanker *Oiltrader* was bombed and sunk in March 1941 while in an east-coast convoy. Captain McLeod reported that: 'Everyone behaved very well, including the Chinese crew who first put on all their best clothes and then proceeded quietly to their boat stations. When the water supply failed they formed a human train to pass buckets of water to fight the fire.'

Such large ships sailing in large convoys of predominantly smaller vessels, was both a reminder of the wider maritime war, and of the distinctions of theatre. There was an alleged exchange between a foreign-going ship-master and a coasting master. 'What would you do if you lost sight of the land, skipper?' the deep-water man asked. To which his home-trade colleague responded: 'The same as you do when you come in sight of it, shit myself.' Such stories reflected social differences as well as exposing the very different environments in which each worked. Both were dangerous, but for different reasons, as the deep-water men appreciated when obliged to join a coastal convoy. Similar differences existed between the mercantile and the naval sides of convoy work, as has been briefly mentioned in respect largely of the practical challenges in handling merchantmen in convoy. But there were other problems arising from the collision of cultures and, as in the First World War, strains and stresses appeared in the relationship between the two sea services.

The difficulties arising from employing superannuated admirals as convoy Commodores has been mentioned. These hiccups were ironed-out early in the war; the retired admirals were men of good sense, settled in with their new hosts and left the defence of the convoy to the active and younger men in the escorts. On the coastal convoys it was rather different. In the first place the naval escorts were harassed and hard pressed; and in the second, the convoy Commodores were rarely regular naval officers. For good reasons coastal Commodores were always RNR men, reservists whose professional roots lay in mercantile shipping and who, it was felt, would get on better with the coasting masters and mates. This was an aspect of coastal operations that Owen Rutter exposed after taking passage with Commodore Mills aboard the *Kronan*, when the two men discussed the running of the convoys and the responsibilities of the commodore and the senior officer of the escort.

> I had several talks with Mills about this divided control. It was a matter on which he felt keenly, as a merchant officer. His point was that the RN escort had no experience of commercial waters and could not realise that a Commodore, by getting a convoy into port earlier than the ETA might save 20 ships a tide, expedite their loading, and so enable 60,000 tons of coal to reach London a day earlier than schedule. Therefore the Commodore's idea is to push on all he can, while the E[scort] O[fficer]'s only idea is to keep to schedule.

Mills attributed this lack of willingness to understand his point of view to 'professional snobbishness' on the part of the escort commander. More tellingly he considered this dysfunctional attitude worse than it had been in the previous war, of which he had had experience and to which reference was made in the preceding volume. Rutter adds that Mills 'admits the same feeling [on the part of regular naval officers] does not exist against the RNVR ... therefore it must, apparently, be due to social snobbishness'. The point Rutter is making is that the officers of the Royal Naval Volunteer Reserve were invariably drawn from the same social class as that of Royal Naval officers, and while they were rank amateurs, their adoption of naval manners and naval practices was often 'more navy than the navy'. It was not so much that merchant officers, whether they were serving in their own company's ships or were commissioned Royal Naval Reservists in men-of-war or – as in this case as convoy Commodore – were not from the same class, because many of them were, but that their professional background was in commerce. It was not quite a gentlemanly thing to do, even if one was in command of a trans-Atlantic liner, so that the master of a 900-ton collier plying her trade within the official home-trade limits of Brest and the Elbe was very small beer. This produced a mild contempt on the one hand, and resentment on the other, and naturally it was the latter that was the more destructive. Such a lack of integration between the Royal Navy and its merchant counterpart was felt by all ranks and in varying degrees. Much of it arose from the inadequacy of the navy's protection, particularly in its failure to kill U-boats. Merchant Jack felt badly let down and paid a heavy price while the Royal and the Royal Canadian Navies re-engaged with a formidable enemy they thought they had mastered twenty years earlier. The navy was also weak in air defence and although the death toll was much reduced over time, sinkings of merchant ships continued to the very end. For most of the time, of course, the two sea services rubbed along reasonably well, nursing their mutual antipathies as the British generally do, with a suppressed irritation. The job was too important to do otherwise and, for much of the time, it was the navy's fate simply to fuel the merchant seaman's ancient right to grumble. Inevitably, the Royal Navy had the upper hand, but the extent to which the resentment penetrated the skin of the Merchant Navy found its voice in the *débâcle* of Convoy PQ17, the echoes of which were to last long after the war.

To place the post-PQ17 situation in context this account of PQ7B by Third Officer George Russell of the *Empire Redshank* – formerly the *Braddock* – is of interest. The ship had loaded a cargo of cased petrol and carbon black – used to reinforce rubber – in the Texan ports of Houston and Beaumont. This was marked for Vladivostock but at Sydney, Nova Scotia, they discovered the deception and headed for the assembly anchorage at Reykjavik, aware that their destination was Murmansk. Russian convoys had yet to acquire their infamous reputation as they joined their convoy which:

comprised just nine ships and set off from Hvalflord anchorage ... on Hogmanay 1941. There were three other *Empire* ships in addition to our own, one being an ex-Italian prize whilst another was a new ship from Lithgow's and managed by Raeburn & Verel of Glasgow. Two other British ships were the *Jutland* owned by Glen & Co of Glasgow and the *Botavon* managed by Smith's of Cardiff [on behalf of the Board of Trade – hence her name, though she had formerly been the Blue Funnel liner *Eurypylus*]. An elderly Russian and two Panamanians completed the convoy. I recall that we had two H.M. trawlers as escort for the first part of the voyage, which was made around the inhospitable looking sheer black lava cliffs of the west coast of Iceland, to its northern extremity on the Arctic Circle from whence we took a departure towards Bear Island standing in 74° North latitude. Once clear of the Icelandic coast our escort was relieved by two destroyers which remained with us for the rest of the voyage ... [We] were relatively unprepared for what lay ahead, other than we knew it would be cold! The convoy route from the north of Iceland was laid to pass as far north of the German occupied Norwegian coast and North Cape as the southern extremity of the ice pack allowed. In winter this meant steering a NE'ly course towards Bear Island thence east into the Barents Sea and thereafter SE and South to the Kola Inlet and Murmansk.

Unused to the prevailing conditions, the difficulties of navigating in high latitudes were soon encountered.

> Strong winds, squalls, thick weather and snowstorms were frequent. The sky was almost always overcast making observations rare. Constellations took on an unfamiliar appearance and when partly obscured their stars appeared only momentarily making identification almost impossible. With the sun always below the horizon in the far northern winter giving just three to five hours of twilight around midday, the nights seemed interminable. Nevertheless, like all good sailors we soon learned to adapt to these conditions and made our way without enemy interference to arrive off the Kola Inlet on 11 January 1942, being met by a single torpedo boat of the Russian Navy as their contribution to the escort.

Nor was their destination particularly welcoming.

> The bleak snow covered grey granite cliffs guarding the 2 mile wide entrance to the Kola Inlet was a very real indication of what lay within. It is a long and narrow inlet which runs in a Sly and SWly direction for 25 miles to Murmansk, where the width is less than a mile. It is enclosed by steep barren hillsides of modest height which remain snow covered all winter long. It has ample deep water reducing from 150 fathoms inside the entrance to some 15 fathoms in the approaches to Murman**sk**, but with ample anchorage space and depth in the bays for ships awaiting berths or assembling for homeward convoys. Although the inlet remains ice-free, the bays and shores and spaces between the jetties become frozen over, and are only prevented from thickening by the rise and fall of the tide and by the constant movement of shipping. The normal daytime temperature in January is minus $1°C$ and minus $15°$ at night. Steam winches and windlasses have to be kept turning to prevent their freezing up. Unfortunately our voyage was made without any of the special protective clothing which later became standard issue on Arctic convoys, and we certainly felt the cold … Murmansk['s] quays and jetties and many of the town buildings were of wooden construction. By 1942 most of these buildings had been razed to the ground by frequent incendiary raids of the *Luftwaffe*, and with the German front line only 50 miles distant most of the population that we saw appeared to be military rather than civilian … and with most if not all of the cargo sheds destroyed, any cargo not immediately removed by rail or truck was left on the quay and soon buried by snow. Discharge of our cargo was made by gangs of women who arrived and departed marching like soldiers and obeying commands from men with whistles. These women frightened the life out of us when we saw them slinging our drums of aviation spirit with steel chains, causing sparks in the hold. There were no recreational or shoreside facilities for crews, which I suppose was understandable with almost everyone in uniform and Mother Russia then fighting dearly for her very existence.

The *Empire Redshank* departed from Murmansk on 24 January, one of the six-ship returning Convoy QP6.

Initially our escort comprised two Russian destroyers and two British minesweepers, but the latter being based at Kola turned back after the first day at sea. Some days later when to the south of Bear Island the Russian destroyers were relieved by ... [the] cruiser *Trinidad*, plus a Tribal-class destroyer and two minesweepers. Only a day later, however, the convoy was dispersed and all ships directed to proceed independently to destination, which was given as Loch Ewe. We learnt later that the *Tirpitz* was thought to have been in the area and about to attack the convoy. In later years much was made of the infamous PQ17 being scattered and left to its own devices, but our convoy suffered the same fate although not with the same disastrous results.

At our full speed of 10.5 knots we soon left the other ships of the convoy behind and all went well until some 160 miles north of the Shetlands, when we sighted an enemy aircraft. This was identified as an Heinkel He111 bomber, which began to circle us and continued to do so, out of range of our anti-aircraft guns, for the next forty minutes. During this time the Radio Officer dashed up to the bridge and excitedly informed us ... he was planning our demise by directing some of his friends on to us. Sure enough two other Heinkels appeared ... [These] circled for a while until one came down to a very low altitude and flew towards us from the port beam, aiming amidships at the funnel. These He111s had a very prominent and clear perspex bubble shaped nose with the pilot visible from all around. He flew directly over us, virtually at mast height and dropped a stick of eight bombs whilst our gunners blasted away for all they were worth. Some of the bombs fell short and others went wide on the starboard side but one was a direct hit on the boat deck, which left its fins there while the bomb itself passed down and clean out the starboard side without exploding. At this point I felt a stream of water on my head and shoulders and on looking up, noticed it was coming from the 20 mm gun mounting supported on top of the starboard bridge wing. The gunner had been so frightened he had inadvertently relieved himself! However as a baptism of fire it proved a good luck omen. The second Heinkel now attacked in a similar fashion but with somewhat less enthusiasm. An identical stick of eight bombs narrowly missed but our gunners scored a hit on this aircraft, which was last seen with smoke emitting from its port engine, heading back towards Norway. We often wondered if it ever made it.

The Master, Captain Davitt, had sent off a distress call at the beginning of the attack, but did not acknowledge subsequent enquiries as to our well being, in the hope that the enemy would assume we had sunk, which unfortunately caused the Admiralty to reach the same conclusion. However ... the many near misses had caused leaks in the double-bottom fuel tanks allowing water to contaminate the fuel. After steaming onwards for about an hour we had to stop and separate the water and fuel, then steam away for another hour or so until we had to stop again. In this fashion we eventually put into Kirkwall in the Orkneys, where of course we were not expected but were able to report our safe arrival to the Admiralty. It took a couple of days at anchor to sort out the fuel problem, whence we joined a coastal convoy to Methil Roads and thence to Blyth for dry docking.

Russell makes light of this passage but after paying off on 10 February 1942 he nevertheless 'finished up in hospital with pneumonia, a direct result of having insufficient and proper clothing for the Arctic winter.' In the following months the Germans turned their attention increasingly on the now established and accessible sailings to North Russia and by mid-summer the war in these high latitudes was to reach crisis point. In May the largest convoy thus far, PQ16 had successfully fought its way through to Archangel and the Admiralty's apprehensions were somewhat eased. The following month a similar number of merchantmen began assembling at Hvalfjordur for what was to become the most notorious convoy of the war.

Convoy PQ17 was a signal strategic defeat but it possessed a complex political dimension all of which gave the outcome the sharp twist of tragedy. The details of the operation must be sought elsewhere,[45] but the bones of the story are as follows. When on the 21 June 1941 Hitler turned upon his ally and invaded the Soviet Union, Churchill had immediately inaugurated a series of convoys to the ports of North Russia to supply the Red Army with arms and *matériel*. Keen to encourage any ally, Churchill's commitment was bold, both in terms of what he could offer, bearing in mind that the British were rearming after Dunkirk, and in view of the strategic situation with German forces occupying Norway. Insofar as the Admiralty staff were concerned, the plan to run convoys through to Russia with ice to the north, German airfields to the south, U-boats able to operate out of Norwegian bases and the heavy units of the *Kriegsmarine* also in Norwegian waters, was little short of foolhardy. The First Sea Lord, Admiral Sir Dudley Pound, assessed it as 'a most unsound operation with the dice loaded against us in every direction'. Tragically, Pound was himself to play a key role in turning an unsound operation into an unmitigated disaster.

Notwithstanding this, with the early convoys assembling at Hvalfjordur in Iceland – they would later run north from Loch Ewe – and taking a route as far north as the ice would allow in the summer and hoping that the short Arctic winter days would compensate for more southerly tracks in the winter, the new supply route functioned. Certain contingency plans could be put in place: a mine-sweeping force was sent to the Russian Naval base at Polyarnoe near Murmansk, to provide local escorts to meet incoming convoys and see homeward convoys well out to sea; in addition to the close ocean escort, a cruiser squadron provided supporting cover in the offing, at least for part of a convoy's passage; and finally the battle-squadrons of the Home Fleet would sail and give 'distant support' should there be any danger of German capital ships emerging from the Norwegian fjords. With the Germans preoccupied elsewhere, it was not until PQ12 that any serious attempt was made to intercept them. Even then a sortie by the battleship *Tirpitz* and a covering force of destroyers was seen off in classic style by the Home Fleet, but from this point onwards the scale of the forces ranged against the PQ convoys grew steadily, most significantly in the way of air attacks.

By the summer of 1942, with the United States transformed into a fighting ally, an increasing number of American merchant ships were loading for Russian ports and leaving the trans-Atlantic convoys under escort to assemble at Hvalfjordur where they joined British and a few Russian vessels. For PQ17 the naval forces assembled to protect it were considerable and included some American warships serving under Rear Admiral Hamilton in his cruiser squadron. This was the first time the United States Navy had permitted its ships to come under British operational control, for unlike the Atlantic convoys which by this time had become a joint operation, the Arctic convoys were left to the British Admiralty to control.

Convoy PQ17 consisted of thirty-six merchant ships, predominantly American and including a number of the then new Liberty-ships, but with some British, Russian and Panamanian vessels. They contained an immense quantity of goods: 297 aircraft, 594 tanks, 4,246 military vehicles and over 150,000 tons of military stores and general cargo. The destruction of one laden vessel with a single torpedo was the equivalent of a military defeat in term of lost *matériel*. Apart from one American Liberty-ship, the convoy sailed in good order on 27 June. It had a powerful ocean escort including destroyers and the two anti-aircraft ships HMSs *Palomares* and *Pozarica*; Hamilton's cruiser squadron was in support and heavy units of the Home Fleet provided distant cover. It also had three rescue ships in attendance. A homeward sailing was to run at the same time, as had become established practice, and the course of Convoy QP13 lay between PQ17 and the Norwegian coast. The two convoys passed on 2 July and next day part of the escort of QP13 detached to sweep to the southwards, on the lookout for the *Tirpitz* which was reported missing from her moorings. Being high summer with no darkness, PQ17 could be seen for miles in the crisp, cold air. Passing north of Bear Island and through loose pack-ice a second American ship was obliged to turn back, her master using his radio too readily and frustrated by Commodore Dowding's stoic radio silence. The senior officer of the escort, Commander Jack Broome in HMS *Keppel*, used the first days of the passage to work up his ocean-escort with a series of exercises while refuelling operations took place.

Convoy PQ17's early encounters with the enemy on 4 July were fought off with some loss, but spirits were high and a cheery exchange of signals between the American warships and Hamilton in HMS *London* recognised American Independence Day. By noon Hamilton was approaching the point at which he was supposed to turn back, but the Admiralty gave him discretionary powers to continue if he thought it advisable. In view of the rather vague intelligence that *Tirpitz* was not secured to her customary moorings in the Altenfjord, Hamilton considered his duty to 'remain with the convoy as long as possible'. Hamilton was subject to two masters, Admiral Tovey commanding the Home Fleet from which he was detached, and Sir Dudley Pound in London, who theoretically had more up-to-date intelligence information. Hamilton's cruisers closed with the convoy in anticipation of an attack, sending the USS *Wainwright* to refuel from the accompanying fleet-oiler *Aldersdale*. The destroyer approached the *Aldersdale* just as the first serious air attack developed, hauling out of the convoy to demonstrate her impressive anti-aircraft capability, adding a certain *brio* to the occasion. In the aftermath of this attack, although several merchant ships were hit and two lost, Broome was quietly confident, as was Commodore J.C.K. Dowding in the *River Afton*. Dowding was not a retired admiral, but a captain in the RNR and had served in Russian convoys previously.

In London, Pound relied upon several sources for information about German movements, one of which was a line of patrolling submarines. The most eastern of these were Russian and from one of these emanated a signal that indicated the *Tirpitz* was heading north. In fact the Soviet commander had fired a torpedo at the

German battleship and hit her, though the damage was slight, but in the absence of aerial reconnaissance, Pound sent a signal to Hamilton ordering him to withdraw the cruiser force to the west at high speed. A few minutes later Pound signalled Broome to disperse the convoy 'owing to [the] threat from surface ships'. PQ17 was ordered to proceed to Russian ports. A few minutes later Broome received another signal ordering the convoy to scatter. This was sent by Pound as an amendment of the dispersal order because it had been pointed out to him that the dispersal manoeuvre would not spread the merchant ships sufficiently quickly. However, to Broome, Dowding and Hamilton, it appeared that the situation was escalating. As Hamilton turned west and ordered Broome's destroyers to join him, the naval officers on the spot thought that within a few minutes they would see the superstructure of the *Tirpitz* and her battle-group break the sharply defined horizon.

But aboard the scattering merchant ships and the slower escorts – the anti-aircraft ships, anti-submarine trawlers and some minesweepers on their way to Polyarnoe – it looked very much as though the Royal Navy was running away. The same perception began to dawn on the bridges of Hamilton's warships as they drew off but found the sea ahead empty. The commanders of the U-boats that had been trailing the convoy could not believe their eyes as they dived to avoid detection, allowing the naval force of cruisers and destroyers to pass overhead. Once they had gone, the U-boats surfaced and increased speed in pursuit of the helpless merchant ships. The first radio signals of distress now reached the naval forces. On the destroyer *Oribi* there was a near mutiny as the officers discussed reversing course and going to the assistance of PQ17, but it was too late. The convoy was no longer. Instead the Barents Sea contained thirty laden merchant ships, a handful of small warships and three overburdened rescue ships making their way to Russian ports. Those on the port wing of the convoy ran up into the ice and escaped that way; others pressed ahead, hoping to reach the coast of Novaya Zemlya before turning south and coasting down towards the White Sea. Those in the starboard columns were easy prey and soon succumbed. In the succeeding days the remnants of the convoy reassembled in the Matochkin Strait, one American master running his Liberty-ship aground on Novaya Zemlya claiming he had delivered her to a Russian port! Although the Admiralty transmitted a subsequent signal to those naval vessels that had remained with the convoy, chief of which were the *Pozarica* and *Palomares*, to attempt to gather together and protect any ships with which they were in contact, it was too little, far too late.

In the event twenty-four merchant ships – two-thirds of the convoy – were destroyed by aircraft and U-boats, including Dowding's. In terms of lost *matériel* 210 bombers, 430 tanks, 3,350 vehicles and a little under 100,000 tons of munitions, explosives and raw materials lay on the sea bed. The naval aftermath was complex and beyond remarking that its effect upon American naval opinion may be imagined, it does not lie within the scope of this work. Suffice it to say that efforts were made to stem the swirl of rumours among the ratings of the various warships: Tovey took the unprecedented step of boarding the American cruiser *Wichita* when she returned to Scapa Flow, to apologise for the losses among American merchant seamen; Hamilton, who was unjustly tainted by the affair, cleared the *London*'s lower-deck and explained to his crew what had happened.

The political consequences require a brief mention, for they are part of the legacy of PQ17 insofar as they affected morale throughout the British merchant seafaring community, notwithstanding the fact that the majority of the lost ships were American not British. In London, Soviet Ambassador Maisky asked when, in view of the losses, the next convoy would be run? He was informed that it was impossible until the nights closed in again. In the Commons Emmanuel Shinwell asked the Financial Secretary to the Admiralty, George Hall, if he was 'aware that a recent convoy proceeding in a very important direction was denuded by Admiralty [of] protection ... and that a large number of vessels were lost?' Hall remained silent. There was a long series of inquiries, official and unofficial. The British assumed silence in the hope that the matter would die, but it did not. The reporter Godfrey Winn, who had sailed in the convoy, accurately warned Sir Dudley Pound that such silence would breed mistrust on the part of the Americans and cause much mischief elsewhere.[46] Pound assumed the full responsibility, admitting his errors at a War Cabinet meeting on 1 August in Churchill's presence, though the latter maintained in his *History of the Second World War* that he knew nothing of the rationale of the order to scatter. He had been stung by a remark made in Moscow by Stalin where the two men had been conferring at the time. 'Doesn't the British navy know how to fight?' Stalin had asked, and on his return home Churchill ordered that a further convoy be despatched immediately. Convoy PQ18 fought its way through to Russia in a series of spirited actions, though not without loss. It brought the PQ convoys to an end. When they resumed after Operation TORCH – which had required the redeployment of the Home Fleet – a new JW/RA series would be established. These were an unqualified success, but this did not wipe-out the stain left by PQ17.

The majority of the survivors of PQ17 returned in Convoy QP14. On arrival in Glasgow they were forbidden to go home, but were marched to St Andrew's Hall and addressed by Philip Noel-Baker, an Under Secretary of State in the MoWT. As a damage-limitation exercise his speech was a dismal failure. 'We know what the convoy cost us. But I want to tell you that whatever the cost, it was well worth it'. His weary audience howled with derision. It has been claimed that the cost of PQ17 has been exaggerated, that the loss of 153 Allied merchant seamen from twenty-two merchant ships was light in comparison with the 4,000 lost in the preceding months by the Royal Navy from the same number of warships. Such comparisons are invidious; one can only compare like with like and the effect of those 153 deaths, the majority of which were avoidable had, sad to say, a far greater impact than that of 4,000 naval personnel. War is full of such savage inequities. Besides the immense loss of the cargoes, the perception that the Royal Navy had 'run-away' acted as a catalyst upon the bitterness resulting from social divisions, injustices – real and imagined – of misunderstanding, mistrust and mutual ignorance that were harboured by many merchant seamen.

Sir Dudley Pound's fateful and ill-informed decision, compounded in its effect by an injudicious amendment, was contrary to what every thinking sailor knew in his bones: that a convoy *always* stuck together. Besides its powerful ocean-escort, PQ17 had been covered not only by Hamilton's squadron, but by the Home Fleet in the offing, Tovey's flagship, HMS *Duke of York*, the aircraft-carrier *Victorious* and all the might, dominion and power of the King's ships. As one *naval* participant pointed out 'in strong and emotional language,' not a single naval ship was lost in the defence of PQ17. It was the failure of this unwritten covenant between the two sea services – so brilliantly exemplified elsewhere time and time again – that caused the trouble. The destruction of Convoy PQ17 gave life to an inchoate conviction long embedded within the embittered folklore of the British Merchant Navy.

Sadly, however, the point seemed repeatedly justified. Many men and boys were left in Russian hospitals, some suffering from wounds, most from the effects of the cold. Amputations were common and men – and boys – returned home alive, but badly disabled, often to find that their wives had not been paid allotments, that while they languished in hospital their pay had been stopped. The convoys to Russia were beset by personal tragedies, which is one of the reasons the veterans consider themselves entitled to a separate campaign medal, and the government's steadfast refusal to this day to grant them one only reinforces this feeling.[47] In due course, with the renewed JW/RA convoys, matters improved and later Russian convoys were models of co-operation between the sea services, with proper protection, including local air cover provided by escort aircraft-carriers. The medical facilities in Russia were also being improved by the establishment of a British naval hospital at Vaenga, while merchant crews were issued with Arctic clothing.

No other single convoy had such an impact upon the conduct of the war at sea from the perspective of the merchant seafarer, even though PQ17 was not quite alone in being disastrous. Perhaps the convoy most qualified for this epithet was OG71 which, even in remnant form, failed to make its destination. The twenty merchant-men forming up on the commodore's ship, the Yeoward Bros' *Aguila* as they passed the Mersey Bar on Wednesday 13 August 1941 were bound for Gibraltar, by way of the Tagus. The *Aguila* was a medium-sized cargo-passenger-liner owned by the Yeoward Bros and designed to run to Northern Spain, Portugal, Morocco, Las Palmas and Teneriffe. In consequence she had not only Vice Admiral Patrick Parker embarked as Commodore with his signals staff, but ninety service personnel on their way to postings in Gibraltar, twenty of whom were young members of the Women's Royal Naval Service, better known as 'Wrens', under Second Officer Christine Ogle. The *Aguila* under Captain Arthur Frith was something of a veteran in her own right, having driven off an Italian submarine, the *Barbarigo* under Capitano di Corvetta Ghiglieri, after a running fight the previous August. Although most of the vessels were small, short-sea traders, a larger tramp, the Cardigan Shipping Company's *Grelhead* was making a ballast passage, and two neutral Irish ships of the Limerick S.S. Co., the *Clonlara* and the *Lanahrone*, were conspicuous in their peace-time colours. The convoy had been routed 200 miles closer to the Biscay coast of Occupied France since to the westward a fast convoy, WS10X consisting of the P&O liners *Strathmore* and *Strathnaver*, Orient Line's *Orion*, the Blue Star Line's *Brisbane Star*, the Royal Mail liner *Palma*, and Port Line's *Port Jackson*, was outward bound for the Middle East.

The 5th Escort Group protected Convoy OG71. Led by HM Sloop *Leith*, Lieutenant Commander E.C. Hutton, supported by HNorMS *Bath* – one of the fifty former American destroyer escorts handed over to Britain and her European allies – and by an anti-submarine trawler and six corvettes. Aware of the convoy from aerial recon-naissance provided by a Condor from *Kampfgeschwader 40*, Dönitz mustered a wolf-pack of which three, *U-559* (Heidtmann), *U-204* (Kell) and *U-201* (Schnee) made contact on 19 August, shortly after the convoy had beaten off an attack by Ju88s. There was a strong wind blowing and a high sea running when Schnee torpedoed the *Aguila* with fearful loss of life. Captain Frith – it is Firth in some accounts[48] – along with six of his crew, two passengers and one naval signaller were rescued by HM Corvette *Wallflower*, seven more by the tug *Empire Oak*,[49] leaving a toll of Parker, four of his signalling staff, five DEMS gunners, fifty-eight of the ship's crew and eighty-nine passengers, including some of the Wrens. Almost simultaneously Kell torpedoed the *Bath*, Kaptein-löytnant F. Melsom, just then making a counter-attack on another U-boat contact. She sank with heavy loss of life. He then attacked MacAndrew's *Ciscar* which was carrying military stores for the garrison at Gibraltar. While thirteen men died with their ship, Captain E.L. Hughes and thirty-four of his crew survived, being picked up by the General Steam Navigation Co.'s *Petrel*. Heidtmann also struck, sinking Glen & Co.'s *Alva* of Glasgow and her 2,300 tons of coal. One man was killed in her engine room but Captain C.S. Palmer escaped with the remaining twenty-four of his crew, rescued by the *Clonlara*.

Despite the loss of the commodore, OG71 struggled on, the 5th Escort Group – less the *Bath* – driving off further U-boat contacts during the 20th, but the Admiralty ordered the destroyers *Legion* and *Gurhka* to reinforce Hutton. Intermittent sightings were made by the Germans in the following hours, but it was not until Oberleutnant Suhren in *U-564* spotted OG71 to the west of Portugal on the afternoon of the 22nd that the convoy was again attacked. Vectoring the pursuing Schnee in *U-501* onto the convoy, along with Topp in *U-552*, the U-boats attacked that night. Towards midnight Suhren torpedoed the *Empire Oak* and the *Clonlara*, both laden with survivors. Captain F.E. Christian and seven of his crew were picked up by HM Corvette *Campanula*, but the *Aguila*'s survivors, including some Wrens, were drowned. The *Clonlara* took six of her own people and all the survivors from the *Alva* to the bottom. Captain J. Reynolds and just half a dozen of his own men were rescued by the corvette *Campion*. In torpedoing the General Steam Navigation Co.'s *Stork*, Schnee had ignited her cargo of cased petrol. Captain Williams and all but three of his crew survived the inferno, rescued by *Wallflower*. Schnee's next victim was Captain H.W. McLean's *Aldergrove*, owned by the Grove Line of Glasgow. She was carrying 2,650 tons of patent fuel for Lisbon and this went to the bottom with a naval rating, embarked for the passage to Gibraltar. McLean and his crew managed to scramble aboard the *Campanula* which had picked up some of the Wrens' bodies. Suhren also torpedoed, damaged and set on fire the Norwegian cargo-vessel *Spind*, compelling her crew to abandon ship. They were rescued by the escorts and, in the small hours of the 23rd, Topp came upon the burning *Spind* and sank her with a torpedo and gun-fire. Suhren remained in contact with the convoy, firing several more torpedoes ineffectually until as a faint trace of dawn illuminated the eastern horizon, he struck the corvette *Zinnia*. She was commanded by Lieutenant Commander Charles Cuthbertson RNR, an 'old-*Worcester*' who in 1939 had been second officer in the Union-Castle liner *Caernarvon Castle*. His first lieutenant, Harold Chesterman, though born in Australia and at twenty-four, eleven years Cuthbertson's junior, was another former *Worcester*-boy who had been serving with Shaw, Savill & Albion before the war. Both were Master-Mariners and were engaged in changing stations with another of the escorts when torpedoed. In the prevailing conditions Suhren's U-boat was almost invisible on the surface. The *Zinnia* sank rapidly with heavy loss of life though Cuthbertson and Chesterman were, among a handful of others, later picked up by the *Campion*.

Despite the failure of several torpedoes, to the frustration of the German U-boat commanders, the night's toll was terrible, over 400 lives, eight merchantmen and two escorts.[50] Such destruction in the face of not only the 5th Escort Group but with the extra reinforcements, including powerful fleet destroyers, was a defeat for the British. As OG71 approached neutral Portuguese territorial waters the escorting warships turned away for Gibraltar. In Lisbon German spies and newspaper reporters converged on the banks of the Tagus to contemplate the battered merchantmen as they anchored on Sunday 24th. Captain John Klemp of the *Petrel*, all but overwhelmed by the demands of the survivors on the slim resources of his small ship, found little support from either the Portuguese authorities on a Sunday or the British Embassy officials, for whom there was no excuse. A press conference was organised for the following day and *The Daily Telegraph's* reporter gleefully wrote to confound German claims that the convoy had been destroyed, admitting to the loss of seven merchantmen, but suppressing that of two escorts. As Bernard Edwards comments:

> the *Telegraph's* correspondent gave such an up-beat version of the running battle for OG71 that it could have been construed as a major victory for the Allies. It must have delighted the Ministry of Information in London, hence its immediate approval for publication.
>
> In reality, the assault on Convoy OG71 resulted in a very convincing victory for Admiral Dönitz. Although protected by an unusually strong escort force, eight merchantmen, 36 percent of the convoy, had been sunk, along with two of the ships guarding them. And all this without loss or damage to any German U-boat or aircraft ... [I]t could not be denied that the U-boats had brought off a coup of major proportions ... for the first time in the war they had forced a British convoy to abandon its voyage and seek refuge in neutral waters. For the Royal Navy it was the ultimate humiliation.[51]

This was how the operation was regarded at L'Orient, where decorations were handed out to the victorious U-boat commanders by Dönitz himself, but in Lisbon and Gibraltar matters wore a different complexion. Seeing the remnants of OG71, the waiting Irish crew of the *Vassilios Destounis*, newly acquired by Irish Shipping of Dublin, who had been ordered to join a north-bound British convoy, flatly refused to sail.[52] Preoccupying many at Gibraltar was the fate of the twenty-two Wrens. One alone was thought to have been picked up by the *Empire Oak*, but she had not survived the tug's torpedoing; no one was ever to know precisely how they died.

Amid the carnage and the courage of the war at sea there were instances of fine seamanship. By one of those odd conjunctions of fate Captain D.L.C. Evans, formerly of the *Aeneas* and the *Phemius*, and Commander Scurfield of HMS *Broke* who had both taken part in Convoy OA178, were destined to co-operate in one of these. Evans's next ship was the Glen Line's new cargo-liner *Glenartney*, and on 5 April 1941 she was outward bound from Birkenhead for the Middle East with a cargo of military stores. As a measure of her importance she had been assigned an escort of the destroyer HMS _Lincoln_ and the AMC HMS _Comorin_. Since she had been built for P&O, the _Comorin's_ accommodation was full of naval personnel on their way out to Freetown and she had on board some 400 people. That afternoon the group of ships were off Oversay, heading out into the Atlantic in a south-easterly gale, accompanied by a lowering overcast and a heavy sea when Evans was called to the _Glenartney's_ bridge. A signal had just been received from Acting Captain J.I. Hallett of the _Cormorin_: 'Have serious fire on board. Stand by me.'

From his experience in the _Phemius_, Evans brought _Glenartney_ close up on the _Cormorin's_ windward side and pumped oil over the side to flatten the sea. Also on his way to assist at 18 knots was Scurfield's destroyer _Broke_. Aboard the _Cormorin_ the fire was being gallantly but ineffectually fought by Chief Engineer W.F. Lee and his staff, but it was soon raging out of control, leaving the _Comorin_ rolling in the trough of the sea and drifting to leeward with smoke and flames pouring from her. Hallett had given orders for those not actively fighting the fire to muster at their boats stations, but their prospects of survival did not look promising, notwithstanding Evans's efforts to minimise the effects of the heavy seas. In defiance of the conditions, the _Comorin's_ crew managed to lower two boats and seven rafts but the _Comorin's_ leeward drift was greater and these were exposed, enabling Evans to bring _Glenartney_ up to windward of them and, using his own leeway, drop down onto them and pick up 109 survivors while his own ship rolled through a tremendous arc of 60°. The _Lincoln_ also assisted; having got a line across to the _Comorin_ and attached a raft mid-way, her crew were painstakingly and intermittently hauling this back and forth, picking up a number of men willing to risk jumping into the raft. After dark the _Broke_ arrived and Scurfield carried out a most daring manoeuvre, running his destroyer repeatedly alongside the starboard quarter of the burning _Comorin_, allowing men to jump directly from the larger liner onto the slippery steel foredeck of the much smaller destroyer. Here help was offered by the _Broke's_ first lieutenant, the young Peter Scott, but not everyone made it. Two men fell into the sea and only one was recovered; one man fell between the two vessels and was crushed; another landed astride the _Broke's_ guardrail, another astride the barrel of her B-gun – an indication of the relative motion of the two vessels – both of whom survived. The last man to leave the _Comorin_ was Captain Hallett but he was caught up in a dangling rope and spun round as the _Broke's_ deck dropped away in the trough of a wave. By some chance the captain landed as the destroyer rose, sitting on her guardrail from where he rolled inboard onto the hammocks spread there by Scott and his men. With great aplomb he got to his feet and replaced the monocle that had dropped from his eye. As a model of sang-froid, this matched the earlier evacuation of a former P&O steward, signed-on under the T124 arrangement. Awaiting his moment, 'with his raincoat folded neatly over one arm and a cigarette in his mouth,' he 'swung his legs over ... and stepped casually from one ship to the other'.

It was after midnight on the 7th before Scurfield ordered his engines full astern for the final time, signalling the _Lincoln_ to put a torpedo into the _Comorin_. The two destroyers made for the Clyde, the _Broke_ with 180 survivors, the _Lincoln_ with 121, leaving the *Glenartney* to proceed to Freetown independently with her complement of survivors. Incredibly only twenty of *Comorin*'s 400 had perished. Evans's report to the Admiralty was terse, the laurels for the night's work properly belonging to the Royal Navy.[53] He did not wish to be thought of as 'blowing our own trumpet', he wrote to Lawrence Holt, but his own contribution in a much larger and less manoeuvrable vessel than the two destroyers, had been worthy. In order to recover the *Comorin*'s people from the lifeboats and rafts, members of Evans's crew had not only thrown ladders and cargo-nets over the side, but had gone down them to help the survivors scramble aboard. Given the violent and heavy rolling of the *Glenartney* this required a cool nerve and Evans drew particular attention to Assistant Engineer R. Scott and Quartermaster Chen Siao Chuen. 'The Chinese crew,' he wrote:

> were truly excellent, working to the point of exhaustion … As an illustration of the spirit prevailing, the Chinese boys made it clear that any attempt on the part of the survivors to offer any reward or gratuity would be most offensive to their feelings, and would be met with disdainful refusal. I can only say with all the sincerity I possess that I am proud to have been in command of such a ship, manned by such excellent officers, midshipmen and crew.

Though in far less extreme conditions, a similar exploit had been carried out between two merchant ships in the same waters on 15 November 1940 when a Liverpool-bound convoy was attacked by a lone German bomber. One of the two bombs dropped smashed through No.3 Hatch of the Elder, Dempster liner *Apapa* where it burst and ignited the oily palm kernels with which the hold was full. The fire spread rapidly and it was clear that the ship was doomed, but another of the company's ships, the *Mary Kingsley*, was in convoy and her master brought her stern-first close up to the *Apapa*'s stem where many of the latter's crew and passengers were able to transfer in comparative ease from one ship to the other before the blazing *Apapa* broke in two and sank.

Mercifully, despite the harshness of the war at sea, there were few repeats of the blatant atrocities against merchant seamen that had occurred in the previous conflict with Germany. Contrary to public perception there was only one actual conviction of a U-boat commander for a war crime, and that was the sentence of death passed on Kapitänleutnant Heinz Eck of *U-582* who, on the evening of 13 March 1944, torpedoed the Greek steamer *Peleus* in mid-Atlantic twenty-miles-south of the Equator. The *Peleus* was on charter to the British MoWT, was bound in ballast from the convoy dispersal port of Freetown towards the Rio de la Plata and had a detachment of British DEMS gunners on board. Having sunk his target Eck, aware that four of his sister-submarines had recently disappeared 'without trace', cruised about among the survivors and removed the life jacket from the *Peleus*'s third mate as it had the ship's name on it, thereby proving his 'kill'. The U-boat then motored away and the survivors were attempting to organise themselves when Eck returned and shouted to the men in the water and on rafts to make their way towards his U-boat. Then *U-582* was driven through the pathetic assembly of floating debris while machine-gunfire was opened on the bobbing heads, and grenades were flung at the rafts until whatever was left was abandoned to the sharks. However, the extermination had been botched and three men survived, Chief Officer Liossis, Seaman Argyros 'and one Rocco Said, a British subject, who in 1941, had given up his peacetime and peaceful employment as a furrier and returned to the sea he had followed as a boy'. The third mate had survived badly wounded for twenty-five days but died before the Portuguese steamer *Alexandre Silva* rescued this trio on 20th April. By this time Eck's U-boat had been destroyed off the Somali coast by two RAF aircraft of 621 Squadron and all fifty-nine of her crew taken prisoner. After the war, Eck and four of his officers were brought to trial at Nuremburg and all but one executed.[54]

Among the more extreme incidents is the horror that followed the sinking of the Cunard White Star liner *Laconia* when she was torpedoed north-east of Ascension Island on her way home from the Middle East by Korvettenkapitän Hartenstein in *U-156*. The *Laconia* had on board a total of 2,732 people consisting of a crew of 463, British service personnel numbering 286, eighty civilians including women and children and 1,793 Italian PoWs guarded by 103 Polish solders.

One of a group of large, long-range U-boats code-named *Eisbär* and sent to operate in the South Atlantic, *U-156* had, a few days earlier, sunk the Clan Line's *Clan Macwhirter* with the loss of her master, Captain R.S. Masters, ten men and 2,000 tons of manganese ore, 3,500 tons of iron ore, 3,500 tons of linseed and a quantity of general cargo all of which was on its way from India to Britain. Hartenstein torpedoed the *Laconia* silhouetted against the last of the sunset on 12 September 1942, just as the second sitting for dinner was taking place and the ensuing chaos was terrible as the ship listed and half the boats could not be launched into a heavy sea. The Italian prisoners panicked and turned on their Polish guards, adding to the confusion. As the ship sank, taking with her the bodies of Captain Rudolph Sharp (formerly of the *Lancastria*), 138 of his crew, 551 passengers and 1,378 prisoners, the *Laconia's* boilers exploded, adding to the terror and injuries of those floundering in the water, struggling to pull lifeboats clear, or struggle onto rafts and floats. Some of those who survived could not, in those first moments, come to terms with what had happened. They felt light-headed, even optimistic, detached from reality as all about them others thrashed helplesly.

Hartenstein surfaced, shocked to hear Italian voices and, overcome by remorse, ordered his men onto the U-boat's casing to drag aboard as many as possible. He also transmitted a signal, *en clair*, declaring the position, his need of assistance and making it plain that he would not attack any Allied shipping prepared to assist. To deter air attack, Hartenstein had a large red cross painted on a white sheet, ready to spread conspicuously across *U-156's* deck. In distant L'Orient, Dönitz was not hostile to this act of humanity and the nearest *Eisbär* U-boats were ordered to help, request also being asked of an Italian submarine, the *Commandante Capellini* (Revedin) and any vessels from Vichy French West Africa. Twenty-one Britons were among the 263 survivors picked up by *U-156*, or left in their lifeboats towing astern by the time that *U-506* (Würdemann) arrived during the night of the 15th/16th. Würdemann took aboard 132 Italians and by dawn had recovered more than 200 survivors. Meanwhile Schacht's *U-507* had picked up the women and children out of four more of the *Laconia's* lifeboats, which she had taken in tow. Around noon on the 16th an American Liberator overflew the scene and Hartenstein spread his red cross. An RAF officer aboard the U-boat sent a message explaining the situation and the Liberator flew off. However, half an hour later it returned, having been ordered to attack and destroy *U-156*. Two bombs were dropped, both missing the U-boat, but as Hartenstein ordered the towed lifeboat cast adrift 'the aircraft dropped a bomb in the middle of these ...'. *U-156*'s War Diary records that:

> One boat capsized. Aircraft cruised round in the vicinity ... then dropped a fourth bomb some two or three thousand yards away ... Another aircraft. Two bombs, one of which with a few seconds' delayed action, exploded directly beneath control room ... Control room and bow compartment reported making water. Ordered all hands to don life-jackets. Ordered all British to leave the boat. Next – all Italians ... 13.11: sent out war emergency message ... Returned to the life-boats, to which I transferred all remaining survivors ... [The American aircraft had been] unequivocally ordered to sink the submarine.

It is thought that in the air attack two lifeboats were affected, the second being destroyed. One of the British nursing sisters on board *U-156*, Miss Doris Hawkins, recalled that:

> Six bombs were dropped, and each was a very near miss. The submarine shivered and shook, and one end compartment was damaged. It was a dreadful sensation; we knew that one direct hit could send us to the bottom. The explosions through the water were tremendous.

In consequence of this callous act, Hartenstein left the area, Miss Hawkins among those who 'found ourselves once again swimming for our lives.' It took them over an hour to reach the lifeboats and several did not long survive. At dusk Revedin arrived in the *Commandante Capellini* and took aboard all the Italians, remaining among the bobbing lifeboats throughout the night, while a distant Dönitz continued to encourage the rescue. In the next few days several vessels came to assist, meeting the Italian and two German submarines that had already embarked a large number of survivors and relieving them of their burdens. One of the U-boats – *U-506* – had also been bombed when towing lifeboats but had resumed doing so when the Liberator disappeared. The submarines were met by the Vichy French cruiser *La Gloire*, the sloop *Dumont d'Urville* and minesweeper *Annamite* which took aboard a large number of the survivors, including fifty women and children. Dönitz later claimed that the British failed to respond to Hartenstein's humane message and while no British vessel actually reached the scene in time, the merchantman *Empire Haven* and the Ocean Boarding Vessel *Corinthian* were in fact both ordered to assist.

The sixty-eight souls left in Miss Hawkins's boat relied upon the *Laconia*'s doctor, a young man named Geoffrey Purslow who had a rudimentary knowledge of sailing, and an army officer, to take charge. They had little in the way of sailing gear and improvised a rig out of oars and blankets but headed for land, 600 miles away. The *Laconia*'s fourth engineer, William Henderson, fashioned a rudder and worked tirelessly to ease their sufferings in any way he could until, 'one morning, we found he was no longer breathing'. The following days 'passed in dreadful monotony' and the early promise of reassurance from a lamp flashing from an American aircraft yielded nothing but despair. The shortage of water became acute and they were subject to the dreadful torture of extreme thirst. Their pores closed, their tongues hardened, their lips cracked, their nails grew brittle, they hallucinated. Saltwater sores became infected; eyes, fingers and toes grew septic. Purslow and Hawkins used a pen-knife to keep wounds open and drained to head off gangrene while the touching of any soft flesh against the boat's structure brought pain. Sightings of unresponsive ships eroded dwindling mental resilience. Then Purslow developed septicaemia and, knowing he was a danger to them all he wished them goodbye and went overboard. After twenty-one days they ran out of water altogether. Next morning it rained heavily and they were able to masticate their rations properly. Finally, on Thursday 8 October, they fell in with the land and although unable to get ashore through the surf they were spotted by a patrolling RAF flying-boat. Two days later they were thrown ashore through the breakers, just sixteen alive of the sixty-eight who had originally been in the boat. They had arrived on the coast of Liberia where, after a less excoriating but no less arduous boat voyage of over 1,000 miles, part of the crew of Sir William Reardon Smith's *Quebec City* were also washed ashore; she had been Hartenstein's next victim.

After several days living with hospitable Liberians, both parties were embarked by British anti-submarine trawlers and taken to Freetown where, as already remarked, the aftermath of the disaster combined with the influx of other survivors of Dönitz's southwards extension of operations to confront the British naval authorities. In due course the survivors were repatriated aboard the AMC, HMS *Carnarvon Castle*, late of the Union-Castle Line, which anchored off the Tail o' the Bank in the Clyde on 29 October. The following day – most of them broke and few of whom had any documentation or suitable garments – they were given clothing and told to queue up.

Two thousand men had to be questioned individually about where they lived and their nearest railway station and to sign three official forms before they could receive their [rail travel] warrant and £3 [to assist with subsistence] … It was 19.00 before we began disembarking, on a dark night, in black-out conditions, onto Clyde ferries. These conveyed us to Greenock Pier where we boarded special trains for Glasgow Central Station, where we arrived at 22.00. the station was under armed guard and civilian passengers barred from its forecourt and platforms. Five special trains had been laid on – for the Midlands, East Coast, London, West Coast and Wales/ South West respectively – and we were escorted to our places by army personnel … Under close army supervision the first to be loaded were the stretcher-cases. Then the walking wounded … The women of the W[omen's] V[olunteer] S[ervice] and Red Cross were everywhere, helping us to board our trains, ensuring that we were as comfortable as possible, offering cups of tea. It was midnight by now and word came through that the *Luftwaffe* had been bombing the sidings in the East Kilbride area and all rail movement had been suspended. It was 01.30 before my train eventually moved out.[55]

The result of the American bombing of *U-156* was the issuing by Dönitz of his notorious *Laconia Befehl*, which henceforth proscribed assistance of any kind to survivors. It was justified by a reminder that German women and children were being bombed in their homes by Allied air forces and was central to the accusations made against Dönitz at Nuremburg. In a double irony it was an American who rescued Dönitz from the gallows; the affidavit of Fleet Admiral Chester Nimitz confirmed that submarines 'as a general rule … did not rescue enemy survivors'. It was a final sinking of the last vestige of the Prize Regulations.

The indiscriminate slaughter inherent in unrestricted submarine warfare had been clear from the first day of the war, when the *Athenia* was torpedoed, and only emphasised by such events as the sinking of the *City of Benares*. The involvement of enemy nationals, ironic though it was, was not unique to the *Laconia*. Earlier, in July 1940, Prien in *U-47* had torpedoed the 15,500-ton *Arandora Star* some seventy-five-miles west of Bloody Foreland. The ship, under Captain Edgar Moulton, was sailing independently from Liverpool to St John's, Newfoundland, zig-zagging at 15 knots. She was carrying eighty-six German PoWs, 479 male German alien internees, 734 male Italian internees accompanied by 200 soldiers acting as guards, besides a large crew. Moulton and his officers did their best to evacuate the ship, successfully launching several boats, but the numbers of terrified internees 'greatly hampered' the work and the consequent loss of life was heavy, altogether 805 of the 1,673 on board. Although the survivors were rescued by the Canadian destroyer *St Laurent*, Moulton and fifty-five of his crew, ninety-one military guards, 713 Italian and German internees and PoWs were lost, many of the latter refusing to get into the boats. Prien slunk away, leaving many of his own countrymen to drown.

There were other comparable slaughters. On 28 November 1942 Furness, Withy's Johnston Warren intermediate liner *Nova Scotia*, Captain Alfred Hender, was torpedoed by *U-177* (Gysae) off Lourenço Marques when bound from Egypt to Durban and sailing independently. Besides her crew, she had on board six passengers, eleven military and naval officers, and 130 South African soldiers guarding 780 Italian PoWs. Only seventeen of the ninety-six strong crew, one of the ten DEMS gunners, three of the military officers, forty-two of the guards and 130 Italians were rescued by a Portuguese frigate, Hender being lost with his ship. West of the Azores nine days later *U-515* (Henke) torpedoed Shaw, Savill & Albion's *Ceramic*, Captain Herbert Elford. With a crew of 295, she was on her way to Durban and Sydney with 378 passengers and troops, and 12,362 tons of Government stores and general cargo. There was only one survivor, Sapper Eric Munday, who, rescued by Henke, became a PoW.

With U-boats favouring the torpedo, there were far fewer gun-duels than in the previous war, though one was notable for its duration. On 25 November 1942 the Dutch-flagged Blue Funnel liner *Polydorus*, Captain H. Brouwer, was approaching Freetown on an independent voyage from Liverpool. She bore an Anglo-Dutch crew of sixty-six plus eleven DEMS gunners and carried two passengers. That afternoon a heavy explosion was heard and a fountain of water erupted off the ship's starboard quarter, which Brouwer judged to be the premature detonation of a torpedo fired at his ship. Sending his crew to action stations and transmitting the SSSS signal, Brouwer cracked on speed, altering course after dark to due east. The *Polydorus* was betrayed by a rising moon and at 21.05 first tracer and then heavier shellfire began falling close to her. Fire was returned by the ship's Oerlikons, smoke canisters were dropped and a rain squall briefly hid her from the pursuing U-boat. One shell had damaged the engine-room skylight and near misses had caused leakage in the main-engine fuel system, but no one was hurt. Unbeknown to Brouwer, Kapitänleutnant Dierksen of *U-176* had already been frustrated in two attacks, hence his decision to chase on the surface.

Zig-zagging intermittently, it was daylight before there was any further sign of the enemy, when Brouwer saw a torpedo track in time to take evasive action. Despite the damage to the fuel lines, Chief Engineer E. Beymerwerdt and Second Engineer W. Flight, managed to raise the steam pressure to 250 psi and 'the ship responded splendidly'. Brouwer managed to open the range to five miles when gun-fire resumed, with both *U-176* and *Polydorus* racing eastwards. The two exchanged shots for about half an hour when the action was broken off until 07.25, when Dierksen attempted to close the range. More smoke canisters were dropped, but at 08.15 *U-176* came clear of the smoke and *Polydorus*'s 4-inch stern-gun maintained fire under the command of Second Mate Salomons, its gun-layer being Midshipman George King. After a few minutes the enemy fell astern and seemed to have given up, so once the U-boat was out of sight, Brouwer turned north-west in an attempt to throw off his pursuer for good. The *Polydorus* had suffered superficial damage, and two of her lifeboats were wrecked, but thus far she had avoided destruction. During the evening Brouwer brought her head back to the eastwards; he was now within 800 miles of Freetown and could expect support from the naval force there. However, fortune did not favour the brave and in bright moonlight at 03.00 on the 27th, the tenacious Dierksen succeeded in sending two torpedoes into the *Polydorus*'s port side. Even as she sank and her boats were lowered, her radio officers were transmitting to Freetown. All of her crew escaped and when Dierksen approached the boats asking for the master, Brouwer's presence was denied. Satisfied after expending eight torpedoes and numerous shells, *U-176* made off. At 05.00 the gallant *Polydorus* sank 'in a cloud of dust'.

Gathering his boats, Brouwer discovered that one of the Chinese firemen had died of injuries sustained in the attack. They were able to augment their stores from an abandoned RAF air-sea rescue launch found nearby and, carefully provisioning and manning the three best boats, they set sail in good heart at 09.00 on the 28th. Before dawn the following morning they had attracted the attention of a passing ship, the neutral Spanish *Eolo*, Captain Urgelles, which landed them at Las Palmas. In his report Captain Brouwer paid particular tribute to his engineers who had enabled him 'to frustrate the submarine for so long. The fact that the engines ran under heavy pressure without any breakdown after three years strenuous service speaks volumes for the care … given to them'. He also commended 'little Midshipman King' who had taken over the sight-setting of the gun and 'won our hearts by his quietness, stubbornness and great courage under heavy stress and I bring him to notice as a youngster with the makings of a fine man in him'. The *Polydorus* was later honoured by Queen Juliana of the Netherlands and the teenage King was decorated with a Dutch award. Captain Brouwer was not wrong in his assessment of 'little Midshipman King' who went on to have a distinguished career, becoming the Managing Director of BP Tankers.

The German effort to destroy British shipping was largely concentrated in the North Atlantic, with early surface commerce-raiding and some later submarine activity in the South Atlantic, off the Cape of Good Hope. However, the Japanese onslaught of December 1941 reinforced the Axis campaign in eastern seas by a devastating effect upon British shipping. An hour earlier than the attack on Pearl Harbour, but on the 8th December owing to the International Date Line, the Japanese launched heavy air attacks and invaded Hong Kong and Malaya, storming ashore at Kota Bharu. That day in Hong Kong the China Navigation steamers *Nanning* and *Soochow* fell to the Japanese; elsewhere in Chinese ports, British ships were seized, many owned by British-flagged Chinese firms, or Sino-British companies based in China. China Navigation's large river steamer *Fatshan* was seized at Canton, and the *Siangtan* at Inchang. Here too the Ching Kee Co.'s *Kia Wo* and the Indo-China S.N.Co.'s *Hsin Chang Wo* were captured. Other tugs were lost at Hangkow and the Shanghai pilot cutter *Ling Kong* was seized off Woosung. In the Whang-pu and Shanghai, the China Navigation Co. lost the little *Kintang*, the *Chekiang* and the *Wantung*, their sister-ship, the *Shasi*, being taken in the Yangtze itself. A number of coasters were taken and the *Hsin Tseangtah* owned by the China Import & Export Lumber Co. also fell into enemy hands. N.J.Asquith & Co. lost the *Sui Tai*, a ship of about 1,800 tons at Shanghai and the *Kong So* at Tinghai. The Shanghai Tug & Lighter Co. lost two tugs, the *Scot I* at Shanghai, and the *St Dominic* off Saddle Island. Moller's tugs *Merry Moller*, *Diana Moller* and *Christine Moller*, their salvage vessel *Jessie Moller* and their cargo-ship *Mary Moller* were all seized at Shanghai, as were the *Marie Moller* at Ningpo and the tugs *Ready Moller*, *Carmen Moller* and *Elsie Moller* at Amoy.

The Imperial Japanese Navy scoured the China Seas intercepting China Navigation's 2,100-ton *Hsin Peking* on her way between Tongku and Hong Kong and further offshore their larger vessels, the *Woosung*, *Wenchow* and *Wuhu*.[56] Seven ships owned by Wheelock & Co., the *Analock*, *Deslok*, *Hatterlok*, *Federlok*, *Munlok*, *Vitorlok* and *St Quentin*, were all interdicted; as were the Indo-China S.N.Co.'s *Kiang-Wo*, *Paowo*, *Kut-Wo* and *Loongwo*; the *Tung On* owned by the Tung On S.S.Co., and the Kin Hong Co.'s *Sagres*.

A number of vessels went missing in the China Seas, namely the Hong Kong, Canton & Macao Steam Boat Co.'s river steamers *Kinshan* and *Taishan*, the Yuen On S.S.Co.'s *Kwong Tung*; the Shiu On S.S.Co.'s *Kwong Sai*; the Tai Sang S.S.Co.'s *Kau Tung*; and China Navigation's *Changsha*. Further afield in the eastern seas Lau Wa Ping lost the *Chung On* and *Fook On*; the Chuen On Steam Boat Co. lost the *Chuen Chow*; the Ming San S.S.Co. the *Kwong Fook Cheung*; Sze Lap the *On Lee* and the *Tai Lee*; the Sang Wo Co., the *Tai Hing* and the *Tai Ming*; the Fook On S.S.Co., the *Tin Yat*. Owned and manned by Chinese from Hong Kong or Shanghai, all had British masters and officers and wore the red ensign. Next day, the 9th, the *Bennevis*, Captain D.J. Wilson, was captured off Hong Kong and taken by her Japanese captors to Hainan where she was renamed *Gyokuyo Maru*. A War Emergency ship built in 1918 as the *War Ostrich*, she had been acquired by Ben Line in 1928. Wilson had been ordered by the naval authorities at Hong Kong to tow a large, 800-ton lighter to Singapore. Although aware of the tense situation, he had no knowledge of the actual outbreak of war until two Japanese destroyers approached and ordered him to strike his colours, precipitating several years of imprisonment for Wilson and his crew, three of whom died in captivity.

The following day, 10 December, British prestige suffered a bitter blow when the *Prince of Wales* and *Repulse* were bombed and sunk in the South China Sea. On the periphery of these events, British merchantmen continued to be lost, the Tai Yau S.S.Co.'s *Hareldawins* being sunk by a Japanese submarine off Luzon, on her way to Singapore. Carrier-borne Japanese aircraft ranged at will and on the 24th they bombed and sank the *Forafric* in the Celebes Sea, though her company escaped with their lives. Her owners, Williamson & Co. of Hong Kong, exemplify the small shipping companies operating coasters on the China coast with a fleet of nine second- or third-hand tramps ranging between 2,900 to 5,450 gross tons, the oldest of which, the *Asian*, had been built in 1900. These were divided between seven subsidiary firms, the 3,475-ton *Forafric*, of 1909, being owned by the Wing Ning S.S. Co.[57]

In Burma too, the year ended disastrously for the British, resulting in the complete destruction of the Irrawaddy Flotilla, only two tugs and one motor barge escaping to India out of 650 riverine craft operated by the Flotilla Company. The first casualty was the river steamer *Nepaul*, commanded by Commodore Coutts. She was lying at Botatoung Depot, loading for Manadalay, when bombed by the Japanese. The relief commander, Captain Ferns, was killed and Chief Engineer George Watt was mortally wounded. The Flotilla's vessels did what they could to support the army but as it fell back before the relentless advance of the Japanese, its craft were either sunk or scuttled. Captain Rea was awarded the Military Cross for carrying a Commando raiding party downstream from Prome to Henzada in the Creek Steamer *Hastings*; Captain Railston's *Mysore* was used as a Casualty Clearing Station as General Alexander ordered a general retreat. Elsewhere, Second Class Master Bassa Meah of the *Sinkan*, towing several barges and flats, remained on his exposed bridge as his vessel was bombed and machine-gunned. To expedite the movement of troops above Mandalay a class of officer-cadets undergoing training at Maymyo were hurriedly drafted as deck-hands and firemen, and 'literally took off their shirts and got down to stoking boiler furnaces and handling ropes' until the general break-up at Katha. Here, the paddle-steamer *Taping* was bombed, killing a very popular Chittagonian *serang*, Abdul Hakim.

Amid fierce fighting in Hong Kong a number of ships were scuttled, among them the *Cambay Prince*, owned by the Hong Kong based John Manners & Co., the *St Vincent de Paul*, owned by C.W. Gordon & W.M. Reeves, and the Fleet oiler *Ebonoil*. Another tanker, the Asiatic Petroleum Co.'s small *Sumatra* was captured by the Japanese, but sunk by the guns of the Royal Navy. On the capitulation of the crown colony on the 25th, a number of British-registered merchantmen fell into Japanese hands: the Po Hing S.S. Co.'s *Apoey*, China Navigation Co.'s *Chengtu* and *Kanchow*; the Indo-China S.N.Co.'s *Hinsang*, *Fausang*, *Ming Sang* and *Yat Shing*; the Sing Hing S.S. Co.'s *Shun Chih*; the *Ariadne Moller* and *Joan Moller*, along with five of Moller Ltd's harbour craft and a tug of the Shanghai Tug & Lighter Co. Offshore, G.L.Shaw's steamer *Shinwa* was also captured. Meanwhile in Bangkok another China Navigation ship, the *Kalgan*, had been seized. Across the South China Sea in Manila Bay the Blue Funnel liner *Tantalus* was bombed, set on fire and sunk by Japanese aircraft. The next day the Douglas S.S. Co.'s steamer *Seistan*, the Asiatic Petroleum's *Hai Kwang* and the Chinese Engineering & Mining Co.'s *Kaiping* were destroyed from the air. Further south at Kuching in Sarawak the *Shinai*, owned by G.L. Shaw, had been seized, along with the little coasters *Margaret* and *Rejang*, *Gladys* and *Kim Chin Seng*. A few days later at Labuan the Straits S.S. Co. lost the *Subok* and the *Jitra*.

As the Japanese army advanced towards Singapore many of the small coasters of the Straits S.S. Co. were commandeered as naval auxiliaries and, embarking machine-gun parties of marines and blue-jackets, hoisted the white ensign and attempted to save what could be saved before heading south for the waters of the Dutch East Indies. They were harried by warships and aircraft, bombed, machine-gunned and sunk. Bigger ships fell foul of the onslaught, the China Navigation's *Kwangtung* was caught south of Java by a Japanese submarine on a circuitous route from Hong Kong towards the sanctuary of Colombo, and the *Wulin* was bombed and sunk in the Muar River, near Johore. A submarine accounted for the Bombay-based Scindia S.N.Co.'s *Jalarajan* in the Malacca Strait as she made her way towards Calcutta from Singapore on 14 January, two days after the Japanese entered Kuala Lumpur. A fortnight later Scindia lost the *Jalatarang* and the *Jalapalaka* off Madras to gunfire from the Japanese submarine *I-164*. Another submarine patrolling off the Irrawaddy delta had torpedoed the Indo-China S.N.Co.'s *Chak Sang* on the 22nd and her sister, the *Tai Sang* was lost approaching Singapore on the 24th.

Singapore was now all but lost. In the last days of January and the first of February 1942 many ships were either caught in the Lion City or trying to escape from it, laden with civilians. They included the Shell tankers *Harpa* and *Pinna*, Maclay & McIntyre's *Loch Ranza*, the *Norah Moller*, the Straits S.S.Co.'s *Katong*, the China Navigation's *Wanyuan*, the Asiatic S.N.Co.'s *Subadar*, McCowen & Gross's *Derrymore*, Indo-China's *Hosang* and the Hua Khiow S.S. Co.'s *Hua Tong*. Off Singapore, the Canadian Pacific liner *Empress of Asia*, carrying 2,300 troops, was bombed and set on fire on 5 February, though all but fifteen soldiers were evacuated, only soon afterwards to become PoWs of the Japanese.

Several merchantmen other than the small Straits coasters had been armed and commissioned as naval auxiliaries[58] and one merits mention here, for she had belonged to Jardine & Matheson's Indo-China Steam Navigation Co. and she had been commissioned under the command of Lieutenant Commander T.S. Wilkinson of the RNR. HMS *Li Wo* was only 700 tons and bore a single 4-inch gun, but Wilkinson 'engaged a vastly superior force bound for Sumatra'. The *Li Wo* rammed a transport before sinking and Wilkinson was awarded a posthumous Victoria Cross.

As Singapore fell and Japanese forces ranged throughout the China and Indian seas the Sarawak steamer *Vyner Brook* and the Straits steamer *Kamuning* were sunk, as were the Thai Navigation Co.'s *Redang* and the British India managed *Johanne Justesen*. On the 15th, along with 64,000 British and Indian troops, the few merchant ships remaining in Singapore fell into the hands of the Japanese. Chief of these was the Blue Funnel liner *Talthybius*, which had been badly bombed while discharging military stores. Captain T.A. Kent and his crew laboured valiantly to save her but were overtaken by *force majeure*.[59] They escaped aboard the small naval auxiliary *Ping Wo*, thought to have been the last ship to escape capture as the Japanese took the city.

Shortly after his country entered the war, the Japanese ambassador in Berlin, Oshima Hiroshi, conferred with Hitler. Among other things they discussed attacks on Allied merchant shipping and in particular the fate of captured merchant seafarers. Oshima shared Hitler's attitude that a policy of extermination would weaken the enemy seamen's morale and compromise the Allied supply train. Initially Dönitz had disagreed until the *Laconia* affair when Order 154, the *Laconia Befehl*, was promulgated. 'Rescue no one and take no one on board. Do not concern yourself with the ship's boats ... We must be hard in this war.' If survivors were to be abandoned, the best that can be said about the *Laconia Befehl* is that a ship's boats were to be left alone, but Oshima passed Hitler's ruthless opinion to Tokyo, the nub of which was annihilation. Oshima's coded dispatches were simultaneously read at Bletchley Park and their import was appreciated in London. Although never high on the War Cabinet's agenda, some staff officers became increasingly concerned about the morale of the Merchant Navy. These fears were, as we shall see, justified in the aftermath of Convoy PQ17 but it was some time before Oshima's doctrine became clear. A year later, in March 1943, Sho-sho (Rear Admiral) Mito Hisashi commanding the submarines operating from the Marshall Islands ordered his commanders to 'totally destroy' Allied shipping. 'Do not stop with the sinking of enemy ships and cargoes; at the same time carry out the complete destruction of the crews ... if possible seize part of the crew ... to secure information about the enemy'.

Whether this emanated from a higher source is unclear but, given the hierarchy of the Imperial Japanese Navy, probable. The policy had certainly been adopted a year later when Tai-sho (Admiral) Takasu Shiro ordered a cruiser squadron to capture Allied merchant ships, the consequences of which follow, by which time Mito's order had been discovered by the Americans when they took the Marshall Islands early in 1944. They did not share it with the British until March 1945, fearing requests for convoy escorts which they could not spare from their offensive against Japan, by which time it was too late.[60] Evidence of Japanese atrocities had long been circulating among British seamen following the sinkings of the *Centaur* and the *Daisy Moller*.

The Blue Funnel liner *Centaur* was requisitioned as an Australian Hospital Ship and commissioned in March 1943. She was one of three small vessels designed for Holt's Singapore to Western Australia service, her strong hull capable of sitting on the bottom at Broome and Derby where the tidal range is large. Specially fitted out for the carriage of livestock, which was embarked on the hoof through side doors, her capacious 'tween decks commended her for her new role. After requisition, Captain George Murray, a Scot who had settled in Australia, remained in command, as did his officers and engineers, though her Chinese ratings were replaced by Britons, Australians and a handful of Scandinavians, a total complement of seventy-four men. To these were added sixty-four medical staff, a dozen of whom were female, and 193 members of a Field Ambulance Unit. In accordance with international protocol, the *Centaur's* new role had been notified to the Swiss government who had promulgated it to the world. To make this clear she was painted white, with a broad green ribband interrupted by large red crosses, her identification number, '47', conspicuously painted on her bow. She steamed fully illuminated and floodlit at night.

On 12 May the *Centaur* left Sydney on her second voyage to recover the battle-wounded from Port Moresby, Murray having the assistance of sixty-seven-year-old Richard Salt as pilot for the Great Barrier Reef. At about 04.15 on the 14th the *Centaur* was fifty miles off Brisbane when Chu-sa (Lieutenant Commander) Nakagawa Hajime in submarine *I-177*, lying between the floodlit *Centaur* and the coast, torpedoed her. Penetrating the engine room and the forward bunker tank, the torpedo sent a fireball of burning oil into the air, searing the face of Chief Officer Harold Lamble on the port wing of the bridge. Having shortly before handed over to Chief Officer Lamble, Second Officer Gordon Rippon had inspected the illumination of the red crosses on the ship's side and made his way to his cabin. He had just settled in his bunk when:

> there was a most almighty crash and I was picking myself up from the floor. I got up … and saw a sight I will never forget, and which has since been flashing through my mind … The ship was way down by the head. All the forepart was one vast sheet of flames, and it was raining drops of burning oil. At first I thought I was cut off but I grabbed my life-jacket and dashed outside.

He found Murray, a badly burned Lamble and a few others including the fourth engineer and some stewards trying to launch two boats when water surged along the deck as the *Centaur* foundered. Rippon and Fourth Engineer Cairnie jumped for their lives. In his letter to his father, Rippon continued: 'I learned later that Captain Murray, Chief Officer Lamble and two doctors had been clinging to a raft which had sunk under them because the drums had been pierced'. They were supposed to have been filled with kapok, but the contractors had skimped on the job. Others escaped, including a group of nurses, though only one survived, Sister Ellen Savage being pulled onto some wreckage by Private Thomas Malcolm.

Rippon dragged himself onto the precarious refuge of the *Centaur's* wheelhouse top. Looking around at daylight he thought about 200 people had escaped, many burned and all of them near naked. He encouraged them to gather together. Australian Steward James Watterston took a rope and swam to the debris upon which Savage and Malcolm were clinging, and they were drawn towards Rippon's makeshift raft; throughout the day, others came together of their own volition. Despite her internal injuries, Sister Savage and Dr Leslie Outridge, himself badly burned, did what they could for the injured. Taking charge, twenty-nine-year-old Rippon gathered all salvable provisions and flares, dividing them up for four days and putting them in the charge of Sister Savage. Their hopes were raised when a patrolling flying-boat was seen in the distance, but it failed to respond to their flares, as did several others later in the day. The appearance of sharks further dejected them.

If the day had been hot, the night was cold and during its long hours the badly burned Ambulance Driver Jack Walder died. His body was slipped respectfully over the side at daylight. Early the following afternoon a RAAF aircraft on anti-submarine patrol spotted them and summoned help from a passing American destroyer. The USS *Mugford* picked up the sixty-four survivors, including Ordinary Seaman Robert Westwood, at sixteen the youngest of them and Richard Salt, the oldest. Nakagawa's action had killed 268 people, among them Murray, Lamble, the *Centaur's* Swedish Boatswain, Gustav Brandin, and eleven women. The sole female survivor,

Ellen Savage, was awarded the George Medal and she survived her injuries, as did Salt, Chief Engineer Ernest Smith, Fourth Engineer Cairnie and Third Officer Ernest Banks, for whom it was his fourth torpedoing. Second Officer Rippon continued to serve Alfred Holt, retiring in 1974.

The 4,087-ton tramp *Daisy Moller* had been built in 1911 as the *Pindos* and could manage little more than 8 knots. In mid-December she was on passage from Colombo to Chittagong laden with 'military supplies required for the front' in Burma, including the Royal Engineers' annual quota of twenty-two steam-rollers. She had become something of a joke to the naval authorities. Admiral Sir James Somerville, the Commander-in-Chief, Far East, writing to Admiral Cunningham in London that she made more reports of sightings of Japanese submarines than any other vessel. When Vizagapatam radio received yet another, transmitted by Radio Officer Patrick Healy at 04.20 on the 14th, Somerville's staff 'concluded it was probably just another scare; unfortunately the wolf was there this time and what was worse her boats were rammed and machine gunned by the submarine'. For fear of Japanese submarines from Penang operating in the Bay of Bengal, Captain Reginald Weeks had been ordered to hug the coast and keep in shallow water. At the time of the torpedoing the *Daisy Moller* was approaching the Godavari delta, no more than three miles offshore, a small consolation as the ship began to sink, struck in way of the two forward holds. All seventy-five on board escaped, most in three lifeboats, the gunners aft by rafts. As they gathered their wits and watched their ship submerge amid a welter of bubbles and white water, *R-110* surfaced a short distance away. Weeks afterwards deposed that the enemy submarine, commanded by Chu-sa (Commander) Ebato Kazuro, then:

> approached my boat after firing tracer bullets at us … approximately three minutes later the sub, rammed my boat at an approximate speed of 16 knots, opening fire with machine guns directly after. I swam to a raft about one and a half miles away. The submarine then rammed the other two boats and machine gunned the water over a large area.[61]

When a tug arrived in answer to Healy's distress signal it found only fifty-five corpses floating in their bullet-riddled life jackets. Weeks and a dozen men on the rafts had vanished, having paddled clear and hoisted makeshift sails they landed three days later to the southward. On the same day three lascar seamen were found by fishermen clinging to a capsized lifeboat.

A few months later, in February 1944 Nakagawa was back on patrol, this time off the Maldives in *I-37*. On the 22nd he torpedoed the British Tanker Co.'s *British Chivalry*, Captain Walter Hill, which was in ballast. The explosion in the engine room killed six people but fifty-three got away in two lifeboats. While Chief Officer Payne in the motor lifeboat collected the two floating but empty rafts, the submarine surfaced a mile away and opened fire with her deck gun, concentrating upon despatching the *British Chivalry* whose empty tanks remained intact after the torpedo strike. Closing his quarry, Nakagawa was obliged to fire a second torpedo at short range before approaching Payne's boat and motioning it alongside. Payne answered in the negative when a voice asked for the master and he was ordered to tow Hill's boat alongside. Having done so, Payne watched Hill clamber onto the casing before his boat back-watered away in the charge of Second Officer Mountain.

As *I-37* moved away, Payne ran alongside Mountain's boat and passed a line and began to tow in the opposite direction. A moment later he was aware that the submarine had swung round and was coming up astern fast. As it did so, machine guns opened fire and most of Payne's men jumped overboard, though several of Mountain's failed to do so as they came under a withering fire. For over an hour Nakagawa quartered the area, indiscriminately shooting at anything that moved. Those in the water feigned dead, or were too terrified to move, treading water in a dread of instant death. As Nakagawa withdrew, Payne gathered the survivors together, thirty-nine in all, though five were in a bad way. Plugging the bullet holes as best he could, Payne garnered all he could, then hoisted sail and headed west, maintaining his course for thirty-seven days. He lost only one more of the wounded men before being seen by the British motor-vessel *Dulane* on 29 March.

Meanwhile, on the late evening of 26 February, Nakagawa had sunk James Nourse's *Sutlej*, Captain Dennis Jones, on her way from Kosseir towards Fremantle with a cargo of 9,700 tons of rock phosphates.[62] The torpedo struck the ship between Nos 1 and 2 Holds, sending a choking cloud of phosphate dust high into the air and causing the ship to begin a rapid descent to the seabed. The crew had insufficient time to launch any lifeboats, but several rafts floated free onto which Chief Engineer Richard Rees, among others, managed to struggle in the darkness. Rees was surrounded by a considerable number of bobbing life-jacket lights, estimating that a good number of the seventy-three crew and gunners had escaped. Many swam towards the rafts and Rees was hauling them on board when they were suddenly illuminated by a searchlight as *I-37* approached, a voice asking for the *Sutlej*'s master. Learning that he had been lost with his ship, Nakagawa washed aside the raft in an attempt to ram, before beginning to strafe the area with machine gun fire. There were other rafts with survivors on them and Nakagawa cruised among these for an hour, firing at them.

Captain Jones, forty of his crew and nine DEMS gunners were lost with the ship. Richard Rees, ten crew and one gunner endured forty-six days on their raft before being sighted by a patrolling flying-boat operating from Diego Garcia. They had drifted some 650 miles by the time they were hauled aboard HM Sloop *Flamingo*, by which time Third Officer Francis Newall, Third Engineer Arthur Bennett, nine crew and one gunner had been picked up by HM Whaler *Solva* within sight of the Madagascan coast and only ninety miles from Diego Suarez towards which Newall, without compass or charts, had been making. Bennett was awarded Lloyd's War Medal for bravery at sea.

While his victims struggled to survive, Nakagawa had returned to Penang at the end of his war patrol. On the way, shortly after noon on 29 February, he fired a torpedo at the *Ascot*, a tramp steamer owned by Watts, Watts & Co. She was on a voyage from Calcutta and Colombo to Diego Suarez and Port Louis, Mauritius, laden with linseed oil, gunnies, wax, pig-iron, coconuts and fibre, part of a general cargo of 9,000 tons. Although the torpedo explosion in the engine room wrecked the *Ascot*'s starboard boats and caused a heavy list, she came upright as she foundered and Captain James Travis and most of his men abandoned the ship by way of one port lifeboat, others taking to a single raft. Again Nakagawa surfaced and shelled the sinking ship before turning his attention to the crew, asking for the master. From the raft Apprentice Harold Fortune watched Captain Travis stand up and make himself known, whereupon the boat was ordered alongside and Travis climbed onto *I-37*'s casing. Here he was confronted by an officer, thought to have been Nakagawa who, appearing displeased, slashed at Travis's hand with his sword before having him thrown overboard. The lifeboat's occupants pulled Travis from the sea, by which time *I-37* was under way and turning in an attempt to ram Travis's boat, while machine-gunning indiscriminately before firing some more shells into the *Ascot*, which was now ablaze and settling fast. Nakagawa cruised among the wreckage for some time before disappearing, leaving Travis, thirty-nine of his crew and seven gunners dead. On the rafts Fortune, another apprentice, two seamen, the cook and two gunners remained alive, though one of the last was wounded. Next morning they saw a drifting lifeboat but it was not until the following day that they succeeded in paddling alongside, to discover it contained a wounded gunner, Sergeant Hughson. On the following day they were picked up by the Dutch ship *Straat Soenda* and landed at Aden on 3 March.[63]

By the spring of 1944 Japan was desperately short of shipping of her own. Relying, for their war machine, upon imports of raw materials from Manchukuo, China and their conquests in South-East Asia, the Japanese High Command had never bothered to organise their merchantmen into convoy, a fact exploited by American submarines. Consequently the Japanese determined to seize as many Allied merchant ships as possible and in February Tai-sho (Admiral) Takasu Shiro, Commander-in-Chief, South West Area Fleet, ordered Chu-sho (Vice Admiral) Sakonju Naomasa with his flag in the heavy cruiser *Aoba* to carry out a sweep through the Indian Ocean in quest of ships. With *Aoba*, Sakonju had under his orders the cruisers *Tone* and *Chikuma*. Takasu's instructions to Sakonju included specific orders to destroy any captured ships' crews, excepting only the masters and radio officers from whom it was thought intelligence could be gleaned. On 28 February the three cruisers cleared the Sunda Strait and entered the Indian Ocean, carrying out a wide sweep towards the Cocos Islands and cutting the India – Australia trade-route, but to no avail. Sakonju turned north, his warships advancing well apart in line abreast, and on the forenoon of 9 March, despite a low mist, the lookout high in the *Tone* spotted the low silhouette of a British merchant ship.

This was the *Behar*, a virtually new ship, owned by the Hain S.S. Co., P&O's tramping subsidiary.[64] She was unusual in having been constructed not as a war-standard ship, but under special licence to her owners' specifications. The twin-screw motor-vessel had been completed the previous year by Barclay, Curle & Co. on the Clyde, and had a service speed of 16.5 knots. Fitted with accommodation for twelve passengers, she had nine on board that morning, including two ladies, a retired Australian bank manager, three Royal New Zealand naval officers, one RAF Flight Sergeant, Dr Lai Young Li, and Captain P.J. Green, a master in Jardine, Matheson's Indo-China S.S.Co. She was also unusual in being heavily armed with a dual-purpose 4-inch, and a 3-inch gun, besides Oerlikons, a Browning machine-gun, rocket-projectors, Asdic (sonar) and depth-charges. To serve these she bore fifteen members of the Royal Artillery Maritime Regiment and DEMS Organisation gunners, besides two Asdic operators. Her crew comprised eighteen British officers and engineers and sixty-seven lascar seamen and firemen, commanded by Captain Maurice Symonds.

At about 10.00 Third Mate James Anderson was astonished to see a heavy cruiser loom out of the low mist a couple of miles away, flying the international signal to stop instantly. As Anderson hit the alarms and Symonds ran to the bridge, shouting for Radio Officer Cumming, then on watch, to transmit a distress signal. The 'RRRR' prefixed position and ship's name told anyone listening that the *Behar* was under attack by a surface raider. The instant the signal was intercepted aboard the *Tone*, Tai-sa (Captain) Mayazumi Haruo opened fire. If this was to intimidate his victims, it succeeded; if it was to capture the *Behar*, it did not. Within seconds the *Behar* was on fire from end to end, and even before her gunners could loose a shot, Symonds ordered the ship abandoned. The boats were lowered under bombardment but both Symonds and Chief Officer Phillips searched the accommodation before leaving the ship, aware that some of the passengers were missing. Three were found dead, but five, including the two women, were alive and were escorted over the side, all shortly afterwards being picked up by the lifeboats.

As the *Tone* swept up to the burning *Behar*, the lifeboats were motioned alongside and the survivors scrambled aboard. Captain Green recalling that:

> Arriving on deck I found myself facing six to eight men armed with rifles ready to shoot. Other Japanese sailors removed most of our clothes, leaving us only in shirts and trousers. My hands were then tied tightly behind my back … My arms were forced up behind my back and the rope put round my throat.

The women's hands were also tied, at which Chief Officer William Phillips, 'a heavily built, robust man,' protested. He was savagely beaten with a base-ball bat for his pains. All were then forced to sit in the hot sun before being confined in a small, airless and ill-lit compartment where, apart from short exercise periods, they remained until the *Tone* arrived at Tanjong Priok on 15 March.

Sakonju had been extremely displeased to learn that Mayazumi had sunk the *Behar* and was furious when he learned that he had captured enemy personnel. Not only had a fine ship been needlessly lost to the Japanese war effort, but Sakonju was now encumbered with 108 prisoners. Mayazumi was ordered to dispose of them but had not carried out the order when the squadron arrived off the Javan coast. He reported to Sakonju aboard the *Aoba* and pleaded for clemency. Mayazumi was a Christian, but Sakonju's wrath could not be turned aside: a select number might be taken for intelligence purposes, but the majority must be executed. Unhappily Mayazumi returned aboard the *Tone* where his sympathetic second-in-command, Chu-sa (Commander) Mii refused to carry out the order, obliging Mayazumi to go over Mii's head. The prisoners who were to be taken into captivity were selected: Symonds, Phillips, Chief Engineer Weir, Radio Officer Walker, DEMS Petty Officer Griffiths, the two Asdic operators, twenty-one lascars and six passengers, including Green, Dr Lai and the two women. These were put aboard the *Aoba* on the 18th before the *Tone* weighed anchor and proceeded to sea on her grim task. That evening Mayazumi ordered Tai-i (Lieutenant) Ishiwara and some other junior officers to carry out Sakonju's order. The prisoners were brought on deck, lined up and then each was felled by a blow to the stomach, kicked in the testicles and beheaded.

The reprieved were landed from the *Aoba*. Symonds, Green and Walker were separated and sent to Japan where other merchant seamen and Allied PoWs were obliged to work in the mines. The two women were sent to a women's interment camp. The rest were taken to a camp outside Batavia, isolated from the other PoWs and suffered privation, beatings and interrogation. William Phillips was placed in solitary confinement in a small wooden hut. 'Bound hand and foot, with a bamboo lashed across his throat to prevent sleep ... Phillips kept his sanity ... by forcing himself to do intricate feats of mental arithmetic and studying a young plant seen growing through a tiny window'. Eventually Phillips and the others joined other Allied PoWs, finally being liberated and reaching home in October 1945, to call upon the widow of Second Mate Gordon Rowlandson and the mother of Apprentice Denys Matthews to express his condolences.

Earlier on the day that Ishiwara executed the *Behar* survivors, 18 March 1944, Sho-sa Shimizu Tsuruzo, commander of *I-165*, torpedoed the *Nancy Moller*. She had been laden with South African coal at Durban and was heading for Colombo when the torpedo struck her at around 08.30 that morning. The *Nancy Moller* was about 600 miles short of her destination and settled quickly, taking about one minute to sink. Thanks to the hour, many of her fifty-three crew jumped overboard and one lifeboat floated free, though capsized. Captain James Hansen[65] and Chief Officer Neil Morris were lost and the senior surviving deck-officer was Second Mate Chu Shih Kao from Hong Kong. Chu struggled onto the upturned lifeboat and observed the surfaced submarine approach a pair of rafts onto which several survivors clung and ask for the master. No one knew Hansen's whereabouts, so DEMS gunner Dennis Fryers, the two Chinese and three lascars on the rafts were dragged aboard the submarine. The Chinese were shot in the back and thrown overboard, the two Indian ratings simply kicked into the sea while Fryers was taken below. Shimizu then circled the area machine-gunning any sign of life. Surprisingly thirty-two men survived, though at least one was wounded. Gathering them together on the liferafts Chu ordered them to paddle north. Four days later they were rescued by HM Cruiser *Emerald* and landed at Port Louis, Mauritius, on the 26th.

Further atrocities were committed that day by Chu-sa Ariizumi Tatsunosuke, commander of *I-8*, who sank the Dutch Royal Interocean liner *Tjisalak* some 600-miles south of Ceylon. The ship, though commanded by a Dutch master and officers, had a crew of British Chinese from Hong Kong, her armament was manned by British DEMS gunners and with her passengers she had over one hundred people on board. The DEMS gunners opened fire and this may have precipitated the outrage that followed. All but three of those on board got into the boats but these were ordered alongside *I-8* and all the survivors were ordered aboard the submarine to squat on the forward casing.

[T]he Captain and an American Red Cross nurse were ordered below and not seen again. The boats were cast off and the crew ordered to fall in before and abaft the conning tower with strict instructions they were not to look toward the conning

tower or they would be shot. The Japanese then began to tie the men together
in pairs; on realising what this meant, one of the DEMS crew resisted and was
promptly shot; this was a signal for a general massacre and the unfortunate crew
were killed with tommy guns, axes, swords, crowbars and hammers. The mate [Frits
de Jong], one Lascar [Dhange] and 2 other Europeans fell overboard wounded ...
and after swimming 5 miles regained the boats ... [66]

Admiral Sir James Somerville was mistaken in the precise numbers, as three Dutch
officers escaped, but Ariizumi had submerged *I-8* and only the last lascar on the rope,
the man named Dhange, managed to escape and join the others. Two days later they
saw a ship approaching; it was an American Liberty-ship, the *James A. Wilder*, whose
Armed Guard were characteristically trigger happy and assumed the lifeboat was a
submarine, subjecting the five survivors from the *Tjisalak* to a shelling before realising
their error and rescuing them.[67]

During the War Crimes Tribunals held after the war in Hong Kong, Nakagawa was
arraigned for sinking the Hospital Ship *Centaur*. He attributed the action to the dead
commander of another Japanese submarine known to have been patrolling in the vicinity and since incriminating Japanese documents had gone missing, the case against him
could not be proved. Following the torpedoing of the ship a rumour had been rife that it
was in reprisal for the sinking of a Japanese hospital ship in Rabaul by American aircraft,
but such rumours were, as Stephen Roskill points out, 'impossible to substantiate'. In
1942 the Japanese High Command had issued definitive orders to respect hospital ships
and nothing in Nakagawa's blaming of a dead colleague for the action, suggests otherwise. Nevertheless, he escaped the full rigour of International Law, being sentenced to
eight years' hard labour for his actions against the *British Chivalry*, *Sutlej* and *Ascot*, though
he served only six and lived to the ripe age of eighty-four. Sho-sho Mito received the
same sentence for issuing his extermination order. Sakonju and Mayazumi were also
tried in Hong Kong; the court sentenced the former to death but showed a degree of
leniency to Mayazumi who was imprisoned for seven years. Shimizu Tsuruzo escaped
trial and rose to the rank of Sho-sho (Rear Admiral) in the post-war Japanese Defence
Force. Ariizumi shot himself and Ebato was killed in action. Most of their surviving
victims returned home. Phillips' fate we know, Captain Hill of the *British Chivalry* and
Gunner Fryers of the *Nancy Moller* were interned, Fryers in Changi Gaol, but both lived.

The humane Somerville was rightly concerned when he learned of the frightful
fate of the *Tjisalak*'s people. The following day he forwarded a list of the atrocities
committed by the Japanese 'on the crews of torpedoed ships,' expressing 'the view
that when the news of these ... leaked out there might be a reluctance on the part
of crews to sail in unescorted ships.' The matter of morale among merchant seamen
had been a touchy matter, ever since the disaster of PQ17 in July 1942 and as the war
dragged on it became increasingly acute.

Small things helped improve the lot of the merchant seamen. The 'Merchant Navy
Comforts Service' initiated by Mrs Margaret Watts, wife of Edmund Watts, the manag-

ing owner of Watts, Watts & Co. and promoted through The Marine Society, ensured books, socks, sweaters, scarves and other amenities reached the otherwise neglected merchant seamen. Not all were well received, particularly when bizarre coloured wools were used, or inappropriate designs supplied, particularly to seamen on their way to Russia. Before the war, to increase the public's awareness of merchant shipping, Edmund Watts had founded the Ship Adoption Society which linked a school with an individual ship. But in wartime it gained the additional purpose of keeping-up morale. Letters were exchanged and, occasionally, visits were undertaken. A master, chief engineer or some among the other officers visited schools during their brief leaves, giving lectures and generally raising the profile of 'the Merchant Navy'.

One of the more remarkable of such schemes was initiated aboard Captain Bone's *Cameronia* when she lay at Pier 45 in Manhattan in the spring of 1940. Bone, a long-time visitor to New York, was entertaining American friends when the second officer brought the ship's binoculars into his cabin for safe-keeping whilst in port, a standard procedure on most ships as they were easily stolen. Shortly thereafter word was brought that the *Queen Elizabeth* was coming up the harbour. The brand new Cunarder had arrived in secret, with none of the:

> advance publicity, no excursion steamers to meet her, no convoying aeroplanes overhead, no flurry of newsmen and photographers, no civic receptions, when the huge grey ghost emerged from the Atlantic mists off Sandy Hook on the morning of 7th March 1940 and berthed quietly and efficiently at her up-town pier ... she bore no streaming flags at her mastheads ... Grim and grey, she wore only the Red Ensign of the British Merchant Navy on the staff above her massive stern.

Bone and his guests went on deck to watch her, several of them picking up binoculars from those laid down a few moments earlier. What they thought of the new liner, Bone does not record, but their opinion of the binoculars he does: they were poor. Bone explained that the officers usually had their own, and these were those supplied by the company, excusing their quality by saying that despite frequent requisitioning indents, there was a shortage of binoculars in Britain owing to the pre-eminent demands of the Royal Navy. Long before the American government agreed Lend-Lease a private arrangement, known as 'the Binocular Scheme' was initiated from a bookstore in New York which, through the British Consul-General in New York, arranged for loaned binoculars to be supplied to British masters on the understanding that they would be returned in better times. Bone had a pair lent by a Senator to replace his own worn-out Zeiss glasses, and in 1945 returned them from Singapore.

> I have the thought of having them reconditioned before sending them back to you. The lenses have been well looked after, only the rounds are scratched a little by the rub-rub of uniform buttons. But perhaps you would prefer to have the sentimental (and even historic) interest in the binoculars preserved, for they have seen much since 1940.[68]

In the early part of the war the British public had little appreciation of the Merchant Navy's contribution to the war effort, indifference that played upon the merchant seafarer's inherent self-image of an underdog. There were many examples of poor treatment, disregard or insult, many of them petty but many of which stung the victim and not all were as forgiving as Ronald McBrearty.

> I remember once in the early days in a period known as the 'phoney war' I was almost elbowed out of a bus queue by some young army recruits because I was not in uniform. I wasn't so old myself, at twenty-four, but I had been at sea since 1931 and made a few wartime crossings of the Atlantic at the time. Still, they were not to know.

What hurt most were the real injustices, particularly those based on the ancient dictum that freight was the mother of wages, such as the stoppage of pay when a ship sank, and the consequent failure to maintain allotments to dependants. And while such disregard for a man might be considered as no more than one could expect of a capitalist shipowner, the indifference of some trade unions to real hardships was incomprehensible. Far worse was the state's occasional inability to understand the torpedoed mariner's predicament. One young man who, having been frost-bitten whilst adrift in a lifeboat in the Barents Sea, subsequently suffered amputation for gangrene in a Soviet hospital. He was not repatriated for many months but when he did return home he was dismayed to find an income tax demand on wages he had never been paid. What made this so hard to bear, he said years afterwards in a radio broadcast, was the subsequent failure of the Inland Revenue to apologise for an error.

Over time things changed. Second Radio officer Eric Ranalow had found he had transgressed by wearing his Merchant Navy uniform in a smart swimming club in colonial Singapore in 1940; later 'the Merchant Navy became more "respectable" and was welcomed in places where they would not have been allowed in previous years'. Ranalow also extols the virtues of the mail service that ensured letters reached seamen often in remote places, particularly when their ships were being used as transports on charter to the MoWT in support of military operations. On the other hand the reception accorded to survivors who had left their ships without papers and in the clothes they either stood up in or had been sleeping in, depended entirely upon where they were landed. Perhaps the most extreme example was that of Cadet David Jones who had been taking a shower when the *Quebec City*, mentioned earlier, had been torpedoed. He was naked when he left his ship and remained so for the fortnight his lifeboat took to sail 1,000 miles before pitching up on the Liberian coast. Here, confronting native fishermen, a shipmate handed him a scarf to wear as a loincloth. Once Jones and his fellows reached Freetown, Sierra Leone, they had to be processed and issued with papers to establish their right to British nationality prior to repatriation. Others landing with little or nothing, found their reception cold and unfeeling; some complained that too much burden was thrown upon the charitable missions and other Christian or socialist organisations and that, although every man got a fortnight's survivor's leave, the monetary compensation to refit himself with clothes, uniform and, in the case of masters and mates, re-equip with new sextant, binoculars, nautical tables and so forth, was quite inadequate. However, once the

Left: Wearing the unusual insignia of a torpedoed mariner, Captain F.J. Hunter wears the cap-badge of Stephenson, Clarke, collier owners, for whom he worked after the First World War. (© Courtesy of Robert Hunter)

Below: The tramp-steamer *Glenroy* of which Captain Hunter had previously been in command. Lost during the First World War, she was a typical of her type. Painting by Robert Lloyd. (© Courtesy of Robert Hunter)

necessity for proper support was established – and it was this that was tricky – matters were generally better attended to. Most impressive were the arrangements made in the repatriation of large numbers of survivors, such as arrived *en masse* in the aftermath of the *Laconia* affair and has already been related.

The often difficult interaction between the seafarer and his shore-going counterpart was only exaggerated by war, not created by it. The shore officials, from the Shipping-Master supervising his local Mercantile Marine Office at the signing-on, to the Customs Officers who performed the last rites of discharge following a foreign voyage, were all in a sense Merchant Jack's traditional 'enemies'. He was used to their miserable strictures and took them in his stride; they were evils necessary to the pursuit of his calling and had little effect upon his self-esteem. What he found difficult was the perception of himself as a second-class citizen *vis-à-vis* the Royal Navy, a perception etched deep by war's propinquities and which found its confirmation and articulation in the rumours surrounding the disastrous Convoy PQ17.

The excoriating effects of PQ17 upon the relationship between the two British sea services had a long-lasting effect, building upon the mutual indifference arising from complex social causes largely based upon class and that English vice, snobbery – along with its complementary inversion as mentioned earlier. It predominated where the contact between the two services was most distant and most anonymous, and where personal relationships could never flourish. When professional ship-masters and naval commanders worked together there was rarely any friction, both parties understanding the tasks and demands of their counterparts. The commanders of large liners perfectly comprehended the distinction granted by a King's commission which placed a naval officer in a functionally superior post, even though his ship might be larger and his crew of equal size. What usually irked were the assumptions of disdain experienced by the mercantile part, with or without justifiable grounds. The social cachet and close-knit *brüderbond* enjoyed by naval officers, had no equivalent in the merchant service where masters, officers and men were mere employees and even joked about their fellow shipmates as mere 'Board of Trade acquaintanceships'.

Among the ratings, nothing equated to the job-security enjoyed by the three-badge blue-jacket for the mercantile jack so recently affected by the Depression. True the naval rating had had his pay dropped to below a living wage, but he had had *something* when thousands of merchant seamen trod the streets for work. *That* was always forgotten when the naval rating complained his merchant cousin received a higher wage and, in war, additional danger-money. And it was long remembered by the men who held certificates of competency as master-mariners and who had been forced to sail as able-seamen in squalid forecastles that no such demotions prevailed in the King's service; while not since 1748 had a naval rating's pay ceased the day his ship was sunk.

Such a dog-in-the-manger attitude was hard to dispel in the face of the rumours that spread after PQ17. That these were misunderstandings did not signify, and the necessary silence of officialdom only seemed, in the collective and aggrieved state-of-mind of many merchant seafarers, to validate their worst opinion of the Admiralty and all its works. What had been inchoate was no longer so. This was a great pity and stemmed as much from the secrecy which prevailed in all the Merchant Navy's doings. Men did not know where their ships were going next, or the purpose of the special operation that they knew they were part of from the increased security or the unusual cargo, or some other special or peculiar circumstance of their voyage. And while the masters, mates and engineers had sufficient work to occupy them and absorb their intellectual energies, the ratings, who were not necessarily innately less intelligent men, could only speculate. Naturally when the hazards of convoy and the horrors of sudden torpedoing loomed large in every man's imagination, such speculation found fertile ground and in its flourishing it spawned conspiracy theories, wild and unfounded grievances and a general disaffection. This took greatest root in the younger men, those who were at sea because of the war rather than those who had been at sea prior to its outbreak. They were unused to their social obloquy; it ran counter to the propaganda about 'keeping the life-line open'. The Merchant Navy was not alone in suffering a serious dip in its morale towards the end of hostilities; there was a similar mood abroad in the Royal Navy where full-scale mutinies took place. The fact was the nation was weary after five years of war. Unfortunately the case of PQ17, like the oyster's irritant, allowed a mood to accrete and grow into a mighty grievance.

This was a tragedy, for in fact the close working relationship that had been operationally necessary in certain ships had increased the Admiralty's confidence in a considerable number of merchant masters. In the first months of the war when a large merchantman was requisitioned for special service she was usually taken over to become a commissioned ship, flying the white ensign and commanded by a naval post-captain. As the demands and exigencies of war increased, this became more difficult. Masters remained in command when their ships were designated as HM Transports, hoisting the blue ensign and keeping their crews. This integration became even closer-knit when ships were converted to such role as LCI(L)'s – by which was meant Landing Craft Infantry (Large). Such vessels had landing craft slung on either side in place of lifeboats; they embarked a division for the purpose of landing its soldiers upon an enemy-held shore and they were remarkably successful. Captain Bone commanded one such vessel, HMT *Circassia*, taking part in Operations TORCH, HUSKY and BIGOT, this last on the Vichy French Riviera. While the human cargo he brought to the front-line came from the army, the men who carried them from the ship to the beach in the fourteen landing-craft *Circassia* bore, were all naval, some thirty officers and 200 ratings. Bone wrote of the experience with his customary insight and good sense.

> With over two hundred naval shipmates aboard, it was well we had the advantage of a shake-down cruise; for, when we returned to the Gareloch to await the next turn of the adventure, there was reasonable amity below decks between the lions and the lambs of our large joint manning. It would be invidious to mention who was who in that connection, for there was nationality and its ancient grudges in the admixture. The merchant crew were Clydesiders to a man and the bulk of the naval party came from the South of England. It was only natural that there should be claim and counter-claim, but it was the comparison of service that provoked most of the controversy. The naval seaman was envious of the merchantman's greater wages and had his understandable gibe for the 'danger money' in current effect; he saw preference too in the statutory comforts of the fo'c's'les as compared with the bare troop-decks

in which he had to sling his hammock. On the training period we did not long have troops embarked and doubtless, seeing idlers amongst the catering staff, he had his ideas about the sharing of ship-work. On our part we were inclined to look upon the navy men as passengers, not dissimilar to the drafts we had so often trooped abroad. We did not know then that we would be teamed together for nearly two years.

Our relations with the naval officers were good, but it was undeniable that many juniors had reason for complaint about their quarters ... and it was unfortunate that nothing could be done to relieve the pressure ... The division of authority was quite another matter, and there were points upon which argument arose. What was done by or in the landing craft when away from the ship was in no way my business, but it was as well to be agreed on the manner of their approach when returning alongside. The flotilla officers and cox'ns were all young and impetuous, which is as it should be for such a special service, but they had their way of boring into my ship with their awkward square bows ... There were too many bumps and bruises ... and I thought it opportune to read a riot act concerning such over-hearty boardings. It was ... agreed that craft making alongside should come under ship's orders and, for a time, the old-fashioned hand megaphone was used. Old fashioned merchant-ship profanity burst from it on occasion ... [and] we and they toned down in the course of exercises.

When, eventually, the *Circassia* ceased to be a LCI(L) and returned to the task of ordinary trooping towards the end of the war, there was an air of sadness as the naval party departed. The bosun's pipes summoned them:

with perhaps a special flourish [and they mustered] to embark in the [landing] craft for the last lowering from the ship they had served in. They were in high spirits ... From the bridge and for the last time I spoke 'Lower aa-way' in the loud hailer and they were quickly gone ... The ship looked strangely lean and narrow with the empty falls dangling overside and the landing craft that she had nursed for so long gone away into the rain and mist.[69]

Besides their traditional role of carrying cargoes, the important part merchantmen played in combined operations, in the re-supply and support of many fighting fronts almost beggars belief and can hardly be overemphasised. Their roles were extensive, whether they were partially adopted by the Royal Navy as specialist vessels like the *Circassia*; or as transports such as the *Melbourne Star, Brisbane Star, Port Chalmers, Rochester Castle, Glenorchy, Waimarama, Deucalion* and *Dorset* and the borrowed tanker *Ohio* whose participation in Operation PEDESTAL of August 1942 prevented the surrender of Malta. There were many other diverse roles, such as the *Anglo-African* which was specially fitted out to handle mule-pack divisions of the Indian Army, landing them on beach-heads in the Lebanon, Italy and the French Riviera. All contributed to deny the enemy having his way and are among the forgotten elements of victory.[70] But they were nevertheless elemental in all senses of the word.

The exploits of these ships all merit mention, but this is impossible; instead, the brief tales of four lonely merchantmen will perforce suffice to illustrate the dependence

placed upon them in the extraordinary circumstances of war. The difficulties in supplying Malta are obvious once France had fallen and Italy had entered the war. Unlike
the trade convoys of the North Atlantic, every convoy forced through from either
Gibraltar or Alexandria required a major naval presence often outnumbering the small
selected fast cargo-liners being escorted. However, maintaining a regular run of such
scale was impossible and expedience led to the notion of periodically despatching
individual ships, an idea which appears to have come, at least anecdotally, from the
owner of Stanhope Shipping, the young and enterprising Jack Billmeir. As noted in
an earlier chapter, Billmeir had made a fortune during the Spanish Civil War, having
founded his company in 1934. It is thought that he had a measure of tacit approval
from the British Government and that this had given him the ear of the Establishment.
In 1940 he acquired the Pyman Brothers' ageing steamers *Welcombe* and *Parracombe*
and in April of the following year the latter lay in Leith after sustaining some mine-
damage. She was generally in a poor state of repair having made a bruising voyage
across the Atlantic and one cannot escape the conclusion that, with his history of successful arms-running, Billmeir sought to repeat this enterprise and profit from Malta's
extremity. Given the rather different circumstances, this was an appalling gamble but it
chimed well with the desire to run supplies to the beleaguered island fortress.

At this time the *Parracombe*'s master was Captain David Edward Jones. He had previously commanded the *Stanwell*, one of Billmeir's blockade-runners during the Spanish
Civil War, and had endured the heavy aerial bombardment in Tarragona in March
1938 previously narrated. Some confusion appears to have occurred in the Admiralty
where it was thought that this Captain Jones was none other than the famous 'Potato'
Jones whose exploits had earned a price being put upon his head by Franco. In the
event this was of no consequence since he was replaced as master of the *Parracombe*
by Captain David Llewellyn Hook, another veteran blockade-runner of the Spanish
war. Only Hook knew of the importance of the voyage he was about to make under
Admiralty orders and which Their Lordships had designated Operation TEMPLE.
Better informed, the knowing dock labourers assured the joining crew that they were
off somewhere dangerous, adding that they would probably be blown-up long before
they reached their destination. The *Parracombe* was loaded with a military cargo, including twenty-one crated Hurricane fighters, anti-aircraft gun-barrels and ammunition,
while the ship's decks were encumbered with boom-defence equipment.

Leaving Leith, the *Parracombe* sailed to Oban where six RAF ground-crew signed-
on as shilling-a-month supernumeraries. Also joining was the anti-fascist Spanish
merchant master Luis Diaz de Lassaga who, having found himself in Britain during
the final months of the Spanish Civil War, decided to remain. The *Parracombe* left
Oban in Convoy OG59, but when west of Gibraltar, in accordance with his orders,
Hook left the protection of the escorts and steamed on alone. It was now that he
assembled the crew and told them what they were up to. Their ship, he assured
them, was sufficiently nondescript to arouse few suspicions as she posed as a neutral Spaniard, a subterfuge given greater credibility that night when the *Parracombe*
was stopped, stages were rigged and a Spanish name along with the red and gold of
the Spanish national ensign were painted on the ship's rusty topsides. Capitano De
Lassaga conned the vessel through the Strait with the Spanish ensign flying, keeping

her close to the Moroccan shore and the Spanish enclave of Ceuta, under the bee-
tling mass of Sidi Musa. That night, as they approached the border with Vichy French
Algeria, the ship was again stopped, the Spanish flag overside was painted out and the
tricolore hoisted. Her name was changed to *Oued-Kroum* and this seemed to disarm the
suspicions of a questing Italian aeroplane that buzzed them later in the day.

By 2 May the *Parracombe* was approaching Cape Bon and Hook assembled his
officers to explain that they would double the Cape and set course as if making for
Sfax in Tunisia. Under the cover of darkness the stokehold would be double-manned,
speed increased, and the *Parracombe* would head for Malta, 200 miles away. He withheld the information that the area was heavily mined and he only knew of the British
minefields, brushing aside any argument that the *Parracombe*'s boilers might not stand
the strain. In the event they encountered a fatal mine which exploded the ammunition in her holds and this 'tore the bottom out of her and carried away the bridge
and killed those left on the boat-deck'. The *Parracombe* sank rapidly, 'with a screaming
crowd hanging on her starboard rail aft,' recalled Able-Seaman Stanley Sutherland.
'Our appeals for them to jump were all in vain. They went down with her,' a total
of thirty men. Eighteen, including Hook and Diaz, were left struggling in the water
and several were severely wounded, including Sutherland's step-brother and Second
Mate John Wilson whose right arm was hanging by a strip of flesh. Several found
refuge of sorts on a boom-defence flotation tank that had broken free of the sinking ship, others scrambled aboard a raft. Thirty-six hours later they were picked up
by Vichy French seaplanes and flown to Bizerta where an Arab fireman died. They
were then moved on to Tunis and, having been vilified and spat upon, the survivors
were interned at a Vichy camp at El Kef, near Sfax and endured months of miserable boredom, poor food and indifferent treatment, sustained largely by the popular
Hook's sing-songs. Later they were joined by survivors from other ships sunk during
operations to maintain Malta and in due course moved to Sfax. Sutherland and others
proved unruly prisoners, suffering reprisals for the problems they caused their guards
and being moved to Bordj le Boeuf, eventually escaping by stealing a train to make
contact with the Allied forces coming ashore as part of Operation TORCH. They
were repatriated aboard the troopship *Orontes*.

News of the *Parracombe*'s fate reached London by way of the American Embassy,
though the details were kept from the crew's relatives for some time and even Lloyd's
were obliged to suppress the information of her loss. Churchill, learning of it, penned
a curious note to the First Sea Lord, Admiral Sir Dudley Pound.

> This is a pretty humble role for the Admiralty to play. I should like to know the
> reason why merchant seamen in a poor little tramp steamer carry out Hurricanes
> vitally needed by Malta, while the Royal Navy has to be kept far from these dan-
> gers. I never thought we should come to this.[71]

As evidence of the confusion caused by the Welsh surname Jones, Churchill later
wrote, 'I was never an enthusiast for this project. I trust "Potato" Jones is saved'. This is
Churchill at his disingenuous best, for not only were two more operations mounted
to supply Malta in this way, but the method was transferred to Arctic waters. Insofar as

Malta was concerned, a subsequent solitary passage by the *Empire Guillemot* made that September did prove successful, but a follow-up in November made by the *Empire Defender* and *Empire Pelican* was a disaster, both ships being sunk. The two ships were owned by the MoWT but had been placed under the management of Dene Shipping of St Helen's Place, Bishopsgate.

Churchill certainly knew of a later but similar plan which, after Convoy PQ18, in the hiatus in regular convoys caused by the drawing off of warships to support Operation TORCH, attempted to keep a nominal quantity of supplies flowing to North Russia. Roosevelt wanted PQ19 to run, but this was impossible, so, mindful of Stalin's attitude to the Royal Navy after PQ17 and the insistence by the Russians that their own ships be returned to them, it was decided to send some merchantmen singly through the Barents Sea. Two Soviet ships, the *Friedrich Engels* and the *Belomorcanal* had made it safely in August, but by October the season was far advanced. However, any ships trying to run the gauntlet would be able to proceed under cover of the long periods of darkness in the high Arctic. Moreover, a crisis of the war was forming around Stalingrad, and anything that supported the Soviet Union at this juncture had to be attempted. Thus the project, the burden of which fell entirely upon British, American and Soviet merchant ships, was unequivocally politically motivated, and went under the innocuous name of Operation FB, predictably translated by some taking part as 'Foolish Bastards.' In explaining why Operation FB was to be mounted in place of PQ19, Churchill cabled Roosevelt in early October 1942 to state, incorrectly, that all the ships involved would be British 'for which the crews will have to volunteer, the dangers being terrible, and their sole hope if sunk far from help being Arctic clothing and such heating arrangements as can be placed in the lifeboats'. These two assumptions were crass. The only 'Arctic clothing' available to merchant navy crews at this time were pullovers, scarves, hats and gloves knitted by the good women of Great Britain and collected and shared out by the Merchant Navy Comforts Service. The 'heating arrangements' were, of course, non-existent.

As for the potential crews, the rumours and half-truths that had swirled around accounts of PQ17 remained uppermost in the minds of many. Volunteers only came forward when bonuses were offered of £100 for each officer and £50 per rating, not from public funds as one might expect in the circumstances, but from the eccentric Jack Billmeir who had himself accompanied one of his ships to North Russia by way of 'fact-finding'. In the event, in the last days of October and first few of November, at roughly twelve hourly intervals alternating British and American merchant ships with an additional Russian, the *Dekabrist*, set off from Iceland. In all thirteen sailed, 'protected' by submarine patrols and a handful of anti-submarine trawlers strung out along their route. Astonishingly five ships arrived safely, but four were lost to the enemy and one, the *Chulmleigh*, ran aground on Spitsbergen's South Cape, afterwards being despatched by *U-625*.[72] The loss of life was heavy, only a few surviving from the sunken ships, and in view of this three further ships, two British and one American, were recalled.[73]

The ordeal of the tramp-steamer *Chulmleigh*, however, emphasises the desperation of the plan and the fatal intervention of distant management, once again that of the Admiralty. Owned by W.J. Tatem & Co, whose chairman was the self-made Lord Glanely, the *Chulmleigh* had been loaded at Philadelphia for the cancelled Convoy PQ19. Her master was Captain D.M. Williams and although he was thirty-five years old, this was his first command. In addition to his regular crew, Williams had a mixed complement of eighteen gunners, part naval from the DEMS organisation to man the after 4-inch, part from the Marine Regiment of Artillery to handle the single 40mm Bofors guns, the four 20mm Oerlikons and two Marlin machine-guns fitted to the *Chulmleigh*. The ship was to be routed north of Jan Mayen, then thirty-miles south of Spitsbergen before swinging south towards the White Sea, which was already icing up. It would mean a passage of 2,500 miles, most of it in darkness or crepuscular gloom and speed was urged on him at his pre-departure briefing by the naval control officers at Hvalfjord.

The weather was against the *Chulmleigh* from the beginning; overcast skies, haze and snowstorms deprived Williams of anything other than dead-reckoning from the outset and he made his alteration of course off Jan Mayen on this basis, shortly after midnight on 3 November. An azimuth of a star taken during a brief break in the scud to determine the error of the compass showed that this was 8° out, unsurprising in such high latitudes, but scarcely reassuring and constantly compounding the errors inherent in dead-reckoning. In addition the airwaves were alive with distress calls coming from the FB ships ahead and at 01.00 on the 5th the *Chulmleigh* received a signal from the Admiralty ordering Williams to maintain a northerly course until he reached the 77th Parallel before turning east to pass south of Spitsbergen. Anxious about his position, Williams delayed obeying for four hours in the hope of getting a decent fix. At 11.00 a BV138 flying-boat suddenly loomed out of the cloud, adding to Williams's anxieties and initiating the fear of air attack among the crew. An hour later the noon dead-reckoning position indicted they had reached a latitude of 77° North and Williams altered course to the south-east. The daylight had vanished by mid-afternoon, shut in by thick snow and a rising southerly gale presaged by an increasingly heavy swell. Considering himself clear of Spitsbergen's South Cape, at midnight Williams brought his ship's head up to due east.

The *Chulmleigh*'s actual position was, in fact, only twenty miles distant from where the dead-reckoning of Williams and his mates put her, but it was twenty-miles *north* and at 00.30 on 6 November, the *Chulmleigh* ran aground on a reef extending a few hundred yards from the South Cape of Spitsbergen, driving so far over the rocks that only her stern was aground when she came to a standstill. It was the worst kind of misfortune; at any moment the ship might break her back and this possibility unnerved some of the crew when Williams ordered the boats launched as a precaution. The third mate's was lowered carelessly, one fall ran away and the two men in the boat were needlessly pitched into the freezing sea. The other boats were lowered successfully, despite the surge of water alongside, and only Williams, Ernest Fenn the mate, and Second Engineer Middlemiss remained on board. Fenn began sounding round the ship, the confidential books were ditched and at this point Williams heard the cries of the two men thrown out of Third Mate Clark's boat. The boats had difficulty manoeuvring until Williams called one of them back alongside, clambered into it himself and with the aid of the boatswain and an apprentice, hauled one of the swimmers to safety; the second was already dead. Climbing back aboard the *Chulmleigh*, Williams consulted Fenn and Middlemiss with a view to raising steam. By recovering some of the men from the boats, an attempt was made to drive the ship ahead, over and off the reef but this failed. In the extreme conditions the ship offered more shelter than the boats, but the men were unwilling to reboard and, in the knowledge that the bond attaching them to the ship ended with her loss, they were not anxious to stay. In a sense they were justi-fied for, having lain close to the ship until a little light showed them a way clear of the breakers, they were pounced upon by five Ju88 dive-bombers which set the ship on fire.

Williams knew that a mining settlement existed 150 miles to the northward, so course was set accordingly. One boat proved slow, so all hands were gathered in two boats, twenty-eight in Williams's and twenty-nine in Fenn's, but darkness soon separated them. Williams's boat made progress until the 8th when a brief calm was fol-lowed by a gale, obliging them to heave-to under a sea anchor. Williams was driven to bullying his men to prevent them falling into the lassitude that comes over men suf-fering from hypothermia. When daylight returned they found themselves out of sight of land, but the boat's motor was started and shortly afterwards they again sighted not only the inhospitable coastline but Fenn's boat. This put new heart into everyone and it was decided that, since the master's boat possessed an engine, Williams should pro-ceed and get help. Nightfall brought a fierce wind and a deathly chill. Freezing spray covered the boat. In the early hours of the 10th Chief Steward Islwyn Davies, aged thirty, died and was slid overboard. Later they sighted the entrance to the Icefjord but when the engine died, so did morale. The donkeyman began to rave and Williams slipped into unconsciousness. Matters devolved onto the shoulders of twenty-year-old Third Mate David Clark who was himself suffering from frost-bitten feet. Shortly before noon on the 11th, the wind being favourable, Clark ordered sail hoisted; it took a long time, the men's minds numbed by the cold, their frozen hands unre-sponsive, thirst and hunger consuming what little resolution they had left. At last it was done and Clark headed east, closing the shore but unable to find a landing place before the pitiless dark returned. It was now that Clark rose to the occasion, staking everything on a desperate gamble. Ordering the sails dowsed, the oars were shipped and the men made to pull directly for the land. He was rewarded by the distant glitter of the lights of the Russian mining settlement at Barentsburg.

At about 03.00 on the 12th in a confusion of oar looms and breaking waves the boat rode over a reef on a swell, wallowed briefly and was then thrown up a stony beach. Men and gear tumbled about, oblivious to the damage being done to their nerveless extremities. The conscious dragged the unconscious clear of the wreck and the freezing sea. Three dead men were abandoned in the shallows. Unbelievably, a row of seal-trappers' huts confronted them in which they sought shelter from the bitter wind and fell instantly asleep. Next morning Clark discovered a small stock of tinned food and coffee; added to the stores remaining in the lifeboat, this made a passable meal, restoring a measure of hope. Driftwood provided a fire but the thawing effect revealed gangrene and its accompanying stench: they were all suffering from frost-bite and immersion foot, Clark particularly so, and during the following four days, thirteen men died of gangrenous septicaemia. Williams began a slow recovery, encouraging the fittest men to forage. Meanwhile Clark and one of the MRA gunners, Richard Peyer, decided to make for Barentsburg. Blizzards drove them back three times, though during the last attempt they did discover further dry stores in another hut. Christmas now approached; they were supine, exhausted by the cold, gangrenous and stinking;

all hope had dwindled as they ran out of food. Only water and a little blubber oil remained and it was now a desperate Williams who overcame his weaknesses. With a small, hard-bitten gunner and former Liverpool docker named Reginald Whiteside, Williams took up the task of reaching Barentsburg. Within hours they too had returned and all seemed utterly lost. Another man died on Christmas Eve and, with his anxieties for Fenn – whose fate had already been sealed – Williams determined on another attempt to reach help, leaving with Peyer and Whiteside. They did not get far.

On 2 January 1943 Whiteside left the hut in search of fuel. They were now burning the adjacent huts and only nine men remained alive, their stinking limbs putrescent. A moment later Whiteside barged into the hut, apparently demented. He was shortly afterwards followed by two white-clad Norwegian soldiers on a routine patrol. Emptying their knapsacks for the wretched seamen, they went for help. Early on the 3rd two sledges arrived and evacuated Clark and Boatswain Hardy. They left a doctor with the others until more sledges arrived on the 4th. That evening the remaining survivors arrived at Barentsburg, only twelve miles away, to be hospitalised. The nine survivors had endured fifty-three days but at a terrible price. Clark did not live to see the arrival of two cruisers, HMSs *Bermuda* and *Cumberland*, to replenish the Norwegian garrison four months later. The survivors were landed at Thurso on 15 June while the wrecked *Chulmleigh* was bombed again and finally torpedoed by Benker in *U-625*. There had been no heating in the lifeboats and the bones of some lie, like those of their ship, in the bleak and terrible beauty of the high Arctic.

The Russia-run provides two more examples of the extremities to which war put British merchantmen. The first was that of a another tramp, the *Empire Starlight*, one of a handful of *Empire*-type steamers built for the MoWT in the Taikoo Dockyard before Hong Kong fell to the Japanese. She was placed under the management of the well-known tramping firm, Ropner & Co. of West Hartlepool and commanded by Captain William Stein, also of West Hartlepool, who had passed for master in 1930. Her crew consisted of seventy-seven: fourteen British officers, twelve DEMS gunners and fifty-one Chinese and she had sailed to Murmansk as part of Convoy PQ13 in March 1942 after a dreadful passage during which an Arctic storm had scattered the ships. When the weather abated, Stein found his ship isolated with a handful of others but without escort. They were attacked by Ju88s on several occasions and their passage was further obstructed by ice. Stein pressed on alone and finally reached his destination, though several of the others were not so fortunate.

Murmansk was only a few minutes flying-time from the front-line and the *Empire Starlight* had hardly secured to her berth on 3 April before her ordeal began with a heavy bombing raid. Along the quay the cargo of ammunition aboard the *New Westminster City*, owned by Smith's of Cardiff and commanded by a Captain Harris, was detonated by four bombs. Near misses close to the *Empire Starlight* strained her plating and started several leaks. The engineers began pumping operations, the Chinese crew working tirelessly to plug the leaking seams. Next day, while engaged in discharging cargo, another air raid began. A heavy bomb burst in No.1 Hold, killing six Russian dockers and starting a fire in No.2 as four more bombs detonated alongside. Eight army lorries and three Hurricane fighters were destroyed, though the ship's guns were manned and formed part of the defences of Murmansk. Unusually, the Soviet authorities accredited the ship with the destruction of a German aircraft. By the morning of the 5th the fire had been extinguished and the crew toiled to save the *Empire Starlight* as she again came under attack but without any further damage. Two more air raids were made the following day and most of the survivors from the *New Westminster City* were taken on board.

Next day the ship's discharge was completed and she endured further attacks on the 8th, moving off the berth to anchor in the river until the 13th when she returned alongside to begin loading a homeward cargo of pit-props and timber. The attacks on her now occurred daily. Cargo continued to be worked and repair parties made good the damage, keeping her afloat until the evening of 15 April, when eight bombs straddled her and one exploded in No.2 Hold. The damage was severe, with the bilge-line fractured and flooding the hold, open seams admitted water into the fore-peak, No.3 Hold and the engine room. The crew, assisted by Russian divers, strove to save her, for she had become a symbol of their combined defiance against the common enemy. They resorted to exertions of heroic optimism; softwood plugs, cement boxes, tarpaulins, rags and cotton waste were pressed into use and water was pumped out of all spaces save for No.2 Hold.

On the 14th they were joined by the survivors of the *Lancaster Castle*, bombed while anchored in the stream. It was now doubtful if there was any purpose in continuing to load the *Empire Starlight*. As a precaution she left the berth and was moved upriver to Michakov where a measure of peace was found for a few days but on the 23rd the *Luftwaffe* again paid a visit but were met by the ship's gunfire. Two raids were beaten off the next day with still more the following morning, another at noon and a third in the evening, when three Ju88s maintained a 'criss-cross running attack'. The cumulative damage from near misses and straddling bomb-bursts now proved increasingly serious. The *Empire Starlight*'s bottom plates began to fail, the bulkhead between Nos 4 and 5 Holds began to collapse, but the ship's furious barrage brought down a third Ju88. On 24 April she was again straddled, after which she was left alone until 5 May when the attacks resumed. Four air raids followed on the 6th and the ship's company began to show signs of exhaustion. Throughout this whole period, while the DEMS gunners and their assistants manned their guns, the ship's engineers under Chief Engineer Morgan, attempted to plug leaks and pump the ship out. Despite the success of the German bombers, they failed to kill any of the *Empire Starlight*'s crew except for one poor Chinese steward who was ashore in an air-raid shelter when it sustained a direct hit, but the constant struggle to keep the ship afloat and the increasing impossibility of this, sapped their will. By the 17th the pumps could not contain the water pouring into Nos 1 and 3 Holds and Stein moved his ship into shallower water. Further help from the hard-pressed Russians was not forthcoming. The *Empire Starlight* was bombed daily on the 18th, 19th and 20th and on the 21st further bombs from seven separate air raids started new leaks. Two attacks came on the 22nd and the 23rd and on the 24th five raids damaged the shaft tunnel. At 17.00 on the 25th, six bombs straddled the ship and, with a roar, the bulkhead between Nos 1 and 2 Hold gave way, allowing water to flood through from No.2 to No.1 Hold. The *Empire Starlight* began to settle by the head.

There were five raids on the 26th. At 11.00 the bombing increased the leaking forward so that water poured into No.3 Hold. Shortly after 17.00, a 'sustained and heavy attack was deliberately aimed at the *Empire Starlight'* by six Ju88s, three unidentified but four-engined bombers and three Stuka Ju87s. The ship's air-barrage was superb and not one bomb hit its target but the near-miss effects of an estimated forty bombs proved fatal. The ship began to sink and Stein ordered the crew ashore. Incredibly, they returned the following day to resume their efforts to save her. For a while these were partially rewarded by a failure of the *Luftwaffe* to return, but on 1 June this hiatus came to an end. A stick of six bombs burst along the ship's port side and were followed into the water by the aircraft dropping them: the gallant ship had had her day. The crew removed everything they could and abandoned the *Empire Starlight* on 16 June. The survival of all but one of her crew and the exceptional and persistent anti-aircraft defence were outstanding but, after their return home, on 20 January 1943, Stein and Morgan received only OBEs, civilian honours and not comparable with the DSCs with which Captain Hook and Second Officer Wilson of the *Parracombe* received because she sailed under Admiralty orders. None of the *Empire Starlight's* crew were honoured as two of the *Parracombe's* able-seamen had been, both receiving Distinguished Service Medals. Stein took over the *Fort Rampart* early in 1943. Homeward bound from Vancouver in convoy, the ship was torpedoed. Six men were lost and Stein went on to command the *Fort Coulonge* in which he remained until the end of the war.

Extraordinary though the ordeals of the *Chulmleigh* and the *Empire Starlight* had been, perhaps the oddest adventure endured by a British merchantman in the war was that of the *Hopemount*. The only tanker owned by the Newcastle firm of Stott, Mann and Fleming, she had been loaded with fuel and gas oil and chartered as a fleet-oiler, forming part of Convoy PQ14. Although attacked by the enemy, she suffered no battle damage, but sustained injury from the ice. Nevertheless she discharged the oil destined for the thirsty convoy escorts and the Royal Naval minesweepers based at Polyarnoe. She was now high enough out of the water to tackle the ice-damage. The sprung plates of her forepeak were drawn together with long bolts and welded, which cured the forward leak, but her bent propeller blades presented a different challenge. The Russians brought to bear 'an enormous blow-lamp, shrouded by canvas curtains to contain the heat' mounted on rickety wooden scaffolding and the bent blades were brutally beaten back into a semblance of their proper shape by Russian labourers who 'worked like hell', the *Hopemount's* chief officer, Arthur Nunn recalled. 'They didn't get it quite right and we always had a period of critical revs when the ship shook, but it worked,' so well, in fact, that the repaired tanker was selected for special service.

Relieved of her duty as a British fleet-oiler, the *Hopemount* was now chartered to the Soviet government and escorted to Molotovsk on the White Sea by HM Minesweepers *Hazard* and *Leda*. Here she loaded oil and her crew were issued with Arctic clothing, including *papenkas*, fur hats bearing the red star of the USSR. She then moved on to Archangel and on 29 July she joined a mixed force of Soviet and British warships, Russian icebreakers and merchantmen. The convoy headed east towards the Kara Sea where the Soviet destroyers, British minesweepers and corvettes all turned back and the *Hopemount* continued in company with the three ice-breakers and the merchantmen. Their task was to penetrate the North East Passage, meet Soviet vessels coming west from Vladivostok and to pass their merchantmen through the Bering Strait bound for Russian Tartary.

This was an annual event and had been pioneered only a few years earlier in 1932 when the ice-breaker *Aleksandr Sibiryakov* had successfully negotiated the ice-strewn passage. In view of this achievement the Germans had fitted a long-range BV138 flying-boat for reconnaissance over the region. Determined to wound Russian pride in what the Soviet Union regarded as *mare nostrum*, the Kreigsmarine despatched *U-601* and *U-251* to intercept the convoy in the Kara Sea – hence the heavy escort of Allied men-of-war. The *Admiral Scheer*, under Kapitän sur Zee Meendsen-Bohlken, was also sent after the Russian convoy and her seaplane located it passing through the Vilkitski Strait on 16 August. Mist and ice detained the *Admiral Scheer* so that the convoy escaped. Instead she encountered the *Aleksandr Sibiryakov* under Kapitan Kacharev and although the ice-breaker put up a furious fight, she was no match for the German guns and was sunk with heavy loss of life off Ostov Belukha. On 27th Meendsen-Bohlken reached Dikson where the convoy, having heard on the 25th when off Ostrov Hansen, of the pursuing German *Panzerschiff* and of the sinking of the Russian freighter *Kujbysev* by *U-601* east of the Yugorski Shar, had taken refuge. Meendsen-Bohlken shelled the ships and shore installations damaging the Soviet patrol ship *Dezhnev* and the freighter *Revolutsioner*, but came under unanticipated heavy fire from the shore batteries. The German capital ship was struck aft and several of her crew were killed and wounded; Meendsen-Bohlken withdrew to the westward and the convoy continued its interrupted voyage.

By this time the *Hopemount's* master, Captain W.D. Shields, was a sick man and much of the burden of conducting the tanker eastwards fell on Chief Officer Arthur Nunn. He assiduously drew sketches of the coastline in a manner reminiscent of the running surveys of Dalrymple, well aware than no British ship had ever previously penetrated these forbidden and forbidding waters. On the 31 August the convoy reached Tiksi Bay, in longitude 134° East. Here they anchored and the *Hopemount* loaded more oil and took aboard some fresh water. On 16 September three Russian destroyers arrived from Vladivostok and were refuelled by the *Hopemount*. Two days later a fresh northerly wind began to close the ice, causing anxiety to the captains of the ice-breakers *Krassin* and *Lenin* so, with the prospect of more ships arriving from the Pacific diminishing, the convoy began the long haul back to the west. When the *Hopemount* reached Dikson on the 26th she was short of supplies and symptoms of scurvy were evident. She left in company with the other vessels on 6 October, passed the Yugorski Shar on the 11th where the British minesweepers HMSs *Halcyon*, *Sharpshooter* and *Hazard* cleared their route of a number of mines laid by aircraft. With the ice forming rapidly, the minesweepers did not linger as the convoy was now caught in the freezing sea and remained in the strait until the 21st, when the ice-breakers broke the ships out. Finally, on 20 November the *Hopemount*, slowed by her damaged propeller, again reached open water and nine days later she anchored close to the British minesweepers at Iokanka on the Kola Peninsula. She was visited by the young surgeon from HMS *Harrier* who diagnosed scurvy while the food and medical supplies provided by HMS *Bramble* saved several of her crew from seriously impaired health. The subsequent sinking of the *Bramble* in action with the *Admiral Hipper* affected many of the *Hopemount's* crew, particularly Nunn.

The *Hopemount* went to Murmansk where she was dry-docked and her propeller was again knocked into shape before she returned home as part of Convoy RA51, arriving at Loch Ewe on 11 January. She reached Methil on the 16th, sustaining a slight collision, and in due course she crossed the Atlantic and underwent full repairs in the United States. While British merchant ships detained in Russian waters awaiting return convoy made coasting voyages within the White Sea, the *Hopemount's* experience was unique. Her penetration of the North-East passage to the 134th Meridian on the 84th Parallel was both unprecedented and unsurpassed by a British ship navigating on the surface, while the fact that her crew contracted scurvy added another historical footnote to the voyage. With this in mind the 'very low-key report' made by the ship's master has led at least two historians to conclude that 'he must have been a remarkable Master with a first class crew …'.[74] While Captain Shields complimented his ship's company by saying they 'behaved very well … it was a case of all pulling together' this was a formulaic assessment and included the significant clause, 'but nobody was outstanding'. The facts were that Shields had been ill for much of the voyage and one man *had* been outstanding and exceptionally so, though he suppressed the details of the voyage being made public during his lifetime. In bearing the brunt of the voyage, Chief Officer Nunn, afterwards a Trinity House pilot, mitigated its effect upon his indisposed captain. That he was denied the praise that was his due, is itself telling.

To the aggressive acts of the enemy and those hazards and Acts of God that bedevil the seafarer's life at any time, the conduct of the war exposed the merchant mariner to 'accidents' that might otherwise have been avoided. Among these disasters the worst were those at Bari and Bombay. For fear the enemy would use it, both the Americans and the British held stockpiles of poison gas which, although never deployed, was shipped overseas. In 1941 consignments of mustard-gas shells, bombs and canisters were sent to Singapore in the *Silver Beech* and the *Medon*. Prior to the surrender they were dumped at sea, being largely recovered post-war. Only the ships' masters and chief officers had been made privy to the precise nature of the 'munitions' on their manifests. This procedure was followed by the United States Army when 2,000 mustard-gas bombs were loaded into the American Liberty-ship *John Harvey* and sent to Italy. The *John Harvey*, Captain Elvin Knowles, arrived off Bari on 28 November 1943 only to find the port choked with shipping discharging military supplies for the Allied advance. Despite the crucially secret nature of part of Knowles's cargo, he was kept waiting at anchor until 2 December, when the *John Harvey* secured alongside Pier 29.

In addition to Italian ships, there were over thirty Allied merchantmen at Bari: American, Polish, Yugoslav, Dutch, Norwegian and seven British. Bank Line's *Teesbank*, Captain Herbert Jones, was full of munitions and lay astern of the American ammunition-ship *John L. Motley*. The *Fort Athabaska*, Captain Walter Cook, was under the management of J&C Harrison and nearby lay other MoWT-owned ships, the *Fort Lajoie*, the former Danish tramp *Lars Kruse*, Coast Line's *Devon Coast* and *Britanny Coast*, and the small motor-tanker *Crista*, owned by Shell Oil's Anglo-Saxon Petroleum Co. At this stage of the war they were well armed and their complements large and varied. The *Testbank* was manned by Indian ratings and the larger ships had apprentices and ordinary seamen below military age, several being sixteen.

That morning the Commander, Allied Tactical Air Forces, had announced to the press that he had total air supremacy over southern Italy, but at 19.30 that evening a force of one hundred German bombers raided Bari and in twenty short minutes they had sunk seventeen ships and damaged eight. A direct hit on the *John L. Motley* caused her part-discharged cargo to explode, detonating the lading of the *Testbank.*. The *Lars Kruse*, with a cargo of aviation spirit, was hit, exploded and caught fire, her cargo mixing with burning petrol from the bombed American tanker *Aroostock*. The *Fort Athabaska*, also carrying munitions, received a direct hit and blew-up and the *Devon Coast* caught fire and sank. The *Fort Lajoie*, *Crista* and *Britanny Coast* were also damaged. The devastation was widespread. One Yugoslavian, six American, three Italian, three Norwegian and two Polish ships were destroyed, with many others badly hit. But amid this carnage it was the direct hit on the *John Harvey* that did most damage, for she caught fire and her master, mate and the US Army officer responsible for the consignment of 100lb gas-bombs were all killed. As the Liberty-ship blazed she spewed mustard-gas out over the harbour which, lurid and hellish from the mixture of petrol and avgas burning on its waters, the air punctured by secondary detonations and thick with smoke and raining debris, defies the imagination. Hundreds of people, in the docks and the surrounding town, their eyes streaming, their respiratory systems traumatised, were ignorant of the cause of their agony. An American destroyer, moving into the harbour to rescue men from the water, withdrew to Taranto to land the casualties. On arrival, all her executive officers had gone blind and it was some time before the inexplicable cause of these terrifying symptoms was revealed. The death toll exceeded 1,000, over 800 people were hospitalised and 628 of them were found to be suffering from mustard-gas poisoning. The heaviest casualties aboard the British ships occurred to the *Testbank*, in which seventy men were killed, including Captain Jones, her three apprentices and forty-four lascars; thirty-nine including Cook died aboard the *Fort Athabaska*, others lost among the other ships bringing the total of British dead to 118 merchant seamen and DEMS gunners.[75]

The explosion of the *Fort Stikine* at Bombay on 14 April 1944 was equally devastating. Allocated to the management of the Cunard subsidiary Port Line by the MoWT she was under the Command of Captain N.J. Naismith and had loaded a cargo of cotton, 900 tons of TNT and about £1 million in gold consigned from the Bank of England to the Reserve Bank of India. Whilst discharging in Victoria Dock, Bombay, the cotton caught fire and, despite the best efforts of the Bombay Fire Brigade and the ship's crew led by Chief Officer N.D. Henderson and Second Officer N.H. Harris, the fire gained a terrific hold. Naismith ordered the *Fort Stikine* abandoned. Having carried out a search of the ship and ensured no one remained on board, Naismith and Henderson were hurrying along the quay when a tremendous explosion occurred, killing them both. Shards of red hot steel and blazing wads of cotton were blown skyhigh, adjacent buildings collapsed and the shock-wave travelled through the ground. The ship astern, Scindia's *Jalapadma*, was lifted bodily 60ft into the air, swung through a right angle and then fell back, her stern on the warehouse alongside. Half an hour later there was a second explosion which flung hot debris up to 3,000ft into the air and caused immense collateral damage. Besides ships and buildings, the human cost was appalling: about 700 people were killed or were missing, approximately 2,500 were injured, some 960 seriously. In recognition of his gallantry for his part in leading the fire-fighting Harris was awarded the MBE and Lloyd's Silver Medal but the ferocity of the fire consumed most of the gold, although an ingot was dredged out of the dock during routine operations in the 1960s.

Amid all this destruction many ships survived to ensure Allied victory. Among these survivors perhaps the oddest is the *Baron Forbes*. Unusually for a vessel owned by Hogarth & Co., a Scots tramping company notorious for its tight-fisted management, the *Baron Forbes* had, since 1922, been on a regular run between the Clyde, Huelva in Spain and Lisbon. Her outward general cargo always included a large consignment of Scotch whisky, while her homeward lading included a reciprocal quantity of port and this routine remained inviolate until May 1944. The 3,061-ton ship herself had been acquired from Germany as part of post-1918 war reparations and had been built for the Hamburg-Amerika Linie in 1917 as the *Hamburg*. It was widely supposed that her German build made her readily identifiable and thus secured her immunity from attack as she regularly joined Gibraltar-bound convoys, creeping through neutral waters to reach Huelva and Lisbon before creeping back again to rejoin a homeward convoy in the shadow of The Rock.

Certainly she seemed safe from harm, and on at least one occasion a Fw200 Condor flew round her before attacking another vessel in the offing. Whatever the truth of this, it was common knowledge to her crew that most of the whisky she discharged in Lisbon went aboard trains ultimately destined for Germany. Throughout this period her master was Captain Lachlan McPhail and it is probable that his ship was used to carry more than whisky and port. Certainly McPhail played an incidental part in one of the war's most successful deceptions, for when the *Baron Forbes* lay in Huelva one day he was asked by British consular officials to represent his country at the burial of a Major Martin. The corpse of this marine officer had, with his briefcase attached, been mysteriously washed ashore, having been discharged previously from HM Submarine *Seraph*. In Major Martin's briefcase were secret papers leading the enemy to conclude that forthcoming operations against Sicily – Operation HUSKY – were only a feint and that the main Allied attack would be on Sardinia and Greece. Thanks to German sympathisers in Spain, Berlin were made aware of these details and appear to have believed the subterfuge made by the corpse of 'the man who never was'.[76]

The first casualty of the war had been the liner *Athenia* and within hours of the armistice it was another British merchant that proved to be the last. The *Avondale Park* was owned by the MoWT and managed by Witherington & Everett of Newcastle-upon-Tyne. She had arrived from Hull on her way towards Belfast and joined a coastal convoy, EN91, at Methil. The convoy's twenty-five ships weighed and proceeded from Methil Road on the evening of 7 May. At 22.40, in the vicinity of the Isle of May, the *Avondale Park* was torpedoed. Her assailant was *U-2336*, and she was Kapitänleutnant Emil Klusmeier's second victim that day, for he had already sunk the Norwegian steamer *Sneland I*. The *Avondale Park* began to sink, the bulkhead between No.3 Hold and the engine room having collapsed, drowning her chief engineer and donkeyman. Captain James Cushnie, thirty-nine of her crew and four DEMS gunners escaped, though not without difficulty for she foundered fast and the explosion had destroyed her starboard lifeboat. Although the Carley rafts were released, several jammed and proved useless. Nevertheless, the survivors were quickly rescued by the escorts. Klusmeier returned to Kiel and surrendered a week later, six days after the German capitulation on 8 May.

The exact number of casualties suffered by the British Merchant Navy in the Second World War remains uncertain. The Registrar-General of Shipping and Seamen states the losses as 31,908 with a precision that defies doubt. In her official assessment, Miss Behrens estimated that of fewer than 145,000, about 39,000 were either killed or 'permanently damaged'. What is certain, if little appreciated is that the proportion of personnel lost was greater than in the armed services of the Allies: about 1 in 4. While that vague allusion to permanent damage may seem of less importance than loss of life, it was to play its tragic aftermath in the years of peace that followed.

As after the First World War there were the grandiloquent words of praise and comfort. Churchill, with his strong sense of history sought to embed the contribution of merchant seamen in the nation's consciousness: 'We never call upon the officers and men of the Merchant Navy in vain,' he wrote, long after darker days when, for fear of their wavering, he had rallied them with the words quoted earlier, 'We are a seafaring race and we understand the call of the sea.'

Nor did he forget, in the hour of victory, 'that when our minds turn to the North-Western approaches we will not forget the devotion of our merchant seamen … so rarely mentioned in the headlines'. Others realised the importance of the Merchant Navy's contribution. Invited to speak to the Chamber of Shipping, Field Marshall Viscount Montgomery stated unequivocally that:

> victory was … not only by the courage and skill of our Fighting Services, but also the quality of the ships and men of the Merchant Navy who transported us to our overseas bases and battlefronts, and maintained us there until the job was done. All this is quite apart from the fact that our country could never have survived either of the two world wars if our imports from overseas had not been maintained, and they were maintained in spite of the most determined attacks by the enemy to disrupt our sea communications.

While victory could only be achieved on land, without success at sea, triumph on land was impossible. After the war, in July 1950, a sick and depressed Admiral Horton considered that the war had given the Royal Navy no great naval victories. This was a perceptive assessment from the viewpoint of the naval purist, despite the successes of the Plate, Taranto and Matapan, the Barents Sea and North Cape. Important though these actions had been, they were not on the awesome scale of Leyte Gulf, Midway, or the Battle of the Philippine Sea. Nor, for that matter, did they possess the impact of Quiberon Bay, Camperdown, Trafalgar or even of Jutland. Horton was, however, too hard on himself and his little ships, and that other extemporised navy which lacked the bull of the King's service though it flew his red duster, for there is little doubt that the Royal Navy's great victory of the Second World War, perhaps greater in real importance than Trafalgar itself, was that battle 'of groping and drowning, of ambuscade and stratagem, of Science and Seamanship'[77] that was the Battle of the Atlantic.

The German naval historian Jürgen Rohwer wrote that:

The Allied victory in the Battle of the Atlantic was the result of the vastly superior resources on the Allied side in shipbuilding and in aircraft production, and in the superior development of anti-submarine detection equipment and weapons, and their superiority in the field of signals intelligence.

But that is only a part of the picture, the material part of the audit of war. There was also the moral element. According to the Napoleonic maxim, the moral is to the material as three is to one, and there was that steadiness of purpose evinced by the patient progress of those unremarkable grey-painted merchant ships – a navy by circumstance, but a navy nonetheless – that sustained Great Britain, held the line, and enabled the surging tide of war to be met, contained, turned and flung back in the enemy's face.

NOTES

1. Problems associated with convoy were outlined in Chapter Three but for a fuller description see *More Days, More Dollars*, Chapter Four.
2. Those lost to the enemy were the *Huntsman, Counsellor, Scientist, Astronomer, Scholar, Planter, Diplomat, Tribesman, Statesman, Craftsman, Logician, Dalesman, Auditor, Designer, Merchant, Traveller, Observer, Contractor, Director, Wayfarer, Arica, Daytonian, Colonial, Davisian, Inanda, Inkosi* and *Empire Explorer*.
3. The loss of the third Harrison ship, the *Magician*, was similarly an error in navigation made in April 1944. Bound for London from the West Indies and in convoy to Methil in the Firth of Forth in dense fog, Captain G.H. Howard missed sighting a buoy on his way south from the Pentland Firth. The ship went aground near Peterhead, broke-up and became a total loss.
4. See Cubbin, G., *Harrisons of Liverpool*, p207 *et seq.*
5. Conversations with the late Captain E.V. Parry, *c.*1974.
6. Roberts used the phrase 'the cruel sea' in his final address to naval officers at the completion of the course he ran at Derby House, Liverpool.
7. This anonymous account is held in the Imperial War Museum's Department of Documents (Misc. 3869) and I am indebted to Dr Roderick Suddaby for drawing it to my attention. The writer opens his 'Memo' by saying, 'I have just lived through the most thrilling and terrifying adventure of my career, and to whom it may interest I am taking this opportunity of putting on paper their nature and true facts. Readers must realise however, that for obvious reasons, positions, certain names of places, etc, must be omitted ...'. It is difficult to determine the writer's age for, although the junior of three radio officers, he is married, so is more likely to be in his early twenties and it is clear that this is not his first voyage, though he has not been at sea long – lifeboat falls do not 'snap'. After a little sea-time, even a radio officer would in time pick up the seaman's jargon and use the verbs 'part' or 'fail'.
8. I much regret being unable to record the name of the *Ensis*'s master or any of her crew. Her exploit, as far as I know, warrants no mention elsewhere. Clay Blair, *Hitler's U-Boat War, The Hunters 1939–1942*, maintains on p306 that after being damaged: 'In retaliation, *Ensis* turned on *U-46* and rammed her, knocking out the attack periscope. Endrass put *Ensis* under with a finishing shot, then aborted to France.' On his way home with his 'damaged' attack-periscope Endrass apparently 'sank a 5,300 ton freighter ...'. This is clearly not quite what happened. From the account I quote, the *Ensis* neither 'retaliated' by hitting *U-46*'s attack periscope, nor was sunk by Endrass. Nor were Endrass's torpedoes all dud, as is also suggested. All this hints at some creative log-keeping by Endrass, who was bedevilled by defective torpedoes. He may, of course, have damaged his attack-periscope in some other way, and found in the *Ensis* a convenient scapegoat. The *Ensis* was certainly not 'put under ...' though it helped Endrass to claim sufficient tonnage sunk to secure oak leaves to his *Ritterkreuz* by saying so. Blair later contradicts his claim that the *Ensis* had been sunk when, on p539, he devotes a short paragraph to Heinz Hirsacker's later (29 February 1944) 'lackluster small-gun attack on the 6,200-ton

British *Ensis*, which escaped with slight damage.' We know that the *Ensis* survived the war and was not replaced. While these conflicting accounts emphasise the 'fog of war' and the difficulties confronting the historian, they also demonstrate the lack of precise information about merchant shipping – an additional reason for including this anonymous account at some length. That said, I am in no way censorious of Mr Blair and am only conscious that this anonymous account makes a significant contribution to the detail, better determining the fate of one British tanker.

9. See Roskill, S., *The War at Sea*, Vol. 2, p211.

10. The shuttle was not quite unbroken, for the *Queen Mary* was to make another voyage to Sydney in the spring of 1943.

11. After the war Brooks, being Jewish, fought for the foundation of an Israeli state against the British mandate in Palestine before returning to London.

12. P. LeQ. Johnson to the author, 1964.

13. After returning to Britain the *Memnon's* Fourth Officer Eric Casson joined the Royal Naval Reserve and served in the Far East. He had learned Japanese and was an interpreter at the end of the Pacific War. After the war he returned to the Blue Funnel Line and rose to become Chief Officer, but in 1955 he took Holy Orders and became a popular padre in the Anglican Missions to Seamen at Yokohama where he was particularly kind to young midshipmen in his former company's ships. Another member of the *Memnon's* crew, Midshipman Curtis, returned to sea to be sunk twice more.

14. Peter Le Quesne Johnson's memoir, written in October 1968, is in the Imperial War Museum (89/5/1). For further details see the author's *The Real Cruel Sea*, p313, *et seq*, and p701–703.

15. The statement was signed: N.T. CLEAR, ex Chief Engineer s.s. *Criton*. Chief Engineer (Retired), British Tanker Co.

16. Later that day he sank the Swedish ship *Trolleholm* on the pretext that she was chartered to the British.

17. See Taylor, L., Gordon-Cumming, H., and Betzler, J., *War in the Southern Oceans*, p73.

18. The German *Hilfskreuzers* were invariably fast cargo-liners with relatively low profiles and were therefore capable of being easily disguised.

19. See Slader, J., *The Fourth Service*, p134.

20. Of the remaining *Hilfskreuzers*, the *Orion* and *Widder* reached Axis ports in Europe. The *Thor* was destroyed by fire at Yokohama. The *Komet*, after making a voyage from the then friendly port of Murmansk through the North-East Passage into the Pacific, was sunk in the English Channel. The *Michel* was sunk by the US Submarine *Tarpon* near Yokohama, the *Togo* was damaged by aircraft and recalled to Germany, and the *Stier* was destroyed in a classic single-ship action with the American Liberty-ship *Stephen Hopkins* on 27 September 1942 in which the *Stephen Hopkins* was also sunk. The adventures of their supply-ships were almost as extraordinary.

21. The former King Edward VIII had been made Governor of the Bahamas after his abdication, largely to remove him and his wife from Great Britain.

22. Karl Muggenthaler in his *German Raiders of World War II* claimed that: 'it was an impression many frightened survivors in many wars, shocked by their ordeal, ducking from fragments of flying steel and deadly ricochets, retained even after much of their hatred had worn off, but it was one usually impossible to substantiate.'

23. Robert Tapscott died in 1963. The *Anglo-Saxon's* jolly-boat survives and may be seen today in the Imperial War Museum in London.

24. From Third Officer Covell's Report to Alfred Holt & Co., February 1943.

25. Allen's account, written after the war, is in Stephen Roskill's *A Merchant Fleet in War*, p265 *et seq*. Allen's refusal to identify Eccles was a selfless act that warranted recognition. I am unaware that he received any.

26. See *The Milag Story; The Enemy – A Paradox*, by William Mutimer, published in the *Journal of the Honourable Company of Master Mariners*, Vol. XVIII, spring, 1993, No.213. Having lost his right arm, William Mutimer had to give up his chosen career at sea and worked for the British Legion and War Graves commission. His post-war attempts to trace his benefactor, Sister Elisabeth, proved fruitless. He died in 1997, his working career ending as Personnel Manager at the British Legion's Poppy manufactory at Richmond, London.

27. Though not exclusively so. The camp included volunteers of the International Brigade captured during the Winter War in Finland and some commandos from the raids on Dieppe and St Nazaire.

28. Bird, A., *Farewell Milag*, p87.

29. After the war under the auspices of the Commonwealth War Graves Commission, the Merchant Navy dead were reburied at Becklingen War Cemetery at Soltau.

30. See Elphick, P., *Life Line*, p89.

31. Long after the war Donald Stewart declined to take part in a French television programme in honour of the *Atlantis*'s captain, Bernhard Rogge. He died, aged eighty-five, in 1991.

32. Bird, A., *Farewell Milag*, p43.

33. The late Stan Hughill became something of a legend, a popular shanty-man who sang at various folk-song festivals and, as a musicologist and author produced a number of books. His compendium of sea-shanties, *Shanties from the Seven Seas*, is the standard work on the subject, and his study of the social history of the windjammer seaman, *Sailortown*, makes a unique contribution to the history of British mercantile seafaring. Both are illustrated by the author whose intelligence was spotted by his employers. After the war Alfred Holt & Co., in concert with the Seafarers' Education Service, obtained a place for Hughill at London University where he was granted a degree in Oriental Languages. Holts intended him to take up agency work on their behalf in the Far East but he went instead to the Outward Bound Sea School at Aberdovey and served as boatswain. Here he inducted would-be Blue Funnel midshipmen and young men from all walks of life into basic sea-skills and self-reliance. One of his large paintings, entitled *Outward Bound*, showing a four-masted barque under full sail, graced the main assembly hall at Aberdovey.

34. Originally the *Leicestershire*, the *Zamzam* had been sold and converted to an exhibition ship after the First World War, intended to promote British goods. However, the slump ended this project and she was sold for the Red Sea pilgrim trade under the Egyptian flag.

35. The Swedish national airline Aktiebolaget Aerotransport ran a joint service with the then newly formed BOAC who had been tasked to undertake the mission by the British Government in February 1941. Diplomatic mail and mail for PoWs in Germany were the main outward freight, with ball bearings predominating on the homeward run. People were carried in both directions for a variety of reasons. Initially Hudson, Lodestar, Whitley, Lockheed and Dakota aircraft were used by BOAC, but in 1943 they received some fast Mosquitoes which were flown at night. After December 1941 the Swedes used ten B-17 Flying Fortresses that had made forced landings in Sweden. These were given to the Swedes on condition they released and did not intern their aircrews. The Boeings were converted by SAAB to transports and airliners and operated after 1943 by the new Swedish national airline Svensk InterKontinental Lufttrafik AB, established to operate internationally and leaving domestic flights to Aktiebolaget Aerotransport. The ten-hour flights were made crossing hostile Norwegian territory where it was narrowest in the far north.

36. The five Norwegian ships were the *Elizabeth Bakke*, *John Bakke*, *Taurus*, *Tai Shan* and the tanker *Ranja*. Operation RUBBLE, which took place between 23 and 25 January 1941, was covered by cruisers and destroyers of the Home Fleet and No.18 Group, Coastal Command.

37. A mere sixteen Swedish ball-bearings could make one Bristol aircraft engine available, and every 143 an air frame for the badly needed torpedo dive-bomber, the Barracuda. See Hampshire, A.C., *On Hazardous Service*, p161.

38. The SOE officers attached to Operation BRIDFORD as 'chief officers' were: W.H.L.P. Wentworth-Fitzwilliam, eighth Earl Fitzwilliam (*Hopewell*) an ex-Guards officer'; Lieutenant Ruffman of the R.A. (*Nonsuch*); Peter Thorneycroft of the boat-building family (*Gay Corsair*); one Brian Bingham whose real name was Sylvanus Brian Reynolds, lately an agent in Finland (*Gay Viking*); and A. Reynolds-Brown (*Master Standfast*).

39. To take the longest of the trans-Atlantic series as an example, of the 377 HC convoys only fifty-six were successfully attacked. In total these consisted of 17,744 ships of which the total of actual losses, including stragglers, was 206 vessels.

40. This vessel is not to be confused with the Blue Funnel liner of the same name.

41. The Admiralty had the surviving senior officer of all merchant ships interviewed in order to study the enemy's method and to improve defensive measures if at all possible. This and Williamson's testimony are from ADM199/2133.

42. National Archives, ADM 199/2133, quoted Hewitt, p98.

43. National Archives, ADM199/42, CW Convoy Reports, quoted Hewitt, p110.

44. This account of the *Highlander*'s action with He115s is drawn from the ship's Official Log Book and the formal report Gifford submitted to the Admiralty.

45. For a fuller account of Convoy PQ17, please see the author's *Arctic Convoys, 1941–1945*.

46. Winn's manuscript account of PQ17 was suppressed, though it made a post-war best-seller, *The Story of a Ship*.

47. The recent (2008) awarding of a lapel badge for veterans of the North Russian convoys did little to ameliorate their feelings about this. The official attitude that their entitlement to an Atlantic Star

is sufficient commemoration of their services is at variance with the granting of campaign medals elsewhere.

48. Many convoy accounts contain wrongly spelled names of people and ships, evidence of the tiredness of the compiler. The *Aguila* is occasionally wrongly rendered as *Aquila*.

49. The ocean-going salvage tug *Empire Oak* was managed by the United Towing Co. of Hull on behalf of the MoWT and was being deployed to Gibraltar as part of the Ocean Rescue Service to assist merchant and naval vessels disabled by the enemy, one of the most under-rated and little-known contributors to ultimate victory in the Battle of the Atlantic. Although some were commissioned and armed, flying the white-ensign, others wore the blue ensign of an auxiliary service and were manned, like the rescue ships, by officers and ratings drawn from the ranks of the Merchant Navy Reserve Pool. One such rescue epitomising many was the salvage of the Port Line managed *Empire Treasure*, Captain R.B.Linklater, which had shed her propeller blades and dropped out of a North Atlantic convoy in January 1944. The weather was appalling and the ship, loaded with explosives, rolled alarmingly for three days until radio bearings established her whereabouts and HMRT *Bustler* – which later laid PLUTO, the fuel 'pipeline under the ocean' between England and Normandy – was able to get a line aboard the casualty. In seas described as 'precipitous' and with winds of hurricane force the *Bustler* towed slowly for two days until a moderation allowed her to crack-on and bring the *Empire Treasure* safely into Newport in the Bristol Channel after a tow of 1,094 miles.

50. The effect of the dead Wrens on the *Campanula*'s first lieutenant, Lieutenant Nicholas Monsarrat RNVR, was to gestate into his masterpiece, *The Cruel Sea*, turning him from a pre-war journalist into a post-war novelist.

51. See Edwards, B., *The Cruel Sea Retold*, p74 *et seq*.

52. In the event the *Vassilios Destounis*, due to be renamed the *Irish Poplar*, sailed alone and arrived safely in the Liffey.

53. If Captain Evan's handling of the *Glenartney* was commendable, Commander Bryan Gouthwaite Scurfield's manoeuvring of HMS *Broke* was exceptionally masterful, given the circumstances and the sea conditions. It is a matter of regret that I mis-spelled his name in my book, *The Real Cruel Sea*. This gallant officer was later taken prisoner after the destruction of HMS *Bedouin* in the Mediterranean and was killed by his own aircraft strafing a column of marching PoWs who were unfortunate enough to have been handed over by the Italians to the Germans. Happily in my account of the *Bedouin*'s actions in Operation HARPOON in Malta Convoys, I spelled Scurfield's name correctly.

54. For full details see *Trial of Heinz Eck, August Hoffman, Walter Weisspfennig, Hans Richard Lenz and Wolfgang Schwender (The Peleus Trial)*, William Hodge, 1948, Edited by John Cameron with a Foreword by The Rt. Hon. Sir David Maxwell Fyfe, from which is quoted the description of Rocco Said. There is anecdotal evidence alleging that Wolfgang Lüth may have been involved in a similar incident in which the survivors of a French vessel were summarily despatched.

55. See Jones, D.C., *The Enemy we Killed, My Friend*, p81.

56. The China Navigation Co. almost simultaneously lost a ship, the *Shuntien*, on government charter in the Mediterranean.

57. Williamson's other subsidiaries were the Douglas S.S.Co., the Lena Tramp Ship Co., the Ling Nam S.S.Co., the Shun Hong S.S.Co., and Foreign Investments Ltd, Williamsons owning the 1905-built *Ashridge* in their own name.

58. Other companies whose ships were hurriedly commissioned as auxiliary warships included Shanghai-based Moller & Co.

59. The *Talthybius* was later salvaged and repaired, to become the *Taruyasu Maru*. She was located, sunk, in Japanese waters at the war's end. Refloated and renamed the *Empire Evenlode* she steamed to Singapore to load scrap, bringing 10,000 tons of that much needed raw material on a voyage lasting almost six months, after which she too was scrapped and broken-up.

60. It seems that the British ambassador in Washington, Lord Halifax, was aware of the order but regarded the information best suppressed. See Elphick, *Life Line*, p185.

61. Quoted by Elphick, *Life Line*, p187.

62. The *Sutlej* was also carrying diplomatic mail in a special steel box on deck. This was intended to go down with the ship, rather than risk capture as had occurred aboard the *Automedon* earlier in the war. This is what the Admiralty assessed had happened.

63. It is not clear whether one man died, one record showing that only seven survived, four crew and three gunners. Elphick is more specific, detailing eight. See *Life Line*, 190.

64. Unusually the Hain S.S.Co. had eschewed their usual prefix of *Tre* … for the *Behar's* name, suggesting that she had been ordered by the P&O board to be built as a cargo-liner and placed under Hain management for the duration.

65. One authority quotes Captain Hansen as surviving.

66. Admiral Sir James Somerville's *Desk Diary*, 31 March 1944. See *The Somerville Papers*, p535.

67. Somerville thought they had been recovered by HMS *Emerald*, but see Peter Elphick's *Life Line*, p193. I am indebted to Captain Elphick for much of the information regarding Japanese atrocities.

68. See Bone, D., *Merchantmen Rearmed*, p66.

69. See *Merchantmen Rearmed*, pp194–5 & 265. David Bone's narratives of his experiences in both wars are particularly evocative, giving a real feel for his era. The several transformations through which ships such as the *Circassia* went during the years of war, so essential at the time, seem ephemeral now and to lose these insights seems almost criminal. My thanks to the Bone family for permission to quote at length.

70. The *Anglo African*, Captain Caradog Thomas, belonging to the Nitrate Producers' S.S.Co., managed by Lawther, Latta & Co., also landed the Texas Rangers and their mounts in Italy and withdrew an Italian cavalry division from Corsica to Civitavecchia on the surrender of the island. This was landed in full parade order. See Jones, D.C., *The Enemy We Killed, My Friend*, p85 *et seq.*

71. Quoted Elphick, P., *Life Line*, p109.

72. The five ships that arrived were the Americans *Hugh Williamson*, *Richard H. Alvey*, and *John Walker*, and the British *Empire Galliard* and *Empire Scott*. Those lost were the Russian *Dekabrist*, sunk by aircraft on 4 November 1942; the American *William Clark* sunk by *U-345* the same day: and the British *Empire Gilbert*, Captain William Williams, torpedoed by *U-456* (von Esch) on 2 November and the *Empire Sky*, Captain Thomas Morley, sunk by *U-625* (Benker) on 4th. The *Empire Gilbert* was managed on behalf of the MoWT by Turner, Brightman & Co., owners of the 'Z' Steamship Co., and the *Empire Sky* by Claymore Shipping of Cardiff.

73. The recalled ships were the British *Briarwood* and *Daldorch*, and the American *John H.B. Latrobe*. During the period 29 October to 24 January 1943, the Russians successfully passed twenty-three ships westwards, to return to Archangel later fully laden.

74. Bob Ruegg and Arnold Hague in their *Convoys to Russia, 1941–1945*, World Ship Society, 1992, p19. The late Arthur Nunn was interviewed by the author in 1992 whilst writing *Arctic Convoys*. In accordance with his wishes, his name has been withheld until after his death. His modesty was typical of many merchant seafarers whose conduct merited better recognition.

75. As a post-script to the uncomfortable story of poison-gas, among its final post-war acts the Ministry of War Transport requisitioned the 1917-built *Glennevis* from Furness, Withy, renaming her *Botlea* and placing her under the management of Reardon Smith & Sons of Cardiff. In December 1945 she was loaded with poison gas shells and bombs and in December 1945 she steamed out into the South Western Approaches and was scuttled.

76. To which might be added a further note concerning Spain. At the beginning of the war when British shipping losses began to mount and before Lease-Lend had come into play, a plan was hatched between London and the British consul in Majorca, Captain Alan Hillgarth RN. Hillgarth had contacts with Juan March, a Majorcan millionaire and entrepreneur who had bank-rolled Franco during the Spanish Civil War. It was intended to purchase for the British merchant fleet as many interned German ships as lay in the neutral ports of Spain. In the event the plan came to nothing but March was later contacted by the British ambassador to Madrid, Sir John Sloane, who had gained Churchill's support to offer bribes totalling £1 million to several Spanish generals with influence over Franco to keep Spain out of the war. However, although Spain, weakened by her divisive Civil War, never joined the Axis Powers, not only did her ports – particularly those in the Canaries – provide refuge for German ships, but these refuelled U-boats, thereby extending their war-patrols.

77 This was Churchill's description of the Battle of the Atlantic.

FIVE

'AN ADVERTISEMENT FOR THINGS BRITISH'

Post-War Ship-owning and Seafaring, 1946–1965

Despite enormous losses in men and ships,[1] the economic position of the British shipowner in 1945 was relatively strong. There was, naturally enough, a shortage of tonnage, but this, along with reconstruction programmes, meant good freight-rates. However, the expectation of a post-war slump as had occurred in 1921 made some British owners nervous. The worn-out state of the British shipyards made replacement of losses with new ships difficult, not least because prices rose steeply and the limited but competitive demand was high. Instead of meeting this new challenge by raising new capital, many owners chose to spend capital by repaying debts. At the same time the MoWT was dissolved, handing over the remaining ships it had chartered during the war to the peace-time Ministry of Transport which wished to disencumber itself, making relatively cheap replacement tonnage available by the passing of the 1946 Merchant Marine Sales Act. Among the war-built tonnage both the British and the American governments were disposing of were some 2,000 surplus ships. American buyers snapped-up about 800 – re-registering them in Panama under a flag of convenience, or 'of-necessity' if one was an American eager to remain competitive. While the remainder were sold to others, mostly Greek operators, 200 were acquired by British owners. Among these were the faster, more sophisticated American-built Victory-class steam-turbine ships which, with the Liberties and Canadian-built Forts and Parks, and British-built Ocean-class freighters, adequately stopped the gaps in not only tramp tonnage, but in cargo-liner fleets. The standard-built T-2 tanker performed a similar function in the field of oil transportation. The Americans nevertheless retained a large number of such vessels, laid-up in reserve, notwithstanding which, in 1953, Britain could still boast of having 'the largest fleet afloat under any single flag'.[2]

This post-war restoration of 'normal' trade-routes took time and required immense effort. Although shipyards had full order books the pressure left them no time for re-equipping: already outdated facilities carried on, increasingly anachronistic. The ravages of war were not over with the coming of peace and the short-fall of shipping delayed recovery everywhere. People died of starvation, particularly in the Far East, where the once thriving coastal trade had been completely destroyed. Writing in late 1950 and referring to the newly built Blue Funnel liners serving North Borneo, one observer remarked: 'In addition to a few new Empire ships which occasion much admiration when they arrive in port, anything that floats is still used for shipping – and occasionally something that doesn't float'.[3]

In the aftermath of war it took time for the MoWT to release ships back to commercial service but the delays were less than had occurred after 1918 although many liners were utilised for repatriating PoWs. Restoration, which in the case of requisitioned passenger liners could be extensive, took some time, and diverted shipyard resources from new construction. Although given priority, it was not until Wednesday 16 October 1946 that James Bisset, now Commodore Sir James,[4] took the *Queen Elizabeth* out of Southampton bound for New York with 2,288 fare-paying passengers on board on what was officially styled the great liner's 'Maiden Voyage'.

While there was less predation by shipowners in the late 1940s than had occurred during and after the First World War, a certain levelling occurred. In 1944 Lord Vestey's consortium, led by the Blue Star Line, bought Lamport & Holt and the Booth S.S. Co. two years later. In 1952, the Austasia Line was formed to run between Australia, north by way of Indonesia, to Singapore and Malaya. Other mergers included that of the Clan and Union-Castle Lines in 1956, producing British & Commonwealth Shipping, and in the following year the New Zealand Shipping Co., Shaw, Savill & Albion and the Port Line joined forces, establishing Crusader Shipping to extend their services to Hong Kong and Japan, to run in competition with the P&O Group's Eastern & Australian Co., and services run by Alfred Holt & Co. Finally, in 1965, Holt's Ocean Group secured full control of Elder, Dempster in which they had for many years been the major shareholder.

Elsewhere there were new enterprises afoot. In addition to the war-built merchant ships of the MoWT, other redundant vessels came on the market in the aftermath of hostilities. A Colonel Frank Bustard, recalling wartime developments in beach-landing and sensing the opportunities offered by the presence of a post-war British Army of the Rhine, acquired three new Tank Landing Craft (LCTs) for his Atlantic S.N.Co. Renamed the *Empire Baltic*, *Empire Cedric* and *Empire Celtic*, these initiated the first roll-on, roll-off ferry service between Tilbury and Hamburg. This success led in 1948 to a further four vessels being acquired to serve Preston and Ulster, an initiative establishing a new type of ship, the roll-on, roll-off, or RORO. The remaining redundant LCTs were laid-up in the Clyde and recommisssioned for service during the Suez Crisis of 1956 and subsequently deployed to Malta, Aden and Singapore under the management of the Atlantic S.N.Co. By 1960 the laid-up LCTs in eastern waters had been transferred to the management of the British India S.N.Co. and, retaining their 'Empire' names, flew B.I.'s red saltire house-flag. This company was to be entrusted with their eventual replacements, the army's Logistic

Support Ships, until between 1968 and 1970 all these were taken over by a reforming Royal Fleet Auxiliary.

Other eyes were on ferry services. The former River-class anti-submarine frigate *Halladale* was bought by the Townsend Bros Ferries Ltd and converted to a ferry under the management of European Ferries Ltd. This company expanded, using further redundant military tonnage, acquiring a LCT in 1958 and later developing into the Townsend-Thoresen group. Meanwhile several shipping companies with war-built tonnage available, offered them to the Government as naval auxiliaries in emulation of the war time practice in the face of a continuing call for naval deployments worldwide. In the event the Government decided to custom build tonnage for the Royal Fleet Auxiliary which, although it was to run for many years yet as a state-supported, but mercantile-regulated, logistical force in support of naval and military operations, would slowly acquire a naval formality as the fleet itself shrank.

These naval commitments were many and varied, and involved not merely the Admiralty's own auxiliary, but the wider Merchant Navy. Still possessing a large empire, there remained a requirement for troopers, a requirement that increased as independence movements in various colonies and mandated territories became increasingly violent, while the United Nations intervention in Korea in July 1951 provided employment for troop-ships.[5] To fulfil these obligations the British India S.N.Co. provided the Government with three troop-ships, the ageing *Nevasa*, the *Dunera* and *Dilwara*, and managed on its behalf the *Empire Orwell*, a German war-prize formerly called the *Pretoria*, for the state. Another former German liner, the *Potsdam*, was managed by P&O as the *Empire Fowey* and, after a new steam plant was installed, she carried the 8th Hussars to Korea, ending her days carrying pilgrims as the *Safina-E-Hujjaj* under the house-flag of the Pan-Islamic S.S. Co. of Karachi. British India also employed three smaller vessels, the *Sirdhana*, *Santhia* and *Sangola* to convey the Ghurka Rifles from Calcutta to Malaya and Hong Kong. Nearer to home the maintenance of the British Army on the Rhine was not only served by Colonel Bustard but by the former L.N.E.R. steamer *Vienna* which, at 4,236 tons, had been taken up for trooping in 1939, evacuated the B.E.F. from Dunkirk and was retained post-war under the management of the newly nationalised British Railways to run between Harwich and the Hoek van Holland in support of the B.O.A.R. The company most notably associated with trooping was the house of Bibby which in 1951 had, with B.I., agreed a trooping contract with the Government and accordingly ordered a new purpose-built troopship. Over-ordering and shipyard inefficiencies delayed her construction and it was not until 1957 that the *Oxfordshire* was commissioned. In 1945, with two pre-war troopers still serving as hospital ships, only three Bibby liners had been available for trooping and these were either phased out, or sold when the *Oxfordshire* eventually entered service. B.I. acquired the former *Devonshire* as the *Devonia* and she joined a newly built *Nevasa* in 1956 as the last troopers under their flag, the *Nevasa* always being commanded by the company's Commodore, or senior master. It was this ship that Bibby's *Oxfordshire* joined the following year while the surplus tonnage was sold, the *Dilwara* going to the China Navigation Co. as the pilgrim-ship *Kuala Lumpur*, while in 1961 the *Dunera* became an educational cruise ship for schools, a service long provided by B.I. The *Empire Orwell* was returned to the state and acquired by Alfred Holt & Co. in 1958 as will be seen. By this time the days of trooping by sea were over. National Service was abolished, overseas commitments falling away as former colonies gained independence. In October 1960 the Government had introduced the Air-Trooping Plan, the first casualty of which was the *Vienna*. The plan was soon extended and the new distant deployment troopers *Nevasa* and *Oxfordshire* were prematurely retired, the latter ship arriving from the Orient at Southampton on 18 November 1962. After two years laid-up in the River Fal, the latter was sold to the Sitmar Line of Italy to become the emigrant-carrying *Fairsky* serving Australia, while the *Nevasa* became an educational cruise ship.

Other merchantmen were periodically requisitioned for a variety of purposes, some connected to Britain's retreat from Empire, itself by no means a simple matter, others with British military operations. Among these were Operation MUSKETEER, the Anglo-French invasion of the Suez Canal Zone in 1956, and the nuclear weapons tests in the Pacific that took place between 1952 and 1960, during which several tramps and cargo-liners were chartered by the Ministry of Supply.[6] They reached a crescendo in Operation CORPORATE, the retaking of the Falkland Islands in 1982, after which there were too few traditionally manned and operated British merchant ships to call upon, which was one reason why the Royal Fleet Auxiliary became increasingly integrated with the Royal Navy. One influence on the decision to detach the navy's logistical support from a semi-mercantile ambience was the changing nature of British merchant tonnage which was itself less and less essentially 'British'. Indeed, in these years – prior to the fall of Communism in 1989 – one British admiral conducting an exercise under the auspices of NATO, was outraged to discover that the BP Tanker Co.'s vessel which had been chartered for the purpose, whilst being officered by Britons, was manned by Poles.[7] While the presence of Maltese and Chinese had long been accepted in civilian roles even in Her Majesty's Ships, let alone British merchantmen, this seemed a step too far. In the light of the immediate post-war years, this wholesale change was astonishing.

The ethnic and national origins of the British mercantile rating had undergone a series of changes since 1945. With the demobilisation of naval seamen flooding the market and a reduction in mercantile tonnage with the relinquishing of the Ministry of War Transport's own shipping, there was a huge surplus of seafarers. Consequently many among the ethnic minorities then serving in merchantmen were forcibly repatriated. Many lascars, confronted with turmoil in their own country as it gained a divided independence, found themselves caught between two evils. So too did the Chinese, many of whom had settled in Liverpool and London's Limehouse, married English wives and had families. Such was the appalling nature of this ruthless act that many wives never knew what had happened to their husbands, assuming they had been deserted, while children never saw their fathers. Events in China following the triumph of the Communists in 1949 imposed an absolute separation which was a tragic and terrible end to years of loyal service. Notwithstanding this callous inhumanity, many British companies continued to employ non-British nationals as seamen, firemen and stewards, maintaining a long tradition that would persist for many years yet to come.

Ironically, in an entirely different economic position, many young Britons serving as junior mates in the last years of the war turned away from the sea, evidence of the

Sunset Industry: Arthur Burgess's nostalgic image of two anachronistic sailing barges being passed by the inward-bound Harrison motor-vessel *Herdsman* in the lower reaches of the Thames in the 1950s, is redolent of a passing age. No longer the world's largest port, by the end of the century, the old docks were redundant. (© Courtesy of The British Mercantile Marine Memorial Collection)

new and challenging attitude of youth to tradition. Insofar as those who remained in what was now unequivocally termed the Merchant Navy, conditions began to improve incrementally. The new Labour Government under Clement Attlee, did not abandon all the good intentions of wartime in the face of commercial reality, and in March 1947 the Merchant Navy Reserve Pool set up seven years earlier was replaced by the Merchant Navy Established Service Scheme. Guarantee of continuous service was unsustainable in peace-time but the new scheme enabled a seafarer to secure a two-year contract, contingent on his good behaviour and satisfactory service recorded in his, or her, Discharge Book. The following year the wartime interest in the quality and morale of the nation's merchant seafarers which had led to the appointment of Welfare Officers led to the setting up of the Merchant Navy Welfare Board.

Among the Labour Government's well-intentioned reforms was the nationalisation of the nation's railway system. Distribution by road was also consolidated into British Road Services and these, plus the rise in private motorised transport, tended to reduce the commodities being sent round the coasts. There was little revival in post-war passenger traffic, though a few excursion steamers remained, while oil and coal for the power stations of the south of England provided adequate lading for coastal tankers and the fleet of colliers which would in time include some large vessels run by the Central Electricity Generating Board and companies like Stephenson, Clarke & Co. But a general erosion of the coastal trade took place over the next quarter-century, by which time Britain's motorway system had killed coastal traffic and was leaching goods from the inefficient British Railways. Many small firms vanished and not a few of the larger companies went into decline, among them the General Steam Navigation Co., although Fred. Everard & Co. continued trading by moving with the times, acquiring tankers and generally operating increasingly sophisticated vessels. By the end of the century, that 'nursery of seamen' that had extended from the Tyne to the Thames, was almost denuded of British coastal shipping.

Strapped by debt and faced with considerable economic difficulties not helped by a cold and protracted winter of 1946/47, Attlee's Government was desperate to feed the population. So acute was this crisis that the Government was compelled to reintroduce wartime rationing in 1948 and it was to be 1954 before matters had sufficiently improved for its abolition. However, helped by the enforced moratorium of war, which had enabled fish stocks to recover, fishing enjoyed a post-war boom very necessary to feed a hungry population. Other sources of cheap protein were sought and 'expeditions' annually sailed south for the Austral summer to hunt whales in the Southern Ocean, mounted by Salvesen & Co. whose fleet of whale-factory ships, each with a number of fast whale-catchers and occasionally supported by the newfangled helicopter, slaughtered Rorquals, Right and Blue Whales. Based on South Georgia, where a trying-out factory and support base had been set up at Grytviken, the factory ships and their attendant catchers worked along the ice edge of the Weddell Sea in a complex commercial operation involving several hundreds of men. Although never very popular, whale meat provided a rich source of nourishment until better times and a rising objection to the extinction of these species dissuaded the British from the hunt and it was left to others.

Despite the policies of austerity imposed upon the British people by the country's war-debt to the Americans, Attlee's well-intentioned reforms extended across the entire shipping industry. In 1947 a National Dock Labour Scheme was introduced to improve the working conditions and job-security of the dockers. Although they had produced prodigies of effort during the war, the dockers had nevertheless flexed their muscles and struck on occasion. Increasing unionisation led to a fierce resistance to any modernisation in cargo-handling techniques that would reduce the numbers of men employed and this stranglehold empowered the dockers to take random industrial action, often on the flimsiest of pretexts. In 1949, while food remained in short supply the London dockers struck. Troops were drafted in to handle cargo, particularly vital consignments of frozen meat such as that in the *Port Lincoln*, which was discharged by the 1st Battalion, Irish Guards, who had just returned back from duty in Tripoli and a troubled Palestine. Strikes now became a commonplace; some were short-lived, others such as the London Dock Strike in the autumn of 1954 which was long, caused expensive delays to the liner companies. Port Line, for example had several ships detained for weeks, the *Port Pirie* and *Port Auckland* with stalled cargoes from Australia, *Port Halifax* from America and *Port Phillip* partly loaded for Australia. Such delays lost more than revenue, they lost trust and the cumulative effect of such industrial action had one inevitable consequence – the end of labour-intensive, break-bulk cargoes. The ineluctable change took time, but its impact would be profound; it required new methods and investment but the great imperial ports of the kingdom – Glasgow, Hull, Liverpool and London – would be changed forever. Their societies

Dockers handling cases in the 'tween-deck of a cargo-liner. This drawing by Frank Brangwyn shows the slow methods that had hardly changed since the days of sail. Brangwyn casts his subjects in heroic mould. (© Courtesy of Lloyd's Register of Shipping)

Handling small casks of spirits, Brangwyn's drawing depicts dockers carry their loads past the tally clerks who ensure the precise number are landed and no pilfering, for which the dockers were notorious, took place. (© Courtesy of Lloyd's Register of Shipping)

would be sundered by upheaval and the dockers' collective 'enemy' capitalism would, once again, triumph. Elsewhere this vast change would mark the landscape of the nation and it would prove one more nail in the coffin of British shipping.[8]

Social change of another kind was occurring simultaneously. In a shattered, exhausted country with an increasingly politically empowered population demanding a better life, shortages of labour occurred as Britain rebuilt herself. In 1948, following the passing of the Nationality Act, the *Empire Windrush*, managed on behalf of the Ministry of Transport by the New Zealand Shipping Co. and commanded by Captain T.L. Maltby was on her way back from the Far East via the Panama Canal. Calling at Kingston, Jamaica, she embarked ex-Servicemen willing to rally to the need of the Mother Country a second time. The profound social consequences which her voyage initiated are beyond the scope of this work, but it is important to recognise that once again a merchant ship played a hugely influential part in our history when she arrived at Tilbury on 21 June 1948.

Although the industrial woes of the docks would in time play their part in the decline of British shipping, such troubles were a back story in an era of global turmoil and realignment. If the anticipated post-war slump failed to materialise, there was sufficient political uncertainty in the Middle East, the Indian sub-continent and Burma, Malaya, Africa and China to daunt the faint-hearted. Other troubles, equally political but of wider influence, possessed a more immediate impact and for many years provided the British shipowner with opportunities to profit. Moreover, the long hegemonic domination of the United States in the so-called Free World which, committed to liberal world trade, might have eclipsed Britain's maritime power entirely after 1945 and prior to the oil crisis of 1973. Instead American shipping and shipyards proved uncompetitive and instead American capital underwrote flags of convenience which 'soon gave them indirect control of world bulk-shipping'[9] ending the British tramping trades. Nevertheless, in the short term, the unscrupulous had ample opportunity to profit.

With the Royal Navy enforcing a strict blockade to prevent Jewish refugees landing to settle in Palestine and establish the state of Israel, British merchantmen were chartered by Jewish agencies acting on behalf of thousands of would-be *kibbutzim*. Many old ships were bought-up by London-Greek owners, some as unsuitable as those designed for the Canadian Great Lakes. An anecdotal source alleged that one London-Greek shipowner still managing tonnage on behalf of the Government, purchased a strengthened 'Laker' for this purpose but that 'she caught fire before she could do anything'. With many cheap vessels available, their fitting-out for numerous indigent passengers was minimal, for the ships were not expected to accomplish more than one voyage, even supposing they were fortunate enough to run the British naval blockade. Most, denied any port for disembarkation, were likely to end up run-ashore on a beach near Haifa or Acre. Usually these blockade-runners took aboard their excited human cargo at Sète and then ran down through the Messina Strait before heading for the eastern Mediterranean. While the shipowners profited, the would-be citizens of the new Israeli state were more likely to find themselves in the hands of the British navy, their ships diverted to Cyprus where the intercepted refugees were put into internment camps. As the numbers of displaced persons grew alarmingly, the British Foreign Secretary, Ernest Bevin, was obliged to ship many back to Poland in several of the ships still retained under charter to the Ministry of Transport, the post-war legacee of the MoWT. One of these, the *Ocean Vigour*, was attacked by Zionist terrorists who attached a small limpet mine to her hull whilst she was lying off the Cypriot coast, though they failed to sink her.

Such amoral opportunities were fleeting and eschewed by all but the unscrupulous. The most significant of these geo-political events for the British was Indian independence in August 1947. The partition of the sub-continent into a Muslim Pakistan and a Hindu India resulted in the horrors of wholesale dispossession and movement of people. In the immediate aftermath of partition such oddities such as the transport of a large detachment of the Royal Indian Army Service Corps from India to Pakistan occurred, but thereafter the Indian state reserved its coastal traffic to its own flag. Although this had the effect of removing at a stroke the trade carried by the Asiatic S.N. Co., its overall impact was partial. The larger carriers, B.I. and P&O, simply adapted. British India, for example, although maintaining their Bombay – Persian Gulf run, cut their Calcutta service to focus on the East African route where independence for the British colonies was yet some years away. Indeed, as with the colonial bush-wars of the previous century, the bloody uprising of the Kikuyu people's Mau-Mau organisation which erupted in 1952 and outlasted Kenya's independence in 1963, provided employment for British India's ships.

Immediately following India, Burma broke away from the imperial fold and, declining to join the Commonwealth, in 1948 severed all connections with Britain and its shipping almost overnight. There had been warnings of this. In 1947 the small British India coaster *Sir Harvey Adamson* employed on the Burma coast disappeared without trace. She was presumed to have detonated a mine, 'a relic of the war against the Japanese' but given the political heat of the day, the deep-rooted connection of the British India S.N.Co. with the *Raj*, her fate may have been otherwise. Burma's retreat into an isolationism that exists today, affected other companies, such as the Asiatic S.N. Co., the Anchor, Henderson, Harrison and Nourse Lines, several of which moved closer to the engrossing P&O Group by chartering some tonnage to the giant consortium and were, in time, incorporated by it. Bibby, however, managed to maintain a service to Rangoon despite the hostility of the Myanmar regime until 1971 when, after a prolonged struggle – the passenger service having terminated in 1965 – all cargo services ended and the ships were chartered to the Bristol City Line. Circumstances were similar for Bibby in Ceylon (Sri Lanka) where Colombo had become a 'politicians' playground, with continuous strikes, stoppages and holidays and consequent congestion …'. With tea shipped from Galle and Trincomalee, Bibby left it to others, notably the Glen Line whose homeward-bound vessels would fill any available space.

Despite the outbreak of the Mau-Mau rebellion in Kenya in 1952, the immediate prospects for South and East Africa looked good. Both North and South Rhodesia possessed apparently limitless mineral resources, while all the colonial economies in the area relied upon vast quantities of agricultural produce. Attlee's Government conceived the idea of providing a Great Britain impoverished by war, indebted to the United States and with her industrial plant run-down and her population exhausted, with a cheap source of vegetable oils and fodder. The scheme would also provide an inducement to white emigration to Tanganyika (Tanzania) and Kenya where groundnuts would be grown for export to Britain. The notion was badly planned, and the agricultural techniques almost as unsuited as the droves of white emigrants who sought to recapture the voluptuous extremes of the imperial age when its day was already over.[10] The Groundnut Plan intended that vast tracts of land would be divided into 30,000 acre farms connected by a new railway and about £25 million was set aside. A new port at Mtwara in southern Tanganyika would be built at a cost of £4.5

million and a mighty hydro-electric plant constructed at Owen Falls in Uganda. The cost of this alone was another £4.8 million and, begun in 1948, it took six years to complete.

Nevertheless, whatever its failings, the rich ethnic mix of indigenous Africans, along with a more mobile population of Arabs and Indians, combined with the influx of thousands of Britons, provided shipping with huge opportunities. Apart from the raw materials and produce of the colonies carried to Britain, great qualities of general cargo, from factory plant to vehicles, railway lines to personal effects were carried out to the three colonies, Uganda, Kenya and Tanganyika. By 1952 the immigration rate to Kenya alone was three times what it had been before the war, the numbers of 'Europeans' doubling between 1949 and 1952, and the number of Indians trebling between 1939 and 1962. This was hugely encouraging for the British India S.N. Co. entirely compensating the company for its losses from Indian and Paksitani independence.

Violent though the partition of the Indian sub-continent had proved, it was not to be compared to the horrors about to engulf Indo-China where France had been the colonial power.

The conflict in Indo-China between the French and the Communist-inspired Vietminh who, under Ho Chi Minh, sought independence from Paris and had been part of the Allied opposition to Japanese occupation, provided employment for the London-Greek shipowners. Companies such as Chandris Lines, who owned 'an old passenger ship called the *Carlton Star* under the British flag … spent many years trooping … chartered to the French government to carry French troops to Indo-China'. Counties Ship Management also picked up work from the French government, their *Sycamore Hill* being among a number of their tramps chartered to the French liner company that had traditionally served Indo-China, Compagnie des Messageries Maritimes of Marseilles. They took 'military cargoes out' from Marseilles and Algiers to Saigon (now Ho Chi Minh City), and by the end of the war they brought 'some wrecked equipment [back] to Algiers and Marseilles. All the ships were wartime Canadian-built Parks that still belonged to the [British] Government and were only under [Counties Ship] management'.

Such chartering could prove lucrative as Captain Aris Finiefs recalls of his days as an apprentice with Counties Ship Management.

When I joined them, the vast majority of the fleet of twenty-eight ships were on charter to the [Communist] Chinese Government on what were, and are still, Zhongzu-charters. We traded between Europe and China with mostly bags of fertiliser, and some ships stayed on the coast bringing coal from Chinwangtao to southern Chinese ports, mostly to Canton. The Chinese had no shipping then, except for some small American craft built for the invasion of Europe. It was said that the red 'C' that Counties had on the funnel of the ships was changed to a red star to appease the Chinese. How true it is I do not know … [but] the London Greeks were very popular with the Chinese, and the brother of a Mate in the company, who had fought in the Korean War, told me that British troops could not understand why British ships were loading and discharging in Chinese ports while they were fighting Communists.

The unsatisfactory partition of Vietnam proved temporary and British merchant ships were to become involved in the later conflict in Indo-China, the Vietnam War (1964–1975). Once again the tramps of the London-Greek shipowners picked up the inevitably available charters. London and Overseas Freighters, for example, placed four ships on charter to the States Marine Lines who were themselves keen to profit from their own government as the United States became increasingly and disastrously embroiled in the war for South Vietnam.

American hegemony in the Far East had been challenged first by the triumph of the Chinese Communists. Having occupied Japan in 1945 the Americans also dominated the Philippines, while the Guomindang was driven out of China and retreated to Taiwan, leaving the victorious legions of the People's Liberation Army to takeover China and the Communist government to root out what remained after Japanese occupation and civil war of the red barbarians and their foreign investment. Gone were the International Settlements, the Treaty Ports and the British ships on the China coast. Butterfield & Swire's China Navigation Co., were barred under a treaty signed in 1943 with the Guomindang government. However, residual services remained on a much-reduced scale and insofar as the Chinese authorities tolerated their utility.

In October 1954 three British banks and the old Taipan's firm of Jardine, Matheson entered into negotiations with the new Communist government of China to surrender their assets. Although Jardine, Matheson continued to own the Indo-China Steam Navigation Company their ships would, like those of the China Navigation Company of Butterfield and Swire, be infrequently seen in Chinese waters and their close association ended on 26 July 1955 when Mr T. Beesley arrived in Kong Kong from Shanghai. The firm had had 'extensive interests in 14 major Chinese cities and Shanghai was the last to be liquidated'. Alfred Holt & Co. had already lost its wharf at Pootung, though the Glen and Blue Funnel Lines were to maintain a tenuous but regular liner service with Red China, their ships and their complements exposed to danger, as we shall observe in the following chapter, but henceforth the British could trade *with* China, but not *in* it. Within half a century the position would be reversed with crypto-capitalistic Chinese conglomerates owning *British* ports.

'The memory of the Opium War with China is branded indelibly on the minds of all Chinese and it is the starting point of every history of modern China', wrote *The Times* correspondent covering affairs in China at the time:

> It was industry that invaded China in the nineteenth century; the bruises left by the gunboats are still felt. Less than a century ago the first Chinese statesmen began to think of building their own arsenals and coming to terms with these heavy-gunned barbarians from the west.

Thus what goes around, comes around.

Peripheral logistical support would be provided to British forces operating not only under the mandate of the United Nations during the Korean War (1950–1953), but in the 'Confrontation' between Indonesia and the newly formed Malaysia (1963–1966) and in the ineffectual anti-Communist SEATO alliance which, having failed to intervene collectively in Vietnam, Laos and Cambodia, was dissolved in 1975.[11]

The post-war schisms in the Far East were, of course, mirrored in Europe by the descent of the iron curtain that divided the continent. The new Satellite countries of the Soviet Union – Poland, Yugoslavia, Czechoslovakia, Bulgaria, Roumania and East Germany, together with the annexed Baltic States of Estonia, Latvia and Lithuania – were now obliged to co-operate with Moscow under the terms of the Warsaw Treaty. This economical union, or 'Comecon' produced substantial national fleets of merchant-cum-military sealift ships which, although nominally under the aegis of 'companies' were under no obligation to show a profit and could therefore undercut the freight-rates of the open market.[12] Since they apparently espoused the creed of brotherly love and had no connections with the old imperial powers, they found customers in the newly independent states, particularly in Africa where the post-colonial democracies rapidly metamorphosed into new dictatorships, or in promoting ancient tribal differences, strove to suppress rebellions and required arms, *matériel* and 'advisers'. These were readily available courtesy of Comecon shipping.

Amid all this change, some things remained much as they had been pre-war. In 1948 Alfred Holt & Co. converted six of their new Mark 2 'A'-Class Blue Funnel cargo-passenger-liners for the carriage of pilgrims from Malaya and Indonesia to Jeddah, joining the ex-troopers mentioned earlier and the *Tyndareus*, a stalwart veteran of the First World War which had picked up the trade as soon as peace returned. Ten years later they acquired the *Empire Orwell*, renaming her the *Gunung Djati* after a holy mountain in Java, converting her specially to give a multi-class service to the growing number of Muslim pilgrims from Indonesia wanting passage to Jeddah. This released the 'A'-class liners for normal service and replaced the *Tyndareus* which, despite the scantlings which had resisted a mine off Capetown, was now worn-out after forty-four years' service.

Emigration to Australia continued with cheap non-return inducements of a £10 passage for families, young people and tradesmen willing to make their lives 'Downunder', and in 1948 the Children's Act initiated a renewal of the forced emigration of orphans from the voluntary societies following the recommendations of the Curtis Report. This had been encouraged by a movement in Australia to increase its ethnically white population by any means. Consequent upon Japanese military successes which culminated in the bombing of Darwin in the north of Australia, a xenophobic fear of the 'teeming masses of Asia' began to dominate Australian politics. The wholesale export of unwanted children who found themselves in the hands of Christian voluntary societies which had been initiated in 1922, now found a post-war impetus. They were embarked, largely from the south of England, in vessels such as the Orient Line's *Otranto* and despite the damning but suppressed report of the Ross Committee investigating the transportation of orphans.

Between 1951 and 1960 the New Zealand government employed the Donaldson Line to manage their steamer the *Captain Cook* employed on an assisted-emigrant scheme. She was the former Donaldson Liner *Letitia* and was not only the sister ship of the *Athenia*, but commanded by the aptly named Captain James Cook who had been master of the *Athenia* on 3 September 1939.

With the large liner companies rebuilding their fleets, the smaller firms struggled. For some, like Butterfield & Swire's China Navigation Co., ejection from their traditional routes led to a complete shift of emphasis and location, from Chinese coastal carriers to world trading based on the south-west Pacific, a shift from Shanghai to Sydney. Firms like the Asiatic Steam Navigation Co., were subsumed by others, in this case P&O. Others adapted less dramatically. With only six ships left in 1945 the United Baltic Co. bought three German-built Hansa A-class standard ships as a temporary measure until a post-war fleet rebuilding programme was launched. When this began the old *Baltannic* was sold to Imperial Chemical Industries' Nobel Division and for nine years lay at moorings in Loch Riddon as an explosives store, being finally broken-up at Troon in 1958. Despite the post-war incorporation of Eastern Europe into the Soviet Bloc, services were resumed to Poland and Soviet Russia, as well as to the Scandinavian countries and extended to Finland. In due course the Hansa ships were sold to resurrected German shipping companies and new-built vessels acquired, largely from German yards overlapping their service with their partners MacAndrews & Co. After the war UBC ships fitted with fridge-space inter-changed with those of MacAndrews and a joint Anglo-German operation was launched as the Sloman Mediterranean Line, two ships being assigned to this service which ran from German and Dutch ports to peninsular Italy, Sicily and North Africa.

MacAndrews' post-war rebuilding, like that of its fellow Weir subsidiary UBC, benefited from German shipyards and UBC innovations, but new ships were also built at Sunderland and some second-hand tonnage was acquired. Several of the new ships were fitted with special steel tanks for the bulk carriage of wine and like UBC an engine-aft configuration was adopted for some of them. While the company continued to import fruit and wine, nuts, olives, cork and other Mediterranean produce, outward cargoes consisted of manufactured goods and general cargoes for Iberian and Italian ports, and government stores for Gibraltar.

By 1960 seven UBC ships serviced Finnish ports, two ran to Gdynia, one to what was then Leningrad and Polish ports. Occasionally the *Baltic Swift*, which was fully refrigerated and usually employed on the Helsinki run, carried frozen cargoes worldwide, visiting ports as diverse as Buenos Aires, New Orleans, Casablanca, Colombo and Hsinkiang, a newly opened port in North China near Tientsin. At this time the company's board represented the continuing Anglo-Danish union established after the First World War. Chaired by Lord Inverforth, the Vice Chairman was Prince Axel of Denmark with board members from both countries and including another Weir.

As one manifestation of the post-war disaffection of youth, the scions of many ship-owning families showed little disposition to continue in the business, admitting to company boards others whose interest lay not in ship-owning as a means of making money, but in simply making money by any means. This lack of hereditary will in the younger generation combined with an exhaustion in the older to produce one insidious cause of decline in British ship-owning. Their remained sufficient traditional owners, even among the increasingly expensive liner operators, to conceal this encroaching disinterest for some time, particularly on the Ben Line board, where the Thomson family remained in power, but also in other companies such as the Andrew Weir Group, parents of MacAndrews, UBC and the Bank Line.

Like many others, Bank Line's post-war reconstruction relied upon the purchase of a dozen redundant Liberty-ships from the Americans. The first new-build was the

Eastbank, handed over by her builders, Wm Doxford & Sons Ltd of Sunderland in December 1947. Thereafter new tonnage followed steadily, including the outright purchase of three ships which Weir had had on charter. The main fleet rebuilding continued throughout the 1960s and by 1970 stood at sixty ships.

However, by 1956 Japan had displaced Britain as the world's leading shipbuilding nation. In the face of increasingly fierce foreign competition and with British yards retaining many of their primitive methods and working practices, which included building in the open air, British shipbuilding was approaching a long foretold crisis. Three years earlier it had been pointed out to the ageing and anxious Prime Minister, Sir Winston Churchill, that Britain still owned the world's largest merchant fleet but that her shipbuilding industry might require Government intervention 'as they did in the thirties'. The success of a Liberty-ship replacement, the SD14, did not save British shipbuilding as it might have done and the story of the building of these vessels typifies that of the decline of a great industry (see Appendix One). The woeful tale was symptomatic of a great malaise endemic among the senior management and direction of much of British manufacturing, which failed to address, let alone moderate, the excesses of the demands made by unionised labour, or to invest in modernisation comparable with German and Japan.[13] There ensued consequent deep and irresolvable industrial unrest in which capital, whilst inevitably beating labour, did so by seeking investment opportunities unconnected with shipping. This extraordinary rejection of new ideas, of self-deception, the undermining of morale and the rejection of new talent, which looked elsewhere, is historically an un-British aberration, but it was powerful enough during these years to encompass enormous industrial vandalism upon which, in 1989, the fearsome eye of Margaret Thatcher fell. This was to have a knock-on effect on the merchant fleet of a dying industrial giant.

The Ben Line of Leith invested in innovative new tonnage, emerging as an increasingly serious threat in the 1960s to Alfred Holt & Co.'s hold on the Far East trade with its Blue Funnel and Glen Lines. Encroachment on Holt's traditional preserves was relentless, Ben Line entering the Borneo trade where in 1953 the *Benrinnes*, Captain J.S.R. Grassick, gave her name to a newly discovered reef.[14] With shippers of homeward cargoes seeking both low freight-rates and speedy delivery, the Far East trade became a test bed for fast cargo-liners, a challenge eagerly taken up by the Thomson-led Board in Leith. This was a period during which the designers of cargo-liners in all maritime countries produced some elegant, even beautiful, ships. Ever since the introduction of their pre-war diesel-powered 18-knot *Glenearn*-class, Holts had enjoyed a pre-eminence among British owners, though it was constantly challenged by Japanese, German and Dutch owners. In 1959 Ben introduced the 20-knot, steam-turbine-driven *Benloyal*, the fruit of a secret project between the company and William Connell & Co.'s chief naval architect William Paterson. Incredibly finelined, the *Benloyal* suffered a number of problems, not least her lack of stability which required 500 tons of permanent concrete ballast, but alterations made to her halfsisters *Bengloe*, *Benvalla* and *Benarmin* overcame these. Instead of steam-plant, the trio were powered by Sulzer diesels. On the introduction of the *Benloyal* the palm in the monthly rivalry between Glen's mature *Glenearns* and Ben's new ship's passage time on their Singapore to London-direct invariably went to Ben Line Steamers. In

Fast and fine-lined, Brocklebank's *Markhor* was one of the last generation of versatile cargo-liners that were barely fit-for-purpose, being built on the eve of the container revolution. (© Courtesy of the artist, Robert Lloyd)

Liverpool Holt's chief designer, Harry Flett, immediately put pen to paper and in the winter of 1962 the first of Glen Line's four *Glenlyon*-class entered service. Flett died during their construction, but the prominent funnel that had become his and his principal's signature belied the fine lines of the *Glenlyons'* hulls. Like their predecessors and their competitors, these ships were highly versatile with overwhelming self cargo-handling derricks, and heavy-lift, fridge and liquid-cargo capabilities. Flett also incorporated bulbous bows and weight-saving though expensive aluminium superstructures. Against such innovations there had to be set ominous signs of threat, most notably but not yet significantly, the increasing use of unitised cargo shipments in steel boxes – the first manifestation of the container revolution which would render all these ships redundant within a few short years – but more pressingly, a serious delay in the completion of the *Glenogle*. She and the *Glenfalloch* had been ordered from a British yard, Fairfield's on the Clyde, whereas the *Glenlyon* and *Flintshire* (the name a reminder of the old Welsh Shire Line) had been built in the Netherlands. Nevertheless the *Glenogle*, 11,918 tons, managed over 22 knots on trials, a reserve that was concealed from the opposition which swiftly responded. Ben Line added a further four vessels to their fleet for express service, the *Benledi* of 1965, followed by the *Benwyvis* and *Benalbanach*, all three being diesel-engined and capable of a service-speed of 21 knots. The fourth, the *Bencruachan* of 1968, incorporated limited space for containers and reverted to steam turbines, but this is to anticipate and we shall encounter her in a later chapter.

   In following the fortunes of several representative British shipping companies in detail, it is possible to sketch a more general history of British seafaring. One such firm, the diligent reader will recall was that established by Captain James Nourse for the carriage of 'indentured labour' which, by the early 1920s, had ceased this but retained services between Calcutta and the West Indies, carrying rice and gunnies, or coarse jute sacking. Return cargoes did often carry passengers, Indians who were returning home permanently or on leave. Company expansion was blighted by the Depression but when trade again to pick up new ships, the *Jhelum* and *Johilla* were built and, with B.I. funnel colours, chartered to British India which company had acquired the personal shares in James Nourse owned by Lord Inchcape on his death in May 1932. New tonnage was affected by the outbreak of war when the company's ships were requisitioned and came under the direction of the Liner Division of the MoWT and several ships were lost.[15]

In 1945 Nourse took delivery of the *Tapti* which was briefly under MoWT requisition before returning to the company's service. Unfortunately she ran aground on a reef off the Hebrides on 17 January 1951; refloated a few days later she finally sank on 24th. In the post-war years new tonnage was added. Although the Hampton family continued to hold directorates, the strategic fate of the company lay in the lap of its principals, British India as part of the P&O Group. By the summer of 1955 the company passed entirely into the hands of P&O and the last Hampton, Robert, retired. This affected the fates of the ships and the fortunes of their crews. The *Kallada*, for example, built in 1946, was sold to P&O in June 1957 but returned to James Nourse two months later, only to be sold out of the group in 1964. The *Marjata*, also a 1946-built ship, suffered a similar fate, being sold in 1963. She went missing and was presumed overwhelmed by a typhoon the following year.

By the time the company marked its centenary in 1961 it had disposed of several of its oldest ships as the traditional trade between India and the West Indies folded. Other P&O subsidiaries were also in trouble, among them the old tramping firm of Hain & Co. of St Ives in Cornwall, and the Asiatic Steam Navigation Co. whose smart ships operating in the Bay of Bengal had for years maintained contact with the Andaman Islands and the penal colony there. In due course Nourse assumed responsibility for the Asiatic S.N.Co.'s ships. In 1961 the P&O board, having invested in a tanker registered as being owned by the Charter Shipping Co. of Bermuda, placed the new *Foyle* under the management and colours of James Nourse. In the following year a second tanker, the *Erne*, came into service. Although delivered for Hain-Nourse – a new ship-management company formed by P&O by combining their tramp and general-cargo fleets with their new venture – the *Erne* swiftly passed to a new P&O subsidiary, Trident Tankers Ltd, in May 1963. However, she was returned to Hain-Nourse in October 1965 before being transferred again to Trident Tankers on 1 April 1969.

Trident Tankers came to specialise in the carriage not just of oil, but of bitumen and liquefied petroleum gas (LPG), but this constant change was bewildering to the personnel involved and caused a good deal of confusion and disillusion, particularly among the officers. Several who had joined P&O to escape the tedium, long voyages and lack of opportunities to go ashore, suddenly found their tanker expertise invoked. Offered promotion, they found themselves chief officers to masters with no tanker experience and therefore stuck for some time in a career cul-de-sac. At the same time officers who had served their time with, say, Hain's tramps, discovered their futures were to be in tankers of considerable complexity. But this was not the end of the complicated story.

James Nourse took delivery of its last 'traditional' cargo-vessel in 1962. The *Jumna*, a handsome 16-knot motor-vessel of some 7,118 gross tons, was built to a stand-ard tramp-ship design, and was transferred to the Hain-Nourse Management on 1 October 1965, when actual registered ownerships was vested in the Hain S.S. Co., in turn part of P&O's Bulk Shipping Division. Exactly six years later, thanks to another reorganisation, she transferred to the General Cargo Division of the P&O Group and was caught up in events outlined in the following chapter but in 1975 she lost her Nourse name to become the *Strathnaver*. Two years later she was disposed of to Singapore buyers and, after knocking about under the Singaporean, Liberian and Greek flags, she went to the breakers in 1985. Hers was the fate of many ships, particularly the smart, post-war British tramps and smaller cargo-liners. Not only had Hain's and Nourse's fleets been subsumed by the giant, but so too had Moss, Hutchison & Co., and Frank Strick's fleet.

While the P&O Group had long been in possession of a vast tonnage such as the British India and Federal Steam Navigation, and the New Zealand Shipping Companies, they had retained a little of the outer trappings of independence, those odd distinctions that motivated seafarers, binding them to one identity before another, inculcating an odd, inexplicable loyalty to *their* company. More than anything else these shifting expedients, howsoever logical in distant boardrooms where balance-sheets and profit-and-loss accounts reminded company directors of their obligations to shareholders and themselves, sent out a signal to their employees. Their predeces-sors had noted it in the heat of war and reversed their '*M.N.*' badges to read '*N.W.*' – 'Not Wanted'. Slowly it dawned on a new generation that neither were they. The signs had been there for some time.

A mere six years after the end of the Second World War the cash-strapped British Government regenerated a war-devastated site on the south bank of the River Thames as a large exhibition centre. Here was held the Festival of Britain, an attempt to echo the Great Exhibition of 1851 and to celebrate the industrial, social, scien-tific and economic progress of Great Britain which remained an imperial power, if a fading one. One pavilion was devoted to 'The Sea and Ships' and the official guide begins with the rather extraordinary claim that:

> Our ancestors came by sea and found here natural havens for their craft. We still live of the sea and by it, using this same coastline as the childbed of our inheritance – the building of ships for the world and for ourselves.
>
> Several nations have had their spell of pre-eminence at sea. The British tradition has been continuous.

The pavilion contained exhibits showcasing British shipbuilding, its associated tech-nologies and resources, and sea-fisheries, culminating in:

the sterns of three very different types of vessel … a whale factory ship, a passenger liner and a large tanker for British oil. The central exhibit is a model of a floating dock, containing a modern liner. Around this are examples of twenty-four different vessels, all specialised for a particular kind of duty.

'British discovery at sea' occupied a whole section of 'the Dome' while 'The great business of operating these and other types of ship is the subject of the Sea section in the neighbouring "Transport" building.' Here it was admitted, without clarifying the precise nature of the explicit alternative, that:

> Without the enterprise of our ship owners and their associates in the vast business of operating shipping lines, the growth of the British Commonwealth would have followed very different trends. Without a mercantile marine such as we have now, we people of Britain and our industries would starve.

By 1951, only six years after the sacrifice of the war the term 'Merchant Navy' did not feature in a celebration of the nation's achievements. There are many who would argue this was a good thing, an accurate reflection of the actual status of many private fleets gathered under a national flag. However, the point is, that despite the official wartime adoption of the term enshrined within the rope loop and its abbrevia-- tion: '_M.N._', and despite the legitimisation of a 'Merchant Navy' within the ambit of the Establishment, the 'hands-off' attitude of the shipowners and the preference for _laissez-faire_ on the part of an impoverished Government had, once again, cast the mercantile marine adrift upon the chilly waters of market forces. A mercantile marine is not a possession -- is not even a perceived asset -- of the state; it is but a manifesta- tion of British genius and enterprise. Not all of that genius and enterprise resided in its owners' boardrooms; some might be found upon the bridges of its ships and the platforms of its engine rooms. This might seem a small, even a sociological, point, but its importance lies in the consequences that flowed from this early cementation of the official and the public perception. Merchant shipping was admitted as an integral part of the nation's global transport system, but it was not regarded as important as the railways – which were then just nationalised. The pros and cons of this product of post-war socialist ambition would in time be deemed a failure. Its weakness lay not in its conception, but in its realisation. This was in the hands of its management, the British Railways Board, and its overlords, successive British Governments. The same could be said of British shipping, even though its managers – the large shipping con- sortia – were not operating on behalf of that lumpen mass of 'the people' but in their own and the interests of their shareholders. These men were not quite the overlords of shipping, for their possessions remained subject to requisition in time of national crisis and were subject to Government regulation.

In February 1952 the death of King George VI had brought Queen Elizabeth II to the throne and with her the dawn of what the newspapers and publicists thought of as 'a new Elizabethan Age.' Ironically, Queen Elizabeth's long reign was to be a reverse of her namesake and where English sea power had risen, Elizabeth II was to see it decline. In the following year, while the Royal Navy painted its ships and prepared for a Coronation Review, merchant seamen then awaiting berths on ships, their names being 'on the Pool', were engaged and sent to London where, using their skills with bosun's chairs, *soogee-moogee* and paint, they cleaned and painted buildings on the route of the Coronation procession.

Most British shipping companies were invited to send ships to participate in the Fleet Review in the Solent and a number did. It was rumoured that the managers of Alfred Holt & Co. declined to send a Blue Funnel liner on the grounds that it would disrupt their schedules. A similar – and probably apocryphal – rumour circulated that they had also declined a request to provide Her Majesty with a ship to use as a Royal Yacht, an old tradition but one which had always previously involved the Union-Castle, Orient or P&O Lines. The Royal Yacht, the third to be named *Victoria and Albert*, had been deemed unseaworthy some time previously and was, in any case, unsuitable to undertake a world cruise. A new yacht capable of that role had been ordered and was under construction, but would not be completed in time. Instead the Shaw, Savill & Albion liner *Gothic* was chartered and taken in hand, a timely benefit to a company facing over-capacity on the Australasian service. The Queen and her consort, Prince Philip, embarked in the *Gothic* which was under naval command and flew the white ensign as a commissioned ship for the duration of the cruise. The royal couple returned home, not in the *Gothic*, but aboard the new Royal Yacht *Britannia* to which they transferred at Malta on their way home.

During the Royal Cruise, Ellerman's City Line built the last of its fine, large capacity passenger-cargo liners, four vessels of which the celebratory *City of Port Elizabeth* was the first. Ironically, however, it was in this year that the company ended its passenger service to India owing to the traffic being lost to BOAC – the British Overseas Airways Corporation, forerunner of British Airways. Nevertheless, the Ellerman fleet still numbered more than ninety ships. Twenty years later only thirty-six flew an Ellerman house-flag. There was an irony in all this for, in 1955, as air travel had made serious inroads into the numbers of passengers travelling by sea, British liners covered more routes than any other national mercantile fleet – and this in spite of the rapid shedding of colonies and establishment of independent states within a British Commonwealth of Nations. Such apparent security of tenure was an illusion, but for a brief boom British shipping thrived.

In the early 1960s the post-colonial network of British passenger services remained extensive. Ten liners ran to Canada, namely three Cunarders, three Canadian Pacific, two Donaldson and two Donaldson Warren liners. Six Cunard liners, joined by the *Caronia* when she was not cruising, ran to New York; two Elders & Fyffes passenger-cargo liners serviced the West Indies, supported by the traffic passing through the Panama Canal. The Blue Star Line ran four, and the Royal Mail Line three liners to South America, while the Booth Line continued to penetrate 1,000 miles up the Amazon to Manaus, with the P.S.N.C., owners of the *Reina del Mar*, maintaining contact with the west coast of South America. Provision for passengers to the west coast of Africa was provided by five Elder, Dempster and four former Bullard King ships; the distant Cape continued to be the fiefdom of Union-Castle, supplemented by accommodation aboard eight Ellerman City liners. Two large British India liners served East Africa and were supported by the large number of B.I. ships operating the

Midshipman John Hunter on the boat-deck of a Blue Funnel liner in the 1960s wearing the customary shore-side rig of a blazer bearing the badge of the naval crown that had become the symbolic device of a national 'Merchant Navy'. (© Courtesy of Robert Hunter)

trans-Indian Ocean routes mentioned elsewhere. Direct passenger contact with India, Pakistan and Burma was maintained by the Anchor, Henderson and Bibby Lines with nine vessels. Eight Glen liners carried passengers to the Far East, as did a similar number of Blue Funnel ships and four large P&O liners, supplemented by lesser accommodation on their cargo-liners. The long-haul route to Australasia still absorbed a large number of passenger liners: four of the *Strath*-class plus the *Arcadia*, *Canberra*, *Himalaya* and *Iberia* plus five of their subsidiary, the New Zealand Shipping Co., made up P&O's contribution. The Orient Line retained five passenger liners joined by the new *Oriana* on the route, Blue Funnel maintained four and Shaw-Savill six.

With tourism increasingly popular as the wage of the British worker rose, Shaw, Savill and Albion commissioned the revolutionary one-class passenger liner *Southern Cross*, followed later by the *Northern Star*. The following year Canadian Pacific introduced the *Empress of Britain* but she lasted as a liner for only seven years before being chartered for cruising and then sold. In the face of the obvious takeover of passenger traffic by air lines British shipbuilders continually sought the ultimate, viable passenger-cargo ship, seeking a mix of prestige accommodation for the rich able to indulge themselves with long periods of luxurious and pampered living at sea with more pragmatic accommodation for tourists and one-way emigrants, particularly on the run from Britain to Australia.

The Orient Line, for example, had ordered a number of large new passenger ships after the war for their service to Australia. The *Oronsay*, *Orcades* and *Orion* were all around 29,000 tons, capable of speeds that reduced passage time to four weeks, but the company failed to take sufficient notice of the growing power of air travel, despite the investment in the world's first jet airliner, the de Havilland *Comet*. Once again when passenger traffic slumped, passenger-liner owners turned to cruising and other expedients; the Orient Line decided to bypass Capetown in 1954 and re-route their large ships westwards through the Panama Canal. Despite these developments both Orient and P&O ordered new large tonnage in the late 1950s. By 1960 the former had reduced the passage from the United Kingdom to Australia to three weeks with their new *Oriana* which carried 2,100 first and tourist-class passengers at over 27 knots. She was the last liner to wear distinctly Orient livery and fly the company's house-flag. The company's great rival, P&O, had produced their own new liner, the *Canberra* and in that same year the two merged into the tautologically awkward P&O-Orient Line. In 1964 the distinctive, corn-gold hulls of the Orient Line were abandoned in favour of P&O's white livery and *Orcades* and *Oronsay* shifted to P&O ownership. Two years later the *Orsova* and *Oriana* followed and with them went any pretence that the Orient Line existed at all, the name being dropped. Henceforth it was as P&O that the company would be known. Neither of the expensive, steam-powered new liners, *Oriana* nor *Canberra*, enjoyed a long period on the run for which they were conceived and constructed and by 1974 were increasingly engaged in cruising. However, in deference to that residual company loyalty of which mention was made earlier, on the last voyage before her retirement in March 1986, the *Oriana* made her last voyage under her original house-flag. Economically redundant, she was to remain afloat as a floating tourist attraction until 2005. Her name was given to a new super-cruise ship in 1995 and she, with her successors in the P&O cruising fleet, retain the red, gold, blue and white colours of Arthur Anderson and Brodie McGhie Willcox's original company, though few now know their derivation from the royal colours of the ruling houses of Spain and Portugal.

Meanwhile, the Union Castle Line maintained a fast passenger and mail service to the Cape, building new tonnage to service it, such as the *Pendennis Castle* of 1959. This was the last long-distance, traditional liner service, surviving in a reduced form until 1977 by which time the best-known passenger carrier under the British ensign, Cunard, had moved its large ships into cruising following the slump in trans-Atlantic travel. Since more passengers crossed the North Atlantic by air in 1960, the numbers had steadily dwindled as the cost of air travel fell. There had been no lack of foresight; several companies had attempted to invest in air transport – Holts in the late 1940s in Malaya – and Cunard and BOAC had attempted to combined service offering the benefits of both methods during the early 1960s though without success. Unfortunately both the British and American governments discouraged any such combinations for fear of monopoly. Furness, Withy, however, along with P&O, did invest in civil aviation, though the most conspicuously enduring link between the old and the new was that of Swire, with its acquisition of Cathay Pacific.

A few companies maintained specialist passenger ship services, where possible underwritten with cargo contracts. In 1964 Alfred Holt commissioned the Blue Funnel liner *Centaur*, built on Clydebank by John Brown & Co, to replace two old and pre-war ships, *Charon* and *Gorgon*, on their Singapore–West Australia service. An innovative design incorporated accommodation for 190 passengers and extensive pens in her 'tween decks for either cattle or 4,500 sheep as well as for general cargo. She was diesel powered and fitted with twin screws to give a service speed of 20 knots. This specialised trade – she had to dry out at Broome in north east Australia where the tidal range is huge – gave the ship a long life and although her overall managers transferred her from one subsidiary to another within their fleet, she remained in service until 1981. The following year, as a consequence of the chartering of their own supply-ship, the *St Helena* by the British Government for service in the Falklands campaign, the St Helena Shipping Company Ltd in turn chartered the *Centaur* as a substitute. She thus supported that lonely British possession in the South Atlantic until relieved, whereupon she was sold to the Chinese in May 1983. Though this was regretted by many old hands, she enjoyed a reincarnation as first the *Hai Long* and later the *Hai Da*.

In reality economically profitable international sea-travel was petering out from the late 1950s onwards. When the former Prime Minister Sir Anthony Eden, leaving office in the wake of the Suez *débâcle* in 1956, travelled to convalesce following surgery, he did so in the New Zealand Shipping Company's *Rangitata* where one of his stewards was a future politician, John Prescott.[16] But by 1960 such a passage by a statesman, even a sick and retired one, was increasingly unlikely. Although passenger ships continued to be built, even for scheduled runs, after this date most cargo-passenger liners lost their passenger accommodation, another sign that profound changes were under way.

The post-war resumption of trade under the British-inspired Conference system soon came under attack from a number of sources, the first of which – newly independent former colonies, particularly those of India, Pakistan and Burma, but which soon included Ghana and Nigeria – has already been touched upon. These states now aspired to possess national deep-water merchant fleets, an ambition which was shared elsewhere, the states of Latin America, for example, adopting protectionist policies in emulation of their giant neighbour to the north. Attempt to co-operate with some of these were made, particularly with Ghana and Nigeria. Companies like Palm Line and Elder, Dempster – aboard whose *Calabar* her passengers had celebrated Nigerian Independence on 1 October 1960 – undertook the training of young officers in the pious hope that this would ring concessions from new governments eager to flex their muscles and operate flag-preference in favour of their own national companies. Much of the goodwill extended to these states evaporated as democratic institutions foundered and gave way to autocracies of one sort or another, a dysfunction exacerbated by widespread corruption. With the Ibo people's attempt to seceded and establish an independent Biafra, Nigeria descended into civil war (1967–1970), affording these companies a brief boom supplying the Nigerian government with arms and munitions from Britain, but such experiments failed. Pressure was also felt from American owners who, operating under a flag of convenience, nevertheless used anti-trust opinion to discredit the Conference System. In this milieu few liner companies attempted to develop new trades which, given their worldwide network was not surprising. One that did succeed was Furness, Withy's subsidiary Manchester Liners which inaugurated a new Great Lakes commerce with the opening of the St Lawrence Seaway in 1959.

By 1960 the liner groups were much as they had been, dominated by P&O which in 1964 possessed assets of over £100 million grossing 2.4 million tons, but also comprising Furness, Withy, Cunard, Ellerman, Holt's Ocean, British & Commonwealth, Vestey's Blue Star and Weir's Bank Line groups. Together they owned eight-tenths of British liner tonnage and also, as will shortly be seen, a number of tankers.

The steady post-war rise in world trade and increasing use of mechanised transport conferred benefits on oil tankers whose size increased rapidly. The British tanker fleet was largely in the hands of BP and Shell, though Chevron, Regent, Hunting,

C.T. Bowring and Eagle Oil retained some of the share, while tramping companies and later cargo-liner owners, also broke in. Athel Tankers remained specialist carriers principally of molasses, but it was the oil majors that led the way and in 1950 Shell produced the *Velutina*. With a deadweight tonnage of 28,000 she was regarded as the world's first 'super-tanker' but was quickly surpassed, with tonnages passing 100,000 tons by the end of the 1960s. However, the rise in demand for oil outstripped the nation's tonnage and while British Petroleum had striven to carry nine-tenths of its production pre-war, by 1957 it carried only 57 per cent, allowing independent foreign owners to charter tonnage, a fact that in the case of Greek owners like Stavros Niarchos and Aristotle Onassis, encouraged the construction of ever larger tankers to corner this market. Such ownership further engrossed the flag-of-convenience registers, particularly that of Liberia which was actually a Liberian government agency run by Americans in New York. Here a number of Greek shipowners had spent the war, familiarising themselves with the oil industry and able to finance new tonnage from these charters. The shipowners collectively known as the 'London Greeks' also took up this challenge, in particular Mavroleon and Kulukundis whose establishment of London & Overseas Freighters in 1948 was designed to carry bulk cargoes of both dry-bulk and oil. By 1960 London & Overseas was the largest independent tanker owner with 190,000 gross tons at its disposal, followed by Hunting with 172,000 grt.

Among those others emulating this during the 1950s were the tramping firms of Ropner, who owned two tankers one chartered to each of the oil-majors, BP and Shell; Turnbull Scott, Hadley and Evan Thomas Radcliffe who accepted deals of new tonnage – two tankers each – along with Shell charters; and Common Bros who built-up its own tanker fleet and managed the Lowland Tanker Co. for BP. Even the P.S.N.C. were tempted by such a deal, taking one tanker. Other liner operators were attracted, particularly Scottish Tankers, a subsidiary of Cayzer, Irvine, owners of the Clan Line, which began investing in tankers in 1951. Five years later, faced with diminishing passenger traffic, the P&O Group weighed in and by 1960 possessed almost 160,000 gross tons of tanker capacity, consolidating their vessels in Trident Tankers. Notwithstanding all this, in 1960 three-quarters of the British-flagged tanker fleet was owned by the oil-majors and all this comprised only a third of the world's tanker fleet, so the overall impact was not huge.

Concurrently the British tramp continued to decline, the emerging and larger bulk-carrier making inroads into her traditional trades and undercutting her economically. There was a substantial lack of interest by the old owners whose fleets and ships were too small to compete. This lack of invigoration was almost systemic; innovation was regarded with suspicion, investment and imagination was absent and, with the Korean War creating a boom in the demand for tonnage, many owners simply sold-out. With many liner companies picking up more of the smaller tramp cargoes, often simply as part cargoes otherwise made up of break-bulk stows, only a few British owners reversed the trend by building fast, modern tramps vessels which could be chartered to the liner companies. The ever-flexible Bank Line was among these, but so too were others. The Britain S.S.Co., owned by Watts, Watts & Co. of London who in 1949 had introduced a class of three 14-knot, Doxford-engined, 5,393-gross-tonnaged tramps of such superiority in their accommodation and other features that they warranted a visit by the Prime Minister, Clement Attlee, prior to sailing on their maiden voyages. Sadly Watts, Watts & Co.'s vision was not copied by others for the *Wanstead*, *Wendover* and *Woodford* were to enjoy lives profitable not only to their owners, but to the liner companies later chartering them. In 1957 the *Wanstead* began three years on charter to Port Line as the *Port Wanstead*, followed by nine months as Lamport & Holt's *Raeburn* in 1964 when she was demise-chartered to China Navigation as the *Wanliu*. At the same time the *Wendover* was chartered as the *Wenchow*, along with the *Woodford*, which had also run a voyage for Lamport & Holt as the *Rossetti*, now renamed *Woosung*. When Watts, Watts sold the Britain S.S. Co. to Bibby, the three ships were offered for sale and snapped-up by China Navigation. The *Woosung's* service with the company was to suffer a tragedy narrated in the following chapter.

As industry demanded larger consignments, few British tramp-operators moved into the large, single-deck bulk-carriers with easily accessible holds, leaving this to others, mostly foreigners. Like the oil-majors, the British Iron & Steel Corporation attempted to stimulate investment into the new ship type, but with little success, although there were notable exceptions. The Glasgow firm of Denholm founded Scottish Ore Carriers in 1949 and in 1956 Common Bros also acquired bulk-carriers, cutting a deal with British Iron & Steel known as Vallum Shipping. The same year Lyle Shipping also took up an offer from the steel giant, taking up time charters with the corporation. One of the largest companies involved was Furness, Withy who set up Ore Carriers Ltd to pick up British Iron & Steel charters. Elsewhere there was little interest and where there was the ships proved too small so that when a shipping depression occurred in 1958 companies like London & Overseas Freighters and Hunting converted their tankers to bulkers and undercut others with much larger ships offering economies of scale. Insofar as the traditional tramping firms were concerned it was a case of external competition and internal incompetence which could have only one consequence, even in a world of rising volumes of trade. Even the innovative Billmeir, doyen of entrepreneurial tramp-owners, gave up, selling out in 1963, though to be fair he was no longer a young man and there were now other more attractive projects in which to invest capital.

The modest returns available from shipping no longer matched expectations, at around 10 per cent, roughly half of the best investment available in British industry as a whole between 1950 and 1957. And while overall returns fell to 13.6 per cent thereafter, those from shipping plummeted to 3.5 per cent, much of this caused by the failure of passenger shipping, though tankers and bulk carriers – though not tramps – fared better, but an inexorable expansion of the world fleet also had an effect, leading to the over-capacity that caused the slump of 1958. The Tory Government, feared a return to the 1930s fuelled by foreign protectionism to which the liberal, free trade ideals of the British seemed as out of date as had once their insistence on the imposition of the Navigation Acts. Indeed, in January 1964, J. Hughes-Hallet of the Shipping Advisory Panel proposed a revival of the Acts but the die had been cast three years earlier when the Panel had been established to encourage greater competitive efficiency. It considered that 'there can be little hope that the trend away from free competition in world shipping will be reversed in our lifetime,' which damnation did not prevent the Minister of Transport, Ernest Marples from informing the Commons in February 1962 that 'the greater part of world shipping is still open to free competition. It is not all dominated by flag discrimination. The prize goes to the most efficient.' Scandinavian owners were held up as exemplars ready to adopt new ideas, unlike their fuddy-duddy British counterparts. The consequences of all this were to lead to a further study of foreign protectionism rather than a serious inquisition into British method, producing Hughes-Hallet's proposal while a series of official enquiries was initiated into Britain's maritime industries. It began in 1960 with the Fleck Report into fishing and was followed by the first Rochdale Report of 1962 on ports, the Devlin Report of 1965 on dock labour and the Geddes Report of 1966 to which reference has already been made. More were to follow, but the vicissitudes of trade versus industrial relations created an artificial boom-and-bust cycle which overlay that of the world at large. During the autumns of 1960 the London tally clerks had gone on strike; when they returned to work in November, a brief boom occurred as cargo-liners lifted the thousands of tons of exports held-up by the strike.

The Conservative's ineffectual establishment of the Shipping Advisory Panel was swept away by the Labour victory in late 1964; the new Government abolished the panel and turned its attention to shipbuilding, a poorer investment opportunity into which it was to pour millions of tax-payers' money.

As we have seen in the example of the *Glenlyon*-class, British shipowners – apart from the Royal Navy practically the only source of new orders – were increasingly disenchanted with British shipbuilding and this in turn led to a falling off of investment in shipping generally. This was just at a time when reinvesting in fleets was becoming increasingly necessary, not merely in terms of combating foreign vessels, but in the integrated transport system pioneered in 1958 in the Pacific by the American Matson Line and taken up two years later by Malcom McLean's Sea-Land Services Inc. Rising above the British shipowner was now the spectre of the container revolution.

In 1964 the Shipbuilding Credit Act was passed, releasing £75 million of credit and leading to the ordering of over 950,000 tons of shipping. With a cargo-liner such as the 12,000-ton *Glenlyon* costing around £2 million this was tempting, but the ship-yards barely rose to the challenge, and when the credit was exhausted the orders dried up. British owners turned to European yards, or looked further east. Just as it had in the 1930s with its first scrap-and-build scheme, the Japanese government intervened directly in their own shipping, equally affected by the slump whereas unlike the 1930s, the British Government failed to follow suit. To failing shipyards must be added the more pressing obstacle of failing ports where outmoded practices, and a refusal to adopt faster cargo-handling methods in the mistaken belief that this provided realistic job-protection, caused unacceptable congestion. Delays cost not merely money, but customer's ships had to sail with their British-consigned cargoes still on board, tran-shipping them into coasters in European ports for final delivery to their destinations at the expense of the shipowner and the frustration of their consignees.[17]

Nevertheless, for the young Briton growing up in a post-war world and seduced by the specious glamour of a life at sea, the twenty years between 1945 and 1965 represented something of a Golden Age, gilded perhaps through the spectacles of reminiscence and not without hardship and challenge but, for the seafarer, a high-water mark after which all flowed at the ebb. For the canny British shipowner the culmination of *his* tide had occurred half a century earlier and his prospects looked increasingly bleak. But for Young Merchant Jack, who as Third Officer in a cargo liner could earn in 1965 just over £1,000 a year, the future looked rosy. Britain was an island nation; her Merchant Navy had saved her twice from a mortal enemy and held its head high; the Royal Navy was shrinking, but an island nation that depended upon trade would always require merchant ships and seafarers, would it not? Certainly that is what those going to sea in the post-war period thought. So too did the Government which in 1965 produced a report on the future of British shipping, 'the ubiquity' of which 'is in itself a world wide advertisement for British industry and commerce, and for things British generally'.

After the war, the relief with which the British seafarer found his life restored to what he considered normal was almost palpable. Harry Wright, cook on MacAndrews' *Cid*, recalled running from London as a contrast to the late war.

> During the season we collected Seville oranges, just a few donkey cart loads from each of a dozen tiny Mediterranean ports, the Iberian Peninsula was a lovely unspoilt place then and the people were great. The fiestas were always so colourful and gay ... On other trips we would load Port wine and visit the little sardine ports in Portugal. However, the highlights would be Seville collecting bales of cork and Cadiz picking up Sherry. Apart from the iniquitous fascist police it was by far my favourite area of the world. ... I landed in jail a couple of times, they would round up anyone looking the worse for wear and about five in the morning we would all be given brooms and have to follow the water-cart and scrub the streets under armed guard ... The tourist exchange was very favourable for us both in Spain and Portugal, we could draw £5 worth of currency on board, go ashore, buy five £1 notes and have enough left for an evening's entertainment. We were lucky enough to get tickets for the Carl Rosa Opera Co. at the Lisbon Opera House, performing *Cavaliera Rusticana*, starring Beniamino Gigli ...

Nevertheless, the detritus of war took some years to clear, with minefields a danger for years afterwards and law and order absent in many places. In 1952 the coast of Java was less than exotic to Midshipman Ian Johnston of the *Ulysses*.

> Palembang was our next port of call. Here we unloaded our cargo of oil drilling machinery and food into lighters ... Little did we know that the bone fide lighters had been hi-jacked and that we had loaded the whole lot into lighters that disappeared into the night never to be seen again. After that it was a series of ports one after the other with only a few hours spent at each. The names Semarang, Tjeribon, Tegal Pascuran, Probolingo, Banjuwangi, Balik Papan and Macassar all seem exotic, but to us they were just names on the chart ... visually they were just distant lines and smoky smudges on the horizon from which the lighters appeared to take or deliver cargo to us. Most of the coast had been mined by the Japanese during the war and we could only go into special swept areas. Not quite like the coast Conrad knew so well.

Happily these minefields did less damage than they might have, though one or two ships encountered them. On a coasting voyage loading cargo for a voyage to the Pacific coast of North America the Royal Mail cargo-liner *Pampas* was on her way from Bremen to Liverpool having loaded pipes for a new oil pipeline from Alberta to Vancouver when, in thick fog early on 23 March 1953, the ship detonated a mine. Second Engineer Robert Blackmore had just come on watch.

> At 04.15 there was an almighty crash and the whole ship seemed to lift up. The generators had been knocked off the switchboard and the emergency lights cut in … I ran round the back of the main engine to fin water cascading down all over the place from fractured pipe fittings … We also found the four middle propeller shaft bearing covers were broken. The shaft must have lifted out …

Fortunately the damage was not fatal and the ship was towed into dry dock at Schiedam where the split rudder suggested to the Admiralty experts that examined the damage that the *Pampas* had activated an acoustic mine astern of her at sufficient distance to save her from destruction.

Post-war political upheavals made trading with many places difficult and, at times, dangerous. The independence of Indonesia from the Dutch in 1949 did not bring peace and amity to the new country. Years of turbulence followed and in 1958 the Eagle Oil tanker *San Flaviano* became embroiled when on a voyage with crude oil from Mina Al Ahmadi to Balik-Papan. On berthing Captain J. Bright was advised that a rebel faction in Celebes (Sulawesi) had obtained former American aircraft and discharging might be interrupted by air raids and for some hours every day the ship would be required to move off the terminal jetty and anchor in the river. Before dawn on the third day, 28 April, with only 1,500 tons left in the ship and the emptied tanks full of gas, the *San Flaviano* moved into the river to anchor close to Shell's *Daronia*. At 07.20 the chief officer, then on bridge anchor watch with his wife for company, saw an aeroplane approaching fast and low over the Balik-Papan signal station. As the Mitchell B-25 roared overhead it dropped a stick of bombs, one of which hit No.7 Starboard Tank and another detonated some distance off the port side. However, the gas in the empty tanks erupted in a rapid series of explosions, ravaging the *San Flaviano*'s hull and setting her ablaze. She listed to starboard while her port topside bulged outwards as her people rushed to the only boats capable of being launched, those on the port side. Fire separated those struggling on the boat-deck of the midships superstructure from those doing likewise with No.4 boat on the poop. This caused overcrowding of the after boat and it took some time to get her clear. Bright, the chief officer and his wife were among those who got away in No.2 Boat. The Second and Third Officers both got out of their cabins through portholes, ran forward and, entering the hawse-pipes, slid down the anchor cable into the river. They were picked up and both boats were pulled ashore to watch the *San Flaviano* burn and break her back.

The victory of the Chinese Communists in 1949 made Chinese waters hazard-ous, as the Nationalist Guomindang forces retreated to Taiwan. British ships in the area spread tarpaulins painted with large union flags on forward and after hatches, and hung boards similarly decorated over their sides. In 1947 Captain J.E. Watson, master of the brand new Blue Funnel liner *Anchises*,[18] wrote of his impressions to the school that the ship had adopted under the Ship Adoption Scheme as the tide of war receded, and the Japanese were driven out of China.

> Shanghai appears to be in a chaotic state. The city is now … in Chinese hands … The Chinese monetary system has depreciated to an abysmal level and people … talk of millions of dollars … The essentials of life are very meagre and expensive, consequently destitution is rife and widespread. The export market … has dwindled … and imports mainly consist of materials consigned to relief organisations, as in our case. Chingwantao in North China was a coal-exporting port, but *Anchises* found no coal, the mines then being in the hands of Communist rebels fighting the Nationalist government. A little cargo came from Taku Bar [near Tientsin] (bristles, goat and camel wool and straw-braid), and then on to Japan … [In Yokohama the American occupation forces] control everything – labour, ship's movements, quarantine, sentries, policy – in fact soldiers everywhere … Kobe in pre-war days was a hive of industry, but today it looks as if all the bees have been 'smoked-out'.

Two years later, on 21 June 1949, Watson's *Anchises* was the first Blue Funnel liner to maker her way upstream to Shanghai since the city had fallen to the 'Communist rebels'. The *Anchises* passed the quarantine station and headed up the Whang-pu and, half an hour later she was under starboard helm in the Astra Channel when a Mustang fighter-bomber with Nationalist markings attacked by bombing. In contrast to his letter to 'his' school, Watson's report to India Buildings reflects the terse professionalism required of a Holt master.

> Aircraft also made one run over the ship with machine-gun fire. Bomb struck water very close to port side and appears to have exploded under the surface. Blast extensive and ship immediately began to list to port; helm was put over to get ship out of channel and was beached on the Shanghai side of river-bank. Starboard anchor let go … [I]nspection revealed extensive damage to plates and frames in vicinity of engine-room. The following day the spare bower was carried out by sheer-legs on the insurance wire, help being received from Holt's Wharf. She received further bombing and machine-gunning in the afternoon, a bomb falling on shore on each quarter giving ship a distinct shock. A tug carried out … an anchor … and the kedge was put out by sheer-legs also on port quarter. With a tug assisting the ship was hove nearer the bank. Diver commenced and worked all night on patch, port side; great difficulty … in keeping Chinese in sampans away from ship's side whilst diver at work. These people are salving oil leaking from damage. Police gave good assistance but had to open fire on several occasions to enforce authority.

No one was killed, though water entered the engine room, three of the crew sustained minor injuries and an eighteen-year-old deck-boy was seriously wounded by bomb splinters from which he subsequently recovered. There was 'quite a rush' to get *Anchises* out of China owing to the complications surrounding the extrication of

HM Sloop *Amethyst* which had been shelled by the Communists and ran aground on
her way up the Yangtze-Kiang to relieve the destroyer *Consort* on protection duties.
Her commander was preparing to make a dash for the sea and there was a fear that
Anchises could be seized against the fate of the sloop. 'Towed by a Moller's tug which
managed to part the towing wire twice when trying to get underway', *Anchises* had
cleared Chinese waters when the *Amethyst* started downstream, and finally arrived
at Kobe for repairs.[19] Other ships were strafed by nationalist aircraft when passing
through the Taiwan Strait, including a Glen liner, but it was to be the new rulers of
China who posed the greater threat to personal safety. Having sequestrated Holt's
Wharf at Pootung, their complex immigration process, fuelled by anti-British indoctrination justifiably based upon the outrages of the Opium Wars, sought to inflict a
humiliating loss of face on British ship's companies. However, their xenophobia and
fear of spies was dangerous and all ships were boarded by both pilots and soldiers of
the Peoples' Liberation Army when in port limits. In 1952, Third Mate John Woodger
of the *Astyanax*, Captain F.M. Wilkes,[20] could not read the ship's draught marks without an armed guard. The ship was in Tsingtao on Christmas Eve and:

> we were allowed to visit a night club, the Hwai Hur, where we were assured by
> the Commissar that the happy workers would be delighted to welcome us. This
> turned out not to be so. However, after a couple of hours of music and a few drinks
> we returned to the ship. One of the stewards became separated and lost his way.
> Climbing over a wall he ended up in a prison cell having found himself in the Naval
> Dockyard and accused of spying. Following this the Master was also arrested and
> confined ... Fortunately the [Chinese] Agent was able to persuade the authorities
> that there was no espionage involved and the Master and steward returned to the
> ship just in time for Christmas Dinner.

A less clear-cut circumstance arose when the mates took bearings as was the case for
Third Mate Alston Kennerley of Holt's *Atreus* at the end of 1953 when she ran from
Hong Kong to Whampoa, the port for Hong Kong.

> It's a dramatic run up the Pearl River ... during which, on duty on the bridge, I was
> charged with noting the positions of the navigation marks, surreptitiously so as not
> to be noticed by the bridge guards, basic navigation data being something that the
> British authorities needed to up-date charts.

Accusations of espionage were to put Alfred Holt's officers at the centre of a diplomatic incident sixteen years later, and one recalled being asked in Shanghai why a
named naval officer had been aboard the ship in Hong Kong. By and large, however,
cargo-liners were less vulnerable to minor *contretemps*, unlike tramps which occasionally spent many weeks in Chinese waters awaiting cargo or on charter for many
weeks. The Communists swiftly closed-down anything resembling a night club, sub-
stituting International Seamen's Clubs where beer and king prawns could be had
along with a strong dose of indoctrination. Such a lack of traditional entertainments
where Merchant Jack could let off steam could land him in trouble. Similarly, whereas

details like flag etiquette were usually observed with a nod to naval practice in cargo-liners, it was more casually approached in tramps where the red duster was usually neglected. The bright new and potently iconic red flag of the People's Republic flown as courtesy ensign *had* to be respectfully hoisted and lowered, and *never* suffered to trail even accidentally on the deck. Such 'ceremonies' were carried out under the eyes of the armed guards and woe betide any tramp-ship apprentice who did not obey the regulations to the very letter. Even the most basic acts were capable of mis-interpretation, as Apprentice Goddard in the *Sudbury Hill* discovered when fishing for a length of removeable railing which had been lost overboard when Goddard slipped on an icy deck in Shanghai. Caught by the army guards for illegally 'taking sound-ings,' the apprentices were arrested and 'had to write a confession, apologising for our actions against the People's Republic of China.'

The Counties Ship-Management Co.'s tramp *Sudbury Hill* was a Fort-class vessel and an unhappy ship. Prior to her arrival on the China coast in July 1959 she had discharged scrap at buoys in Kobe, Japan. The master cut everyone's advance of wages for their shore leave by half and would only allow one boat ashore daily. Kobe was renowned for its bars, girls and cheap shopping, so the master's parsimony went unappreciated by all.

> On Sundays at least we had some respite, as we were able to convince the Chaplain from the Missions to Seamen of our religious fervour … The Chaplain threatened to report the Old Man [to the owners in] London if an additional boat was not provided … for us to go to church, a move that infuriated the Old Man and forever endeared the Mission to me. We found that the Mission chapel was also used by the local British community in Kobe, so the Sunday morning service also proved to be a friendly social gathering. They also took us under their wing so … we were whisked off to various homes for a good square meal and pleasant conversation … The Old Man extracted his revenge … by ordering us three apprentices to each write a long letter to a school in London that had adopted the ship.

Unlike Watson's Anchises, the *Sudbury Hill* did find coal at Chinwangtao and was chartered by the Chinese government to carry this and other produce on the coast, cargoes now denied the old firms like China Navigation. 'It proved to be a rotten trade that further compounded the low morale already reigning aboard the *Sudbury Hill*. Thus started what was probably the most miserable time of my life at sea, some eight months on the China coast.' The prolonged inspections by the Border Guards for which the Communists were notorious proved tedious, required four times every round voyage. Mustered on deck under armed guard, usually during the small hours, each crew member had to identified against his papers. While this was in progress the guards searched the ship for anything considered subversive, including 'the much read magazines supplied by the Mission in Kobe' and American magazines – *Playboy* was an especial favourite, evidence of the decadent West – along with anything else considered capable of corrupting, perverting, or being politically incorrect.

> On one trip a map of the world in the radio office was confiscated because Tibet, recently invaded by Chinese troops, was marked in a different colour from China;

on another occasion our charts showing Taiwan as Formosa [its name when part of the Japanese Empire] were removed ...

The process was prolonged, taking up to three or four hours during which no one was allowed to return to their cabin and was carried out by 'very tall north Chinese dressed in padded winter uniforms' as being 'very intimidating'. On the *Sudbury Hill's* arrival at Hsing Kiang, a new port established in 1952 near Tientsin:

> The cabins were searched, the Mate's especially, which he said was literally stripped. The annoying thing about these ... is that the guards don't know what they are looking for. They just say it is regulations. Yesterday there was one of the security police walking about in the cabins just looking around and reading letters ...

Besides taking coal at Chinwangtao to Shanghai, the *Sudbury Hill* loaded stores at Hong Kong and ran between Shanghai, Tsingtao and Dairen, where sawn timber and bulk maize were loaded. Round-the-clock cargo working was noisy enough, but the accompanying blare of martial music and exhortatory broadcasts to cheer 'the ant-like hordes of coolies' was exhausting.

> [T]he methods of loading were stone-age. On the wharf gangs of coolies enveloped in dust shoveled coal out of railway trucks into closely woven cargo nets to be lifted aboard by the ship's derricks. In the hold the coal was tipped out and the empty net [sent ashore again] ... Each lift weighed about one-and-a-half tons though frequently the Chinese would overload them causing [damage to] ... our runners and guys ... since any instruction to reduce the loads were totally ignored. We normally resorted to immobilising the winches by shutting off the steam supply. This always produced an uproar from the Chinese and threats about our 'non-co-operation' from the resident commissar.

This expedient was also used to prevent coal observed 'steaming' being loaded for fear of spontaneous combustion. But it infuriated the Chinese since the necessary spreading on the wharf, allowing it to cool, upset their planned – and demanded – loading rate. While the *Sudbury Hill's* master cut their advances and the drab, politically charged Seamen's Clubs proved depressing, what Goddard and his colleagues did achieve:

> after six months of endeavour, was the opportunity to visit the Great Wall of China which was only a short drive north of Chinwangtao. In spite of the grey day it was a delight to get away from the ship and the port area, and venture out into rural China ... we were tremendously impressed ...

Less impressive was the cold of a North China winter where the sea was often frozen.

> We waddled round the ship wearing our entire wardrobes ... The fire-main froze solid and the heavy steel pipe split in several places. The rigging and fittings were festooned with icicles ... [and we] had to take special care of our winches to ensure

they were not immobilised by the cold … Normally … [they] were kept turning slowly … which didn't please the engineers who had to tour the deck and keep an eye on them. Usually this was a job done by the Indian greasers, but due to the low temperatures, our crew had long since refused to turn out for all but the most essential duties … On our … final call in Dairen we found the intense cold had frozen the spray round our bows and the anchors were solid in the hawse-pipes … we had to steam round in circles waiting for tugs to come out and take us to our berth.

As the foregoing shows, life in British tramps could be basic and even miserable, notwithstanding the wartime improvements in conditions. Despite the huge war losses, there remained a few survivors of an earlier period. Seventeen-year-old Jim Scott joined Headlam's *Fylingdale*, of Whitby in 1947 as a deck-boy. The vessel loaded china clay in Fowey for Philadelphia, after which: 'It took ages to cross the North Atlantic'. The ship was fitted with rod and chain steering which had to be dismantled to work the after hatches, over which it ran, and required reassembling before the ship could sail. When he signed-on Scott asked if the ship was new. 'Practically,' he was told. She had been built in 1924. On joining he was issued with a knife and fork, a tin plate and mug, a bucket, sweat rag, bar of soap and – incomprehensibly – a tin of cheese. Fresh water was severely limited to a bucketful a day and for hot water it as necessary to go below to the engine room where, if one wanted a thorough wash, one stripped off and had a scrub on the engine-room gratings. The food, however, was 'quite good' and better than that enjoyed at home, where rationing had just been reintroduced.

Such was the poverty of post-war Britain that food rationing was reintroduced in 1949 and charters for cargoes, particularly of frozen and chilled meat from Australasia and South America continued to be awarded by the Ministry of Food into the early 1950s. A healthy young man with a good appetite was to find the food at sea, particularly in passenger and cargo-liners, far better than he could expect at home. Nevertheless, food could be a contentious issue, especially aboard the aptly nicknamed tramps of Hungry Hogarth's of Glasgow. When asked by a member of the Hogarth family why so few of their apprentice returned to the company after obtaining their Second Mate's certificates, one of their chief mates responded that it was because of the appalling way they were treated while serving their 'time'. Food and living conditions in this company, according to one of its apprentices, Robert Fullarton, were appalling and little better, it seems, than had pertained before 1914. Required to report to the master after working cargo aboard the B*aron Herries*, Fullarton found:

Captain Ewing sitting in his cabin with coal dust around his eyes, in his ears and around his nose … I decided, there and then, that once I finished my time and passed for Second Mate, I would never again sail on a coal burning or a coal carrying ship. What was the point of … studying and rising through the ranks to live in conditions like this[?] [21]

Fullarton had gone to sea in 1944 and had been in the *Baron Herries* since the end of the war. While Ewing was 'a real gentleman,' his predecessor had been 'a young master determined to make a name for himself with the owners and so secure a shore job in the Glasgow office'. Fullarton did not enjoy the experience of serving under so mean-minded and penny-pinching a man and unsurprisingly the *Baron Herries* was an unhappy ship. Ewing proved a more congenial master, transforming the vessel. Although only built in 1940, the *Baron Herries* might have belonged to an earlier era, her owners sparing no effort in keeping her fitments to a minimum, in sharp contrast to the environment of the American-built war tonnage which many men had experienced or at least heard-of. The voyage undertaken by Captain Ewing in 1946 was long, tedious and typical of post-war tramping. The ship left Middlesbrough in ballast for Safi, Morocco, where she loaded phosphates for Capetown. Proceeding light-ship to Durban she loaded coal and proceeded through the Suez Canal towards Ancona in an Italy ravaged by war and now gripped by the coldest winter for many years. This was a United Nations relief cargo and the women and children were allowed on board to pick up coals which spilled onto the deck. The cold was so bad that every evening the apprentices had to run the derrick wires off the winch drums so that they could be kept revolving slowly all night to prevent them freezing up. From Ancona the *Baron Herries* returned in ballast to Lourenço Marques to load South African coal for Mombasa, a short run but one which guaranteed a return to Lourenço Marques for another cargo of coal to the French colony of Djibouti. Here the holds were cleaned and cotton-seed was loaded for Alexandria and once discharged the *Baron Herries* proceeded to dry-dock in Bombay. Indian independence in August 1947 had split the sub-continent into two with consequent mass migration and a tense atmosphere prevailing. Having had her bottom cleaned and painted and all absolutely necessary repairs cleared by her class surveyor, the *Baron Herries* steamed to Calcutta, embarking a Hughli pilot at the Sandheads.

> In those days a Hughi pilot, whether British or Indian, was a very grand gentleman. He did not climb a pilot ladder, the full accommodation ladder had to be ready to receive him, his leadsman and his luggage. He was rowed over [from the pilot cutter] pulled by six uniformed seamen and steered by a *Serang* with a silver chain and bosun's pipe. The Pilot, dressed in spotless white and wearing a topee, sat on a white cushioned seat in front of the *Serang*. When he arrived on deck he had to be met by a deck officer who escorted him to the bridge to meet the Captain while his leads-man with the luggage was shown to the Pilot's cabin by an apprentice. The 90 mile passage up the Hughli could take a day or more, depending on the amount of water in the river, with spells at anchor waiting for the tide.

At Calcutta, coal was loaded within the Kidderpore dock system, so waiting ships were secured between the buoys on the Hastings Moorings, an eight-hour task even when helped by the Indian mooring gang that came aboard for the purpose with the port pilot. While lying in Calcutta security was a problem and Ghurka guards were engaged. These men wore military uniforms, topped off by their pill-box hats, and were armed with kukris. They were punctilious at saluting the deck-officers, but ignored the engineers. While at Calcutta the *Baron Herries'* lascars were signed-off and a new crew entered the ship ready for her passage to Colombo where her coal cargo was dis-charged. Another ballast passage followed, across the Indian Ocean, cleaning her holds, towards Victoria where a part cargo of flour was taken in. Topped off in Fremantle, the

Baron Herries headed back for Colombo and then proceeded light-ship towards Aden, the crew cleaning the holds in preparation for a cargo of salt. However, on approaching Cape Guardafui she received orders to divert to Durban where, to Fullarton's fury another cargo of coal awaited her. To do this she needed both fresh water and bunker coal which was taken aboard at Mombasa. From Durban she hauled another cargo of coal north to Massawa in Eritrea which remained littered with the hulls of ships scuttled by the Italians. Here one of the shore labourers lost control of a winch and several of the labourers discharging coal from No.2 Hold were severely injured when the heavy steel buckets dropped on top of them. Back in Durban the *Baron Herries* loaded coal again for Mombasa, then took more coal from Lourenço Marques to Aden. Another coal cargo from Lourenço Marques was loaded for Port Said from where the weary ship headed west to La Goulette, near Tunis, where a conveying system dumped thousands of tons of iron ore into the *Baron Herries*. With this she headed for the Manchester Ship Canal and the steel works of Irlam. Here the British crew was paid-off after a voyage just sort of the full-Articled time of two years. Robert Fullarton had long since completed his apprenticeship. He had served four and a half years and had had twenty-six days leave in that time. Neither he nor Captain Ewing returned to Hogarth's employment.

If 'Hungry Hogarth's had a bad reputation, others like Bank Line retained loyal sea-staff. Service in their ships was not universally popular, however for, in common with all deep-water companies, Bank Line signed-on their crews for two years, but whereas most cargo-liner companies broke Articles at the end of a voyage of, say, four months, granted leave and signed-on again at the beginning of the next voyage. Bank Line, with their extended and sometimes irregular trading pattern – especially if the ships were tramping – often retained crews for the full two years. Absence from home for such a long period, tolerated in the harsh pre-war years, became increasingly unacceptable as the liberated society of the sixties demanded greater personal liberty. Sexual freedom for women destroyed the social norms that provided a distant husband with a faithful wife. Long-service appealed to a certain breed of young man but was tough on the married and also on the young apprentices who, for all their tough talk, remained between the ages of sixteen and twenty. As we have seen, conditions in many older ships remained primitive. Writing of his experiences as 3rd Mate in 1956 aboard the *Irisbank*, Alan Rawlinson recalled 'having to pump water by hand from the lower forepeak into a bucket and then negotiate the heaving foredeck back to the accommodation [where] the water was boiled by putting a ... steam jet into the bucket'. Supervision of correspondence courses was patchy, as it was almost universally throughout the British merchant fleet, and entirely dependent upon the diligence of the ship's master and his deck-officers. Consequently 'the courses were rarely completed [even] over [the] four years' of an apprenticeship. At this time Bank Line usually followed the tramp company's practice of taking on boys at sixteen for a full term apprenticeships, eschewing the eighteen year old who had had some schooling at a nautical training-establishment and thereby earned some remission of his qualifying sea-time for the Second Mate's examination. Four years was, neatly enough, two two-year contract periods. Bank Line, Rawlinson goes on to say:

> had their share of miserable and unhappy apprentices, not to mention drunken and
> suicidal masters. The plain, and perhaps unpalatable, truth to romantic shiplovers like

me is that, apart from a few truly suited individuals, the majority of senior officers and masters, in the time honoured way, were there because they had not the drive nor gumption to succeed ashore ... Perhaps my happiest memory is that of serving aboard the *Inchanga*, one of the Bank Line passenger vessels ... During 1952 we traded between Calcutta and Durban on a three- to four-month trip, calling at East Coast ports like Zanzibar and Dar-es-Salaam, and to the Bay of Bengal ports at the other end. We carried an assortment of species, apart from the ubiquitous bales of gunny sacks, and the huge, open-cowled vents opening onto the wide, wood-sheathed decks gave out pungent and spicy smells which, when experienced today, are an instant reminder of that long gone vessel.'[22]

Until being superseded by bulk-carriers in the 1970s, many British tramp-companies retained their disreputable image. Despite Rawlinson's harsh judgement, many men of all ranks settled into this raffish existence as happily as William McFee had done a generation earlier. As for the itinerant Marconi radio officer, hired by his employer to whatever shipping company required a 'Sparks,' exchange into such a ship could mean a radical change of culture, as Norman Freeman found out in 1961.

Up to this time I had had an extremely good run of ships; clean, well run vessels, with excellent food and accommodation and companionable colleagues of my own age. Three years had been spent on the deck-passenger ships of the British India Company, a proud and aristocratic survivor of the *Raj*. Goan servants solicitously attended all one's needs, laying out the spotless white uniforms one donned before going down to the festooned promenade deck. There might be a dance or a film show. One could sit in the comfortable bar, feeling glamorous, eyeing the exposed brown midriffs of the silk-sari-clad Indian ladies travelling first class.[23]

For the radio officer of a tramp-ship duties were light. In port a contracted Marconi man had few obligations, though he might be asked to help tally a valuable consignment of cargo.

Only at sea did the radio room come into being. With the long aerials hoisted high, the receivers pulled in the twittering tin-whistle orchestra of the Morse-world wavebands. Here thousands of jostling streams of dots and dashes sped ... between earth and ionosphere. The ship's radio room was a floating outstation of this universe of communication, whose language, the fluting sounds of Morse, whistled from loudspeakers and earphones ... On a three month voyage there would not be much more than forty incoming and outgoing telegrams to handle ...

Nevertheless, a considerable amount of time was spent by the 'Sparks' in raising high-frequency stations, sending or receiving one such telegram, and listening to the traffic lists that announced whether any messages were held at any of these stations for one's own ship. Messages also had to be sent when the ship arrived at, or departed from, a port, not only to the port concerned, but to a Commonwealth radio station, opening or closing the ship-radio station as she entered or left international waters. But the Marconi Sparks enjoyed a lifestyle denied to others of similar age. As a first-trip eighteen-year-old he might be one or two years junior to the senior apprentice, yet enjoyed the full benefits of manhood, with status as an officer and the entitlement to a bar account. Moreover, by remaining in one ship he could, with the master's compliance, take off on unofficial leave until the ship was ready to sail, a particular advantage in a tramp with a large, homogenous cargo to discharge. Such 'captain's leave' entitled him to accumulate 'a store of Marconi-leave, which could provide him with nine months or a year's holiday when he felt like it.'[24]

Many young officers found life less satisfactory. Having left the *Worcester* as a prize-winning cadet late in 1947, Donald Wright found the penny-pinching of Lord Vestey's Blue Star Line and its lack of prospects intolerable. He left soon after obtaining his Second Mate's Certificate, to join Athel Tankers.[25] He knew nothing about tankers.

> They were never mentioned at the *Worcester* – infra dig? – as if they did not exist
> … It was a different world: they ploughed their own half-submerged way, to their
> own places, on their own routes, with their own expert crews. I did know that their
> voyages were long and boring, their stay in port short and miles from anywhere. For
> all these disadvantages, in return, the pay, food, and accommodation were known to
> be the very best, and the saying was 'once a tanker-man, always so'. The Companies
> were reliable and trusted – during the war they had not stopped a sailorman's
> money the moment his ship was sunk …

Brian McManus served his time with Cunard and having obtained a Second Mate's Certificate in January 1947 joined Cunard's Mediterranean 'brig' *Bantria* as Third Officer on £30.5 a month. Feeling this was insufficient he was persuaded by a friend to join the War Department's Royal Army Service Corps' tank landing craft referred to earlier. 'It was only standard rates of £28.5 a month for a Third Officer and more-or-less dead ships with no galley staff or stewards. The chief and second officers had been demobbed from the RNR. I stayed six weeks'. He then joined Bibby's *Somersetshire* as Third Officer, exciting no little envy from the master and chief officer who had had to obtain their master's certificates before the war to obtain a junior officer's post. Pay rates were similar to Cunard but in Bibby's McManus discovered 'the highest standard of navigation'. He also enjoyed something else: 'It is surprising what incentive is a young girl waiting on deck for making one proficient at taking and working out four stars in twenty minutes … The Bibby troopers and hospital ships, with no cargo-work, and plenty of girls to flirt with were a soft easy life'. However, he did not get on with all his masters, one of whom he described as 'a trembling wreck' when in sight of land despite – or perhaps because of – having been in command of an assault ship during the war. When the Bibby fleet contracted, McManus was dismissed and joined Elder, Dempster, to whose trade he took to like a duck to water.

There were many factors that affected a man's attitude to the life at sea. The necessity of greasing palms and offering douceurs to port officials was a problem of which the Royal Mail Line 'were well aware of'. In a South American port aboard a 'a passenger ship' of which he was second officer, Jack Le Brecht recalled encountering:

several local dockside loafers approaching the gangway along the main-deck with large cardboard cartons on their shoulders. When challenged in my South American Spanish they looked shifty and I ushered them into the purser's office to establish their authority to unload whatever was in the cases. The purser looked concerned and sent for the chief officer who, on his arrival, became very red in the face, took me aside and ordered me to let the party ashore. About an hour later I was summoned to the head of the gangway to find the chief officer, the purser and the chief of police for whom the toilet preparations were destined and who suggested that a run ashore for me would not be a good idea.

The security of a merchant ship and her cargo in port was a problem, particularly in the east where destitution for the majority of the population made of a British ship, fair game. From desirable items of general cargo, by way of mooring ropes and hatch tarpaulins to the personal effects of her crew, all had a value. General cargo-liners were particularly vulnerable, having a huge variety of goods on board in open stows, but even in ships like the *Baron Herries* where the crew had very little, theft could mean deprivation of a relatively serious nature, hence the employment of Gurkhas. Elsewhere other minorities provided security guards and Sikhs were employed in Singapore and Hong Kong. Occasionally word of a cargo's utility to those ashore got out, sometimes with serious consequences.

In 1951 the *Javanese Prince*, on a west-about round-the-world service plying from New York, was lying in a Flippino anchorage 'a few hours south of Manila' where she was boarded by local thieves. Among her cargo was a stow of cartons of toy plastic guns, loaded in the United States for consignees in the Philippines. These were in the forward 'tween decks but their presence on the ship's cargo plans had been entered in abbreviated form: 'guns'. This information had clearly been noted by one of the tally clerks on the ship's arrival, and interpreted for the real thing. A state of chronic insurrection pertained ashore and the tally clerk's loyalties clearly lay with the communist 'Huk' rebels, to whom he communicated this inaccurate intelligence.

Accordingly the *Javanese Prince* was boarded, the marauders making directly for the forward hatches. Their approaching boats had been seen as soon as they came within the ambit of the ship's floodlights. The officer-of-the-watch, Mr Anthony Uden, quickly seeing the men in the boats were armed, called the master, Captain Jones, who immediately ordered all his officers to turn out, distributing small arms. These, held in the master's cabin, consisted of two Winchester rifles and a dozen Colt revolvers and the armed mates ran out and confronted the raiders, their aggression surprising the Huks and resulting in the capture of nine. One man jumped over the ship's rail and Uden shot at him, wounding him in the shoulder. Immediately realising the winged man might drown, Uden promptly dived in after him. The thieves were handed over to the civil authorities. Afterwards, Uden was given a cash reward by Prince Line and awarded its Silver Medal by the Royal Humane Society for this extraordinary double act.

Most voyages passed off, of course, without such excitements, pre-war trade patterns rapidly re-emerging. Joining Dutch, German, Scandinavian companies, Elder, Dempster dominated the trade with West Africa. These companies, together with John Holt's Guinea-Gulf Line and the United Africa Co.'s Palm Line formed the conferences necessary to serve the coast that before the war had still been blighted by yellow-fever and malaria. However, although inoculations against the former and prophylactic paludrine tablets removed the threat of these, something of the past lingered along the littoral, cargo still being worked by way of surf-boats at the several open anchorages. Elder, Dempster's cargo-liners were nicknamed 'the monkey-boats' from having once been the source of this sailor's pet on the Liverpool waterfront. Their outward cargo consisted of 'more or less anything that could be bought in a department store,' plus a great deal more, as Captain Brian McManus recalls:

> In Liverpool 32lb white cotton and 1 cwt hessian bags of salt, bales of printed cotton, cigarettes, Guinness, lager, whisky, cases of soap, baled sacks of dried cod, corrugated iron and asbestos were the main commodities loaded. In the case of the white bags of salt, the bag was worth more than the contents. In London similar cargoes were loaded with gin replacing whisky and cars being about equal in numbers from Liverpool and London.
>
> Full cargoes of cement were a big export from the cement wharves on the London River, sometimes with lorries stowed on top. At one time Brazil had been Britain's best customer for cement but in the 1950s it was West Africa.

To this might be added chemicals, cables, pipes, steel, aluminium, rubber tyres, paper, dyes, iron pots, sugar, glue and margarine. Cargo was also loaded in Hamburg, Bremen, Rotterdam and Antwerp, ports served by many British lines from all over the world. Manufactured goods, Volkswagen cars, cases of German and Dutch lager and beer, even cement from Hamburg, supplemented the British exports. Prior to the independence of Nigeria, the Gold Coast, Sierra Leone, the Gambia and the Cameroons, the Crown Agents for the Colonies were the 'big-shippers supplying their needs'. When the ships reached their first port, Freetown, Sierra Leone, seventy men from the Kroo tribe – 'the best sailors in West Africa' – were embarked, a tradition dating from the slave trade.

> There were four gangs to work the cargo, six engine-room hands, three washmen who did the ship's laundry, four tally-clerks and a cook. They lived aboard the ship and worked the cargo at the ports of call along the coast. At the larger ports such as Takoradi and Lagos, extra gangs would be employed.

Sometimes the coast labour was embarked at Takoradi, in which case the men were Beribis. The engine-room hands attended to maintenance while the deck-labourers handled the cargo and cleaned a ship's deep-tanks for a homeward lading of palm and ground-nut oils from Nigeria, and latex from Monrovia, Liberia. These men were also 'skilled experts at loading logs' which formed part of the homeward cargoes which were, besides their oils, ground-nuts and palm cocoa and kernels, coffee, cotton, rubber and sawn timber.

Reminiscent of an earlier age there remained navigational challenges, the 1,200 miles between Monrovia and the Cameroon's being largely featureless, 'making soundings of utmost importance and the echo-sounder the most valuable navigational aid' owing to the constant change in depths over the bars and alongside the wharves.

Some of the older masters who had sailed along the coast in the 1930s claimed that by using 'bush' navigation they could navigate along parts of the coast by recognising the trees. Fishtown, on the Liberian coast, was one example. It was identified by three prominent trees ... [A]t Liberia's eastern boundary with the Ivory Coast there was a huge prominent tree [and] when looking for Tafu Point lighthouse [during daylight] the 'Tafu tree' was sighted first. About 1955 the tree was struck by lightning and reported in the weekly Notices to mariners [issued by the Admiralty]. This marked the end of 'bush navigation'.

Navigation in the creeks of the Niger Delta, hedged in by monotonous and indistinguishable mangrove swamps was slow to develop from the practice of relying on a local fisherman who was embarked to guide a ship to her destination:

by literally pointing to the correct creek to enter. The second and third mates were stationed in the bridge wings. Their job was to watch the bow wave as it fanned out. If it stopped breaking, or what they called 'making a fuss,' they called to the master. He then knew that on that side of the ship the water was shallowing and sheered the ship away into deeper water. Another indication of the depth of water was the actual mangroves. It the trees were high at the water's edge there was insufficient depth close to the bank. On the other hand if the bank was fringed with low scrub it was deep enough to go almost alongside. With regular contact aboard ship the fishermen were taught to steer. They soon learnt where the deep water lay and were able to give the master a break from conning the ship. As their knowledge grew they were able to offer their services as pilots. They progressed into bringing a son as helmsman and gave their orders in the Iwaw language: *Komobra* – port, *Amanbra* – starboard, *Zeemassin* – amidships, and *Tiyemowery* – steady.

During the 1920s the colonial Nigerian Marine made a complete survey of the delta's creeks and at this time some masters continued navigating the creeks alone. With the conference lines owning the wharves and lighters, 'Even in the 1960s John Holt's Guinea-Gulf Line masters still went to their company's wharf at Warri without pilots'.

In 1959 Elder, Dempster and Palm Line took a 40 per cent stake in the new Nigerian National Line, the remainder being Nigerian-state owned. The partnership did not last long, the British companies withdrawing as problems arose.

No coastline could contrast more with the low West African littoral than that of western South America, which rose to the summits of the Andes and was to fascinate Third Officer Richard Lothian of the Pacific Steam Navigation Co. He had served as a cadet, joining the company's *Pizarro* in October 1963, shortly afterwards running into a hurricane on his first Atlantic crossing. The company's ships were all meteorological reporting ships which submitted observations every six hours and the *Pizarro* was among those vessels awarded for the accuracy and regularity of her reports by the United States Coastguard. In the early 1960s a P.S.N.C. cargo-liner left Liverpool every Friday night, calling first at Bermuda, then the Bahamas, Santo Domingo, Puerto Rico and Jamaica, skirting the United States naval blockade of Cuba. Having left the Panama Canal at Balboa, Lothian recalls then 'being with the pelicans' as the ship headed south, her first port of call Buenventura in Colombia. 'Always a dangerous place,' it was a tropical port where the midday rain was heavy and predictable. The ship was now 'on the coast' an expression all liner companies used for the coastlines they regarded as their own special preserve. For the P.S.N.C. this was the long spine of South America which, lying on a north-south axis took a ship directly through each successive climatic zone. Tropical vegetation prevailed from Balboa south to Peru's northern headland of Cabo Blanco, so that Ecuador's Guayaquil, situated ninety miles up a river surrounded by dense jungle, proved a mosquito-infested ordeal, while the shifting shoals in the estuary provided a navigational hazard.

Beyond Cabo Blanco, where the warm water is invaded by the cold, northerly Humboldt current, the coast is bleak desert and the ships coasted south to Callao, towards the port for Peru's capital, Lima. 'Because of dead plankton [Callao] had a strong, lingering smell that turned all brass green and silver cutlery was left very tarnished'. Small ports were visited, but few other than Callao, Salaverry and Matarani allowed ships to berth alongside, so cargo was brought off to the anchored vessel by lighters and small craft. One feature of the entire coastline was:

the distinct lack of wind, no rain and the sea was always calm. So-much-so that the ships always sailed from northern Peru almost as far south as Valparaiso, with all hatches open and just covered by a tent. This saved an immense amount of time. You normally arrived at a different port each day, sometimes two and even three within twenty-four hours.

Peru and northern Chile had at this time the world's biggest fishing industry: anchovies, which were turned into fish-meal, thousands of tons of which were brought back to Europe each week, for fertiliser and animal-feed, much of it going to Poland and East Germany. Vast armadas of fishing boats worked from several dozen ports while the islands you passed looked black in the morning, totally covered by cormorants and when they took flight, the islands turned white from the guano they had deposited. Although the weather was always hot and dry – a most agreeable climate – the sea was always freezing on all the beaches.

On arrival in Arica, the first Chilean port, one could always see, proudly flying on the Morro, the national flag flying over land won from [its neighbours] … Tocopilla and Iquique were the old nitrate ports – holiday places now – but copper was still exported through Antofagasta, Chanaral and San Antonio. It was loaded either for a specific port or 'on option,' bought and sold in transit like oil.

The climate began to change in Coquimbo, becoming 'Mediterranean' which produced good wine … One or two ships a year went south to Punta Arenas, normally during the summer, and for this a Chilean naval pilot was embarked at Valparaiso. He remained with the ship for however many weeks one was in the south … [Despite the season] the weather could never be trusted south of Puerto Montt, and a decision had to be made whether to go 'outside' in the open ocean, or 'inside' through the *canales* … [In the] *canales* the scenery was the most stunning I have ever seen. Sheer mountains rising from either side of the ship. No human habitation, [only] dense forest, with the huge Andes, majestically there. The ship generally anchored at night, sometimes after searching for a sunken mountain top on which to drop the anchor. Tides and currents were notoriously strong, particularly so in certain narrows. Many tiny, isolated ports lay along this southern coast, all surrounded by lush vegetation. On arriving in the Magellan Straits and making for Punta Arenas the weather might be a pleasant summer's day, [but] on approaching the anchorage, within five minutes, it could suddenly change, with hurricane force katabatic winds coming down from the mountains.

There was always a long swell over the entire length of 'the West Coast'. Ships always rolled at anchor, and even alongside berths in port, they would always roll slightly, no matter how the breakwaters had been designed, but more particularly a vessel would continuously range [up-and-down] her berth, despite having heavy rope and wire springs.[26]

Fourteen years earlier in September 1949, Richard Goss had visited the eastern seaboard of South America in the Prince liner *Scottish Prince*. A future academic, Goss was 'impressed by Buenos Aires, its squares, streets, cafes and restaurants. As a comparatively penniless cadet I could make only limited use of these, but I have always enjoyed walking about a new city, and this can cost very little.' Loading was intensive as they lay alongside a wharf with barges outboard.

Working both sides of the ship ... we discharged and loaded simultaneously. It took four days to load the tung [wood] oil, which was pumped aboard from barges and road-tankers [into deep-tanks] ... Elsewhere we had sunflower seed expeller, cottonseed cake, hooves and horns, bone-meal, horse-hair, sheepskins and wool, corned and brisket beef (in tins), tallow, honey, salted casings (for sausages) and sinews ... We then set off homewards with all hands busily cleaning and painting ship ... replacing the rope guys on the [twenty] derricks ... all cut, spliced and properly whipped.

After refuelling at Las Palmas the *Scottish Prince* berthed in the Surrey Commercial Dock on 13 October and Goss went home for a week's leave, rejoining on the 21st when the ship sailed for Avonmouth.

The new Chief Officer, Gale, had brought his wife and small daughter on board. She became quite frightened when the ship rolled heavily in Force 8 winds off the Scillies and cried. We were, therefore, the only ship with two howling gales at the same time ... At Avonmouth we loaded unboxed cars, some China clay and stone for Montreal, sailing on 30 October. Some pieces of stone weighed up to 7-tons, so we moored port-side to the quay, where our 10-ton derricks were and used them ... with wire guys led through snatch-blocks to the windches at a near-by hatch. This occasional re-rigging of derricks for special purposes was interesting and was a skill which needed to be known by the Chief Officer ...

In mid-Atlantic the humdrum routine of the voyage came to a dramatic end.

The wind was Force 10 ... and the ship was rolling heavily when the engine stopped with a bang at 05.15 on 4 November. The piston-skirt had fallen off inside No.1 cylinder and the piston rings were broken into several pieces, breaking the lower cylinder liner and lower scavenge-belt. Pistons, cylinder liner, etc, were removed with the engine-room crane and, to reduce the rolling, steadying sails were made by folding tarpaulins into triangles. They were hoisted up the mast with a derrick-runner secured to a corner folded back, a sheet was secured in the same way and the luff was made fast round the mast with several pieces of one-inch rope passed through eyelets. We had one sail forward of the bridge and another aft. When No, 1 cylinder was dismantled the engine was started, to the Chief Engineer's surprise, on Nos 2 and 3 cylinders. We thus achieved steerage way and Captain Proctor then leaned over the bridge-rail and shouted: 'Brail up the foresail!'

A tug was summoned from St John's, Newfoundland, but on the 8th the wind rose to Force 11 they were unable to maintain steerage and ran off before the wind:

at about 8 knots with the wind on the port quarter and [in] very high seas. The tug arrived after dark … and, at first light next morning, fired no less than five lines across our bow before getting one properly aboard us. We had caught an earlier line, but they paid out so much that the messenger parted. We were not impressed with their seamanship.

Having detached one anchor and fished for the cable in preparation for the tow which at one stage parted, they arrived at St Johns on 14 November where the ship underwent expensive repairs, a new piston-skirt being flown out from Britain – though that was not the end of the story – before eventually reaching Montreal ten days later. Here it was freezing cold:

and a tug steamed round the dock each morning to break the ice which had formed overnight. Physically, however, this was very exhilarating, since the air was very dry. The windlass forward and the warping winch aft were kept going all the time to prevent the steam system from freezing and the three cadets were put on continuous watches to keep them lubricated. As the work was not strenuous we took the unusual pattern of working 12 hours on and 24 hours off. This gave us a good opportunity to explore the city. However, I was asleep when two 38-ton transformers were loaded from a lighter with a floating crane. Despite the heavy weather and rolling there had been no damage to our inward cargo. We loaded cars, trucks and tinned milk, mostly for Rio.

We left Montreal on 29 November, being glad to escape from an increasingly ice-bound port, called at Quebec for a cargo which … included bagged asbestos and at Sydney for coal before leaving for New York, where we arrived at our usual Brooklyn terminal on 11 December but our voyage to Rio was interrupted by another engine breakdown. There were six engine stops at sea, varying from one hour to fifteen hours and eventually we diverted to Recife in the Brazilian state of Pernambuco, arriving on 30 December and leaving on 9 January 1950. the cause of our breakdown was that running the engine in mid-Atlantic on two instead of its normal, three cylinders had distorted the engine bearings. All cross-head and crank bearings had to be removed and sent ashore.

Richard Goss later remarked that when submitting himself for examination for a certificate of competency he had 'always hoped that I could work some reference to these events into a reply at my 'Orals', since I knew the examiner would be so interested that he would have no time to ask me anything else. But I had no such luck.'

As the foregoing shows the life at sea remained as full of hazard as ever, as the British public had been reminded with the loss of the American grain-laden freighter *Flying Enterprise* in the English Channel in January 1952.[27] In November 1954 a similar fate overtook the Hain tramp *Tresillian* off the Cork coast when her cargo of Canadian grain shifted. Fortunately the Shell tanker *Liparis* was on hand to rescue her people. Eleven months later a curious document was produced by the Ministry of Transport referring to the 1928 loss of the Furness, Withy's *Asiatic Prince* (see Chapter Two) when between San Pedro, Los Angeles and Yokohama. There had in the interim been much idle conjecture about the causes of the ship's loss, including speculation over her cargo which was said to have contained bullion. This was fuelled by the by then public knowledge that Prince Line had, as related, carried substantial shipments of bullion during the war, and pirates were blamed for hi-jacking the vessel. In fact an SOS had been heard eight days after the *Asiatic Prince* left San Pedro but although mentioning a 'terrific storm' the call-sign, though similar to the *Asiatic Prince*'s was not unequivocally hers. Although a search was instituted, including units from the United States Navy, nothing was found of Captain Duncan and his forty-eight men and the ship was Posted Missing at Lloyd's. Besides the piracy theory, an asteroid strike was considered, while other barmy scenarios were advanced. The precise reason why the MoT considered it necessary to issue a statement in October 1955 is unclear, but this said that a Board of Trade Preliminary Inquiry in 1928 had not proceeded to a fuller Formal Investigation on the grounds that since there were no survivors, there were no witnesses and therefore no useful conclusions could be drawn from the event 'which might lead to the prevention of similar occurrences in the future'. Such 'occurrences' were rare enough, though the *Asiatic Prince*'s disappearance was followed only two years later by the small London Midland and Scottish railway steamer *Calder* vanishing on passage across the North Sea from Cuxhaven.

The most likely cause for the loss of both ships was extreme weather or the now better-understood rogue-wave (see Chapter Six). The celebrated survival of the *Phemius* mentioned earlier was not unique and the Harrison liner *Tactician* was so suffer a similar ordeal. An unlucky ship, she had been built in 1961 and was an 8,844-grt, engines-aft general-cargo motor ship fitted with a 110-ton Stülken derrick, and was to suffer three fires, one of which was caused by an engine-room explosion that killed two engineers. On her maiden voyage under Captain W.S. Eustance she was in Belize City in British Honduras in late October 1961 when Hurricane Hattie struck. As with the hurricane that hit the *Phemius*, the late season Hattie proved one of the most devastating of the decade. Like Evans before him, Eustance had received a forecast indicating the tropical revolving storm would pass well to the east and, having completed loading fruit in Stann Creek, had proceeded to load timber at Belize, some thirty miles away. By noon next day, however, the hoisting of storm-warnings over the signal station on Fort George ended cargo work, the lighters being towed away and the *Tactician*'s hatches covered. As an additional precaution, her derricks were stowed and lashed. Anxious not be caught against the surrounding reefs, Eustance shipped a pilot, Mr Locke, weighed anchor and sought the security of an anchorage under the lee of Grennell's Cay to the southward of Belize. By midnight the *Tactician* was safely anchored in a rising gale.

An hour later she began to sheer and a second anchor was dropped as the ship was scoured by a wind of incredible violence and the engines were run at slow speed to ease the weight on the cables. Still the wind increased and the *Tactician* sheered even more and began seriously straining her cables, so that there were signs of dragging the anchors. The wind stopped the radar scanner and was so filled with spray, sand and coral dust that it stripped paintwork, while the turbulence of the sea caused so much aeration under the surface that the echo-sounder failed to function and the cooling-water intakes were choked with weed and required endless clearing by the engineers. About 05.10, with the barometer low at 924.5 millibars, the wind suddenly dropped and the ship was overwhelmed with exhausted birds. Nevertheless, in such shelter the sea rapidly dropped, the radar and echo-sounder were operating and Eustance and Locke weighed both anchors and securely re-moored the vessel to two anchors. The master then went round the ship and encouraged the crew. By the time he returned to the bridge it was daylight and, with a mighty roar, the wind rose again from the opposite direction and the whole process was repeated for a further six hours.

As the weather cleared the effects of the hurricane were all around them on islands bare of trees. At 13.00 Eustance weighed again and *Tactician* headed north for Belize where even worse scenes of destruction greeted the ship. Anxious to reach his home, Locke was put ashore by a ship's boat manned by volunteers appreciative of the service the pilot had rendered. The boat, in the charge of Second Officer Gordon Oxley, reached shore to find the place ruined. The harbour was littered with the wrecks of fishing boats and local schooners, buildings were razed and even Government House was destroyed. In fact about seven-tenths of Belize and nine-tenths of Stann Creek had been wiped out. Of Belize's population about half were homeless, many were injured and all were hungry. Later some 340 people were known to have been killed. The year's crops of citrus fruit and bananas were ruined and there was a threat to civil order.

Oxley made contact with the Governor, Sir Colin Thornley, and brought back to the ship his appeals for aid, for Belize's radio station had been destroyed and *Tactician*'s radio was the only means of communication. Next day the ship's boats landed cooking utensils, meat, rice, flour, canned goods, tea and medicines, chiefly antibiotics, all from her own stores and in the hands of Chief Steward Tom Pim assisted by his staff, an engineer, the purser and a cadet. They were met and assisted by immaculately turned out scouts and guides, and backed up by quantities of loaves that had meanwhile been baked on board. Co-operating with the harbour-staff, Oxley and Chief Officer Roy Simmons assisted in the making and laying of makeshift buoys to replace the lost buoyage and facilitate the entrance of relief ships. Two US Destroyers, unfamiliar with the port, were anxious to help but could not approach through the unmarked reefs, though HM Frigate *Troubridge* came straight in. Meanwhile the actual work of buoying the approach was carried out by the *Tactician*'s Third Officer Gwilym Jones and his lifeboat's crew of seamen. Meanwhile refuge had been given to a number of people whose lives were thought to be in danger. By this time the *Tactician*, virtually stripped of anything useful, was relieved by the Royal Navy and released by Thornley to continue her voyage, leaving for Corpus Christi on 2 November. On her arrival at New Orleans, she was given a heroine's welcome and Eustance, a veteran of the war, was awarded the OBE. Sadly, however, a strike by port workers marred the ship's next visit and a Governor's reception planned to honour Eustance and his ship was cancelled when boycotted by leading, anti-colonial politicians. No cargo consigned to Belize, beyond some British army supplies, was unloaded, although some was discharged at Stann Creek where normal lighterge was available until this too was brought to a halt by flying pickets from Belize. On trying to clear outwards at the Customs House the anti-British feeling ran so high that this was refused and specious headlines alleging customs evasion appeared in the news. Eventually tempers cooled and the cargo was discharged. Eustance's rueful telegram to his owners summed up the situation; referring to a famous speech made by Prime Minister Harold MacMillan referring to anti-colonial 'winds of change', but this embittering incident, and similar events elsewhere in the West Indies, would ultimately prove fatal to Harrison's operations.

In July 1968, by which time she was under Captain H.G. Skelly, the *Tactician* was on passage from the Bahamas towards Dublin. On the evening of 4th, a fire broke out in the engine room when a fuel pipe fractured and No.4 generator burst into flames. Before this could be shut down by the duty fourth engineer and the engineer cadet, this had ignited the main engine, the electrical power failed and the space filled with smoke and fumes. At risk to his life, Fourth Engineer D. Hughes gallantly stopped the main engines and did what he could to shut off the fuel to No.4 generator but had been driven out of the engine room, his lungs seared. Having ensured the engine room was evacuated and sealed, the carbon-dioxide smothering system was activated.

Skelly transmitted a request for assistance to which a number of vessels responded, including the British tanker *Asprella* and the US Coastguard Cutter *Hamilton* then acting as an Ocean Weather Ship, the Italian liner *Raffaello* and Ellerman's Wilson liner *Rapallo*. Skelly accepted the assistance of a working party equipped with breathing apparatus from the *Hamilton* and it became clear that the *Tactician* was disabled and required a tow. With the *Raffaello* relaying messages a Lloyd's Standard Agreement was swiftly made between Harrison's and the Wilson Line. Half the size of the *Tactician*, the *Rapallo* reached the scene and prepared to take the casualty in tow at daylight on the 6th. In an minor classic of latter-day seamanship, Captain Metham of the *Rapallo* manoeuvred his ship under the bow of the *Tactician* and both crews toiled until her insurance-wire,[28] shackled onto a chain snotter over the *Rapallo*'s stern was in turn shackled on to the *Tactician*'s port cable from which the anchor had been detached and 'hung-off'. The *Rapallo* then headed for Punta Delgada in the Azores, Metham fending off offers of assistance from a Greek salvage tug which had appeared, and arrived after a tranquil tow of six days.

Such near catastrophic failures were increasingly rare with the passage of time, which makes the rendering of effective assistance all the more remarkable when compared with uncertainties of the sea life half a century earlier. That they called forth initiative, ingenuity and resolution in a later generation spoke volumes for the quality of seamanship still practiced. The *Tactician*'s experience was not, therefore unique, nor was Captain Metham's admirable expertise.

In June 1957 the Henderson liner *Captain Hobson* suffered a serious breakdown. Built in 1920 as the *Amarapoora*, she had served as a Hospital Ship during the war and in 1946 had been acquired by the Ministry of Transport carrying many sick French from Saigon to Toulon, remaining under Henderson management. She had then taken Muslim pilgrims from the Levant to Jeddah and repatriated German PoWs from North Africa. In 1948 she had been converted to carry displaced persons from Italy to Australia on behalf of the International Refugee Organisation and on her return, she had repatriated Dutch nationals from Indonesia to the Netherlands. She was also used as a troop-ship by the British army. In July 1952 she had been made available to the New Zealand government which was then encouraging settlement. Undergoing further conversion work and a change of name to that of the first Governor of New Zealand, she embarked 580 emigrants and began a traffic in which she was still engaged five years later when, about 570-miles east of Auckland, her main engine broke down.

Ahead of her the *Port Macquarie* turned round and came to her assistance, along with a sloop of the Royal New Zealand Navy. Captain R.C.H. Webb and his crew successfully coupled up a tow and brought the *Captain Hobson* into Auckland, earning themselves high-praise, a salvage award of £4,000 to which the Port Line directors added another £1,000. It was unfortunate that two further towing exploits involved engine trouble on a single Port Line cargo-liner, but fortunate that in both cases the company's ships were not far away and could thus reduce the costs of rendering assistance.

On 29 October 1960 The *Port Townsville*, Captain J.M. Reid, broke down between Levuka and Dunedin. A connecting rod in her main engine had broken and after a remarkable attempt to lash the whole thing together failed after some hours running, she was taken in tow by the much older, pre-war, *Port Fairy* and brought into Auckland, 170 miles distant. Five years later, on 21 November 1965, her main bearings and top ends gave way, leaving her adrift off Cape Hatteras. In New York the *Port Alfred*, Captain R.H. Finch, was completing her cargo. Embarking the local marine superintendent, Captain J.R. Peek, Finch sailed and headed for the casualty at 18 knots. Having married the *Port Alfred*'s insurance wire to one of the *Port Townsville*'s anchor cables, the tow commenced. Having entered Chesapeake Bay, the wind freshened, causing the *Port Townsville* to sheer wildly and part the tow, which was completed into Newport News by local tugs.

Despite the increasing use of radar, the dangers of collision in fog continued. Indeed it was found that failure to appreciate relative motion as displayed on a radar-screen led to 'radar-assisted collision' the worst of which occurred between two trans-Atlantic liners, the Italian *Andrea Doria* and the Swedish *Stockholm*. When two Blue Star liners collided the Vestey board decided to remove the radar sets installed in their ships, considering they bred a false sense of confidence and the maintenance of high speeds, though they rescinded the decision some years later. The Ministry of Transport bestirred itself and introduced Radar Observer's training courses for deck-officers, since when both radar and their sea-going operators have improved exponentially to the extent that it is the duty of plain lookout that is now neglected. Despite its benefits, many masters required calling before radar was used which, as a Royal Mail Line officer, Jack Le Brecht points out, 'was a problem for junior officers with no wish to call him in the silent hours'. But collisions occurred in conditions other than fog, affecting P&O shortly after the Suez Canal was reopened following the Egyptian-Israeli War and Anglo-French intervention of 1956.

On the evening of 22 October 1957 the P&O cargo liner *Shillong*, outward bound from London to the Far East, was approaching the Strait of Gûbàl at the southern end of the Gulf of Suez. She was commanded by fifty-one-year-old Captain Eric Spurling, brother to the marine artist Jack Spurling and had on board six passengers, a crew of twenty-six British officers and sixty-one lascars. Besides a valuable general cargo, the ship was carrying thirteen thoroughbred horses destined for Singapore. The night was dark, the wind fresh and the sea rough when she was in collision with the Belgian-flagged tanker *Purfina Congo*, on her way to Europe from the Persian Gulf with crude oil. The *Shillong* settled rapidly and Spurling immediately ordered her abandoned. Two lifeboats and a single raft were launched and all but two of her crew escaped, some like Fourth Officer G.R. Yeatman jumping directly into the sea. Most were rescued by the Danish tanker *Skotland* and landed at Suez. One of the two men lost was the middle-aged chief steward, John French, a man who had been at sea for thirty-four years and had survived two previous collisions in P&O ships, the *Corfu* and the *Bendigo*. The other loss was that of eighteen-year-old Derek Palmer, a cadet on his first voyage to sea, a voyage he was so eager to make that he defied the family doctor who wished him to remain at home on account of his health.[29]

As tankers grew larger a new danger emerged, inexplicable explosions. Improperly understood for some time the build-up of static in a tanker's empty tanks could, under certain critical circumstances, ignite a minimal residue of gas causing major damage. Not understanding the cause and fearful of creating diverse problems, the authorities attempted to hush things up, instructing affected crews to remain silent though, of course, the facts leaked out. Douglas Renton recalled serving in the Shell tanker *Serenia* when on the way from Bonny, Nigeria, for Europe. On 14 December 1969 'a ship was reported off the port bow as having just exploded. On looking through the telescope I realised it was one of our own *M*-Class. We took off all the survivors, and a couple of days later she disappeared, the largest ship in the world to sink – 207,000 tons deadweight'. This was the Dutch-flagged *Marpessa* which had exploded off Dakar two days earlier. At the end of the same month the Shell VLCC *Mactra*, closely followed by the Norwegian VLCC *Kong Haakon VII* blew-up while washing their tanks using automated equipment.[30] Although the *Mactra* was capable of steaming under her own power she had a colossal hole over 400ft long blown in her deck. Third Officer R.W. Gardner and Seaman J.S. Lincoln had been killed and several others seriously burned, including the wives of two engineers. Both of these VLCCs were repaired, but of greater importance was that, following inquiries in which 'there was 'no Government pressure to find a solution,' subsequent prolonged and exhaustive investigations led to understanding the cause of these 'spontaneous' explosions. The potential difference created in a tank being cleaned by an electrically charged water mist which, combined with an explosive mixture of residual oil-gas and air, required only the ignition of a build-up of static electricity to detonate. The proportions of the air-gas mix were critical, which was why few previous incidents had attracted notice and a spate of almost identical and simultaneous explosions in December 1969 had done so. The solution was the displacement of air by inert gas, which became the industry standard.

Such hazards were routinely run, but in times of turmoil the sheer spread of British shipping attracted deliberate and outrageous acts. The fate of the British India's cargo-passenger liner *Dara* is long forgotten in a world inured to terrorist atrocities. The ship had sailed from Bombay on her regular scheduled round voyage to Karachi, Pasni, Muscat, Dubai, Umm Said, Bahrain, Bushire, Kuwait, Mina Al Ahmadi, Basra, Korramshahr, Kuwait and Bahrain, reaching Dubai again on 7 April 1961. Anchored off Dubai she had loaded and discharged cargo and embarked her new passengers as necessary. These were accommodated in first and second-class cabins and 'unberthed' on the main deck where space was available to poor passengers under the Simla Rules of 1931 which was spatially 'more generous … than [that] provided in cross-Channel services, though of course it was for slightly longer voyages'. Altogether there were seventy-six cabined passengers and 537 'unberthed,' in addition to which there were seventy-four 'friends seeing the passengers off, stevedores and hawkers in search of business, besides the crew of 132 British officers and lascar ratings. During the afternoon the weather deteriorated and the *Zeus* of Panama, anchored close by, dragged her anchors and ran into the *Dara's* bow, doing a small amount of damage and Captain C. Elson, 'having regard to the holding ground, prudently decided to put out to sea'. There was a superfluity of life-saving equipment on board for this purpose so the ship was hove-to to the northward until 04.00 on the 8th, when a moderation permitted the vessel to return to Dubai. Having seen the ship onto her new course Captain Elson retired to his cabin, leaving Second Officer Alexander on watch. Forty minutes later there was an explosion on the port side of the upper deck which blew holes in the adjacent bulkheads, ruptured pipe work, ignited a fire, began to fill the ship with smoke, and disabled the electrical power and the steering telemotor. Cadet Tew was woken by the alarm bells. 'I jumped down from my top bunk and went out into the alleyway … The ship was rolling heavily and it felt as though she was stopped. The shocked face of the third officer appeared in the dim light of the emergency lighting …'. Tew woke his cabin-mate and they went to their emergency station. Meanwhile Chief Officer Jordan and Chief Engineer Cruickshank assessed the damage and reported to Elson on the bridge. It was initially thought that the fire was seated in the engine room and, once the space had been evacuated, measures were taken to inject carbon dioxide. In the engine room itself, Second Engineer Birrell thought the same and shut down the main engine to avoid major damage, but an inspection with the fifth engineer could see nothing wrong until they encountered thick smoke around the top platform and heard passengers screaming. It was now clear to the engineers that this was something extraordinary. As the emergency alarms rang they and the greasers and firemen in both engine and boiler rooms evacuated the space. Cruickshank and Birrel went to start the emergency generator by which time there was chaos in the passenger accommodation where the ship's officers were concluding the seat of the explosion and fire lay. Suspicion fell on the first-class smoking room which was partially over the engine room but had, in fact been ignited from the baggage room on the deck underneath the port side.

Meanwhile Birrell and the two cadets, Grimwood, aged eighteen, and Tew, a year younger, proceeded to set off the carbon-dioxide smothering system. Dense smoke required that Grimwood donned breathing apparatus to do so but was driven back by the smoke and intense heat. Elsewhere the Extra Third Officer had attempted to get a hose into play but there was no pressure on the fire-main and as Alexander and Jordan returned to report to Elson on the bridge it was clear that events had overtaken their capacity to fight the fire and 'the situation was hopeless'. Elson ordered an immediate distress message to be transmitted and the boats swung out but by this time the extreme rapidity of the fire's spread made all but the after two boats on the starboard side inaccessible.

In those first moments as the alarms rang the passengers suffered a spreading sense of abandonment by the ship's officers. After the explosion there had been a silence as the throb of the engines died away, broken only by the strain of rivets and plates. As the passenger emerged on deck 'the only sounds were from the rush of the sea and the violent wind blowing across the decks. Then suddenly pandemonium, shrieks of 'Fire!' and doors slamming preceded a flood of fugitives, some clutching children and all in their night-clothes. Clouds of smoke poured out of the first-class accommodation 'huge puffs shooting outwards where they were caught by the wind and thinned out over the dark crests of the waves'.

Power was briefly restored by the emergency generator but this soon failed and the decks rapidly filled with a terrified throng. P.J. Abraham recalled that:

> We were all in pyjamas or night clothes of some description; most of the women had put saris over their skirts and undergarments. I cannot remember seeing anyone with a life-jacket. Shortly after we arrived with the main crowd standing against the wind on the port side we saw a beam of light from a torch approaching. A European officer walked rapidly past, darting the beam here and there as if looking for something. 'Everyone stay where you are,' he said, 'Don't move from here – there is no danger.' [Then] … He was gone. And our attention was drawn to a man who had just come up from … below. He was walking in a peculiar sideways fashion, shuffling one leg behind the other and moaning. The whole of the left side of his body was dark with blood and grime … [31]

It was an appalling situation and could only deteriorate further as the officers and ratings attempted to the launch the boats in a heavy sea and the bewildered and terrified passengers crowded the rails. The two cadets had by now made their way to their boat station. 'It was chaos,' recalled Tew:

> People were shouting and screaming and running around, some already in the lifeboat and some trying to get in, although it was not properly turned out, let alone lowered … we were alone among the passengers. The boat was incredibly heavy, and no one took any notice of us. I grabbed a man to help me turn the boat out, as did Jos [Grimwood], and we managed to get her hanging over … 'You get in and take charge,' shouted Jos. 'I will lower.'
>
> I climbed up and in and fought my way aft to the rudder. I found the tiller under a passenger and pushing him out of the way, I shipped it … I [then] pushed and shoved my way through many legs to the bottom of the boat and found the … plug …
>
> Jos lowered away and stopped at the embarkation level. More and more passengers got into the already overcrowded boat, with people shouting and screaming …
>
> 'Lower away,' I heard a voice shouting … People were still jumping in as she went down the side of the ship, the rolling making the boat hit the hull of the burning

Dara with sickening jolts … making the already panicked people more frightened. My efforts to calm the passengers were a complete waste of time.

The lowering slowed and then went down with a rush. The lifeboat hit the water with a splash and the lifting hooks swung clear both fore and aft. We were lucky. But then unfortunately a nearly empty boat appeared in the glow of the fires raging in the accommodation. The passengers saw it and made a rush to the side of my lifeboat, heeling her over. And then I was in the water. My boat had capsized … I began to swim. I was not wearing a lifejacket … After the bedlam and noise in the lifeboat it was suddenly quite quiet. What had happened to all the passengers in my boat? I could still hear shouting and screaming but it was becoming faint as the *Dara* drifted away, surprisingly quickly. It was rough, and waves were breaking over my head. I tried to swim back … but it was no use and I soon gave up, treading water … It became darker as the *Dara* moved away. I was alone.

The official Inquiry determined that: 'Six life-boats, five from the port side and one from the starboard … were … launched, most of them over crowded … despite the efforts of the officers and crew …', efforts which were laced with 'the best language of the sea … [until] one of the officers switched from English oaths into a pidgin Hindi to try and make his point.' The Inquiry found that despite the initiative of the cadets Grimwood and Tew in handling the lowering of No.8 Boat, it and another subsequently capsized which:

in the case of No.8 Boat … was due to the fact that another boat, which was not overcrowded came alongside … and a mad scramble ensued … [I]n the case of No.10 Boat it probably capsized because it was so heavily over-laden with the weight unevenly distributed …

Abraham's evidence is more vivid.

One second there was a boat below us crowded with living, moving people, the next moment only its white, rounded bottom wallowing alongside … A few people were clutching at the sides, some were trying to scramble on top of the slippery surface. I saw an old Sikh with a flowing beard succeed in drawing himself up by the keel where he lay prostrate for a second until a sea swept him away. All around the boat we could see white bundles through the waves. Some stayed near the boat for a short while, tossed about like flotsam; we could see others going straight down, shivering paler and paler as they went below the dark, translucent surface. White bundles – these were people. For the first time I realised we were all going to die.

Many among both passengers and crew had to jump into the sea. Some of the buoyancy units unaffected by the fire were thrown overboard, along with anything else that would float and support life but for the passengers crowded at the rails, the jump into a wild sea was intimidating. Daylight dawned and Tew caught sight of a crowded lifeboat to which he swam and was met by the purser who told him to take charge. Tew had the oars manned and kept the boat head to sea. 'The rolling was much reduced and it was much more comfortable. It became much warmer as the morning wore on and the sun rose higher.' By now ships were arriving, the first of which was the old B.I.-managed tank landing craft *Empire Guillemot*, Captain Godley, followed by the Norwegian tanker *Thorsholm*, the Japanese tanker *Yuko Maru No.5*, the BP tanker *British Energy* and another British India ship, the *Barpeta*. Boats were lowered and a rescue operation began, Tew laying his lifeboat alongside the Japanese tanker.

> In the result, 584 persons were rescued by these means. Unfortunately, one man died in one of the life-boats before reaching [safety] … and two persons died subsequently of their injuries, shock or exposure. The total number of lives lost … was 238. [A subsequent effort was made by the ship's company led by Elson and Cruickshank to fight the fire] 'but a sudden puff of heavy smoke and oil on fire issued from the port side of the vessel about amidships and it was feared that an explosion in the oil tanks might occur, and the party hastily left the vessel.

That evening HM Frigates *Loch Ruthven*, Captain Desmond Law RN, *Loch Alvie* and *Loch Fyne* arrived but freshening weather prevented anything being achieved beyond playing hoses on the ship during the following night. They were joined next morning by the US Destroyer *Laffey* which was soon afterwards 'recalled by her own superior authorities'. A British naval fire-fighting party boarded the ship and were joined by a salvage officer, Mr Cowasjee, in the *Ocean Salvor* and the *Dara* was taken in tow for Dubai. During the fire-fighting the naval ratings came across 'bones and charred bodies and in the No.2 'tween decks the bodies of about a couple of dozen persons lying in neat rows who had apparently been asphyxiated in their sleep.'

Before the *Dara* could be beached at Dubai 'she rolled over and sank' owing to the quantity of water that had been pumped into her. Later naval divers determined the seat and cause of the fire as 'an explosion of an explosive of a high order'. It was, in the opinion of the Court of Inquiry held in London in the spring of 1962 under Mr J.V. Naisby, 'practically certain that this was detonated deliberately probably by a detonator with a time device. What individual or individuals was or were responsible for placing this explosive there was no conclusive evidence to show'. All normal precautions, fire rounds, boat drills and safety routines had been complied with and, despite the understandable misgivings of the passengers – fifteen of whom gave evidence – over the conduct of the ship's crew, the Court found that:

> There was no evidence that any member of the crew of the *Dara* did not know what his duties were in case of fire or the sounding of the Emergency Signal, though there was evidence that some did not carry out those duties. No officer of the deck, engine or catering staff, neither of the cadets, nor most of the senior ratings in the deck or engine staff seem to have left the vessel by boat except in the proper execution of their duty and, in some cases, when specifically ordered to do so by the master or one of the senior officers. So far as efforts to fight the fire are concerned, there was evidence that some few members of the crew attempted to fight the fire when they encountered it with hoses or extinguishers without waiting for any orders. How many others may have done so is unknown.

> In considering the actions of those on board … both crew and passengers, after the explosion, the whole circumstances must be considered … a high-explosive bomb in peace-time is something which no one would expect. The instantaneous fire and its extremely rapid spread accompanied by dense and suffocating smoke and the absence of lights must have been terrifying …

The Court addressed the lack of life jackets being worn by the survivors. In the case of the crew this was because they had begun fighting the fire. Most of the passengers abandoned their life jackets in their cabins when they left them. In both cases, the fire prevented any later return to individuals' accommodation but the Court was critical both of the passengers' negligence to aquaint themselves with the notified procedures and that many were also illiterate or unable to read the notices in Urdu which was unintelligible to many of the 'unberthed passengers' who spoke either 'uncultured Urdu' or other dialects or languages. The question of educating passengers in emergency procedures in such circumstances 'is one of great difficulty'. Nevertheless, the Court recommended that it be addressed, adding this to a number of other recommendations concerning the disruption of the ship's fire-fighting system which had been effectively disabled by the explosion, but was critical of the practice of locking away the valuable non-ferrous fire-hose nozzles which had 'been subjected to regular pilferage'. The reference to some members of the crew failing to execute their duties was 'particularly true in the case of those … who had to deal with passengers' the training for which was considered inadequate. The Court was also critical of aspects of the engine-room management and the Court was 'certainly of [the] opinion that an immediate attempt should have been made to restore the main lighting … but whether or not this … would have been successful it is impossible to tell. Nevertheless, all the engineer officers played their part in getting the boats away and in rescuing the passengers'.

It was also considered that:

> One of the things that militated against the control of the passengers was the fact that this sudden explosion in the very early morning found most of the officers out of uniform. It is hardly to be expected that an officer roused from his bed by a sudden emergency, the nature of which is not known, should do other than grab the first clothing to hand, and the same remarks probably apply to the crew …[32]

During the proceedings, Counsel for the Ministry of Transport stated that:

> The Court has heard of instances of very courageous and highly responsible behaviour … and [referring to the cadets in lowering No.8 Boat] in particular perhaps on the part of some persons still in their teens, and some perhaps not very much older, who can said to have upheld the highest traditions of the Merchant Service, and appear to give the lie to persistent present-day criticisms of our young people …

As for those whose who 'didn't put up an absolutely perfect showing,' this was attributed to the circumstances of the situation.

Although it was impossible to determine the perpetrators of the deliberate and wrongful act that destroyed the *Dara* and so many lives, it was widely believed – then as now – that they were Omani rebels. The dreadful incident was exacerbated by the nature of the *Dara's* variety of passengers and their origins, the complexities of her schedule and embarkation arrangements combined with the unreality of establishing principles to regulate such a disparate and polyglot population, many of whom were only on board for a few days, took little notice of broadcast announcements and could not read safety notices.

After the dangers of fog, fire rates as high a hazard in modern times as it did in the past. Although the frigates recognised the dangers of pumping too much water into the ship and after a while confined their actions to 'boundary-cooling' her topsides, the instability to which a ship can be reduced by fire-fighting in her superstructure was a nightmare. The worst victim was the Canadian Pacific's *Empress of England* which caught fire in Liverpool at this time and capsized in Gladstone Dock. At the end of 1964 the Blue Funnel liner *Phyrrus* caught fire while loading for Japan in Vittoria Dock, Birkenhead. In order to avoid a similar fate, holes were cut in her sides to drain the water directly out of her hull.

Among those from the *Dara* pulled out of the water was the youthful cadet Ian Tew. He was one of an expectant generation of young men who went to sea in those post-war decades of the 1950s and 1960s. Many cadets and apprentices still began by attending pre-sea schools such as the *Conway* or *Worcester*, the School of Navigation at Warsash, Devitt and Moore's foundation at Pangbourne, or King Edward VII Nautical College in London's East End, thereby earning remission of actual sea-time to qualify for sitting the Second Mate's examination. Although promotion remained slow in the liner companies thereafter, opportunities offered in Hong Kong where China Navigation and the Indo-China Navigation Co., in which Tew later served, occupied the 'top-dollar' places. Other companies were also eager to get hold of young men with British qualifications, such as John Manners & Co., one of whose ships became embroiled in alleged arms smuggling to Algeria. Promotion was rapid, but service in such ships did not come without a certain sacrifice, as Fraser Stuart discovered when serving in the *Thames Breeze* not long after the Cuban Missile Crisis of October 1962. The ship was time-chartered to Sinofracht, the Chinese government.

> We loaded general cargo in Shanghai and Whampoa for Singapore, Conakry in Guinea, Dakar, but mainly Havana. We then loaded bagged sugar for China via the Panama Canal. Relations between Cuba and [the] USA at this time were rather strained and the Panama Canal authorities including the pilots treated us like social lepers. The only time the pilots spoke to us was to give the necessary orders.

The shake-up among companies in later years could see an apprentice who joined a tramp company like Hain of St Ives, part of the P&O Group, survived its amalgamation with James Nourse and then find himself in the P&O Bulk Carrier Division aboard bulk-carriers or specialised product carriers. One such was Captain Andrew Smeeton who went to sea with Hain in 1960, served in bulk-carriers and rose to command the liquefied petroleum gas-carrier *Gazana*, launched from Cammell Laird's Birkenhead yard in May 1971.

Such transformations were not obvious in the late 1940s and 1950s. Traditional tramps still flew the red ensign and took five weeks to discharge a cargo of gunnies in Buenos Aires. A cargo-liner spent roughly half her life in port and, if the demands of cargo-work permitted, it was still possible to see a little of the world before the days of mass travel. Across the globe the Seamen's Missions of the Missions to Seamen and Apostleship of the Sea, provided refuges and, usually, a bar, swimming pool and perhaps a weekly dance. Among the beneficial consequences of the war were the British Apprentices, and British Merchant Navy Officers' Clubs in New York. Both were located in central Manhattan hotels, the latter in the Sheraton Astor and were much appreciated by their beneficiaries.

A young cadet's experiences remained rich. Joining the Blue Star Line's *Pacific Star* in July 1947, Donald Wright found her to be 'anything but romantic; a rusty Liberty-ship' plugging the company's war losses.

> The crew could be said to be non-standard too. Poor old Captain F., kindly, frail and tired, worn-out by two World Wars, could barely keep his eyes open when he was (occasionally) on the bridge. The Mate, a small-pox scarred Welshman, a fine a sailor as any could find, rows of medals from two wars, sunk twice, [a veteran of Convoy PQ17] but mentally scarred because his wife and daughter had been killed in a

Cadets at the School of Navigation, Warsash, 1955. The cadet captain, with drawn cutlass, is escorting the Lady Mayor of Southampton as she inspects young men being imbued with ideals that transcended mere commercialism: they were to become Merchant Naval officers first, servants of their shipping companies second. (Courtesy of Louis Roskell)

Cardiff bombing raid. He got DTs about fortnightly. Strangely, I have no memory of the 2nd Mate, but the 3rd Mate saved the day, wise, older than most, an ex-Able Seaman who got his certificates by self-study. He and the Mate taught us (two cadets) so much, and the tough Geordie bosun did the rest.

Such 'self-study' was encouraged by the Seafarers' Education Service and the College of the Sea from its Balham headquarters, where, under the able directorship of Dr Ronald Hope, it provided – besides ship's libraries – courses in a wide variety of subjects. It was possible to take formal qualifications under properly invigilated conditions and Hope gradually formulated the means of improving both the social and the academic standing of the Merchant Navy's officer corps. This resonated with the Merchant Navy Training Board and others among enlightened shipowners like Lawrence Holt, though the Ministry of Transport resisted any rapid modernisation of the syllabuses of certificates of competence. Since no shipping company considered it necessary for a young deck-officer to sit for Extra-Master-Mariner – indeed many were actively in favour of dissuading any such attempt – the three grades of foreign-going certificate remained unchanged. They remained vocational qualifications only, devoid of any pretence to equate to a degree, a level of intellectual development to which the Extra-Master's certificate was supposed to aspire.

Officers taking the certificates of competence studied at various nautical colleges scattered round the country. These were often attached to a larger technical college, though a few stood alone or were part of a pre-sea training school. Former apprentices and cadets for examination in London, for example, crammed for their Second Mates' certificates at King Edward VII Nautical College in Limehouse where pre-sea course were also running, whereas their older colleagues, candidates swatting for First Mate or Master, attended the Marine Department of Sir John Cass College in Houndsditch. Other establishments were at Plymouth, Cardiff, Lowestoft, Fleetwood, Glasgow, Leith, Aberdeen and South Shields. Up until the 1950s there remained one of the old private crammers run by the Nellist brothers, reminiscent of the former 'navigation schools' of earlier times.

Undeterred, Hope and his like-minded allies established a new BSc in Nautical Science and persuaded several universities which, under successive educational reforms gradually subsumed these nautical colleges, to run courses to which he encouraged enlightened owners to send their young cadets and apprentices. This revolutionised the old-fashioned apprenticeships system and after 1962 new-entrants no longer spent their 'time' aboard ship accruing 'sea-time' but enjoyed a period of academic rigour undergoing mid-apprenticeship release courses in technical colleges around the country, contributing to a youth's eventual degree.

Most cadets, who tended to be attached to cargo-liner and tanker companies, and apprentices who were indentured to cargo-liner companies or tramping firms, were still used by ship's officers as cheap labour. This old abuse remained firmly in place owing to the unwillingness of mates to run-up heavy overtime bills employing the ship's able-seamen, when a gang of four apprentices could be turned-to for nothing. There were also numerous jobs considered too dirty or awkward for European deck-hands to undertake without argument or extra pay, and the easy solution lay to hand among the denizens of the half-deck. In November 1948 after pre-sea training John Ager joined the Prince Line's *Arabian Prince*, Captain G. Lindsay, only to find that all he had learned of navigation he 'forgot during my time at sea as such knowledge was not necessary when one's work consisted of chipping, scraping, occasionally painting and always cleaning brass'. At the end of the voyage Ager returned home to Eastbourne where his father managed Barclays Bank, 'two months older in age and twenty years older in experience'. He did not stay at sea and left before completing his time. Another, Ian Johnston, one of Holt's midshipman aboard the *Ulysses* in 1952, thought that 'I suppose we learned a bit about ship-construction from the painting of all those frames and beams.'

It was such an abuse that Ronald Hope sought to undermine, but it was a difficult nut to crack, even in smart companies such as Blue Funnel, whose chief officers did not always practice what the company preached. The young aspirants were customarily put on day-work at sea, or if in the latter half of their time, on watch with a good chance that if the ship demanded it, their off-duty watches might be spent working on deck or cleaning holds and bilges. In port they assisted the officers on deck while cargo was being worked. Wherever there was a risk of pilfering – which was universal – this might consist of six hours at a stretch sat in a hold guarding a valuable consignment from theft. Even when one caught a thief, justice could be skewed. One of Holt's midshipmen apprehended a pilferer and was assaulted and knocked from the 'tween-deck into the lower hold where, fortunately, he landed upon bales of hemp and suffered nothing worse than the loss of his front teeth.

'Even by stretching one's imagination it is very difficult to raise much enthusiasm for cargo-work while loading a straightforward cargo,' wrote one young Anchor Line deck-cadet of his arrival at Karachi.

> The dockers were waiting like an army. As soon as the gangway was aboard they advanced on the ship, opening the hatches and swarming over the ship in a manner which at first sight would appear quite unorganised, but once the cargo started pouring on board, the gangs disappeared into the hatches and began stowing the bags and bales at a great rate … [so that] apart from going round the hatches to see that they are properly dunnaged there is very little to do unless some emergency arises. The temptation is to leave the decks and read a book or gossip with someone, with the good intention of having a look round at regular intervals. It does work out though and although it does become irksome, it is best to keep on deck the whole time and try and forget about everything except the cargo.

Such were the conditions in almost any port handling general cargo. Seafarers were obliged to share their ships with such necessary shore-labour during the long periods that cargo-liners and many tramps spent in port during the course of a voyage. Along with the manual labourers, came tally clerks, security guards, tank and hold-cleaners, not all of whom attended solely to their employer's affairs which, in the tropics aggravated the living conditions of a crew and wore tolerance thin. Tramps loading a homogeneous cargo were often less encumbered by this passing population, especially when doing so under automatic plant, such as grain elevators, but the situation of a busy cargo-liner, with scores of various consignments to handle, frequently resembled a scene from bedlam. Alongside a wharf it was much the same, while ships often worked both sides, inboard from the wharf and outboard from small craft of one sort or another. In open anchorages these consisted of coasters, barges, lighters, junks, *lorchas, tongkangs, praus, gallivats, pattamars* and all manner of craft depending upon where in the world the ship lay. Queues of men and boys each clutching the 'boat-note' supplied by the shipping agent and assigning his little argosy's consignment to the loading cargo-liner, would crowd outside the chief officer's cabin awaiting the appointed place of stowage before running to the *cranis'* office to consult the chief tally clerk and have the goods checked aboard. As these nippers dodged about the decks the ship's derricks, swung out over the sides, their wire runners humming on the winches, hove sling after sling aboard, the united runners able to heave and veer so that each load rose from the lighter, slewed across the deck until above the hatch and then disappeared below. The hum of electric winches, or rattle and hiss of steam plant, the calls of the watchers guiding the slings, the shouts of the gangs down below, or the tally clerks disputing some numerical discrepancy amid which the harassed duty *malim-sahib*, or *tuan*, or *tze-foo* went from hatch to hatch checking and supervising, conveyed an impression of utter chaos. Remarkably this apparent muddle resolved itself; one by one the craft alongside were discharged; one by one the coolies, the dockers or the long-shoremen came up on deck and drifted ashore, the tally clerks cleared up their papers, the wharfingers retreated and the final flurries of paperwork in the chief officer's office concluded the ship's business. By now whatever passengers were boarding would appear on deck, aghast at the apparent disorder.

Meanwhile the hatches were closed, the tarpaulins pulled over and the carpenter and his mate could be heard knocking the wedges in as the able-seamen lowered or secured the derricks for sea. On the bridge the second and third officers checked steering gear and made the necessary navigational preparations, readying the engineers for the forthcoming movements of the engine, while the fourth officer and a cadet concluded the measurements of all available space in the rapidly filling holds so that the ship's free capacity could be made known by way of the agent to head office and the next port. The last formalities were concluded by the master, the agent's runner and the port officials. Finally the pilot came aboard and the master ascended to the bridge to be informed by his officers that all was ready for departure. After the ship had cast off and was moving slowly towards the sea the crew, stood-down from harbour stations and armed with wash-deck hoses, drove the filth of the shore from her decks, tearing down the makeshift shanties the winch-drivers had erected from dunnage timber and coconut mats to shade them from the sun or rain and lowered and lashed the derricks and any deck cargo. After the pilot had been discharged and 'full-speed away' rung on the engine-room telegraph, the ship set her first course and casting off 'the trammels of the shore,' as Conrad noted, settled into 'the balm of the ship's routine'.

Insofar as marine engineering was concerned, some reformation had occurred in 1952 when the Ministry of Transport introduced the Alternative Entry Scheme for Marine Engineers. This allowed entry without the former full apprenticeship having been served in a heavy engineering works or a shipyard before going to sea as an assistant engineers, or 'junior'. Many did so to avoid National Service in the armed forces, service in the Merchant Navy being an acceptable alternative. The issue of National Service had little effect upon boys wishing to become deck-officers, the recruitment which at this time remained as steady as ever. This was not true of potential engineers and after the state conscripted its last intake of reluctant warriors in 1960, it was sea-going that became unpopular. Many companies found it difficult to attract junior engineers and sought to recruit outside the traditional sources which boosted alternative cadet schemes such as engineer cadet-ships, allowed under the Alternative Entry Scheme of 1952.

After the war a number of cargo-liner companies had commissioned cadet-ships for deck-cadets. These supplemented the customary two or four-berth half-decks that most ships – tramps, cargo-liners and tankers – provided for their trainee officers. Cadet-ships carried around thirty aspirants and the appropriate instructors, officers nicknamed 'schoolies' who were seconded to the duty of teaching navigation, seamanship and the related subjects. The *Chantala* and *Chindwara* fulfilled this purpose for British India, the *Rakaia* and *Otaio* for New Zealand Shipping and the *Durham* for the Federal Steam Navigation Co., all of which were P&O subsidiaries. All these ships otherwise carried full crews and operated a two-voyage scheme of 'seniors' and 'juniors' where the curriculum alternated between classroom lessons and practical experience on deck. In port most enjoyed organised runs ashore, inter-ship regattas pulling and sailing lifeboats and other benefits looked upon askance by the apprentices on conventionally manned vessels.

As might have been expected of them, Alfred Holt & Co.'s Blue Funnel Line did it differently. In establishing the *Calchas* as the company's cadet-ship in 1951, Lawrence Holt negotiated a deal with the Seamen's Union whereby apart from a bosun and carpenter, no white ratings were carried. Instead twenty-two midshipmen did the work of the deck-hands but the overtime earned by the midshipmen during a voyage was paid into The Calchas Fund from which were drawn bursaries for able young seamen who could not otherwise advance their careers to study, sit and take examinations for certificates of competency. Holts thus funded a means of promoting these otherwise disadvantaged men 'through the hawse-pipe'. After 1952 Holt extended the system to include fourteen engineer cadets, but this system was not particularly successful; uptake appears to have been unencouraging and trouble often broke out between the two tribes of oil and water. When the *Diomed* was built in 1956 she took over the role, but without any engineer cadets who joined the six-man half-decks in some of Holts other vessels alongside four midshipmen.

Such cargo companies offered a first-class training which was also undertaken by the large British oil-tanker operators. Among these the British Tanker Co. and Shell Tankers were the leaders in terms influence and fleet size, but the Eagle Oil Co. had a particularly good reputation having from the start of the company in 1912 taken particular care of their personnel.[33] Having taken over the direction of the Seafarers Education Service in 1947, Ronald Hope, began his initiatives intended to improve the status and standing of the officer corps of the Merchant Navy. A committed and convinced socialist, a talented economist, economic historian and Fellow of Brasenose College, Oxford, Hope had served in the Royal Navy during the war, emerging with a commission and a deep appreciation of merchant shipping. He possessed rare talents, not he least of which was the ability to make friends and gain the ear of the influential. Thanks to alliances forged by Hope and others, a future deck-officer's apprenticeship was after 1963 punctuated by the mid-apprenticeship release course, adding a much-needed intellectual dimension to a young man's training with which he was able to gain the BSc in Nautical Science mentioned earlier.

The importance of cadet training was recognised by all the principal shipowners at this time and although P&O itself did not have a dedicated training ship, leaving that to its subsidiaries, its justification was explained by P&O's long-standing chairman, Sir William Currie. 'This method,' he said, 'inculcates in these boys an esprit de corps and an atmosphere of tradition which is invaluable in later years'. Currie's objective of generating company loyalty, which he shared with other owners, paid-off handsomely in the post-war generation of cadets. He retired on 30 March 1960 after forty-four years' association with the Group; few of his eventual successors on the P&O or any other board considered such an abstract quality of much value. The avuncular, popular septuagenarian left a company of declining profitability[34] confronting a period of unparalleled challenge and was succeeded by the decisive and imposing patrician Sir Donald Anderson, 'a daunting and frightening man, seemingly distant and autocratic,'[35] who recognised that 'when misfortune comes to shipping, it comes as an epidemic'.[36]

Oblivious to the coming deluge, the young post-war merchant seafarers looked forward to full careers. For those at the end of working lives that had endured the vicissitudes of Depression and World War little seemed to have changed. Mr Harrison had served as Alfred Holt & Co.'s engineer superintendent at Singapore for twelve years prior to his retirement on a fixed pension in 1959. Unfortunately a period of rapid inflation ensued and Harrison found he had to work into his seventies, teaching at HMS *Conway* and recruiting for his old company. 'He was of the old school, a workaholic,' his daughter Vanessa recalled.

> He hardly ever took a day off and loved his job. When he retired they replaced him with three people. He was greatly saddened in his later years by what he saw as the decline of merchant shipping. But I have wonderful memories – of those beautiful ships; paint and varnish and brass all gleaming, with their kindly crews and delicious food.

NOTES

1. In 1918 Britain had lost 41 per cent of the merchant fleet she possessed in 1914. In 1945, she had lost 62 per cent of the shipping she had had in 1939. Losses in capital equipment and labour exceeded those in any other British industry.
2. By 1950, for example, Bank Line had restored its fleet to its pre-war strength of fifty ships.
3. See A.N. Keith, *White Man Returns*, p293.
4. Bisset had already been awarded the CBE. His passengers embarked from the Ocean Terminal from four special 'boat-trains'.
5. The policing role of the British Army in these years included combating – besides the *Mau-Mau* in Kenya – the *Eoka* movement in Cyprus, anti-terrorist attacks by the Zionist Irgun and Stern Gang in Palestine, the suppression of the Communists in the Malayan Emergency, the Aden Emergency and Confrontation between Malaysia and Indonesia.
6. Operation MUSKETEER was a military success but a political disaster. It followed the nationalisation of the Suez Canal by the Egyptian government following disagreements with the west

over loans to finance the Aswan dam. Acing in secret concert with the Israelis, Britain and France resolved to take back what they had title to, but the United States refused its support and Egypt was driven into the Soviet camp.

The nuclear tests in the Pacific of first an atomic and then a hydrogen bomb were held at Christmas Island. Among the merchant ships chartered in 1957 were Ben Line's *Benwyvis*, Ropner's *Somersby* and a Bank Line ship.

7. This incident astonished those in merchant ships too, not by the presence of the Poles in a British tanker, but that the admiral was surprised.

8. The end of traditional dock labour, linked as it was with decline in shipbuilding, had massive impact on Liverpool and Glasgow. Hull was to suffer too, but as the capital London was better able to survive. Nevertheless, the end of intensive employment cargo-handling on the Thames not only caused hardship and near destitution, it ended a tradition of pilfering which was easily accomplished with commodities in open stows and was a tacitly accepted price paid by shipper and consignee on the one hand, and a beneficial supplement to a docker's income on the other. As early as 1802 Patrick Colquhoun had described the institutionalised theft on the Thames as 'a system of matured delinquency,' its exponents euphemised as 'tier-rangers', 'light horsemen' and 'scuffle-hunters'. Pilfering was not merely a perquisite, it became an assumed 'right' and a weapon in the old war between labour and capital. In the late 1950s it was entrenched, but largely contained within the culture of the docks, the riverside wharfs, and the serving systems of lighterage, road-transport and – to a far lesser extent – on the nationalised railways. In these circumstances *not* to indulge required a stronger moral sense than many working-men possessed, which led to widespread abuse. Almost no one involved was immune from the taint (ship's personnel, including officers, occasionally being dismissed for pilfering), while the dock police – although maintaining a constant war against flagrant manifestations – nevertheless applied their own mulcts. Of wider and more lasting implication, the social diaspora caused by the clearing of London's Docklands of its settled population may well be seen as one contributory factor to a late twentieth-century crime-rise, underlying the more sociologically assumed causes of unemployment and drugs.

9. See Jamieson, A.G., *Ebb Tide in the British Maritime Industries*, p6.

10. It was ironic that the Groundnut Plan, so typical of the organised and central conceived schemes of left-wing governments, produced such a right-wing consequence.

11. SEATO, the South-East Asia Treaty Organisation was formed in 1955 and comprised Australia, France, Great Britain, New Zealand, Pakistan, The Philippines, Thailand and the United States of America.

12. In the 1960s Soviet and satellite merchant ships invariably voyaged in pairs while considerable fleets of 'trawlers' a-bristle with aerials and antennae could be encountered manoeuvring with the precision of warships and were always in the vicinity of NATO or SEATO warships.

13. On Clydeside the militant and highly unionised workforce at John Brown's, faced with falling orders and the closure of the yard that built, among many other warships and merchantmen, the *Queen Mary*, *Queen Elizabeth* and *Queen Elizabeth 2*, formed a partnership which for a few months subsisted amicably on donations and deliveries that ought to have put its woeful management to shame had it succeeded. Unfortunately the shipyard was too out of date to compete with modern foreign builders. See also A. Holt & Co.'s experience in Chapter Six.

14. Such serendipitous discoveries were the subject of Hydrographic Notes, submitted by masters of British ships to the Hydrographer of the Navy who would issue a Notice to Mariners correcting the current edition of the Admiralty chart of the area. The oceans of the world are littered with rocks and shoals found by the chance afforded by taking precautionary soundings. Sadly this practice of using the discovering ship's name as an eponym is no longer permitted.

15. The *Saugor*, Captain J.A. Steel, outward bound for the Cape and Calcutta via Freetown in Convoy OS4 was attacked by *U-143* and *U-557* (Paulshen) when west of Ireland in heavy weather in the small hours of 27 August 1941. The loss of life was heavy, but Steel and fifteen of his crew were picked up by a Rescue Ship. The *Jumna* was sunk on Christmas Day 1940 by the German cruiser *Admiral Hipper* when dispersing from Convoy OB260. The *Jhelum* was torpedoed by *U-105* on 21 March 1941 when in Convoy SL68. Nine men died in the attack, the surviving forty-six escaped in the boats, landing on the Senegal coast on 3 April to be interned by the Vichy French authorities. Along with the older *Hughli* and *Megna*, the *Johilla* survived the war to be sold in 1960, but the *Bhima*, *Ganges* and *Indus* were also lost.

16. John Prescott was destined to become, *inter alia*, Deputy Prime Minister in Blair's 1997–2007 Government which was responsible for a similar Middle East disaster. In his office Prescott

requested a picture of his old ship to be hung in his office and a portrait of her by Burgess in the Government's collection was roused-out for the purpose.

17. The author was on one such ship at this time, which took a large London-bound quantity of sawn Borneo timber to Rotterdam after failing to discharge it in time in London's Royal Docks. Occupying wharfage twice the length of the vessel, she discharged the timber which was trans-shipped into three Dutch coasters astern for onward shipment to – London. On another vessel in Liverpool the dockers stopped work when they discovered that the sacks they were discharging were full of whole peppers from Sarawak. These had a pleasantly faint odour but the information caused a sudden and violent outbreak of entirely phoney sneezing, whereupon work stopped. After haggling, an additional two shillings and sixpence per hour was agreed and work resumed. In Glasgow, loading whisky, at least one case fell mysteriously from a sling each shift so that a number of bottles were 'lost to breakage,' just one example of the endemic corruption and pilferage referred to earlier. Such amusing yet commonplace anecdotes had a powerfully cumulative economic effect.

18. The *Anchises* had been known as the 'Bronchitis' when she was building at Caledon's Dundee yard in the bitter winter of 1946/47. She was the first of a new, post-war, Flett-designed class, but her completion was severely delayed, so that the first to be delivered was the *Calchas* built by Harland & Wolff, Belfast.

19. Additional information from Captain Patrick Duff. The bombing of the *Anchises* by a Guomindang aircraft preceded the 'Yangtze Incident'. HM Sloop *Amethyst* had been badly damaged by artillery of the People's Liberation Army in April, her captain and several of her hands killed or wounded shortly before she grounded near Rose Island below Jiangyin on her way up to Nanking to relieve *Consort* and protect diplomatic staff. *Consort* broke out under fire and attempted to tow *Amethyst* clear but was unable to do so. *Amethyst* was blockaded for over three months while attempts were made to extricate her and other Royal Naval ships were fired upon in a delicate and uncertain situation. With a new captain, Commander Kerans, she made her dash downstream in July to rejoin the fleet. The Communists repudiated all agreements to permit foreign warships access to the Yangtze, restoring the *status ante* to 1842. The humiliation of the Royal Navy was clearly a matter of some importance given the strength of feeling against British arms after the Opium Wars.

20. Captain Frank Wilkes was the first of Holt's midshipmen. See *More days, More Dollars*.

21. See Robert A. Fullarton, *Still Tramping*, Part 2 of *Going Tramping*, typescript autobiography.

22. See letter from Alan A. Rawlinson, *Ships Monthly*, May 1996.

23. Freeman, N., *Seaspray and Whisky*, p2, *et seq*.

24. *Ibid*, p205.

25. Owned by Tate & Lyle, Athel Tankers specialized in carrying molasses in season, otherwise they carried oil. Wright served aboard the *Athelsultan* for one year until March 1953 then left the sea.

26. Correspondence with Richard Lothian, September 2009.

27. The ordeal occupied the BBC Home Service news for several days as the Admiralty Rescue Tug *Turmoil* and the Trinity House Vessel *Satellite* stood by the *Flying Enterprise*. Her grain cargo had shifted in heavy weather and her list gradually increased so that although the *Turmoil* put her mate aboard to assist Captain Carlsen of the Isbrantsen-Export Line, who was alone on the ship, to connect up a tow, she foundered before she could be brought into Falmouth, both men escaping from her horizontal funnel.

28. All ships carried 110 fathoms of heavy wire, in this case of 5-inch circumference, as an insurance against requiring or being required to tow.

29. A number of other collisions occurred at this time, attracting attention owing to the popular belief that radar should have obviated such hazards. One of these was that of the Sugar Line's *Crystal Jewel*, sunk in collision in September 1961.

30. VLCC signified a Very Large Crude-oil Carrier and they superseded the 30,000-ton deadweight 'super-tanker'. The Shell *M*-class was forty-one times larger than Marcus Samuel's *Murex*.

31. See Abraham, P.J., *Last Hours on Dara*, p16 *et seq*.

32. Extracts from *The Report of the Court (No.8024)* on the loss of M.V. *Dara*, HMSO.

33. See *More Days, More Dollars*, Chapter Three.

34. The P&O Group's pre-tax profits in 1960 were £5,800,000, compared to £17,600,000 in 1957.

35. See Howarth, D., and Howarth, S., *The Story of P&O*, p168.

36. Quoted *ibid*, p168.

SIX

'SUNSET INDUSTRY'

The Decline of the Merchant Navy, 1966–2010

The year 1966 was portentous for British shipping. In its events may be perceived something monumentally tragic; in its consequences a lost opportunity of national significance. Although huge sums of public capital had provided support for fishing,[1] dock labour and shipbuilding, shipping itself had received little public money as trading conditions seemed to be improving. Encouragingly, although the Americans were inaugurating trans-Atlantic and trans-Pacific container services,[2] British boardrooms were meeting the new challenge in the full knowledge that what was afoot would entirely revolutionise the carriage of the general cargo in the so-called liner trades. Large new ships would be needed; no longer capable of independent operations, they would require dedicated terminals and, while economies of scale offered – fewer hulls and far fewer seafarers – the necessary investment would be enormous. Raising such facilitating capital could only be done through co-operation, in recognition of which, on 4 May 1965, Sir John Nicholson, Chairman of the Ocean Group, wrote to Sir Donald Anderson of P&O suggesting a conjoint operation. To some extent the ground had been prepared by Viscount Rochdale's Report into the adequacy of Britain's ports which had recommended, *inter alia*, the establishment of new port facilities at Tilbury and Southampton, but such developments would take time and in order to maintain confidence, competitiveness and trade the shipowners needed to move faster. Anderson replied two days later and a meeting was arranged in Brooks Club, St James, between the 'four knights'. Ocean's Nicholson and P&O's Anderson conferred with Sir Nicholas Cayzer of British & Commonwealth and Sir Errington Keville of Furness, Withy.

As the grandees of British shipping organised this new opportunity for their capital, on 16 May 1966 British merchant seamen were called out on strike by their

Capable of lifting 22,530 deadweight tons of bulk-cargo, the *Sir Charles Parsons* of 1985 was built for supplying coal to the power stations of her owners, PowerGen plc. She was managed on their behalf by Lothian Shipping Services (London) Ltd. Specially drawn by John Morris.

The agile Bibby Line moved into bulk-carriers such as the 29,171-ton deadweight *Cheshire* of 1989. One of their larger bulkers on charter to the Seabridge Consortium, the 169,000-ton deadweight *Derbyshire*, became Britain's greatest loss at sea during a typhoon in 1980. Specially drawn by John Morris.

trade union, the National Union of Seamen. The strike was part of widespread social discontent throughout the nation, but although the later miners' strike of 1984 is held to have engineered profound change in British society, that of the seamen in 1966 was arguably of greater consequence. However, it was barely justified; its demand of an increase in pay of 17 per cent on a basic pay of £14.00 for a fifty-six-hour week looked fair on the news-placards, particularly as other working people were paid for a forty-hour week, but the claim was unsustainable in the wider global context. In fact, few seamen earned as little as was claimed owing to the then practice of augmenting pay by complex allowances for such things as overtime and Sundays at sea, so much so that conditions at sea in most British ships had never been better. Alas, excessive emphasis was laid upon traditional norms; as elsewhere in Britain's traditional industries, her mercantile marine had become complacent, a victim of its own success.[3] Everything was out of date, from its training methods, its regulation, its ship-design and building, its management and its distance in psychological terms from

Government, maintained by many owners who resisted interference, and politicians who seemed less and less able to understand shipping.

Among these union activists was a future Secretary of State for Transport, John Prescott, who claimed, with some justification, that seafarers' conditions lagged far behind those pertaining elsewhere in British industry and that the merchant seaman remained a second-class citizen, unprotected by certain industrial legislation that affected the worker ashore. Prescott was among those who maintained that the Merchant Shipping Act was the only legislation on the statute book that retained the anachronistic master–servant relationship long discredited in wider society. In this fundamental he was correct, but the time for changing this was long past. What should have been reformed years earlier had been so neglected that the change itself was counterproductive and in the interim there had been an improvement in actual conditions.

As far as the Government was concerned the heirs of those merchant seamen who had saved the country a quarter of a century earlier were an enemy of the state. 'We are under attack,' claimed Harold Wilson, the Prime Minister, writing later that 'the moderate members of the seamen's executive were virtually terrorised by a small professional group of Communists, or near Communists, who … were able to impose their ideas …'. Both sides dug in, but elsewhere in the world things were stirring: British shipping had for over a century attracted the green eye of jealousy and aroused the competitive spirit of others. As one shipowner expressed it, 'the higher the national baboon climbs up the economic tree, the more his unattractive bits are exposed to his competitors'. The National Union of Seaman's assumption that the shipowner remained a fat enough cat to be reduced in the crucible of industrial action was a fatal miscalculation.

Taking place in a period of seriously disruptive social upheaval and political instability, and appearing as one more manifestation of what had become known as 'the British disease', the strike's consequences were dire. In the short term the immobilisation of the British merchant fleet, still a major world carrier, had an immediate and serious impact on Britain's economy. Among many traditional but failing industries the ability of British ships to earn 'invisible' revenue remained relatively strong and was an important economic prop, but in consequence of the seamen's action Wilson, who ironically enough led a Labour Government, was compelled to devalue the pound sterling.[4]

On Wilson's promise of an inquiry, the strike ended on 28 June and although, by the end of the summer, British merchant ships were back at sea, a fatal wound had been sustained. The folly of striking at a time when shipping was poised on the brink of revolutionary change was not long in becoming obvious. The British merchant fleet, rebuilt after the Second World War on essentially traditional assumptions, was now ageing. To this were added a growing number of influential factors that were under-mining the national fleet's power base. To the growing inefficiency of British shipyards, the immense inroads made on traditional passenger traffic by increasing air travel, the undercutting of the British tramping trades by new and foreign bulk-carriers, the frequent unrest in the labour-intensive and outmoded docks, growing competition from the national fleets of former colonies and other countries including the subsidised merchant fleets of the Soviet-Russian-led Comecom Alliance, and soaring and unpredictable costs, the strike of 1966 added, if not the final straw, then one of the last. The camel's back had never been over-tolerant. In its nineteenth-century successes Britain had bred a new aristocrat in the British shipowner and he could already feel the chilly wind of change and recognise the coming of discomfort. Remote in person, global in influence, patrician in outlook, and establishment in status, these grandees had had enough. Even those whose acceptance of social respon-sibility had not entirely separated them from their workforce and who, while they might believe in their own right to enjoy the fruits of capitalism, believed equally and reciprocally in a duty to their employees, now lost patience. The subtle bond that bound all together was, among the permissive and hedonistic social imperatives of the 1960s, a fragile concept.

While the Government commissioned yet further enquiries – the Pearson Report of 1967 and the conditionally promised second Rochdale Report into the shipping industry in 1970 – the shipowners were wrestling with a consequential paradox. While larger more mechanised ships required fewer crew, the introduction of container-liners took some time. And while a reduction in overall manpower was the logical outcome, there were in these transitional years, sufficient conventional vessels in use to produce a shortage of crews, particularly masters, mates and engineers. This led to a hike in the wage and salary bill, set against a changing market in which it was increas-ingly necessary to react to demands for specialised carriers. Tankers now ranged from small coasters to super-tankers of increasing deadweight, including highly technically complex liquid-gas and chemical tank-ships. The closure of the Suez Canal in 1967 and subsequent diversion of tonnage round Africa encouraged even greater size, pro-ducing the Very Large Crude Carrier, or VLCC. The tramp's replacement by equally gigantic bulk-carriers, some even more versatile and capable of loading ore, oil or grain, was matched by larger versions of the roll-on, roll-off short-sea road-vehicle or railway-ferry producing the long-haul RORO, while the extraordinary boom in motoring engendered the specialised car-carrier, arguably the ugliest of these new models. Many of these dedicated ships required their personnel to receive specialist training and this in turn coincided with an accelerating obsession by the state to leg-islate and interfere with day-to-day operations. This gathered momentum during the following two decades and all these factors ate away at the margins from which profit was extracted, driving the shipowner to search for cheaper and cheaper options. As for the cargo-liner, her fate was sealed by containerisation.

But, as the meeting of the four knights demonstrated, the will to meet challenge remained and retreat was not yet inevitable. As one British shipowner admitted, how-ever, there was a lack of energy among many post-1945 British shipowners, some of whom ignored the changes going on around them. The diminishing and irregular returns on investment failed to attract: there were easier ways of satisfying share-holders and banks, and they lay outside shipping. There was, according to Martin Barraclough, an element of 'clogs-to-clogs in three generations,' although some family names remained in shipping, if less conspicuously than hitherto.

It was an irony that at this time of transition several of the liner operators were bringing into use some of the fastest – and many would argue, most elegant – con-ventional diesel-powered cargo-liners ever built. The Ben liners have already been mentioned, but in 1965 Union-Castle took delivery of two Tyne-built, Sulzer-engined vessels designed to operate a 22.5-knot service to Capetown alongside their mail-liners. The *Southampton Castle* exceeded 27 knots on her trials with anecdotal evidence that she could top 30 making her and her sister, the *Good Hope Castle*, the most powerful cargo-liners ever built. Oddly, accommodation for a dozen passengers was added in 1967 to cater for travellers to and from St Helena and Ascension, but the ships' lives ended when the Cape mail service was terminated.

Possessing the multi-functionality for which their predecessors were well known Alfred Holt's Ocean Group also produced its last conventional Blue Funnel, Glen and Shire liners in 1966 with the *Priam*, first of a class of eight ships designed by Marshall Meek, Flett's successor. Intended as the answer to Ben Line's *Benledi* and her derivatives, their story was an unhappy one and, as so often with this company, exemplifies a wider narrative. Four, the *Priam*, *Peisander*, *Prometheus* and *Protesilaus*, were intended to wear Blue Funnel colours and were, with the *Radnorshire*, ordered from Vickers Naval Yard on the Tyne. As a gesture John Brown's on the Clyde were contracted to build the *Glenfinlas*, but the *Pembrokeshire* and *Glenalmond* were ordered from Mitsubishi at Nagasaki, a contentious decision but soundly based on evidence provided by Sir Stewart MacTier and fully justified by the outcome.

Japanese shipbuilding 'was viewed very sympathetically by their Government' and Mitsubishi had orders exceeding those on the books of the entire British shipbuilding industry. Mitsubishi did not find it easy to meet Ocean's exacting specification, but Ocean's contracts with the two British yards were, as Marshall Meek points out, 'a golden, although belated opportunity to learn from the Japanese, but such was the ineptitude and torpor in UK management that they lost the chance,' and disastrously so. Not only were the class-ship and her British-built sisters delayed between seven and eleven months by inefficiency resulting in a loss of earnings of £4 million, but at £3 million each they were a tenth more expensive. 'What was particularly galling,' Meek concludes, was that, 'as we were taking delivery of the belated *Priam*-class ships in 1967, we were well on the way to building the containerships which were to sound the death-knell for all cargo-liners …'.[5] In the end, the *Glenalmond* was the first to be delivered in September 1966. The last was the Vickers-built *Radnorshire* in 1967, by which time, such was the Ocean Board's disgust with Vickers, that there was no formal launching.

Nevertheless, the *Priam*-class were solid 21-knot ships of 12,094 gross tons with capacious insulated and tank space, six rail-mounted cranes, a 60-ton Stülken heavy-lift and twelve lesser derricks. Later attempts to carry containers on a round-the-world service were only partially successful, but in 1970 the *Peisander* loaded a record cargo of 16,500 space-tons[6] worth £183,000 in Japan. As it was Chinese New Year in Hong Kong the *Peisander* had proceeded directly to Yokohama, reserving two deep-tanks and the space above them for homeward cargo from Singapore. In addition to her normal discharge ports of Liverpool and Glasgow, she loaded cargo for Lisbon, Leixoes and Dublin. But it was a last hurrah! In the complex fleet adjustments following Ocean's taking over full control of Elder, Dempster, the class enjoyed bewildering name changes and inter-line exchanges within the Group, and their lives under Ocean were short. Six were sold to the Hong Kong owner C.Y. Tung in 1978.

The *Glenfinlas* (renamed *Phemius*) and the *Radnorshire* (renamed *Perseus*) continued to fly the red ensign after their sale to China Navigation as *Kwangsi* and *Kweichow* that same year. In 1982 the *Phrontis* (formerly the *Pembrokeshire*) and the *Patroclus* went to owners in the Persian Gulf. All thereafter had chequered histories: both the former *Prometheus*, by then Tung's *Oriental Importer* and his *Oriental Champion* (ex-*Priam* and fully converted to carry containers) being hit by a missile during the Iran-Iraq War in 1985 and subsequently scrapped. Others followed them, along with a score of the company's older ships and the loss of hundreds of jobs. By the time the *Kwangsi* and *Kweichow* were broken-up in China in 1984 and the former *Protesilaus* followed them two years later, all had been sold on. In 1974 a joint service had been arranged with the old rival firm of Thomson's Ben Line. Ben Ocean Services ran the *Benledi* and *Glenlyon* classes in tandem for a few years but in 1978 the Glens had been sold and ten years later Ocean sold its freehold in India Buildings in Liverpool, its six remaining ships operating elsewhere. Having been bought by the Shanghai Ocean Shipping Co. in 1979, a rumour circulated at the end of the millennium that one of the previous class, the *Glenfalloch*, lingered on under the Chinese flag; tentative ideas were bruited that she should be preserved but these petered out with her removal from Lloyd's Register in May 2002. There was something appropriately mysterious in her disappearance behind the bamboo-curtain which her forebears had penetrated over a century earlier. The great Odyssey conceived by Alfred Holt when he had found that pot of ethereally blue paint aboard the *Dumbarton Youth* 140 years earlier had run its course.

Shaw, Savill & Albion built two large 19-knot refrigerated ships *Majestic* and *Britannic* in 1967 retaining their management when, in 1974 the New Zealand government established a new national line in which Furness, Withy took a quarter-share. A commensurate holding in the ships was retained until *Majestic* was sold in 1978, and *Britannic* in 1980. From the same yard of Alexander Stephen, which became part of Upper Clyde Shipbuilders during their deliveries in 1967 and 1968, came Port Line's 21.5-knot *Port Chalmers* and *Port Caroline*. Built with an odd, flattened sheer to enable palletised cargoes to be stowed by fork-lift trucks in their long 'tween-decks they were fitted with a mix of deck-cranes and derricks. Port Line did not entirely lose their faith in the extreme form of cargo-liner, for three further vessels were to be built, the *Port Huon*, the *Port Albany* and the *Port Burnie* 'which were very different from anything that had gone before, not least their builders with the first two from Caledon in Dundee, and the third from Barclay, Curle, another unfamiliar yard for the company'. Ordered in 1962, the *Port Huon* was delivered six months late in March 1965, the *Port Albany*, due in January was not delivered until September 1965, causing trouble between Caledon and Port Line, with the *Port Burnie* following in January 1966. They were fast and fine-lined, designed to do two round voyages a year carrying Australian fruit, filling-in elsewhere as required. As Michael Grey, a former Port Line officer and later editor of *Lloyd's List* records:

> They reflected a lot of the ideas of Captain Ian North, who was lost in the *Atlantic Conveyor* [off the Falklands in 1982, see below], and who was a very clever master, whose views registered with the directors. The ships were 19-knots, were notoriously wet and rolled like pigs, One of them shipped a vast quantity of water on

the foredeck from an 'extreme' wave and set down the forecastle before they could get speed off her, Captain David Sinclair reported that the *Port Albany* heeled like a destroyer on her trials and was dangerously hazarded off the Nantucket, when three road graders carried away [their lashings] and bulged out the shell plating in No.3 'tween-deck. They were expensive, never made any money, because of all the sophisticated gear in them, and were flogged to the Greeks in 1972, although they ran for a further 20 years as reefers [refrigerated ships].

By this time there only two ships remained, the *Port Chalmers* and the *Port Caroline* which by 1979 were displaced by the behemoths of Associated Container Transportation to which Port Line had signed-up in 1966. In the following years the MANZ line was run down to cease operations in 1969, at which time Port Line's proprietors, Cunard, were bought-out by the construction company, Trafalgar House. In 1978 the Port Line ceased to exist, these two remaining ships being transferred to Cunard, itself now reconfigured as Cunard Shipping Services. Three years later they were put under Brocklebank colours as *Manaar* and *Matra* respectively, after which they were laid-up. Plans to convert them to other roles were shelved and, after a brief life under a foreign flag, they too were scrapped.

The most durable of this mid-sixties vintage were Blue Star's 21-knot, 11,300-ton *Scotland Star* and *New Zealand Star*, which were the first of their type to have engines capable of being remotely run. In 1977, a year before the company terminated its passenger services to South America, both were returned to their German builders and converted to fully cellular container ships, the latter emerging renamed as the *Wellington Star* but both continuing under the distinctive Vestey livery – and the red ensign – as part of the ACT consortium until their break-up at Chittagong in 1993.

The foregoing offers a peep show of the swirl of mergers, consortia and rationalisations engulfing the all-important liner companies in this short but influential period. The acquisition of two of the *Priam*-class by the China Navigation Co. draws us into a brief review of a firm that survived the gathering death-throes of others. In January 1943 Britain and America had signed an agreement with the then Chinese government ending extra-territoriality, the Treaty ports and of western navigation on the Yangtze-Kiang and the China coast. This prevented the China Navigation Co., among others, from resuming their traditional services after the war. Moving head office from Shanghai to Hong Kong proved prescient in view of the coming to power of the Communists in 1949, by which time roughly concurrent with their move into air transport mentioned in the previous chapter, the company joined the Australia and Far East Conference, making a shift to deep-water shipping. To this end in 1949 they built two 7,410-ton cargo-liners, the *Changsha* and *Taiyuan*, far larger than anything previously owned but they did not altogether abandon their interest in China and, despite heavy war losses, their fleet was substantial. Having established a Hong Kong to Canton ferry, in 1950 they ran the *Tsinan* through the Nationalist Guomindang blockade of Shanghai, though the ship was damaged by a mine in the Yangtze. For a few years thereafter a small and ageing 'beancaker' might still be seen in these waters, but it was the Hong Kong, Philippine, New Guinea, Australia route that rapidly replaced the lost China traffic, carrying general cargo and replacing beancake with copra. The company invested in a nine-ship *Chungking*-class for Pacific Services in 1955, a joint service with Blue Funnel between south-east Asia and Western Australia in 1958 and, two years later, acquired the *Kuala Lumpur* as a pilgrim-ship mentioned earlier.

Expansion in the wool trade between Australia and Japan led to the purchase of second-hand tonnage, while the offer of other cargoes, particularly nickel ore from New Caledonia, Indian iron ore, or Philippine timber, encouraged the chartering of suitable tramp-ships. The outright purchase of the three Britain S.S. Co. tramps renamed *Wanliu*, *Wenchow* and *Woosung* in 1969 was noted in the previous chapter. Under the terms of the demise charter, in addition to the ship, the charterers acquired the master and ship's company, enabling these people to transfer to China Navigation, an opportunity taken by Captain W.F. Grist of the *Woosung*, then engaged in the Filipino timber trade. The ship was loading at Buguey, a small logging port in northern Luzon, when, in disagreeing with the shipper's agent over cargo-gear arrangements for which he was responsible, Grist was shot for his pains. With no local medical help, it was overlong before the poor man reached hospital, whereupon the second trauma of surgery killed him.

These three tramps underwent considerable modification during their time under charter and Swire ownership. Some 40,000 cubic ft of refrigerated space was created in No.4 Hold, deep-tanks were installed for the carriage of liquid cargoes and modifications enabled them to carry palletised cargoes, making all three effectively cargo-liners.[7] They were sold out of Swire service in 1975 and broken-up three years later but demonstrate their owner's flexibility and vision. The Swire board was, like that of Bibby and Weir, among the most agile of the traditional British operators and, like Bibby and Weir, still included members of the founding family. It headed a number of parent companies operating in diverse fields and moved into container-shipping in 1968 linking with their old Holt partners, Ocean, as part of the Australia Japan Container Line, or AJCL. These *Eredine*-class vessels were owned by John Swire & Co. and managed by China Navigation. A similar consortium was formed with old rivals, the Japanese Mitsui-OSK Line, to form the New Zealand Unit Express Line a year later and in 1971 the rump of the old Crusader Shipping Co. (see below) which had been jointly owned by Blue Star, Port Line, P&O's New Zealand Shipping Co., and Shaw, Savill & Albion, was rationalised into a joint Swire/P&O venture, Crusader Swire Container Services. Similar deals were done with Korean and Dutch interests and in 1974 the partnership name of Butterfield was dropped. By the end of the century only a few Swire ships retained the old 'beancake' Chinese names, but these had been kept for nine ships of the *Chekiang*-class ordered in 1990 for charter work, though their names altered according to the terms of the charter parties. A plethora of subsidiary interests blossomed under the auspices of the Swire Group which in 1995, a few years prior to the return of Hong Kong to China, moved its headquarters to London. By this time Swire, which owned fifty-seven vessels, had moved into tankers and one-class cruising catering for the Japanese with the *Coral Princess*. Many of the ports on the Pacific Rim served by Swire lacked the facilities for containers, so that self-handling lifting gear remained in many of their ships for the handling of containers and palletised cargoes while the tonnage of their ships grew steadily. The company

One of Great Britain's last real success stories at sea, the cellular container-liner *Providence Bay* of 1994 grossed 50,350 tons with a deadweight of 59,093 tons. She had a service speed of 22 knots and was owned by P&O Containers Ltd. Specially drawn by John Morris.

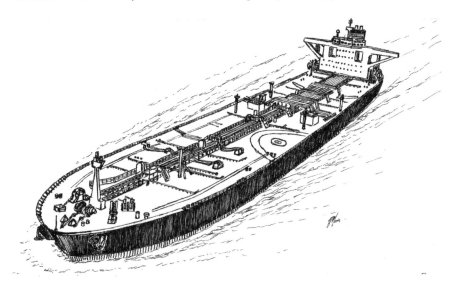

The vast bulk of the BP tanker *British Pioneer* of 1999. With gross tonnage of 160,216, this vessel could load 306,397 tons of crude oil and carry it at a speed of 15 knots. Specially drawn by John Morris.

had changed radically but this evolution ensured its survival. Curiously, some if the old evils remained. Between October 1991 and April 1992 three of the company's ships had been subject to piratical robberies; all had occurred in the Malacca Strait and on two occasions, both aboard the *Chekiang* – then chartered under another name to the Danish giant Maersk – either the chief engineer or the master had been seized and tied up.

The management flexibility of Swire's brought them into contact with others like Maersk, enabling new alliances. During the conversion work of the *Wanliu*,

Wenchow and *Woosung* at Swire's Taikoo Dockyard in Hong Kong the three ships had been relieved by the time-chartered Bank Liner *Cloverbank*. The relationships would prove durable. Bank Line had been quick to relinquish many of its traditional regular liner sailings to concentrate on chartering, bulk-cargo shipments and spot-market opportunities. With competitive threats from elsewhere, British liner services underwent reductions and realignments. Joint service, almost to the point of integration, became common. As another example of this versatility the *Willowbank*, a motor vessel built by Smiths Dock Co. Ltd on the River Tees, was delivered in July 1980 and immediately chartered to the Bank & Savill Line, a combined operation which ran a trans-Pacific service in Partnership with the Columbus Line between Australasia, Central America and, by way of the Panama canal, the Caribbean and American ports in the Gulf of Mexico. The *Willowbank* operated with two other cargo-liners, the *Dunedin*, owned by Shaw, Savill & Albion Co. Ltd, and the Shipping Corporation of New Zealand's *New Zealand Caribbean*. Where opportunity offered, however, Bank Line was significant among the shrinking numbers of British shipowners in retaining its opportunistic flair. A liner service between the eastern seaboard of the United States and South Africa was revived in April 1980 with the *Roachbank* loading for Capetown, Durban and Port Elizabeth in New Orleans.

Another joint service was that entered into with the Columbus Line of Hamburg arising from Bank Line's traditional shipment of copra, the dried kernel of the coconut which when pressed yields an oil used in foodstuffs and soap, lifted from the islands of the South Pacific. This was a one-way cargo but developments in both chemical substitutes for the natural oil and the burgeoning economies of Polynesia and Micronesia reduced shipments of unprocessed copra and increased the demand for manufactured goods. Contributing four vessels to a six-ship service, Bank Line inaugurated a sailing every twenty-four days from British and Continental ports in Germany, the Netherlands and France, to the South Pacific. The ships engaged in this trade were multi-purpose, having refrigerated ('reefer') space, deep-tanks for the carriage of coconut and other oils and capacity for break-bulk general cargoes and deck space for containers. To this end they were fitted with cranes and derricks and thus free to work cargo wherever it was available. Built originally for Soviet owners, they were also fitted with a heavy-duty stern ramp.

One such converted Russian vessel was the *Foylebank*, measuring 18,663 tons gross, registered in the Isle of Man under the island's defaced red ensign and, being on charter to John Swire & Co., wearing Swire's colours. On a voyage in 2007 Captain John Gunson was joined in Auckland by Dennis Richards, taking passage to Singapore; both had trained with Ocean and Richards, a former second mate, recalls the cargo as:

> Mainly heavy machinery, army trucks and earth-moving equipment, drums of steel-cables, etc. The rest of the space taken up with containers of various sizes including Reefer. On deck there was a large luxury yacht and one container had been ingeniously converted for the carriage of four horses from Auckland to Noumea. Two grooms accompanied us on this leg. Cargoes loaded through the islands, other than containers included bagged cocoa beans, coconut oil, palm oil and 4,000 tons of bulk copra, which in turn was off-loaded on arrival in the Philippines

and Pasir Gudang. That space in turn being filled with sawn-timber in Sandakan and Kotakinbalu. The ship, said to be in its last four years of life, has been hard-used and running repairs were aided by having an AB and fitter both of whom doubled as qualified welders.

At the end of June we arrived at Singapore after a fascinating seven-week leg of the voyage via New Caledonia, Vanuatu, Solomon Islands, Papua New Guinea, the Philippines and Sabah. Fourteen ports in forty-eight days.

The *Foylebank*'s crew consisted of thirty-one officers and ratings, including four cadets; Gunson and the second mate were British, but 'the rest of the crew, which includes three stewardesses and a lady chief and second-cook, are Russian'.

The Weir dynasty proved remarkable. The first Andrew Weir, Lord Inverforth, saw his company's seventieth anniversary before his death aged ninety-one in September 1955. He had been a remarkable shipowner, eulogised in his lifetime as 'an exceptionally alert, capable, honest personality; boasting, justly, that his firm never undertake anything they cannot carry through'. Succeeding to his father's title as the second Baron Inverforth of Southgate, The Hon W. Morton Weir took over the company and was in turn followed by his son, who died suddenly on his fiftieth birthday in June 1982. The third baron had steered the group through troubled waters and was esteemed in London's small shipping fraternity where he, like his forebears, had held office in the Chamber of Shipping, The General Council of British Shipping and the Baltic Exchange. He had also underpinned the Weir Group's shipping interest with diversification into insurance, travel, hotel ownership and the acquisition of companies like Spink & Son, the numismatological and fine art dealers. Inverforth's chair was inherited by his brother and the Andrew Weir Group continues in business.

Perhaps the most adept of the older firms embracing 'diversification' with imaginative enthusiasm was the house of Bibby.[8] Having lost its traditional trade with Burma and its role as a trooping contractor to the Government in 1966 this former liner company purchased the first of four liquefied petroleum gas carriers, the *Wiltshire* and by 1975 its fleet of over 1 million tons deadweight comprised LPG, bulk and general cargo-carriers, mostly on charters, trebling its overseas earnings but the ensuing depression caught Bibby with a new ship, the *Staffordshire*, and falling world markets. In 1978 four vessels were sold during a crippling twelve months, a fifth going in 1979, with the four Dart line vessels disposed of in 1980. This was a fateful year for Bibby, with the loss of the bulk-carrier *Derbyshire* (see below) followed by a disastrous financial background. Changes in tax laws, falling freight markets, low inflation and the debts accrued from earlier expansion led to a string of ship sales and redundancies. By 1982 the Bibby fleet was reduced to nine vessels, a situation that would have caused despair among shareholders except that Bibby were held together by some remarkable people rooted in shipping led by Sir Derek Bibby. Three years later wellmanaged diversification had secured interests outside shipping.

With many ventures on the fringes of oil exploration and extraction from submarine sources,[9] Bibby took diversification to new extremes chartering floating accommodation vessels, or 'coastels' to the Government to provide barracks in the Falklands and in 1987 it sent two of these across the Atlantic on the deck of the Dutch heavy-lift ship *Super Servant* to become a 'chartered detention facility,' or prison. This restored Bibby's financial position and led it to acquire a new LPG carrier, the *Cheshire* in 1989, followed by two chemical carriers, but the survival of these enterprises necessitated joint-ventures and management deals with foreign companies, emphasising, if emphasis were needed, of the deconstruction of successful commercial shipping from any tacitly implied national asset. Two hundred years after its original founding in 1807, Bibby Line was part of a large and successful group with diverse, if marine related, interests which included a ship-management company based in the Isle of Man, offshore production and storage units, diving support vessels, a technical consultancy, distribution and financial services.

Such admirable versatility lay beyond the horizon of public regard which required more obviously glamorous eye-candy. Despite now being the subsidiary of a building-conglomerate, Cunard maintained its own image alongside the illusion that British seafaring remained a mainstream industry by building the *Queen Elizabeth 2* at John Brown's ailing yard in 1969. Designed by Dan Wallace she, like others among the last British liners, incorporated aluminium in her superstructure to save weight and reduce maintenance. Wallace's brief fortuitously required a ship capable of operating as a conventional Atlantic liner and a cruise ship able to transit the Panama Canal so that she was an early example of a vessel whose dimensions became known as 'Panamax'. Cunard were obliged to seek state assistance in funding the construction which went to Brown's on the cheapest tender. In fact the new ship was to be built at cost in a yard that was already disrupted by labour disputes, crippled by outdated working practices and poor management, as Ocean had discovered. Although the result was a handsome ship that lasted until 2009 she had a chequered career and had long since had her British steam turbines replaced by German diesels.[10]

The *Queen Elizabeth 2* was launched by Queen Elizabeth II on 20 September 1967 and erroneously referred to by an increasingly maritime-ignorant media as 'the flagship of the British Merchant Navy'. While she was fitting-out the following year her predecessor, the *Queen Elizabeth*, made her last voyage and was sold to C.Y. Tung of Hong Kong. Renamed *Seawise University* and converted for cruising she caught fire and sank in Hong Kong Harbour in January 1972. Her half-sister, the *Queen Mary*, had also been sold to find a permanent berth in Long Beach, California. The rise of the long-range air-liner meant that the new '*QE2*' could only attract trans-Atlantic passengers for part of the year, but even this income stream dried up and she was soon switched to full-time cruising. Other late British passenger liners had already made the change: P&O's *Canberra* and *Oriana*, for example, took advantage of a rising prosperity among retired but still active British pensioners, who wished to indulge in cruising. Later British passenger ships, such as P&O's *Oriana* of 1995 and *Aurora* of 2000 – both built in a German yard – and Cunard's French-built *Queen Mary 2* of 2005, though still almost lovingly but quite wrongly referred to as 'liners', catered for the huge boom in this sector.

Behind the scenes of the Seamen's Strike of 1966 the 'four knights' had concluded their deliberations and that August formed a consortium in Overseas Containers Ltd, or OCL, with a working capital of £45 million. OCL was to be supported by Australian subsidiaries to handle the new traffic and to establish container terminals at

Sydney, Melbourne and Fremantle. In March 1967 six container-liners were ordered to serve Europe and Australia and on 18 September the New Zealand Shipping Co.'s conventional cargo-liner *Piako* lifted the first OCL containers containing photo-copy paper and bagged chemicals. A month later the now obsolescent *Mystic* proved briefly useful on a time-charter to Shaw, Savill & Albion, leaving Melbourne bound for Hull with containers full of wool and fruit.

To be able to service the forthcoming container-liners which lacked the cargo-handling gear of their predecessors, the new container terminals required huge container cranes, straddle carriers, automated cargo-handling facilities and extensive container parks backed up by road and rail networks in the wider hinterland beyond. Once these facilities became available, a single first generation container-liner replaced three or four conventional cargo-liners like the *Mystic*, a factor which increased with successive new tonnage.

Impetus was given to this revolution by world-changing events elsewhere as the Suez Canal was again was closed. On 5 June 1967 the 'Six-Day War' between Egypt and Israel caught fourteen ships passing through the Suez Canal, of which four were British, the remainder being two each from Sweden, West Germany and Poland, one each from France, Bulgaria, Czecholslovakia and the United States. Fierce fighting at Port Said prevented the south-bound ships from leaving, but the north-bound convoy was ordered to leave Suez by the Egyptian authorities for reasons of their own.[11] It was led, as was usual, by tankers laden with Arabian crude and it was not long before those aboard the north-going ships were extremely anxious and increasingly aware of their predicament as Israeli Mirages screamed overhead at mast height. On arrival at the Great Bitter Lake where the convoy customarily anchored to allow the south-bound ships to pass, it became clear that something other than a desperate attempt to pass the ships through the waterway was in train. With no vessels approaching from the north, the tankers steamed on towards Port Said but the cargo-liners were ordered to anchor in the Great Bitter Lake. Two Soviet Russian vessels immediately turned round and steamed straight back to Suez, thus escaping the entrapment that was in progress. Like the tankers filled with Saudi, Kuwaiti, Iraqi and Iranian oil, the Russian ships were seen to be 'friendly' towards Egypt, since the Soviet Union supplied arms to the Egyptians. The detention of these politically well-favoured vessels would have weakened the Egyptian position, whereas the case was otherwise with the remainder which could be played as pawns in an attempt to implicate state-governments not directly involved.

The following day the Egyptians blocked the canal by scuttling dredgers and trapping the anchored fourteen cargo-ships. For several days all on board remained ignorant of events, retaining pilots, mooring-boats and their crews that each carried during the canal transit, but eventually these were withdrawn and the masters were informed that all navigation in the canal had been suspended indefinitely. The reality was brought closer when the Egyptian airfield beyond the Kabret signal station was bombed and retreating Egyptian soldiers appeared on the eastern shore of the lake, 'hungry, thirsty, bootless'. In an act of humanity a number of the ships, the British among them, lowered lifeboats and after dispensing water, conveyed the soldiers in overcrowded boats six miles across the lake to land them among friends.

When it became clear that a stalemate existed and the Egyptians were going to do little to assist, the various ship's companies fell back on mutual self-help. They were all moored in pairs in the Great Bitter Lake, stem to stern, each ship laying two anchors out ahead. The four British ships were all cargo-liners: two Blue Funnel liners, the *Agapenor* and the *Melampus*, made up one duo, the Blue Star Line's *Scottish Star* and Port Line's *Port Invercargill* making a second, their companies having that year formed a joint manning and management company – though not an ownership merger. The ships lay closer to the Egyptian shore than the Israeli-occupied eastern side of the lake but initially their isolation was complete. All supplies, especially water, were withheld and of necessity these privations made common-cause among the crews, developing a remarkable spirit of co-operation from their common misfortune and led to a system of bartering between the vessels which in due course welded them into a community. When it became clear that the ships were likely to be incarcerated for some time, their cargoes were written-off and their crews, by then reduced to standby status, were allowed to make use of them. On the first Monday of every month they went shopping, swapping frozen Japanese trout, hake and shark from the Swedish East Asia liner *Nippon*; fresh meat, butter and eggs from Hamburg-Amerika Linie's *Münsterland*; canned fruit and chilled apples from the *Scottish Star* and *Port Invercargill*; sugar, tea and rice from the Blue Funnel ships; frozen shrimps and prawns from the Messageries Maritime liner *Sindh*, and so on. Among the others, the American Farrell Line's *African Glen*, and the Bulgarian-flagged *Vassil Levsky* were flying light in ballast.[12]

In due course, having been trapped while in transit of their canal and with the ground fighting over, relations with the Egyptians thawed and water and other essential services were supplied. The ships' agents began to do rather well out of the retention of their clients, in contrast to the Israelis who were unsympathetic. When a boat worked loose from her moorings alongside the gangway of one of the British ships and washed up on the Israeli-occupied shore, the boat's crew sent to retrieve it were arrested and interrogated before being directly repatriated and not allowed back aboard their vessel. Crew members were each paid £2 *per diem* danger and hardship money, though the war was confined to the occasional 'shoot-out once a week (usually on a Saturday night) – and jet fighters and bombers roared overhead – we watched with an air of detachment.' Nevertheless, an armed Egyptian guard was allocated to each vessel, and although use of the radio was forbidden, news of events in the outside world, particularly the occupation by Warsaw Pact troops of Czechoslovakia to suppress President Alexander Dubcek's 'Prague Spring' percolated through, to cause mourning aboard the *Lednice* and the lowering of her ensign to half-mast. However, with the conviviality and resource natural to seafarers they made the best of it all, forming the Great Bitter Lake Association, printing stamps, engaging in social events, inter-ship sports and fiercely competitive regattas between unorthodoxly rigged lifeboats. In emulation of the Olympiad of 1968 they organized their own improvised mini-Olympics.

By the time the canal was reopened in May 1975 most of these fine vessels had been abandoned, only the two Germans leaving under their own power. The rest were towed to Port Said and all four British ships were sold to Greek owners and overhauled for further service despite having been written off as constructive total losses by their underwriters in February 1969. Of far greater significance than the fates of these ships was the increase in tanker size precipitated by the closed canal and the fact that, by the time it reopened, the increased passage times between Europe, the Middle East, the Orient and Australia were further complicated by the quadrupled price of bunker oil following the Oil Crisis of 1973/4.

Meanwhile the new OCL consortium had progressed with the new Europe-Australia container-trade under the subsidiary Container Fleets Ltd – CFL. The joint Swire-Ocean venture, the Australia Japan Container Line, had been set up to pick up the trade between east Australia and eastern Asia; a year later in 1969 similar arrangements had been set up to extend the original service to New Zealand, and to establish a new route between Europe and the Far East.

Some efforts had been made under the provisions of Lord Devlin's report to mitigate the impending effects of containerisation upon the dock-labour force in Britain, including a redundancy scheme and better pay for those remaining in a more skilled employment operating the new plant, but such was the militancy among the dock workers at Tilbury that the OCL board were obliged to resort to their contingency plans for trans-shipping cargo from Harwich and Ipswich to load at Rotterdam on OCL's first new vessel. This denied the *Encounter Bay* 'the send-off this mighty British enterprise had hoped for or indeed deserved'.[13] Similar problems were met in Australia, but these were overcome, largely because of a wider societal interest – from the Government to the press – which greeted the new ship with enthusiasm. At home, however, the prolonged industrial action in London delayed the full service into Britain for fourteen months.

On 6 March 1969, the new – German-built – *Encounter Bay* sailed from Rotterdam with 1,300 containers 'filled with goods ranging from toothpaste to caterpillar tractors' under the command of Captain Michael Champneys, former staff-captain of the *Oriana*, with Mr Ian Stewart as his chief engineer. Both were P&O men and they led a new regime in which, with small complements, the chief engineer now assumed responsibility for all maintenance. Under a General Purpose arrangement, British deck and engine-room ratings were interchangeable, leaving the caterers in their traditional role, while the officers' embraced an entirely new system.[14] Although initially 'operations at Australian terminals still proceeded slowly and three or four days in port was not unusual,' the new *modus operandi* introduced some uncomfortable truths for those at sea, as we shall see.

For those directing this revolution there were many matters to address. Such were the expenses and capacity in the rising container terminals that besides the co-operation of the companies within OCL, that of others must needs be sought. Over a two-year period OCL joined forces and resources with Associated Container Transport, or ACT, a rival consortium of Cunard's subsidiary Port Line, Vestey's Blue Star and Ellerman, which secured an arrangement with the Australian National Line. ACT built three container-liners, running *ACT 1* and *ACT 2* under the British flag and the third, *Australian Endeavour* under that of Australia. Although of small capacity by comparison with what was to come, these nine vessels displaced twenty-eight conventional hulls. There was a similar impact on personnel, the initial six *Encounter Bay*-class requiring a total complement of 250 against 1,250 in the twenty cargo-liners they made redundant.[15]

In the meantime R.B. Stoker, the chairman of Furness, Withy's Manchester Liners, had moved his company centre-stage on the North Atlantic with the departure of the first British fully cellular container liner. The *Manchester Challenge*, Captain P. Fielding, left Manchester bound for Montreal in November 1968. Others followed, forming consortia with former foreign rivals. Cunard, under Philip Bates, joined forces with French, Dutch and Swedish firms to establish the Atlantic Container Line, or ACL. This specialised in hybrid container and RORO ships with Bates running the Cunard component from Southampton. A rival on this high-volume route was the Dart Container Line composed of a Canadian, Belgian and a British shipping company, the Bristol City Line, whose four ships and interests were soon afterwards subsumed by Bibby, as already noted. By 1971 the British merchant fleet possessed fifty-one container-liners, second only to the pioneering Americans with seventy-five, out of world total of 231.[16]

This commanding position failed to save the mercantile marines of either countries. An ominous marker occurred in 1967 when Liberia replaced Britain as possessor of the largest flag-fleet, having itself exceeded the tonnage of Panama in 1956. As the major liner consortia raised capital and replaced their fleets, others sold or scrapped old ships, crews were trimmed, costs over-hauled, extraneous assets disposed of and dead-wood cut out. Some invested in bulk-carriers and some small tanker companies either disappeared or were subsumed by the oil-majors, enabling tankers to rapidly increase in size as the Suez Canal closure seemed irreversible.

These processes did not have to proceed very far to reveal a number of facts: the brave new world of modern shipping required fewer ships and these would need not only smaller crews, but could manage with men recruited from Third World countries where labour was significantly cheaper and vastly more tractable than the traditional manpower sources in Britain. Fewer Britons went to sea, and fewer families had a maritime connection. Moreover, as with the distant oil terminals, container ports not only dispensed with the organised and intransigent port labour forces, they began to occupy new sites, downstream and miles from the old port centres where they could draw on small numbers of local manpower. In so doing they drew merchant shipping with them, so that it passed out of the sight of the British public and as a consequence, out of mind.

To these immense changes were added further factors outside the control of any shipowner. In the first place, and against the optimism of the directors of OCL and ACT, it had long been obvious that Britain could not rely upon trade with the Commonwealth as it had done with the Empire in the 1930s. In shrinking from her former role as a world power, Britain's economic links with Europe grew stronger and in 1973 Britain joined the European Economic Community, forerunner of the European Union which would by the end of the century also lay siege to her political independence.[17] There were major consequences for both Australian and New Zealand trades, with both countries having, over time, to find new markets for goods which had traditionally filled the 'Commonwealth liners'. Unfortunately, what opportunities were to be had from these seismic shifts, were largely ignored by British owners. The large container terminals, or 'hubs' became the new *entrepôts* from where smaller 'feeder-ships' distributed 'boxes' to their final destinations and collected outward freights by the reverse process. While such 'feeders' could be manned and run profitably locally, few British owners took up the challenge, a missed opportunity when set against a rapidly congesting road network and a less than optimally efficient railway system. Although several European mercantile marines specialised in this niche in the new integrated transport system, there was no revival in British coastal shipping. This was inhibited by the National Dock Labour Scheme, which tended to blight ports under its control and dissuaded owners from using them to ship containers in feeder-ships.

Nevertheless, in one of those statistical anomalies that reflect the past rather than the present, these container consortia and an increase in the unit size of other ship types under the red ensign, such as tankers and bulk-carriers, combined to produce in 1975 the British merchant fleet's greatest post-war gross registered tonnage of no less than 33 million. Unfortunately, during the decade between Nicholson's letter to Anderson and this peak, much else had occurred. To cope with the fiscal demands of containerisation, co-operation was not enough: the companies needed to restructure. Like others, the P&O Group's shipping needed radical overhaul. In 1971, under the new chairman Ford Geddes, the entire combine was reorganised into divisions, sweeping away the old company identities. Along with the lost liveries and the traditional names went that keen *esprit* that gave seafarers their own identity; what was logical, even imperative at the board table was not so comprehensible on the bridge to the career sea-officer, still less to the lascar on deck. For those involved in these upheavals the impact could be devastating, careers came to abrupt ends, expectations underwent radical changes and morale slumped.

In this context, the fate of the subsidiary British India S.N.Co. is of interest. Having lost much of its traffic with India following the independence and partition of the sub-continent in 1947, it had concentrated, *inter alia*, on services to east Africa. By the early 1970s the regular and coincident arrival of several B.I. ships in Kilindini Harbour had for years been declining from its peak on Sunday 16 September 1951 when no less than seven cargo-passenger liners were working cargo alongside.[18] In May 1971 the end of British India's east African service came a step nearer. This had in part been caused by the introduction of a combined B.I.-Union-Castle service which required a reduction in tonnage, and the encroachment of air travel, but was also accelerated by political upheaval in the area. The first of the company's post-war passenger liners reached the breakers at Kaohsiung, Taiwan. The *Kampala*, Captain V.P. Harvey, had completed 179 voyages and carried half a million passengers. Her sale was followed by that of several of the 'once ubiquitous' C-class, the *Chupra, Chanda, Chantala* and *Chindwara*, the last two of which had been cadet-ships. On 1 October the few liners retaining a separate identity were absorbed into the P&O General Cargo Division. Fortunately the *Karanja, Rajula, Sirdhana, Dwarka* and *Dumra* were not obliged to adopt the white P&O logo of the blue funnel, but retained the traditional funnel design and house-flag, as did the 'school-ships' *Uganda* and *Nevasa*. In the following two years the rest of the cargo-ships were fully subsumed into the General Cargo Division of P&O, adopting the new-age colours which did little for their looks, or their crews' self-esteem. Gone were the old symbols; all must be new, corporate and image conscious. Meanwhile the older vessels were scrapped piecemeal:

the *Sirdhana* being broken-up in late 1972. That year, following the *Tairea's* departure in January, the *Chilka* closed the London-East Africa run, leaving the Royal Albert Dock on 18 May and reaching Mombasa on 14 June from where she headed for Taiwan and the acetylene torch. Only the *Karanja* was left, running between India, Pakistan and East Africa, but already her days were numbered.

The company's East Africa service was dealt what would prove a mortal-wound in 1972 when President Idi Amin expelled Uganda's Asian population, thus removing at a stroke all potential passengers. When an international airport was opened at Mahé in the Seychelles in 1974, rendering the regular call of the B.I. service redundant, and the Portuguese abandoned their overseas territory of Mozambique leaving it to an uncertain future, it was clear that the inevitable end had arrived. Reluctant to give up the service the lone *Karanja* lingered on until 1976 when, on 19 April, she departed from Ballard Pier, Bombay, on her 173rd voyage. She called at Karachi, Mombasa, Dar-es-Salaam and Lourenço Marques (now renamed Maputo), arriving at Durban on 14 May. Three days earlier the *Edinburgh Castle* had departed that port for a breaker's yard in Taiwan and the *Karanja* sailed on the 15th, calling at Beira, Dar-es-Salaam, Mombasa and Karachi before reaching Bombay on 9 June. Two months later she was handed over to the Shipping Corporation of India, renamed *Nancowry* and served in the Bay of Bengal between Madras and Port Blair until 1988, the last of a proud and distinguished company.[19] Only the old *Uganda*, heroine of the Falklands Campaign and recalled by a generation of children who had cruised aboard her for educational purposes, cheated the ship-breakers by foundering and capsizing in a typhoon whilst awaiting destruction at Kaohsiung in 1986.

As redundant tonnage was disposed of to Third World owners or the scrapyard, the remaining conventional P&O tonnage was divided among the Passenger, General Cargo or Bulk Shipping Divisions. This optimistic reshuffle was blighted by the Oil Crisis created by the oil-producing OPEC nations' decision to raise oil prices four-hold in 1974 and which had a profound affect worldwide. Since the closure of the Suez Canal in 1967, P&O had been among those acquiring vessels of tremendous size, so that when the company built their largest oil/ore carrier in 1972, the *Lauderdale's* deadweight tonnage of 264,591 was not exceptional. In reaction to the Oil Crisis the P&O Group fleet was rapidly cut, shrinking to half, from 178 to eighty-nine hulls by 1980, helped by sales and improved new ship-design, particularly in larger ferries. Of greater import was the drift of group investment out of shipping into safer sectors, Inchcape remarking ominously to his shareholders in 1980: 'We will certainly remain in some areas of shipping'. In addition to its conspicuous cruise ships, P&O derived much of its economic drive from its interest in OCL, which it was progressively acquiring in its entirety.

The predatory instincts of city capitalists were excited by these container consortia and their component companies came under attack. The construction company Trafalgar House had acquired Cunard in 1969 and Ocean, with its substantial reserves, was scrutinised by the Rank Organisation in 1972. A boardroom battle ensued at P&O over plans to diversify and acquire Bovis, another construction company, but the rebels won and Ford Geddes was obliged to relinquish the chair to the current Lord Inchcape. Nine years later Inchcape's imminent retirement sparked interest in a takeover which was resisted and from which Jeffery Sterling emerged as the Chairman. Sterling was not a shipping man, but a skilful financier and he simultaneously took the chair of Overseas Container (Holdings) in which P&O had the largest share of the original partnership with Ocean, British & Commonwealth, and Furness, Withy.

Sterling received a knighthood in the New Year's Honours of 1984 by which time P&O owned 47.5 per cent of OCL. Apart from ferry services in the Irish and North Sea, drawing the company closer to the Swedish firm Stena, Sterling now bought-out Ocean's stake in OCL which became P&O Containers and sold the Group's Liquid Petroleum Gas (LPG) tankers to Bergesen of Norway, retaining a fleet of bulk-carriers. In 1987 the Group owned seventy-six ships grossing 1.7 million tons, had a turnover of £2.68 billion pounds, employed 42,000 people and celebrated its 150th Anniversary with a gala dinner aboard the cruise ship *Pacific Princess* at Greenwich in the presence of HM Queen Elizabeth II. Five months later in November, following the *Herald of Free Enterprise* disaster in March (see below) in which the death toll was heavy, Sterling, having just bought Townsend-Thoresen, expunged the sullied brand to form European Ferries. There followed a prolonged strike among a militant work-force at Dover, but the prospect of a cross-Channel tunnel and the damage done by the disaster at Zeebrugge weakened the strikers' case. Sterling steered the Group to a record operating profit the following year, 1989, of £442 million after the purchase of Sitmar Cruises for £215 million. In 1990 P&O moved into the North Atlantic in a joint slot agreement with the Dutch company Nedlloyd and the American Sea-Land Corporation. This was further enhanced in the following year by a buy-out of Trafalgar House's Cunard-Ellerman's container interests, with Andrew Weir Shipping taking over the combine's Mediterranean container services – the rump of Cunard's 'brigs' and Ellerman's Pappayani Line – along with Ellerman's cargo rights for the eastern Mediterranean, Red Sea and East Africa.[20] P&O also purchased the container-liners owned by ACT and sold them to Blue Star for operation in the Pacific, building new bulkers, and ordering larger new container-ships.

Three years after acquiring a half-share in Rowbotham's coastal tankers, P&O took over the firm in 1993 and sold it on to James Fisher & Co. of Barrow-in-Furness, operators of specialist carriers of nuclear waste. New container-liners and cruise ships followed, of which the *Oriana* of 1995 was the jewel but in 1995 the container operation was merged with Nedlloyd, making P&O Nedlloyd a huge operator. The combined Anglo-Dutch board of eight directors commanded 112 wholly owned or chartered vessels, but derived savings from a reduction in the workforce from 9,400 to 8,000. The original six *Encounter Bay*-class liners were switched to the trans-Pacific service when they were superseded by the new vessels. These burned only 120 tons of fuel against the *Encounters'* 156-ton daily consumption, and had a capacity of 6,673 20ft equivalent container units (the industry standard measure known as 'teu'), an increase of 5,373, making them extraordinary vessels. Further ferry acquisitions by P&O were followed by recovery of the Blue Star container-liners and the commissioning of the gigantic cruise ship *Star Princess* of over 100,000 gross tons.

In the opinion of one industry expert, however, the merger with Nedlloyd was flawed.

[T]he way that [the] company was run is open to criticism. No one knew who was in charge: the Dutch or the British ... Because of the structure of the P&ONL [operation] they were not agile enough in the market, their costs were too high and profits were poor.[21]

Joint-operations were entered into in other sectors, creating a plethora of name changes and complex arrangements such as the formation in 1996 of the Associated Bulk Carrier Fleet from P&O's Bulk Carrier Division working in conjunction with the Norwegian Naess fleet. These huge vessels, the descendants of the humble tramp, no longer reacted to the lifting of discrete homogenous consignments on voyage, or spot charters, but entered into Contracts of Affreightment whereby the 'just-in-time' delivery of hundreds of thousands of tons of ore or coal, or regular seasonal quantities of grain, ensured steady employment for the ships. Integration of the supply of these commodities reflected the practice in oil delivery and the scheduled services of containerisation, and marked a greater culminating globalisation of shipping. However, its efficiency was so ruthless that – subject as always to the vicissitudes of world trade and the fluctuations of freight-rates – competition for such contracts in the bulk-markets was fierce. The customer favoured the cheapest deal, leading to cost-cutting advantageous to foreign-flagged, cheaper-manned and maintained ships. By 1998 the ABC Fleet had merged with another partner, Shougang of China, with Filipino crews and British officers, to satisfy China's growing demand for coal and iron ore. This period also marked the merger of P&O and Stena's ferry operations in the Dover Straits, though four years later, in 2002, P&O bought-out the Stena share.

By this time, however, other developments were emerging. In 2000, half P&O's bulk-carrier fleet was sold to the Israeli owner, Samuel Ofer, the remainder following three years later, leading to heavy redundancies. A further shake-up occurred on 18 April 2003 when, at an Extraordinary Annual General Meeting, following the Board's recommendation, a 98 per cent vote found in favour of Carnival Cruises of Miami taking over P&O Cruises. The arrangement was complicated, with the now Lord Sterling becoming life president of Carnival plc, and Carnival's principal, Mickey Arison, being appointed chairman and chief executive. Such international ownership, a consequence of the globalisation of finance, deracinated the company's British cruising fleet; henceforth registration and flagging were matters of fiscal shrewdness, ships losing any pretence at 'nationality'. Such arrangements were by this time widespread, affecting vessels of many types, a reversion to polyglot manning driven by economical imperatives and the cupidity of shareholders.

Most conspicuously, cruise ships now epitomised this globalisation of so-called human resources, being frequently commanded by British masters, but run by officers of several nationalities, usually European and many from the now liberated Comecon countries from whence came well-trained but cheap officers. Ratings were commonly recruited in South-East Asia, particularly the Philippines whose government had embraced a policy of sea-training. Despite all this, at the time of writing, internationally flagged cruise ships continue to offer opportunities for British officers, even juniors and cadets.

The unprecedented trading conditions prevailing at the turn of the century gave P&O further opportunities. A major replacement of the fleet was undertaken in 2002 with seven new liners and 23,000 teu containers. It was operating 157 vessels on eighty-four routes with 235 ports of call including new terminals in developing countries like Brazil while serving those in a China now in the throes of the massive export boom that drove world trade. 'Helped by the best market ever,' the industry expert quoted above remarked, the company was 'turned … round' to become profitable. 'But the shareholders (at least the British) had a hidden agenda which was to sell out'. With Lord Sterling announcing his forthcoming retirement in 2005 and a new chief executive in Robert Woods, then also Chairman of the Chamber of Shipping, a flotation of shares in P&O Nedlloyd initiated the 'hidden agenda'. The British shareholders defied the lessons of history and sold to the Danish giant Maersk. Writing of his former company, Jim Davies remarked:

> It is simply sad that by selling the cruising activity to the Carnival Corporation the venerable P&O S.N. Co. once indisputably the greatest brand name in shipping, became reduced to a middle-sized global port company … Let us remember that Carnival and even the mighty Maersk were comparatively small companies a little while ago … It could have been so very different.[22]

With its unprofitable tankers sold and the gas-carriers following, the exit of P&O from deep-water ship-owning in favour of becoming a cruise ship, port and ferry operator was an event of major significance, the implications of which were lost on the wider public. It begged the question articulated by one commentator: 'If Denmark can have the largest line in the world, why can't the British?' Maersk, among a handful of other European shipping enterprises, remained controlled by a few highly motivated 'individuals [who] had a vision of a highly concentrated industry …'. The British response had been short-sighted and subject to the powerful voracity of shareholders; it was, alas, a comment upon the times.

Money could still be made by managing ships on behalf of others, but for many either selling out altogether or registering their vessels under foreign flags came with the powerful inducement that by 'flagging-out' they could employ cheap and docile crews from the developing world. The search for costs driven down to global minima had been accelerated by the continuing political turmoil in Britain that in 1979 had produced the neo-conservative government of Margaret Thatcher. Thatcher was a moderniser possessing a complex mixture of old-fashioned ideas – which were articulated for public consumption and produced the personal greed-culture referred to above – and an enthusiasm for the Chicago-school economics of Milton Friedman. These she put into operation with confrontational effect combined with a Friedmanesque indifference for the social consequences. In her drive to move the British economy towards the wholesale provision of service-industries she effectively destroyed Great Britain's greatest of these. Her global hands-off policy excoriated British shipping which she famously declared 'a sunset industry'. And so it became.

The P&O Group was the greatest of all the great British shipping houses and its contraction from ship-owning is the most important marker in tracing the decline of the red-ensign fleet. Others, having tumbled into its lap, thereafter fell into its wake. Lord Vestey's distinctive Blue Star, for example, may still be found painted upon the side of a 'box-boat's' superstructure and she may still have a British master, but the ship will be registered in Germany and be operated by the gigantic Maersk conglomerate of Denmark. Cunard became a shadow of its former glory, and a mere brand of the giant Carnival empire, though it heroically maintained its image in the cruising world with a new *Queen Mary 2*. Ellerman had long since sunk, as had T&J Harrison, which had never fully recovered from the Second World War. Poor port-performance in the West Indies had affected the company's schedules, the Harrison board recognising it was more efficient to charter foreign ships or hire capacity than to operate under the red ensign. Like other British and European companies, various expedients were tried, most of them short-lived, since their rights were bought-out by the larger consortia. In the end the house of Harrison was subsumed by P&O in October 2000 to die with it, a fate typical of many firms. A few lingered on, old names under complex ownership, manning and management arrangements, often under foreign ensigns, odd names and unfamiliar logos. Weary ships ended their days usefully in distant places, though few, if any, had a British seafarer aboard.

Among the wreckage lay the Ocean Group, called Ocean Transport & Trading in its final years.[23] Back in 1965 the managers had decided to make Alfred Holt & Co. a publicly quoted company, abandoning the strict familial paternalism with its interests and expertise vested in shipping general cargo, its skilled workforce and enviable capital reserves. The new entity of Ocean began to diversify with the acquisition of Cory, handling bulk-fuel and road transport, and the complete takeover of Elder, Dempster's fleet which, at a stroke, destroyed morale in the Blue Funnel and Glen Line vessels as personnel were made interchangeable. The next major development was the Group's joint-venture – OCL.

The OCL operation was managed by men drawn from several companies. Its technical director, for example was John Newton, who had been Furness, Withy's very first engineer cadet, but initially many came from P&O which supplied the sea-staff manning the *Encounter Bay*-class liners on the Autralasian route. It was therefore Ocean who, with the later 26-knot steam-turbine-powered *Liverpool Bay*-class, manned and operated the Far East container service. 'It is difficult to believe how different were the styles of management between Ocean and P&O,' recalled Captain Ken Owen, an old Blue Funnel man. With its huge cargo-liner fleet now swiftly becoming redundant, Ocean now embarked upon a venture which was to prove fatal, abandoning the precepts of financial conservatism and tight control that had been the great Holt legacy. With no experience of tanker operations, Ocean involved itself with all manner of ship types, VLCCs, OBOs, gas and chemical tankers, offshore supply vessels, ferries and ocean-going ROROs. With the exception of its container-liners, which capitalised on the excellence and expertise of its original sea-staff and shore management, its ventures into other unfamiliar areas were unsuccessful, in the case of gas and oil tankers, disastrously so with the huge 113,551-grt *Titan* and 120,787-grt *Troilus*. These were both steam-powered and commissioned on the eve of the Oil Crisis; they lost money and were sold as soon as possible. The company that had once built its ships to a standard far exceeding those of the classification societies,[24] whose sea-staff possessed an *esprit de corps* analogous to a Guards Regiment, had, after its sell out of its OCL interests to P&O in 1986, little more interest in shipping than a handful of small tugs.

Neither the pioneering containerisation initiative of the *Manchester Challenge*'s trans-Atlantic voyage of 1968, nor their stake in OCL, ultimately secured Furness, Withy's fortunes either. By 1965 the Furness, Withy Group owned 160 ships totalling 1,300,000 tons gross, second only to P&O, far in excess of all other British shipping companies and making it highly influential. However, from this apogee, increasing costs, technical developments and economic factors led to rationalisation as the slow unravelling of complex minority shareholdings progressed. Between 1965 and 1972 the ship-management of the group's companies was combined, Furness Ship Management drawing together the Furness fleet with those of Royal Mail and P.S.N.C., by which time Furness, Withy's five bulk-carriers had joined Bibby, H. Clarkson, C.T. Bowring, Hunting and Silver Line to form the Seabridge Consortium. Later adverse freight market conditions, coupled with some ill advised decisions by the consortium managers, caused Furness, Withy to withdraw and operate their ships independently. The circumstances surrounding this event were a matter of some internal dispute between Furness, Withy Bulk Shipping and another subsidiary, FW(Chartering) formed in 1971. By this time Furness Ship Management had been supplanted by two divisions: Furness, Withy General Shipping into which all the dry cargo trades were subsumed, and Furness, Withy Bulk Shipping which managed all bulk-carriers, tankers and gas carriers whatever their ostensible ownership; but by 1979, with the overall fleet size decrease to sixty vessels, these divisions were amalgamated into Furness, Withy (Shipping).

Furness had entered the 1970s regarded, however unfairly, as a 'sleepy, asset-rich under-performing group'. Almost always profitable, the average annual profit of perhaps £20 million against an asset base of nine or ten times that figure was regarded with derision by young financial Turks in the City and the group was considered ripe for asset-stripping and breaking up. Hostile shareholders managed to place their nominees on the board and much of the next ten years was spent in fending off various predators and seeking suitable partners. In the former the company was successful but, despite talks with Cunard and Ocean, no partner was found.

Three significant events marked the 1970s. First, the sale of twenty-three conventional cargo-liners in November 1970 marked the end of Furness, Withy itself as an active shipowner. Several routes were abandoned or truncated under the pressure of containerisation, and the remainder left to subsidiaries. Secondly, a takeover was mounted by a large shareholder in Manchester Liners (which was quoted separately from its parent on the London Stock Exchange) who bought into Furness, Withy and directly challenged the Furness board. For the last time – and in a pallid reminder of the Kylsant affair – the Government regarded a British shipping company of sufficient importance to the national interest to have Shirley Williams, the then Secretary of State, refer the matter to the Monopolies and Mergers Commission, which reported in October 1976. Furness called-in many favours from shippers, unions and others during the hearings, rebuffing their opponent's planned merger and deconstruction. The Furness board emerged victorious from the Annual General Meeting of May

1979, but was exposed to further approaches. Thirdly, under the guidance of John Houlder, Furness became the premier British company in the offshore contracting field, developing and operating dynamically positioned semi-submersible diving support and sub-sea construction vessels, oil-rigs and sea-bed diving units. The heavy investments made were repaid within two to three years in the early days of the North Sea oil-boom and Houlder Offshore acted as a useful anti-cyclical asset to counter the generally poor shipping markets at the start of the 1980s.

Then, in 1980, Tung Chao-Yung, better known as C.Y. Tung, the Hong Kong ship-owner, purchased Furness, Withy for £112 million, somewhat less than asset value, after satisfactory assurances had been obtained on the ring-fencing of finance and retention of British control. Tung almost immediately received £28 million from the three erstwhile partners of Furness, Withy in OCL because the Furness integration with a major competitor (Tung's Orient Overseas Container Line) triggered a 'get-out' clause written into the OCL Articles of Association. Many sea staff were transferred to the Hong Kong-registered ships, particularly to man bulk-carriers and, despite adverse conditions, FW traded profitably overall, especially on the oil side, recording profits of £11 million the year after takeover.

George Swaine[25] explains events after Tung's death in 1982:

Towards the end of 1985, his heir, C.H. Tung, was forced to reveal to his bankers that he was going to have to default on scheduled loan payments in the then enormous sum of US$2.8 billion, eventually to peak at US$3.5 billion. The majority of the losses were the costs of over forty new building orders, whose financing had been supported (as it turned out) by worthless paper companies, some privately owned. Most major banks were creditors and a consortium of seventy of them was formed following a decision not to liquidate the group, but to reconstruct it. Discreet but significant financial support was given by the Chinese Government through a front-man in Macao, their favour eventually being called in by insistence that Tung be appointed as the first Chief Executive of Hong Kong after the British withdrawal in 1997.

Furness was a major asset of the Tung group and whilst perfectly able to finance its own loans, was prevented from doing so in order to assist its parent. Many assets including insurance, offshore oil and gas, hotels and other assets were sold off, reducing the size of FW considerably. Furness continued to trade profitably but it became clear that capital required for expansion or renewal would not be forthcoming from the Tung group. Accordingly negotiations took place with the German Oetker group in 1990, leading to the purchase of Furness for $130 million. Oetker ... a large (if not the largest) private German family concern with interests in food, brewing, banking, insurance, hotels and many shipping companies, headed by Hamburg-Sud, a well known liner concern ... was interested in the major share of conference rights on both coasts, held by Furness through its ownership of Royal Mail, Houlder Brothers and P.S.N.C.

The 1990s saw Furness providing profits to their new shareholder, paying off the purchase cost within ten years. This was achieved by an extremely entrepreneurial activity based on contracts for the supply and storage of liquid petroleum gas to Ecuador ... Significant contributions were made also made from Furness Withy (Chartering)'s time charter and cargo contract operations, primarily in the large bulk-carrier market with commercial management under the aegis of British trained staff, many with seagoing experience – the last gasp of empire.

By 2005 it was clear that the required authority and the necessary critical mass required to back funding of future ventures (by necessity of a complex technical nature) were lacking in these factors, together with the absurdly short pay-back times usually stipulated by bankers, brought about a decision that the company no longer had a viable future. Everything was wound up in a careful and systematic way and 134 years after Kit Furness' first venture, netting £50,000 in an adroit exploitation of the French blockade of the Elbe during the Franco-Prussian War, FW went into voluntary liquidation on 15 March 2005, leaving Furness Withy (Chartering) and its Australian subsidiary as the sole remnant of what in 1912 had been regarded as a 'great Imperial asset.' *Sic transit gloria mundi.*

Others followed. The Union-Castle Line – part of Cayzer, Irvine's British & Commonwealth Group which included the withering Clan and King Lines – had in 1973 combined its services to South Africa with the South Africa Marine Corporation. In 1975 the *Pretoria Castle* went to Taiwanese breakers, the *Rothesay Castle* and *Rotherwick Castle* were sold, with four Clan liners transferred under Castle names to replace them. Other ships were disposed of, including the *Windsor Castle* and the two fast cargo-liners *Southampton Castle* and *Good Hope Castle* mentioned earlier. Only the four renamed Clan liners remained and in 1979 they lost their revised names, the '*Castle*' being displaced by '*Universal*'. This residual fleet dwindled and, in the early 1980s, had become little more than a memory, followed by that other mighty enterprise that had opened up West Africa to better possibilities in the aftermath of the slave trade. The company's regular passenger run had ended with the withdrawal of the *Aureol* in 1972 and by 1990 Elder, Dempster's fleet had dwindled from fifty to a dozen 'combos', capable of self-handling a combination of break-bulk, liquid and containerised cargoes. Gradually they too ceased their regular runs and sought charter work elsewhere.

In this decline the insular British dependencies of Ascension and St Helena became isolated. Cometh the hour, cometh the man, and into the breach stepped Andrew Bell to open a service between Avonmouth, Las Palmas, Ascension, St Helena and Capetown. Bell had begun his sea career as a midshipman in Alfred Holt's Blue Funnel and Glen Lines. He established Curnow Shipping and secured the Government's contract to provide a mail and passenger service to the lonely South Atlantic outposts with the RMS *St Helena*. Unfortunately, towards the end of 1999, at an extraordinary general meeting the managing director was voted off the board, an action which had all the hallmarks of a conspiracy. Bell felt compelled to resign, whereupon – hey presto – the board installed a new managing director who had, until a few months previously when he had left Curnow for bigger things, been both Bell's protégé and his likely successor.

Some weeks later the *St Helena* suffered a major breakdown and although possessing twin engines, made for Brest. She was in danger of breaching her mail and passenger contract and at this difficult juncture the newly installed managing director resigned and Curnow Shipping forfeit the contract. There was, however, an unpleasant aftermath in which Andrew Bell and four directors were charged with fraud, a case which was brought to an abrupt end by a Crown Court judge ruling that there was no case to answer. The shipping service contract and the *St Helena's* operation were bid for and awarded to Andrew Weir Shipping in 2001.

Shortly after the brief moment of military glory conferred by the retaking of the Falkland Islands in 1982, the recession in world shipping deepened and its impact upon the British merchant marine was appalling, the number of ships owned and registered in Britain declined sharply, the fleet dropping from 13th to 33rd in world ranking. The post-war peak of 1,614 ships in 1975 had made up 8.8 per cent of the world's tonnage, but the fall to 1,143 vessels in 1980 amounted to only 5.3 per cent, and five years later the remaining 627 ships, represented a mere 2.5 per cent of the total. The Chairman of Bibby Line, Sir Derek Bibby, described 1984 as 'the most appalling year for operational problems in my thirty-eight years experience in shipping,' not least because the Iran-Iraq War endangered shipping in the Persian Gulf owing to the indiscriminate laying of mines, bombing raids and torpedo attacks. In addition the freight market was poor, there were bad debts, third parties collapsed into bankruptcy and charterers were slow in paying-up. To cap it all, changes made in the Finance Act of that year 'found shipowners paying tax despite making trading losses'.

Throughout, the level of our imports by sea remained – and remains – roughly constant at 97 per cent so, with only one-fifth of this arriving in British ships by 1989, it was clear that by paying for the services of foreign ships, a balance of payments surplus turned into a deficit. That year there were 601 'British' ships claimed by the Chamber of Shipping, of which two thirds were on the Isle of Man or the Gibraltar registers. The decline in hulls was matched by a decline in seafarers. In 1975 there were 41,257 officers and 39,551 ratings at sea in British ships, showing the rapid imbalance caused by a requirement for technical skills in modern shipping, the use of greater mechanism on deck and a decline in the necessary standard of seamen. In 1980 the figures were 32,315 officers and 30,812 ratings. By 1990, however, these figures had fallen to 7,194 and 10,442 respectively. Significantly, far fewer cadets were under training, all of which created a skills shortage, threatening the maritime infrastructure as a whole since it produced a serious short-fall of pilots, harbour masters, ship surveyors, fleet managers and superintendents. This entirely rules out any provision for either a rapid expansion of the fleet if conditions favoured this, or a reserve of maritime skills should a future national emergency occur.

Misleadingly, even in 1990 'shipping' was among the top three invisible earners for the British economy, adding £4 billions to the national coffers, but most of this was enshrined in 'maritime services' centred on London and was not earned by vessels on the high seas. Thus, when John Major's Conservative Government went to war to clear Iraqi forces out of Kuwait in the First Gulf War in 1991, there was little British mercantile tonnage available to charter for military transport. One consequence of this was to increase investment in the Royal Fleet Auxiliary, which, although flying the defaced blue ensign of the state's service, employed officers and men trained in the mercantile ethos and this soon constituted the largest entity in Britain's remnant Merchant Navy.

Despite this parlous state and a rise in world trade in the following years, Britain's merchant fleet was neglected, and while over seventy foreign governments supported their own mercantile marines which provided two thirds of the world's tonnage, the British Government did little, content to see about £1 billion added to its balance of payments deficit and disregarding the employment opportunities a renascent fleet might have offered. True, there had been a brief flurry of anxiety in 1989 over the fact that while in a national emergency shipping might be chartered, the rather less certain reliability of their crews begged the question of a national 'Merchant Navy Reserve'. On 27 May a statute offered an annual bounty of £150 to existing or former merchant seamen willing to volunteer for call-up. It followed an announcement in the Commons on 4 April by Norman Fowler, Thatcher's Employment Minister, abolishing the National Dock Labour Scheme which had since 1947, in its guarantee to the dockers of a job for life, enabled their restrictive practices to frustrate the modernisation of the traditional ports. A feared dock strike never materialised, though the ultimate impact of abolition on wider society may have been worse (see Chapter Five, Note 8). Instead, container handling grew apace in non-Scheme ports such as Felixstowe which was union-free and destined to be Britain's main container terminal. Faced with the inevitable, new terminals were developed in Southampton, Tilbury and Liverpool and while Thatcher's reform of the docks swept away half a century of protected employment, the Merchant Navy Reserve scheme quietly expired.

Despite its political emphasis on service industries and shipping's 'invisible' contribution to the exchequer, the Thatcher Government had shown little love for the Merchant navy itself. Even after the salutary wake-up call of the Falklands, the 1984 budget abolished the meagre capital allowances on new tonnage, whereupon the removal of these modest benefits placed British owners at a disadvantage, as Peter Le Cheminant, then Director-General of the Council of British Shipping pointed out to the Government without effect. At a trade meeting at the British Embassy in Tokyo the Minister of Trade and Transport, Nicholas Ridley, an arch-Thatcherite and a man of individual and intemperate style, was asked by Peter Ryder, the principal surveyor of Lloyd's Register of Shipping in Japan:

> what the Government proposed to do about the serious decline of British shipping … [Ridley] was almost abusive in his reply, that they would rather see it disappear than offer any subsidy. So much so that the embassy staff rang Peter next morning to apologise for the way he had been spoken to.[26]

After she was out of office Captain Kenneth Owen met Margaret Thatcher at a dinner in Manchester where she was the guest speaker. 'Do you think you might have been able to revitalise British shipping if you had continued as Prime Minister?' he asked.

> I had introduced myself as a captain in P&O, Lord Sterling's company, and she seemed exceptionally friendly and attentive. She said: 'You know the trouble was with the *unions*, they were *so* inflexible.' I was hurried on by her minders before any further explanation was forthcoming.

The decline continued until, in the wake of Blair's landslide election victory of 1997, a certain John Prescott re-emerged as Secretary of State for Transport in a New Labour Government, the significance of which was that, despite Prescott's presence in its ranks, New Labour had charmed the electorate by adopting largely Tory policies and made no attempt to reconnect with the now marginalised 'Old Labour' movement. Prescott grasped something of the importance of shipping to the country and, after lobbying from disparate quarters, he sought a way of reviving some form of merchant fleet. Among the anxieties aired were the obvious lack of a strategic asset upon which the country might call in times of dire necessity, and the worrying lack of young people under training already referred to. In an attempt to attract shipping to the British flag a Tonnage Tax was introduced in 2000 which, by shaping a joint policy among the various 'stake-holders'[27] in the industry, offered the benefits of well-regulated British registry, under the auspices of the Maritime and Coastguard Agency, in a 'business-friendly' environment to any owner willing to undertake certain obligations, one of which was the training of British national cadets. Britain would offer shipowners a place on the United Nations' 'white-list' of countries running efficient and well-regulated ships which in turn would attract freights. The price of flying the red ensign would be simplified to a predictable levy on tonnage. By 2005 the results were promising, though the fleet was only fractionally beneficially British-owned and in most cases the obligation to train British cadets was inadequately observed.[28]

One all-British initiative under the Tonnage Tax was the establishment of Foreland Shipping which was conceived to provide a 'strategic sealift capability' for a Ministry of Defence contract by a consortium consisting of Bibby, Andrew Weir, Fisher & Co. of Barrow-in-Furness and the Hadley Shipping Co. The contract required six purpose-built, Ice Class 1A, 18 to 21-knot ROROs able to load tanks; four ships were to be committed full time, and two to operate commercially, on the understanding that they could be recalled for Government service in certain limited circumstances at twenty to thirty days' notice. The *Hurst Point*, *Eddystone*, *Longstone* and *Beachy Head* were built at Flensburg, the *Hartland Point* and *Anvil Point* were constructed under licence at Harland and Wolff's at Belfast, the last ships to be built at the Queen's Island yard. The two allocated to commerce are, at the time of writing, operating on a Finnish charter between Finland and Germany. The four working for the Government chiefly support the army, restocking the Falklands garrison and supplying major exercises in Belize and Canada. The eighteen-man all-British crews are recruited by Bibby International of the Isle of Man, the technical management of the ships being handled by Andrew Weir.

Anxiety about the loss of maritime skills for the wider maritime infrastructure encourage various institutions in the City of London to launch their own cadet-training schemes, subsidising the costs and placing individuals in various companies, a system that did at least offer the aspiring young sea-officer a variety of experience from which he – or she, for young women were encouraged to join – might make their final choice. The most successful of these was that run by the Corporation of Trinity House which, thanks to its property portfolio, was able to muster sufficient funds.

These successes were, however, somewhat illusory. In 2005 the British celebrated the bi-centenary of the Battle of Trafalgar amid a multi-national review of

Foreland Shipping Ltd was formed by a consortium of traditional ship-owning names, to answer the contractual needs of the Ministry of Defence for a strategic sea-lift capability. The *Eddystone* of 2002 is one of six roll-on, roll-off ships available, though two are operated commercially until required. Specially drawn by John Morris.

foreign warships and British merchantmen at Spithead.[29] This was an extension of the International Festival of the Sea held in the Royal Naval Dockyard at Portsmouth, which was the culmination of 'The Year of the Sea,' the intention of which was in part to address what was increasingly called 'sea-blindness' and raise awareness of our reliance upon sea communications. Although several British merchant ships participated in the review, few British merchant shipowners committed ships to open-days in Portsmouth. An exception, F.T. Everard & Sons whose yellow-hulled coasting fleet had been synonymous with London's River for a century and more, sent a state-of-the art vessel and generated interest, but the firm soon afterwards sold-out to Fisher & Co. of Barrow. The Chamber of Shipping did its best to 'market' the Merchant Navy to the public, but the question arose among the perceptive as to whether what the Tonnage Tax had yielded was in fact a Merchant Navy as had been conceived in 1920, or a mere mercantile marine under a flag of convenience – even if of relative excellence?

Although, largely thanks to residual expertise and the revolution in global communications, the state of British merchant shipping has yet to seriously damage London as a centre of 'marine services' such as insurance, ship-broking, classification and disputatious litigation – still a major earner of invisibles – there are signs that this state of affairs is no longer so certain.[30] As for those ships presently supporting Britain, as Alan Jamieson so appositely pointed out in 2003:

> Originally the creation of American business interests, the flag of convenience ships can only thrive under the *pax Americana*. Only if war, terrorism or piracy render the major ocean trade routes insecure will flag of convenience ship-owners suddenly find the security offered by the national flag of a naval power attractive once again.

In the intervening years neither terrorism nor piracy have abated, and the signs are that both are increasing.

Of the native Britons most affected by this rapid decline in British merchant tonnage and whose fate, if not personally tragic might be argued as a national tragedy, was the officer corps; most especially the deck-officers for whom no subsidiary career lay open, as was – to some extent – the case for engineers, radio officers and catering staff. For many of the last group and some fewer of the deck-officers the huge growth of the cruising market had provided welcome opportunities. The boom that grew out of the fierce recession of the early 1980s gave even more people in the Western World disposable income, expanding this sector and attracting new and ever-larger cruise ships. Beyond the vacancies in these ships, many British officers were either driven out of the industry, or compelled to work for foreign owners. For some years British masters remained in demand, but many ended up in command of ships in which they were in a minority, or even the only native Briton. Some few, however, clung on and enjoyed prominent and successful careers, benefiting from tax regimes that no longer crucified a workforce obliged by definition not to enjoy the fruits of the shore for which they paid. Some few, attaching themselves to the giant enterprises of the oil companies or container conglomerates, did well. But the endgame was not without interest or incident, and carries with it strange reversed echoes of the beginning, when the plight of individuals reflects the fate of James Lancaster and others of his day.

Despite the first tremors of cataclysmic change that were then rumbling, it was still possible to enjoy a lifestyle reminiscent of the past in the early 1970s. The 'Long Jag' of service in a ship engaged in a cross-trade or a branch line such as were run north from Australia by the Austasia Line could be an addictive delight to those who did not mind extended absences from home. A combined first-class passenger service carrying American, British, Burmese, Thai, Japanese, Indian and even Russians, was maintained between Malaysia, Singapore, Indonesia, New Guinea and Australia in such ships as Austasia's *Malaysia* and *Australasia* – the former Booth Line's 1955-built *Hubert*, the latter once the Belgian liner *Baudoinville*. The P&O subsidiary, Eastern and Australasian, kept two ageing Victory-ships on the service, their intermediate ports varying slightly from their competitors. Another part of the P&O Group, the New Zealand Shipping Co., had in the late 1950s combined with Port Line, Blue Star and Shaw, Savill & Albion, to form Crusader Shipping. Three ships, the *Crusader*, *Saracen* and *Knight Templar* were acquired and manned by Shaw, Savill & Albion with British officers and Chinese crews. When demand required it, the other parent companies contributed a vessel, and they all maintained a service from New Zealand round the Pacific Rim by way of Hong Kong and Japan, across to the West Coast of North America and the Caribbean. However, by 1971, when Captain Alexander Kinghorn commanded the *Caledonia Star* on a voyage under the Crusader house-flag, it was a prelude to her going to the breakers at Kaohsiung, Taiwan. On a similar run between Malaysia, Singapore and Western Australia, Blue Funnel had in 1964 replaced the *Charon* and the *Gorgon* – half-sisters of the torpedoed *Centaur* – with a new *Centaur* capable of carrying livestock and of taking the bottom at ports like Broome where the tide ebbed and left her high and dry.

Elsewhere there were ships whose daily round was redolent of an earlier age and which offered careers outside the ordinary run of cargo-carrying. Cable-ships, particularly those on distant stations such as Singapore or Fiji, enjoyed a long twilight until takeovers and satellite communications reduced them. The ships of the National Environmental Research Council and British Antarctic Survey provided long but stimulating deployments, while until May 1996 Ocean Weather Ships offered posts for men happy to wallow a-hull in the North Atlantic.

Ian Tew, who had escaped the burning *Dara*, had joined the Indo-China Navigation Co. owned by Jardine, Matheson, and still enjoyed a privileged life with a personal steward 'even as third mate ... [We had] silver service for breakfast and lunch and dinner ... There was always a boy on duty, always dressed up properly ... Food was excellent,' and the master had 'table-money for wine at dinner'. However, by 1967 many of the company's ships were effectively tramping and their hitherto quiet Chinese crews had been increasingly influenced by communism and touted the infamous 'Little Red Book' of Maoist aphorisms. Undeterred, Alfred Holt's liners maintained a tenuous liner-service through the 1960s with the then almost hermetically reclusive Communist China. Although a number of tramps visited Chinese ports and suffered at the hands of zealous Chinese officials, it was Holt's operations that attracted attention. Ships of the Blue Funnel and Glen Lines were the only British cargo-liners to call regularly at Chinese ports, maintaining their traditional routes which were, by the late 1970s, scarcely to the company's advantage with freight-rates remaining at their 1948 level. Nevertheless, in the waning hope that matters would improve, the Holt management held on, although this exposed their sea-staff to a variety of humiliations. Loss of face was the chief weapon of the Chinese authorities and while their exercise of such tactics were usually no more than ritual, especially where Holt's Chinese crews were concerned, the effects upon the officers could occasionally become more serious, particularly when Mao Tse Dong launched his zealous and obedient young people upon the Cultural Revolution.

The practice of monitoring the position of ships when undergoing pilotage was standard practice, but the effect upon the indoctrinated, xenophobic peasant soldiery of the People's Liberation Army was to rouse their suspicions when they stood on a ship's bridge. These actions of the duty officer seemed to cast aspersions on the diligence of the Chinese pilot giving his helm orders alongside the ship's master, while the marking of the chart and the necessary scanning of the riverbank through binoculars, appeared to be blatant espionage. In February 1968 Second Mate Peter Crouch of the *Demodocus* was arrested for spying and was taken ashore with the master, Captain W. Richards. Both men were treated impeccably to begin with, but were subjected to prolonged interrogations which sought to extract confessions. Denying any wrong-doing, the authorities increased the pressure and at one point the two detainees were exposed and denounced to an angry crowd. Captain Richards was in fear for their lives. Separated from Crouch, he was allowed back to the *Demodocus* and ordered to sail. Thereafter Holts decided that only one of the company's ships would be in Chinese waters at any one time.

By 27 February 1970, when the *Anchises* arrived in Shanghai on a routine call to discharge 230 tons of cargo and load 1,800, nothing had been heard of Crouch, but accusations of espionage were now made against Captain James Ray. To observers the move against *Anchises* and her master seemed a deliberate one, a calculated humiliation 'as she had always been held in high esteem by the Chinese having been bombed by the Nationalists when approaching Shanghai'. Captain Ray was taken ashore, along with the marked charts and a pair of binoculars. As Patrick Duff explained: 'There had been considerable Seaman's Union trouble in Hong Kong at this time, Ray was convinced that this had some bearing on his arrest at the time.' A later revelation claimed that about 100 armed Chinese militiamen were filmed storming aboard the *Anchises* shouting Maoist slogans. After Ray's arrest on 5 March, the crew was mustered and, to make him lose face, Ray was vilified in front of them. They were then photographed and each was given the *Thoughts of Chairman Mao* – the 'Little Red Book', a charade allegedly arranged on the orders of a senior officer of the Shanghai Security Service. The ship was released under command of Chief Officer John Brunskill and headed for Singapore.

Meanwhile, on 2 March, the *Glenfalloch* arrived in Shanghai. Prior to any news of Ray's arrest, it had been thought in Liverpool that 'atrocious weather' in China had delayed the *Anchises'* departure. In consequence the decision had been made to waive the restriction on one ship being in Chinese waters and allow the *Glenfalloch* to enter the port but on the 8th, just as the *Anchises* sailed, she was placed under arrest. The *Glenfalloch's* crew consisted of Captain Plenydd Edwards, twenty-one British officers – two or three of whom had their wives on board – eight Chinese petty-officers and thirty-four Chinese ratings. Captain Edwards was fifty-seven and had thirty-four years sea service behind him. Accused of harbouring spies, he refuted all charges, but this did not satisfy the Chinese authorities. Chief Officer Brian Hood was attending to cargo-matters after berthing when:

> Four uniformed frontier guards came into my cabin and read a declaration in Chinese, which they translated to me and which alleged I had broken Chinese law. When I asked what law they said: 'You know too well.' [Hood tried to attract attention as he was marched off the ship and driven away in a jeep.] They interrogated me three times a day for three days [for six to ten hours in what Hood thought was the chair-filled ball room of an old hotel where for three days he was questioned for six to ten hours a day before being released.] I was given a temporary bed in a small room and allowed to use a bathroom. They were very proper and shared tea and cigarettes with me. They said I had broken the law by marking the ship's position as we sailed up the river to Shanghai. I told them this was normal practice every time we approached a port but they kept on asking me why I had done it and preaching a lot of the thoughts of Mao at me. [He signed a confession after each session.] 'I did not argue, I just signed. I knew it was the only way out.

Hood was unaware that anyone else had been seized until he returned to the *Glenfalloch* as she was about to sail to discover that Second Officer Patrick Duff and Third Officer Christopher Gofton had also been arrested. Gofton had signed a confession as a condition of release, but Duff had only just been taken off the ship. Edwards afterwards reported that:

> We were ready to sail at midnight on March 9, and were loaded with general cargo – rice frozen rabbits, prawns and cotton piece goods. That afternoon the guards

came for Mr Duff and took him ashore for questioning. I was not able to speak to him before he left. That was the last I saw of him.

Retaining Duff, the Chinese ordered Captain Edwards to sail within two hours of the return of Hood and Gofton, leaving Duff behind. 'In China you do not argue, you do as you are told. I had been in touch with our agents over Duff and we tried to send him a letter of advice and encouragement.' After the *Glenfalloch* cleared Chinese territorial waters Edwards was able to use his radio but by now the world was taking an interest.

On Thursday 12 March John Brunskill brought the *Anchises* into Singapore where the agencies were avid for news from China, but Holts were tight-lipped. To protect both Ray and Crouch, Reuters were told by a spokesman for the company, 'the less said about it, the better,' but behind the scenes Brunskill was debriefed by George Holt who, on a visit to Indonesia, had flown from Djakarta. The matter was now taken up in London where in the Commons on the same day the Foreign Secretary, Michael Stewart, said that the British Chargé d'Affaires in Peking, Mr John Denson, had expressed grave concern over the incident to the Chinese government. It was thought that both Duff and Ray had been accused of plotting changes to the river and the approaches to Shanghai. Elsewhere charges of breaching Harbour Regulations were alleged, but on arrival in Kobe where he met George Holt who had flown on from his meeting with Brunskill, Captain Edwards had reiterated that Duff's actions had been consonant with normal chart plotting. The ship had carried two armed Chinese Red Army guards on the bridge during the passage up river which was under the direction of a local pilot, and this too was quite normal. For its part, the Chinese Mission in London had, according to the *South China Morning Post* on the 22nd, 'suggested that British seamen have been trying to pinpoint the location of military installations being built in Shanghai and Tientsin because of the threat of war with Russia'.

A slightly more parochial spin was put upon the incident on 16 March when *The Daily Express* quoted Commander John Kerans RN, a former Tory MP for The Hartlepools who in 1949 had commanded HM Sloop *Amethyst* during her famous dash down the Yangtze-Kiang. Having previously served as naval attaché in Nanking, he was by this time an acknowledged expert on Chinese affairs. 'These current troubles have just sprung from internal politics,' Kerans explained, 'Shanghai wants to prove it is as pro-Mao as Peking. It is an internal political game and it can't do any harm to confess and be released.' Kerans explained that an extracted confession saved Chinese face and that 'face is a very important thing in China.'

'When first incarcerated,' Duff wrote:

I was told that being a 'Running Dog and Lackey of the British Imperialists,' I was to reflect and record my crimes against The Chinese People, a ream of paper being provided. My interpreter spoke flawless English … Quite early on when we were alone I asked what I should write in my 'confession'. 'Oh, it is far too early for that,' he replied.

Meanwhile, the Ocean Group's board had taken decisive action. The *Anchises'* predominantly British crew was ordered to remain silent over what had happened, to avoid problems for Crouch and the other Britons in Chinese hands. Seven of the company's vessels were diverted from Chinese ports, cancelling all further trade with China, while even those proceeding directly to Japan were forbidden to pass through the Taiwan Strait. In the opinion of an editorial in the *South China Morning Post* of 29 March it was this, rather than any diplomatic pressure, that resulted in the sudden release of Duff and Ray, against whom no charges were actually laid. Even with the release of the two officers, eight Britons remained detained in China and the newspaper dismissed notions that diplomatic pressure had played any part in the matter. Instead 'it would be perhaps nearer the truth to give the credit to Chinese pragmatism and the Ocean Steamship's suspension of service to Shanghai'.

> The Glen and Blue Funnel Lines are the only two regular western liner services to China. What proportion of Sino-British trade (estimated last year at almost HK$1,260 million) they carry is hard to tell but it is possible that with the current Soviet tension China is not willing to lose a useful shipping link with the outside world, for this would leave her largely dependent on ships from Poland, East Germany and Japan, countries which enjoy no wide esteem in Chinese eyes at the present time. If the Chinese wanted to follow up the release of Ray and Duff to demonstrate their goodwill there are still people like the 26-man crew of the *Eternity*, Mrs Constance Martin and Mr Peter Crouch (another Blue Funnel officer) whose release would be widely welcomed.

Ray and Duff crossed the bridge at Lowu into Hong Kong territory on 26 March. Here, Duff recalled, 'Ray and I received our last indoctrination from the Little Red Book. It [was] made clear I was exonerated and could return to China. Ray, on the other hand, was being expelled. I crossed the bridge but had to wait a further half-hour for Ray to join me.' The two men were put on a BOAC flight for London that evening. Since 5 March, Captain Ray had been held 'in a certain degree of solitary confinement and under interrogation'. There was no question of brutality, the Chinese 'attitude was totally correct.' Asked why he had signed a confession admitting violation of Chinese laws, Ray said: 'When somebody tells you they are prepared to accommodate you for thirty years, you are quite prepared to sign.' Duff said of his arrest on 9 March: 'I didn't really know what was happening. I had to sign a summons, but I didn't know what the hell I was signing. I had to admit I had committed a crime against the law. If I confessed my crimes I would receive leniency – if I refused I would be dealt with with the utmost severity.'

But Crouch remained in captivity and was not to be released for many months to come and that May, Sir John Nicholson, Ocean's chairman, announced:

> Our enterprise originated and grew with the trade between Europe and China. But in recent years this has brought us little profit, dislocated other operations and caused hardship to our ships' crews, whose endurance deserves much respect. We have, therefore, decided to suspend our calls in China ports and are pro-

foundly sorry that we can no longer maintain this service between our respective countries.

Throughout the incident the British Government's attitude had been disingenuous. It was claimed that 'there appeared to be considerable uncertainty about the harbour regulations which the two officers were alleged to have infringed, there could well have been a genuine misunderstanding.' The matter must be let drop because, although the conduct of these officers had been entirely consistent with their ordinary duty, a potential embarrassment lay in the fact that some of the mates in Ocean's ships held commissions in the Royal Naval Reserve. Therefore, although the Chinese Chargé d'Affaires in London had been summoned and interviewed by the Deputy Foreign Secretary, Mr George Thomson, Michael Stewart squared the circle by restoring the *status ante*. 'There was no question of Britain breaking off diplomatic relations with China following the detention of the two officers.'

In the midst of it all, on Friday 13 March, *The Daily Telegraph* had been trenchant:

Whereas Russian policy, in between power-struggles, is a straightforward one of Soviet imperialism abroad and missiles before butter at home, China seems to stagger along from one phase of hysteria to another. For the past few years the recurring arrests, humiliation and callous incarceration of British sea captains, crew members, businessmen and others seemed to be a product of the 'cultural revolution' combined with China's traditional and deep-rooted xenophobia.[31]

As far as can be seen on the present occasion, involving the arrest of two British captains and several officers and crew members, including the wives of a captain and an officer, the current brand of hysteria seems to arise from fear of a Russian invasion. For months the country has been almost on a war footing, with trenches being dug, air raid shelters built and troops shuttled around. Now a whole lot of fresh security measures seem to have been imposed in harbours. So far as can be gathered from the usual combination of propaganda and official silence, the arrests are connected with these measures.

Both of the captains concerned are men with long experience of the many hazards, navigational and political, of occupying their business in Chinese waters and harbours. The extreme improbability that either of them should have been guilty of any offence is increased by a whole string of cases of utterly unwarrantable and uncivilised behaviour by the Communist Chinese against others. In any case, if accusations are to be made, then they should be made by process of law. Mr Stewart has expressed 'grave concern' through the British Chargé d'Affaires in Peking, but for all the good he is allowed to do, on this and on other occasions, he might just as well not be there. As to the Chinese war-scare, developments in the Sino-Soviet dispute are so unpredictable that the West has no grounds whatever for lowering its guard.

Howsoever personally unpleasant, such hazards never displaced the ancient dangers of the sea, among the worst of which is fire. On Friday 2 August 1968 the Shaw, Savill & Albion's ageing *Gothic* – the ship which had conveyed the Queen on her Coronation Tour of much of the Commonwealth in 1953 – was 1,800 miles out of Bluff, New

Zealand, homeward bound for Liverpool with a cargo of butter, meat, cheese and general, when fire broke out. The ship's thirty-five-year-old master, Captain Brian Agnew remained at his post even though the fire consumed the bridge, radio room and much of the centre accommodation. Such was its intensity that glass melted, steel buckled and the ship's main steering was destroyed within a few minutes of the fire breaking out at 02.25. Steering was shifted to the after emergency position and the boats were lowered to the embarkation deck ready for launching in the heavy seas and strong winds then prevailing. Fortunately, however, a determined three-hour effort by the ship's company succeeded in first controlling and then extinguishing the inferno which 'stripped complete areas of every vestige of combustible material', a heroic achievement by all concerned. Sadly, engineers Daniel Mulcahy and Paul Goldfinch, and electrician Edward Skelly died, along with all four members of the Halliday family who, as passengers, were fast asleep in a cabin immediately above the seat of the fire. Several attempts were made to rescue them but the fire proved too fierce, driving them back. Agnew brought the *Gothic* back into Wellington, his crew loud in their praises: 'It was the Old Man who saved us. We were heading into a gale when it started and if he hadn't kept his head and turned the ship round so the flames were blown ahead of us we wouldn't be here today,' one told the *Otago Times*' reporter.

The crew of the Houlder Bros' *Royston Grange* was not so fortunate. Some nine miles off the Argentine coast in the darkness before dawn on 11 May 1972 the British cargo liner was passing through the Indio Channel in the estuary of the Rio de la Plata, on her way from Buenos Aires with a refrigerated cargo of beef for the United Kingdom. By the time the *Royston Grange* reached No. 15 buoy she was in dense fog and it was here that she collided with the *Tien Chee*. Both vessels had their port sides torn open by the impact and were instantly engulfed in a huge fire-ball. The Liberian-registered tanker was loaded with crude oil but her configuration saved many of her crew; two lifeboats were quickly launched from her after superstructure, carrying half of her people to safety aboard the Argentine coastguard vessel *Delfin*, to be landed at La Plata, south of Buenos Aires. The *Royston Grange*'s midships bridge and accommodation was rapidly filled by dense smoke and utterly consumed by a fire fed by the oil and gas pouring from the *Tien Chee*'s ruptured tanks. The two ships lay drifting, their tangled plates and torn frames locking them together. As the sun rose and burned off the fog they could be seen from the distant shore, lying under an immense pall of smoke in the heart of which a dense fire burned.

The arrival of the *Delphin* to rescue the *Tien Chee*'s Chinese crew was accompanied by other vessels, but attempts to render further assistance was frustrated by the ferocious heat, dense smoke and the heavy slick of crude oil surrounding the crippled ships. Fire-fighting tugs arrived from both sides of the estuary so that by sunset, after the action of the tide had separated the two vessels by about a cable, the deluge of water spray had reduced the intensity of the fires and the heat of the ships' hulls. Nevertheless, it was late that evening before parties from the Argentine and Uruguyan coastguards, port officers and fire-fighters, could board the *Royston Grange*. All they found of the master, seventy-three crew, ten passengers, the Argentine pilot and his small staff, were charred bodies. Still burning, the British vessel was taken in tow by two tugs and towed to within two miles of the wreck of the *Admiral Graf Spee* where emergency moorings had been laid. Here she was secured by her stern as her forepart was inaccessible and all but destroyed.

By the 14th most of the fires aboard the *Royston Grange* were extinguished, though some, dampened down, still smouldered in her forward holds. The engine room was found remarkably undamaged and here the only recognisable corpse was recovered from the engine-room plates, that of Engineer Cadet James Craddock. The following day an explosion shook the ship and she was evacuated, but later a number of charred bodies were removed in coffins. The ship was not considered worth repairing by her owners who, in addition to the tragedy, were confronted with the increasing use of containers rendering their cargo-liners obsolete. In due course the *Royston Grange* was towed to Barcelona where, on 20 May 1974, she was surrendered to breakers.

With little available evidence, the subsequent Inquiry in New York considered the collision had been due to the close proximity of the two vessels in a narrow navigable channel. This caused complex changes of pressure between the two hulls where the overriding low pressure drew them both together, a phenomenon better understood today, which had caused the *Royston Grange* to veer to port and strike the *Tien Chee* a little forward of amidships. There was, of course, no one to argue to the contrary, but her rudder was found hard over to starboard and her engine-room telegraph set to full astern. Although both vessels had local pilots on board, it was thought that invasions of the channel by soft mud had occurred unbeknown to the pilots and the *Tien Chee* was likely to have been 'ploughing through the mud on the bottom of the channel.' The *Royston Grange*, entering at a lighter draft and thus more susceptible to lateral influences, was also thought to have had her port bilge keel in contact with the mud. The master of the *Tien Chee* received a reprimand for 'not waiting for more favourable tidal conditions before getting under way in the shallow channel with a deeply laden vessel'. For many the Inquiry's conclusions were unsatisfactory. The annihilation of the *Royston Grange*'s entire complement was considered by many to have been 'engulfed in a fireball from the ignition of the tanker's crude cargo' as verifiably occurred in subsequent similar collisions.[32] The dead, who could tell no tales, are commemorated in the British cemetery at Montevideo and by a stained-glass window in All-Hallows-by-the-Tower, near the Merchant Navy War Memorial in London on Tower Hill.

Few Britons at sea in these years expected war to affect their lives unless it was the great cataclysm of Mutually Assured Destruction that seemed probable during the Cuban Missile Crisis of 1962. The aspirations of new nations were more likely to offer opportunities to convey *matériel* and arms to trouble spots, rather than otherwise, but this was to be far from the case. In December 1971 the Bengalis' desire to secede from their union with Pakistan provoked a war between India and Pakistan in which an Indian naval offensive blockaded Karachi. Leaving supporting forces off Dwarka Point at sunset on 4 December, three fast attack craft approached Karachi Roads towards midnight and targeted their missiles on radar-echoes, sinking the Pakistani destroyer *Khaibar* and the Liberian-registered *Venus Challenger* loaded with rice and steel rails from Texas, killing all hands. A second attack was made on two vessels awaiting berths on the 8th. One was the Panamanian *Gulf Star*, sunk with the loss of four lives, the other was the British tramp *Harmattan*, owned by the Gowland S.S. Co. and

managed by J&C Harrison of London, which had arrived from Gdansk with a full
cargo of 12,500 tons of bagged fertiliser. Seven of her crew were killed and seven
wounded. Captain H. Houston, himself slightly injured, ordered her abandoned and
the crew took to the boats, carrying their wounded with them. The *Harmattan* did
not sink, but she was so badly damaged that she was afterwards broken-up at Karachi.

Although Harold Wilson kept British troops out of the Vietnam War (1964–1975),
British ships became involved, particularly British-flagged Shell tankers. Service in
such theatres could be lucrative for owners and crews, with a declared 'war zone'
producing high charter rates and bonuses to augment pay. 'Unlike World War Two
merchant seamen, we got double pay in Vietnamese waters,' one Shell officer admitted. An early British casualty was the *Amastra*, which suffered a large hole in her
engine room caused by a limpet mine attached to her hull by a 'swimmer' as she
discharged at a buoy-mooring and pipeline off Nha Trang in March 1967. No one
was hurt, but the *Amastra* settled and was thought to have been lost until the assistance
of a US naval salvage vessel and the Dutch Shell tanker *Kara* enabled her to be saved,
completing her discharge before being towed to Singapore for repair. In December
1968 the *Helisoma* suffered an identical attack, though the mine blew a hole in the
Fore-Hold and No.1 Cargo-tank. This was full of jet fuel but it did not ignite, no
one was hurt, and the vessel was lightened before proceeding to Singapore for repair.
Thereafter a practice was adopted which entailed, as Douglas Renton recalled:

> running in at dawn to buoy moorings, pump like hell, and out at dusk, repeating the
> process daily until the cargo was all discharged. The 'swimmers' could and did, come
> out at night and plant limpet mines. If bubbles were seen in the water we called the
> armed Vietnamese guards, and they threw percussion grenades into the water to
> blow the swimmer out. It was effective as I saw a photograph of a dead swimmer
> found by a previous ship visit.

But even this precaution did not entirely outwit the enemy.

> Our out-turn figures for cargo were queried by the Singapore office, as they were
> always substantially more than the Vietnamese received. One theory was that the
> [Communist guerrilla] Vietcong tapped into the pipe-lines in the jungle as we dis-
> charged.

Nha Trang, Robert Bushnell wrote, 'was in a land-locked bay surrounded by densely
forested hills. A nearby US Air Force Base provided nightly entertainment with
Hercules aircraft flying very close overhead in cloud – just ghostly lights and lots of
noise'. Apart from Nha Trang, Shell's tankers called at Quinhon and Danang to discharge at buoy-moorings, and carried oil up the Mekong to Saigon. Renton recalls
the *Hermisinus* bouncing over the bar at full speed to catch the tide up to Saigon and
meet her escort, an American warship which she usually overtook.

> We weren't going to hang about and we did little damage to the river-banks as
> they had already been defoliated by the Americans. The bridge-staff all wore

body-armour, trusses and tin hats during the river passage ... Mind you, trouble was nothing new at Saigon, in the fifties our ships travelled up-river with a sand-bagged machine-gun emplacement on the bridge, manned by the French Foreign Legion ...

A month before the attack on the *Helisoma*, on Monday 18 November, when in the Long Tau River thirteen-miles south-east of Saigon, her sister-ship the *Halia*, Captain Jack Booth, 'came under rocket, grenade and automatic weapons fire,' the *Daily Sketch* reported next day. 'One rocket – it failed to explode – passed through the deck house on the vessel's stern.' It was the forty-second attack against 'allied merchant shipping on the main channel' in 1968. Apprentice Peter Gill's account is vivid.

We were carrying a cargo of mixed white oils from Singapore – jet fuel, petrol, diesel and the like. The ship was not full, as we were draught-restricted in the river and I remember the aftermost tanks being empty of cargo but, of course, full of gas. We were in a convoy, with a small armed motor patrol-boat both ahead and astern and being followed by an American Lykes Lines' ammunition ship. At about ten minutes to noon we rang slow ahead as we were approaching Coral Bank Corner, a long port-hand bend. I handed over to fellow first-tripper apprentice Alistair Wallace and made my way down aft for a beer with the Fourth Engineer before lunch. At 12.22 I was sitting in his cabin ... when there was an Almighty bang. After a few moments we opened the door to the alleyway which was slightly smoky, to see the Mate ... running towards us telling us to take cover as we had been hit by a shell ... We rapidly headed across to the starboard side and hid behind the capstan on the poop ... We could see the patrol-boat astern immediately responding, turning and accelerating towards, and firing at, the river bank a few hundred yards away. The river banks which should have been lush green jungle, were completely bare mud-flats as a consequence of the defoliation by ... 'Agent Orange'. We could see two men in what must have been a hollowed-out pit, some 100 yards from the water, with what I was told was a rocket-propelled grenade launcher. The patrol-boat made short work of them. In the meantime the Lykes Lines ship astern, not wanting to be too close to us, overtook at an increasing speed down our starboard side, heeling over to starboard as she did so, around the outside of the bend. Only one shot was fired. It struck [a sailor's cabin] ... There was a small, 4-inch diameter hole in the ship's side, but the alleyway bulkhead was badly smashed and some shrapnel had entered the engine-room, putting a small hole in one of the domestic steam-pipes. The sailor's cabin was wrecked. Fortunately the occupant was on the wheel at the time and the only casualty was the A.B. in the adjacent cabin ... who was sewing his working shorts with a palm and needle – which he put clean through his left hand. He was also temporarily deafened ... Up on the bridge, the captain ... leaned over the aft side of the bridge-wing to watch the action – somewhat powerless in the situation ... Had the RPG struck fifty-feet forward and ten feet lower it would have been a different matter. I recall there were three sets of bullet-proof vest and cod-piece, plus helmets, one each for the Master, O.O.W. and Helmsman. None of these were ever used.

Another of Shell's *H*-class, the *Hatasia* discharged first at Vung Tai at the mouth of the Mekong, where her cargo of fuel oil was required for power genera-tion in two beached wartime turbo-electric tankers, one of her officers, Robert Bushnell remembered.

> *Hatasia* was too deep-draughted to go alongside, so we anchored close-in and dis-charged 1,000 tons at a time into an ex-US Army coaster operated by a Bristol Greek dipsomaniac we named Archimedes. It was June or July and the south-west monsoon had set in. Dark green, broodingly beautiful, humid, but corrupt country. It remained overcast and mostly rained heavily throughout our two weeks on the coast. [Off Nha Trang] a small tanker anchored about a mile from us was mined and blew up one night. The anchorage seemed to ignore it! Gunfire regularly crack-led in the distance and on the one clear night we experienced, we were treated to a tracer-bullet show from a US [helicopter] Gunship firing into tropical rain-forest. We kept [deck] watches by day, discharging our cargo, parcel by parcel, into Archimedes' bath-tub. At night it was anchor watches with armed patrol launches circling the assembled ships. *Hatasia* rarely visited Vietnam so we had no protection. The regulars didn't get much – tin hats and sand-bagged bridge-wings. I remember being slightly on edge the whole time we remained at anchor.

One consequence of the final phase of the Vietnam War was the terror induced by the Vietcong victory. Long after the end of the conflict, thousands of desperate refugees escaped the country by embarking in anything that floated and the South China Sea became dotted with these 'boat-people' helplessly adrift. This posed a moral dilemma for many masters. The humanitarian instinct is strong among seafarers, but the ultimate destination of these refugees became a huge and acute problem over several years.

Thirty-eight refugees were rescued by Captain A.N. Watson in Weir's *Sibonga* (actually the *Firbank*, but on charter and carrying an old Natal Line name while doing so), but this modest operation was eclipsed on 21 May when the same ship, now commanded by Captain Healey Martin, picked up almost 600 desperate souls from a badly leaking vessel on 21 May 1979 as the *Sibonga* made her way from Bangkok towards Hong Kong. That same morning another craft was sighted con-taining another 300. Relief was given by the ship's company led by Mrs Martin who toiled indefatigable to attend to their needs. On arrival at Hong Kong the *Sibonga* disembarked no less than 895 men, women and children, part of what would become a human flood pouring into the British Crown Colony. The desperate straits to which the boat-people could be reduced by privation was emphasised two days later when the *Roachbank*, Captain J.A. Applebey, recovered a further 393 mal-nourished and dehydrated refugees ranging in age from a ten-day-old baby to an eighty-five-year-old woman. These were landed in Kaohsiung in Taiwan but were not the last. When off Subi Island approaching Shanghai on 4 August, after a pas-sage from Bilbao, the *Ruddbank*'s lookout spotted a small, overcrowded sampan. The *Ruddbank* was stopped and the boat came alongside. It had been at sea for eleven days and eight of its original occupants had died. There were 124 people embarked, one baby was found to be dead, another child died subsequent to rescue and one adult required urgent medical help. The *Ruddbank*'s master, Captain C.B. Davies, aware that he would receive little sympathy from the Chinese authorities whose immigration procedures were at that time difficult enough for crew members, altered course for Hong Kong. Even here the ship was barely welcome. The small and already populous Crown Colony was overstrained by this human tide and *Ruddbank* was confined to an extra-territorial anchorage. Here two refugees were taken off for treatment but, with a typhoon warning coming into force and his owners pressing him to proceed, Davies left for Shanghai. Here he was obliged to accommodate his guests on board and they were eventually landed into the care of the United Nations' Commission for Refugees and accommodated in a transit camp.

Once in such a holding camp, refugees could apply to enter a country of their choice but, if they were not accepted they remained the responsibility of the flag-state of the rescuing vessel. Other British ships picked up boat-people, some of whom had drifted far from Vietnam but, as Captain Overland explained, 'some owners were very reluctant for their masters to pick up refugees because of the great difficulty in finding a country that would accept them. We were lucky in that we were on course from Hong Kong in a Hong Kong registered ship'. Overland commanded the *Poyang*, owned by the China Navigation Co. then trading between Hong Kong, Singapore and the South Pacific Islands. At 11.10 on Monday 29 June 1981 Cadet Wong Ting Yeun, the *Poyang*'s Acting Third Mate, spotted two small boats off the port bow and reported to the master the occupants of one were 'waving frantically'. Overland immediately slowed the *Poyang* and manoeuvred her alongside, throwing the pilot ladder over the side. An English speaker, Mr Willy Ho, climbed aboard and informed Overland that there were forty-three sea-sick people in the boat, including twelve children, and they had run out of food and water after six days at sea. The *Poyang*'s gangway was lowered and 'all the refugees boarded safely'. The other boat was empty, its occupants having already been rescued. The survivors – seventeen men, thirteen women, six boys and six girls – were generally healthy, apart from some minor injuries. They were accommodated in the crew's mess room and given food and drinks, blankets, mattresses and pillows, and issued with life jackets. 'By five in the afternoon they were all washed and dressed in a variety of clothes provided by the ship's officers and crew. The children were now all fast asleep'. Next day Overland interviewed Willy Ho and another man who had been a South Vietnamese naval officer. They had sailed from a small village on the Mekong River delta.

> They possessed a US Navy chart of the South China Sea but no compass or navigation aids. Their express intention was to be picked up by a ship, as their boat was not capable of a sea voyage and they carried little food or water. On Saturday 27 June a large fishing boat approached them and to their horror they realised the boat contained armed Vietnamese pirates. They all panicked and threw their identity papers overboard, and two young men swallowed their gold rings. The pirates robbed them of all their possessions, their few valuables and their … money … [and] refused to give them any food or water … The Captain reports … [they] came mostly from the Saigon area. They all stated that the main reasons for leaving Vietnam were denial of basic human rights and government persecution of South Vietnamese.

Some time after the refugees were landed at Hong Kong, Mr Ho wrote to Overland to tell him that most of those rescued were settling in San Francisco. However, the next of Swire's ships on the route also 'came across a boatload of people but only found two alive out of about thirty'. Such incidents were typical and became commonplace. In May 1984 the crew of the Shell tanker *Gastrana*, Captain Douglas Renton, pulled thirty-seven survivors from a boat adrift off Palawan in the southern Philippines and landed them in Japan.[33] 'A Norwegian vessel on the next pier landed a few at the same time, more or less fifty in a day.'

During the Iran–Iraq War (1980–1988) the hostilities occasionally implicated international shipping as each side sought to damage the enemy's vital oil exports in what came to be called the 'Tanker Wars'. These events embroiled a few of the dwindling number of British tankers, or tankers under British masters driven by economic necessity to 'go foreign-flag'. Something of the complexities of British shipping in this period are illustrated by the plight of the *Altanin*, 39,100 deadweight tons, which was among seventy vessels trapped in the Shatt-al-Arab waterway in mid-October 1980. Formerly the *Athelqueen*, belonging to Athel Tankers, a company traditionally employed in the carriage of molasses, she had been purchased earlier in the year by the Vlasov Group of Monaco, renamed *Altanin* and placed under the management of their British subsidiary Silver Line, which Vlasov had taken over in 1975. The *Altanin* therefore flew the red ensign and had a British master, Captain Beverley Dyke, aged thirty-three, six British officers, three of whom had their wives on board, and a Filipino crew. She carried a cargo of soya bean oil, the largest then lifted in a growing 'vegoil' trade and worth some $50 million. This was consigned from Brazil to the Persian Gulf and the loading took some weeks at several ports in Brazil which proved more congenial to her crew than conventional tanker ports. Fortuitously in view of the outcome, in anticipation of the discharging process taking some time, the ship had been well provisioned at Capetown, but on her arrival in the Shatt al Arab waterway in early September bound for Korramshahr, near Basra, the *Altanin* became one of some sixty vessels quite literally caught in the cross-fire of the Iraq-Iran War.[34]

By 4 October the *Altanin* lay anchored fifty miles up the waterway between two machine gun posts on the Iranian shore, one of which was uncomfortably close when the tanker swung on the tide. In consultation with Chief Officer Peter McGuigan and having been dissuaded from an attempt to break-out to the open sea, Captain Dyke decided to move his ship to a safer position. Banking on an early morning when the tide served, Dyke accomplished this without interference and all on board settled down to await events. The *Altanin* had acted as a radio relay station for some of the ships caught up in the fighting and, as had occurred in the Great Bitter Lake thirteen years earlier, her people now assisted an adjacent Peruvian naval auxiliary, the *Mollendo*, with much-needed provisions. They also helped out 'some of the impoverished children from the riverside villages with occasional food parcels,' taking advantage of the ability of some of the villagers to speak a little English, to pass messages. This was not particularly successful, though they received in return a bag of dates and a charming if stilted letter. Having reconnoitred a small creek on the Iraqi shore offering a landing place for a lifeboat, Dyke now determined on an evacuation of all but essential personnel, as he later reported. 'A list was drawn up of those who should go ashore. Obviously the wives were the first priority. They had been very good for the ship and had done a marvellous job in keeping everyone's spirits up ...'. In the meantime, however, on 13 October the *Altanin* had been manoeuvred alongside the *Mollendo* and food and water had been exchanged for bunker-fuel before the two ships separated. It was now arranged that the second officer, the third officer and his wife, two engineers and their wives, and seventeen Filipino ratings would leave the ship at the first opportunity. 'Everyone who was asked to stay willingly agreed to do so,' Dyke wrote. 'Everyone did exactly as they were asked. They were an excellent team. No man could have wished for better'. Retaining McGuigan, Chief Engineer A. Hills, the second and third engineers, the electrical officer, chief steward, the chief fitter, storekeeper, pump man and two hands, Dyke next needed a local agent.

Silver Line's Khorramshahr agency had been bombed out and in London, Captain James Punton, Silver Line's Fleet Director, had failed to get help from the Foreign Office. However, having seen the *Altanin* on the television news it was decided to contact the Independent Television News reporter on the spot, Jon Snow, and recruit him as the company's agent. This was accomplished by Silver Line's Chairman, Robert Crawford, who gave Snow full control. The arrangement offered Snow and his colleague Robert Fisk of *The Times*, a real scoop, and they set about the organisation of an evacuation with the help of the Iraqi Navy. Fisk and Snow, assisted by an official of the British Foreign Office, exploited their local connections, obtaining their own chart of the Shatt al Arab from another trapped ship further up the waterway, and established communications with Dyke thanks to the co-operation of the Iraqi military. In a guarded conversation Dyke and Snow concerted a plan involving a 'fibre ascent,' a phrase thought incomprehensible to any listening Iranians.

Although the time difference between the ship and the shore threatened at one point to compromise the plan, the co-operation of a discreet team of Iraqi naval divers enabled them to reach the *Altanin* after a hard paddle in their inflatable against the tidal stream, make their 'fibre ascent' up Dyke's lowered rope ladder and assure the *Altanin*'s people that their landing would be unopposed. Fisk's report of the evacuation appeared in *The Times* of 15 October, describing the moment at 'four o'clock in the morning' as he and Snow waited on the banks of the creek with some Iraqi soldiers. 'They came towards us in a lifeboat whose little engine made far too much noise, startling the stray dogs in the over grown date plantation and carving on the calm river ripples of light which the Iranians really should have seen.' As the boat nosed into the muddy bank of the creek, the appearance of a young English woman asking if someone would help her ashore defused the tension. 'It was,' wrote Fisk, 'one of those quintessential moments so dear to Anglo-Saxons: the British were cheating danger again, landing on a tropical shore under a quarter moon with the possibility of a shell blowing them to pieces and three young women to protect'. Fisk later described the Iraqi Navy as having performed 'a genuinely humanitarian act with courage and enthusiasm'[35] while of Captain Dyke and the thirteen left on board, Fisk said that they 'took it all very much in their stride'.

What they had to take in their stride in the days to come was a worsening of the situation. Khorramshahr fell and heavy artillery moved south on the east bank. The *Altanin* was shaken by the daily barrage that ensued, while the Iranian gun-emplacements in turn attracted Iraqi air-strikes. As mortar shells passed overhead, the daily routine helped; they all mucked in hoping that negotiations between the United Nations and the warring governments on behalf of the international shipping caught in the cross-fire would bear fruit. These, protracted though they were, came to nothing; the same fate awaited an initiative made by the International Red Cross. Dyke and Hills now had to confront a new situation: their ship's bunkers were running down. If sufficient fuel was to be retained for a passage to the sea, the ship had to be moored more securely, then shut down and evacuated, for her ability to sustain life was finite. Again Captain Dyke's planning was meticulous. The *Altanin* was moved and remoored using a head and stern anchor, a difficult technical task given the large size of his ship and his skeleton crew. It nearly went wrong when one of the heavy mooring ropes being used to transfer one cable from bow to stern fouled, but one of the Filipino ratings unhesitatingly dived overboard to clear it. With the ship secured, all papers, tools, navigational equipment and surplus personal effects were locked away. Steel doors were locked and where necessary vulnerable entrance points were covered with steel sheets fabricated on board. These were then welded-up and the welding gear was lowered through a vent-trunking out of the reach of looters. When all preparations were completed, on 22 November, Dyke and his dozen men enjoyed a drink of champagne on the after-deck before taking to a lifeboat and, using the bulk of the ship as cover from the Iranian gun batteries, chugged into the creek on the Iraqi side. Tying their boat up to an adjacent palm tree they made their way to an Iraqi position and were taken into Basra by bus where Edward Joseph, the Silver Line representative from Kuwait, and Jack Simmons of the Foreign Office, attended to their repatriation through Kuwait.

Captain Dyke had maintained the morale of his crew and earned warm praise from the Chairman of the General Council of British Shipping, Sir Adrian Swire, who wrote to Robert Crawford, commending Dyke's conduct as having been 'in the highest traditions of the British Merchant Navy' and his own 'admiration for the way in which he conducted himself and for the leadership he gave to his crew in what were clearly most difficult, dangerous and trying conditions'. The *Altanin*, however, had been abandoned and Sir Adrian concluded his letter with a degree of dry ambiguity. 'I trust that in the end you will be able to get the ship safely out of the Shatt.'

In 1982 the first deliberate attack offshore in the Gulf occurred on a Saudi tanker in which one man was killed and the ship declared a constructive total loss. In January 1984 Iraq announced an exclusion zone round Iran's Kharg Island oil terminal 'because it was losing the land war' and Saddam Hussein hoped by attacking Iran economically he would secure a victory. His forces therefore sought to deter international shipping from loading at Iranian terminals and in August 1986 an Iraqi air-strike on the Sirri Island oil terminal destroyed two tankers killing twenty seafarers. This compelled Iran to move its exporting facilities to Larak Island in the Strait of Hormuz with a loss of production, while attacks on Kharg Island reduced the loading berths available there from fourteen to three. Iran responded by attacking shipping beneficial to Iraq and trading through the Gulf states, particularly arms moving through Saudi-Arabia and Kuwait. Between 18 April 1984 and 18 May 1987, 227 vessels – including 253 oil-tankers – were attacked, 137 by Iraq and the rest by Iran.

Over the longer period between May 1981 and May 1987 no less than 211 merchant seamen were killed, most aboard tankers.

One British master involved was Captain David McCaffrey of the *Caribbean Breeze*, a large VLCC, which was hit by an Iranian missile off Doha, Qatar. McCaffrey was wounded – his arm shattered as the missile struck the bridge structure. Interviewed in hospital in Doha the fifty-four-year-old master who had begun his working life in the cargo-liners of Alfred Holt said that he would 'like to castrate … [the pilot] with a blunt knife.' In December 1987 the huge 412,000-ton deadweight ULCC *World Petrobras*, which was providing static oil-storage off Larak Island, was transferring oil into the *British Respect* when the two tankers were bombed by Iraqi jets. Fortunately no one was hurt aboard the British vessel, but the *World Petrobras* was hit and the hose connecting the two vessels had been damaged, the leak feeding a blazing fire. Both vessels were running their inert-gas plants, thereby avoiding an explosion, but it was necessary that the *British Respect* cast-off quickly and allow approaching fire-fighting tugs alongside the ULCC. The master of the *British Respect* did so, parting the hose and increasing the flow of oil to fuel the fire which now spread on the surface of the sea. Although the fire did some damage, it was soon brought under control and finally extinguished after eleven tugs had fought the blaze for seven and a half hours. Two days later the *World Petrobras* was busy loading another ship. The last major incident of the war was also at Larak the following year when the world's biggest ship, C.Y. Tung's Hong Kong-registered *Seawise Giant*, was bombed when acting as a static storage-tanker. She was consumed in a fierce fire-ball with heavy loss of life, though afterwards repaired and returned to service.

Few British seafarers expected their own country to go to war, or for their services to be called upon as a matter of national necessity, but the decision of the Argentine *junta* to invade the Falkland Islands in the spring of 1982 changed that. Not content with a United Nations' resolution demanding the withdrawal of the invaders, Margaret Thatcher's Government issued orders to the Chief of the Defence Staff to retake the islands, initiating what was to become Operation CORPORATE. The enemy had a large and capable air force, an aircraft-carrier and a well-equipped navy, most of which had been obtained from the Royal Navy. However, before a single soldier's boot could be put on a Falklands beach, 8,000 miles distant from Aldershot Barracks, there loomed a major demand for logistics support. The resources of the state – which included the Royal Navy, the Royal Fleet Auxiliary, or RFA, and some vessels of the Royal Logistics Corps – could not meet this without help.

Within hours Government ship-brokers sought suitable merchant ships to be chartered in and taken up from trade, a policy that acquired the apt acronym STUFT, while naval planners worried over practical measures to adapt them to what would be a difficult task. No alongside berths would be available and the merchantmen would have to imitate naval and auxiliary vessels operating in an 'offshore' scenario. Among the vast list of requirements was a bewildering variety of oils, heavy boiler fuel for the older warships, diesel and aviation fuels for jets and helicopters. The naval staff officers were well aware that the demands on all ships taking part would be severe as the Austral winter approached, but probably less so that the British merchant fleet was contracting fast. On 4 April P&O's cruise-liner *Canberra* and North Sea ferry

Elk were taken up and rapidly passed into dockyard hands for the fitting of helipads and other crude modifications considered necessary for war. The manning operations were complex but essentially the same as during the Second World War, with the company crew remaining to run the ship, supplemented by key naval and military personnel to handle the military stores, flight operations and tactical and strategic liaison. Some of these came from the armed services, some from the Royal Fleet Auxiliary. As these enthusiasts joined, there was a certain amount of 'them-and-us' about the inter-relationship, some naval liaison officers condemning mercantile practice as was usual – and had ample historical precedent – and while matters did not run smoothly, outcomes were no less competent in the supporting merchantmen, for whom the task was completely unfamiliar, than in the navy and its fleet auxiliary service that trained constantly for it. Although Ascension would be used as an advanced base, one of the most pressing requirements would be fuel for the warships and while the RFA could and did undertake this task, supplementary fleet-oilers were provided by several of BP's 16,000-ton River-class tankers for which demountable transfer-rigs were available and soon fitted.[36] Besides troopships and tankers, the operation required other auxiliary support such as heavy transports, a repair ship, tugs and rig-supply vessels to act as salvors, even a squadron of minesweepers derived from Marr & Sons' deep-water stern-trawlers underemployed after the Cod Wars and eager to be commissioned HM Ships for the duration; to these the *St Helena* acted as a depot-ship.[37] Other oil tankers were chartered from P&O, Shell, Esso, Silver Line and Canadian Pacific, which also provided a water-tanker, along with a number from Scandinavian firms, with Rowbotham providing their coastal tanker *Orionman*. Heavy sea-lift was shared between a number of large and medium-sized ROROs besides the *Elk*, including Cunard's *Atlantic Conveyor* and *Atlantic Causeway* (both of which carried Harrier fighter-bombers and Chinook helicopters concealed behind barriers of loaded containers), Stena Line's *Atlantic Ferry*, Townsend-Thoresen's *Europic Ferry*, *Nordic Ferry* and *Baltic Ferry*; and general-cargo and reefer-ships. These consisted of Cunard's *Saxonia*, Ocean's *Lycaon* and Geest Line's *Geestport*. Joining the *Canberra* as a troopship was the *Queen Elizabeth 2* and the *Norland*, while the old BI liner *Uganda* was taken up as a hospital ship and was adapted at Gibraltar dockyard.

The planning was meticulous and took into consideration as many problems as could be envisaged, so that the *Stena Seaspread* and *Stena Inspector*, fitted with dynamic positioning, were equipped with extensive workshops to repair battle damage. The little North Sea supply vessel *Wimpey Seahorse* was to lay moorings as required in the windswept anchorages and the British Telecom cable-ship *Iris* was ready to assist. With a lack of aircraft-carriers, the Royal Navy's *Hermes* and *Invincible* were supported by supplementary flying-platforms provided by the *Atlantic Conveyor* and Sea Container's *Contender Bezant* which, besides helicopters, carried Harrier 'jump-jets'. Normal charter rates were paid, plus a further sum for 'consequential losses' incurred through lost earnings, and although the crews received war bonuses as the Government declared a war zone round the disputed archipelago, they came under the Naval Discipline Act. By 9 April, 3 Commando Brigade were embarked in the *Canberra* and with 'a great deck-full of containerised war stores, and a huge shipful more on the accompanying *Elk*,' the two vessels left Southampton amid a blaze of publicity.

After a rapid conversion for trooping the North Sea Ferries' *Norland* left Portsmouth on 26 April carrying 2 Para south. Thereafter the others followed until they were 'strung out in a long line' down the length of the Atlantic. A total of fifty-two merchant ships, the majority of them British, were sent south to assist the RFA in its support of the Royal Navy and to undertake military duties. The two iconic and best-known of these were the *Canberra* and the *Queen Elizabeth 2*, but the *Norland* was to be the longest serving British merchantman in the campaign and was the first into San Carlos Water where she landed the Parachute Regiment on 21 May. She survived several determined air assaults by Argentine Super Etendards on the 22/23 before leaving for South Georgia to embark more troops from the *Queen Elizabeth 2*, which remained there out of harm's way. Back on 3 June *Norland* landed a trans-shipped Ghurka Brigade before taking 1,046 Argentine PoWs to Montevideo on the 11th. A further 2,047 were later taken home and disembarked at Puerto Madryn, in Argentina. Her trooping duties were completed in July when she landed the Queen's Highlanders to garrison the recaptured islands.

The Harwich-Hook Sealink ferry *St Edmund* was a late departure, not being requisitioned until 12 May under Section 4 of the Compensation Defence Act, 1939, and left Harwich for Plymouth to be converted. After her departure a volunteer crew mustered in Harwich under Captain Michael Stockman and entrained for Plymouth on the 16th. Here they found their ship almost unrecognisable.

> The mainmast had gone, and she now carried two helicopter decks. Below, even more of a transformation had taken place, converting her from a ferry with a duration of little more than twenty-four hours, to a deep-sea troop-carrier and support vessel capable of sailing great distances and sustaining a full complement of 1,500 passengers and crew for months at a time. Electronic equipment, pipe-work, steel-work, a fresh-water plant, containers full of frozen food, vast quantities of dry goods, all were installed or were being installed and the noise and apparent confusion of the whole operation was almost overwhelming.
>
> By Thursday 20 May *St Edmund* was completely ready, the intervening days having been taken up by sea and helicopter trials of all descriptions. For the first time, a Sealink Ferry under way, had connected with a Royal Fleet Auxiliary tanker whilst fuel-oil was pumped across the narrow gap separating the two vessels. The bosun had never concentrated so hard … as he did so on that occasion, steering *St Edmund* a she steamed parallel to the *Grey Rover* – lifting occasionally to the gentle swell of the Western Approaches. The Royal and Merchant Navy crew members already working as a team and, although their close association would not be entirely free from minor friction, a pattern was established which was to last the coming four-and-a-half months.
>
> As *St Edmund* finally sailed from Plymouth Sound, she carried with her personnel of 5 Brigade, together with various RAF detachments including No, 1 Squadron (Harrier fighters) and Chinook helicopter crews whose aircraft were aboard the *Contender Bezant*, a converted container-ship which was to sail in company. Passing Plymouth Hoe, nearly everyone was on deck as sirens sounded and groups of spectators ashore waved. Morale was sky-high as one patriotic young lady raised the

hem of her dress in a particularly patriotic gesture to the cheers and whistles of everyone lining the rails on the port side. Soon, for the first time in her life, *St Edmund*
left home waters by rounding Ushant and heading out into the Atlantic.

Although Captain Stockman was in command, *St Edmund* carried a Naval Party led
by Lieutenant Commander Andrew Scott RN, who tactically 'directed' the ship's
movements. 'The chain of command, although more complicated than usual, seemed
to work well enough under the circumstances and seemed appropriate for the task
ahead,' recalled the Senior Second Officer, Louis Roskill. The ship was crowded, camp
beds being placed 'in every conceivable space, including the bar and even the Ladies'
toilet'. On the voyage south Stockman announced the ship would be placed under
the Naval Discipline Act, the necessity for which became apparent as they learned of
the landing at San Carlos and the losses of HMSs *Ardent*, *Antelope* and *Coventry* which
followed that of *Sheffield*. They also heard the sobering news of the destruction of
Atlantic Conveyor, with all but one of her desperately needed Chinooks, by a missile.

The *St Edmund* arrived at Freetown, Sierra Leone, on 28 May, by which time

each department was busy at its own task, but in a more intense way: for example
the twelve galley-staff were preparing four thousand five hundred meals each day
without any prospect of respite in the foreseeable future. Deck staff were overhauling
safety equipment and the engine-room staff were ensuring that everything electrical
or mechanical was in first-class condition. The Royal Naval flight-deck crews were
kept busy with frequent helicopter operations between *St Edmund* and *Contender
Bezant* and the call 'Hands to Flying Stations! No smoking on the upper-decks! No
Rubbish to be ditched!' soon became a familiar ritual, especially at meal times.

By the last day of May she lay at anchor in Clarence Bay, Ascension, her crew painting
over her name and funnel insignia, the flight deck busy with helicopter movements and
the boats shuttling to and fro to other vessels with supplies, personnel and equipment.
She left at noon on 3 June in company with the *Contender Bezant*. A shadowing Russian
warship was driven off by the naval guardship and that night they proceeded without
lights and 'their newly acquired armament manned constantly during daylight'. On
9 June they fuelled on rendezvous with the RFA *Appleleaf* and encountered the grey
skies and chill of the Roaring Forties, though the wind remained moderate. Rumours
of damage inflicted on the Logistics Ships *Sir Galahad* and *Sir Tristram* at Bluff Cove
filtered through and on 12th a Lynx from HMS *Brilliant* was their first contact with
the Battle Group itself. The destroyer escorted them south and they were joined by the
Europic Ferry, 'an old rival ... looking tired and salty ...'. Stockman now announced
that no further drills would be held: from now on any alarm would be 'the real thing'.
The Chinooks began to fly off *Contender Bezant*, heading for *Hermes*, Rear Admiral
Woodward's flagship, but were disrupted by bad weather on the 14th. One Chinook
was badly damaged in the heavy 'forty-foot waves and Force 11 winds' which at one
point threw *St Edmund* on her beam ends until they hove-to, no longer able to maintain
station. Although the news of the Argentine surrender came through on 15 June, it was
17th before the weather enabled the *St Edmund* to enter Port Stanley Harbour.

[T]he persistent drizzle … carried with it the stench of conflict. Smoke still hung over the settlement and, silhouetted against the skyline, long lines of figures could be seen trudging along the airport road. The streets of the little town were strewn with rubbish … including live ammunition, weapons and uniform clothing, much of it trodden into the black, peaty mud by the side of the road. Warily watched by British soldiers, groups of Argentine prisoners were being herded onto the jetty and ferried out to the … *Canberra* … waiting for them in the outer harbour. Military vehicles, mostly captured, were everywhere and … the sound which dominated Port Stanley … the clattering roar of the 'choppers' … filling the grey overcast sky as they flew to-and-fro on their various tasks.

Soon afterwards Scott's Naval Party disembarked and, with the lessening tension, morale took an inevitable dip. The *St Edmund* next went to Fitzroy and embarked the Scots Guards for a period of rest. Oily smoke still rose from the wrecks of the *Sir Galahad* and *Sir Tristram*. Back in Port Stanley *St Edmund* acted as accommodation for ten days, a haven for battle-weary troops and a holding place for senior Agentinian officers, including the Commander-in-Chief, General Menendez and his staff. The ship also hosted a party for the children of Port Stanley for whom 'men whose families were on the other side of the world … pulled out all the stops'. On 30 June *St Edmund* entered San Carlos Water and anchored in Ajax Bay.

It was difficult to equate the peaceful scene with what had happened a week or so before. Known to our forces as 'Bomb Alley,' the Argentine pilots referred to it as the 'Valley of Death'. The derelict freezer factory was now in use as accommodation for the remaining 500 or so professional elements of the Argentine Army of Occupation. Here the Scots Guards finally left us to take up duties at Port Howard and the PoWs were embarked in their place … some were still found to have arms hidden in their clothing and so very tight security was implemented … *St Edmund* then returned to Port Stanley … while the diplomats and politicians played their parts and obtained some sort of guarantees from the Argentine Government. The Welsh Guards had now been embarked, many of whom were survivors from the tragedy at Bluff Cove, but were now engaged in the intense but tedious business of guard duty.

On 9 July the *St Edmund* took stores from the *Avelona Star*, Captain H.K. Dyer, which was acting as a floating food and supply store to the Task Force. Finally, on 12th she left Port Stanley, arriving at Puerto Madryn two days later under escort of an Argentine warship met offshore. By mid-day Menendez and his men had all been landed to 'a quiet but dignified reception'. The ship returned to Port Stanley to embark military and civilian personnel, sailing for Ascension on the 17th during which two children were baptised. By this time 'the crew were very much hoping for a relief, particularly as they were mostly used to getting home regularly' and the news that she was returning to Port Stanley to provide accommodation indefinitely was demoralising. For thirty-eight days:

the crew were faced with the prospect of having very little action or change of scenery. For the catering-staff, the pace continued as before and everyone on board concentrated on making *St Edmund* the cleanest and most comfortable accommodation in the Falkland Islands.[38]

The crew were eventually relieved and sailed to Ascension in the *Norland*, the first group flying home and arriving at RAF Lyneham on the evening of 28 September. Sadly, however, as Michael Grey was to comment long afterwards:

> The sweet home-coming for the crews of the merchant ships very often turned bitter, with the UK shipping industry in free-fall. They may have been heroes, but it didn't stop the brown envelopes arriving on the doormat as the ships were sold, the great companies becoming shadows of their former selves and the cheap and cheerless taking over the maritime world.

This was true of the *St Edmund*, which never returned to the Harwich-Hook route, her refit being blighted by 'a welter of industrial trouble' as she became the focus of agitation by the National Union of Seamen. In the end she was acquired by the Ministry of Defence, renamed and placed under Blue Star management to shuttle between Ascension and the Falklands. The campaign proved a feat of arms and amid the carnage the lives of those lost from the merchantmen was mercifully small. Captain Ian North, master of the *Atlantic Conveyor* did not outlive the attack on his ship. He had twice survived being torpedoed as a teenager, once when in a tanker loaded with benzene. North was, as Admiral Woodward recorded, 'a real old sea dog,' symbolising the symbiotic union of the Task Force, as Woodward noted with appreciation.

> All the way south from Liverpool he [North] had made himself increasingly popular with the young seamen in his ship from both branches of the Navy, regaling them with stories of the sea and occasionally, late at night, to the delight of everyone, playing his trombone. When they 'crossed the line', the short, chunky Ian North, with his snowy beard, played the part, inevitably, of King Neptune.
>
>   The senior Royal Naval officer on board, Captain Mike Layard ... adored the old boy, for his humour, his complete professionalism and for his wisdom. He also admired him for his philosophical outlook, remembering that Captain North was probably the only senior officer who actually *knew* what it was like to be hit, possibly the only man in the entire operation who had no illusions about what to expect in the event of a bomb, missile strike.[39]

The *Atlantic Conveyor* had brought fourteen Harriers, four Chinooks and five Wessex helicopters to the war zone. She 'was of incalculable value' and, as far as helicopter operations were concerned, became 'a third aircraft-carrier'. By 25 May, Argentina's National Day, all the Harriers had been flown off, along with one each of the Chinooks and Wessexes but she was 'still loaded to the gun-whales with stores and ammunition ... including all of the equipment to construct an airstrip for Harriers in the beach-head area in San Carlos Water.' That morning Woodward had ordered her to move forward from her 'safe' position in rear of the Battle Group prior to making a fast delivery run to San Carlos to discharge after nightfall. This inevitably exposed the ship 'to some small risk of air attack for a few daylight hours, but granting them more hours to unload in the dark …'. Woodward had, however, taken the precaution of stationing her 'at the likely "safe" end of the line of auxiliaries while she waited for the light to fade' and behind what was left of the Royal Navy's defensive picket line of warships screening the Battle Group's carriers. That evening, unbeknown to the British, two Etendards had made a long sweep northwards from their base at Rio Grande, refuelled in the air and attacked the Battle Group from the north-west: far from being 'safe' the *Atlantic Conveyor* was almost directly in harm's way. The incoming jets were detected forty miles out by HM Destroyer *Exeter* which raised the alarm. HM Frigate *Ambuscade* picked them up 'within a minute' at twenty-four-mile range, as did *Brilliant*, stationed 'further back' at 28.

> At 18.38 the two Argentinians released their Exocets, both at the same 'blip', the first they came across … *Ambuscade*, from which the [defensive anti-missile] chaff-rockets had already been launched. The two French-built missiles swerved past her and hurtled through the chaff cloud [of metal foil designed to decoy the missile] deceived but still looking ahead for a target.

The grey mass of the *Atlantic Conveyor* lay just four miles away and both Exocets immediately detected her and trimmed their trajectories. She had no chaff but her crew were already at Emergency Stations and North had wisely turned his ship away from the threat, presenting *Atlantic Conveyor's* 'very strong stern to the incoming missiles'. At 18.41 the two Exocets penetrated her port quarter 9ft above the water-line and exploded. The crew immediately fought the fire with hose-parties, sprinkler systems and carbon-dioxide smothering, but it was hopeless. Behind thick smoke, fire had taken a fierce hold and the decks were rapidly turned red hot as it crept inexorably forward towards 'thousands of gallons of kerosene and the huge consignment of cluster bombs … Eleven men were already dead'. At 1920 North informed Layard that if any of them were going to survive they would have to abandon the ship before she exploded. Others were already coming to the *Atlantic Conveyor's* assistance as minor detonations began occurring and a fire-party of thirteen men was cut off. These were plucked from death by a Sea King from *Hermes*, but the remaining 134 men began to clamber down the ship's side by way of rope ladders into the life rafts bobbing on their painters alongside. Already the ship's side was hot, parts of it glowing in the twilight, and from within the hull the explosions grew in frequency. Captain Layard went over the rail and down a ladder, to drop the last 10ft into the icy Atlantic. Behind him, the last man to leave, a dog-tired Captain Ian North dropped alongside him with a splash. Layard immediately realised something was wrong, North 'was floating too low in the water'. As he struggled to save North, Layard felt the ominous tug of an under-tow drawing them under the overhang of the stern as the hull rose in the swell and then pressing down on top of them, driving them deep. The life rafts were having similar trouble getting clear of the ship's side.

Michael Layard struggled heroically and, still holding onto North, reached a life raft where, summoning all his strength, he thrust the master towards it. But a wave broke over them, Layard lost the older man and, although he dived in search of him, Ian North had gone. Having rendered assistance to another in trouble, Layard was finally dragged into the life raft where he lost consciousness. Later he was grief-stricken over the death of a respected colleague who had become a friend. The survivors, pinned alongside the burning ship, were rescued by another act of heroism. Unfazed by the imminent possibility that the burning *Atlantic Conveyor* might explode, Commander Christopher Craig brought the frigate *Alacrity* close in and his seamen fired life-lines over the rafts. These were grabbed and clung onto, whereupon Craig gently went astern and drew them all clear before embarking their survivors. Among those killed aboard the *Atlantic Conveyor* in addition to Captain North were six other mercan-tile personnel, the remainder being service-men. The loss of the *Atlantic Conveyor* – 'Down goes another £100 million worth,' a troubled Woodward wrote in his diary that dreadful night – placed the operation in some jeopardy, not least because now the Marines would have to walk from San Carlos to Port Stanley, an achievement which added the verb 'yomp' to the English language.

Unsurprisingly, the Task Force in the South Atlantic had found that, in spite of the bravery of the Argentine air force, it was the weather that proved the inveter-ate foe. Even today, with all the advantages of modern materials and techniques, sea conditions arise which confound us. Earlier, mention was made of a Port liner suf-fering damage inflicted by an 'extreme' wave and verifiable reports of these were inclining oceanographers to believe what had hitherto been considered seamen's tall tales. Among seafarers, however, it had long been understood that one such wave had overwhelmed the Blue Anchor liner *Waratah* in 1909, since the locality of her disappearance off South Africa where the strong Agulhas current meets a prevailing westerly wind can, when the wind is strong, produce huge breaking seas.

In February 1956 Captain Douglas MacKenzie, of the elderly Union-Castle mail liner *Arundel Castle* which had shortly before left Durban, had been:

> taking his ease on the bridge wing on a fine sunny morning … when, glanc-ing ahead, he was astonished, terrified in fact, to see the sea opening up into one almighty hole – right under his ship's forefoot. Immediately, as he saw it, she started to plunge into this abyss. She was at full speed of some 18 knots or so. She went down quickly. The whole of the foxcle (sic) head went under and the sea flooded across the foredeck as she struggled to rise. Eventually she crossed the hole and started to rise on the other side. After see-sawing a bit, the ship evened-up, her speed increased and away she went … No one was lost … and the only damaged or miss-ing fitting was the jack-staff …[40]

In the early hours of 3 May 1973, the fast Ben liner *Bencruachan* was less fortunate. At this time the vessel was sixty-miles south of Durban, homeward bound from the Far East in the joint BenOcean service under Captain D.S. Sinclair, steaming at speed into a 'moderate south-westerly gale'. In the darkness of the small hours the *Bencruachan* surmounted a large sea and pitched downwards into a long trough. As she began to lift to the approach of the next wave it rose high above the ship – an estimated 75ft – and broke over the ship's long forecastle and No.1 Hatch, a sudden burden she threw off with difficulty. The damage was extensive: the whole forepart of the ship was 'set-down' so that her long forecastle 'drooped' some 15ft at the bow. Her forward bottom plating was compressed into folds and No.1 Hatch was 'torn open'.

Sinclair stopped the ship and at daylight the passengers were winched-up by helicopter before the *Bencruachan* was towed, stern-first, into Durban. Here she was patched-up, a careful note being taken of the damage. She was then sailed, her bow still drooping, to the United Kingdom. British yards having by then 'priced themselves out of the market,' she departed for Rotterdam where, thanks to the meticulous measurements taken in Durban, a prefabricated bow section restored her to service 'with the minimum of delay'.

The confirmed incidence of such cumulative waves now increased and began to explain the steeply increasing number of disappearances of bulk-carriers. Following the *Bencruachan* incident, the *Neptune Sapphire* suffered tremendous damage off East London and, in 2001, the German cruise ship *Bremen* had her bridge smashed. Other German vessels became implicated, the huge German LASH-carrier *München* vanishing in the North Atlantic in 1978.[41] Better satellite surveillance began to gather data about such waves, and when in 1995 Cunard's *Queen Elizabeth 2* encountered one estimated at 95ft, no one doubted Captain Ronald Warwick's assertion that it was 'like going into the white cliffs of Dover'. A series of German studies concluded that waves of 120ft, or 40m were perfectly possible and contributed to the loss of about 200 super-carriers, or bulk oil/ore bulkers of over 600ft in length in the last two decades of the twentieth century.

By this time most of these were not British-flagged, but one that was was destined to become a *cause célèbre*; her name was *Derbyshire*. Apart from the opposition of wind and current off South Africa, extreme waves were most likely to occur in the vicinity of a tropical revolving storm,[42] such as Typhoon Orchid which the *Derbyshire* ran into while crossing the North Pacific in September 1980. Built in 1976 by Swan Hunter on Teesside as the *Liverpool Bridge*, a 91,655 grt – and 169,000 tons deadweight – the ore/oil/bulk-carrier, or OBO, owned by Bibby Line was chartered to the Seabridge Consortium. In 1978 she had had her name changed in 1978 and her last voyage was from Canada towards Kawasaki, Japan with iron-ore concentrates. On the 9th she reported her position some 230-miles south-east of Okinawa. Six hours later Captain Geoffrey Underhill signalled the *Derbyshire* would be delayed owing to having run into a severe storm. Thereafter nothing was heard from her and she was posted missing, presumed lost with all hands: forty-two officers and ratings, and two wives.

She became a *cause célèbre* only because of agitation on the part of the families of the crew who formed an association to determine what had happened, otherwise, as in the case of the *Asiatic Prince* lost in 1928, the Department of Transport refused to hold an Inquiry for lack of witnesses. There was nevertheless, substantial evidence from other similar super-carriers that they suffered from a defect in that their hulls were prone to crack in way of Frame 65, just forward of the bridge. Many bulkers had been lost from unknown causes where the circumstantial evidence nevertheless suggested such a fundamental weakness may well have been the root cause of disaster, to which had to be added the battering they took loading ore and a lack of reserve buoyancy in a design that lacked a forecastle head. In 1986 a sister-ship, the *Kowloon Bridge* went ashore off Ireland and cracked in way of Frame 65, sharpening the families' appetite for a proper Inquiry but when in January 1989 they finally had their way, the verdict concluded: 'That the *Derbyshire* was probably overwhelmed by the forces of nature ... possibly after getting beam on to wind and sea ... the evidence does not support any firmer conclusion'.

If the Government thought that such a whitewash would satisfy the families, they were to be disappointed. Demanding an underwater search and survey, the families were denied this on the grounds that the competent technology did not exist, but matters now gathered their own momentum. A television documentary spread the news of the disaster and the Government's apparent indifference; Edward Loyden MP, pressed for action as the families submitted a petition with 47,000 signatures. In 1994 the International Transport Federation paid for an American expedition that located the wreck. A second expedition was agreed to, funded by Britain and the European Union which collected an enormous amount of evidence from the sea bed using remote units. Instead of failure at Frame 65, it seemed that a forward hatch had been left open, allowing water to flood a huge void space from which the bow-heavy *Derbyshire* became increasingly vulnerable to seas breaking on board and sank rapidly under unimaginable stresses. Such implied negligence on someone's part was a bitter blow for the families.

The formal Inquiry was reopened on 5 April 2000 under Mr Justice Colman and a great deal of technical evidence was considered, expert opinion consulted and argument heard. The upshot of this revealed the probability was vastly more complex and dismissed the expedience of blaming dead seamen as contemptible. It was inconceivable that the hatch had been left open and that no one had spotted it when the ship was aware she was heading for heavy weather. Evidence from other operators suggested that the stresses to which the *Derbyshire* had been exposed had induced complex reactions in her hull and that precedent could be found for the hatch-toggles becoming dislodged if struck by debris or shaken by pounding. In sinking, the *Derbyshire* had produced at least 2,500 separate items of wreckage and studies undertaken by the Universities of Liverpool and Glasgow corroborated expert opinion to provide the most likely scenario. This argued that a fatal interaction had occurred in which the length of the ship and the wave-length of the seas coincided. This created an onslaught upon steel hatch covers which, though fabricated to international standard, proved inadequate to resisting the stresses imposed upon the ship's hull as it worked in 'remarkably consistent wave patterns over many hours'.

Unbeknown to anyone on board, to whom the ship would appear to have been behaving satisfactorily – hence the lack of any distress message – once these stresses had done their damage the break-up of the ship would be catastrophic, so rapidly progressive as to seem all but instantaneous. In short the hatches had yielded in sequence from forward to aft following 'sustained green water' flooding the forward void spaces after the ventilation pipes had been destroyed by the heavy seas. Thereafter No.1 Hatch-cover failed and sea-water poured into the huge ullage space above the ore, depressing the ship's bow so that within a matter of seconds No.2 suffered the same fate and so on, whereupon 'the *Derbyshire* was irretrievably lost'. With an ore-cargo's weight and the huge space it left in each hold, the *Derbyshire* would have driven herself into the abyss below her before anyone was aware of what was happening. The crew were exonerated, but it was a terrible end.

Elsewhere less consequential events indicated some things had changed little in five centuries. In December 1969 the *Phyllis Bowater* was on passage from Liverpool, Nova Scotia, to Montreal and her master decided to take:

> a short-cut through the Strait of Canso. There is one small lock to pass. We locked-in but the Lock-Keeper would not let us out till we had paid cash (he had been let down so many times with ships saying [the] agent will pay, but they never did.) As the Phyllis didn't carry cash the Master, M.P.R. Turner, had to muster all the Officers to borrow enough to pay the Lock-Keeper. Luckily, we did get our money back ...

In 1976 – ten years after the Seaman's Strike of 1966 – Cadet Simon Robinson recalled the poverty and desperation of the dead-beat crew joining the Sugar Line's *Sugar Transporter* in London from the Canning Town Pool. Improvident as ever, they were ill-equipped for a winter voyage across the North Atlantic. With threadbare clothing only fit for a tropical voyage they found themselves in a cold Quebec, shivering in their additional clothing improvised from the cleaning rag-bag and including balaclava helmets made from mutton cloth. Two of them were consequently hospitalised with frost-bite.

A revival in the late twentieth century of the practice of an earlier era allowing wives on board was intended to retain officers in their jobs, but it was viewed by many as a mixed blessing. Not a few marriages ended, the predictability of the ship's routine favouring a philandering wife. Others found the privilege illuminating, even shocking. In 1984 Rosie Thurston accompanied her husband to sea in the bulk-carrier *Newforest*, then newly acquired from Spanish owners by P&O. The vessel, which had been built in 1972, was 957ft long, could lift 155,760 deadweight tons and was loading coal in Osaka. Mrs Thurston found that 'his extra long working hours in port mean we hardly see each other, except to sleep.' Once the vessel was in sunny climes sunbathing was a favourite pastime for the several wives on board:

> ...it felt heavenly to stroll round in just shorts and a bikini top. I felt rather embarrassed each time we met one of the [British] crew, because of my state of undress. I am acutely aware that they are all 'jack-the-lads' and think themselves real lady killers. Some are built like power-houses and all have an excellent command of slang. The bosun is said to be a temperamental chap! When in a bad mood, he resorts to grunting and obscenities, and you can practically see the black cloud hanging above his head. Needless to say, I'm staying well out of his way. All the same the crew seem very friendly.

The presence of one gay man on board enlivened things: 'He really is very nice but I can't forget for long that he likes the other men! He is very clothes conscious and complimented me in a feminine sort of fashion ... He ... is very friendly and a lovely person'. The same could not be said of the wives who often split into factions. Meeting a newly arrived mate's wife, one young spouse reacted:

> She seems very educated and rather a snob. [Her husband] was rather amazed when she started discussing engineering, as though it was her forte! I'm sorry to have formed such a negative attitude so quickly, but she seems rather full of herself. [A few days later] the wives split into two groups. There are too many of us to all want to do the same things, but the atmosphere was electric ashore this morning. It's hard to say what caused the rift, but … the Mate's wife is very bossy and irritated the others … It's a silly situation. Although very little has actually been said, the tension and 'camps' remain.

Perhaps worst was to have a master's wife on board especially if:

> her reputation has gone before her, of course. Her arch enemy seems to be … the Mate's wife … It seems she loves to know everything that's happening on board and makes the Captain's life a misery to effect this. He is said to become a different person when his [own] wife is on a ship. She also is reputed to only speak to officers and wives of senior rank … This we can now verify as truth! … Upon arrival, the Captain tried to introduce us all, but his wife stayed on the opposite side of the bridge, looked straight ahead and said nothing! They came and went without any proper introductions being made. It was quite incredible. Had I not have seen it happen, I would never have thought it possible.

Unused to the ship-board ethos, wives had an objective view of things. The master of a P&O bulker amazed a mate's wife who had been cajoled into running the officers' bar. Her 'biggest worry is that we will run out of beer or whisky one night. The Captain drinks whisky (doubles) and gets through about at least eight tots a night. I know this from serving behind the Bar … Every five minutes, literally, I was getting up to fill his glass'.

It was still just possible to undertake a sea voyage as a passenger, even when the accommodation used was the 'owner's' and the pilot's, two cabins retained for the company's service. Elizabeth Hodges, her son and husband – who had family connections with Brazil – made a voyage up the Amazon in the summer of 1985 aboard the *Benedict*, last of a pair of Booth liners.

> Our voyage was from 27 June to 20 August, sailing out of Liverpool's Alexandra dock to Bridgetown, Barbados (two days), and Port of Spain, Trinidad (four days off, two days in port). We entered the northern mouth of the Amazon for Porto Santana and on to Manaus (three days); then down river to Belem (eight days) and finally back to … Heysham with a cargo of 500 tons of Brazil nuts from Manaus and 5,000 tons of hard-wood from Belem, a voyage of 10,660 nautical miles. [Mrs Hodges observed of the master] Captain Glyn Round came from Flint; very hands-on, always kept the 8 a.m. to noon watch … Approachable, ready to explain, frustrated by delays. Liked activity and kept his exercise bike just outside the bridge … I haven't mentioned the food – it was wonderful, prepared by the Bajan crew – and always something

for the officers to look forward to ... The officers were uncertain what the future would bring ... the Captain said the Danes were trying to muscle in and with a crew of ten (master, mate, two engineers, cook, steward, four seamen) compared with about twenty-four on the *Benedict*, were much more competitive. We saw stern loading ships with a much quicker turn-round, while the *Benedict* loaded containers by ship's derrick or dock-side cranes for heavier items, but the Brazil nuts came on in sacks and the timber in individual lots. Amidst the larger scale activity at Belem a few motorised canoes would pull alongside at dawn and wait patiently in the heat for their timber to be unloaded. A slow, interesting process, but not very competitive.

Besides this obvious lack of edge and innovation, disastrous events seemed to dog the dwindling merchant fleet in these years. In 1982 two ferries, the *Speedlink Vanguard* and *European Gateway*, collided in the approaches to Harwich Harbour; the latter sank, with the loss of four lives. Another Townsend-Thoresen ferry, the *Herald of Free Enterprise*, capsized with heavy loss of life as she left Zeebrugge for Dover on the evening of 6 March 1987.[43] She was increasing to full sea-speed but her bow doors had not been secured and water poured into the car deck. Free-surface effect took over and the vessel rolled over on her beam ends, to sink in shallow water. The subsequent Inquiry blamed lax procedures on board and complacent management ashore. Even Britain's maritime infrastructure proved vulnerable in the heart of the City of London when an Irish Republican Army bomb destroyed the Baltic Exchange in 1992.

By the end of the twentieth century the Merchant Navy had declined to an insignificance reminiscent of the early 17th. In May 1981, some years before this nadir, it was assumed by the Thatcher Government that small wars were a thing of the past and that any future major conflict was insured against by nuclear weapons and the NATO Alliance. A *national* strategic sea-lift capability was no longer required and if matters came to push-of-pike then, as the Parliamentary Under Secretary of State wrote to a concerned citizen: 'In the event of hostilities, the merchant fleets of NATO countries would be pooled and allocated to tasks in the best interests of the alliance'.[44] The certainty of this doctrine was disrupted almost immediately by the Argentine invasion of the Falklands in the spring of 1982, and the Task Force sent to the South Atlantic comprised both warships and auxiliaries deemed redundant and actually in the process of sale to other countries. But even this timely reminder that events have a habit of surprising us failed to interest the Government in the wider merchant fleet, even though its contribution to the Falklands campaign had been vital. The empirical evidence that in even notionally predictable circumstances, the law of unforeseen consequences is ever present, seemed not to trouble the thinking of ministers. Preoccupation with Friedmanite principles led to a faith in the global market ensuring a steady and constant supply of necessities, even though increasing reliance on foreign carriers surrendered the nation a hostage to fortune.

There had been 30,000 British ratings at sea in 1980. By 2005 there were only 9,000, most of them aboard Royal Fleet Auxiliaries or ferries, a few remaining on the books of crewing agencies. In 2004–5 – the Year of the Sea – only fifty people came forward for training as ratings. The augmentation of the European Union by the accession of several former Soviet satellite states provided cheaper and well-trained officers and by flagging-out owners could easily evade the EU Directive that European sea-farers should be paid the rate of the flag-state. Moreover, when the New Labour Government was, according to one of Prime Minister Blair's own MPs 'addressing this [maritime] sector of British life, which had been excluded from the basic laws of civilised society as we know it ... [T]he government created the bizarre situation in which discrimination on the basis of ethnicity was outlawed but discrimination could continue on the grounds of nationality'. The extension of the national minimum wage from buses and trains to ferries remains outstanding.

Surprisingly therefore, despite its failings in the matter of training young offic-ers, by 2005 the Tonnage Tax had increased the size of the commercial fleet that was registered in the United Kingdom and its Crown dependencies, doubling its capacity and more than quadrupling its size. By this time shipping itself – as opposed to the maritime service-industry – had a turnover of £5.12 billions, compared with that of aerospace of £18.5 billions, but those employed in shipping proper were a fifth of those in aerospace. At the inception of the Tonnage Tax scheme a mere 896 British officers were employed in what the then shipping minister, Dr Stephen Ladyman, was pleased to call 'tonnage tax *boats'* and this number had increased by 2,000 over the five years to 2005, the number of British ratings increasing from 449 to 1,460, although some 26,500 British seafarers were at sea under foreign flags in the wider world.

William Whatley, a former Trinity House cadet who later served as third officer in the Royal Research Ship *Bransfield*, wrote that:

> The majority of people have never heard of the Merchant Navy ... [It] was an obvious choice for me as a keen yachtsman and I have not been disappointed. A career in the Merchant Navy offers opportunities to travel and receive a high-level of training. It is hard work but enjoyable and the periods of leave allow for other interests to be pursued.[45]

Heather Cowan, an engineer officer, echoes Whately's sentiments. 'I was attracted to marine engineering for the variety of the job and the attraction of seeing the world.' Seafaring remains a predominantly young person's career and technology has improved conditions so that although crews are small and contentment relies upon an individual's inner resources, a change for the better was experienced by Cowan during thirteen years. 'These days the trips are shorter and the communications on board greatly improved. My last two vessels had internet in the cabins so you could stay in touch with home ... every day ...'.

As always, a seafaring background eased entry. Whately was 'a keen yachtsman' and both Cowan's parents had been at sea; 'being brought up with ships' was 'very much part of daily life' and included 'getting tied to ships' railings by my reins as a child'. What drew her to engineering, and ultimately to service as a watch-keeping engineer in oil and liquefied petroleum gas-carriers, was her school's placement for her work experience in a local shipyard.

> It wasn't my first choice by a long shot and having your mum make cakes for lads and accidentally dyeing your boiler suit pink didn't help ... I got a week with the

fitters and then a week with the platers and got to go home with the contents of the swear-box every week … But it wasn't an easy ride. There were plenty of ups and downs throughout my cadetship, ranging from never wanting to see another ship ever again, till I'm not sure I want to go home, I'm having such fun. And then some plain interesting times, like finding the steward is stealing your shoes, finding a large cockroach resting on your tooth-brush, to realizing the scavenge space isn't really the best place to be with a hangover, but all character-building stuff … [46]

But what the reality of all this meant in terms of ships was something inconceivable to seafarers of even a generation earlier for – though there were many who asserted the British flag had long been in part a flag of convenience – it had undergone full conversion by this time. In January 2007 a modestly sized container ship, the *MSC Napoli*, on charter to the Italian-Swiss Mediterranean Shipping Company, found herself in difficulties in the English Channel. Outward bound she ran into exceptionally heavy weather and her hull cracked. She had been aground earlier in her life and was no longer a new ship, but the cracks disabled her, and her engine room filled with water. Under the auspices of the British Maritime and Coastguard Agency, which by this time was the controlling authority for both the old regulating 'Board of Trade' and the Coastguard, naval helicopters removed her crew. There was little consideration given to them remaining to help save the ship, which was undertaken by salvors who succeeded in beaching her in Branscombe Bay, off the coast of south Devon. In the brouhaha that followed the public – and wilfully criminal – looting of some of her containers which washed ashore, other details of the ship were obscured. Few among a population marvelling at the bonanza of motor-bikes and personal effects spread out upon the beach, understood that this was technically a *British* ship – at least she was a British-registered ship – and flew the red ensign. She was actually owned and managed by Samuel Ofer's Zodiac Shipping. Ofer, it will be recalled, had purchased much of P&O's tonnage and Zodiac's ships constituted the largest fleet then under the British flag. In fact the *Napoli*'s master and officers were Ukrainian, her crew was Filipino and only her two cadets – carried to fulfil Zodiac' obligations under the Tonnage Tax – were British. Charming youngsters, Michael Grey recalled, 'their experience everything they wished about seafaring and more, and [they] could hardly wait to get back to sea and get ship-wrecked again'.

The following year the last trans-Atlantic Cunarder, *Queen Elizabeth 2*, long a cruise ship, left British shores to become an hotel at Dubai, in the Middle East. She left Southampton for the last time on 11 November 2008, under the command of Captain Ian McNaught, a Younger Brother of Trinity House. Somewhat notorious for groundings in her long career, she seemed reluctant to relinquish the habit and had touched bottom on her approach to the port, an embarrassment that delayed her and only added to the sense of things awry. Thanks to the systemically inaccurate British-press labelling her as 'the flagship of the Merchant Navy,' her going rang down the curtain on the final act, though it failed to merit a mention on the BBC's main television news bulletin that night.[47]

There was something truly tragic in the end of the British Merchant Navy, that its replacement by a multi-nationally owned, if British-flagged, merchant marine

– as exemplified by the *MSC Napoli* – can never mitigate. That so small an island could have produced so large and universal a public service provider for so many years would have been remarkable enough, but it was made the more so since it had saved the world from the ambitions of tyrants more than once. That it did so in the face of danger, social obloquy and public indifference, made it somehow quietly heroic. Those of us who knew it in its last flowering, in the aftermath of a war which conferred upon it a dignity never before afforded to its humble servants, watched its disintegration with disbelief. The great asset was squandered, first by Government whose faith in *laissez-faire* proved misplaced, next by the seamen who failed to realise that labour has both value and price, and finally by the many shipowners. Once fiercely independent, so many private firms went public, opening their dealings to the selfish rapacity of shareholders interested only in self-enrichment and with little notion of wider implications. Ownership became collective, fragmented, disinterested in the core-business and its patriotically beneficial but intangible elements. Profits in shipowning have never been made quickly though they are cumulative and, in the hands of the skilled and patient few, can be immense. On the back of this others can earn and prosper, but reactive versatility and a degree of autocracy is essential, so that advantage may be taken of sudden shifts in market demand. Such astute agility was inimical to modern governments for whom shipping diminished as part of a Cabinet Minister's portfolio, not even rating cabinet status as successive 'shipping ministers' were reduced to mere Under Secretaries of State waiting in the wings for promotion elsewhere. No ambitious politician would countenance such a poisoned chalice: between 1990 and 2009 Major's Conservative and the Labour Governments of Blair and Brown saw no less than ten such ministers.[48] The gulf between shipping and Government yawned wider, both sides retreating, the shipowner giving up and seeking easier and more profitable returns on his capital, the Government simply losing interest.

    In the neutral ground between them the much put-upon seafarer struggled. His options shrank and if he stayed at sea he joined an International labour market with no national pretensions. Although openings for British mates and engineers exist, there are far fewer for British ratings. A handful of seamen, stewards and greasers remain in short-sea ferries, but the raffish, indomitable, querulous rough diamond who cursed God, the shipowner and the master who logged him his day's pay for the offence of drinking himself into oblivion, who nonetheless could and did heed his country's call for help, is long a thing of the past. Amid the disintegration of its great shipping-companies many of the men it had produced remained at sea, their *curricula vitae* evidence of the changes the industry had undergone. Typical of them was that of Christopher Sturcke, an ex-*Worcester* boy, who served a traditional cadetship with Royal Mail Line's general cargo, passenger and refrigerated ships, running from Britain to South America, the West Indies, the west coast of the United States and Canada. Having obtained his Second Mate's Certificate in 1957 and continued with Royal Mail as a watch-keeping officer, he passed his First Mate's and Master's examinations and was appointed Second Officer in Royal Mail's A-Class intermediate passenger ships, the *Amazon*, *Arlanza* and *Aragon*, running between London and Buenos Aires. When in 1967 the company was integrated into the Furness, Withy Group, Sturke became chief officer in general-cargo and refrigerated ships servicing

South and Central America. In 1973 he transferred to a cruise ship before stand-ing-by new tonnage being built in Poland for the Cairn Line. Promoted to master in 1980, Captain Sturcke commanded ships employed between the Mediterranean and Iceland, Scandinavia and the Baltic; three years later he was in command of a refrigerated container ship running to the United States, Australia and New Zealand. When Furness, Withy was acquired by C.Y. Tung, Captain Sturcke continued in their container-liners on the North Atlantic, but by 1988 the process of 'flagging-out' was completed, with the fleet directly managed from Hong Kong, and six years later, Sturcke swallowed the anchor and retired, having become a Younger Brother of Trinity House in 1983.

He was one of thousands emerging from the half-decks of British merchantmen which had produced a steady stream of competent and dutiful seamen. Among them men of remarkable stamp, some numbers of whom achieved public notice. Several Polar explorers, some soldiers of field rank, both civil and military aircraft pilots, the commander of a nuclear submarine along with several other naval officers of distinc-tion, a wartime Commander-in-Chief of Coastal Command, a remarkable number of distinguished academics and lawyers, a few authors and men of letters, a Poet-Laureate, even a Viceroy of India, all began their lives as apprentices or cadets. Among those produced by the Merchant Navy in the 1960s was Robin Knox-Johnston who, as a junior officer in the British India Steam Navigation Co., had had a small yacht named *Suhaili* built in Bombay. After serving as Second Officer in the *Santhia* – on the Persian Gulf service replacing the lost *Dara* – he sailed *Suhaili* home in late 1965 for some leave, arriving at Gravesend in 1967. He had been obliged to 'refill his cof-fers' in South Africa where he sailed as master of a coaster and worked as a stevedore *en route*. He returned to serve B.I. as chief officer before undergoing training in the Royal Naval Reserve in HM Frigate *Duncan* during the early months of 1968, by which time he had become interested in the single-handed, non-stop round-the-world race then being proposed. At 14.20 on 14 June 1968 he left Falmouth in *Suhaili*, something of an unknown outsider, returning 313 days later and crossing the finish-ing line at 15.25 on 22 April 1969 to find himself the winner.

Navigating in the pre-GPS age, Knox-Johnston attributed his success to his train-ing in the British India S.N. Co. 'There was nothing to beat a cadet-ship like mine,' he has said. British India, like the other blue-chip companies of his day were still training their cadets in accordance with the principles laid down by Francis Drake at the dawn of the British maritime era. Drake, whose roots lay in the mercantile tradi-tion of exploitation and privateering, whatever his later ambitions brought him by way of a Vice Admiral's flag, had admonished his ship's company on that ruthless and unquestionably commercial first circumnavigation by an English ship: 'I must have the gentlemen to haul and draw with the mariner, and the mariner with the gentle-man. I would know him that would refuse to set his hand to a rope, but I know there is not any such here'.

But by this time the *Worcester*, having in 1954 lost her consort *Cutty Sark* to a Greenwich dry dock where she became a tourist attraction, was disposed of. For a while training facilities were maintained ashore at Greenhithe but the sharp decline in young men wishing to follow the sea forced eventual closure. Shortly afterwards similar facilities folded on the Menai Strait where HMS *Conway* had moved ashore after the tragic loss of the ship on her way to dry-dock twenty years earlier. In charge of two tugs, she had sheered across the stream, grounded and her back broke as the tide fell, causing widespread lamentations. Other pre-sea training establishments went the same way, from King Edward VII's College in London to the *Mercury* on the River Hamble. Among the survivors Devitt and Moore's foundation, Pangbourne College, is today but one more private educational establishment, no longer encouraging its alumni to go to sea, leaving charitable institutions to provide bursaries and cadetships for young people like Cowan and Whately, both of whom are former beneficiaries of Trinity House. Without such foresight, there would be few avenues open to youthful ambition and even this is limited by the resources available and does not compare with the intake of cadets a generation earlier.

With the depletion of the old pre-sea training schools, the establishments offering degree, specialised and pre-examination courses for certificates of competency are now faculties of wider academic campuses. The Warsash School of Navigation is today part of Southampton University and similar institutions exist elsewhere in such locations as Glasgow, South Shields and Fleetwood. Although much altered in character, there remain both facilities and opportunities, but they are no longer as close to the mainstream as they once were. Mercantile sea service remains undervalued much as it always has been, sometimes to the detriment of many. In 1748 a merchant master wrote to the Admiralty 'out of a sense of duty,' that he found that lemon juice mixed with French brandy always cured scurvy. The Sick and Hurt Board dismissed his claim, stating that 'trials have been made of the acid of lemons ... on board several different ships ... the surgeons of which all agree ... the rob of lemons and oranges were of no service, either in the prevention, or cure, of that disease'. Like that connection made by a merchant master between malaria and the mosquito mentioned in *Neptune's Trident*, one cannot escape the conclusion that had the opinion of a practical tarpaulin seaman been heeded, many lives may have been preserved.

In writing this history I have read a hundred memoirs, from Barlow to Britten. Coming from merchant seafarers these are patchy in historiological terms. The intelligent, much put-upon Barlow waxed vitriolic about the conditions of his day, while the score or so memoirists who manned the last British sailing vessels tended to retrospective lyricism as they told of their harsh and Spartan lives. But there was another cluster of men, those whose fortunes rose on the short-lived crest of public approbation to command great liners. They inevitably stare sternly from their frontispieces: Hayes as Commodore of the White Star Line wearing his sword, his cuffs adorned with the intertwined braid of a Captain in the Royal Naval Reserve; Britten, also a Captain R.N.R., but in his Cunard uniform on the bridge of RMS *Queen Mary*; and Bone, a brilliant author and brother to a brilliant war artist, Muirhead, whose portrait of Brother David as Commodore of the Anchor Line adorns his memoirs. They were among a small but select number of mercantile knights; Sir Bertram Hayes a Knight Commander of the Order of St Michael and St George; Sir James Bisset not merely a knight, but an honorary graduate of Cambridge University, men whose command of well-known large passenger-liners brought them into the public eye. From their portraits one might think them proud and haughty; after all each commanded a huge ship, a crew of 800 to 1,000 officers and ratings – women as well as men – with the responsibility for these lives and perhaps those of 1,800 passengers. To command their great ships, regularly ploughing their way across the Western Ocean, driven by steam-plant of enormous power, required a degree of hauteur one might think.

They were, of course, the successful tip of a demographic iceberg at the bottom of which there were the drunken failures: the men who had lost their ships or their souls and perhaps both. And in between a numerous population of forgotten but largely competent men who did their work well and followed what that most introspec-tive of master-mariners, Joseph Conrad, called 'a useful calling'; men whose ships were not glamorous: big four-masted barques; dirty British coasters; short-sea traders and ferries; underpowered tramp-steamers; vulnerable bulk-carriers; huge oil-tankers; smart cargo-liners and their successors, container-ships. Many masters and officers manning these later, newer ship types, all of whom had been trained in balmier, less hurried days when sea-going was in itself a way of life, found the necessary changes difficult. A Port Line master, joining his first container-ship in 1973 admitted:

> We were all very reluctant to change to containers because the whole concept of living changed and our fishing rods and our guns and our golf-clubs stayed at home. Instead of weeks in port you barely had time to take lunch. The routes stayed the same but it was a totally different world to the extent that, as a junior officer in the conventional world there was no better. In the container world it was terribly boring because you did the same thing all the time … The cargo-plans were done ashore … all we had to do was to make sure the containers went in the right place and the freezer containers did not go on deck.

Other routes were more complex, especially in smaller container ships like those of the Prince Line running from Manchester down to the Mediterranean which:

> only had two watch-keeping officers, so you worked six hours on and six hours off … you would go into port [under the gantries] in the morning, and sail in the afternoon … We all had Master's tickets … These small ships only carried 120 containers. You had the [ship's] stability to consider. When, for example, you were loading in Piraeus you would be loading containers full of currants and they would be very heavy … [so] when you're doing seven or eight ports … it is quite complex.

Nevertheless, there was another disincentive to add to that of the transfer of most of the cargo-management to the terminal ashore. In many container-liners the tradi-tional maintenance function of 'the mate/chief officer' was transferred to the chief engineer. Although, 'at the end of the day the ship's command had responsibility for the safe condition of the ship' this tended to induce a sense of being a scapegoat if matters went awry. Even at sea the steady encroachment of satellite navigation reduced 'the arte and mysterie' of conducting a ship across the ocean to a matter of kindergarten simplicity, depriving it of professional satisfaction. Everything seemed diminished, as one large container-liner commander summarised:

Because no cargo gear was fitted in container ships the need to maintain derricks, blocks, shackles and wires meant there was less for the deck crew to do. Similarly the containerised nature of the cargo reduced the need for lengthy hatch cleaning operations and so the numbers of sailors were reduced to a minimum. I suppose that the need for crew cuts for economic reasons and the development of more sophisticated container vessels happened at much the same time. It always seemed to me that container ship crews were much smaller than those found in general cargo vessels. I found the catering department had virtually disappeared and in the end was reduced to one cook and no stewards. Thus the Master having enjoyed, in older ships, the luxuries of pursers, chief stewards and the like, found himself with a tighter schedule, the victualling to organise, the crew wages to calculate and the ship's accounts keeping him out of mischief when he became bored!

By far the biggest difference I found was the need at all times to keep the schedule. From time to time this could be stressful and occasionally lead one into taking calculated risks such as passing through ice infested waters at night and in poor visibility. Also the definition of 'a safe speed' had to be modified when navigating in fog in high density traffic areas.

In my last years the improved communication through satellite and modern electronic equipment generated a daily heap of interfering signals from an office on the far side of the world. These frequently failed to appreciate local conditions and made one feel more the branch manager than the master of your own ship.

Another master commented on the changes wrought in an officer's personal life in small container-ships:

The officers' cabins were tiny ... there was a communal bathroom; the Captain's cabin was minuscule compared with what had been the case in the past. There was a mess-room, where the Cook passed the officers' food through the hatch. [The ship] ... did a three-week round-trip to Israel ... and they had to do two or three of these ... before they got any leave. The vibration on them was so bad that you couldn't fill in the log-book on the bridge at the end of your watch, you had to come down to the mess-room ... otherwise it would be illegible. These are the conditions that the men from the cargo liners were put into. This was in 1969. The officers had effectively been de-skilled, because the container operation is simple ... with that goes one's pride in the profession. It was a culture shock, an utter culture shock.[49]

In contrast, Commodore Ronald Friendship described conditions on board the tanker *British Respect* in 1970, 'every man, except deck and engine cadets [who were accommodated in pairs], has his own cabin complete with toilet and shower ... all air-conditioned.' Even on modern coastal colliers, the accommodation could be 'absolutely fantastic'. The master of the *Amberley* considered her quarters to be 'beautiful ... panelled in dark wood as though it had come from a passenger ship. The master had a day cabin ... immediately below the bridge ... [and] a sleeping cabin with a double bed so that you could take your wife with you'. Such comforts and privileges were increasingly rare, though younger men proved more adaptable, as

Second Officer Nicolas Lampe recalls discovering when he joined OCL's *Botany Bay* at Fos-sur-Mer on January 1975.

> I well remember the long car journey across the flat landscape from Marseilles airport. The ship and the huge container gantries could be seen from miles away, confirming fears of the remoteness of the berths from 'civilisation'. I was soon changed into a boiler-suit and learning the intricacies of how the deck container lashing rods were secured and the vagaries of the pneumatic 'flip-flops' that were used to guide containers into the hold cell-guides.

The *Encounter Bay*-class were well appointed and the ambience was less formal than Lampe had experienced in P&O's traditional ships.

> Efforts were made to break down the ancient divides between 'oil and water,' and between officers and ratings. Officers still dined in their saloon, and the meals were of a high standard. However, meals had to be consumed fairly quickly to avoid over-time payments ... An engineer from Shell Tankers joined *Botany Bay* with me. The first evening at sea, seated with the captain and senior staff, he asked the steward to serve coffee at the end of dinner. The steward explained that coffee was available in the Officers' lounge. 'I'd like it here, please.' 'Sorry, we don't have coffee to serve here ...' he became known as 'Shell-shock' and left at the end of the voyage.

The privilege of saloon-dining was much valued and was one of the incremental privileges that made life tolerable, but it attracted attention. Michael Grey recalled:

> a confused conversation with a celebrated British ship-owner who thought it incredible that a British ship-master of a large internationally trading ship should have the services of a steward who would clean his cabin and make his bed and enjoy silver service in a saloon rather than sit with the crew in a canteen wearing a boiler-suit. 'He doesn't get that treatment when he is home,' said this seer. 'So why should he enjoy this service at my expense?'

Perhaps nothing demonstrates the decline in status so eloquently as the erosion of the professional, and particularly the senior, officers' privileges, nor the shipowner's parsimony and misperception in comparing home life with that at sea. There was no comparison, as Dea Birkett noticed aboard Elder, Dempster's *Minos* in 1990.

> The married younger officers ... had passport-sized photographs of their wives pinned up above the desks in their cabins ... It was as if Keith kept the photograph ... to remind him what she looked like ... Keith ... also had pictures of ... [his] children ... end-of-term school photographs, and they both wore grey uniforms with crimson piping ... 'My family,' Keith had said, pointing proudly ... For eight months out of twelve, Keith's family was no more than these strained pictures. Steve hadn't seen his daughter until she was almost four months old.[50]

Silver service seems a modest price to pay to secure hearts and minds in order to further one's own private venture. The extent to which its removal troubled men is a measure not of their desire for the privileges of rank, but the ease by which they might be soothed and reconciled to their ship-bound existence. Mealtimes and food perform an important social function on board ship, possessing a ritual quality which placed value on an officer's service by playing on his vanity and securing his loyalty. A study of conditions at sea showed this when:

> the standard of accommodation was very good but the silver service in the saloon had gone. It wasn't self-service, but … [t]he days when you all put uniform on and sat down had gone; it didn't quite fit in with the style of working. As far as the food itself went, some of it was diabolical. One ship I sailed on called the *Oceanic Crest* we had four months at anchor off port because of strikes ashore, the cook could not cook anything British at all, so I lived for at least two months, without exaggeration, on a bowl of rice with a fried egg on top as my only meal of the day, with lots of soy sauce, and possibly sometimes a fried egg for breakfast. That was all that was edible. In hindsight it must have been a fiddle. What was ordered and what was delivered was not the same and the saving was split between the Old Man and the Chief Steward. For those two months we were also down to one bucket of water a day each, but you soon learn to cope with a bucket of water …

Which only goes to emphasise the importance of good food.

Such were the conditions possible under ensigns of foreign states, even when an officer worked for a British company. 'Going foreign-flag,' as many did, was lonely and unenviable, as one master admitted in the same study.

> The ship … had a complete Chinese crew apart from myself, as master. The officers were from Hong Kong, the crew from the P[eoples'] R[epublic of] C[hina], it was registered in Liberia and it was a real wreck … running for a company … out of Abidjan … a slow, old ship not good for fending off pirates. I could not believe what had happened to me. There I was in … Africa, with a Chinese crew, most of which could not speak English, there were no knives and forks on the ship, there were no cups, it was completely and utterly Chinese.

By contrast with this isolated soul, some officers and masters 'displayed an astonishing lack of flexibility in coping with a changed world,' George Swaine recalled.

> Perhaps it was not their fault. I remember interviewing one senior master from the South American and Australasian trades for command on a new bulk-carrier. I told him that we expected him to make every effort to ensure his ship traded profitably and gave him a few examples of what our Scandinavian and Greek masters would do. Indignation was not too strong a word for his response. How dare I tell him how to run his ship? I fear the transit from the comfortable world of a classic liner company … to a world full of bill of lading swaps, crooked charterers, all important lay-up time calculations, etc., was not for him.

For those who did adapt and met the challenge, it was possible to succeed. A British master working for a German subsidiary of a Danish company in 2008 had good leave, a salary of £70,000 and paid little tax, but for those flagging-out under less congenial ensigns their sole *raison d'être* was their British certificate of competence as master-mariner.

It was a far cry from the days of Hayes, Britten, Bone and their peers, in spite of their harsh apprenticeships in sail. The accolade of their knighthoods and their great ships mark the apogee of it all. One turns the pages of their memoirs and that first impression of hauteur fades: here are the reminiscences of boys matured by responsibility; humorous, honest and often remarkably humble. Not afraid to speak their minds when they observed things wrong or unjust; autocratic certainly, but fair-minded and, above all, dutiful. Strapped with a heavy burden of responsibility, devoid of the stern sanctions of a naval captain, they ruled 'by the Act' and the force of their own character. As the sequel has shown, the days of their personal glory were short and their successors became an endangered species. Not long after their passing the British Merchant Navy, as a national asset that combined a wholly commercial viability with an unquantifiable reserve of public benefit, dwindled into sudden extinction. In 1920, at the beginning of the long decline, the shipowner William Forwood perceiving something awry, wrote of the 'serious national danger … [to which] we may some day awake' of losing 'beyond recovery the industry that is above and beyond all others' pre-eminent. Ninety years later the consequences of this great squandering are all too obvious and, to paraphrase the seaman's lament, *Fiddler's Green*, the British seafarer is no more on the docks to be seen. The consequences await the verdict of history.

But what of the shipowner himself? Why exactly had he sold his fleet, diversified, taken his money elsewhere? Not all had, of course. Some few moved offshore and carried on. Since merchant shipping must exist in an open, global market, the owner whose ships carry the world's good about the oceans is the owner who does it cheapest. It is of no interest to the shipper or the consignee what flag the cheapest ship carries, nor what wages are paid to her crew, nor that in her rusty state she *might* prove a risk; he is insured against all that. What he wants is service at the minimum cost. That is what globalised ship-owning provides and therefore advanced nations wanting a national carrying fleet for any purpose whatsoever, whether as an insurance against a national emergency, or to train harbour masters, pilots and so forth, have to pay a premium price, or protect their trade in some way, such as was once the case with the English Navigation Acts. There simply is no other way.

While the Seamen's Strike of 1966 had its impact in the short term, one shipowner admitted that it 'does not occur to me as very significant. These things happen and often crafty owners recoup the outlay and more with rate adjustments shortly after[wards]. Creating a macro-climate which was unattractive for the industry was much more relevant.' And that is what had happened. It was, in the end, the state itself, in the form of successive British Governments, that effectively engineered the decline of the British Merchant Navy. After the war the Labour Government of Clement Attlee, desperately short of money though it was, with its immense debt to the United States, recognised the absolute necessity of rebuilding the damaged merchant fleet. The same attitude prevailed in the succeeding Conservative administrations of the 1950s. A series of measures favouring ship-owning were introduced, some deliberately vague so that, at their face value, these did not disturb the delicate relations between Britain and others, particularly the United States. 'United Kingdom shipowners were allowed to obfuscate profits completely by transfers to and from reserves without providing detail in their accounts,' a shipowner of the time explained. As long as this tacit co-operation prevailed, underwritten as it was by an understanding by ministers of the national importance of a modern mercantile marine, British shipping made its very considerable contribution to the Exchequer by way of invisible earnings. This state of affairs, however, was systematically destroyed by a series of measures which withdrew such benefits, successive governments attempting to manipulate circumstances, rather than formulate a shipping policy.

As William Thomson, a partner in the Ben Line puts it, it was the fiscal measures which resulted in 'the wholesale removal of incentive to take the risk of ship-owning'. This began in 'the ridiculous Wilson/Dennis Healey era' of Wilson's Labour Government of the mid-1960s and was compounded by the Oil Crisis of 1973/4 which coincided with a manpower crisis that led to an increase in the wage-bill. Many shipowners had not greatly concerned themselves about running costs until a rising wage-bill was added to a quadrupled fuel account. With their accountants and financial directors telling them that a better return on their investment could be had elsewhere and with far less trouble, they began to pull out. As the distinguished maritime journalist, Master-Mariner and sometime editor of *Lloyd's List*, Michael Grey, put it, 'the tramp fleet, which was the most vulnerable went first'. Larger liner companies sought solutions elsewhere:

> Flagging out was an option that appeared quite attractive and many would go down this road. Diversification consisting of extraordinary efforts by companies like P&O and Blue Funnel just did not seem to work, possibly they were too short term in their approach and all these new ventures seemed to come to nothing. There was also a growing appreciation that shipping was no longer valued by Government. The Thatcher Government did not appear remotely interested in the industry's problems – 'special case' pleading was treated with contempt, and it did not actually seem to be very important anymore that the contribution to invisibles was still quite substantial. Important shipping folk, who in an earlier age had been used to a polite reception from Government Ministers found that they were quite simply regarded as unimportant, and could not even get their telephone calls answered.

William Thomson agrees that the work of discouraging the British shipowner:

> was completed by ... [Margaret] Thatcher ... Refusing owners the opportunity to hold tax free reserves in good times and taxing all the edges (from crew to unworkable capital allowances) simply drove people out of the business. Some ship-owners went bust as they always do in good times or bad, but what was noticeable is that the solvent ones just stopped investing in tonnage and took their money elsewhere.

The irony of Margaret Thatcher, eager to reform the British economy and play to its strengths by encouraging service industries, actually conniving in the destruction of the nation's greatest by doing nothing to support it was in line with the Friedmanite philosophy. Michael Grey recalled Lord Sterling:

> who had battled tremendously for the industry over many years put[ting] the problem quite succinctly. 'When I build a cruise ship costing $300 million,' he said, 'the share price goes down and there are critical articles in the City press, even though that ship will be earning for the next thirty years – when I sell some part of the P&O empire, I am praised to the skies by the teenage scribblers of the City, and the share-price goes up.' This inordinately short-term attitude, which along with the failure of the politicians, press and public to understand the value of the Merchant Navy, contributed to its eventual demise.

As Britain emerged from recession and upheaval in the 1980s and Blair's 'New Labour' Government inherited a blissfully high-revenue-earning economy in 1997, goods flowed into British supermarkets at a cheap rate in foreign ships. In this atmosphere John Prescott's Tonnage Tax revival was of less importance than what was of greater interest to the Government: the preservation of London as a centre of maritime services – insurance, broking and so forth. Michael Grey recalled 'a shouting match' between an advocate of shipping and the then chairman of the Baltic Exchange. The latter:

> insisted that the British merchant fleet was unimportant compared to the 'one-stop-shop' represented by London's maritime infrastructure. This was a view that has persisted even within the Chamber of Shipping, whose biggest members are now [in 2009] foreign-owned shipping companies who treat the red ensign as the flag-of-convenience it has now become.

William Thomson concludes:

> For what it is worth the situation is no better now [2009]. The UK still has plenty of expertise ([marine] brokers, bankers, lawyers underwriters, etc.) but UK-based tonnage owners will not return until the Government makes it worthwhile. There is no sign of this happening …

What the British public did not appreciate was that the cheap transport system that loaded their supermarket shelves bore down upon the wretched seafarer. Stories of unpaid crews, ships abandoned by their owners, or the foundering of numerous aged bulk-carriers all failed to make their newspapers.[51] Surprise greeted the old news that piracy was thriving in certain quarters of the world, notably the Indian Ocean. Thus, at the end of the first decade of the twenty-first century and in the wake of Islamist terrorist attacks on the West, the international seafarer – no less useful than he had been before – found himself back where others had started: abused, poorly paid, ignored and subject to piratical seizure. But it is no longer a British story and its telling must be left to others.

Matters have run their course.

NOTES

1. Including the commitment of the Royal Navy to protect traditional British fishing 'rights' off Iceland whose government incrementally increased her claim to exclusive access, precipitating three 'Cod Wars' between 1958 and 1976.

2. Malcom McLean's Sea-Land Services Inc. undertook a trans-Atlantic container service and in the Pacific the Matson Line planned an extension of their early container service to Hawaii to Japan in 1966.

3. Examples of hard-lying conditions were often exaggerations based upon a traditional mythology, resurrecting images of the 1920s. It was true that none of these issues had been properly addressed when they should have been, but by 1966 most of the awful, ancient pre-war tonnage had disappeared. Indeed archived 'evidence' of wives complaining about their husbands' living conditions suggest that the remedy lay in their own hands and the application of a bucket of *soojee* and some hot water.

4. Wilson gambled upon the United States backing the pound if he remained in tacit, but militarily inactive, support of the United States' war in Vietnam. This acted as one more provocation to the left and their allies, the peace activists, who rioted in London, particularly outside the US Embassy in Grosvenor Square. Thus Wilson's unusual political reticence in failing to denounce the war brought about his downfall.

5. See Meek, M., *There Go the Ships*, p138 *et seq*.

6. A space-ton represented 40 cubic ft of cargo-space and was used in general-cargo ships where occupied capacity, rather than weight, dictated voyage economics and profitability.

7. In 1964 China Navigation also chartered the Glen & Shire Line's *Monmouthshire* from Holt. She had been built in 1943 as the *Telemachus* for Blue Funnel, transferred to Glen & Shire in 1957 and spent a year as *Glaucus* before changing her name to *Nanchang*. Under C.N.Co.'s house-flag she ventured as far south as New Zealand. She was scrapped in 1968 after a career typical of the last generation of conventional cargo-liners.

8. Diversification could backfire. The Court Line's move into mass travel agency wrecked the company's shipping interests – mainly bulk-carrying – when it went bankrupt.

9. These are beyond the scope of this history, but most of the major shipping companies defied American expertise which sought to dominate the North Sea oil and gas-fields by forming rig-support and supply companies with their rugged tenders and anchor-handling vessels. One such combination was between P&O and Ocean, forming Ocean Inchcape Ltd, or OIL, and such new fleets formed a refuge for ambitious young officers made redundant from their original deep-sea cargo firms. Diversification extended into rigs, such as the alliance between the old rivals Ben and Ocean which produced BenOcean, which also saw Ben Line ships like the *Bencruachan* loading on Holt berths and wearing twin blue funnels, and Glen liners wearing Ben's buff. It also led these old shipping giants into 'logistics'.

10. She was not entirely a lucky ship and her career embraced some difficult moments. Although taken up from trade as a troopship for the Falklands Campaign in 1982, the *Queen Elizabeth 2* transferred her troops to other vessels in South Georgia for onward passage to Port Stanley. The official reason for keeping the *Q.E.2* away from the front line was that she was too valuable and prestigious a ship to expose to and risk of attack; the circulated scuttlebutt was that she was unreliable and the official lack of confidence might have made her an even more vulnerable target. This was based on the cogent fact that her departure from Southampton had been delayed by engine trouble and in many ways she was an unlucky ship, suffering several groundings during her career. See Rentel, P. *Master Mariner, A Life Under Way*.

11. Anecdotal evidence exists that the master of a British tanker leaving Port Said in the final hours of 4 June was told, rather enigmatically, by the departing pilot that there would not be many tankers following him, the import of which became clear next day.

12. The *Vassil Levsky* was a relic of the Second World War and had been British-built in 1944 as the *Empire Mackendrick*, a Merchant Aircraft Carrier, or MAC-ship.

13. For full details of this complex matter and the background against which it was achieved, see Bott, A. (Ed), *British Box Business, A History of OCL*, p64.

14. Under the Master, a First, Second and Third Officer designated with the symbol (N) after their rank, maintained bridge watches. The First Officer (N) doubled as medical officer. Under the Chief Engineer Officer, the First Officer (E) was a supervising day-worker. Engine-room watches

were kept by the Second and two Third Officers (E); a Second Officer (L), (F), (R) and (C) were respectively electrical, refrigeration, radio and catering officers. The Bosun and storekeeper for the entire ship (except for foodstuffs) became Petty Officer (N) and there were two petty Officers (E). There were nine GP Ratings who operated a rotating system of three on bridge watch, three on engine-room watch and three on day-work as directed by the Chief Engineer Officer. To feed the crew there were a Chief Cook, Second Cook & Baker, Second Steward, two Stewards and a Galley Boy. In addition four Cadets, usually two deck and two engineering, were carried.

15. The first-generation of steam-turbine-powered container-liners, like the similarly fitted *QE2*, had to be refitted later with large diesel engines to remain economical.

16. The aggregate world gross tonnage was 2,780,681 of which the USA owned 1,067,468 and Britain 627,448. (Quoted Jamieson, p38).

17. By 1986 58 per cent of British exports went to western Europe, most (48 per cent) to EEC countries and 66 per cent of her imports came from the same source, mostly (52 per cent) from the EEC.

18. The seven British India ships were *Kampala*, Captain C.R. Polkinghorne; *Karanja*, Captain C.B. Mitchell; *Kenya*, Captain D.G. Gun-Cunninghame; *Mombasa*, Captain R. Trimble; *Modasa*, Captain W.A. Busby; *Mantola*, Captain R.R. Stone; and the little coaster *Tabora* commanded by Mr A.B Stephens. It was the new *Kenya's* maiden voyage and among her passengers was Lord Inchape. The *Kenya's* predecessor outlived her by a year, having been sold to Italian interests she ran emigrants to Australia as the *Castel Felice* until 1970. Polkinghorne afterwards transferred into her sister-ship, the then new *Uganda* which left Tilbury on her maiden voyage on 2 August 1952.

19. Until 1982 the *Karanja* had been one of two ex-BI ships run by the Indians, the other being the *Dwarka* which was employed on the Mumbai – Persian Gulf service and was broken-up in Karachi.

20. Faced with heavy losses Ellerman had been sold in 1983, ten years after the death of the second John Reeves Ellerman, the rodent expert. The company's fleet had reduced from fifty-odd in 1953 to just five. Cunard-Ellerman was formed in 1987 when Trafalgar House, Cunard's parent company, purchased Ellerman's residual interests.

21. Correspondence with Chris Bourne, November 2009.

22. See Davis, J., *You and Your Ships*, The Memoir Club, Stanhope, 2006.

23. As early as 1961 Alfred Holt & Co. had partly abandoned their practice of carrying their own risk, a low level insurance predicated on minimal losses having been taken out by the Ocean Group. Odyssey Insurance was established in Bermuda in order to take advantage of certain tax-breaks and to cover the rising costs of building ships, but this move was not made common-knowledge for fear of under-mining the company's traditional standards of conduct. 'We have taken this step,' Sir John Nicholson confided in his ship-masters, 'simply as a matter of practical convenience and … it represents no kind of departure from the policy which we have inherited and intend to perpetuate for ever of assuming the fullest possible collective and individual responsibility for the consequences of our mistakes'. The reference to eternity was misplaced.

24. Ocean's disgust with British shipbuilders combined with their desire to have intermediate container and general cargo-ships, had led them in the late 1970s to order tonnage from Japanese and Soviet yards. The Group went into partnership with the Barber Line of Oslo and the Swedish East Asiatic Co. of Gothenburg (with which they had long run a round-the-world service) to form the Barber Blue SEA Line. The once distinct Blue Funnel, Glen and Elder, Dempster fleets became indistinguishable in these last years.

25. George Swaine began his career in 1958 as a sixteen-year-old deck-cadet with Furness, Withy & Co., passing for Master Mariner in 1969. A year later he joined the Baltic Exchange and moved into management, later becoming Contracts and Operations Manager for Furness, Withy (Chartering). Besides holding a directorship with FW(Chartering), he thereafter moved into wider shipping circles, including insurance, arbitration, etc., becoming Managing Director of FW(Chartering) in 1993 and director on the main board six years later, concurrently holding other directorships including that of the Standard Steamship Owners' Protection and Indemnity Association. He is now retired.

26. Correspondence and conversation with Captain Kenneth Owen.

27. The use of contemporarily fashionable buzz-words in this context is almost obligatory. In a broadcast in 2009 John Prescott, well known for his conflated and rather garbled style of oratory, declared the 'customer orientation' of his initiative.

28. At the time of writing, the red-ensign fleet has recovered its 1980 level. Since the introduction of the Tonnage Tax the number of ships has reached 900, increasing the national fleet by three times

and the wider flag-fleet (that is beneficially owned elsewhere) by a factor of five.

29. During this there was a hideously 'politically correct' re-enactment of the battle of Trafalgar not between mock British and a mock Franco-Spanish fleets, but between a 'blue' and an 'orange' fleet.

30. Particularly in the wake of the banking crisis of 2008 and the wholesale undermining of confidence on the probity of fiscal management in London.

31. The journalist Anthony Grey was cooped-up in Beijing for two years.

32. The Inquiry concluded the fire-ball derived from the *Royston Grange's* refrigeration plant probably releasing a cloud of highly toxic gas which in a matter of moments would have flooded the bridge, accommodation and engine room, rapidly asphyxiating all who inhaled it. Others thought it more likely that the fire-ball was caused by the ignition of the crude oil, as occurred in the *Dona Paz* casualty which killed some 2,340 people in the Philippines in 1987, and all 141 people aboard the *Moby Prince* in 1991, after the ferry collided with the *Agip Abruzzo*, laden once again, with crude oil.

33. The *Gastrana* was chartered to the Sultan of Brunei and running Brunei-produced oil to Japan.

34. These ships were caught at Khorramshahr, Basrah and Abadan and several in the two southern ports were damaged by the fighting. Many were abandoned in consequence, the British ship *Red Fisher* being one such.

35. See Fisk, R., *The Great War for Civilisation*, p241. Further details from Martin Barrclough and Silver Line's *Group News Letter*, No.91, December 1980.

36. These were the *Esk*, *Trent*, *Avon*, *Dart*, *Tamar*, *Test* and *Wye*. The smaller *Fern* and *Ivy* were also chartered. Other tankers were Shell's *Eburna*, Panocean's *Anco Charger*, Canadian Pacific's *GA Walker* and Parley Augusstson's *Balder London*.

37. Marr's trawlers were the *Northella*, *Cordella*, *Farnella* and *Junella*.

38. I am indebted to Louis Roskell, Senior Second Officer of the *St Edmund*, for access to his account of Operation CORPORATE.

39. Woodward, S., and Robertson, P., *One Hundred Days*, 1992.

40. Correspondence between Malcolm MacKenzie and Philip Wake of the Nautical Institute, August 2002.
My thanks to both. Malcolm was nephew to Captain Douglas MacKenzie and he met his uncle on the *Arundel Castle's* arrival at Capetown where he was an apprentice aboard Shaw, Savill & Albion's *Cymric* and heard the account first-hand. Another Union-Castle liner to encounter an extreme-wave in this area and at this period was the *Kenya Castle*. The wave swept the bridge and passenger decks. In another such incident a wave hit Reardon Smith's tramp *Atlantic City*, smashing the bridge windows and thereby blinding the chief officer.

41. A LASH-carrier – meaning 'lighter-aboard-ship' – was a large vessel capable of taking in a number of steel barges, lifted out of the water over the stern and carried to their stowage by a gigantic gantry-crane, thus connecting inland waterways with ocean navigation. Designed in the USA and favoured by the Germans, the idea did not become widespread.

42. Captain Bryan Boyer encountered a large wave estimated to peak at 120ft which showed first on the radar of his container-liner which was hove-to in wind of 100 knots on passage from Vancouver to Yokohama. The wave did not break and he concluded that it was a tsunami. See *Seaways*, September 2001.

43. If there were those who viewed these events as symptoms of some malaise, there was always the sinking of the *Rainbow Warrior* to indicate declining greatness. Contentious though her purpose might have been, she was registered in Aberdeen, flew the red ensign of Great Britain and was sunk by the French. On the night of 9/10 July 1985 the *Rainbow Warrior* was in Auckland, prior to her protest at a French nuclear test at Mururoa. She had been in the South Pacific for three months protesting against American and French nuclear testing as part of the campaign mounted by the protest-group Greenpeace. At about 23.45 she was wracked by an explosion and began to settle. Two minutes later, a second detonation took place. An 8ft-wide hole had been blown in the vessel's side and many of the crew ended up in the harbour. Fernando Pereira, a Portuguese-born Dutch citizen was drowned, trapped in his cabin as the vessel sank. Two bombs or mines had been placed by the French Secret Service. A couple were later apprehended and imprisoned in New Zealand. They had been passing themselves off as Swiss nationals but were in fact French army officers, a major and a captain, the latter a woman. Initially the French government denied any allegations that the sinking of the *Rainbow Warrior* was the work of its agents, but in due course Admiral Pierre La Coste, head of the French Secret Service, and the French Defence Minister both resigned. Although

$8.2 million was paid to Greenpeace in compensation and an undisclosed sum was paid to Pereira's parents, neither of the perpetrators served their full terms of imprisonment. The French never apologised and the British Government never protested over the sinking of a British-flagged vessel.

44. The concerned citizen was the father of a deck-cadet serving in the RFA which, under Secretary of State John Nott's Defence Review would be severely cut. See Puddefoot, G., *The Fourth Force*, p90.

45. Correspondence with William Whately, September 2009.

46. Correspondence with Heather Cowan, September 2009.

47. It was the ninetieth anniversary of the 1918 Armistice and much had been made of the occasion, though no mention had been made of the loss of merchant seafarers. It was an irony noted by those who cared, but made Laurence Binyon's immortal memorial lines ring a little hollow. Far from being remembered, the Merchant Navy had been not merely forgotten, but eclipsed. The BBC had slowly eroded its own connection with the Merchant Navy. For years it transmitted The Merchant Navy programme, with features of interest to the mercantile seafarer and his family, including requests for music. Later this adopted a magazine format as the Seven Seas Programme presented by Malcolm Billings until, with shipping failing to excite the executives, this too was dropped.

48. They were Lord Brabazon, Viscount Goschen, The Earl of Caithness, Lord McKay (all Tory); Glenda Jackson, Keith Hill, David Jamieson, Stephen Ladyman, Jim Fitzpatrick and Paul Clark (New Labour).

49. These transcripts are excerpts from a paper entitled *Voices from the Bridge, 1960–1980*, presented at the Greenwich Maritime Institute by John Johnston-Allen, and are reproduced here with his kind permission.

50. See Birkett, D., Jella: *A Woman at Sea*, p155, *et seq.*

51. Though not the American press. *The New Yorker* contained articles on the subject in the 1990s.

AFTERWORD

WHITHER, OH SHIP?[1]

Epitaph or Epilogue?

It might be argued that this history has contained too many references to China, and Britain's trade and shipping links with that vast country; that this has been at the expense of other aspects of British shipping. This may well be true and, as was laid before the reader in the introduction to *Neptune's Trident*, some imbalance in such a varied and extraordinary history is inevitable. However, it is no coincidence, for the correlations and consequences of the Sino-British relationship are arguably greater for the future than any among the others of our trading partnerships.

Whereas the situation of Great Britain in the Great War called onto the world stage an alliance with the United States, bringing that nation in the peace negotiations of 1919 from comparative isolation to the forefront of affairs, so has British commercial policy made a contribution to the rise of China. Napoleon may well have remarked that China should be left to slumber, for when she woke the word would tremble, but it was the likes of the iron-headed old rat, William Jardine, who compelled China to trade with the western world, using opium as amorally as the Chicago-trained economists have more recently forced economic and political meltdown upon states they wished to dominate and exploit by means of shock and awe. What Jardine and his ilk achieved was off less impact when compared with what we have seen in our so-called post-modern world, but the present success of the Chinese model in no small way owes something to its architects – chief among them Mao-Tse Dong – having been made aware of what can be achieved by determined men without scruple as to method. History – and certainly the history of the British Mercantile Marine – has no moral dimension but, notwithstanding this, there remains a power within commerce to transform lives, to raise from poverty, to reduce tension and to realise perhaps mankind's most collectively beneficial aspiration: equality of opportunity. For this, in its diversity, shipping is a powerful tool.

The British, our competitors had believed for two centuries, had had it too good for too long. Like encircling wolves they only awaited an opportunity while the internal body politic grew turgid with disinterest. The post-war assurances given by Aneurin Bevan that continuing economic prosperity could be enjoyed by British workers who were fortunate enough to live on an island of coal surrounded by an ocean of fish, were short-sighted and proved false. The first was destroyed as Iceland asserted its rights to trawl its own waters to the exclusion of others and Britain surrendered its own seas to the dictates of the European Commission, the second fell foul of Thatcher's modernising and produced civil unrest of almost warlike proportions in the face of a Middle East which, ten years earlier, had stirred from its slumbers, woken by the rush of oil rising out of the desert sands. Science and technology meanwhile provided new, easily accessible answers to the problems of ocean navigation, to the handling of larger and larger ships, rationalising the carriage of complex and varied cargoes. Gradually the hard-learned expertises and experience-base of the traditional seafarer were whittled away – they were no longer so vital: armed with the new tools others could do the work as well and ask less for doing it. Tradition, vocation, loyalty and service withered; 'going to sea' lost its appeal to all but a few young Britons. Other opportunities beckoned: hedonism and easy money – for a while at least – seemed assured; there was no need to immolate oneself on a distant ship, dreaming of home and beauty. Let others, less fortunate, endure all that.

Globalisation has enabled money to slide across national boundaries uncontrolled, unseen, eroding the power of the nation state. Our appetites increased, becoming voracious, immoderate. We bought and no longer manufactured. Our moral compass lapsed; we became inconsiderate, unrestrained. World affairs shaped by the destruction of the twin towers of the World Trade Center in New York on 11 September 2001, while mourning the 3,000 souls who perished, ignored the 25,000 human-beings lost that same day to the effects of contaminated water, besides those elsewhere dying from pestilence, starvation and war. In 2003 a former Astronomer Royal, Martin Rees, concluded that: 'The odds are no better than fifty-fifty that our present civilisation ... will survive to the end of the present century ... unless all nations adopt low-risk sustainable policies ...'. This point is made even more cogently by Ronald Wright.

> If civilisation is to survive, it must live on the interest, and not the capital, of nature. Ecological markers suggest that in the early 1960s, humans were using about 70 per cent of nature's yearly output; by the early 1980s we'd reached 100 per cent; and in 1999 we were at 125 per cent. Such numbers may be imprecise, but their trend is clear – they mark the road to bankruptcy.[2]

Britain's rise to become the world's first power capable of global influence managed this not by her Royal Navy, a debit on the state, but by her revenue-earning mercantile marine. In the 1480s, seeking to secure his power base by enrichment, King Edward IV knew, like Henry VII later, that he must himself take up trade, as the *Croyland Continuato* tells us: 'Having procured merchant ships, he put on board of them the finest wools, cloths, tin, and other productions of the Kingdom, and, like one of those who live by trade, did exchange merchandise for merchandise by means of his agents'. Such trade could enrich more than a king: 'It is not our conquests, but our commerce; it is not our swords, but our sails, that first spread the English name ... over and about the world,' Lewis Roberts wrote in *The Treasure of Trafficke* published in London in 1641. Our subsequent naval power grew upon its back, as Sir Horace Mann MP pointed out when he wrote in 1779 that 'the source of our power and greatness [is] our trade and commerce, the consequent number of our seamen, and our naval superiority, which all *inseparably* [my emphasis] give us riches and power.' There was, of course, a cost to all this, paid with in seamen's lives, but there was an amoral dynamism which drove it, a fact pointed out at this time by the former slave Ignatius Sancho in a letter to John Wingrave in 1778. 'I say it with reluctance,' Sancho wrote, 'but I must observe that your country's conduct has been uniformly wicked ... the great object of the English navigators, indeed all Christian navigators, is money, money, money.'

And it was money, money, money that ended it. The short-sightedness of ship-owners who failed to adapt to change, ensured the loss of competitive edge when compounded by trade-union intransigence and the entire lack of understanding by the Thatcher Government. British investors largely lost interest in shipping: quicker and easier bucks could be made elsewhere. The remaining shipping companies were thereafter brought down by the greed of shareholders and thus the sun finally set on the red ensign.

What remains is uncertain; since the introduction of the Tonnage Tax, owners have proved predictably fickle, though a tiny rump remains loyal. The national asset of a Merchant Navy – a great service industry – has been squandered and our maritime fortunes brought to a low ebb. Today the basis of our economy relies largely upon financial services and that too is worm-eaten by greed and teeters upon the edge of an abyss. Its rise went hand in hand with trade and the carriage of goods by sea and what we did once, we might yet do again. In this history have we traced our narrative to what – at this time – seems to be its concluding epitaph. But shipping is a cyclical business and we have been in similar circumstances before. 'Only a poor country can afford to send its sons to sea,'[3] and we are impoverished by our current budget deficit, so this state of affairs may be merely an epilogue, marking a low-water before the flood tide begins to make again. If it ever does, however, it will require effort, investment and expertise. In the meantime, Kipling's prescient *Recessional* expresses it best:

> Far called, our navies melt away
> On dune and headland sinks the fire,
> Lo, all our strength of yesterday
> Is one with Nineveh and Tyre.

NOTES

1. Walt Whitman.
2. See Wright, R., *A Short History of Progress*, Canongate, Edinburgh, 2005, p129. He also quotes Rees's *Our Final Century* (2003) on p125 *et seq*.
3. An old Swedish saying.

APPENDIX

THE SD14 AND THE DEMISE OF BRITISH SHIPBUILDING

The designer and principal builder of the SD14 was Austin & Pickersgill in their spacious yard at Southwick near Sunderland five miles from the mouth of the River Wear which had been cleared and redeveloped in 1958. The yard was owned by Basil Mavroleon of London Overseas Freighters and specialised in general cargo vessels and bulk carriers. Further downstream, at South Dock near the river's mouth, lay the shipyard of Bartram & Sons. The yard was out of date and under-capitalised but was nevertheless building 'comparatively complex' refrigerated cargo-liners for the Blue Star Line and the New Zealand Shipping Co., ten of which were delivered between 1958 and 1966, together with 'their staple diet of conventional but non-standard dry-cargo vessels'.

In response, the Government's Geddes Report sought to:

> rationalise the ship-building industry and offered substantial financial incentives in return for a programme of mergers and take-overs of like-minded yards, and this encouraged Austin & Pickersgill and Bartram & Co. to work together, marketing and building the SD14, a no-frills 14,000 tonne standard dry-cargo tramp designed by A&P specifically for the Greek market to replace the ageing Greek fleet of Second World War Liberty ships. Bartram would build the SD14 for two years, but thereafter A&P would acquire the company … Based on previous production records, initially it was thought that the Bartram yard would have a maximum capacity of somewhat less than 250 tonnes/week, equivalent to four-plus ships per annum and the A&P yard 350 tonnes/week, or six-plus ships a year.

At the very start of the SD14 programme in 1967, by a quirk of contract switching, the very first SD14, one of over 200 built worldwide, was launched from the Bartram yard in December of that year, but the honour of delivering the first completed vessel in the spring of 1968 went to A. & P. and their major shareholder/ ship-owner partner London Overseas Freighters.*

The benefits of series production of standard ships realised by the Americans and Canadians in the shipbuilding programmes of the recent war now manifested themselves on the River Wear. Familiarisation with the new methods increased production. Bartram turned out 330 tonnes/week, Austin & Pickersgill managed 430, a joint capacity of fourteen SD14 hulls a year rather than the programmed ten. 'Of overwhelming significance, little or no increase in the labour-force was required' to achieve this and therefore direct costs and overhead contribution per unit were reduced substantially, 'with obvious implications for profitability and the acid test of the various financial ratios'. The modernised Southwick yard of Austin & Pickersgill and the outdated South Dock slipways of Bartram were now in friendly competition. Under young dynamic management the Bartram yard used both manual and computer-based project-planning and production control techniques which controlled the location and movement of each individual plate and component of a hull. This was:

an absolute necessity, without which the production process in such a limited space [as was available in this old yard] would have been reduced to a grinding halt. The A. & P. Yard, on the other hand, with all the space in the world, was not thought to require such detailed control techniques.

With the Austin & Pickersgill yard the dominating partner, its top management tended to scorn the use of these techniques, insisting that the Bartram shipyard abandoned its *nouveau* notions and – against all common-sense – 'should dispense with all this unnecessary fancy planning and do things the way we do!' Experienced junior management resented the ruling 'but with one exception it was a taboo subject amongst A&P directors'. The 'one exception' was a new financial director new to the industry who quickly realised that the Bartram yard with a quarter of the ground area of A&P produced three-quarters of the senior partners' output. A&P also carried up to three times more investment at any one moment in work-in-progress steelwork, 'a huge variable overhead penalty to be taken into consideration in making any cost comparisons'. Moreover:

Bearing in mind the obvious major discrepancies between the two establishments in terms of plant, equipment, and facilities in general, why were direct labour costs on individual vessels showing little or no positive advantage in favour of the modern yard over the very much smaller ill-equipped yard?

Unfortunately, however:

With the introduction of a new, wholly inappropriate direct cost allocation system covering both yards by an outside consultant with no experience whatsoever of the

---

* These opinions are drawn directly from correspondence with Robert Hunter, formerly of Bartram & Sons Ltd, dated 15 June 2009.

ship-building process, this potentially embarrassing set of statistics was buried and left unexplained.

This self-deception proved disastrous. The board of Austin & Pickersgill now planned to close the Bartram yard after six successful years, subsuming the labour-force and expanding their own Southwick yard. The intention was to increase through-put to 1,000 tonnes/week, or sixteen SD14s a year, which was never achieved, in order to justify £100 million of the Government's investment of public money.

> Not surprisingly, direct costs per vessel rose dramatically, the allocation of a hugely increased overhead burden was now spread amongst fewer ships than in the past and which had been intended for the future; the opportunist profits which had been made in previous years derived from the two separate yards and the friendly competition disappeared overnight, morale declined, and with it industrial relations between an increasingly militant labour-force and an increasingly elderly introspective management looking to the supposed saviour of nationalisation; after which, of course, total closure and despair.
>
> Behind the scenes a tale of lost opportunities and a clash of cultures, with tragic results for all the Sunderland families involved in the industry; in contrast to the transitory image of success which had previously been presented to the public and Government alike.
>
> The shareholders, on the other hand, received compensation based on asset value at the time of nationalisation, which ironically included the full notional value, including the contribution made by Government, of the enhanced production facilities which had contributed significantly to their demise.

The young Bartram management who were able to do so, took their skills and transferred them, along with their modern project-management techniques, to the burgeoning North Sea oil industry.

BIBLIOGRAPHY

PUBLISHED MATERIAL
All published in London unless otherwise stated

Abraham, P.J., *Last Hours on Dara*, Peter Davies, 1963
Allison, R.S., *Sea Diseases*, John Bale Medical Publications, 1943
Anderson, J., *Coastwise Sail*, Percival Marshall, 1948
 Last Survivors in Sail, Percival Marshall, 1948
Anonymous, *History of the Union Steam Ship Company of New Zealand, 1875–1940*, Published by the Company, Wellington, New Zealand, 1940
Anonymous, *Seventy Adventurous Years, The Story of the Bank Line, 1885–1955*, The Journal of Commerce and Shipping Telegraph, Liverpool, 1956
Barraclough, M., *Looking for the Silver Lining*, Bound Biographies, 2009
Barnes, H.C.B. *Troopships and Their History*, Seeley, Service, 1963
Beattie, N.R., *East with a Blue Funnel*, Merlin Books, Braunton, 1985
Behrens, C., *Merchant Shipping and the Demands of War*, HMSO, 1955
Bird, A.H., *Farewell Milag*, Literatours, St Leonards-on-Sea, 1995
Birkett, D., *Jella: A Woman at Sea*, Gollancz, 1992
Bisset, J., and Stephensen, P.R., *Commodore: War, Peace and Big Ships*, Angus & Robertson, 1961
Blake, G., *The Ben Line*, Thomas Nelson, Edinburgh, 1956
 B.I. Centenary, 1856–1956, Collins, 1956
Blake, R., *Jardine Matheson – Traders of the Far East*, Weidenfeld and Nicolson, 1999
Bone, D.W., *The Lookout Man*, Jonathan Cape, 1923
 Merchantmen Rearmed, Chatto & Windus, 1949
 Landfall at Sunset, Duckworth, 1956
Bonwick, G.J., and Steer, E.C., *Ships' Business*, The Maritime Press, Fifth Edition, 1963
Boothby, H.B., *Spunyarn*, G.T. Foulis, c.1935
Bott, A. (Editor), *British Box Business, A History of OCL*, 2009
Boughton, G.P., *Seafaring*, Faber and Gwyer, 1926
Bouquet, M., *South Eastern Sail, from the Medway to the Solent, 1840–1940*, David & Charles, Newton Abbot, 1972
Bowditch, N., *American Practical Navigator*, Defense Mapping Agency Hydrographic/Topographic Center, Washington, 1984
Bowen, F.T., *The Men of the Merchant Service*, Macmillian, 1900
Britten, E.T., *A Million Ocean Miles*, Hutchinson, c.1938
Brooks, L., and Ducé, R.H. (editors), *Seafarers, Ships and Cargoes*, University of London Press, 1951
Brown, C.H., *Nicholls's Seamanship and Nautical Knowledge*, Brown, Son & Ferguson, Glasgow, 1958
Brown, R.D., *The Port of London*, Terence Dalton, Lavenham, 1978
Bullen, F.T., *The Men of the Merchant Service*, Macmillan, 1900
Burn, A., *The Fighting Commodores, Convoy Commanders in the Second World War*, Leo Cooper, Barnsley, 1999
Bushell, T.A., *'Royal Mail', A Centenary History of the Royal Mail Line, 1839–1939*, Trade and Travel Publications, 1939

Butterfield and Swire, *The China Navigation Co, 1872–1992*, B & S, 1992

Cable, B., *A Hundred Year History of the P & O*, Ivor Nicholson and Watson, 1937

Cameron, J., *Trial of Heinz Eck, August Hoffmann, Walter Weisspfennig, Hans Richard Lenz and Wolfgang Schwender (The Peleus Trial)*, William Hodge, 1948

Carson, R., *The Sea Around Us*, Readers Union, 1953

Chandler, G., *Liverpool Shipping*, Phoenix House, 1960

Charton, B., and Tietjen, J., *Seas and Oceans*, Collins, 1989

Clarke, I.C., *Ship Dynamics for Mariners*, Nautical Institute, 2005

Clarke, W.V.J., *Cole's Shipmaster's Handbook to the Merchant Shipping Acts*, Brown, Son & Ferguson, Glasgow, 1949

Cole, S., *Our Home Ports*, Effingham Wilson, 1923

Coombs, W.H., *The Nation's Key Men*, J.D. Potter, 1925

Cope, L.C., *A Century of Sea Trading, the General Steam Navigation Company Ltd, 1824–1924*, A. & C. Black, 1924
     The Sea Carriers, 1825–1925, The Aberdeen Line, Published by the Company, 1925

Cornewall-Jones, R.J., *The British Merchant Service*, Sampson Low, Marston, 1898

Course, A.G., *The Merchant Navy, A Social History*, Frederick Muller, 1963
     The Merchant Navy Today, Oxford University Press, 1956

Cowden, J.E., and Duffy, J.O.C., *The Elder Dempster Fleet List, 1852 - 1985*, Privately Published, 1986

Cowen, R. C., *Frontiers of the Sea*, Gollancz, 1960

Credland, A.G., *Harry Hudson Rodmell, Shipping Posters*, Hull City Museums and Hutton Press Ltd, Hull, 1999

Cubbin, G., *Harrisons of Liverpool, A Chronicle of Ships and Men, 1830–2002*, World Ship Society and Ships in Focus, Gravesend and Preston, 2003

Cunliffe, T. (Editor and Principal Author), *Pilots – The World of Pilotage Under Sail and Oars*:
     Vol. 1, *Pilot Schooners of Great Britain and North America*, Le Chasse-Marée/Maritime Life and Traditions, Douarnenez, France, 2001
     Vol. 2, *Schooners and Open Boats of the European Pilots and Watermen*, Le Chasse-Marée/Maritime Life and Traditions, Douarnenez, France and Chatham Publishing, Rochester, 2002

Davidson-Houston, L.V. *The Piracy of the Nanchang*, Cassell, 1961

Davis, S., *You and Your Ships*, The Memoir Club, Stanhope, 2006

De Mierre, H.C., *Clipper Ships to Ocean Greyhounds*, Harold Starke, 1971

De Reya, G., *A Nomad of the Sea*, Andrew Melrose, 1936

Doughty, M., *Merchant Shipping and War, A Study of Defence Planning in 20th Century Britain*, Royal Historical Society 1982

Drummond, C., *The Remarkable Life of Victoria Drummond, Marine Engineer*, The Institute of Marine Engineers, 1994.

Ellacott, S.E., *The Seaman*, Two Volumes, Abelard-Schuman, 1970

Elphick, P., *Life Line, The Merchant Navy at War, 1939–1945*, Chatham 1999
     Liberty, The Ships that won the War, Chatham Publishing, 2001

Ennis, J., *The Great Bombay Explosion*, Berkley Publishing, New York, 1960

Ericson, D.B., and Wollin, G., *The Ever-Changing Sea*, Paladin, 1968

Evans, B. (Editor), *A Lantern on the Stern*, Two Volumes, Countyvise, Birkenhead, 2007

Falkus, M., *The Blue Funnel Legend, A History of the Ocean Steamship Co, 1865–1973*, Macmillan, 1990

Foreman, S., *Shoes and Ships and Sealing Wax, An Illustrated History of the Board of Trade, 1786–1986*, HMSO, 1986

Foster, C., *1,700 Miles in Open Boats*, Martin Hopkinson, 1926

Fox, S., *The Ocean Railway*, HarperCollins, 2003

Freeman, N., *Seaspray and Whisky, Reminiscences of a Tramp Ship Voyage*, Akadine Press, New York, 2001

Gibson, J.F. *Brocklebanks, 1770–1950* (Two Volumes), Henry Young, Liverpool, 1953

Gibb, D.E.W., *Lloyd's of London, A Study in Individualism*, Lloyd's, 1972

Golding, T. (Editor), *Trinity House from Within*, Trinity House, 1929

Gollock, G.A., *At the Sign of the Flying Angel*, Longmans, Green & Co., 1930

Green, E., and Moss, M., *A Business of National Importance, The Royal Mail Shipping Group, 1902–1937*, Methuen, 1982

Greenhill, B., *Merchant Schooners*, Percival Marshall, Two Volumes, 1951

Greenway, A., *Cargo Liners*, Seaforth, 2009

Gunn, G., *Tramp Steamers at War*, Gomer Press, Llandysul, 1999

Hague, A., *The Allied Convoy System, 1939–1945*, Chatham Publishing, 2000

Haigh, K.R., *Cableships and Submarine Cables*, Adlard Coles, 1968

Hall, A., and Heywood, F., *Shipping, A Guide to the Routine in Connection with the Importation and Exportation of Goods and the Clearance of Vessels Inwards and Outwards*, Pitman, 1921

Hampshire, A.C., *On Hazardous Service*, William Kimber, 1974

Hancock, H.E., *Semper Fidelis, The Saga of the 'Navvies', 1924–1948*, The General Steam Navigation Co. Ltd, 1949

Hardy, A.C., *Merchant Ship Types*, Chapman and Hall, 1924

Harvey, C., *RMS* Empress of Britain, *Britain's Finest Liner*, Tempus, Stroud, 2004

Harvey, W.J. and Solly, R.J., *BP Tankers, A Fleet History*, Chatham, 2006

Haws, D., and Hurst, A.A, *The Maritime History of the World*, Two Volumes, Teredo Books, Brighton, 1985

Hayes, B., *Hull Down*, Cassell, 1925

Heaton, P.M., *Booth Line*, P.M. Heaton Publishing, Abergavenny, 1987
    Reardon Smith Line, P.M. Heaton Publishing, Abergavenny, 1984
    Lamport and Holt, P.M. Heaton Publishing, Abergavenny, 2004
    Welsh Blockade Runners in the Spanish Civil War, P.M. Heaton, Abergavenny, 1985

Hendry, F.C., ('Shalimar'), *The Ocean Tramp*, Collins, 1938
    Land and Sea, William Blackwood, 1939
    Ships and Men, William Blackwood, Edinburgh, 1946
    From the Log-Book of Memory, William Blackwood, Edinburgh, 1950
    Down to the Sea, William Blackwood, Edinburgh, 1940
    True Tales of Sail and Steam, Oxford University Press, 1943

Hewitt, N., *Coastal Convoys, 1839–1945, The Indestructible Highway*, Pen & Sword, Barnsley, 2008

Hill, B., *Postage Stamps of the Great Bitter Lakes Association*, Picton Publishing, Chippenham, 1975

Hirson, B., and Vivian, L., *Strike Across the Empire*, Clio, 1992

HMSO, *British Vessels Lost at Sea, 1914–1917 and 1939–1945*, Facsimile edition, Patrick Stephens, Wellingborough, 1988
    The Mariner's Handbook, Sixth Edition, 1989
    Ocean Passages for the World, Third Edition, 1973
    Seafarers and Their Ships, 1955

Home, W.E., *Merchant Seamen, Their Diseases and Their Welfare Needs*, John Murray, 1922

Hope, R., *A New History of British Shipping*, John Murray, 1990
    Poor Jack, Chatham, 2001
    The Merchant Navy, Stanford Maritime, 1980

(Editor), *The Seaman's World*, Geo. Harrap/The Marine Society, 1982

Houlder Brothers, *Sea Hazard (1939–1945)*, An unattributed company history of Houlder Brothers, Published by the Company, 1947

Howarth, D., and Howarth, S., *The Story of P & O*, Weidenfeld and Nicolson, 1986

Howarth, S., *Sea Shell, the Story of Shell's British Tanker Fleets, 1892–1992*, Thomas Reed, 1992

Hudson, J.L., *British Merchantmen at War, The Official Story of the Merchant Navy: 1939–1944*, HMSO, 1944

Hughill, S., *Shanties from the Seven Seas, Shipboard Work-Songs*, Routledge and Kegan Paul, 1984

Humphries, S., *The Call of the Sea, Britain's Maritime Past, 1900–1960*, BBC Books, 1997

Hyde, F.E., *Shipping Enterprise and Management, Harrisons of Liverpool, 1830–1939*, Liverpool University Press, Liverpool, 1967

Jackson, I., Todd, I., and Ormerod, J., *Three Boys in a Ship*, Ian Jackson, Melrose, 1999

Jamieson, A.G., *Ebb Tide in the British Maritime Industries, Change and Adaptation, 1918 –1990*, University of Exeter Press, 2003

Johnson, H., *The Cunard Story*, Whittet Books, 1987

Jordan, R., *The World's Merchant Fleets, 1939*, Chatham Publishing, 1999

Jones, C., *Sea Trading and Sea Training*, Edward Arnold, 1936

Jones, D.C., *The Enemy We Killed, My Friend*, Gomer, Llandysul, 1999

Jones, J.T., *Tramp to Queen*, Tempus, Stroud, 2008

Keble Chatterton, E., *Valiant Sailormen*, Hurst & Blackett, 1936

Kennedy, G. (Editor), *The Merchant Marine in International Affairs, 1850–1950*, Frank Cass, 2001

Kemp, P., (Editor) *The Oxford Companion to Ships and the Sea*, OUP, Oxford, 1988

Kindleberger, C., *The World in Depression, 1929 - 1939*, Allen Lane, 1973-

King, G.A.B., *Tanker Practice*, The Maritime Press, 1962

Kinghorn, A.W., *Before the Box Boats, The Story of a Merchantman*, Kenneth Mason, Emsworth, 1983

Kohler, P.C., *Sea Safari, British India S.N. Co. African Ships and Services*, P.M. Heaton Publishing, Abergavenny, 1995

Lawson, W., *Pacific Steamers*, Brown, Son & Ferguson, Glasgow, 1927

Laird, D., *Paddy Henderson*, George Outram, Glasgow, 1961

Lane, A., *Guiding Lights*, Tempus, Stroud, 2001

Lane, T., *Grey Dawn Breaking*, Manchester University Press, 1986

The Merchant Seamen's War, Manchester University Press, 1990

Long, A. and R., *A Shipping Venture, Turnbull, Scott & Co., 1872–1972*, Hutchinson Benham, 1974

Lucas, W.E., *Eagle Fleet*, Weidenfeld and Nicolson, 1955

Lund, A., *The Red Duster*, Whitby Press, Whitby, 1989

Making, V.L., *In Sail and Steam, Behind the Scenes of the Merchant Service, 1902–1927*, Sidgwick and Jackson, 1937

Mason, M., Greenhill, B. and Craig, R., *The British Seafarer*, Hutchinson/BBC/National Maritime Museum, 1980

Mathias, P., and Pearsall, A.W.H., *Shipping: A Survey of Historical Records*, David & Charles, Newton Abbot, 1971

McBrearty, R.F., *Seafaring 1939–1945, As I saw it*, The Pentland Press, Edinburgh, 1995

McCutcheon, J., *RMS* Queen Elizabeth, *The Beautiful Lady*, Tempus, Stroud, 2001

McLellan, *Anchor Line, 1856–1956*, Anchor Line Ltd, Glasgow, 1956

McLeod, C., and Kirkaldy, A.W., *The Trade, Commerce, and Shipping of the Empire*, Collins, 1924

McLuskie, T., *Harland and Wolff, Designs from the Shipbuilding Empire*, Conway, 1998

McMillan, A.S., *Port Line Story, 1914–1964, A Short History*, Port Line Ltd, 1964

Meek, Marshall, *There go the Ships*, The Memoir Club, Spennymoor, 2003

Mitchell, W.H., and Sawyer, L.A., *Empire Ships of World War 2*, Sea Breezes, Liverpool, 1965

The Liberty Ships, Lloyd's of London Press, Colchetser, 1985

Moore, W.J., *Shanghai Century*, Arthur Stockwell, Ilfracombe, 1966

Moyse-Bartlett, H., *A History of the Merchant Navy*, Harrap, 1937

Munro, A., *Winston's Specials, Troopships via the Cape, 1940 - 1943*, Maritime Books, Liskeard, 2006

Munro-Smith, R., *Merchant Ship Design*, Hutchinson, 1964

Murray, M., *Union-Castle Chronicle, 1853–1953*, Longmans, Green and Co, 1953

Newall, P., *Union Castle, A Fleet History*, Carmania Press, 1999

Newton, A.P., *A Hundred Years of the British Empire*, Duckworth, 1940

Newton, J., *A Century of Tankers*, Intertanko, 2002

Orbell, J., *From Cape to Cape, The History of Lyle Shipping*, Paul Harris Publishing, Edinburgh, 1978

Osborne, R., *Conversion for War*, World Ships Society Monograph No.6, Kendal, 1983

Osborne, R., Spong, H., and Grover, T., *Armed Merchant Cruisers, 1878–1945*, World Ships Society, Windsor, 2007

P&O, *The P&O Pocket Book*, A. & C. Black, 1926

Palmer, S., *Politics, Shipping and the Repeal of the Navigation Laws*, Manchester University Press, 1990

Peppitt, T., *The Crew, A Portrait of Merchant Seamen at the End of the Tramp Ship Era*, Chaffcutter, Ware, 2000

Powell, L.H., *The Shipping Federation, A history of the first sixty years, 1890–1950*, The Shipping Federation, 1950

Puddefoot. G., *The Fourth Force, the Untold Story of the Royal Fleet Auxiliary since 1945*, Seaforth, 2009

Quétel, C., *History of Syphilis*, Polity Press, Cambridge, 1990

Radford, G., *Captain Radford's Diary*, Grant Books, Droitwich, 1992

Ranalow, E., *A Corkman at Sea*, undated self-publication

Read, A., *The Coastwise Trade of the United Kingdom*, George Thompson, 1925

Rentell, P., *Master Mariner, A Life Under Way*, Seafarer Books, Rendlesham, 2009

Rice, A.L., *British Oceanographic Vessels, 1800–1950*, The Ray Society, 1986

Rinman, T., and Brodefors, R., *The Commercial History of Shipping*, Rinman & Lindén AB, Gothenburg, 1983

Robertson, R.B., *Of Whales and Men*, Reprint Society, 1958

Rohwer, J., and Hummelchen, G., *Chronology of the War at Sea, 1939–1945*, Greenhill Books, 1992

Roskill, S., *A Merchant Fleet in War*, Collins, 1962

Russell, A.G., *Port Line*, Published by the Company, 1985

Rutter, O., *Red Ensign, A History of Convoy*, Robert Hale, 1942

Ryder, S.W., *Blue Water Ventures*, Hodder & Stoughton, 1931

Sargent, A.J., *Seaways of the Empire, Notes on the Geography of Transport*, A. & C. Black, 1930

Schofield, B.B., and Martyn, L.F., *The Rescue Ships*, William Blackwood, 1968

Simpson, G., *The Naval Constructor*, Kegan Paul, Trench & Trübner, 1904

Simpson, M. [Ed], *The Somerville Papers*, Navy Records Society, 1995

Slader, J., *The Fourth Service, Merchantmen at War, 1939–45*, Robert Hale, 1994
  The Red Duster at War, William Kimber, 1988
Smith, K., Watts, C.T. and Watts, M.J., *Records of Merchant Shipping and Seamen*, Public Records Office
  Guide No.20, PRO Publications, 1998
Spong, H.C., and Dobson, J., *Port Line*, World Ship Society, 2007
Sproule, A., *Port Out, Starboard Home*, Blandford Press, Poole, 1978
Stamp, D., *The World, A General Geography*, Longmans, 1966
Starkey, D.J., and Jamieson, A.G., *Exploiting the Sea, Aspects of Britain's Maritime Economy Since 1870*,
  University of Exeter Press, 1998
Stevens, E.F., *One Hundred Years of Houlders*, Houlder Bros & Co. Ltd, 1950
Stevenson, D., *Ship and Shore, Life in the Merchant Navy*, Caedmon, Whitby, 2001
Sturmey, S.G., *British Shipping and World Competition*, Athlone Press, 1962
Stewart, J.C., *The Sea Our Heritage*, Rowan Press, Rowan Press, Keith, 1995
Stewart McMillan, A., *Port Line Story, 1914–1964*, Published by the Company, 1964
Strachan, M., *The Ben Line, 1825–1982, An Anecdotal History*, Michael Russell, Norwich, 1992
Talbot-Booth, E.C., *Ships and the Sea*, Sampson Low, Marston & Co., 1941
  His Majesty's Merchant Navy, Sampson Low, Marston & Co., 1940
Taprell Dorling, H., *Blue Star Line, A Record of Service, 1939–1945*, 1948
Taylor, J., *Ellermans, A Wealth of Shipping*, Wilton House Gentry, 1976
Taylor, L.F.C., Gordon-Cumming, H.R., and Betzler, J.E., *War in the Southern Oceans*, Oxford University
  Press, 1961
Tennent, A.J., *British and Commonwealth Merchant Ship Losses to Axis Submarines, 1939–1945*, Sutton, Stroud, 2001
Thomas, D., *The Right Kind of Boy, A portrait of the British sea apprentice*, Phaiacia, Ystradowen, 2004
Thomas, D.A., *The Atlantic Star, 1939–45*, W.H. Allen, 1990
Thomas, G., *Milag; Captives of the Kriegsmarine, Merchant Navy Prisoners of War*, The Milag prisoner of War
  Association, Pontardawe, 1995
Thomas, H. *The Spanish Civil War*, Eyre & Spottiswoode, 1961
Thomas, P.N., *British Ocean Tramps*, Vol. One, *Builders and Cargoes*, Waine Research Publications, 1992
Thomas, R.E., *Stowage: The Properties and Stowage of Cargoes*, Revised Edition, Brown, Son & Ferguson
  Ltd, Glasgow, 1963
Thompson, B, *All Hands and the Cook, The Customs and Language of the British Merchant Seaman,
  1875–1975*, The Bush Press, Takapuna, New Zealand, 2008
Thornton, R.H., *British Shipping*, Cambridge University Press, 1939
Tomlinson, H. M., *Malay Waters*, Hodder & Stoughton, 1950
  The Sea and the Jungle, Penguin, 1953
Tracy, N., *Attack on Maritime Trade*, University of Toronto Press, Toronto, 1991
Tregonning, K.G., *Home Port Singapore, A History of Straits Steamship Company, 1890–1965*, Oxford
  University Press, 1967
Turner, E.S., *Gallant Gentlemen, A Portrait of the British Officer, 1600–1956*, Michael Joseph, 1956
Villiers, A., *Posted Missing*, Hodder & Stoughton, 1956
Watson, L., *Heaven's Breath, A Natural History of the Wind*, Coronet, 1985
Watson, N., *The Bibby Line, 1807–1990*, James & James, 1990
  The Port of London Authority, A Century of Service, 1909–2009, St Matthews Press for the PLA,
  Gravesend, 2009
Wedge, P.L., *Brown's Flag and Funnels*, Brown, Son & Ferguson, 1958
Whitfield, G.J., *Fifty Thrilling Years at Sea*, Hutchinson, 1934
Williamson, J.A., *The Ocean in English History*, Clarendon, Oxford, 1941
Woddis. J., *Under the Red Duster*, Senior Press, 1947
Woodman, R.M., *The History of the Ship*, Conway, 1997
  A Brief History of Mutiny, Robinson, 2005
  Keepers of the Sea, Revised Edition, Chaffcutter, Ware, 2005
Woodward, S., and Robertson, P., *One Hundred Days*, Fontana, 1992
Wright, R., *A Short History of Progress*, Canongate, Edinburgh, 2005
Young, J.M., *Britain's Sea War, A Diary of Ship Losses, 1939–1945*, Patrick Stephens, 1989

UNPUBLISHED MATERIAL

Fullarton, R.F., *Going Tramping* and *Still Tramping*, typescript auto-biography

Johnston-Allen, J., *Rochdale Before and After: British Masters and Mates c1960–1980*, MA Thesis, University of Greenwich, 2008

Sanders, R.E., *One's a'Burning, A History of the River Thames North Channel Pilotage Service* (with thanks to Captains A. Adams and A. Body, literary executors of the late Captain R.E. Sanders)

OTHER SOURCES

Information has been culled over a period of many years from a variety of magazines and periodicals, some of them now sadly defunct. These included *The Windsor Magazine*, *The Marine Magazine*, *The Blue Peter Magazine*, *The Marine Observer*, *Sea Breezes* and Sea Breezes Publications, *Ships Monthly*, *The NUMAST Telegraph* (now *The Nautilus Telegraph*), *The Mariners' Mirror*, *Maritime Heritage*, *Maritime Life and Times*, *The Seafarer* (now just plain *Seafarer*), and *The Journal of the Honourable Company of Master Mariners*. Other information has been sourced from the publications of The World Ship Trust, The World Ship Society and a number of the 'Ships in Focus' Publications. To the producers of these, past and present, I acknowledge my debt.

INDEX

INDEX OF SELECTED SHIPS
British Merchant vessels, unless otherwise indicated.

Visit our website and discover thousands of other History Press books.

www.thehistorypress.co.uk